LAISSEZ FAIRE
AND THE
GENERAL-WELFARE STATE

Laissez Faire
and
the General-Welfare State

A Study of Conflict in American Thought
1865 - 1901

SIDNEY FINE

Ann Arbor Paperbacks
The University of Michigan Press

Fourth printing 1969
First edition as an Ann Arbor Paperback 1964
Copyright © by The University of Michigan 1956
All rights reserved
Published in the United States of America by
The University of Michigan Press and simultaneously
in Don Mills, Canada, by Longmans Canada Limited
Manufactured in the United States of America

To the memory of my mother and father

To the memory of my mother and father

PREFACE

THE term "laissez faire" is employed in this book to embrace the arguments of those who accepted government as a necessity but nevertheless wished to see its functions reduced to the narrowest possible limits. They recognized that government must protect life and property and must provide a few common services, such as education, but essentially they viewed the state in negative terms and were loath to have it assume positive duties in the interests of the general welfare. The theorists of the general-welfare state, on the other hand, believed that the state could benefit society by a positive exertion of its powers and that it should therefore act whenever its interposition seemed likely to promote the common well-being. Although they were unwilling, in theory, to set any arbitrary limit to the scope of government action save the ability of the state to serve the general interest, the principal advocates of the general-welfare state wished government to operate within the framework of the capitalist order and to avoid the extremes of both laissez faire and socialism. Of course, not all critics of laissez faire were, at the same time, advocates of the general-welfare state, but insofar as they helped to discredit the let-alone policy, they facilitated the task of those who were urging the state to play a considerably more important role in the market place and in social affairs as a whole.

A semantic difficulty is occasioned by the present-day use of the term "welfare state." This expression apparently first attained prominence in the year 1949 (see Emmett E. Dorsey, "The Evolution of the Concept of the Welfare State in the United States since 1890," Ph.D. thesis, American University, 1950, pp. 6–14), some years after the research on the present study was initiated, and it has come to be identified in this country with Mr. Truman's Fair Deal and especially with a thoroughgoing program of social security and a firm government commitment to maintain full employment. The advocates of the general-welfare state of the late nineteenth century were proponents, to a degree, of some of the policies currently associated with the welfare state, but I wish to make it clear that I use the term "general-welfare state" to refer to a particular attitude as regards the relationship of government to the common weal and not to connote certain specific functions of government.

It is a pleasure to express here my gratitude to those who aided me in the work on this book. My research was facilitated by a grant from the Faculty Research Fund of the Horace H. Rackham School of Graduate Studies of the University of Michigan. Professor Dwight L. Dumond of the University of Michigan encouraged and assisted me from the beginning of my research to the completion of the manuscript. Professors Verner W. Crane, Lewis G. Vander Velde, and Z. Clark Dickinson, all of the University of Michigan, read the manuscript at one or another stage of its preparation and gave me the benefit of their wise counsel. The staffs of the various libraries and historical societies to which research on the book took me were wonderfully helpful. I am particularly indebted to my wife, Jean Fine, for her unfailing assistance in the preparation of the manuscript for publication.

Permission to quote has been granted by the following: Paul R. Reynolds and Son, 599 Fifth Avenue, New York, 17, N. Y., for matter from William James, *Collected Essays and Reviews;* Yale University Press, for lines from Albert Galloway Keller and Maurice R. Davie (eds.), *The Essays of William Graham Sumner,* Vol. I; and Doubleday and Company, Inc., for material from *A Builder of the New South: Being the Story of the Life Work of Daniel Augustus Tompkins,* by George Tayloe Winston (copyright 1920 by Doubleday and Company, Inc.). The section on Richard T. Ely appeared in a slightly different form in Volume XXXVII (1951) of the *Mississippi Valley Historical Review.*

SIDNEY FINE

CONTENTS

Conclusion: The Years since 1901

INTRODUCTION: THE EARLY YEARS

I

LAISSEZ FAIRE IN AMERICAN THOUGHT
AND POLICY, 1763–1865

THE Englishman James Bryce, commenting in 1888 on the American conception of the functions of government, declared that insofar as the people of the United States had any theory on that subject, the theory was laissez faire. Laissez faire, he maintained, is "the orthodox and accepted doctrine in the sphere both of Federal and of State legislation." [1] When Bryce wrote these words the doctrine of laissez faire was under strong attack, but it had long been a major tenet of the American faith. In theory at least, Americans had adhered to the view that although government was, unfortunately, a necessity, its functions should be reduced to a minimum. Free individuals, left to their own devices, could solve the problems that confronted them without the aid of the state. The state might wage war, protect property, and administer justice, but in the everyday life of the people it was not to interfere.

The doctrine of the negative state was one of singular vitality in that agrarian America which had proclaimed its independence in 1776 but which in 1865 was beginning to recede before a new America of cities and factories. The result both of American experience and of American conditions, hostility to government and to government action was promoted in the sphere of ideas by the doctrine of natural rights, by the faith of Americans in the self-sufficiency of the individual, and, to a lesser extent, by the teachings of classical political economy.

The existence of a "law of nature" that was superior to man-made law had been vigorously affirmed in seventeenth-century England and had been imported thence to the American colonies. Belief in a higher

[1] Bryce, *The American Commonwealth* (London, 1888), III, 272.

law was strengthened in the colonies by the necessity of establishing
the validity of the American case in the struggle with England after
1763. Such colonial leaders as James Otis, Patrick Henry, Samuel
Adams, John Adams, Thomas Paine, and Thomas Jefferson asserted
that there is a law above kings and parliaments that limits the arbitrary exercise of governmental power. They insisted that the individual is in possession of certain inalienable natural rights that no
government can abridge, and that governments had indeed been instituted for the precise purpose of preserving these rights.[2] Belief
in the existence of inalienable natural rights was written into the
Declaration of Independence and into the state constitutions of the
Revolutionary era. Through bills of rights in the state constitutions,
an attempt was made to define the rights of individuals with which
no government may interfere and which it is the duty of government
to protect. Such a bill of rights was eventually added to the federal
Constitution, in itself designed to keep the powers of the national government within strictly prescribed limits. The theory of natural rights,
as Charles Grove Haines has asserted, thus "became the foundation for
the concept of limited government."[3]

The first half of the nineteenth century saw something of a decline in the use of the concept of natural law and natural rights, but
the theory was far from dead. One finds in the writings of such jurists
as James Kent and Joseph Story and in the decisions of state and federal courts evidences of the continued vitality of the doctrine of the
higher law. In defending the vested rights of property holders, judges
sometimes referred to the "principles of natural justice," the "fundamental maxims of free governments," or the "dictates of reason" as
constituting a law above constitutions and the acts of legislatures and
limiting their application. A partial reaction against this attitude
took place in the Jacksonian era, when the courts tended to allow

[2] Charles Grove Haines, *The Revival of Natural Law Concepts* (Cambridge,
Mass., 1930), pp. 52–55; Benjamin Fletcher Wright, Jr., *American Interpretations
of Natural Law* (Cambridge, Mass., 1931), pp. 64–94.

[3] Haines, *Revival of Natural Law Concepts*, p. 58. Carl Becker has stated
that the central conception of the natural-rights philosophy with respect to the
functions of government was "the happy idea that the best way to secure the inalienable rights of man is just to leave the individual as free as possible to do what he
likes, and that accordingly no form of government can secure them so well as the one
that governs least" (*Freedom and Responsibility in the American Way of Life* [New
York, 1945], pp. 15–16).

AMERICAN THOUGHT AND POLICY IN THE EARLY YEARS 5

state legislatures rather wide discretion; but in the 1850's there was a return to the idea of implied limitations on legislatures, and the doctrine of affording judicial protection to vested rights independent of specific constitutional provisions was revived.[4]

Associated with the concept of natural rights and serving as an additional buttress to the edifice of laissez faire was the faith of Americans in the self-sufficiency of the individual. To a great extent the result of the unusually favorable economic conditions that prevailed in the United States, individualism became part and parcel of the nation's democratic faith. Americans placed their trust not in "external government" but in the free individual, who must be kept free from restraints; and it was widely held that as individuals became more intelligent and more attuned to the moral law, there would be a decreasing need for government.[5] Evangelical Christianity, with its emphasis on individual regeneration, and transcendentalism, which identified the individual soul with God, served but to strengthen this faith. It was, indeed, in the writings of the transcendentalists Emerson and Thoreau that the doctrine of the free individual attained its classic expression in mid-nineteenth-century America. To Emerson, the self-reliant individual was more than a match for organized government, and he foresaw the day when the advance of the individual would render the state unnecessary.[6] Thoreau was even more contemptuous of the state, and in his famous essay "Civil Disobedience" carried individualism to a point where it became almost indistinguishable from anarchism.[7]

The teachings of classical political economy, which were brought to America from England and France, also helped to promote the idea of the negative state. Laissez faire was at the very core of the economic doctrines first proclaimed by the physiocrats in eighteenth-century France and more fully developed by the famous English economists, beginning with Adam Smith. It is with the physiocrats

[4] Haines, *Revival of Natural Law Concepts,* pp. 86–103; Wright, Jr., *American Interpretations of Natural Law,* pp. 288–291, 293–298.

[5] Ralph Henry Gabriel, *The Course of American Democratic Thought: An Intellectual History since 1815* (New York, 1940), pp. 4–6, 19–22; "American Political Ideas," *North American Review,* CI (October, 1865), 558.

[6] Ralph Waldo Emerson, "Self-Reliance," *Essays, First Series* (Boston, 1883), p. 87; Emerson, "Politics," *Essays, Second Series,* p. 206.

[7] *The Writings of Henry David Thoreau* (Riverside ed.; Boston, 1894), X, 131–170.

and the classical political economy that the term "laissez faire" is ordinarily associated.[8]

The physiocrats, reacting against the excessive mercantilist regulations of the France of their day, expressed a belief in a "natural order" of liberty under which individuals in following their selfish interests contributed to the general good. Since, in their view, this natural order functioned successfully without the aid of government, they advised the state to restrict itself to upholding the rights of private property and individual liberty, to removing all artificial barriers to trade, and to abolishing all useless laws. New laws, if required, the physiocrats contended, should merely enforce the laws of nature. Beyond these limits, the state should not venture: its policy should be one of "Laissez faire, laissez passer." [9]

The work of the physiocrats was eclipsed by Adam Smith's *Inquiry into the Nature and Causes of the Wealth of Nations*. Writing in 1776, at the dawn of the industrial revolution, Smith struck heavy blows at the prevailing mercantilist regulations. He proclaimed self-interest to be the chief psychological motivation of man in his pursuit of a livelihood and declared this to be not only natural but beneficial; for he, like the physiocrats, assumed the existence of a natural order wherein each man in pursuing his own economic interest unconsciously serves the general interest. The individual, Smith declared, "intends only his own gain," but he is "led by an invisible hand to promote an end which was no part of his intention."

Of mercantilist policies and practices Smith was highly critical. The system of "encouragements and restraints," he asserted, "retards . . . the progress of the society towards real wealth and greatness; and diminishes, instead of increasing, the real value of the annual produce of its land and labour." Although he was not a "doctrinaire

---

[8] Although Gournay, an associate of the physiocrats, is usually credited with having given currency to the expression "laissez faire, laissez passer," D. H. Macgregor ascribes the authorship of "laissez-faire as an economic principle" to the Marquis d'Argenson (1694–1757), a predecessor of the physiocrats. The physiocrats, he points out, rarely used the expression. Similarly, the English classical economists did not employ the term until John Stuart Mill in 1848 "pronounced it a rule of general practice." See Macgregor, *Economic Thought and Policy* (London, 1949), pp. 54–67; and "Laissez-Faire, Laissez-Passer, History of the Maxim," R. H. Inglis Palgrave, ed., *Dictionary of Political Economy* (London, 1894–1901), II, 534–535.

[9] Charles Gide and Charles Rist, *A History of Economic Doctrines from the Time of the Physiocrats to the Present Day* (Boston, n. d.), pp. 8–12, 33–34.

advocate of laissez faire," [10] Smith wished to replace mercantilism with the "obvious and simple system of natural liberty," in which "every man, as long as he does not violate the laws of justice, is left perfectly free to pursue his own interest his own way, and to bring both his industry and capital into competition with those of any other man, or order of men." The sovereign would then be relieved of the duty of directing the economic life of the nation, a task "for the proper performance of which no human wisdom or knowledge could ever be sufficient." [11]

Smith's successors as disseminators of economic doctrine, notably T. R. Malthus and David Ricardo, were much less optimistic than he as regards the beneficent operation of an unregulated economic order. They discovered laws that gave to political economy a pessimistic character, and caused it to be referred to as the "dismal science." Malthus pointed out that there is "a constant effort in the population to increase beyond the means of subsistence," with the result that the "lower classes of society" constantly tend to be subject to distress and cannot look forward to "any great permanent melioration of their condition." Poor laws, in Malthus' view, did not constitute a solution to this problem. The poor, he declared, must be taught "that they are themselves the cause of their own poverty; that the means of redress are in their own hands, and in the hands of no other persons whatever; that the society in which they live and the government which presides over it, are without any *direct* power in this respect." [12]

The wages-fund theory and Ricardo's "iron" law of wages, like the Malthusian law of population, offered little comfort to the laboring classes. According to the wages-fund theory, the general level of wages is determined by the quantity of capital set aside to pay wages as compared to the number of wage earners. Some of the classical economists intimated that the wages fund was at any particular time a fixed and predetermined sum and that therefore workers who suc-

[10] As Jacob Viner has pointed out, Smith "saw a wide and elastic range of activity for government, and he was prepared to extend it even farther if government . . . showed itself entitled to wider responsibilities. . . . He did not believe that laissez faire was always good, or always bad.   It depended on circumstances . . ." ("Adam Smith and Laissez Faire," in John Maurice Clark *et al., Adam Smith, 1776–1926* [Chicago, 1928], pp. 153–155).

[11] Smith, *An Inquiry into the Nature and Causes of the Wealth of Nations,* ed. Edwin Cannan (New York, 1937), pp. 421, 423, 650–651.

[12] Malthus, *An Essay on the Principle of Population* (6th ed.; London, 1826), I, 17; II, 287–288.

ceeded in increasing their wages did so only at the expense of other workers. Indeed, even were laborers to limit their progeny and thus reduce the number to whom the wages fund was distributed, they could not, according to Ricardo's law of wages, expect wages *in the long run* to rise above the level of subsistence.[13] "The natural price of labour," declared Ricardo, "is that price which is necessary to enable the labourers . . . to subsist and to perpetuate their race, without either increase or diminution." Ricardo's law presented a rather bleak prospect to the laborer, but the government was nevertheless instructed not to interfere on his behalf. "Like all other contracts," Ricardo declared, "wages should be left to the fair and free competition of the market, and should never be controlled by the interference of the legislature."[14] Malthus and Ricardo thus replaced the easy optimism of Adam Smith with a bleak pessimism. They were by no means indifferent to the fate of the workingman,[15] but they saw little possibility of altering by legislative reforms the course of the laws that they elucidated.

It remained for the Frenchman Frédéric Bastiat and the American Henry Carey to reassert the sanguine spirit of Adam Smith. Bastiat, for example, maintained that the natural laws of economics are beneficial and that "all legitimate interests are in harmony." So long as government is restricted to the maintenance of order, security, and justice, he asserted, there will be "free play of those laws of harmony which God has provided for the development and progress of the human race." This harmony of interests will result in a constantly rising level of living, for, as capital increases, the relative share going to the capitalist will decrease, whereas the relative share of the laborer will increase.[16]

By the middle of the nineteenth century, classical political economy

[13] Frank W. Taussig insists that the idea of a *rigid* wages fund was not "prominent" in the minds of the classical economists and that it is possible to infer that some of them actually believed the fund to be elastic, but he does concede that both Ricardo and, for a time, John Stuart Mill implied that the fund was fixed (*Wages and Capital: An Examination of the Wages Fund Doctrine* [New York, 1896], pp. 176–181, 214–215, 233–236).

[14] Ricardo, *On the Principles of Political Economy and Taxation* (3d ed.; London, 1821), pp. 86, 101–102. See also Malthus, *Principles of Political Economy* (2d ed.; London, 1836), p. 224.

[15] Lionel Robbins, *The Theory of Economic Policy in English Classical Political Economy* (London, 1952), pp. 70, 78–79, 82–84.

[16] Bastiat, *Harmonies of Political Economy* (London, 1860), pp. 1, 13–15, 183, 293.

consisted of a series of well-defined doctrines, arrived at, for the most part, deductively. The economists concentrated their attention on "economic man," a creature motivated by self-interest and devoted to the pursuit of wealth. "Political Economy," declared the youthful John Stuart Mill, "considers mankind as occupied solely in acquiring and consuming wealth." [17] Man as a social creature and the ethics of distribution were thus pretty much ignored.

The classical economists tended to describe the economic order as controlled by a set of natural laws analogous to those governing the physical order, and although they were by no means unqualified adherents of laissez faire, they were inclined to argue that human interference with these laws would be productive of nothing but harm. [18] The principle of free competition was the essential ingredient of most of the laws proclaimed by the classical economists, and, as Mill declared, it was only by the assumption of this principle that political economy had any "pretension to the character of a science. So far as rents, profits, wages, prices, are determined by competition," he asserted, "laws may be assigned for them." [19] Free competition was thus postulated as the great regulator of economic affairs, and government was advised not to interfere. This principle transcended national boundaries and led the English classical economists to advocate a policy of international free trade. [20]

The doctrine of laissez faire became an integral part of nineteenth-century European liberalism. Just as liberals supported freedom of thought in the intellectual sphere, so were they equally prepared to champion the principles of free trade and free competition in the sphere of economics. The state was to be merely a passive policeman, protecting private property and administering justice, but not interfering with the affairs of its citizens. Businessmen, and par-

[17] Mill, *Essays on Some Unsettled Questions of Political Economy* (London, 1844), pp. 137–138.

[18] For evidence that the classical economists were not completely doctrinaire in their support of laissez faire, see Robbins, *Theory of Economic Policy*, pp. 36–46; Macgregor, *Economic Thought and Policy*, pp. 80–87; and n. 21. Robbins contends that it was only insofar as the market "conformed to the conditions which they postulated" that the classical economists regarded government interference as harmful (*Theory of Economic Policy*, p. 57).

[19] Mill, *Principles of Political Economy* (from 5th London ed.; New York, 1881), I, 306.

[20] The chief tenets of classical political economy in the middle years of the nineteenth century are concisely set forth in Gide and Rist, *History of Economic Doctrines*, pp. 354–366.

ticularly British industrialists, were quick to associate these principles
with their own economic interests. International free trade would,
after all, ensure the preëminence of British manufactures, and laissez-
faire principles could always serve as a convenient excuse for dis-
claiming responsibility for the fate of the laboring class. Sentiments
of this sort produced the so-called Manchester School, made up of
merchants and manufacturers who sought to combat factory legislation and to secure the adoption of free trade. The latter objective
was successfully attained, but the Cobden-Bright group failed to
check the enactment of factory laws.[21]

Classical political economy was not long in finding its way to the
United States. Of special importance in this connection were the
works of Jean Baptiste Say and Harriet Martineau. Say's *Treatise on
Political Economy*, a restatement in polished form of the laissez-faire
creed, was the most widely used economics textbook in American
colleges up to the Civil War.[22] Miss Martineau's popular *Illustrations of Political Economy* set forth the principles of classical economics in story form and carried the doctrine of laissez faire to the
extreme. Social legislation, strikes, and even poor relief were denounced by Miss Martineau as injurious to society, and she entered
a plea for the "unimpeded operation" of the "entire system of commercial exchanges."[23]

Although the American college curriculum before the Civil War

[21] Carleton J. H. Hayes, *A Political and Cultural History of Modern Europe*
(New York, 1936), II, 73; W. Cunningham, *The Growth of English Industry and
Commerce in Modern Times* (Cambridge, England, 1917–1919), II, 630, 737–745;
"The Manchester School," Palgrave, ed., *Dictionary of Political Economy*, II, 678–
680; J. Salwyn Schapiro, *Liberalism and the Challenge of Fascism: Social Forces in
England and France (1815–1870)* (New York, 1949), pp. 60–110, 205–214.
Contrary to popular impression, the British classical economists were not uniformly
hostile to factory legislation and were generally sympathetic to factory legislation
for children. See Kenneth O. Walker, "The Classical Economists and the Factory
Acts," *Journal of Economic History*, I (November, 1941), 168–177; and Lloyd R.
Sorenson, "Some Classical Economists, Laissez Faire, and the Factory Acts," *ibid.*,
XII (Summer, 1952), 247–262.

[22] Anna Haddow, *Political Science in American Colleges and Universities,
1636–1900* (New York, 1939), p. 160.

[23] Martineau, *Illustrations of Political Economy*, Nos. I, II, VII, VIII, XII, XVI,
XVIII (London, 1832–1834); Joseph Dorfman, *The Economic Mind in American
Civilization, 1606–1918* (New York, 1946–1949), II, 708. Another economic
treatise of considerable influence in America was John Stuart Mill's *Principles of
Political Economy; with Some of Their Applications to Social Philosophy*, first pub-
lished in 1848. See Dorfman, *op. cit.*, II, 710–711. Mill, incidentally, thought that

did not generally make provision for political economy as an independent subject of study, but included it rather within the course in "moral philosophy," [24] the United States was not without its own authors of economic treatises. The most influential of such writers, at least within academic circles, was undoubtedly Brown University's distinguished president, Francis Wayland. Wayland's *Elements of Political Economy*, first published in 1837, had, by the time of the Civil War, gone through eighteen editions and was challenging the primacy of Say in American universities.[25] A minister, Wayland tended to associate the laws of economics with the laws of God, but his work did not depart in its essentials from the English classical economics. Wayland insisted that every man must be permitted to use his capital as he desires and that the legislator has no right to interfere. He attacked poor laws as contrary to the fundamental principles of government and as "destructive to the right of property, because they must proceed upon the concession, that the rich are under obligation to support the poor." "If this be so," declared Wayland, ". . . then the division of property and the right of property are at an end." Even the construction of internal improvements, such as roads, canals, and railroads, and the regulation of banks were considered by Wayland to be improper exercises of governmental power.[26]

Wayland was not alone among early American economists in his acceptance of the laissez-faire position of the British theorists; Thomas Cooper, John McVickar, Henry Vethake, Samuel Phillips Newman, George Frederick Holmes, J. Newton Cardozo, Francis Bowen, George Tucker, and John Bascom were similarly convinced that laissez faire was the only safe policy for government to pursue. Some of these men rejected Ricardo's theory of rent, and others among them found fault with the Malthusian law of population; but that in no way altered their view as regards the relation of the state to the individual. "Free

---

Miss Martineau reduced laissez faire to an "absurdity" (Robbins, *Theory of Economic Policy*, p. 44n.).

[24] The social sciences were generally included in the moral-philosophy course. See Gladys Bryson, "The Emergence of the Social Sciences from Moral Philosophy," *International Journal of Ethics*, XLII (April, 1932), 304–323.

[25] Michael J. L. O'Connor, *Origins of Academic Economics in the United States* (New York, 1944), p. 174; Haddow, *Political Science in American Colleges and Universities*, p. 160.

[26] Wayland, *The Elements of Political Economy* (3d ed.; Boston, 1840), pp. 15, 114–121, 126–127, 193–195, 295–306.

competition and denial of state interference was their dogma, economic liberty their slogan." [27]

II

As it expressed itself in Jeffersonian and Jacksonian democracy, the liberal tradition in America before the Civil War, in theory at least, was associated with the concept of the negative state. That government should minister directly to the needs of the people by positive action, that it should regulate to any extent the economic life of the nation, were ideas foreign to the liberals of Jefferson's and Jackson's time. The state was feared as an outside, and possibly oppressive, agency and as the potential tool of special interests. In the relatively simple, agrarian society that characterized the America of that day, liberals thought it best to reduce the functions of government to a minimum. They would entrust such activities of government as were necessary to the state governments, which were close to the people and thus subject to popular control; they would restrict the national government to the functions specifically assigned to it in the Constitution.

Thomas Jefferson was the embodiment of the liberal, agrarian tradition. In the agrarian society he loved so well, he would entrust a maximum of powers to the people, a minimum of powers to the state. He regarded the people as adults who could be relied on to govern themselves rather than as infants who required the care of nurses. On the other hand, as he informed Madison, he was "not a friend to

[27] J. F. Normano, *The Spirit of American Economics* (New York, 1943), p. 61. The thought of these individuals is summed up in Dorfman, *Economic Mind in American Civilization*, II, 516–522, 527–539, 551–566, 731–743, 752–755, 835–844, 920–928. Insofar as political economy was offered as a college subject before the Civil War, it was taught in strict conformity with the principles of laissez faire. Jeffersonians sought to further the study of political economy in the United States, and there is no doubt that mercantile interests in the Northeast found many of the teachings of the laissez-faire economists congenial, but on the whole it would appear that men of affairs and a practical bent of mind were little interested in the abstractions of the classical economists. Daniel Webster was giving voice to a common complaint when he declared that "there is no science that needs more to be cleared from mists than that of political economy." See Haddow, *Political Science in American Colleges and Universities*, pp. 160–161; O'Connor, *Origins of Academic Economics*, pp. 22–26, 56–58, 96–98; Normano, *Spirit of American Economics*, pp. 64–65; and Webster to Jared Sparks, October 12, 1826, *The Writings and Speeches of Daniel Webster* (National ed.; Boston, 1903), XVI, 125.

a very energetic government" because "it is always oppressive." [28]

What then should be the relationship of government to the economic life of the people? Jefferson's answer to this question was laissez faire. "Agriculture, manufactures, commerce, and navigation, the four pillars of our prosperity," he asserted, "are the most thriving when left most free to individual enterprise." He advocated "a wise and frugal government, which shall restrain men from injuring one another, which shall leave them otherwise free to regulate their own pursuits of industry and improvement, and shall not take from the mouth of labor the bread it has earned." Jefferson did not commend such a policy in the interests of property and property rights, but rather because he thought it the program best designed to promote the general welfare. It was for this second purpose, and not the first, that he believed governments were "instituted among men." "The only orthodox object of the institution of government," Jefferson wrote, "is to secure the greatest degree of happiness possible to the general mass of those associated under it." [29]

That other great exponent of Jeffersonian democracy, John Taylor, was no less an advocate of limited government than was Jefferson. Taylor regarded freedom and property as natural rights that are anterior to government and that government must protect. Since it was his contention that the state inevitably interferes with the right of the individual to the products of his labor, he regarded government as necesarily evil to a certain extent, and therefore advocated a policy of laissez faire. "The utmost favour which it is possible for a government to do for us farmers and mechanics," he asserted, "is neither to help nor hurt us." [30]

The Jacksonians were no less devoted than the Jeffersonians to the

[28] Jefferson to Du Pont de Nemours, April 24, 1816, in Dumas Malone, ed., *Correspondence between Thomas Jefferson and Pierre Samuel du Pont de Nemours, 1798–1817* (Boston, 1930), pp. 182–184; Jefferson to Madison, December 20, 1787, in Andrew A. Lipscomb, ed., *The Writings of Thomas Jefferson* (Library ed.; Washington, D.C., 1903–1904), VI, 391.

[29] Jefferson, "First Annual Message," December 8, 1801, *Writings of Jefferson*, III, 337; Jefferson, "Inauguration Address," March 4, 1801, *ibid.*, III, 320–321; Jefferson to F. A. Van Der Kemp, March 22, 1812, *ibid.*, XIII, 135–136. The social aspects of Jeffersonian democracy are interpreted in Charles Maurice Wiltse, *The Jeffersonian Tradition in American Democracy* (Chapel Hill, N. C., 1935), pp. 214–217, 238–267.

[30] Eugene Tenbroeck Mudge, *The Social Philosophy of John Taylor of Caroline* (New York, 1939), pp. 42–51, 161–164.

idea of limited government. Their party organ, the *Washington Globe*, proclaimed their conviction that "the world is governed too much." The Jacksonian drive against monopoly was not inconsistent with this belief: it was a negative rather than a positive approach to the problem of the relationship of the state to business. The Jacksonians would tolerate government intervention to remove monopoly, but such intervention was designed to restore a situation where competition would once again prevail and where government intervention would no longer be necessary. Thus Jackson's solution for the problem of the relationship of the government to the Second United States Bank was not to strengthen control of the government over the Bank, but rather to sever the connection between the two and thus destroy the Bank. The eastern Locofoco wing of the party was in full sympathy with this policy. Such Locofoco leaders as William Leggett believed, no less than Adam Smith, in laissez faire and a "natural order of things." They were certain that all persons would enjoy equal rights if only monopoly and special privileges were eradicated and competition given a free field.[31] The Jacksonians, like the Jeffersonians, were too suspicious of the exercise of state power to conceive of the state as a service agency.

Jackson's successor as president, Martin Van Buren, reaffirmed the hostility of the nineteenth-century liberal to the idea of the positive state. Van Buren did not believe that the people should look to government even during "periods of sudden embarrassment and distress." Government, he maintained, should not interfere with private pursuits. "It is not its legitimate object to make men rich or to repair by direct grants of money or legislation in favor of particular pursuits losses not incurred in the public service. This would be substantially to use the property of some for the benefit of others." The state can do most for the general welfare, Van Buren suggested, by not "assuming . . . such powers as were not designed to be conferred upon it." [32]

III

Opposed to the Jeffersonian-Jacksonian liberal tradition and its concept of the negative state was the Federalist-Whig program for

---

[31] Arthur M. Schlesinger, Jr., *The Age of Jackson* (Boston, 1945), pp. 314–317; William Trimble, "The Social Philosophy of the Loco-Foco Democracy," *American Journal of Sociology*, XXVI (May, 1921), 705–715.

[32] Van Buren, "Message to Special Session of Congress," September 4, 1837,

the positive state devoted to the interests of the business community. The greatest advocates of this program were Alexander Hamilton and Henry Clay.

Hamilton identified the prosperity of the state with that of the business classes. He would employ the government to dispense favors to men of industry and commerce, and the resultant economic benefits, he supposed, would percolate down to the other groups in society. For the latter, however, he would do nothing directly. His trust was placed in the "rich and well born" rather than in a "turbulent and changing" people, who "seldom judge or determine right." The vices of the wealthy he found "more favorable to the prosperity of the State than those of the indigent." He rejected the Jeffersonian idea that industry prospers in direct proportion to the degree in which it is left alone. "In matters of industry," he commented, "human enterprise ought, doubtless, to be left free in the main; not fettered by too much regulation; but practical politicians know that it may be beneficially stimulated by prudent aids and encouragements on the part of the government." [33] Here was the Federalist-Whig program in a nutshell: government aid to business, but no embarrassing government regulation.

To implement his views on the relationship of the federal government to the economy, Hamilton suggested the establishment of a privately owned Bank of the United States, the assumption by the federal government of the existing national and state debts, and government encouragement to manufactures. He proposed to accomplish this last objective by a protective tariff, the offer of bounties and premiums, and the setting up of a government board to promote the arts, agriculture, manufactures, and commerce. But Hamilton was opposed to taxes on profits or capital as contrary to the "genius of liberty" and the "maxims of industry." [34]

Henry Clay somewhat broadened the Hamiltonian scheme, and by his "American System" sought to enlist the support of the farmer

in James D. Richardson, comp., *A Compilation of the Messages and Papers of the Presidents, 1789–1902* (New York, 1903), III, 344–345.

[33] Hamilton, "Speeches in the Federal Convention," June 18, 1787, in Henry Cabot Lodge, ed., *The Works of Alexander Hamilton* (New York, 1885), I, 382; Hamilton, "Speech on the Compromises of the Constitution," *ibid.*, I, 436; Hamilton, "Examination of Jefferson's Message to Congress of December 7 [*sic*], 1801," *ibid.*, VII, 216.

[34] See Hamilton, "Report on Manufactures," *Works of Hamilton*, III, 294–416; and Dorfman, *Economic Mind in American Civilization*, I, 404–417.

as well as of the businessman for a program of government aid. Clay repudiated the idea that the state must pursue a hands-off policy with respect to trade. He thought that "it should be a prominent object with wise legislators, to multiply the vocations and extend the business of society, as far as it can be done, by the protection of our interests at home, against the injurious effects of foreign legislation." Not only would a protective tariff aid industry, but it would also build up a home market for the nonindustrial sections of the country. Clay sought further to win the support of the Western farmer by the second leading feature of his American System: internal improvements. He considered the construction of internal improvements a proper function of government, since a particular road or canal might be necessary before sufficient private capital was available to undertake the task.[35]

Clay, like Hamilton, was willing to use the state to deal out favors, but he was unlike Hamilton in trying to win support for such a program from the farmer as well as from the businessman. Neither man, however, thought the state should act as a regulatory agency. That was an idea alien to the Federalist-Whigs. A Daniel Webster could support the Whig program for a protective tariff and internal improvements and still insist that if great results were to be produced the government must entrust private enterprise "to the effect of fair competition" and must not intervene "under the false notion of protecting the poor."[36] The Federalist-Whigs abandoned laissez faire only in particulars that suited their best interests.

Paralleling the development of a program of economic nationalism in the arena of national politics was the emergence of a national school of political economy. This school was represented by such figures as Mathew and Henry Carey, Daniel Raymond, John Rae, Stephen Colwell, and Willard Phillips. These men rejected the pessimism of Malthus and of Ricardo as inapplicable to American conditions:

---

[35] Clay, "Speech on American Industry in the House of Representatives," March 30–31, 1824, in Calvin Colton, ed., *The Works of Henry Clay* (Federal ed.; New York, 1904), VI, 263–266, 290–293; Clay, "On Internal Improvements," February 4, 1817, *ibid.*, VI, 116–135.

[36] Webster, "The Reduction of the Duty on Coal," February 24, 1837, *The Works of Daniel Webster* (11th ed.; Boston, 1858), IV, 307. Despite his acceptance of the tariff and internal improvements, Webster adhered to laissez-faire views throughout his life. Expediency forced him to make departures from an economic philosophy which revealed "the unmistakable influence of Adam Smith." See Robert Lincoln Carey, *Daniel Webster as an Economist* (New York, 1929), p. 196.

American experience, they believed, had given the lie to the classical theories of wages, rent, population, diminishing returns, and free trade.[37] Repudiation of some of the central propositions of the classical economists did not, however, necessarily involve a wholesale abandonment on the part of these men of the doctrine of laissez faire. Their positive program, like that of Henry Clay, generally embraced little more than a protective tariff and, what was of lesser importance to them, government construction of internal improvements. With the exception of Daniel Raymond, who believed that government must seek to augment the national wealth, to regulate private property in the public interest, and to help those who could not help themselves,[38] when the national economists attacked laissez faire, they were really attacking free trade. They abhorred free trade as a policy designed to promote the interests of English industry at the expense of countries such as the United States, where manufacturing was in the infancy stage of development.[39]

The most important figure in the national school of political economy was Henry Carey, and his work can be taken as indicative of the philosophy of that group.[40] Carey was highly critical of the economics of Ricardo and Malthus and characterized their teachings as "unchristian." The state, he believed, must reject the policy of laissez faire (or, more correctly, free trade) and must exercise its "coordinating power" (by enacting a protective tariff). The protective tariff was to Carey the panacea for the nation's woes. Not only would

[37] Sidney Sherwood, "Tendencies in American Economic Thought," *Johns Hopkins University Studies in Historical and Political Science,* XV (December, 1897), 578–596; Normano, *Spirit of American Economics,* pp. 80–108; A. D. H. Kaplan, *Henry Charles Carey* (Baltimore, 1931), p. 30; Dorfman, *Economic Mind in American Civilization,* II, 566–574, 585–593, 771–826.

[38] Raymond, *The Elements of Political Economy* (2d ed.; Baltimore, 1823), II, 13–14, 29–84, 95–104, 121–122, 200–205. Mathew Carey was particularly solicitous of the needs of the poor, but he looked principally to private charity to cope with this problem. See Kenneth Wyer Rowe, *Mathew Carey* (Baltimore, 1933), pp. 101–102.

[39] "The limit of their Utopia," the Bernards declare of the Carey school, "was a protective tariff for the United States of America" (Luther Lee Bernard and Jesse Bernard, *Origins of American Sociology* [New York, 1943], p. 425). See also Henry C. Carey, *Principles of Social Science* (Philadelphia, 1858–1860), III, 440–442; and Rowe, *Mathew Carey,* pp. 50–106, 114–116.

[40] In his biography of Carey, Arnold W. Green (*Henry Charles Carey, Nineteenth-Century Sociologist* [Philadelphia, 1951], pp. 46 *et passim*) argues that Carey was more a sociologist than an economist.

it serve to increase the productiveness of labor and to diversify the modes of employment, but it "would find husbands for old maids and free the entire sex from an age-old bondage. The tariff would make Southern planters rich, but it would also ultimately free the slave. . . . The tariff would lower the bastardy rate, improve morals, eliminate crime and war." [41] And even the tariff, Carey suggested on occasion, was essential only so long as the United States remained industrially undeveloped.[42]

Like Bastiat, Carey saw a harmony of interests prevailing in the internal life of the nation. He therefore recommended that government action in this sphere be limited to the removal of all obstacles to "association." [43] Such a policy would require the government to construct internal improvements, to provide gas and water, to maintain schools and the post office, and to coin money. But Carey reminded reformers who would go beyond this that nature works slowly, and he declared his opposition to trade unions, to the regulation of hours and wages, and to public aid to the unemployed. As his most recent biographer has declared, Carey "approved of a dog-eat-dog individual competition within national boundaries." [44]

Although Carey and the national economists rejected much of the theory of classical political economy, they can hardly be considered advocates of the positive state.[45] The only major government policy that they recommended was the protective tariff. For the industrial society that they expected the tariff to produce, they had no real program.

IV

Whatever the theory, in practice the federal government and the state governments of the era before the Civil War did not confine

[41] See Carey, *Principles of Social Science,* I, 28–31, 94–233; III, 440–445; and Green, *Henry Carey,* p. 137.

[42] In *Principles of Social Science,* III, 442, Carey flatly stated that protection was only a temporary policy; but see Green, *Henry Carey,* pp. 140–141.

[43] Carey shifted the meaning of this term, but he usually used it to refer to "the progressive and utopian development whereby increasing population, decentralization of power and populations, increased diversity and specialization in the division of labor and its socio-psychological component, individualization, all took place together" (Green, *Henry Carey,* p. 73).

[44] See Carey, *Principles of Social Science,* III, 409–415, 469–470; and Green, *Henry Carey,* pp. 101, 123–127, 186.

[45] Cf. Gabriel, *Course of American Democratic Thought,* pp. 85–86.

their activities within the limits recommended by the advocates of laissez faire. The federal government became the promoter of a variety of economic enterprises. It constructed the National Road and military roads on the frontiers, purchased stock in four canal companies, provided surveys and land grants for wagon roads, canals, and railroads, assigned land to the states for the general purpose of internal improvements, and itself improved rivers and harbors. It appropriated the money for the first magnetic telegraph line in the United States. It sought to aid manufacturers in general by enacting a protective tariff and to aid manufacturers of small arms by advancing them funds without interest on government contracts. It promoted the nation's merchant marine by imposing tariff duties and tonnage taxes that discriminated in favor of United States shipping engaged in foreign commerce, by excluding foreign vessels from the coastwise trade, and by providing subsidies for steamships. To the codfishery it offered bounties on exports and a cash subsidy to owners and crews of vessels engaged in the industry. Also, it provided the states with land for both common schools and state universities.

On occasion the federal government thought it wise to regulate as well as to promote economic enterprise. Not only did it forbid the use of liquor in the fur trade and require the licensing and bonding of private fur traders, but it also set up its own fur "factories" as a yardstick for private enterprise in this line of endeavor. It constructed marine hospitals to care for sick and disabled seamen, and required monthly deductions from the wages of seamen to meet part of the cost of the program. It regulated in detail the conditions under which merchant seamen labored, and by the terms which it imposed on the recipients of the codfish bounty, it determined, in effect, how that industry should operate. In the interests of safety, Congress provided for the regulation of interstate steamboat operations. And although labor failed to persuade Congress to shorten the workday for government employees, President Van Buren in 1840 ordered the institution of a ten-hour day on the public works of the federal government.

Despite the range of the activities in which the federal government engaged in the period before the Civil War, it must be noted that as the era drew to a close the federal government tended to intervene less rather than more in the economic sphere. Although Jeffersonians and Jacksonians did not always adhere to their principles of limited government, it was Jefferson and Madison who allowed the First United States Bank to perish, and it was Jackson who destroyed the Second Bank. Presidential vetoes by Madison, Monroe, and Jackson placed obstacles in the path of federal aid to internal improvements, and under Jackson the National Road was turned over to the states. The Democrats reduced tariff rates substantially in the tariff acts of 1846 and 1857, and they killed steamship subsidies in 1858. Acts of 1815 and 1828 paved the way for the elimination of most of the discriminatory tariff duties and tonnage taxes that favored American ships engaged in foreign trade. The government abandoned its fur posts in 1822, and at the same time it weakened the regulations pertaining to private fur traders. Though importuned to do so, Congress refused to purchase Samuel Morse's patent, and permitted private enterprise to assume control of telegraphic communication. The program of government advances to the small-arms industry was largely abandoned after 1830. In the decade before the Civil War it was the Democrats who were in control of the national government, and they did not generally look with favor on programs of government aid.[46]

The state governments were even less inclined than the federal government to construe their functions in any narrow sense in the era before the Civil War.[47] They emerged from the colonial period and

[46] The account of the federal government's activities during the era before the Civil War is based on the following works: George Rogers Taylor, *The Transportation Revolution, 1815–1860* (New York, 1951), pp. 367–371 *et passim;* Benjamin Horace Hibbard, *A History of the Public Land Policies* (New York, 1924), pp. 228–247, 305–324, 338–339; Emory R. Johnson *et al., History of the Domestic and Foreign Commerce of the United States* (Washington, D.C., 1915), I, 336, and II, 161–163, 295–299, 301, 303–305, 308–310; Henry W. Farnam, *Chapters in the History of Social Legislation in the United States to 1860* (Washington, D.C., 1938), pp. 159–163, 231–251; Felicia Johnson Deyrup, *Arms Makers of the Connecticut Valley* (*Smith College Studies in History,* Vol. XXXIII) (Northampton, Mass., 1948), pp. 38, 41–43, 45–47, 117–119; Caroline E. MacGill *et al., History of Transportation in the United States before 1860* (Washington, D.C., 1917), pp. 12–18, 31–37, 139–142, 523–528, 584–605; and Katharine Coman, *Economic Beginnings of the Far West* (New York, 1912), I, 298–299, 344–346.

[47] This thesis is developed in detail in Oscar Handlin and Mary Flug Handlin, *Commonwealth: A Study of the Role of Government in the American Economy: Massachusetts, 1774–1861* (New York, 1947); in Louis Hartz, *Economic Policy and Democratic Thought: Pennsylvania, 1776–1860* (Cambridge, Mass., 1948); and in James Neal Primm, *Economic Policy in the Development of a Western State: Missouri, 1820–1860* (Cambridge, Mass., 1954). With regard to Georgia, Milton Sydney Heath notes that "the spirit of *laissez faire* was ever pervasively present and

the era of the Revolution with a full complement of powers in the fields of licensing, inspection, and incorporation, and they continued to wield these powers throughout the period preceding the Civil War, although some adaptation to changing economic conditions proved necessary.[48] The state governments did not hesitate to become promoters of economic enterprise. Anticipating large profits from the banking business or seeking to fill local credit needs, they subscribed to the stock of state banks, loaned such banks the credit of the state, or even established their own banks. However, the panic of 1837 produced considerable antibank sentiment, and by the end of the 1840's most of the states had withdrawn from active participation in the banking business.[49]

The states also assumed the initiative with regard to internal improvements. Since private capital was not available in amounts sufficient to develop the arteries of transportation deemed necessary by the public, state governments either furnished aid of one sort or another to companies chartered to build turnpikes, canals, or railroads, or they actually undertook the task of construction themselves. Many states, however, either because they had assumed undue financial risks or because of their own administrative shortcomings, saw their internal-improvement programs end in disaster. This fact caused some states, particularly in the 1840's, to impose constitutional restrictions of one sort or another on state action with respect to internal improvements, but it did not halt all state and local activity in this field, nor did it prevent state and local governments that desired to do so from aiding railroads in the two decades before the Civil War and in subsequent years.[50] The states also subsidized

its influence reflected repeatedly," but "it enjoyed no extended period of ascendancy" (*Constructive Liberalism: The Role of the State in Economic Development in Georgia to 1860* [Cambridge, Mass., 1954], p. 388).

[48] Handlin and Handlin, *Commonwealth*, pp. 67–143; Hartz, *Economic Policy and Democratic Thought*, pp. 6–7, 37–42, 204–207; Taylor, *Transportation Revolution*, pp. 378–379.

[49] Guy S. Callender, "The Early Transportation and Banking Enterprises of the States in Relation to the Growth of Corporations," *Quarterly Journal of Economics*, XVII (November, 1902), 113–114, 160–162; William J. Shultz and M. R. Caine, *Financial Development of the United States* (New York, 1937), pp. 126, 147–148, 182–183, 203–204, 228, 243–244. Missouri was one of a few states that continued to participate in the banking business after the 1840's. See Primm, *Economic Policy in Missouri*, pp. 70–71.

[50] Callender, "The Early Transportation and Banking Enterprises of the States in Relation to the Growth of Corporations," *Quarterly Journal of Economics*,

agricultural and industrial fairs, provided bounties for the growing of certain crops, and, in one case at least, loaned money to farmers on mortgage security.[51]

Impelled by the force of Jacksonian democracy, state governments somewhat cautiously entered the field of social reform. Jacksonians evidently discovered that a certain amount of state action would be necessary before the "natural forces" could hold sway. They consequently helped push through state legislation abolishing imprisonment for debt, prohibiting the liquor traffic, extending the public-education system, exempting homesteads from forced sale in order to satisfy the claims of creditors, and recognizing the responsibility of the state toward the insane.[52] There were even some half-hearted attempts at labor legislation.[53] In this field, however, as in the spheres of

XVII (November, 1902), 112–113, 151–159; Edward C. Kirkland, *A History of American Economic Life* (3d ed.; New York, 1951), pp. 228–230, 254–259; Hartz, *Economic Policy and Democratic Thought*, pp. 82–180; Handlin and Handlin, *Commonwealth*, pp. 183–194; Primm, *Economic Policy in Missouri*, pp. 101–105; Carter Goodrich, "The Revulsion against Internal Improvements," *Journal of Economic History*, X (November, 1950), 147–151; Taylor, *Transportation Revolution*, pp. 25–26, 48–52, 92–94, 381–382.

[51] Taylor, *Transportation Revolution*, pp. 380–381; Percy Wells Bidwell and John I. Falconer, *History of Agriculture in the Northern United States, 1620–1860* (Washington, D.C., 1925), pp. 189–190, 193; Primm, *Economic Policy in Missouri*, pp. 115–120.

[52] Carl Russell Fish, *The Rise of the Common Man, 1830–1850* (New York, 1927), pp. 216–221, 256–267; Arthur Charles Cole, *The Irrepressible Conflict, 1850–1865* (New York, 1934), pp. 160–164, 205–209; Farnam, *Chapters in the History of Social Legislation*, pp. 150–152.

[53] In 1842 Massachusetts enacted a ten-hour law for children under twelve, and by 1860 seven states had enacted some legislation on the subject. The labor of children under twelve was prohibited in Pennsylvania after 1848, and three other states had followed this precedent in some form by the time of the Civil War. By 1851 five states had established ten hours as the working day for female labor in the absence of contracts to the contrary. New York enacted the first mechanics' lien law in 1830. Most of these labor laws were poorly enforced. See John R. Commons and John B. Andrews, *Principles of Labor Legislation* (4th rev. ed.; New York, 1936), pp. 95–96, 100–101, 117, 169–170, 337. That laissez-faire ideas occasionally served as a barrier to legislation of this type is indicated by the report in 1845 of the Committee on Hours of Labor of the Massachusetts House of Representatives. The report acknowledged the existence of abuses and the need for shorter hours and more safety provisions, but declared that the remedy was not in legislation "but in the progressive improvement in art and science, in a higher appreciation of man's destiny, in a less love for money and a more ardent love for social happiness and intellectual superiority" (H. Doc. No. 50, *Documents Printed by Order of the House of Representatives of the Commonwealth of Massachusetts during the Session of the General Court, A.D. 1845* [Boston, 1845], p. 16).

public health and corrections and charities, the states evidenced little recognition of their obligations to their citizens.[54]

Although the doctrine of laissez faire thus appears to have been of relatively slight import in the formulation of state policy before the Civil War, there were indications as the period drew to a close that state activity was on the wane. Private rather than public enterprise had come to dominate banking and transportation, and although the states continued to exercise regulatory functions in both areas and to provide abundant aid to the railroads, they were, everything considered, no longer so conspicuous in either of these fields as they had been before 1840. Moreover, the same state governments that had so boldly assumed the role of promoter of business enterprise evidenced an unwonted timidity when it came to providing legislative assistance to the laboring man. It was an omen for the future that businessmen, rising in power and better able than at an earlier date to carry on without state aid, were talking in the 1840's and 1850's of the necessity of restricting the functions of the state and were beginning to challenge state actions which, in their view, interfered with property rights.[55]

Unfortunately for those who fought the intellectual battle against laissez faire in the decades after the Civil War, the experience of the federal government and of the state governments in the era before Appomattox did not give rise to any important body of thought that would serve to justify extensive government intervention in the economic life of the nation. Those who argued for or against laissez faire between 1865 and 1901 generally spoke little of the earlier, varied activities of government in the United States, and tended to assume that laissez faire had been the determining factor in the formulation of government policy.

V

The United States of 1900 was quite a different place from the United States of 1860, for during the intervening years America was transformed from an agricultural society into an industrialized, urbanized society. In 1860 the total capital invested in manufacturing

[54] Before the Civil War, for example, there were no state boards of health or state boards of corrections and charities. Also, despite the legislation already noted, most states paid very little attention to the labor problem before 1885.

[55] Louis Hartz, *The Liberal Tradition in America* (New York, 1955), pp. 215–216; Hartz, *Economic Policy and Democratic Thought*, pp. 166–169, 309–320; Goodrich, "The Revulsion against Internal Improvements," *Journal of Economic History*, X (November, 1950), 161–162; Taylor, *Transportation Revolution*, pp. 382–383.

was something over one billion dollars; by 1900 the figure had jumped to almost ten billion dollars. During the same period the number of wage earners increased from approximately 1,300,000 to about 5,300,000. By 1900 the total value of the products of manufacturing industries was almost two and one-half times as great as the total value of farm products. And whereas 16.1 per cent of the American people lived in cities of 8,000 inhabitants or more in 1860, by 1900 the proportion living in such communities had increased to 32.9 per cent.[56]

Industrialization and urbanization intensified old problems and brought with them a host of new ones. The American people had to decide what to do about slums and tenements, public health, the wages, hours, and working conditions of standard and substandard labor, unemployment, and increased inequalities in the distribution of wealth, railroads, and industrial combinations. Although, for the most part, the intervention of government was required for the solution of these issues, existing theories with respect to the role of the state constituted an intellectual barrier to the development of any realistic program of state action. Jeffersonian-Jacksonian liberalism was already an anachronism in the America of the years after the Civil War. Its policy of "the less government the better," of laissez faire, was designed to meet the needs of a fairly simple agrarian society; it was insufficient, to say the least, to deal with the social and economic problems of an industrial age. Nor did the Federalist-Whig program of government aid but no government regulation come any closer to being a satisfactory solution for the troubles of the new America. The Republican party, heir to the Federalist-Whig tradition, was in control of the state after Appomattox. With lavish hand it met the demands of the business community for tariffs and land grants. But here its paternalism ended, and it refused to provide in the same fashion for the needs of farmers and laborers. "Whiggery" accorded nicely with the desires of industrial leaders, but it fell far short of being an adequate program for the general welfare.[57]

[56] U. S. Bureau of the Census, *Abstract of the Twelfth Census of the United States, 1900* (Washington, D.C., 1904), pp. 300–301; U. S. Bureau of Foreign and Domestic Commerce, *Statistical Abstract of the United States, 1921* (Washington, D.C., 1922), pp. 862, 868; U. S. Bureau of the Census, *Fifteenth Census of the United States,* I (*Population*) (Washington, D.C., 1931), p. 9.

[57] The most colorful short picture of the philosophy of the Gilded Age is to be found in Vernon Louis Parrington, *The Beginnings of Critical Realism in America* (New York, 1930), pp. 7–26.

Thus in 1865, though Americans saw a new industrial society emerging, they were without an adequate philosophy of state action to cope with the problems of that society. What was needed was a new philosophy of the state, a new liberalism embodying something of the spirit of Jeffersonianism but ready to use government as an agency to promote the general welfare. Industrial America made necessary the evolution of the general-welfare state.

THE ARGUMENT FOR
LAISSEZ FAIRE

PREFATORY NOTE

IN THE period between Appomattox and the accession of Theodore Roosevelt to the presidency, in 1901, laissez faire was championed in America as it never was before and has never been since. Social Darwinists, professional and popular economists, sociologists, political scientists, businessmen, clergymen, and lawyers and judges joined in extolling the virtues of the negative state. Although they differed in the degree of consistency with which they applied their doctrines, the advocates of laissez faire were agreed that that government is best which governs least.

In their definition of the proper functions of the state, the social Darwinists, taking their cue from Herbert Spencer, came the closest among American supporters of laissez faire to the laissez-faire ideal of anarchy plus the constable. There was no place in the social-Darwinist scheme of things for the public school, the state insane asylum, the state poor house, the state board of health, or the state post office. In the state envisioned by the followers of Spencer, the tasks of government could be adequately performed by the policeman and the judge.

Most American academic and popular theorists of laissez faire did not apply the tenets of laissez faire so rigorously as did Spencer and the social Darwinists. The model government in their view was not only policeman and judge, but also postmaster, schoolteacher, and perhaps, to a limited degree, guardian of the "unfit." But if most American adherents of laissez faire were willing to allow the state to do a bit more than intransigent social Darwinists thought necessary, they were rather definitely opposed to any extensive government interference in the social and economic life of the nation. The protective tariff, a managed currency, labor legislation, and social legislation in general were to them anathema.

The businessman's version of laissez faire, unlike that of the social Darwinist or the political economist, was essentially a rationalization of the *status quo*. Identifying his prosperity with that of the nation, the businessman accepted without question such favors as a protective tariff and generous land grants that were extended to him by a sympathetic government, and yet he insisted that it was a flagrant violation of the precepts of laissez faire for the state to concern itself too greatly with the manner in which he conducted his business or to afford legislative assistance to farmers and laborers. Since the successful businessman was the most influential social type of the Gilded Age, existing institutions, and especially the church, tended to endorse his views.

The ideas of laissez faire propounded after the Civil War were dressed up in constitutional garb by bench and bar and made an integral part of the fundamental law. Just as the Federalist view of things remained entrenched in the courts long after the Federalists had been overthrown in the political arena, so laissez faire was to find a last refuge in the courts after it had gone down to defeat both in the realm of theory and in the realm of political practice.

Those who advocated a policy of laissez faire in the years after the Civil War seemingly were conforming to the best traditions of European and American liberalism. But liberalism, although its objectives remain constant, is not "mortgaged to any particular system or method," and must adjust the means that it employs to the existing facts. Since liberalism originated essentially as a protest against an authoritarian order in religion, politics, and economics, it was at the outset a purely negative faith, one aimed at removing the artificial restrictions that blocked human progress. Thus, with respect to government and economics, it became associated with laissez faire and economic freedom. In a complex industrial society, however, if the liberal objectives of individual freedom and equality of opportunity are to be realized it becomes necessary to extend the sphere of social control. The result has been that liberalism, which started out as an essentially negative creed designed to do away with obstructions to individual progress, "has developed as a positive effort to better man's estate by constructive action." [1]

Those who in the industrial order that was emerging in the United

[1] See A. A. Berle, Jr., "A Liberal Program and Its Philosophy," in Seymour Harris, ed., *Saving American Capitalism* (New York, 1948), pp. 41–43, 46; L. T. Hobhouse, *Liberalism* (London, [1911]), pp. 18–19, 138–165; W. Lyon Blease, A

States after the Civil War continued to advocate the laissez-faire brand of liberalism tended to establish economic freedom as an end in itself rather than as a means to an end,[2] and were out of harmony with the true spirit of liberalism. They were blind to the compelling necessity for social and economic reform and refused to recognize that some positive action on the part of the state was essential to assure the effective liberty of the individual. Laissez faire in the years after 1865 was the doctrine of the conservatives.[3]

Short History of English Liberalism (London, 1913), p. 328; and Jacob Hollander, *Economic Liberalism* (New York, 1925), pp. 13–14.

[2] Robert Green McCloskey, *American Conservatism in the Age of Enterprise: A Study of William Graham Sumner, Stephen J. Field, and Andrew Carnegie* (Cambridge, Mass., 1951), pp. 15–16.

[3] Clinton Rossiter, appropriately enough, describes the conservatism of the period after 1865 as "laissez-faire conservatism" (*Conservatism in America* [New York, 1955], pp. 134–135).

II

HERBERT SPENCER VERSUS THE STATE

THE most influential opponent of the state in the America of the Gilded Age was not an American but an Englishman. His name was Herbert Spencer. Today, Spencer is little remembered in the United States, but in the years from 1865 to 1901 his was a name of transcendent importance in the world of thought. Nowhere was he more admired than in the United States, and nowhere did his strictures against the state find a more appreciative audience.

To Spencer, laissez faire was more than just a maxim to be applied to the market place. He would make it the guiding policy in the whole sphere of human activities. "I do not think," he wrote, "that *laissez-faire* is to be regarded simply as a politico-economical principle only, but as a much wider principle—the principle of letting all citizens take the benefits and evils of their own acts: not only such as are consequent on their industrial conduct, but such as are consequent upon their conduct in general." [1]

Descended from a long line of nonconformists, Spencer was throughout his life an opponent of the state. In his first work of any significance, a series of twelve letters written for the *Nonconformist* in 1842 and entitled *The Proper Sphere of Government*, he was bitterly critical of all but the most rudimentary state functions. Six years later he became subeditor of the *Economist* and, as such, came under the influence of the strongly antistatist Thomas Hodgskin, disciple of William Godwin. It was Hodgskin who suggested the title of Spencer's most important work on the state, *Social Statics*, first published in 1851. [2]

[1] Spencer to J. E. Cairnes, March 21, 1873, in David Duncan, *Life and Letters of Herbert Spencer* (New York, 1908), I, 213.

[2] F. C. J. Hearnshaw, ed., *The Social and Political Ideas of Some Representative Thinkers of the Victorian Age* (London, 1933), pp. 58–59.

From 1862 to 1896 Spencer was engaged in the writing of *A System of Synthetic Philosophy*. In ten ponderous volumes he sought to apply the new evolutionary hypothesis to the whole domain of human knowledge. This work brought Spencer to the forefront as an expositor of the theory of evolution, and gained him world-wide acclaim. But with Spencer, this vast undertaking was less an attempt to explore the ramifications of Darwin's theory than it was an effort to find scientific justification for his own social philosophy and prejudices. Spencer himself readily admitted this—in the preface to one of the volumes of the *Synthetic Philosophy* he declared that his *Proper Sphere of Government* had set forth his views on "right and wrong in political conduct," and that from that time forward his "ultimate purpose, lying behind all proximate purposes . . . [had] been that of finding for the principles of right and wrong in conduct at large, a scientific basis." [3] His *Synthetic Philosophy*, by his own word, was designed as "a basis for a right rule of life, individual and social." [4]

Spencer's views on government were first made familiar to Americans in 1865, when *Social Statics* appeared in an American edition. These ideas were restated and amplified, but never materially altered, in a series of essays entitled *The Man versus the State* and in various portions of the *Synthetic Philosophy*. Spencer presented to Americans in these works a new version of laissez faire, one that rested not on economic theory but on "Spencerian" sociology and biology.

Two closely associated laws were at the center of Spencer's analysis of the proper field for state action: the "law of equal freedom" and the "law of conduct and consequence" or of the "survival of the fittest." The law of equal freedom proclaimed that "every man has freedom to do all that he wills, provided he infringes not on the equal freedom of any other man." Spencer at first declared this law to be an expression of the will of God; but he later found a biological necessity for it and associated it with his second law, the law of conduct and consequence. [5]

---

[3] Spencer, *The Data of Ethics* (New York, 1883), p. v. Hearnshaw declares that Spencer was dominated by two ideas, liberty in the sphere of politics and evolution in the sphere of science, but that of these liberty was the more important. "With this love he was born, and his early environment tended to foster it. His intellectual passion for Evolution was a later and acquired characteristic. He saw in Evolution the veritable tree of knowledge; but to him Liberty was the incomparably superior tree of life" (*Social and Political Ideas of Some Representative Thinkers of the Victorian Age*, p. 60).

[4] Spencer, *An Autobiography* (New York, 1904), II, 369–370.

[5] Spencer, *Social Statics* (London, 1851), pp. 77–103. In his later writings on

The law of conduct and consequence derived from the fact that Spencer saw the same struggle for existence going on among human beings as among lower creatures. He insisted that if the human species were to be preserved, it, like any other species, would have to permit the distribution of benefits in proportion to merit, merit being measured by the power to sustain oneself. If conduct and consequence were thus associated, if each person received the benefits or suffered the evil results of his own actions, the individual best adapted to his environment would prosper most, the one least adapted would prosper least, and, as a result, the fittest would survive and progress would be assured. On the other hand, were the superior individual in any way made to assume the burdens of the inferior, the general welfare of the species would be adversely affected; for this would hinder the increase of the superior and encourage the increase of the inferior, the "good-for-nothings," thus halting "that natural process of elimination by which society continually purifies itself." [6]

Spencer therefore considered his law of conduct and consequence but an affirmation of simple justice, and saw no ethical warrant for any interference with its operation. He recognized two elements in the functioning of this law and in any true conception of justice—a positive element and a negative element. The positive element, he explained, involves a recognition of the claim of every individual to pursue without restraint such activities as he desires and to enjoy the benefits he can derive therefrom; the negative element implies that limits are placed on each man's rights by the presence of other men having similar rights. In short, conduct and consequence and survival of the fittest had led Spencer once again to his law of equal freedom as "an ultimate ethical principle having an authority transcending every other." [7]

An additional factor that conditioned Spencer's attitude regarding the efficacy of state action, or, for that matter, of any human effort, was his conviction that society is an organism governed by natural laws that override the human will. Legislators, Spencer asserted, fail

---

the state, Spencer substituted a naturalistic, evolutionary approach for the supernaturalistic approach employed in *Social Statics*. He withdrew his earlier objections to private property in land, but, on the whole, his conclusions remained the same. See *The Principles of Ethics* (New York, 1897), II, x.

[6] Spencer, *Principles of Ethics*, II, 6–7, 17; Spencer, "Sins of Legislators," in *The Man versus the State* (New York, 1885), pp. 64–66; Spencer, *The Study of Sociology* (New York, 1896), p. 315.

[7] Spencer, *Principles of Ethics*, II, 35–61.

to recognize this fact. They look upon society as a "manufacture" rather than as a "growth" and seek to mold it to suit their whims. They do not realize that the evolution of society cannot be changed in any essential way, that institutions are too deeply rooted to permit of great alterations. It is, indeed, an "impious presumption" for "political schemers, with their clumsy mechanisms," to attempt to "supersede the great laws of existence." Although there is a gigantic plan at work in the universe and all things are in harmony, the government official comes with his red tape "to put a patch upon nature." Unimpressed by "the wonders that encompass him," he "dares to announce that he and certain of his colleagues have . . . found out a way to improve upon the Divine arrangements!" [8]

Furthermore, Spencer contended, legislators seem ignorant of the fact that, because of the interdependency of institutions and the complexity of influences operating on the individual and on society, the results of specific political acts cannot be calculated. They are unaware that proximate causes have their remote antecedents and that primary effects are followed by secondary and tertiary effects. Society is so complex that a law, although it rarely produces the result desired, invariably has indirect consequences that were not anticipated. Man must therefore see "how comparatively little can be done, and yet find it worthwhile to do that little." As for great changes, they will have to await the slow changes in the character of the individual. The legislator must sit back and watch nature take its course. By his actions he can hinder the operation of natural laws, but he can in no way improve upon them. [9]

In government Spencer put but little trust. He saw man's history as a progression from more to less government, and he thought it a mistake to believe that the state would last forever. As civilization advances, he declared, government will decay. It is essentially immoral and exists because of evil and by evil: "Its continuance is proof

[8] Spencer, *Social Statics*, pp. 293–294.

[9] Spencer, *Study of Sociology*, pp. 1–21, 245, 365–367; Spencer, "Sins of Legislators," in *Man versus the State*, pp. 74–77; Spencer, *Principles of Ethics*, II, 428. Spencer could not agree with his American friend Andrew Carnegie that America's material progress was the product of democratic institutions. "A large part, if not the greater part, of what you ascribe to democracy," he wrote to Carnegie on May 18, 1886, "is, it seems to me, simply the result of social growth in a region furnishing abundant space and material for it, and which would have gone on in a substantially similar way under another form of government" (Andrew Carnegie Papers, Library of Congress).

of still-existing barbarism." Like Ralph Waldo Emerson, Spencer believed that with the development of the moral sense, society would become harmonious and external restraints unnecessary.[10]

In his later works Spencer distinguished between the military and the industrial types of society. The military society, he explained, is characterized by status, and self-preservation is its primary objective. The individual is subordinated to the state, and government must assume a variety of functions, both negative and positive. The industrial society, on the contrary, is characterized by contract. The individual is no longer subordinated to the state, but is, rather, defended by it. Life, liberty, and property are secure; there is no interference by the state between conduct and consequence; and the survival of the fittest is thus ensured. All public organizations except those for administering justice tend to disappear.[11]

Spencer contrasted the efficiency and vigor of private business with the inefficiency and lack of enterprise of the state. He castigated officialism as slow, stupid, extravagant, unadaptable, corrupt, and lacking in vitality. He feared that state superintendence would result in national enervation, and would destroy the self-confidence of the people.[12] Whatever the people deem beneficial, Spencer insisted, they will do for themselves by "spontaneous co-operation." If they do not voluntarily unite to accomplish some necessary task, it is wrong to assume that a law-appointed portion of them can do the job. Because of the "mediocrity of intellect" that "necessarily characterizes representative government," such government is ill-suited to perform the complex task of regulating the affairs of the nation.[13]

Spencer did not believe that government creates any rights, but, rather, looked upon it as a mere "committee of management" established to protect rights that had already been developed among individuals living in a social state. Government, he argued, must

[10] Spencer, *Social Statics*, pp. 13–14, 206–208, 215–216, 241. The abridged 1896 edition of *Social Statics* contains no mention of the ultimate disappearance of the state. Spencer's views with respect to state activities, however, remained the same as in the first edition.

[11] Spencer, *The Principles of Sociology* (New York, 1880–1897), II, 568–642, 659–662.

[12] Spencer, "Over-Legislation," in *Essays: Moral, Political and Aesthetic* (New York, 1865), pp. 67–72, 99–103.

[13] Spencer, "Representative Government," *ibid.*, pp. 163–209; Spencer, "Specialized Administration," in *Man versus the State,* ed. Truxton Beale (New York, 1916), pp. 317–333.

therefore limit its activity to enforcement of the law of equal freedom, that is, to the administration of justice and to the protection of the citizen from external and internal aggression. It has no ethical sanction for assuming any additional functions. So long as it restricts itself to protecting the rights of its members, it enjoys universal support, but let it assume a single additional duty and it immediately produces dissent among those who do not favor that particular activity and trenches upon their right to do as they please provided they do not injure others. Each extra function assumed brings new dissenters, individuals whose liberty is not provided for by the function in question and who do not want to be taxed for its performance. Eventually, there is scarcely a man to whom the state is not doing, in some degree, the opposite of what it was set up to do.[14]

Each organ, Spencer argued, should perform only the function for which it was designed. Once it assumes additional duties, it dissipates its energy and becomes unable to perform satisfactorily the original task for which it was created. The state, therefore, should concentrate on the "negatively regulative" functions of protection and administration of justice for which it was designed, and should abandon its "positively regulative" controls. If the state is to be efficient in maintaining equitable relations among its citizens, it must abandon all general-welfare functions.[15]

To limit government to the performance of its negatively regulative duties was considered by Spencer to be in the best interests of the individual and of society. The individual whose faculties are fully developed, he believed, needs no aid. When the state does something for him, it prevents him from effectually exercising his powers, and thus diminishes his happiness. State aid is also harmful to the individual whose capacities are not altogether adequate, for it prevents him from making the necessary adaptation to his environment, and thus retards his growth. Social retrogression is the inevitable result when-

[14] Spencer, "The Great Political Superstition," in *Man versus the State,* pp. 92–98, 105–107; Spencer, *Social Statics,* pp. 253–254, 269, 275–278.

[15] Spencer, "Specialized Administration," in *Man versus the State* (1916 ed.), pp. 312–314, 332–336. Confusing laissez faire with anarchism, Spencer on various occasions declared that inasmuch as he would permit the extension of state activity in its special, negatively regulative sphere, his policy was not one of laissez faire. However, no advocate of laissez faire contended that the state should not protect property and administer justice. See "Spencer's Impressions of America," *Popular Science Monthly,* XXII (December, 1882), 273; and Spencer, *Study of Sociology,* pp. 320–322.

ever man is compelled to adjust to artificial conditions that are imposed by the state.[16]

Rigidly applying his laws of equal freedom and conduct and consequence, Spencer condemned all the positively regulative functions that the governments of his day had assumed. Poor laws and sanitary laws, systems of public education, government-owned post offices, government regulation of the currency and of labor conditions, public works, and tariffs were all censured by Spencer as violating the principles of justice and as interfering with human progress.

The state, he insisted, may not, through poor laws, tax individuals to mitigate distress. "If it takes from him who has prospered to give to him who has not, it violates its duty towards the one to do more than its duty towards the other." Poor laws serve but to halt the "purifying process" by which society excretes the unfit. If the poor and the weak cannot adapt themselves to their environment, it is better to let them perish than to encourage their multiplication and thus burden future generations. "The poverty of the incapable, the distresses that come upon the imprudent, the starvation of the idle, and those shoulderings aside of the weak by the strong . . . are the decrees of a large, far-seeing benevolence." [17]

Spencer was equally rigid in his excoriation of all public-health measures. If a man is not intelligent enough to look after himself, declared Spencer, let him die. Inconvenience, suffering, and death are the penalties imposed by nature on ignorance. There is nothing harsh about this. It is merely nature's way of improving the race by "weeding out those of lowest development." Sanitary measures, moreover, lead to greater deductions from a citizen's income than are necessary to maintain his rights and result in the diminution of the "social vitality" (Spencer regarded "the amount of vital force pervading society" as limited and, at any given time, fixed) with which other functions of the social organism are performed.[18]

Even the education of its citizens was considered by Spencer an improper function for the state. Since education, he contended, is

[16] Spencer, *Social Statics,* pp. 280–282.

[17] Spencer, *Social Statics,* pp. 311–329. Spencer considered the unemployed "simply good-for-nothings, who . . . live on the good-for-somethings—vagrants and sots, criminals and those on the way to crime, youths who are burdens on hardworked parents, men who appropriate the wages of their wives, fellows who share the gains of prostitutes; and then, less visible and less numerous . . . a corresponding class of women" ("The Coming Slavery," in *Man versus the State,* pp. 18–19).

[18] Spencer, *Social Statics,* pp. 372–395.

not necessary to maintain the individual's rights, the state has no authority to take a person's property so as to educate either his own children or the children of his neighbor. If all children are to be educated at the public expense, the poor man will not hesitate to marry and raise children and will not exercise the same self-restraint that he would were education not state-supported. It is far better to trust to the discipline of nature than to weaken the character of the parent by removing one of the chief reasons for parental responsibility. Also, if education is limited to the state, the state will decide just what type of citizen its school system should produce and will then seek to make all conform to this pattern. With education, therefore, as with every other commodity, the "interest of the consumer" should prevail.[19]

Spencer believed the right of exchange to be as "sacred" as other rights. All government restrictions on trade, he asserted, infringe on the liberty of the individual. For the state to regulate the currency by making its notes legal tender is for it to violate the law of equal freedom. A government mint interferes with the liberty of the citizen to set up his own mint. Similarly, a government monopoly of the postal function is a violation of private rights. Public works are to be condemned as involving the use of taxes for other purposes than the maintenance of public rights. Tariffs and bounties and laws for the benefit of laborers are likewise unjustified. In all these respects, Spencer found the law of equal freedom and the teachings of political economy to be in agreement.[20]

Spencer would permit the mitigation of "superfluous sufferings" by the exercise of beneficence as a private, but not as a public, function. He recognized two types of private beneficence—negative and positive. The exercise of negative beneficence, he explained, requires that one remain passive when advantage might be taken of a given situation, as in competition or in the making of a contract. Positive beneficence, on the other hand, takes the form of aid to the sick and injured and to the poor, but in such a way as not to permit the "incapable" and "degraded" to multiply.[21]

As Spencer looked out upon the world of the 1880's, he found that,

[19] Spencer, *Social Statics*, pp. 330–356.

[20] Spencer, *Social Statics*, pp. 296–304, 396–406, 459–460; Spencer, "Parliamentary Reforms: The Dangers, and the Safeguards," in *Essays: Moral, Political and Aesthetic*, pp. 355–366.

[21] Spencer, *Principles of Ethics*, II, 263–421.

contrary to his theories, the countries that were most advanced industrially were precisely the ones that were assigning an ever-increasing number of functions to their governments. Spencer was alarmed: he did not know quite what to make of this. Was not government to become less and less necessary as man advanced from militarism to industrialism? Spencer was not certain whether the new trend heralded a return to Toryism or marked the approach of a dreaded socialism or communism. English liberalism, which had abandoned the old liberal faith in laissez faire and the relaxation of restraints in favor of government regulation, he castigated as a revived Toryism. England, he feared, was headed for state socialism, another name for slavery.[22] The United States, too, was gradually losing its freedom. To his American friend Edward Livingston Youmans, Spencer expressed his worst fear: "We are on the highway to communism, and I see no likelihood that the movement in that direction will be arrested."[23] That the various governments, in assuming the new functions that caused him so much concern, might actually be promoting the general welfare of their citizens was, of course, an idea too fantastic to be seriously considered.

In the twilight of his life Spencer admitted that he had been wrong in supposing that the relaxation of government restraints indicated by the adoption of free trade in England would continue. Though he felt a greater contentment with "established governmental forms" than he had previously, he was nevertheless certain that the trend was away from contract and toward status. He still believed that a happier day would come, but he feared that that day was "very far distant."[24]

Convinced that his law of equal freedom was the only safe criterion for state action and certain that the survival of the biologically fit was synonymous with progress, Spencer offered to Americans a design of laissez faire that was but one step removed from anarchism. It was a policy that was to be applied not only to economic problems but to the whole field of human endeavor. And, what was important to a people in the process of acquiring a profound respect for science, this

---

[22] Spencer, "The New Toryism," in *Man versus the State*, pp. 1–17; Spencer, "The Coming Slavery," *ibid.*, pp. 18–43.

[23] See "Spencer's Impressions of America," *Popular Science Monthly*, XXII (December, 1882), 270–271; and Spencer to Youmans, October 3, 1883, in John Fiske, *Edward Livingston Youmans* (New York, 1894), pp. 380–381.

[24] Spencer, *Autobiography*, II, 435–436, 543–544.

version of laissez faire was not some philosopher's idle dream but was the result of scientific investigations in sociology and biology carried on by a man deemed by many Americans to be the greatest thinker of the age.

II

It would be difficult to overestimate Spencer's popularity in the United States during the quarter-century after the Civil War. Henry Holt did not exaggerate when he declared that "probably no other philosopher ever had such a vogue as Spencer had from about 1870 to 1890." It was in this country that he had "his warmest reception and his largest audience." His popularity was, moreover, not limited to a small group of intellectuals. As William James noted, Spencer was a philosopher who could be appreciated by those who had no other philosopher.[25]

Spencer's books enjoyed a wide sale in the United States. Between November, 1860, and December 31, 1903, Spencer's American publisher, Appleton, sold 368,755 volumes of his writings.[26] Sales were, however, rather slow in the early years, and lack of funds almost caused Spencer to discontinue work on the *Synthetic Philosophy*. At this juncture it was his American friends who collected the necessary money to ensure the continuance of the project.[27]

The man most responsible for the propagation of Spencer's thought in America was Edward Livingston Youmans. Youmans was tireless in bringing Spencer's views before the public and in defending them from criticism. His *Popular Science Monthly*, founded in 1872, was little more than a vehicle for the dissemination of Spencer's thought: hardly an issue went by without some contribution from the Eng-

[25] Holt, *Garrulities of an Octogenarian Editor* (Boston, 1923), pp. 49–52, 298; Nicholas Paine Gilman, *Socialism and the American Spirit* (Boston, 1893), p. 147; James, "Herbert Spencer's Autobiography," in his *Memories and Studies* (New York, 1917), p. 126.

[26] Publishers' note in Spencer's *Autobiography*, II, 113. Richard Hofstadter, who has provided us with the best account of the influence of social Darwinism on American thought, calls this figure "probably unparalleled for works in such difficult spheres as philosophy and sociology" (*Social Darwinism in American Thought, 1860–1915* [Philadelphia, 1944], p. 21).

[27] Spencer, *Autobiography*, II, 166–167. In a letter to Carnegie of December 16, 1896, Spencer contrasted the favorable attitude toward him evidenced by the Americans with the unfavorable attitude of the English. The English public, he complained, had "on the whole hindered" the execution of his work (Carnegie Papers).

lish philosopher. Spencer's articles elicited wide comment, and You-mans was only stating the facts when he wrote to Spencer: "I think we could run the Monthly solely on the contributions that are sent us pro and con in relation to your ideas and works." [28]

If Spencer seems somewhat dull and prolix and quite unscientific to the modern reader, this was hardly the case in the last three and one-half decades of the nineteenth century. To John Fiske, Spencer was "as wonderful a man as Newton." Henry Ward Beecher de-clared that Spencer was "meat and bread" to him. William Allen White lists him as one of his "spiritual inspirations" at the turn of the century. Andrew Carnegie considered him a more important thinker than Darwin, and was proud to call himself Spencer's disciple. To Carl Schurz, he was "one of the greatest representatives" of the "democratic tendency" and one of the great teachers of "civilized hu-manity." F. A. P. Barnard thought that only Spencer's philosophy satisfied "an earnestly inquiring mind," and he considered Spencer the "most powerful intellect of all time." John R. Commons writes that his father and all his father's friends in eastern Indiana were followers of Herbert Spencer, and that he himself was "brought up on Hoosier-ism, Republicanism, Presbyterianism, and Spencerism." [29]

The climax of Spencer's popularity in the United States was prob-ably reached in 1882, when Spencer made his long-awaited trip to America. Although ill most of the time and unable to make public appearances, he finally consented to a public farewell banquet in his honor. The list of subscribers to this affair included distinguished Americans from all walks of life and was an impressive testimonial to Spencer's repute in the United States.[30]

It is, of course, virtually impossible to dissociate Spencer's influence

[28] Youmans to Spencer, July 8, 1881, in Fiske, *Youmans*, p. 372.

[29] See John Fiske to his wife, October 23, 1873, in Ethel F. Fisk, ed., *The Letters of John Fiske* (New York, 1940), p. 263; Youmans, ed., *Herbert Spencer on the Americans and the Americans on Herbert Spencer* (New York, 1883), pp. 44–45, 66, 86–87; White, *Autobiography of William Allen White* (New York, 1946), p. 326; Carnegie, *Autobiography of Andrew Carnegie* (Boston, 1920), p. 332; Carnegie to Spencer, January 5, 1897, Carnegie Papers; Carnegie to W. T. Stead, January 2, 1901, *ibid.;* and Commons, *Myself* (New York, 1934), p. 8.

[30] Among the subscribers were William Evarts, David Dudley Field, Carl Schurz, Hugh McCulloch, William Graham Sumner, John Fiske, Abram Hewitt, Lyman Abbott, George Peabody, Chauncey Depew, Henry Ward Beecher, Henry Holt, Benjamin Bristow, Edwin Godkin, Charles A. Dana, and Andrew Carnegie. See Youmans, ed., *Herbert Spencer on the Americans and the Americans on Herbert Spencer*, pp. 22–24.

as a political thinker from his general influence as an apostle of evolution. Spencer's most devoted followers, men like Youmans and Fiske, accepted both his application of the theory of evolution and his political individualism. Others, such as William James, were not particularly impressed by Spencer's philosophy but did look with favor upon his laissez-faire views.[31] A third group, one that included such figures as Frank Parsons, was more receptive to Spencer's general evolutionary thought than to his antistatist views.[32] Certain it is, however, that to the numerous advocates of laissez faire in America, Spencer contributed both the great prestige of his name and an almost inexhaustible supply of arguments against the general-welfare state. No authority was more often cited by the opponents of state action than Herbert Spencer.

Spencer's views appealed to Americans for a variety of reasons. His optimistic presentation of the beneficent operation of nature's laws was thoroughly consonant with the American faith in progress. His individualism, although it went too far for most Americans, was nevertheless in the best American tradition. Above all, his application to society of Darwin's theory suited the tastes of the American businessman.

III

Although the advocates of the negative state made abundant use of Spencer in their opposition to specific state activities, few of them were as intransigent as he in their support of laissez-faire principles.[33] However much they admired Spencer, most American adherents of laissez faire were unwilling, for example, to attack the concept of public education or the assumption by the state of a minimum of responsibility for at least certain categories of the unfit. Only a small

[31] James, "Herbert Spencer's Autobiography," in *Memories and Studies,* pp. 140–141.

[32] Parsons attacked Spencer's views on government action and yet revered Spencer "as the profoundest thinker of his age, and the greatest philosopher the world has ever produced" (*Government and the Law of Equal Freedom* [Boston, 1892], p. 1).

[33] The antistatist position that Spencer took in *Social Statics* was more nearly reflected in the thought of American individualist anarchists than in that of any other group. Although American anarchists could not agree with much that Spencer wrote, particularly during his later years, some of them were sympathetic to his attacks on the state and used such of his arguments as gave support to their own position. See James J. Martin, *Men against the State: The Expositors of Individualist Anarchism in America, 1827–1908* (De Kalb, Ill., 1953), pp. 232–237 *et passim.*

band of the devout, whose principal organ was Youmans' *Popular Science Monthly,* refused to deviate from Spencer's uncompromising position as regards the state.

Like Spencer, orthodox American social Darwinists were rigorously determinist in their attitude toward social reform. The teachings of evolution made it clear, they believed, that legislators should not "aggravate social ills by quack nostrums interfering with Nature's laws": government meddling resulted only in "disturbance and mischief." [34] When Henry George asked Youmans what he proposed to do about the evils of the day, of which he was so conscious, Youmans replied: "Nothing! You and I can do nothing at all. It's all a matter of evolution. We can only wait for evolution. Perhaps in four or five thousand years evolution may have carried men beyond this state of things. But we can do nothing." [35]

Laborers were invited by the social Darwinists "to give in to the decrees of Fate without a murmur." Inequalities in the distribution of wealth were, after all, the result of unequal talents and the survival of the fittest; and since relations between labor and capital, like everything else, were based on natural law, it would be idle to attempt to alter them by legislative fiat. Trade unions were "clogging the wheels by 'strikes'" and "waging war against natural law," and legislation in this area would lead only to unrest and hard times. [36]

The social Darwinists were in essential agreement with the classical economists in their criticism of state regulation of the economic life of the nation. They too accepted competition as the only proper regime for the economic order, insisted that trade should be adjusted by

[34] See Charles S. Ashley, "The Relation of Evolution to Political Economy," *Popular Science Monthly,* XLIV (February, 1894), 461; "The Social Science Association," *ibid.,* V (July, 1874), 368–369; Benjamin Reece, "Law as a Disturber of Social Order," *ibid.,* XXXIV (March, 1889), 631–643; Holt, "The Social Discontent—II. Some Remedies," *Forum,* XIX (March, 1895), 68–82; Holt, "The Social Discontent—III. More Remedies," *ibid.,* XIX (April, 1895), 177–180; Holt, *On the Civic Relations* (3d ed. of *Talks on Civics,* Boston, 1907), pp. vii–viii; and Charles Carleton Coffin, "Labor and the Natural Forces," *Atlantic Monthly,* XLIII (May, 1879), 566.

[35] George, *A Perplexed Philosopher* (Garden City, N.Y., [1911?]), p. 136n. A similar statement about Youmans is contained in a letter from George to Edward R. Taylor, January 21, 1881, Henry George Collection, New York Public Library.

[36] R. G. Eccles, "The Labor Question," *Popular Science Monthly,* XI (September, 1877), 610; "The Recent Strikes," *ibid.,* I (September, 1872), 623–624; Erastus B. Bigelow, "The Relations of Labor and Capital," *Atlantic Monthly,* XLII (October, 1878), 483–486.

the natural laws of supply and demand and not by obstructive tariffs, suggested that trusts could be safely left to the operations of natural law, and informed the state that it was not to favor any economic group.[37]

Spencer's most devout American followers also accepted his criticism of public education as contrary to the law of equal freedom and the law of conduct and consequence. State-controlled education was portrayed by them as inculcating the dangerous idea that the people have a right to look to government for aid, as invading the rights of the family, and as undermining the foundations of society. Advocates of the common-school system were declared to be inclined to socialism, since, like the socialists, they believed that a majority might take from one man to give to another. Even the poor, the social Darwinists asserted, would benefit if they were compelled to provide for the education of their children: "Nothing," indeed, "would tend more to raise the spirit of the poor and enhance their sense of citizenship and of social equality." [38]

Convinced that all government action beyond that necessary to protect the people from internal and external aggression is despotic in character and destructive of the liberty of the individual, orthodox Spencerians in America could only view with alarm the increasing amount of social legislation in the 1880's and the 1890's. To them it seemed as if the people had "found a new toy—the power of legislative action—and were playing with it with a kind of greedy zest." [39] They denounced the appeal to the state as an evidence of the hold that socialism had on American public opinion and as contrary to the teachings of the founding fathers—and of Spencer. The federal government, they feared, was being converted into a "universal beneficence to fit out fools with brains and to render innocuous the virus of indolence and perversity." The legislators of the New World were but reviv-

[37] "Competition," *Popular Science Monthly*, XXXIV (March, 1889), 699–700; "Tariff Legislation," *ibid.*, XXXVII (September, 1890), 696–698; George A. Rich, "Trusts Their Own Corrective," *ibid.*, XLIV (April, 1894), 740–743; George M. Wallace, "Governmental Aid to Injustice," *ibid.*, XXXVI (December, 1889), 191–193.

[38] See Franklin Smith, "Real Problems of Democracy," *Popular Science Monthly*, LVI (November, 1899), 7–9; "Functions of the State," *ibid.*, XXX (March, 1887), 701–702; John M. Bonham, *Industrial Liberty* (New York, 1888), p. 291; "State Education," *Popular Science Monthly*, XXXI (May, 1887), 124–127.

[39] "Encroachments of the State," *Popular Science Monthly*, XXXI (October, 1887), 847.

ing the system of restraints that had crushed individual initiative in the Old World. Americans were becoming a race of barbarians, led by greedy politicians and deluded social reformers. Democracy had become just another form of despotism; the government of the many was proving no better than the government of the one, or of the few.[40] One zealous social Darwinist found that of eight hundred laws passed by the legislature of the state of New York in 1897, only fifty-eight were designed to protect individual freedom; and of a total expenditure of two billion dollars for federal, state, and local governments in the year 1896–1897, only 6 per cent had been devoted to the "legitimate" functions of government, that is, to the maintenance of the police and the courts.[41] What hope was there for a nation that trusted so little in "spontaneous developments" and in voluntary effort, that was so addicted to the "law-making habit," that had so conspicuously abandoned the teachings of Spencer?[42]

To be sure, American individualism and American hostility to government regulation antedate Herbert Spencer. His significance lies in the fact that he powerfully reënforced ideas that were already fairly strong and put them on a seemingly scientific basis. The American advocates of laissez faire were ever ready to use Spencer's arguments and Spencer's language to support their views, even if they were reluctant to go quite so far as he did. In Herbert Spencer the cause of laissez faire in America had gained a major ally.

[40] Franklin Smith to Joseph A. Labadie, November 11, 1899, Labadie Collection, University of Michigan Library; Franklin Smith, "An Object Lesson in Social Reform," *Popular Science Monthly*, L (January, 1897), 311; Smith, "An Apostate Democracy," *ibid.*, LII (March, 1898), 654–674; Smith, "The Despotism of Democracy," *ibid.*, LI (August, 1897), 489–507; Smith, "A State Official on Excessive Taxation," *ibid.*, LVI (April, 1900), 645–659; "A Pernicious Political Tendency," *ibid.*, XXVII (July, 1885), 410–412; "The State and Social Organization," *ibid.*, XXXIII (July, 1888), 411–412. John Fiske was one of the few social Darwinists who retained his sobriety in this matter. See Fiske, *Youmans*, pp. 381–382n.

[41] Smith, "Politics as a Form of Civil War," *Popular Science Monthly*, LIV (March, 1899), 591–592.

[42] The bitter-end social Darwinist Franklin Smith, who was particularly disturbed at the drift of events, concluded that all that he could do was "to preach upon all occasions the gospel of individualism . . . as set forth in Herbert Spencer's works, and wherever possible take such political action as will check the onslaught of the forces of socialism, which are nothing more nor less than the forces of barbarism" (Smith to Labadie, November 11, 1899, Labadie Collection).

III

ACADEMIC AND POPULAR THEORISTS
OF LAISSEZ FAIRE

DURING the years from 1865 to 1901 the cause of laissez faire was championed in America both in the classroom and in the public forum. Arguing from various points of view, academic and popular expounders of economic, social, and political theory joined in the defense of the negative state. None of them, of course, proposed to end all state activities or, indeed, even to reduce them to the point advocated by Spencer, but they were at one in wishing that the state construe its role narrowly and that it eschew all general-welfare functions.

From 1865 to 1885 political economy and laissez faire were virtually synonymous in the United States.[1] Orthodoxy required that an economist be a believer in laissez faire and in free trade; and, as one economist declared, orthodoxy was the criterion to distinguish good and bad. "If you were held to be unorthodox, it was a terrible indictment."[2] If anything, this was an understatement of the case, for as

---

[1] An exception to this statement may perhaps be made in the case of the disciples of Henry Carey. However, like their master, they attacked laissez faire chiefly because it was associated with free trade. Their plea was for a national system of political economy, and this involved the repudiation on their part of some of the basic assumptions of the laissez-faire credo. See E. Peshine Smith, *A Manual of Political Economy* (New York, 1868); William Elder, *Questions of the Day: Economic and Social* (Philadelphia, 1871); Robert Ellis Thompson, *Political Economy* (rev. ed. of *Social Science and National Economy*; Philadelphia, 1882); and Van Buren Denslow, *Principles of the Economic Philosophy of Society, Government and Industry* (New York, 1885).

[2] See Richard T. Ely, *Ground under Our Feet: An Autobiography* (New York, 1938), pp. 126–127; and Ely, "Founding and Early History of the American Eco-

the first president of the American Economic Association asserted: "Here it [laissez faire] was not made the test of economic orthodoxy, merely. It was used to decide whether a man were an economist at all." [3]   After 1885 laissez faire was subjected to vigorous attack by the "new school" of political economy, and its hold on American economic thought was considerably weakened. However, it remained, with modifications, in the forefront of the thought of many American economists.

Professional and popular economists were equally vigorous in promoting the cause of laissez faire. The professionals were led by such men as Francis Bowen, Arthur Latham Perry, Amasa Walker, J. Laurence Laughlin, Arthur Twining Hadley,[4] Julian Sturtevant, and Simon Newcomb; the popular economists included in their ranks such prominent figures as David Ames Wells, Edward Atkinson, Edwin Lawrence Godkin, and Horace White. Although many of these men did not believe that their views mattered much with the general public [5] and although policy was often at variance with their recommendations, the laissez-faire economists were not without influence in the years after the Civil War. The key problems of the age—tariff, currency, labor, railroads, monopoly—did, after all, involve the application of economic principles, and what the laissez-faire economists had to say about these matters—the tariff was a notable exception—was

nomic Association," *American Economic Review,* XXVI (Supplement) (March, 1936), 143.

[3] Francis Amasa Walker, "Recent Progress of Political Economy in the United States," *Publications of the American Economic Association,* IV (1889), 254.   Cf. Arthur Twining Hadley, *Economics* (New York, 1896), p. 12.

[4] Although Hadley regarded laissez faire as a "practical maxim of political wisdom" rather than a "fundamental axiom of economic science," his views on most matters involving state action were not essentially different from those of economists who were less cautious in their acceptance of laissez faire.   Henry Demarest Lloyd regarded him as "by far the most dangerous of all the Bourbon economists."   See Hadley, *Economics,* p. 12; Hadley, "Government by Public Opinion," in *The Education of the American Citizen* (New York, 1902), pp. 19–20; and Lloyd to Henry S. Green, October 14, 1898, Henry Demarest Lloyd Papers, State Historical Society of Wisconsin.

[5] See, for example, J. Laurence Laughlin, "The Study of Political Economy in the United States," *Journal of Political Economy,* I (December, 1892), 1; and Simon Newcomb, "The Problem of Economic Education," *Quarterly Journal of Economics,* VII (July, 1893), 375, 394–396.   "The fact is," Wells wrote to Atkinson on November 29, [1881], "there is no chance for economic reform in this country. . . .   I think I shall dry up and give up any idea of accomplishing anything" (Edward Atkinson Papers, Massachusetts Historical Society).

wholly in keeping with the generally conservative temper of the times.[6]

The laissez-faire economists held many of the key positions in the academic world: Bowen taught at Harvard; Perry, at Williams; Amasa Walker, at Amherst; Laughlin, at Harvard, Cornell, and Chicago; Hadley, at Yale; Sturtevant, at Illinois College, of which he was president; and Simon Newcomb, although principally an astronomer, lectured on political economy at Harvard. The academic economists, moreover, did not confine their work to the classroom. They contributed to the newspaper and periodical press, appeared before Congressional committees, and made their services available to public authorities. Hadley served as Connecticut's commissioner of labor statistics in 1885 and 1886 and on the Connecticut Board of Mediation and Arbitration in 1895. He was also responsible in the 1880's and early 1890's for much of the economic writing in the influential religious journal, the *Independent*. Laughlin contributed important articles on the money question to the *Chicago Times-Herald* and was the author of the final report of the Indianapolis Monetary Commission. Perry was extremely active in the free-trade propaganda; his advice, as well as that of Newcomb, was sought by the Cleveland administrations, and when Cleveland's secretary of the treasury, Daniel Manning, became ill, Perry was offered his post.[7]

The popular economists were even more active than their academic allies. Atkinson and Wells did not become the Cobden and Bright of the United States, as Atkinson would have liked,[8] but they did exert an important influence. Atkinson, a prominent figure in the cotton industry, particularly on the commercial side, and after 1878 the treasurer of the Boston Manufacturers' Fire Insurance Company, was the author of several books, more than 250 pamphlets, many of them widely

[6] Dorfman, *The Economic Mind in American Civilization, 1606–1918* (New York, 1946–1949), III, 49; Albert S. Bolles, *Chapters in Political Economy* (New York, 1874), pp. 11–14.

[7] Morris Hadley, *Arthur Twining Hadley* (New Haven, 1948), pp. 58–60, 260; Alfred Bornemann, *J. Laurence Laughlin* (Washington, D.C., 1940), pp. 42–46; Arthur Latham Perry, *Williamstown and Williams College* (New York, 1899), p. 697; Perry to Francis Lynde Stetson, October 28, 1885, Grover Cleveland Papers, Library of Congress; Perry to Daniel S. Lamont, October 27, 1885, *ibid.*; Simon Newcomb to Secretary of the Treasury, November 29, 1886, Newcomb Letterbooks, Simon Newcomb Papers, Library of Congress; W. W. Campbell, "Simon Newcomb," *Memoirs of the National Academy of Sciences*, XVII (1924), 14.

[8] Atkinson to Wells, November 8, 1884, David A. Wells Papers, Library of Congress.

circulated, and hundreds of letters to newspapers and magazines; and, as his biographer declares, "there was scarcely a time after the Civil War when he did not have friends who were important either in Congress, or in the Administration, or both." Secretary of the Treasury Hugh McCulloch was responsive to his views concerning specie resumption, and President Grant was persuaded to veto the Inflation Bill of 1874 partly as the result of the opposition to the measure which Atkinson did so much to organize. Atkinson's views on such problems as money and the tariff received favorable hearing from Garfield and Cleveland, and in 1887 Cleveland appointed him a special monetary commissioner to study in Europe the possibilities of international bimetallism. Atkinson also helped to frame the provisions of two tariff measures, the ill-fated Morrison bill of 1886 and the Wilson bill of 1894.[9]

Wells served as chairman of the United States Revenue Commission in 1865 and 1866, as special commissioner of the revenue from 1866 to 1870, and as chairman of the New York State Tax Commission from 1870 to 1872. His advice on monetary matters was sought by Secretary of the Treasury Benjamin Bristow, and Garfield apparently considered appointing him secretary of the treasury. A staunch advocate of free trade, he drafted President Johnson's veto of the copper tariff in 1869, and during the Cleveland administrations he advised the White House and members of Congress on tariff and monetary problems.[10]

Godkin wielded his influence mainly through the pages of the *Nation* and the New York *Evening Post*, both of which he edited. William James has testified that to his generation Godkin was "the towering influence in all thought concerning public affairs," that "he influenced other writers who never quoted him, and determined the

[9] Harold F. Williamson, *Edward Atkinson* (Boston, 1934), pp. vii–viii, 66–71, 78–79, 82–85, 99, 138–142, 144–148, 154–162, 178–191, 195–212; McCulloch to Atkinson, November 9, 1867, Atkinson Papers; Atkinson, "Veto of the Inflation Bill of 1874," *Journal of Political Economy*, I (December, 1892), 117–119; Atkinson to Laughlin, November 14, 1892, Atkinson Letterbooks, Atkinson Papers; Garfield to Atkinson, May 21, May 25, June 8, 1868, *ibid.;* Abram Hewitt to Atkinson, May 12, 1887, *ibid.*

[10] Herbert Ronald Ferleger, *David A. Wells and the American Revenue System, 1865–1870* (New York, 1942); Fred B. Joyner, *David Ames Wells* (Cedar Rapids, Iowa, 1939), pp. 25–44, 64–66, 90–91, 95–112, 156–173, 198; Bristow to Wells, October 20, 1875, David A. Wells Papers, New York Public Library; Wells to Atkinson, March 11, 1881, Atkinson Papers; E. McClung Fleming, *R. R. Bowker* (Norman, Okla., 1952), pp. 213–214.

whole current of discussion." He was, said Henry Holt, "an authority with authorities." [11]

During the 1880's and 1890's the policy of the *Nation* and of the *Evening Post* toward the economic problems of the day was determined to a considerable extent by Horace White, one-time editor of the *Chicago Tribune*, business associate of Henry Villard, and student of the money question. In these journals and in his celebrated textbook, *Money and Banking Illustrated by American History*, White championed the cause of "sound money" and attracted much attention.[12]

Although the laissez-faire economists never founded an organization comparable to the new school's American Economic Association, some of them participated in the work of various organizations of a largely conservative bent which sought to educate the public with respect to the economic questions of the day. Thus Wells and Perry were active in the ranks of the American Free Trade League, and Wells, Atkinson, and White contributed their talents to both the short-lived Taxpayers' Union, set up in Washington, D.C., in 1871, to promote the cause of tariff reform and sound money, and the Society for Political Education, founded in 1880 by the publisher Richard Rogers Bowker to provide the public with inexpensive reading matter on the issues of the day.[13] Many of the conservative economists were also members of the Political Economy Club, which Laughlin founded in 1883 and which functioned principally as a discussion and social group.[14] Politically, the laissez-faire economists tended to identify themselves with either the Liberal Republican–Mugwump faction of the Republican party or the Samuel Tilden–Grover Cleveland wing of the Democratic party. For these elements of the two major parties the outmoded negative liberalism of the nineteenth century remained a vital faith.[15]

[11] See Rollo Ogden, ed., *Life and Letters of Edwin Lawrence Godkin* (New York, 1907), I, 221; and Holt, *Garrulities of an Octogenarian Editor* (Boston, 1923), p. 293. For the *Nation*'s devotion to the principle of laissez faire during the Godkin era, see Alan Pendleton Grimes, *The Political Liberalism of the New York Nation, 1865–1932* (Chapel Hill, N. C., 1953), pp. 14–35.

[12] Oswald Garrison Villard, "Horace White," in Allen Johnson and Dumas Malone, eds., *Dictionary of American Biography* (Authors ed.; New York, 1937), XX, 104–105.

[13] Joyner, *Wells*, pp. 147–153; Williamson, *Atkinson*, pp. 87–89; Fleming, *Bowker*, pp. 101–103, 219–220.

[14] Laughlin to Atkinson, April 11, 1882, January 29, 1883, Atkinson Papers; Bornemann, *Laughlin*, p. 9.

[15] Joyner, *Wells*, pp. 113–138, 156–177; Williamson, *Atkinson*, pp. 89–91, 138;

In most respects, the political economy expounded by the laissez-faire economists in the United States was but a carbon copy of European classical political economy, although the qualifications present in the work of the great English economists were often overlooked by their American imitators. Smith, Say, Ricardo, Mill, and Bastiat were the standard authorities; [16] economic man was the chief focus of attention, and the increase of the national wealth, the main desideratum of state policy.

The espousal by the economists of the doctrine of laissez faire derived in large measure from their views regarding such factors as the immutability of the laws of economics, the efficacy of self-interest, the merits of competition, and the inefficiency of government. That the American economists should have believed the economic order to be governed by natural laws which are universally true and with which legislators must not interfere is not at all surprising when one considers the extent to which they were intellectual debtors to the European classical economists. Unlike the English economists, however, many of the American economists, whether clergymen or laymen, were prone to associate the natural laws that they elucidated with the laws of God and to assume, partly as a consequence of this association and partly as the result of the bounty of nature in the United States, that these laws operated in a beneficial manner.[17] Edward Atkinson admitted that one of his preconceptions was that "there must be a higher law" which ensures progress. Anyone who believes in a benevolent Deity, he declared, must have faith that this is the best of all possible worlds and that the operation of a higher law is "steadily, surely, and

---

Fleming, *Bowker*, pp. 92–93, 114–133, 196–224, 257–279; Eric F. Goldman, *Rendezvous with Destiny* (New York, 1952), pp. 16–17, 23–24, 39–41.

[16] Bastiat was the major influence with both Perry and Atkinson. "I had scarcely read a dozen pages in that remarkable book," Perry said of Bastiat's *Harmonies of Political Economy*, "when the Field of the Science, in all its outlines and landmarks, lay before my mind just as it does today" (*Political Economy* [18th ed. of *Elements of Political Economy*; New York, 1883], p. ix). Perry, on the other hand, thought Amasa Walker was "too much in bondage to Adam Smith" (cited in James Phinney Munroe, *A Life of Francis Amasa Walker* [New York, 1923], p. 192). See also Wayland, *Elements of Political Economy* (recast by Aaron L. Chapin; New York, 1881), p. i; Atkinson, *The Industrial Progress of the Nation* (New York, 1890), pp. 11–12; and J. F. Normano, *The Spirit of American Economics* (New York, 1943), pp. 130–201.

[17] T. E. C. Leslie, "Political Economy in the United States," *Fortnightly Review*, XXXIV (October, 1880), 496–498.

slowly working to the benefit of the great mass of the people . . . slowly but surely securing to them . . . a constantly larger and increasing share of a larger and larger annual product."

Francis Bowen declared that laissez faire means " 'things regulate themselves' . . . which means, of course, that God regulates them by his general laws, which always, in the long run, work to good." Perry, who recognized the right of free exchange as the central natural right and saw myriads of benefits flowing from the uninterrupted exercise of this right, asserted that the laws of exchange "are based on nothing less solid than the will of God." W. D. Wilson also regarded the laws of economics as "a part of God's laws" and believed that the observance of these laws would not only have a desirable effect on individuals in this world but would serve to prepare them "for the life that is to come." [18]

Whether the economists described the laws of economics in supernaturalistic or naturalistic terms,[19] they were agreed that the one great disturbing force that had ever marred the operation of natural laws was the legislation of the state. Julian M. Sturtevant, for example, spoke of the domain of economics as being "pervaded by all the contingencies which arise from human legislation, and human ignorance and folly." The history of the ages was replete, he said, with "the disasters, and miseries, and confusions" resulting from the violations of natural law.[20]

Belief that self-interest is a universal motive of human action and that this is not only natural but beneficial served as a second major

[18] See Atkinson, *Industrial Progress of the Nation*, pp. iii, 2; Atkinson, *On the Collection of Revenue* (rev. ed.; New York, 1869), p. 8; Atkinson, *The Margin of Profits* (New York, 1887), p. 7; Atkinson to Richmond Mayo-Smith, June 16, 1890, Atkinson Letterbooks, Atkinson Papers; Bowen, *American Political Economy* (New York, 1870), p. 18; Perry, *Elements of Political Economy* (7th ed. rev. and enlarged; New York, 1872), pp. 93, 97–100; and Wilson, *First Principles of Political Economy* (Philadelphia, 1882), pp. 29–30.

[19] For an expression of opinion as to the existence of natural laws of economics by economists other than those already mentioned, see Sturtevant, *Economics, or the Science of Wealth* (New York, 1881), pp. 1, 18, 193–194; Wayland, *Elements of Political Economy* (recast by Chapin), p. 356; and Newcomb, "The Let-Alone Principle," *North American Review*, CX (January, 1870), 3–7.

[20] Sturtevant, Review of Prof. Perry's *Political Economy*, *New Englander*, XXXVIII (January, 1879), 32–33. See also Amasa Walker, *The Science of Wealth* (2d ed.; Boston, 1866), pp. 4–5; and Wells, *Recent Economic Changes* (New York, 1890), p. 466.

basis for the laissez-faire convictions of the political economists. Production and distribution, it was held, are best conducted by individuals in pursuit of their own interests. The individual is, after all, a better judge of his needs than is any legislator. If not interfered with, he will buy in the cheapest market and sell in the dearest. This tendency of the individual to do what is best for himself leads to his doing that which is best for the community, since the community interest is but the aggregate of individual interests. Not only does enlightened self-interest promote the general welfare, but even unenlightened self-interest serves the same cause. The mere money-getter in advancing his own selfish desires yet occasions an increase in the product and a reduction in the cost of life's necessaries and thus brings better conditions for all.[21]

It was but natural for those economists who tended to identify the laws of nature with the laws of God to attribute to the design of the Lord the benefits deriving from the pursuit of self-interest. It is the "benevolent purpose of the Designer," declared Francis Bowen, which effects "the reconciliation of private aims with the public advantage." Economic man is God's agent. He does the work of the Lord and knows it not. "It might be said by the prophet of the present," asserted Edward Atkinson, "that the Lord maketh the selfishness of man to work for the material welfare of his kind." What need was there for legislative action in the Gilded Age if the Lord was thus converting man's baseness to such noble ends? Society was, after all, threatened not by selfish men but by unwise legislation.[22]

Free competition was a third basis on which economists rested their trust in laissez faire. Competition, the economists asserted, is a permanent law of nature which equitably regulates economic exchange and the distribution of wealth. As long as the state does not interfere with competition, demand and supply can be relied on to bring wages, interest, rent, and profits to their proper level. No class is significantly favored by unfettered competition since it tends to

[21] Wayland, *Elements of Political Economy* (recast by Chapin), pp. 6–7; Sturtevant, *Economics,* pp. 118, 338; Newcomb, *Principles of Political Economy* (New York, 1885), pp. 447–451; Newcomb, *A Plain Man's Talk on the Labor Question* (New York, 1886), pp. 13–21, 189–191; Newcomb, "The Let-Alone Principle," *North American Review,* CX (January, 1870), 11–12; Atkinson, *Industrial Progress of the Nation,* p. 208.

[22] Bowen, *American Political Economy,* pp. 15, 18; Atkinson, *Industrial Progress of the Nation,* p. 208; Newcomb, *A Plain Man's Talk on the Labor Question,* pp. 191–192.

reduce gains to a common standard. State interference with this process is interference not only with man's freedom but also with economic law.[23]

A fourth factor that led the political economists to champion the idea of the negative state was their conviction that government is, at best, an inefficient agency. In the decades after the Civil War, when corruption was rife on all levels of government, the economists had a plentiful supply of ammunition available to them when they attacked the state on this point. Godkin took the lead in demonstrating the folly of entrusting new functions to an inefficient state. He pointed out that human affairs had become increasingly complex and that this required a corresponding increase in intelligence on the part of government. Government, however, had failed to keep pace with progress in science and the arts, and this, Godkin argued, accounted for its inefficiency. Able men were going off into the business world and shunning the tasks of government, and legislative work was passing into the hands of unskilled men. "There is no legislature today," Godkin insisted, "which is controlled by scientific methods, or by the opinion of experts in jurisprudence or political economy." He found the state to be administered by men whom no one would trust with the guardianship of his children or of his property. It was absolutely unfit to do the things that people said it ought to do. The state would have to cleanse itself and attract abler men before it could be entrusted with important economic tasks.[24]

Whereas Godkin pointed out some of the more fundamental causes for the inefficiency of government, other laissez-faire economists were content to assume that economic enterprises administered by the state are always less efficient in operation than those directed by private enterprise. Government policy, they maintained, is based on partisanship rather than on sound economic principles, and, as a consequence, economic tasks should not, as a general rule, be assigned to the state.[25]

[23] Bowen, *American Political Economy,* p. 41; Sturtevant, *Economics,* pp. 52–57, 208–209, 223–224, 280; Wilson, *First Principles of Political Economy,* pp. 216, 238; Wayland, *Elements of Political Economy* (recast by Chapin), pp. 355–356.

[24] Godkin, "Equality," in *Unforeseen Tendencies of Democracy* (Boston, 1898), pp. 29–47; Godkin, "The Decline of Legislatures," *ibid.,* pp. 139–140; "The Growth of Corporate and Decline of Governmental Power," *Nation,* XVI (May 15, 1873), 328–329; Godkin, "Economic Man," in *Problems of Modern Democracy* (New York, 1897), pp. 173–174; Godkin, "The Duty of Educated Men in a Democracy," *ibid.,* pp. 220, 221.

[25] See, for example, Newcomb, "Aspects of the Economic Discussion," in

Despite the fact that laissez-faire economists were inclined to associate economic laws with the laws of God, most of them did not believe that the ethical implications of the laws they expounded were any of their concern. They maintained that they were concerned with what "is" and not with what "ought to be." Political economy, Perry declared, "has no concern with questions of moral right. . . . The grounds of Economy and morals are independent and incommensurable." [26]

For the various reasons enumerated, the popular and professional economists concluded that the state must pursue a policy of laissez faire, of noninterference with the economic interests of society. It could best promote the general welfare by making itself as inconspicuous as possible and by relying on individual initiative both to augment the national wealth and to cope with the social problems of the age. "That country will prosper most," Atkinson asserted, "which requires least from its government, and in which the people, after having chosen their officers, straightway proceed to govern themselves according to their common habit." Hadley argued that "the danger of believing that economic laws can be interfered with by human effort is ten times greater than the danger of an extreme belief in laissez faire" and therefore thought it the function of the economist to act as a check on legislatures by setting forth the limits beyond which state action should not proceed.[27]

The extent to which abhorrence of state action was carried by the laissez-faire economists is indicated in the work of J. Laurence Laughlin. Laughlin denied that the state is a fundamental element in economic principles. He denounced all appeals to the state for aid as socialistic in character, since he regarded the essence of socialism to

---

Richard T. Ely et al., Science Economic Discussion (New York, 1886), p. 65; Amasa Walker, Science of Wealth, p. 409; and Hadley, Economics, pp. 402–403.

[26] Perry, Elements of Political Economy, p. 37. Perry hastened to add that the conclusions of political economy and moral science were nevertheless harmonious.

[27] Atkinson, Industrial Progress of the Nation, p. 79; Atkinson, The Distribution of Products (New York, 1885), p. 21; Hadley, "Economic Laws and Methods," in Ely et al., Science Economic Discussion, p. 96; Hadley, Economics, pp. 12–19, 63; Hadley, "Ely's 'Socialism and Social Reform,'" Forum, XVIII (October, 1894), 184–187. Harvard's Frank Taussig believed that economic science should concern itself only with the phenomena of wealth and should not attempt to chart the course of state action. This view, however, did not prevent him from taking a stand against schemes of social insurance as contrary to the idea of "self-help and self-dependence." See Taussig, "The State as an Economic Factor," in Ely et al., Science Economic Discussion, pp. 34–38; and Taussig, "Workmen's Insurance in Germany," Forum, VIII (October, 1889), 169.

be "State-help as opposed to self-help." State aid, he maintained, "has its origin in shiftlessness and ignorance"; it interferes with individuality and independence of character and lowers self-respect. The functions of the state should therefore be cut to a minimum: state action "should be permitted only when there is an absolute necessity, and even then it should be undertaken with hesitation." [28] Laughlin is said even to have objected to the use of the word "social." [29]

Laughlin revealed his prejudices about state action in his abridgment and editing for use in American schools of John Stuart Mill's *Principles of Political Economy*. Although Laughlin included Mill's chapter on the interference of government grounded on erroneous theories, he omitted the chapter on the influence of government.[30] He also omitted Mill's chapter on the limits of laissez faire, a chapter in which the famous British economist upheld the validity of laissez faire as a general principle but then made wide exceptions to this rule.[31] Laughlin insisted that in order to limit Mill's treatise to political economy he had simply omitted materials that were more properly classified as sociology and social philosophy, and that he had attempted to clarify Mill's "more general and abstract statements by a reference to fresh illustrations of facts all about us," but, actually, his excisions and his biased editing gave to Mill's work a meaning that was hardly intended by its author.[32]

Being opponents of any significant state intervention in the eco-

[28] See Laughlin, *The Elements of Political Economy* (New York, 1887), pp. 263–268; and Laughlin, "Protection and Socialism," *International Review*, VII (October, 1879), 428, 435.

[29] Bornemann, *Laughlin*, p. 90.

[30] In this chapter Mill concluded that "the admitted functions of government embrace a much wider field than can easily be included within the ring-fence of any restrictive definition, and that it is hardly possible to find any ground of justification common to them all, except the comprehensive one of general expediency; nor to limit the interference of government by any universal rule, save the simple and vague one that it should never be admitted but when the case of expediency is strong" (*Principles of Political Economy* [from 5th London ed.; New York, 1881], II, 392).

[31] Mill went so far as to maintain that "in the particular circumstances of a given age or nation, there is scarcely anything, really important to the general interest, which it may not be desirable, or even necessary, that the government should take upon itself, not because private individuals cannot effectually perform it, but because they will not" (*Principles*, II, 558–603).

[32] Laughlin to Atkinson, December 23, 1884, Atkinson Papers; Bornemann, *Laughlin*, p. 12; Laughlin, Preface, in *Principles of Political Economy, by John Stuart Mill* (abridged by Laughlin; New York, 1885), pp. iii–iv; Charles A. Beard, "The Idea of Let Us Alone," *Virginia Quarterly Review*, XV (Autumn, 1939), 500–514.

nomic life of the nation, the laissez-faire economists wished to restrict the activity of the state to the protection of persons and property and to the provision of certain necessities and conveniences which private enterprise could not adequately supply. Most of them sanctioned a system of public education, government operation of the postal service, government construction of highways, public provision for the deaf, dumb, blind, and the insane, and some carefully limited aid to paupers.[33] But for the great economic questions of the day— the relations of labor and capital, the tariff, the currency, the railroads, and the trusts—they had but one answer: laissez faire.

The labor problem was intensified in the United States, as elsewhere, by the progress of the industrial revolution and the consequent growth of the factory system and the increase in the number of wage earners. Such issues as strikes and lockouts, labor organization, and labor legislation came to the fore after the Civil War and pressed for solution. To the laissez-faire economist, however, the labor problem, like all other economic problems, could safely be entrusted to the workings of economic laws.

If there is a place for laissez faire, declared James H. Canfield, of the University of Kansas, it is in the relation of the legislature to capital and labor.[34] The equal rights of employer and employee, the economists contended, are best maintained by permitting both capital and labor the utmost freedom. "If labor and capital are free," declared Aaron Chapin, who recast Wayland's celebrated textbook, "the flow of each under the law of competition towards an equilibrium is as natural as that of the waters of the ocean under the action of gravitation."[35] If the capitalist does sometimes take advantage of the laborer and succeeds in obtaining his services at a rate lower than just relations between the two would prescribe, then, asserted Perry, "the remedy for this is not in arbitrary interference of government in the bargain, but in the intelligence and self-respect of the laborers which shall fit them to insist on a just bargain." In the sphere of exchange,

[33] See, for example, Sturtevant, *Economics*, pp. 295–304; Wayland, *Elements of Political Economy* (recast by Chapin), pp. 139–150; Bowen, *American Political Economy*, pp. 18–19; Wells, *Practical Economics* (New York, 1894), pp. 242, 244; and Atkinson to Wells, August 21, 1896, Atkinson Letterbooks, Atkinson Papers.

[34] Canfield, *Taxation: A Plain Talk for Plain People* (New York, 1883), p. 16.

[35] Chapin, "The Relations of Labor and Capital," *Transactions of the Wisconsin Academy of Sciences, Arts, and Letters*, I (1870–1872), 58. See also Wayland, *Elements of Political Economy* (recast by Chapin), pp. 92–107; and Perry, *Elements of Political Economy*, p. 150.

each party must look out for itself. If laborers "are persistently cheated in the exchange, they have nobody to blame but themselves." [36]

The popular and professional economists attempted to convince the worker that he was better off than he had ever been before, that the capitalist was his ally and benefactor, and that therefore he should remain quiescent and abstain from economic or political action designed to alter the *status quo*. God had indeed brought capital and labor "into a relation of mutual dependence" which could never be overthrown. Amasa Walker asserted that any belief that hatred and strife between capital and labor is inevitable "blasphemes against the harmonies of providence,—is sightless before the glorious order of man and nature." [37] Atkinson told the workingman that he already received 90 per cent of the total annual product as against a mere 10 per cent for the capitalist and that, as Bastiat had pointed out, he was getting a constantly increasing share of an increasing product. This, Atkinson declared, was due in the main to the capitalist. It was the result of his efforts that the worker was earning twice as much for ten hours of work in 1887 as he had been earning fifty years previously for from twelve to fourteen hours of work. Capital, he asserted, serves the worker at a low price. For every cent the capitalist makes, the worker is saved ten cents. "The poor," said Atkinson, "are not poor because the rich are rich. . . . The poor are a great deal less poor and a great deal less numerous than they would be, except for the service of capital, of which they enjoy the greater part of the benefit." Labor and capital are thus allies, not enemies, and they can be expected to coöperate so long as the state avoids unnecessary interference. "The abuse of legislative powers is the most potent cause of conflict between labor and capital." [38]

Atkinson's fellow economists joined him in pointing out to the laborer that the entrepreneur was his ally and the source of his well-being. Sturtevant hoped that workingmen would realize that capital

[36] Perry, *Elements of Political Economy,* pp. 140–141.

[37] Perry, *Elements of Political Economy,* p. 136; Walker, *Science of Wealth,* p. 22.

[38] Atkinson, *Industrial Progress of the Nation,* pp. 137–154, 178; Atkinson, *Margin of Profits,* pp. 12–13, 16–17; Atkinson, *Labor and Capital Allies Not Enemies* (New York, 1879), pp. 97–98; Atkinson to the Committee of the Socialistic Labor Party of Minneapolis, September 25 [?], 1888, Atkinson Letterbooks, Atkinson Papers; Atkinson to Editor of the Socialist Review, September, 1900, *ibid.* For an attack on Atkinson's use of statistics, see Frederick B. Hawley, "Edward Atkinson's Economic Theories," *Forum,* VII (May, 1889), 292–304.

is "held in trust for the general good" not only as the result of a "necessary law of nature, but with voluntary intention and purpose." Newcomb maintained that all the benefits the laborer had received had resulted from the efforts of capitalists. He warned labor that if the owners of capital were not permitted to manage their capital as they pleased, the capital itself would disappear, and all would suffer. Laughlin brushed aside talk of the conflict between labor and capital by asserting that the entrepreneur is merely a high-priced laborer and not a capitalist at all. The conflict, said Laughlin, is not between capital and labor but only between different classes of laborers.[39] In his abridgment of Mill's work, Laughlin omitted Mill's chapter on the labor problem which declared that there is a necessary antagonism between capital and labor.

Attempts to improve the position of the laborer through legislation were generally stigmatized by the laissez-faire economists as economically unsound. The economists approved of labor legislation for children and, perhaps, women, since these groups could not take care of themselves; but they proclaimed their opposition to legislative aid to adult male laborers.[40] It would be an "economic abomination" for legislators to determine how many hours a day a man should work or how much a day his employer should pay him, said Arthur Perry. The idea that the worker should be paid a living wage, rather than the market wage as determined by the laws of the universe, is pure and simple communism, declared Godkin's *Nation*. Advocacy of the eight-hour law and of an anticontract labor law in the Republican platform of 1884 was also denounced as "communistic" by the same journal. To those who, like Perry, accepted the wages-fund theory, labor legislation seemed completely futile. What could government do to increase the wages fund or to decrease the number of laborers? [41]

[39] Sturtevant, *Economics*, p. 338; Newcomb, *A Plain Man's Talk on the Labor Question*, p. 141; Laughlin, *Elements of Political Economy*, pp. 226–231.

[40] Arthur Hadley summed up this view when he declared: "We have to take care of our women and children by special legislation; but any attempt to apply the same policy to men's labor is a different matter" (Connecticut Bureau of Labor Statistics, *First Annual Report* [Second Series], *1885* [Hartford, Conn., 1885], p. 69). In his reports as commissioner of the Connecticut Bureau of Labor Statistics, Hadley evidenced some sympathy for trade unions and sanctioned some minor labor legislation, but his general stand was against the "legislative remedy." See *ibid.*, pp. 73–76, 79, 89–91, 102; and *Second Annual Report, 1886* (Hartford, Conn., 1886), pp. xviii–xxx, lx.

[41] Perry, *Elements of Political Economy*, pp. 138–140, 150; [Godkin], "Labor and Politics," *Nation*, XIV (June 13, 1872), 386–387; [Horace White], "Communistic Features of the Chicago Platform," *ibid.*, XXXVIII (June 26, 1884), 540.

The drive against general working-hours legislation was led by Edward Atkinson. When Samuel Gompers asked him to state his views with respect to the American Federation of Labor's efforts to introduce the eight-hour day, Atkinson gave the categorical reply: "I am opposed to any and all statutes which take from adult men and adult women the liberty to make their own contracts." [42] He denounced the proposal to reduce the number of working hours by law as an attempt to impose morality and secure leisure and prosperity by legislative fiat, as an effort to control "conditions . . . wholly beyond the reach of statute." Production, he declared, depends on the length of time spent at the work bench. The hours of labor can be reduced only as man learns to guide the forces of nature more intelligently. To attempt to shorten the working day by law is to attempt "to substitute a statute for a steam engine." Moreover, workers who seek such legislation are in effect asking to be deprived of their liberty to dispose of their own time. Time is the one element of production that they have in common with the capitalist, and reduction of hours by legislation only serves to make labor and capital unequal in this additional respect.[43]

The laborer's attempt to improve his position by means of the labor union and the strike was also frowned upon by the laissez-faire economists. Trade unions, they insisted, not only increase the antagonism between labor and capital but are potential monopolies which interfere with competition by seeking to prescribe the rate of wages, limit the number of workers who can enter a trade, and fix prices. The worker was advised that membership in a union involved a serious curtailment of his liberty. The union would drag him down to the level of the inferior worker and would check his opportunity to become a capitalist. Indeed, Simon Newcomb could think of no cause that had contributed so much "to the poverty and suffering of the laboring class" as trade unions. [44] Strikes were similarly castigated by the

[42] Atkinson to Gompers, August 27, 1889, Atkinson Letterbooks, Atkinson Papers.

[43] Atkinson, "Inefficiency of Economic Legislation," *Journal of Social Science,* IV (1871), 123–132; Atkinson, "The Eight-Hour Question," *Bradstreet's,* XIII (April 24, 1886), 260–262; Atkinson, "The Hours of Labor," *North American Review,* CXLII (May, 1886), 507–515; Atkinson and Cabot, "Personal Liberty," *Popular Science Monthly,* XL (February, 1892), 433–446. See also [Godkin], "The Eight-Hour Movement," *Nation,* I (November 16, 1865), 615–616; and Amasa Walker, "Legal Interference with the Hours of Labor," *Lippincott's,* II (November, 1868), 527–533.

[44] Sturtevant, *Economics,* pp. 163–166; Perry, *Elements of Political Economy,*

economists. Newcomb referred to them as "a kind of war waged against society." Perry condemned them as "false in theory" and "pernicious in practice," and Bowen believed that they "violate the inalienable right of every individual to dispose of his industry and his property as he pleases." [45]

Little sympathy was evidenced by the laissez-faire economists for the unemployed. Unemployment was pictured as the result of intemperance, ignorance, laziness, incompetence, or unwillingness or incapacity to do the work that was waiting to be done. The roots of the problem were considered ethical and moral rather than economic, and the cure, it was thought, would therefore have to come from that direction. Ultimately, said Laughlin, the problem resolves itself into a return to Christian teachings. If the worker improves his character, he will become a more valuable laborer. The state certainly cannot create character and industrial capacity.[46] State intervention in the form of public work for the unemployed was denounced by one writer as "the compulsory waste of capital that would be productively employed under conditions of freedom" and by another writer as "an utter negation of the right of private property." [47]

For the solution of the labor problem, the laissez-faire economists had little to offer other than a conviction that the unimpeded workings of economic laws would secure justice for both labor and capital. The bankruptcy of the laissez-faire position in the face of this great economic problem is perhaps best illustrated by Edward Atkinson's crusade for the Aladdin Oven, the adoption of which, he contended, would be a ready antidote for all the ills of labor.[48] Atkinson, who on one

---

p. 149; Wayland, *Elements of Political Economy* (recast by Chapin), pp. 111, 175–178; George Frederic Parsons, "The Labor Question," *Atlantic Monthly*, LVIII (July, 1886), 103; Newcomb, "The Organization of Labor. II. The Interest of the Laborer in Production," *Princeton Review*, N.S., VI (September, 1880), 239.

[45] See Newcomb, "The Organization of Labor. II," *Princeton Review*, N.S., VI (September, 1880), 241; Perry, *Elements of Political Economy*, pp. 144–148; and Bowen, *American Political Economy*, p. 114. See also Laughlin, *Elements of Political Economy*, pp. 345–347.

[46] Atkinson, *Distribution of Products*, p. 178; testimony of Atkinson, Senate Committee on Education and Labor, *Report upon the Relations between Labor and Capital* (Washington, D.C., 1885), III, 344; D. McG. Means, "The Dangerous Absurdity of State Aid," *Forum*, XVII (May, 1894), 295; Sturtevant, *Economics*, p. 323; Laughlin, *Elements of Political Economy*, pp. 347–349.

[47] See Means, "The Dangerous Absurdity of State Aid," *Forum*, XVII (May, 1894), 292; and Sturtevant, *Economics*, pp. 315–316.

[48] The Aladdin Oven was "a fully insulated piece of apparatus with heat applied

occasion declared that he did not "believe in philanthropy toward the able bodied that does not pay six per cent," [49] maintained that there were three possible means of improving the lot of the laborer: namely, an increase in the quantity of the product and of the market for it, a change in the existing methods of distribution without an increase in the quantity of the product, or an improved mode of using what was produced.

Increased production, Atkinson believed, was best secured by the forces of competition and invention, and he therefore saw absolutely no reason for tampering with the productive machinery of society. He considered the existing method of distribution eminently fair: the worker, in his view, was already receiving 90 per cent of what was produced, and if the share of the capitalist were reduced any further, Atkinson was convinced that he would withdraw his capital. For all practical purposes, then, the problem of helping the worker by direct action resolved itself into teaching him how to use more effectively what was produced. As the means of attaining this objective, Atkinson offered the Aladdin Oven and new rules of cooking that would enable the worker to cut down on waste in the preparation of food. If the worker were careful, he could save as much as five cents a day by the use of the new stove. And, asked Atkinson triumphantly: "Can the anarchist, the communist, the socialist, the protectionist, the free trader, the co-operator, the paper-money man, the knight of labor, the eight-hour man, or the sentimentalist invent or suggest any other method of changing the direction of the industry of the whole community which would on the whole be so effective in improving the conditions of all, as one which would save five cents a day on food and fuel, the money saved to be devoted to providing better houses in which people may live?" [50]

Jane Addams accepted the gift of an Aladdin Oven at Hull House, and Booker T. Washington used several of the ovens at Tuskegee; but that champion of the laboring man, John Swinton, looked upon Atkinson as "the master in the terrible school of inhumanity . . . which is sustained by all of the forces that seem to me to be working for Evil,"

---

from a common lamp in which a little over two pints of kerosene oil would do the work of 120 pounds of coal burned in an ordinary cooking stove" (Roswell Cheney McCrea, "Edward Atkinson," in *Dictionary of American Biography,* I, 407).

[49] Atkinson to Wells, October 12, 1875, Wells Papers, Library of Congress.

[50] Atkinson, *Industrial Progress of the Nation,* pp. 219–246; Williamson, *Atkinson,* pp. 269–272.

and a workingman referred to him as "a man whom the poor regard and rightly as there [*sic*] mortal enemy." [51]   Atkinson, nevertheless, was completely sincere in his promotion of the Aladdin Oven.   He informed Andrew Carnegie that if he (Atkinson) could save the people five cents a day on food and fuel, he would benefit them more than Carnegie could by giving away his entire fortune.   The oven, he wrote Albert Shaw, was destined to "cause a profound revolution in the condition of the civilized world . . . that is what I am going down to posterity upon.   The epitaph on my monument will be 'He taught the American people how to stew.' " [52]   Thus did an anachronistic laissez-faire brand of liberalism confront a major problem of the industrial age.

Consistent in the application of their views, the laissez-faire economists stood foursquare against the protective tariff.[53]   Free trade was, in a sense, the cornerstone of their whole system.   Once admit the right of the government to regulate the economic life of the nation through a protective tariff, and the whole edifice of laissez faire would crumble.   To the laissez-faire economist, the protective tariff was perhaps the most patent violation of those economic principles that he believed to be universally true.   No other device of government did he criticize so vehemently or denounce with so much moral fervor.

The economists most active in the antiprotectionist ranks were David Ames Wells and Arthur Latham Perry.   Wells, a onetime disciple of Henry Carey, did not become a foe of protection until after 1865, when his service as special commissioner of the revenue and his contact with Edward Atkinson caused him to alter his views regarding the tariff.   His reports of 1868, 1869, and 1870 as special commissioner established him as a foe of the existing tariff and projected him into the forefront of the drive for tariff reform.   He came to look upon the tariff question as the most vital issue of the day, and he won recognition as perhaps the leading intellectual advocate of

[51] See Addams to Atkinson, May 3, 1892, Atkinson Papers; Washington to Atkinson, February 9, 1895, *ibid.*; Swinton to Atkinson, May 9, 1887, *ibid.*; and John S. Bell to Laughlin, June 6, 1895, James L. Laughlin Papers, University of Chicago Library.

[52] Atkinson to Carnegie, January 2, 1890, Atkinson Letterbooks, Atkinson Papers; Atkinson to Shaw, June 6, 1891, *ibid.*

[53] Francis Bowen was an exception: he was able to reconcile the tariff with laissez faire, although he did not entirely approve of the existing tariff in the United States. See Bowen, *American Political Economy*, pp. 20–21, 71–77; and *Nation*, XLVII (November 8, 1888), 367.

free trade in the United States.[54] Perry delivered more than two hundred addresses for the American Free Trade League, and the free-trade controversy came very "near to monopolizing his total economic thought and his teaching of Political Economy." If political economy was to be taught as a science, Perry believed, it must be taught as placing the seal of approval upon free trade. In his classroom at Williams College, the right of men to trade freely was presented "not at all as a part of a current and transient controversy, but as an inherent and immanent part of the nature of man and the purposes of God." Protection, in Perry's view, had not even attained to "the dignity of an Opinion," and he yearned for the emancipation of American industries from what he regarded as "the death-throttle of Restrictions and Prohibitions." [55]

The economists believed that government has no more right to interfere with foreign trade than with domestic trade. International trade, they maintained, is best left to the operations of competition, for under a regime of competition industry springs up where conditions for its development are favorable and dies out where they are unfavorable. The wants of the people and not the whims of a political body, they believed, should determine the course of production.[56]

Free trade and liberty were synonomous to the foes of protection.[57] Wells, for example, regarded the question of free trade as but an aspect of the whole question of human liberty. Once endanger this aspect of freedom, he believed, and all men's freedoms are endangered. He looked upon the protective system as a reaffirmation of slavery, for, like slavery, he declared, it denies to the individual the opportunity

[54] Ferleger, *Wells and the American Revenue System,* pp. 199, 223–243, 313–314; Joyner, *Wells,* pp. 40–44, 59–66, 142–146; Wells to Atkinson, July 14, 1866, May 15, 1884, Atkinson Papers.

[55] Broadus Mitchell, "Arthur Latham Perry," in *Dictionary of American Biography,* XIV, 482–483; Carroll Perry, *A Professor of Life: A Sketch of Arthur Latham Perry of Williams College* (Boston, 1923), p. 10; Perry, "Preparation for Citizenship. IV. At Williams College," *Education,* IX (April, 1889), 517–518; Perry to Stetson, October 28, 1885, Cleveland Papers.

[56] Amasa Walker, *Science of Wealth,* pp. 91–93; Sturtevant, *Economics,* pp. 135–144; Newcomb, "The Let-Alone Principle," *North American Review,* CX (January, 1870), 22–23; Perry, *Elements of Political Economy,* pp. 374–379; U. S. Congress, House, Special Commissioner of the Revenue, *Report, 1869,* 41st Cong., 2d sess., H. Exec. Doc. No. 27 (Washington, D.C., 1870), pp. cvii–cviii.

[57] Francis Lieber thought the time would come when nations would include the concept of free trade in their bills of rights (Lieber to Wells, April 1, 1869, Wells Papers, Library of Congress).

of using the products of his labor as he pleases.[58]   Perry insisted that protection constituted an interference with a "natural and inalienable right."   Not only was it, in his view, antagonistic to liberty but also to morality.   The Ten Commandments, the New Testament, and "the whole influence of Christianity," he maintained, were favorable to free trade.[59]

Protection was further denounced by the economists as an immoral device for promoting special interests.   Congress was accused of prostituting its power on behalf of influential manufacturing concerns. The many were being taxed for the benefit of the few.   "We are not merely compelled by Congress to submit to robbery," asserted Atkinson indignantly, "but we are forced to labor in order to bring into existence, and to support, the organizations which are engaged in robbing us." [60]

The tariff was also feared as the entering wedge for other forms of "paternalism": perhaps, as Laughlin feared, it would lead to socialism. If the government could minister to the needs of the industrialist, why should it not look after the farmer and the laborer?   Was not the worker told at every election that his high wages were dependent on the tariff and thus ultimately on the good will of the legislature? There was but one solution for these difficulties: Congress must have done with all forms of special legislation and must permit all economic groups to rise and fall in a free market.[61]

Congress, however, paid but little heed to the wishes of the free traders: the tariff schedules of the period after the Civil War reflected

[58] Wells, *A Primer of Tariff Reform* (London, 1885), p. 10; Wells, *Free Trade Essential to Future National Prosperity and Development* (New York, 1882), pp. 3–4; Wells, "The Creed of Free Trade," *Atlantic Monthly*, XXXVI (August, 1875), 205–206.

[59] Perry, *Elements of Political Economy*, pp. 392–393; Perry, *Williamstown and Williams College*, p. 692; Perry, "A Free Trade Lesson from the New Testament," 1882, Wells Papers, New York Public Library.   See also Atkinson, *On the Collection of Revenue*, p. 16.

[60] See Perry, *Elements of Political Economy*, pp. 430–431; *Our Revenue System and the Civil Service* (New York, c. 1872), pp. 10–17; Wayland, *Elements of Political Economy* (recast by Chapin), pp. 372–377; Hermann Lieb, *The Protective Tariff* (4th and rev. ed.; Chicago, 1888), pp. 8–14, 241–242; and Atkinson, *On the Collection of Revenue*, p. 33n.

[61] Laughlin, *Elements of Political Economy*, p. 293; Laughlin, "Protection and Socialism," *International Review*, VII (October, 1879), 427–435; Godkin, "Some Political and Social Aspects of the Tariff," in *Problems of Modern Democracy*, pp. 98–122; Sturtevant, *Economics*, pp. 135–144; *Our Revenue System and the Civil Service*, p. 17.

the wishes of the friends of protection rather than those of its foes. The advocates of free trade would gladly have settled for reforms that fell considerably short of free trade, but even such changes were not forthcoming. By the end of 1880 Wells had already concluded that "tariff reform is the deadest of all dead things." [62] But Edward Atkinson could not agree with Wells. Although his position as treasurer of the Boston Manufacturers' Fire Insurance Company, and his disgust with the tactics and with what he regarded as the inaccurate statements of the extreme free traders, had by that time persuaded him to abandon the cause of free trade in favor of a gradualist approach to tariff reform, he was nevertheless convinced that protectionism would eventually die because it had "no intellectual force behind it." [63]

The principle of laissez faire was also applied by the economists to the currency questions that troubled the nation in the years after the Civil War.[64] The economists proposed to reduce the government's role in this sphere to the purely passive one of approving the judgment of the market. What shall constitute money and the value of money, they argued, are not and cannot be the result of legislative decisions, but are rather the "natural and inevitable product of the economic machinery of society," of human judgments as to the desirability of things. The sole function of government in this matter is to adopt the standards of value already worked out in the market, "not to determine what shall be money, but to make and enforce laws to compel the fulfillment of contracts, *in that money* which experience has already established." [65] Legislation which seeks to alter values, Atkinson wrote,

[62] Wells to Atkinson, December 19, [1880], Atkinson Papers.

[63] Atkinson to R. R. Bowker, October 16, 1885, Atkinson Letterbooks, Atkinson Papers; Atkinson to Carnegie, November 1, 1890, *ibid.;* Atkinson to Wells, November 11, 1875, February 21, 1884, *ibid.;* testimony of Atkinson, U. S. Industrial Commission, *Report on Trusts and Industrial Combinations* (Vol. XIII of the Commission's *Reports;* Washington, D.C., 1901), pp. 517–551.

[64] Bowen and Sturtevant carried their laissez-faire views to the extent of opposing the national banking system because it involved government regulation of such matters as reserve requirements and the distribution of national bank notes. Bowen did not wish banks to have the power of note issue since he feared that their possession of this power gave rise to the view that they were subject to legislative control even with respect to their functions of discount and deposit. See Bowen, *American Political Economy,* pp. 367–393; Bowen to McCulloch, December 19, 1867, Hugh McCulloch Papers, Library of Congress; and Sturtevant, *Economics,* pp. 99–102.

[65] See Sturtevant, Review of Prof. Perry's *Political Economy, New Englander,* XXXVIII (January, 1879), 30–32; Sturtevant, *Economics,* pp. 78–84; Bowen, *American Political Economy,* pp. 260–261; Newcomb, "The Let-Alone Principle," *North American Review,* CX (January, 1870), 8–10, 27–30; Newcomb, *The A B C of*

serves but to "obstruct the working of the higher laws with which . . . statutes must be made consistent if they are to have any duration." [66]

Given views such as these, the economists naturally looked with jaundiced eye upon the continued circulation of greenbacks, the irredeemable legal-tender currency issued by the Union government during the Civil War. Amasa Walker spoke of the "pernicious character" of this "fictitious currency" and insisted that so long as such a currency circulated the laws of value would inevitably bring a premium on gold. Sturtevant maintained that the government issue of legal-tender currency was "utterly destructive of the property rights of the creditor." "A government," he declared, "never can make its promises to pay a legal tender in the payment of private debts, without violating the fundamental law of all exchange, the free consent of both parties." [67]

Although a few of the economists were content to meet the problem presented by the greenbacks simply by providing for the redemption of the legal tenders in gold,[68] most of them wished to see the greenbacks expunged from circulation entirely. "The Government," Atkinson advised McCulloch, "cannot assume the functions of a bank by issuing a convertible currency"; and with these sentiments Wells, Laughlin, and White agreed.[69] Wells insisted that the federal government

---

Finance (New York, 1877), pp. 41–44; Godkin, "The Real Problems of Democracy," in *Problems of Modern Democracy,* pp. 297–299; Hadley, *Economics,* pp. 227–231; and Monetary Commission of the Indianapolis Convention of Boards of Trade . . . , *Report* (Chicago, 1898), pp. 101–102 (written by Laughlin).

[66] Atkinson to A. J. Warner, May 20, 1885, Atkinson Letterbooks, Atkinson Papers.

[67] See Walker to McCulloch, February 4, 1867, McCulloch Papers; Walker, *Science of Wealth,* pp. 132–136; Sturtevant, *Economics,* pp. 83–84. Taussig also opposed paper-money issues but only on practical grounds; he saw "no strong intrinsic objection" (Taussig, Supplementary Chapter, in Émile de Laveleye, *The Elements of Political Economy* [New York, 1884], p. 281).

[68] Bowen suggested in 1870 that the Treasury should begin to redeem paper currency in specie at the rate of 85¢ on the dollar (he estimated the value of the greenback dollar at that time as 83¢) and then should advance the price 5¢ every six months until full parity was attained. He later advocated contraction of the greenbacks as well. See *American Political Economy,* pp. 366–367; and U. S. Congress, Senate, Monetary Commission, *Report and Accompanying Documents,* 44th Cong., 2d sess., S. Rep. No. 703 (Washington, D.C., 1877), p. 160 (for Bowen's minority report). See also Newcomb, *A B C of Finance,* pp. 106–111.

[69] Atkinson to McCulloch, November 17, 1867, McCulloch Papers; Indianapolis Monetary Commission, *Report,* pp. 390–392; White, *Money and Banking Illustrated by American History* (Boston, 1895), pp. 226–227.

should "get out of and abandon forever and as soon as possible this whole business of creating and issuing paper money, be it redeemable or irredeemable." Partly to accomplish this objective he proposed what was known as the "cremation theory of specie resumption." The secretary of the treasury, Wells suggested, should destroy by burning on a given day every week a minimum of five hundred thousand dollars in greenbacks and should continue this process of cremation until greenbacks had attained a parity with gold.[70] Amasa Walker, whose own suggestion was that compound-interest notes be substituted for greenbacks, saw nothing in Wells's plan that was "not sound in principle," although he did think that the burning of but five hundred thousand a week was "rather too slow a process." [71] Wells's proposal was not accepted by Congress, which preferred a plan of direct specie resumption.

The successful accomplishment of specie resumption in 1879 did not dispose of the money question, for by that time the battle of the standards was already under way. Once again the laissez-faire economists cautioned the government not to accept the proposals of the inflationists, in this case the advocates of free silver. The silver agitation, Taussig pointed out, was "born of restlessness and ignorance," and he deplored the disposition of so many "to tinker with the currency as a remedy for real or fancied evils." [72] Gold, the economists argued, had through the process of natural selection and survival of the fittest proved itself better suited to the needs of commerce than silver, and it would be "presumptuous [for government] to attempt to interfere with an obviously natural evolution in human affairs." The government, in short, must accept the dictates of natural law by adopting a single gold standard. Were the government to assign to silver a value greater than its bullion value, gold, in accordance with Gresham's law, would be driven from circulation, and an inferior silver standard would replace the superior gold standard.[73]

[70] Wells, *The Cremation Theory of Specie Resumption* (New York, 1875), pp. 5–6, 13, 15–16. In establishing the David A. Wells prizes at Harvard, Wells provided, among other conditions, that no essay was to be considered which advocated "the issue by . . . government of irredeemable notes . . . as a substitute for money" (cited in Dorfman, *Economic Mind in American Civilization*, III, 81–82).

[71] Walker to Wells, February 10, 1875, Wells Papers, Library of Congress.

[72] Taussig, "The Silver Situation in the United States," *Publications of the American Economic Association*, VII (January, 1892), 112–113.

[73] Wells, *Practical Economics*, pp. 39–42, 52–53; White, *Money and Banking*, pp. 27–32, 105–107; White, *Coin's Financial Fool* (New York, 1895), p. 105; Laughlin, *Facts about Money* (Chicago, 1895), pp. 94–95; Indianapolis Monetary

Atkinson announced himself as perfectly willing to sanction the free coinage of silver at 16 to 1 provided that all acts of legal tender were repealed and individuals were permitted to specify in their contracts the metal in which the terms of their contract were to be satisfied. If neither gold nor silver was specified in a contract, payment, he proposed, should be made in the dollar of the greater purchasing power at the time the contract matured. "The more you study the problem," Atkinson wrote Wells, "the more you realize the fact that legal tender acts were born in fraud and have been nursed in corruption; that the remedy is free coinage without alternate or optional legal tender." [74]

The economists did what they could to stem the tide of free silver. Wells argued that the low prices of the period were not the result of gold scarcity (he referred to the "d—— nonsense" of this theory) but to technological improvement and the general influence of supply and demand. The single gold standard, he insisted, would not result in appreciation in the value of gold, for the increased demand for gold would be met by a corresponding increase in the supply. All would be well "if people will only keep their hands off." [75] Laughlin, who after a brief sojourn in the business world had returned to academic life partly so that he "might be of some use . . . in these days of financial heresy," exposed in the popular press what he considered the dangers of free silver and entered into debate with William "Coin" Harvey, who had been so ungracious as to enroll the gold-standard economist in "Coin's Financial School." [76] Horace White also sought to refute

---

Commission, *Report,* pp. 101–102; "Bimetallic Theory," *Nation,* LVII (July 13, 1893), 22–23; Atkinson for the *Voice,* January 15, 1891, Atkinson Letterbooks, Atkinson Papers; Atkinson, "The Philosophy of Money," *Monist,* VI (April, 1896), 341, 349–350.

[74] Atkinson to A. J. Warner, May 23, 1885, Atkinson Letterbooks, Atkinson Papers; "Silver," entry after March 9, 1891, *ibid.;* "Free Coinage 16 to 1,—Why Not?" MS in Atkinson Papers for January–April, 1895; Atkinson to W. J. Bryan, September 21, 1896, Atkinson Letterbooks, *ibid.;* Atkinson to Wells, August 21, 1896, *ibid.*

[75] Wells to Atkinson, May 22, August 15, September 19, 1887, Atkinson Papers; Wells, *Practical Economics,* pp. 52–53.

[76] Laughlin to Newcomb, May 17, 1890, Newcomb Papers; Laughlin, *Facts about Money;* Bornemann, *Laughlin,* pp. 42–46. W. H. Harvey's best-selling *Coin's Financial School* (Chicago, 1894) had as its setting an imaginary school where "Professor Coin" argued the virtues of free silver and demolished the arguments of gold-bug "students" in the class such as Laughlin. Some persons actually believed that Laughlin had attended Coin's "lectures" (see, for example, Edward A. Temple

Coin Harvey with an exposition of his own sound-money views, and he urged President Cleveland to stand firm in his fight to protect the gold reserve.[77] Atkinson, who, unlike Wells, regarded the money question as a far more significant issue than the tariff, threw all his vast energies into the fight against Bryan in 1896.[78] To the immense relief of the laissez-faire economists, Bryan and free silver went down to defeat, and the triumph of the single gold standard was assured.

In the drive for some form of public regulation of the railroads, the economists found it difficult to maintain their laissez-faire position; for, as Arthur Hadley, who was a pioneer in the field of railroad economics, demonstrated, because of the problem of fixed costs, competition could not prevail for any length of time in the railroad industry, and consolidation was inevitable. The absence of competition as a regulating factor did not, however, persuade the economists that government ownership or extensive government regulation was the answer to railway abuses. Hadley, for example, argued that "publicity and responsibility are more important than any set of laws or regulations," and although he favored the establishment of a federal railroad commission, he did not wish it to have any extensive powers.[79] Atkinson, who pointed to decreasing railroad charges as evidence that regulation beyond what was required to secure publicity of accounts was unnecessary, was alarmed at decisions of the United States Supreme Court that confirmed the right of the states to regulate railway fares and, unlike Hadley, at the passage of the Interstate Commerce Act. "I regard the Interstate Commerce Act," he wrote to Henry Demarest Lloyd, "as having stopped the tide of progress in railway corporations, injuring existing corporations and depriving the public of yet more benefit that might have ensued." Interference with the railroads, he

---

to Laughlin, April 30, 1895, Laughlin Papers); and Laughlin felt it necessary to make a public denial. See Dorfman, *Economic Mind in American Civilization,* III, 226–227. Laughlin incidentally had informed Richard T. Ely on October 26, 1889, that he was not "a believer under all conditions in a gold standard." However, he regarded it "as the only expedient" at the time (Ely Papers, State Historical Society of Wisconsin).

[77] White, *Coin's Financial Fool;* White to Cleveland, March 14, 1894, Cleveland Papers.

[78] See Atkinson's Letterbooks for the months of the campaign, and Atkinson to Carnegie, January 12, 1897, Atkinson Letterbooks, Atkinson Papers.

[79] Hadley, *Railroad Transportation* (New York, 1885), pp. 63–81, 136–140, 144–145; Hadley, "American Railroad Legislation," *Harper's Monthly Magazine,* LXXV (June, 1887), 141–150.

advised, should be stopped, and the roads should once again be subjected "to the law of competition of product with product in the great markets of the world which will compel them to reduce their charges to the lowest point possible." [80]

Although the economists were generally willing to sanction a minimum of railroad regulation, they were particularly opposed to the vesting of rate-making power in the hands of public authorities. In this matter, they would trust only to the self-interest of the railway corporation; for if the corporation erred in its judgment, the laws of trade would force corrective action, whereas that would not necessarily be the case if the decisions were made by the state. [81]

The conservative economists who addressed themselves to the problem of industrial consolidation in the 1880's and 1890's did not find in it any cause for real alarm or any reason to abandon their laissez-faire views. The Harvard economist-historian Silas Macvane, an "undiluted follower of the classical school," [82] maintained that in a country which permitted "perfect freedom of industry" there was "no serious danger to be apprehended from 'trusts' or other combinations to interfere with the natural course of production and exchange." Effective combination, he argued, was impossible where there were a great number of producers and the means of production were widespread, and it had yet to be demonstrated that a powerful combination could be maintained even if the sources of production were limited. [83] Edward Atkinson, as might have been expected, had no "special fear of trusts," since trusts could not, in his view, contravene the laws of competition. The trusts that survived, such as Standard Oil, did so because they offered their products to the public at lower prices than had previously prevailed; those that sought to raise prices or effect a monopoly generally contained within themselves "the seeds of their

[80] Atkinson, *The Railway, The Farmer, and the Public* (New York, 1885), pp. 3–41, 57–58; Atkinson to Albert Fink, June 2, 1881, Atkinson Letterbooks, Atkinson Papers; Atkinson to Lloyd, May 9, 1898, *ibid.;* abridgment of Atkinson's remarks at meeting of American Economic Association, appended to letter from Atkinson to J. W. Jenks, January 23, 1895, Atkinson Papers.

[81] Wells, "How Will the United States Supreme Court Decide the Granger Railroad Cases?" *Nation,* XIX (October 29, 1874), 282–284; "Regulation and Confiscation," *ibid.,* XLVII (September 6, 1888), 185–186; "The Granger Decisions," *ibid.,* XXIV (March 8, 1877), 143–144; Wayland, *Elements of Political Economy* (recast by Chapin), pp. 381–390.

[82] Dorfman, *Economic Mind in American Civilization,* III, 244.

[83] Macvane, *The Working Principles of Political Economy in a New and Practical Form* (2d ed. rev.; New York, 1897), pp. 118–119.

own dissolution." If abuses had cropped up, they could be corrected by securing "publicity of accounts." [84]

Hadley recognized that free competition could not be maintained in industries that required the massing of large capital funds under concentrated management, but, as in his treatment of the railroad problem, he did not believe that the absence of competition justified extensive government intervention. He rejected the prohibition of trusts, state ownership, limitation of profits, and control of prices as improper solutions for the trust problem and suggested that what was needed were measures that would secure publicity for the actions of combinations and that would educate the directors of the large concerns to an appreciation of their responsibilities. The "creation of a more enlightened public sentiment" was Hadley's real solution for the trust problem.[85]

The laissez-faire economist believed himself in possession of the ultimate truth insofar as economic affairs were concerned. He wished to consign all economic problems to the operations of economic law and to restrict the government to a few simple functions. It mattered not that the economic life of the nation was becoming increasingly complex and that economic facts did not always correspond with economic theory. Principles that are eternally true do not have to be adjusted to changing conditions.

II

Occupying a middle ground between the economists who accepted laissez faire as a principle eternally true and those who rejected it as a safe guide for state policy was Francis Amasa Walker. Walker's work marks a transition between the old and the new schools of political economy. Walker saw certain significant fallacies in the as-

[84] See testimony of Atkinson, U. S. Industrial Commission, *Report on Trusts and Industrial Combinations*, XIII, 533–534; Atkinson to Lloyd, May 9, 1898, Atkinson Letterbooks, Atkinson Papers; Atkinson to the editor of "Bellamy Review," November 3, 1900, *ibid.*; and Atkinson's reply to questions of Civic Federation of Chicago, attached to letter from Ralph M. Easley and Franklin H. Head to Atkinson, August 12, 1899, Atkinson Papers.

[85] Hadley, "Private Monopolies and Public Rights," *Quarterly Journal of Economics*, I (October, 1886), 28–44; Hadley, "The Formation and Control of Trusts," *Scribner's*, XXVI (November, 1889), 604–610; Hadley, "Some Difficulties of Public Business Management," *Political Science Quarterly*, III (December, 1888), 572–591; Hadley, *Economics*, pp. 165–179; Hadley, "The Good and Evil of Industrial Combination," *Atlantic Monthly*, LXXIX (March, 1897), 377–385.

sumptions underlying the philosophy of laissez faire; yet he was reluctant to repudiate the let-alone policy.   His writings show the heavy
impress of classical political economy, but he was nevertheless selected
as the first president of the new school's American Economic Association.[86]

After having served meritoriously during the Civil War, Walker in
1869 became a deputy of Special Commissioner of the Revenue David
A. Wells and chief of the Bureau of Statistics, and in the latter capacity
he superintended the taking of both the Ninth Census and the Tenth
Census.   He taught political economy at the Sheffield Scientific School
of Yale from 1873 to 1881, and from 1881 until his death in 1897 he
was president of the Massachusetts Institute of Technology.   He was
hailed at his death as "unquestionably the most prominent and the best
known of American writers" in the realm of economics.[87]

"I can not swallow a great many things which have been treated by
the economists of the hypothetical school as axiomatic," Walker wrote
to David Wells in 1874.   "It is high time for us to review the fundamental assumptions of pol. econ." [88]   What Walker found particularly
difficult to "swallow" were the classical doctrines with respect to wages
and profits, and in both of these areas he "hit the Economic Harmonies
pretty hard" [89] and made significant departures from accepted views.
He repudiated the wages-fund theory (he spoke of the "infernal nonsense and nuisance of the wages fund" [90]) and declared that wages
come out of the existing product of industry, the laborer being the
residual claimant after rent, interest, and profits are deducted.   Subject to these deductions, Walker argued, laborers receive all that they
help to produce.[91]

[86] For the new school of political economy and the American Economic Association, see Chapter VII.   Richard T. Ely asserted in 1887 that the beginnings of the
new school of political economy could be dated from the writings of Francis Walker.
His works, Ely declared, had probably been a greater source of inspiration to the
members of the new school than had the writings of any other man ("Political Economy in America," *North American Review*, CXLIV [February, 1887], 117).

[87] He was so called by Taussig in the *Springfield Daily Republican*, January 6,
1897 (cited in Jeannette P. Nichols, "Francis Amasa Walker," in *Dictionary of
American Biography*, XIX, 343–344).

[88] Walker to Wells, June 29, 1874, Wells Papers, Library of Congress.

[89] Walker to Richard T. Ely, April 30, 1884, Ely Papers.   Walker regarded
this as "only destructive" and believed that it "should but clear the way for serious,
careful, productive work in economics" (*ibid.*).

[90] Walker to Wells, February 8, 1875, Wells Papers, Library of Congress.

[91] Walker's theory of wages is set forth in Walker, *The Wages Question* (New

Walker's theory of profits stemmed from his view as to the importance of the entrepreneur. It was the entrepreneur, Walker thought, who was primarily responsible for the gain in American industrial power. It was his task to enforce discipline in the factory, to organize, to furnish technical skill, and, above all, to "assume the responsibilities of production." "The armies of industry," Walker asserted, "can no more be raised, equipped, held together, moved and engaged, without their commanders, than can the armies of war." He felt that English and American economists had not sufficiently appreciated the entrepreneurial function and had tended to confuse the entrepreneur with the capitalist and the entrepreneur's share of the product of industry, profits, with the capitalist's share, interest. Walker, however, regarded profits as governed by the same law as rent. Profits, he held, are due to differences in ability among entrepreneurs just as rent is due to differences in the fertility of land.[92]

Walker, like the classical economists, believed that political economy should concern itself only with wealth. He thought that the student of economics should not "allow any purely political, ethical or social considerations to influence him in his investigations." He has no right to assume the existence of a beneficent natural order; nor is he to concern himself with the equity of existing institutions. What "is," not what "ought to be," is properly his sole consideration.[93]

And looking at what is, Walker found that the perfect competition that appeared so prominently in the theory of the economists unfortunately did not exist in actuality. Walker believed strongly in the efficacy of "free and full, unqualified, unremitting competition." Competition of this sort, he thought, would ensure an equitable diffusion of burdens and benefits throughout society and would lead each individual to the best market for his services.[94] But, unlike the classical

York, 1876), and, in brief, in Walker, *Political Economy* (New York, 1883), pp. 259–268.

[92] Walker, *Political Economy,* pp. 60–62, 76–77, 244–259. Parrington, because of Walker's views on the entrepreneur and profits, refers to Walker as "the self-appointed champion of industrialism, the official economist of the Gilded Age" (*The Beginnings of Critical Realism in America* [New York, 1930], p. 111). Walker, however, was less "conservative" in his views on the relations of the state to industry than were the laissez-faire economists discussed above. For a penetrating analysis of Walker's contributions to economic theory, see Hadley, "Francis A. Walker's Contributions to Economic Theory," *Political Science Quarterly,* XII (June, 1897), 295–308.

[93] Walker, *Political Economy,* pp. 1, 25–27.

[94] *Ibid.,* p. 273; Walker, *Wages Question,* pp. 157–160.

economists, he was ready to face the fact that perfect competition existed in theory only.

Walker was mainly concerned with the effect of imperfect competition on the laboring class. Theoretically, under a regime of perfect competition, the worker would not only know what his best interest was, but would actually seek that interest until he attained it. Walker, however, saw that there was little correspondence between theory and reality. The worker stayed where he was, and either because of ignorance, superstition, timidity, or love of home and friends did not seek the best market for his services. Nor did the employer always act according to the dictates of perfect competition. He seemed prone to look for immediate gain by cutting wages, increasing hours, and neglecting sanitary requirements. This failure of competition to operate satisfactorily resulted in hardship to the laboring class and a consequent deterioration in its quality. Orthodox doctrine held that such injuries were temporary and tended to disappear. Lower wages were supposed to be transformed into lower prices, and excessive profits were to bring increased competition for workers and thus higher wages. Walker, however, saw that the facts were rather different, that injuries of this sort tended to perpetuate themselves and to make the rich richer and the poor poorer.[95]

The failure of an unregulated economic order to secure justice for the laborer caused Walker to question the validity of the doctrine of laissez faire and the assumptions upon which it rested. Individual interests, he found, do not necessarily coincide with the general interest, and economic phenomena do not adjust themselves spontaneously for the common good. It cannot be assumed that competition is perfect, that the individual will seek the best market for his services.[96]

But though Walker questioned the soundness of laissez faire, he also had his doubts concerning the advisability of a program of state control. In this respect he was pretty much in accord with the laissez-faire economists. State action to him meant restraint, and he felt that "there is not and there can never be any positive virtue in restraint. . . . There is no life in it and no force can come out of it." However well-intentioned state intervention might be in its efforts to

[95] Walker, *First Lessons in Political Economy* (New York, 1893), pp. 261–265, 276; Walker, *Wages Question,* pp. 163–164, 357–359; Walker, *Political Economy,* pp. 272–286.

[96] Walker, *Wages Question,* pp. 163–164; Walker, *Political Economy,* pp. 286–287.

deal with evils associated with individual action, it was bound "in some degree to miss its mark, and to work more or less of positive mischief. . . . Legislation is always more or less unwise; administration always falls in some degree short of its intent." "It is only when politicians undertake to direct the nation, that we get into trouble," Walker wrote to Simon Newcomb.[97]

Walker thus found himself in a dilemma: he was unwilling to accept either a program of unqualified laissez faire or a program calling for state action. Of the two, however, he found laissez faire more to his liking. Although he readily admitted that strict adherence to this policy had done a considerable amount of harm, he believed unrestricted freedom of individual action to be so important an element in the operation of industry that there was a powerful presumption in its favor. Walker therefore threw in his lot with the British economists John Stuart Mill, J. E. Cairnes, and W. Stanley Jevons and, like them, concluded that although laissez faire was lacking in scientific authority, it was nevertheless "a practical rule of conduct of wide range and high validity" and a safer guide to follow than the principle of state control. Laissez faire was indeed subject to numerous exceptions and was not to be permitted to stand in the way of any urgently required action on the part of the state or to serve as a check to measures which were certain to bring large gains to society, but the presumption in all cases was in its favor, and a "heavy burden of proof" rested on the advocates of state action.[98] "I believe in general," Walker told a Senate committee, "that that government is best which governs least, and that interference with trade or manufactures is very undesirable. Yet I recognize the fact that evils may and do exist which require correction by the force of law." [99]

A philosophy of "laissez faire the rule, state intervention the exception" is, of course, an elastic one. An individual who was sympathetically attuned to the cause of reform, like John Stuart Mill, could

[97] Walker, *Political Economy*, p. 464; Walker, *Wages Question*, p. 413; Walker to Newcomb, December 14, 1878, Newcomb Papers. See also Munroe, *Francis Amasa Walker*, pp. 145–148.

[98] Walker, *Political Economy*, pp. 286–287, 464; Walker, "Recent Progress of Political Economy in the United States," *Publications of the American Economic Association*, IV (1889), 257–258; Walker, *Wages Question*, pp. 413–414; Walker, "Socialism," in *Discussions in Economics and Statistics*, ed. Davis R. Dewey (New York, 1899), II, 270–271.

[99] Senate Committee on Education and Labor, *Report upon the Relations between Labor and Capital*, III, 325.

start out with such a doctrine and end up with something bordering on socialism. Francis Amasa Walker, however, made no such widespread exceptions to the general rule of laissez faire. His examination of the conditions of the laboring class had originally led him to question the soundness of the assumptions upon which the doctrine of laissez faire was based, and it was therefore chiefly with respect to the laboring class that he was willing to permit deviations from that doctrine. Despite all the defects that he saw in state intervention, he conceded that the "wages class may, in exceptional instances, be helped forward in an important degree towards a real and vital competition, by the exercise of the prohibitory power of the State." The community must indeed intervene to prevent "the permanent degradation of the laboring classes through the operation of economical forces which the individual is powerless to resist." [100]

Factory legislation was justified in Walker's view if it improved the ability of the worker to seek the best market for his services and thus helped to promote competition. Legislation of this sort, "wisely conceived to meet the grave and perhaps incurable infirmities of manufacturing populations," would result in increased production and a more equitable distribution of wealth, and was not to be construed as an interference with freedom of contract. A sound man, Walker contended, may not need a crutch, but one suffering from an infirmity does. "If political economy objects to such legislation, so much the worse . . . for political economy." [101]

Although Walker did not spell out in detail the legislation that he favored for the laborer, he did approve the regulation of the working hours and working conditions of women and children, the prohibition of labor beyond ages where it becomes physically harmful, health legislation, a system of sanitary administration and factory inspection, and compulsory primary education. He obviously did not favor minimum-wage or maximum-hour legislation embracing all employees, nor did he advocate a program of social insurance. Examining the industrial situation in 1888, he expressed the belief that there already was an equilibrium of power between labor and capital and that there was but little more the state need do for the workingman. He disapproved of the campaign for the eight-hour day and considered a

[100] Walker, *Wages Question,* pp. 356–357, 411–414.
[101] Walker, *Political Economy,* pp. 376–377; Walker, *First Lessons in Political Economy,* p. 276.

public-housing program for any but the poorest workers a "monstrous step toward Socialism." [102]

In addition to favoring a modicum of labor legislation, Walker also suggested that the state exercise a general regulatory power over the corporate form of enterprise and that industries tending toward monopoly be subject either to government ownership or to government regulation and control.[103] He was also a bit of a heretic with respect to the money question and, unlike David A. Wells and other laissez-faire economists, contended that gold monometallism was an important cause of the decline in the price level after 1873. He attacked the demonetization of silver in the United States that resulted from the Coinage Act of 1873 and entered a strong plea for a system of international bimetallism.[104]

Francis Amasa Walker had much in common with the laissez-faire economists, and, indeed, he would have liked to advocate a policy of unqualified laissez faire. However, since he perceived that an unregulated economic order did not operate in exact accord with economic theory, he was willing to countenance a limited amount of state intervention. He still considered laissez faire a valid rule for state conduct, but he recognized that the public welfare could, on occasion, be advanced by social legislation. Walker continued to think of state action in terms of restraint, but his partial abandonment of laissez faire was at least a halting step in the direction of the general-welfare state.

III

In the period between the end of the Civil War and the turn of the century the laissez-faire theme was most cogently expressed in the United States by William Graham Sumner. In a series of pungent essays written for the leading journals of the day, Sumner argued effectively for a program of undiluted individualism and established

[102] Walker, *Wages Question*, pp. 414–415; testimony of Walker, Senate Committee on Education and Labor, *Report upon the Relations between Labor and Capital*, III, 325, 330–331; Walker, "The Knights of Labor," in *Discussions in Economics and Statistics*, II, 335; Walker, "The Eight-Hour-Law Agitation," *ibid.*, II, 379–396; Walker, "Socialism," *ibid.*, II, 267.

[103] Walker, "Socialism," in *Discussions in Economics and Statistics*, II, 266; Walker, "Is Socialism Dangerous?" *ibid.*, II, 297; Munroe, *Francis Amasa Walker*, pp. 254–255.

[104] Walker, *Bimetallism* (Boston, 1894); Walker, "The Free Coinage of Silver," *Journal of Political Economy*, I (March, 1893), 163–178.

himself as an archenemy of the advocates of social reform.[105] Sumner's essays were written in a "lean, hard prose" and with profound moral fervor: as his leading disciple, Albert Galloway Keller, has said, they were, in effect, "lay sermons." [106]

Not only was Sumner a writer of great force, he was also a teacher of singular ability. After having served as a tutor at Yale from 1866 to 1869, he occupied himself for a time with religious duties. In 1872, however, he returned to Yale as professor of political and social science, and he continued in that post until his retirement in 1909. From all accounts, he was a marvelous pedagogue, "probably the most inspiring and popular teacher that Yale University or American social science has produced." [107] He exerted a profound influence on his students, and instilled in them his own devotion to an uncompromising individualism. "Those who came under his instruction were grounded in certain principles relating to the state and to citizenship upon which, sometimes consciously and sometimes unconsciously, they acted. Public officials, newspaper editors, lawyers, and business men, although they may have ceased to agree with all of his views, preached and exemplified 'Billy Sumner.' " [108]

Sumner's version of laissez faire was grounded in classical political economy and in sociology. It was Harriet Martineau's *Illustrations of Political Economy* that first gave Sumner his interest in political economy,[109] and his views on that subject were strictly of the orthodox variety. His acceptance of the Malthusian and Ricardian laws of population and of diminishing returns and his conviction that com-

---

[105] John Graham Brooks urged socialists to read Sumner as their "most doughty and competent foe." See Harris E. Starr, *William Graham Sumner* (New York, 1925), pp. 500–501.

[106] See Mortimer Smith, "W. G. Sumner: The Forgotten Man," *American Mercury*, LXXI (September, 1950), 361; and Keller, Preface, in Sumner, *Essays of William Graham Sumner*, ed. Albert Galloway Keller and Maurice R. Davie (New Haven, 1934), I, xiii (henceforth referred to as *Essays*).

[107] Harry Elmer Barnes, "Two Representative Contributions of Sociology to Political Theory: The Doctrines of William Graham Sumner and Lester Frank Ward," *American Journal of Sociology*, XXV (July, 1919), 3–4. See also William L. Phelps, "When Yale Was Given to Sumnerology," *Literary Digest International Book Review*, III (1925), 661–663; and Keller, "The Discoverer of the Forgotten Man," *American Mercury*, XXVII (November, 1932), 262–263.

[108] Starr, *Sumner*, p. 498. Charles and Mary Beard give a similar estimate of Sumner's influence. See *The American Spirit* (New York, 1942), p. 347.

[109] "Sketch of William Graham Sumner," *Popular Science Monthly*, XXXV (June, 1889), 262. This "sketch" is in the main autobiographical.

petition is the great regulator are evident throughout his work. However, since political economy dealt merely with the industrial organization of society, Sumner felt that it gave but partial insight into the problems of social development. He came eventually to favor a broad sociological approach that concerned itself with the entire social organism.[110]

It was Spencer's *Study of Sociology* that convinced Sumner of the existence of a science of society. He was of the opinion that the *Study of Sociology* "rescued social science from the dominion of the cranks, and offered a definite and magnificent field for work, from which we might hope at last to derive definite results for the solution of social problems." [111] Spencer was without a doubt a most important influence on his thought,[112] but Sumner was by no means a blind follower of the English philosopher. He rejected, for example, Spencer's a priori belief in natural rights. "Before the tribunal of nature," declared Sumner, "a man has no more right to life than a rattlesnake; he has no more right to liberty than any wild beast." The only true liberty is civil liberty, liberty under law.[113] Because he did not believe in natural rights and because he could not accept Spencer's "law of equal freedom," Sumner was unimpressed by Spencer's *Social Statics.* The law of equal freedom, he caustically stated, "is only one of those formulas which we get into the habit of using because they save us the trouble of thinking, not because they are real solutions." [114]

Sumner also did not share Spencer's optimistic view as to the inevitability of progress. "Under our so-called progress," he asserted, "evil only alters its forms, and we must esteem it a grand advance if . . . on the whole, and over a wide view of human affairs, good has gained

---

[110] Sumner, "Sociology," in *War and Other Essays,* ed. Albert Galloway Keller (New Haven, 1911), pp. 180–183. "The essential elements of political economy," Sumner declared, "are only corollaries or special cases of sociological principles. One who has command of the law of conservation of energy as it manifests itself in society is armed at once against socialism, protectionism, paper money, and a score of other economic fallacies" (*ibid.,* p. 182).

[111] "Sketch of William Graham Sumner," *Popular Science Monthly,* XXXV (June, 1889), 265–266.

[112] Richard Hofstadter calls him Spencer's "most vigorous and influential American disciple" (*Social Darwinism in American Thought, 1860–1915* [Philadelphia, 1944], p. 37).

[113] Sumner, "The Boon of Nature," in *Essays,* I, 385; Sumner, "The Challenge of Facts," *ibid.,* II, 96.

[114] Sumner, "Liberty and Responsibility," in *Essays,* I, 320. See also "Sketch of William Graham Sumner," *Popular Science Monthly,* XXXV (June, 1889), 265.

a hair's breadth over evil in a century." [115] But though Sumner was "not adapted to discipleship," [116] he did accept Spencer's social Darwinism and much of Spencer's argument in support of laissez faire.

Sumner's brand of laissez faire was in part conditioned by his application to society of the evolutionary hypothesis. Social Darwinist that he was, he saw a struggle for existence going on among men which was similar to the struggle for existence in the animal world at large. This struggle, as Sumner viewed it, was essentially a contest between man and nature, with man constantly seeking to increase his power over nature. Only by so doing, according to Sumner, could man make a direct assault on social ills; he could not attack them through legislative devices.[117]

In the struggle between man and nature, Sumner asserted, nature is neutral, submitting to those who assail her most resolutely. If the state does not interfere, men will be rewarded in proportion to their efforts, and the fittest will survive. The survival of the fittest can be altered only by taking from those who have succeeded and giving to those who have failed, thus lessening inequality. "Let it be understood that we cannot go outside of this alternative: liberty, inequality, survival of the fittest; not-liberty, equality, survival of the unfittest." The former makes for civilization and progress, the latter brings "anti-civilization" and retrogression.[118]

The hardships in life resulting from the struggle for existence are not to be mitigated by state action, by socialistic devices that seek to relieve individuals of the difficulties involved in the competition of life and that, in effect, make some people "fight the struggle for existence for others." Those who fail in the struggle cannot ask for help. "The fact that a man is here is no demand upon other people that they shall keep him alive and sustain him." Everyone is entitled to a chance, but not to success. Those in possession of the necessary virtues—industry, frugality, prudence, and temperance—are, however, bound to succeed. "Let every man be sober, industrious, prudent, and wise, and bring up his children to be so likewise, and poverty will be

[115] Sumner, "The Challenge of Facts," in *Essays,* II, 119.

[116] Keller, Introduction, in *War and Other Essays,* p. xvi.

[117] Sumner, "Sociology," in *War and Other Essays,* pp. 184–187; Sumner, "The Challenge of Facts," in *Essays,* II, 87–93.

[118] Sumner, "The Challenge of Facts," in *Essays,* II, 95–97; Sumner, "Sociology," in *War and Other Essays,* pp. 176–177; Sumner, "The Influence of Commercial Crises on Opinions about Economic Doctrines," in *Essays,* II, 56.

abolished in a few generations." [119]   No sympathy, certainly, need be wasted on the working class.   Since capital has accumulated at a more rapid rate than population, the wage earner has considerable bargaining power; and he will remain in a strong position so long as the man–land ratio favors the workingman.[120]

In the struggle for existence the crucial role is performed by capital.   The development of civilization depends on capital.   It is "the indispensable prerequisite of all we care for and all we want to do here on earth," "the first requisite of every social gain, educational, ecclesiastical, political, aesthetic, or other."   "The savings bank depositor is a hero of civilization." [121]

For capital to be effective it must be aggregated in large amounts under the control of a few persons.   Individuals with the organizing skill to manage great aggregates of capital enjoy a natural monopoly, and wealth is their reward.   The state, on the other hand, is incompetent to run great enterprises: the men who can do the job are "found by natural selection, not by political election." [122]

There is no antithesis between capital (property) and persons. Poor laws and eleemosynary institutions that protect persons at the expense of capital increase the number of people but destroy the virtues that are essential to the creation of capital.   This results in a large but miserable population.   On the other hand, laws that give security to capital and property holders tend to restrict the number of people and

[119] Sumner, "Protectionism: The -Ism Which Teaches That Waste Makes Wealth," in *Essays*, II, 435; testimony of Sumner, U. S. Congress, House, Select Committee, *Investigation Relative to the Causes of the General Depression in Labor and Business, etc.*, 45th Cong., 3d sess., H. Misc. Doc. No. 29 (Washington, D.C., 1879), p. 205; Sumner, "The Abolition of Poverty," in *Essays*, I, 109.

[120] Sumner, "Who Win by Progress?" in *Essays*, I, 460–465.   Sumner regarded the ratio of numbers to resources as the prime condition of society.   Democracy, he thought, is possible only when the means of subsistence outstrip population ("Sociology," in *War and Other Essays*, pp. 173–184).

[121] Sumner, "The Challenge of Facts," in *Essays*, II, 97, 108–112; Sumner, "The Power and Beneficence of Capital," *ibid.*, II, 22.

[122] Sumner, "The Bequests of the Nineteenth Century to the Twentieth," in *Essays*, I, 231; Sumner, "The Absurd Effort to Make the World Over," *ibid.*, I, 97–99; Sumner, "The Power and Beneficence of Capital," *ibid.*, II, 28.   In 1878 Sumner declared: "I am rather inclined to the opinion that we have got to have a struggle with the great corporations before we get through, but I have not any programme for it" (U. S. Congress, House, Select Committee, *Investigation Relative to the Causes of Depression*, 45th Cong., 3d sess., H. Misc. Doc. No. 29, p. 208).   This theme dropped out of his later writings.

to produce a small society but one with a high standard of living. Thus the so-called antithesis between protection of persons and protection of property is in actuality an antithesis between numbers and quality. [123]

Sumner's support of laissez faire was conditioned also by his acceptance of social determinism. In this respect he differed but little from Spencer. No believer in natural rights, Sumner was a firm believer in natural law, a knowledge of which he regarded as "the most important good to be won from studying natural science." [124] Convinced that social phenomena are subject to law in the same manner as physical phenomena, Sumner contended that "the life of man is surrounded and limited by the equilibrium of the forces of nature, which man can never disturb, and within the bounds of which he must find his chances." It matters not whether natural facts are beneficent. "A natural fact *is*, and that is the end of the matter, whether we men give it our sovereign approval or not." [125]

The complex industrial organization, Sumner argued, is beyond man's control. It rests on the constancy of certain conditions of existence that give rise to economic forces such as competition and self-interest. These economic forces act in accordance with immutable natural laws, and nothing can be done to alter this. "We have to make up our minds to it, adjust ourselves to it, and sit down to live with it." [126]

The state, like the industrial organization, is not something artificial that can be molded in accordance with some plan. It is an organism whose life goes on despite everything. It is so complex that it should frighten one inclined to interfere with it. There is, moreover, no truth in the widely held notion that we can improve upon existing institutions. Institutions are the products of growth, and the ability of men to control them is very restricted. We cannot change things to suit ourselves, for if we get rid of one evil we merely incur another. True gain results only from a more effective adjustment to existing conditions. Speculation about better worlds is popular simply be-

---

[123] Sumner, "The Challenge of Facts," in *Essays,* II, 97–98.

[124] Sumner, "Sociology," in *War and Other Essays,* p. 172.

[125] Sumner, "Liberty and Responsibility," in *Essays,* I, 310; Sumner, "Is Liberty a Lost Blessing?" *ibid.,* I, 289.

[126] Sumner, "Influence of Commercial Crises," in *Essays,* II, 46–47; Sumner, "The Challenge of Facts," *ibid.,* II, 99–100; Sumner, "The Absurd Effort to Make the World Over," *ibid.,* I, 94.

cause "it is easier to imagine a new world than to learn to know this one." [127]

Socialists and reformers do not understand the nature of the social order and would shape it to suit their views. They would do away with poverty and misery, which they think exist because society has been badly organized. However, there is as little sense in making plans to change the social order as there is in making plans to alter the physical world. The most that man can do is to mar, by his ignorance, the natural laws that control society. Indeed, social evils are in part the result of the misguided schemes of the reformers and philosophers of the past, and it will take centuries of effort just to eliminate the mistakes these individuals have made. Yet even then all will not be well. The hardships of life will continue even when there is no interference with natural laws.[128]

In society, then, there is no possibility of social reform, of planning —human intelligence is inadequate to deal positively with social problems. Man must sit back and allow the forces of nature free play.

Everyone of us is a child of his age and cannot get out of it. . . . All his sciences and philosophy come to him out of it. Therefore the tide will not be changed by us. It will swallow up both us and our experiments. It will absorb the efforts at change and take them into itself as new but trivial components, and the great movement of tradition and work will go on unchanged by our fads and schemes. The things which will change it are the great discoveries and inventions, the new reactions inside the social organism, and the changes in the earth itself on account of changes in the cosmical forces. These causes will make of it just what, in fidelity to them, it ought to be. The men will be carried along with it and be made by it. The utmost they can do by their cleverness will be to note and record their course as they are carried along, which is what we do now, and is that which leads us to the vain fancy that we can make or guide the movement. That is why it is the greatest folly of which a man can be capable, to sit down with a slate and pencil to plan out a new social world.[129]

---

[127] Sumner, "Protectionism," in *Essays,* II, 369–370; Sumner, "Democracy and Responsible Government," in *The Challenge of Facts and Other Essays,* ed. Albert Galloway Keller (New Haven, 1914), pp. 243–246.

[128] Sumner, "The Challenge of Facts," in *Essays,* II, 107–108; Sumner, "The Absurd Effort to Make the World Over," *ibid.,* I, 93; Sumner, "Sociology," in *War and Other Essays,* pp. 171–172.

[129] Sumner, "The Absurd Effort to Make the World Over," in *Essays,* I, 105–106.

Sumner took a more realistic view of the state than did Spencer, and did not see it as a phenomenon that would disappear once man's moral sense was sufficiently developed. When people are in trouble, said Sumner, they call on the state. But what is the state? As an abstraction it is "All-of-us." In practice, however, "it is only a little group of men chosen in a very haphazard way by the majority of us to perform certain services for all of us." Sometimes it is just an obscure clerk who has the power at a particular moment to perform a certain action. If anyone benefits from state action, it is "Some-of-us." Thus the question as to what shall be done for agriculture, labor, or business is in effect a question as to what All-of-us ought to do for Some-of-us.[130]

History demonstrates that ambitious persons or classes have always tried to gain control of the state so as to live off the earnings of other persons or classes. This is as true of a democracy, where the majority rules, as it is of any other form of government. "No fallacies in politics are more pernicious than those which transfer to a popular majority all the old claims of the king by divine right, and lead people to believe that the notions of arbitrary and irresponsible power are not wrong, but only that they were wrong when applied to kings or aristocracies and not when applied to popular majorities."[131] As a matter of fact, a democratic state is in more danger of becoming paternal and of interfering with property rights than any other type of state because it is so sure of itself and so ready to undertake anything. Rights, especially property rights, are safe only when protected against the exercise of all arbitrary power.[132]

Unfortunately, "the legislative machinery can be set in motion too readily and too frequently; it is too easy for the irresponsible hands of the ignorant to seize the machinery." The legislation that results tends to be essentially "speculative" rather than scientific in character since it does not ordinarily proceed logically from known antecedents, but is rather "invented" to attain certain desired ends. Legislation,

[130] Sumner, "Influence of Commercial Crises," in *Essays*, II, 62–63; Sumner, *What Social Classes Owe to Each Other* (New York, 1883), pp. 9–12.

[131] Sumner, *What Social Classes Owe to Each Other*, pp. 30–31; Sumner, "Bequests of the Nineteenth Century to the Twentieth," in *Essays*, I, 215–220; Sumner, "Democracy and Responsible Government," in *Challenge of Facts and Other Essays*, p. 264.

[132] Sumner, *What Social Classes Owe to Each Other*, pp. 31–33; Sumner, "The Challenge of Facts," in *Essays*, II, 119–122; Sumner, "State Interference," *ibid.*, II, 142–145.

in economic matters particularly, is also invariably based on a compromise of opposing views that rarely rest on anything more substantial than public clamor. Legislators capitulate to this clamor rather than seeking to arrive at a decision through sober discussion.[133]

The victim of all projects of social reform undertaken by the state is the "forgotten man." When something is the matter with X, A and B get together to decide what C shall do for X. C is the forgotten man, the one who pays for the schemes of the reformer, the social speculator, and the philanthropist, the one who is weighed down by social burdens. The forgotten man is the average tax-paying middle-class citizen, who is honest and independent and who asks no favors for himself. "He works, he votes, generally he prays—but he always pays—yes, above all, he pays." Those who seek the best interests of the forgotten man must be skeptical of social reform and philanthropy. The interests of the forgotten man are antagonistic to those of the "poor" and the "weak," for it is he who is asked to shoulder their burdens. To aid the forgotten man the state must reduce its functions and must provide for the security and free use of capital.[134]

Not only do state activities tend to oppress the middle class—they also serve to foster plutocracy. Reformers forget that the creation of agencies for social reform is but an invitation to plutocracy. Reformers optimistically assume that they can control these agencies. However, once the state enters the social and industrial field, it becomes a monopoly of the worst sort, and one that men will fight to control. Its regulatory agencies become prizes for which to strive, prizes that can serve one interest as well as another. Capital will defend itself, and in so doing all the vices of plutocracy will be brought into play. The only way the democratic state can avoid the danger of plutocracy, the danger that wealth will be used as a political power, is to confine itself to the task of maintaining order. If the state merely maintains order, there will be no need for capital to control it, and capital will

[133] Sumner, "Speculative Legislation," in *Challenge of Facts and Other Essays,* pp. 215, 219; Sumner, "Legislation by Clamor," in *Essays,* II, 248; Sumner, "The State and Monopoly," in *Earth Hunger and Other Essays,* ed. Albert Galloway Keller (New Haven, 1913), p. 279.

[134] Sumner, "The Forgotten Man," in *Essays,* I, 466–496. As Robert G. McCloskey has pointed out, although Sumner by temperament favored the hard-working middle-class citizen, the successful businessman really constituted "the anointed elite" of the social order he was describing (*American Conservatism in the Age of Enterprise: A Study of William Graham Sumner, Stephen J. Field, and Andrew Carnegie* [Cambridge, Mass., 1951], p. 51).

show but little interest in the state. Capital will then be forced back upon the laws of the market and will have only that power which it can legitimately extract from the industrial and social order.[135]

Since the state cannot, with justice, intervene in the struggle for existence and cannot alter the course of political, social, and industrial development, since state intervention in the social and economic life of the nation tends to burden the middle class and to foster plutocracy, to what activities should government limit itself? No one, said Sumner, has successfully defined the field of action of the state on the negative side, and it is impossible to do so. Individual cases must be decided on the basis of expediency. However, state policy should be guided by certain general maxims. Most important of these guiding maxims is laissez faire. Laissez faire does not mean, "Do not do anything at all to interfere with nature," but, rather, "Let us manage for ourselves." It does not condemn all interference by man, but, instead, calls for an application of human intelligence to assist natural development. "*Laissez-faire* means: Do not meddle; wait and observe. Do not regulate; study. Do not give orders; be teachable. Do not enter upon any rash experiments; be patient until you see how it will work out." [136]

"*Laissez-faire,*" Sumner asserted, "is a maxim of policy. It is not a rule of science." A scientific law permits of no exception, but the domain of statecraft cannot be regulated by absolutes. Here expediency and maxim prevail. The relevant maxims are based on history and experience, and they embody approximate truths that should guide the statesman. Laissez faire is a "general warning, not . . . an absolute injunction." [137]

Although Sumner thus theoretically sanctioned "meddling" based on intelligent study, in actuality the only type of interference he approved was that designed to undo the work of past reformers and to throw man back upon nature. He was hostile to the idea that legislators should study the problems of society and then devise plans to regulate social action.[138] Study of general facts, he assumed, would convince

[135] Sumner, "Democracy and Plutocracy," in *Essays,* II, 217–219; Sumner, "Separation of State and Market," *ibid.,* II, 240–241.

[136] Sumner, "The State and Monopoly," in *Earth Hunger and Other Essays,* p. 271; Sumner, "Laissez-Faire," in *Essays,* II, 468, 472. On another occasion, Sumner declared that laissez faire, in plain English, means, "Mind your own business" (*What Social Classes Owe to Each Other,* p. 120).

[137] Sumner, "Laissez-Faire," in *Essays,* II, 475–477.

[138] Keller would have us believe otherwise. Sumner, he says, was against

men that they must limit themselves to following custom, to altering the arbitrary features of institutions at the proper moment, and to systematizing and affording sanction to new rights created in the give-and-take of the struggle for existence.

Sumner was not opposed to reform, but to him reform meant greater security for property rights. It did not mean positive action by the state, interference by public authorities to help the underdog in the struggle for existence. Such action Sumner alternately branded as a return to medieval restrictions or as socialism. Echoing Spencer, he declared that if the state assumes new functions, it merely loses its ability to perform its vital function, the maintenance of peace and order. The state, he believed, should give equal rights and equal chances—he presumed that the chances were equal if the state did nothing to interfere—but that is all it need do. "I . . . maintain," Sumner categorically stated, "that it is at the present time a matter of patriotism and civic duty to resist the extension of State interference." [139]

In his treatment of specific problems involving actual or possible state action, Sumner revealed his unmistakable laissez-faire leanings. He did not push his hostility to state action quite so far as Spencer,[140] but he opposed most of the new functions assumed by the governments of his day.

Sumner supported efforts to better the lot of female and child laborers, since he believed that women and children could not look out for themselves; but he opposed any state action on behalf of male workers. As noted, Sumner argued that the workingman was in demand and could get what he wanted for his services without the aid of the state. Factory acts would merely teach him to rely on government and cause him to lose the true education in freedom that was

"ignorant meddling," not "intelligent interference." His advocacy of laissez faire "referred only to the cane-poking crowd, not to the engineer who knows the machinery" ("The Discoverer of the Forgotten Man," *American Mercury*, XXVII [November, 1932], 265). What Keller neglects to say is that Sumner assumed that the "engineer who knows the machinery" would see that laissez faire is the only tenable policy.

[139] Sumner, "The Challenge of Facts," in *Essays*, II, 121; Sumner, "State Interference," *ibid.*, II, 145, 148; Sumner, *What Social Classes Owe to Each Other*, pp. 39, 160–169.

[140] Sumner, for example, was strongly in favor of public education and served for twenty-five years on the Connecticut State Board of Education. Starr declares that "Spencer's doctrine of laissez faire was never Sumner's" (*Sumner*, pp. 197–213).

necessary to support free institutions. In the United States, Sumner declared, "all propositions to do something for the working classes have an air of patronage and superiority which is impertinent and out of place." [141]

The state, Sumner contended, must follow a policy of laissez faire even with respect to industrial warfare. Strikes can no more be stopped by state action than employers can be compelled to pay what employees demand. Man is sovereign in making a contract, and no one can tell him to what conditions he must submit. Industrial warfare, regardless of its consequences, is thus but an incident of liberty, and the questions which it seeks to solve can be solved in no other way. [142]

Sumner's special bugbear was the protective tariff, which he denounced as an "arrant piece of economic quackery." The tariff, he charged, "is a subtle, cruel, and unjust invasion of one man's rights by another. . . . It is at the same time a social abuse, an economic blunder, and a political evil." It is an "effort to win wealth, not by honest and independent production, but by . . . a scheme for extorting other people's product from them." If we are taxed to provide profits for some men, why should we not be taxed to provide public workshops and to maintain schemes of social insurance? The tariff is, indeed, the parent of all abuses connected with legislation. Once the tariff was adopted, other interests were able to threaten to "break the steal if not admitted into it." [143]

Sumner criticized the Interstate Commerce Act as "the most remarkable piece of paternal legislation that has ever been passed." The measure was "opposed to the spirit of our institutions," "wrong in principle," and its effect would be "to destroy the transportation business." Sumner cited the Bland-Allison Act, the Oleomargarine Act of 1886, and convict-labor laws as examples of "legislation by clamor," and he looked with disapprobation on the drive for free silver. [144]

[141] Sumner, "The Forgotten Man," in *Essays,* I, 478–479, 482–483.

[142] Sumner, "Do We Want Industrial Peace?" in *War and Other Essays,* pp. 229–243.

[143] Sumner, "Protectionism," in *Essays,* II, 366–367, 435; Sumner, "The Forgotten Man," *ibid.,* I, 489–490; Sumner, "Why I Am a Free Trader," *Twentieth Century,* IV (April 24, 1890), 8–10; Sumner, "The Bequests of the Nineteenth Century to the Twentieth," in *Essays,* I, 231–232.

[144] Sumner, "The State and Monopoly," in *Earth Hunger and Other Essays,* pp. 275–277; Sumner, "Speculative Legislation," in *Challenge of Facts and Other*

"I find," Sumner wrote to his friend David Wells in 1874, "that I am almost the only man who, although . . . he is convinced that it is of 'no use,' nevertheless thinks it his duty to lay down sound doctrine without any modification." He did not, he said, "expect to do any good immediately," but he nevertheless wanted "to keep up the protest during these dark times in hopes of getting a hearing when some bitter experience has made people ready to learn." [145] Twenty-seven years later Sumner apparently did not yet think the people "ready to learn," and as he looked out upon the new century he had little hope that government would pursue a policy of laissez faire such as he had outlined. He feared that either the state would "degenerate into the instrument of an attack on property . . . and cripple wealth-making" or that "the wealth-making interest, threatened by the state," would "rise up to master it, corrupt it, and use it. This," said Sumner, "is the alternative which the twentieth century must meet. It is the antagonism of democracy and plutocracy." [146] What Sumner failed to perceive was that a middle course would be found between these extremes. Attached as he was to laissez faire, he could not foresee that the liberal-democratic state of the twentieth century would be able to assume vast new powers on behalf of the general welfare without in any degree crippling the "wealth-making interest" and without in itself succumbing to plutocracy.

IV

In the period before the Civil War political science did not exist as an independent subject of study in American colleges and universities, but was taught primarily through courses in moral philosophy, municipal law, political economy, and history. Generally, it was considered a branch of moral philosophy. After the Civil War, however, moral philosophy restricted itself pretty much to ethics, and political science began to emerge as an independent discipline.[147]

Although political scientists, taken as a whole, were much less dogmatic about laissez faire than were political economists, political

---

Essays, pp. 215–219; Sumner, "Legislation by Clamor," in *Essays*, II, 248–253; Sumner, "Prosperity Strangled by Gold," *ibid.*, II, 67–71; Sumner, "Cause and Cure of Hard Times," *ibid.*, II, 71–76.

[145] Sumner to Wells, April 6, 1874, Wells Papers, Library of Congress.

[146] Sumner, "The Bequests of the Nineteenth Century to the Twentieth," in *Essays*, I, 215.

[147] Anna Haddow, *Political Science in American Colleges and Universities, 1636–1900* (New York, 1939), pp. 171–222.

science was not without its defenders of the negative state. Conspicuous among these were A. Lawrence Lowell, eventually to become president of Harvard, and John W. Burgess.[148] Lowell considered the best government to be that which governs least. He believed that personal liberty and private rights are dependent to a large extent on the unrestrained functioning of private enterprise, and insisted that contracts must be observed to the letter and that the individual must feel confident that he will enjoy the fruits of his labor unmolested. Whereas he contended that the system of individual enterprise fosters self-reliance and a sense of personal responsibility, characteristics which are essential to the national prosperity and to the development of strong manhood, Lowell thought that government aid is paternalistic and saps the energy of the nation. He saw the nation facing a choice between individualism and paternal government, and he warned that to accept paternalism would be to take a step backwards, to pass from contract to status.[149]

Most influential among the political scientists who championed laissez faire was John W. Burgess. After studying in Germany from 1871 to 1873, Burgess in 1876 began lecturing on constitutional law and political science at the law school of Columbia College. In 1880 he organized Columbia's School (later Faculty) of Political Science, the first institution of its kind in America, and in 1890 he became its dean. Burgess remained at Columbia until his retirement in 1912.[150]

Burgess' views on the state were first clearly set forth in his *Political Science and Comparative Constitutional Law,* a work which has been referred to as "perhaps the first study of political science since

[148] For an extreme interpretation of the science of government from the laissez-faire point of view, see "Government. Part I," and "Government. Part II," *New York Social Science Review,* I (January, July, 1865), 1–29, 288–308. For the authorship of these articles, see Dorfman, *Economic Mind in American Civilization,* III, xii, n. 11.

[149] Lowell, *Essays on Government* (Boston, 1889), pp. 12–19. Lowell was encouraged by court decisions of the period that struck down state legislation "interfering" with freedom of contract (Lowell to Atkinson, April 9, 1895, Atkinson Papers).

[150] For a brief biography of Burgess and an analysis of his views, see Bernard Edward Brown, *American Conservatives: The Political Thought of Francis Lieber and John W. Burgess* (New York, 1951), pp. 103–167. Ralph Gordon Hoxie's "John W. Burgess, American Scholar. Book I: The Founding of the Faculty of Political Science" (Ph.D. thesis, Columbia University, 1950) is "the first part of a projected life" of Burgess.

the Civil War, which was founded on modern scholarship."[151] Imbued with German political philosophy, Burgess rejected the theory of natural rights as "unscientific, erroneous, and harmful." He considered sovereignty, which he defined as the "original, absolute, unlimited, universal power over the individual subject and over all associations of subjects," the most essential attribute of the state, and concluded consequently that "the state can do no wrong." Burgess, however, distinguished between the state and government. The state, he explained, is the sovereign people behind the government, and whereas it possesses unlimited power, the government, which it organizes, is to be entrusted with only limited powers.[152]

The ultimate end of the state, Burgess declared, is the perfection of humanity, its secondary purpose, the development of nationality. However, the state can attain these objectives only by first directing its activities to its proximate ends: the establishment of government and of a system of individual liberty. To begin with, the state must set up a government to maintain peace and law and must give it adequate power to defend itself against internal disorder and external aggression. Once this has been accomplished, the state must provide for a system of individual liberty by marking out a sphere of private rights upon which it cannot encroach and which it will protect from encroachment from any source whatsoever. This sphere will be narrow at first; but as the people of the state advance in civilization, the area of liberty can be widened, and permission can be granted to individuals to set up voluntary associations to accomplish ends that they could not attain acting as individuals.

In the constitutional state, the state which is organized back of the government limits the powers of the government and restrains it from violating individual liberty. In the United States the guarantee of individual liberty has been incorporated in the Constitution. The Constitution establishes a "system of individual liberty" that is not

[151] Edward R. Lewis, *A History of American Political Thought from the Civil War to the World War* (New York, 1937), p. 185.

[152] Burgess, *Political Science and Comparative Constitutional Law* (Boston, 1891), I, 52–70, 88–89. Burgess contended that critics who claimed he was attacking the principle of individual liberty failed to understand his distinction between the state and the government (*Reminiscences of an American Scholar: The Beginnings of Columbia University* [New York, 1934], pp. 249–255). Brown has suggested that what Burgess understood by the "state" had better been termed "society" (*American Conservatives*, p. 128).

to be encroached upon by the state governments or the national government, and the independent judiciary protects this system against "all merely governmental notions of welfare." [153]

Burgess not only favored a broad interpretation of the Fifth and Fourteenth Amendments to the United States Constitution as guarantees to the individual and to corporations against government interference,[154] but, in keeping with this position, he also recommended a very narrow interpretation of the police power. He described it as an administrative rather than a legislative or judicial power and insisted that it is not coextensive with the whole scope of internal administration but is only a branch thereof. As Burgess saw it, the police power is essentially negative rather than positive, and he therefore advocated its use only to restrain the individual in the exercise of his rights when these are exaggerated by him to the point of endangering the community.[155]

Liberty was to Burgess synonymous with laissez faire. Liberty, he asserted, means to the political scientist the "absence of government in a given sphere of individual or social action." Modern political science, he contended, does not welcome any extension of government activities but, rather, "favors the greatest possible limitation of governmental power, consistent with the sovereignty of the state, the unity, independence and security of the country, the enforcement of the laws and the maintenance of justice. It favors keeping open to private enterprise the widest possible domain of business. . . . In a word," Burgess commented, "modern political science is very suspicious of state socialism . . . ." [156]

Not only did Burgess mark out a sphere of individual rights that he wished to secure against government intervention, but he suggested that similar immunity be afforded to private corporations. He looked upon the private corporation as a defender of property rights against

[153] Burgess, *Political Science and Comparative Constitutional Law*, I, 83–87, 174–183; Burgess, *Reminiscences of an American Scholar*, pp. 254–255; Burgess, "The Ideal of the American Commonwealth," *Political Science Quarterly*, X (September, 1895), 416.

[154] In the classroom Burgess taught that the Fifth and Fourteenth Amendments were designed "to prevent the encroachment of socialistic legislation upon private rights." See Charles A. Beard, *Public Policy and the General Welfare* (New York, 1941), p. 136; and Beard and Beard, *American Spirit*, p. 351.

[155] Burgess, *Political Science and Comparative Constitutional Law*, I, 215–216.

[156] Burgess, "Private Corporations from the Point of View of Political Science," *Political Science Quarterly*, XIII (June, 1898), 210–211.

the encroachments of government, and, in truth, he thought it a more able defender of these rights than the individual. The corporation, Burgess argued, aids in maintaining the sovereignty of the people against the tendency of government to transgress the constitutional limitations which the people have placed upon it so as to protect liberty and property. The government must not be permitted to weaken (by regulation) this bulwark against paternalism under the pretext of promoting the general welfare. "This plea," Burgess insisted, "is and always has been the broad avenue of approach to the inner temple of all liberty." [157]

Burgess' defense of laissez faire and his attack on the assumption by government of general-welfare functions were communicated not only through his writings but also in the classroom. One of his most famous students, Nicholas Murray Butler, has attested that Burgess was "the most convincing, most brilliant and most intelligent" of all his teachers. At Columbia, the Beards declare, Burgess provided instruction for "thousands of young men in the law school and a large body of graduate students who became professors in all parts of the country." For a time "the overwhelming majority of chairs in political science" in the leading American universities were occupied by men whom Burgess had trained. [158]

The political scientist Burgess thus added his voice to that of other academic and popular theorists of laissez faire. Though these men differed in their approach to the problem of state action and in the extent to which they would limit state activities, they were agreed that the state should not become an agency of social control and function positively in behalf of the general welfare. In these sentiments the businessmen of the late nineteenth century heartily concurred.

[157] Burgess, "Private Corporations," *Political Science Quarterly,* XIII (June, 1898), 203–204, 208, 211–212; Burgess, "The Ideal of the American Commonwealth," *ibid.,* X (September, 1895), 413–416.

[158] Hoxie, "Burgess," p. 296; Beard and Beard, *American Spirit,* p. 348. Brown maintains that Burgess was of much less influence with political scientists than with the legal profession (*American Conservatives,* pp. 176–177).

IV

LAISSEZ FAIRE AND THE AMERICAN
BUSINESSMAN

IT IS, of course, extremely difficult to speak in general terms of the views of the business community as a whole with respect to the functions of government. Manufacturers, merchants, bankers, railroad entrepreneurs, and small businessmen in the period after the Civil War did not necessarily regard the problem all in the same light, nor were individuals within these groups equally articulate in the expression of such opinions as they did entertain. One finds among the businessmen protectionists and free traders, friends of hard money and of soft money, opponents of any real government control of corporate enterprise and advocates of government regulation of corporations as creatures of the state. What follows, therefore, is largely an attempt to focus upon what appear to have been some of the dominant elements in the thought of the business community regarding the role of the state and, particularly, although by no means exclusively, the thought of the industrial capitalists.

With the triumph of the North in the Civil War the industrial capitalist became for the first time the regnant figure in American life. No longer did he have to contend with the slaveholding aristocrat for control of the state. The policies he favored—a national banking system, a high protective tariff, generous land grants to railway corporations, and the authorized importation of contract labor—were put into effect during the war years by a government amenable to his will, and after Appomattox the national administration remained responsive to his wishes. As the *Nation* caustically pointed out, what the national government interpreted as the common good was, in actuality, "the good of those . . . rich and powerful enough to make their influence felt at Washington."[1]

Since the businessman was the admired social type of the Gilded Age, large sections of the American public acquiesced in his views. Warren Miller, a former United States senator from New York, expressed a desire to see more businessmen in American legislatures because he regarded them as "more competent to deal with the live questions of the hour than any other class"; and Godkin noted that Americans had "an inordinate respect for the opinions on all subjects of 'successful business men.'"[2] A critic of the contemporary business scene, Henry Demarest Lloyd, thought the popular support given the businessman was less a matter of "respect" than of selfishness. "Every man," he confided to his notebook, "winks at the practice of the business world because he is in the race, and hopes to 'get there,' or hopes as preacher, editor, superintendent of charity to share in the gains."[3]

Not content merely to be the most influential figure on the American scene, the businessman felt the need for a philosophy to explain and to justify his preëminent position. To a great extent, he found what he sought in the precepts of social Darwinism and laissez-faire economics. The businessman, to be sure, did not accept the doctrines of Spencer and the economists *in toto:* he took from their thought only what suited his needs. His version of laissez faire, unlike theirs, was essentially a rationalization of the *status quo.*[4] The theorists of laissez faire were, after all, reformers in their own manner and were opposed to the use of government for the benefit of any particular class. They denounced evidences of governmental favoritism, such as the protective tariff, that were dear to the heart of the businessman. The businessman, for his part, saw no wrong in government activities that

[1] "The New Socialism," *Nation,* XLVIII (June 13, 1889), 478.

[2] Warner Miller, "Business Men in Politics," *North American Review,* CLI (November, 1890), 578; Godkin, "Popular Government," in *Problems of Modern Democracy* (New York, 1897), p. 92. See also Edward Searing, "The Reign of the Huckster," *New Nation,* II (January 2, 1892), 5–9; and W. J. Ghent, *Our Benevolent Feudalism* (New York, 1902), pp. 122–153.

[3] Notebook 16, 1889, Henry Demarest Lloyd Papers, State Historical Society of Wisconsin.

[4] Thomas C. Cochran notes that the railroad entrepreneurs of the second half of the nineteenth century developed "an unformulated pragmatic social 'philosophy' that accorded with their economic interests but not with any existing system of thought" (*Railroad Leaders, 1845–1890: The Business Mind in Action* [Cambridge, Mass., 1953], p. 182).

were conducive to his welfare: he did not ordinarily object to the use of state power to promote business enterprise. He tended to become an opponent of the state only when it sought to regulate his economic endeavors or to cater to the needs of other economic groups.[5] Laissez faire to him meant, "Leave things as they now are." "If asked what important law I should change," Andrew Carnegie declared, "I must perforce say none; the laws are perfect." [6]

One element of the businessman's defense of the *status quo* was a formula for success. The success of the businessman, it was explained, was the result of his possessing certain simple virtues and abilities; the failure of the poor man resulted from his lack of these same virtues and abilities. In his book *The Successful Man of Business,* Benjamin Wood explained that success was "nothing more or less than doing thoroughly what others do indifferently." In a lecture delivered at Cornell University in 1896, Carnegie gave it as his opinion that success "is a simple matter of honest work, ability, and concentration." Another businessman asserted that "wealth has always been the natural sequence to industry, temperance, and perseverance, and it will always so continue." [7] Why did poverty still exist in society? To S. C. T. Dodd, solicitor for Standard Oil, the answer was simple. Poverty exists, said Dodd, "because nature or the devil has made some men weak and imbecile and others lazy and worthless, and neither man nor God can do much for one who will do nothing for himself." [8]

Not only did the businessman equate success with virtue and concentration, but he sought to impress upon one and all the view that there was ample room at the top for those who were willing to make the effort. "The storehouse of opportunity is open to all," proclaimed Benjamin Wood. Henry Wood thought that "examples on every hand" proved how simple it was to move into the "independent class." This

[5] For a similar interpretation of the views of businessmen in a later period, see Beard, "The Myth of Rugged American Individualism," *Harper's Magazine,* CLXIV (December, 1931), 13–22. See also Thomas C. Cochran, "The Faith of Our Fathers," *Frontiers of Democracy,* VI (October, 1939), 17–19.

[6] Carnegie, *Triumphant Democracy* (New York, 1886), p. 471.

[7] See Benjamin Wood, *The Successful Man of Business* (2d ed. rev. and enlarged; New York, 1899), p. 59; Carnegie, "Business," in *The Empire of Business* (New York, 1902), p. 205; and Henry Wood, *Natural Law in the Business World* (Boston, 1887), p. 6.

[8] Dodd, "Aggregated Capital: Its History and Influence," in James H. Bridge, ed., *The Trust: Its Book* (New York, 1902), p. 72. Many of the chapters of this volume were published as articles or delivered as speeches in the 1890's.

was not a matter of theory, but of "universal experience." Wall Street's Henry Clews also emphasized the numerous opportunities for acquiring wealth in the United States. It required neither genius, education, breeding, nor even luck to gather "the nimble dollar"; it was necessary for one only to begin "aright." [9]

The businessman's interpretation of success found popular literary expression in the biographies of William Makepeace Thayer and the novels of Horatio Alger. These two authors were among the chief representatives of a veritable "cult of success" that glorified the self-made man and trumpeted the idea that the road to the top lay open to those with the requisite qualities. [10] The implications of such a version of success were obvious—it would be fatuous to interfere with an economic system that so readily rewarded ability and that provided an opportunity for all to gain riches. This, indeed, was the theme of Carnegie's paean of praise to the system that had made his rise to fame possible, *Triumphant Democracy*, published in the year of the Haymarket Affair. "The publication of it is very timely," George Pullman wrote to Carnegie, "as owing to the excesses of our turbulent population, so many are uttering doubts just now as to whether democracy has been a triumph in America." The St. Paul real-estate and loan agent H. S. Fairchild thought the book "better than a direct argument" against the principles of the discontented. It "makes them hesitate to engage in wild legislation or revolutionary schemes that might endanger a government that offers such opportunities, that has accomplished so much, and on whose success the hopes of humanity rest." [11]

In further support of his position and of the *status quo*, the man of wealth pointed to the teachings of Spencer. That part of Spencer's thought that dealt with the struggle for existence, the survival of the fittest as the result of natural selection, and the inevitability of progress

[9] Benjamin Wood, *Successful Man of Business*, p. 33; Henry Wood, *Natural Law in the Business World*, p. 43; Clews, *The Wall Street Point of View* (New York, c. 1900), p. 44. See also Carnegie, "Business," in *Empire of Business*, p. 205.

[10] For the cult of success and the ideology of the rags-to-riches theme, see Merle Curti, *The Growth of American Thought* (New York, 1943), pp. 644–650; and Irvin G. Wyllie, *The Self-Made Man in America: The Myth of Rags to Riches* (New Brunswick, N.J., 1954), pp. 21–54 ff.

[11] See Pullman to Carnegie, May 5, 1886, Carnegie Papers, Library of Congress; Fairchild to Carnegie, January 9, 1892, *ibid.*; and Robert Green McCloskey, *American Conservatism in the Age of Enterprise: A Study of William Graham Sumner, Stephen J. Field, and Andrew Carnegie* (Cambridge, Mass., 1951), pp. 157–158.

was readily adaptable to the pattern of American economic life and to the needs of the businessman. It took no great imagination to see that Spencer offered a rationale for the business triumphs of the industrial leaders and for opposition to all proposals of state intervention on behalf of the unsuccessful.[12] Upon reading Darwin and Spencer, Carnegie remarked, "I remember that light came as in a flood and all was clear." [13]

Competition, the success of some and the failure of others, and the consolidation of industry into ever larger units were all readily explainable by the businessman in the terms that Spencer had made popular. "Competition in Economics," the publisher Richard R. Bowker proclaimed, "is the same as the law of the 'survival of the fittest,' or 'natural selection,' in nature." [14] The great Southern textile manufacturer Daniel A. Tompkins informed an audience that "in a businessman's every-day life he sees this law of the survival of the fittest at work, thinning out the ranks of his competitors, introducing new material." "Competition, the very essence of business life," Tompkins continued, "puts down some and elevates others. The fittest survive. It must be so, else there is no life, no progress. Whatever the socialist and other sentimentalists may think, the survival of the fittest is, has been, and will always be the law of progress in national affairs, in business and in all other walks of life." It would be "the silliest kind of sentimentalism" to fret about those who were "defeated" in this

[12] Richard Hofstadter, *Social Darwinism in American Thought, 1860–1915* (Philadelphia, 1944), p. 30; Thomas C. Cochran and William Miller, *The Age of Enterprise: A Social History of Industrial America* (New York, 1942), pp. 121–128. Irvin G. Wyllie indicates that the propagandists of self-help did not employ the social-Darwinist theme in their writings (*Self-Made Man in America*, pp. 83–87). Businessmen nevertheless did employ social-Darwinist arguments to justify both competition and consolidation and to combat demands for government regulation.

[13] Carnegie, *Autobiography of Andrew Carnegie* (Boston, 1920), p. 339. Carnegie's motto became, "All is well since all grows better" (*ibid.*). Carnegie's "literary assistant" between 1884 and 1889 was Spencer's one-time secretary, James H. Bridge. See Fritz Redlich, Review of McCloskey's *American Conservatism in the Age of Enterprise*, in *American Historical Review*, LVII (April, 1952), 708–709.

[14] Bowker, *Economics for the People* (New York, 1886), p. 60. Although Bowker contended that "the evils that society has done, society must undo" and that "the community . . . will not accept the extreme *laissez faire* theory, it will not let *ill* enough alone," he nevertheless insisted that it was dangerous to assume that it was possible to overcome completely the "relentless discipline of nature" (*ibid.*, pp. 262, 267–268).

struggle for existence.[15]   "The poor and the weak," the general manager of the Atlas Works informed a committee of Congress, "have to go to the wall to some extent, of course.   That is one of the natural laws that we cannot get over except by providing for them by charity." [16]

Not only did the businessman describe the success of individuals in Darwinian terms, but he was able to explain and justify the consolidation of industry in similar terms.   The concentration of capital, Carnegie declared, "is an evolution from the heterogeneous to the homogeneous, and is clearly another step in the upward path of development."   Carnegie was, moreover, quite certain that "this overpowering, irresistible tendency toward aggregation of capital and increase of size . . . cannot be arrested or even greatly impeded."   Rockefeller, too, explained the growth of the "large business" as "merely a survival of the fittest . . . the working out of a law of nature and a law of God."   It was obviously futile, in the view of business advocates of social Darwinism, for the state to attempt to interfere with the process that brought the fittest individuals and concerns to the fore.   "Yes; they are very shrewd men," William Vanderbilt said of the Standard Oil leaders to a committee of the New York legislature.   "I don't believe that by any legislative enactment or anything else through any of the States or all of the States, you can keep such men as them down; you can't do it; they will be up on the top all the time; you see if they are not." [17]

"If I were able," declared the president of the Chicago, Burlington and Quincy, "I would found a school for the study of political economy in order to harden men's hearts!" [18]   And it is clear that, just

[15] Cited in George Tayloe Winston, *A Builder of the New South: Being the Story of the Life Work of Daniel Augustus Tompkins* (Garden City, N. Y., 1920), p. 299.

[16] Testimony of Thomas Miller, U. S. Congress, Senate, Committee on Education and Labor, *Report upon the Relations between Labor and Capital, and Testimony Taken by the Committee* (Washington, D.C., 1885), II, 25–26.

[17] See Carnegie, "Popular Illusions about Trusts," in *The Gospel of Wealth and Other Timely Essays* (New York, 1900), pp. 89, 91; Ghent, *Our Benevolent Feudalism*, p. 29; S. C. T. Dodd, *Combinations: Their Uses and Abuses, with a History of the Standard Oil Trust* (New York, 1888), pp. 11–12; and New York Legislature, Assembly, Special Committee on Railroads, *Proceedings* (Albany, N. Y., 1879), II, 1669.

[18] Charles Elliott Perkins to John Murray Forbes, February 18, 1884, cited in Cochran, *Railroad Leaders*, pp. 436–437.

as the theories of the social Darwinists were readily adaptable to the needs of the captains of industry, so was there much in the doctrines of the laissez-faire economists that fitted the specifications of a businessman's philosophy. Like the economists, the businessman was prone to talk of the inexorable natural laws that governed the economic order, of competition as the great regulator, and of the virtues of self-interest.[19]

The doctrine of self-interest was particularly attractive to the businessman, for it supplied him with a truly potent argument with which to defend the existing order. If each individual in his pursuit of wealth unconsciously promoted the general good, did not those who were most successful in the quest for economic gain promote the general welfare more effectively than all others? The millionaires, declared Carnegie, "are the bees that make the most honey, and contribute most to the hive even after they have gorged themselves full." The millionaire "cannot evade the law which . . . compels him to use his millions for the good of the people." [20] What need was there then for the state to seek by positive action to promote the well-being of the mass of the people. The captains of industry, said John F. Scanlan, of the Western Industrial League, "are fathers to guide the masses to higher conditions." [21]

Like the laissez-faire economists and the social Darwinists, whose views they found so palatable, businessmen generally cautioned the state to pursue a hands-off policy with respect to economic matters. The Chicago banker Lyman Gage, eventually to become McKinley's secretary of the treasury, informed a committee of Congress that insofar as the industrial affairs of the country were concerned, the legislature should "simply . . . define the obligations of the citizens to each other, and . . . secure the enforcement of individual rights." The state, businessmen thought, should protect property and enforce contracts, but they did not wish it to interfere with prices, wages, or profits. "The more the legislature and the people let these things alone, the better they will work out their own solution," asserted the

[19] See, for example, Bowker, *Economics for the People*, pp. 60, 62, 259; and testimony of Jay Gould, Senate Committee on Education and Labor, *Report upon the Relations between Labor and Capital*, I, 1091–1092.

[20] Carnegie, "Wealth and Its Uses," in *Empire of Business*, pp. 135–140. See also "Wages, Capital and Rich Men," *Popular Science Monthly*, XXV (October, 1884), 794; Wood, *Natural Law in the Business World*, p. 122; and Clews, *Wall Street Point of View*, p. 35.

[21] *Chicago Conference on Trusts . . . , 1899* (Chicago, 1900), p. 187.

president of the Wholesale Grocers' Association of New York City. If trade were untrammeled, the head of the sugar trust informed the United States Industrial Commission, no economic group would enjoy any special advantage, and the country would benefit. Of course, if one concern managed to get rid of its competitors in the process, that was trade, and nothing could be done about it.[22]

The businessman was prone to contrast the beneficent natural laws which, in his view, governed the economic order with the clumsy, artificial laws devised by man. "Oh, these grand immutable, all-wise laws of natural forces," exulted Carnegie, "how perfectly they work if human legislators would only let them alone! But no, they must be tinkering." The president of the American Exchange Bank and the onetime president of the American Bankers Association, George S. Coe, thought the laws of economics "as sacred and as obligatory as . . . those of the decalogue." He spoke of the "impotence and limitations of human law" and insisted that "all material values are governed by influences far beyond the reach of human vision and legislation." In Charles Flint's view, industrial progress was assured so long as "natural conditions" were undisturbed. However, if legal restraints were imposed, then, Flint warned, the "wheels which have been driving all this vast machinery will come to rest."[23] The nation was already "overwhelmed . . . by useless legislation," according to J. G. Batterson, the president of the New England Granite Works, and more was to be gained from the repeal than from the enactment of any law. "The universal law of supply and demand," he averred, "is superior to any law which can be enacted by Congress or any other power on earth."[24]

Not only did the businessman compare man-made law unfavorably with natural law, but he also found virtue on the side of private enter-

[22] U. S. Congress, House, Select Committee, *Investigation Relative to the Causes of the General Depression in Labor and Business, etc.*, 46th Cong., 2d sess., H. Misc. Doc. No. 5 (Washington, D.C., 1879), p. 12; testimony of G. Waldo Smith and Henry O. Havemeyer, U. S. Industrial Commission, *Preliminary Report on Trusts and Industrial Combinations* (Vol. I of the Commission's *Reports;* Washington, D.C., 1900), pp. 69, 105.

[23] See Carnegie, *Triumphant Democracy*, p. 48; Fritz Redlich, *The Molding of American Banking: Men and Ideas, Part II: 1840–1910* (New York, 1951), pp. 434–435; Flint, "Combinations and Critics," in Bridge, ed., *The Trust: Its Book*, p. 8. See also Wood, *Natural Law in the Business World, passim.*

[24] Cited in William E. Barns, ed., *The Labor Problem* (New York, 1886), pp. 108–109.

prise as contrasted to government enterprise. "It is better always," said the merchant Danford Knowlton, "to leave individual enterprise to do most that is to be done in the country." Even the Post Office, Jay Gould thought, should be in private hands, "because individual enterprise can do things more economically and more efficiently than the Government can." [25]

In his approach to such problems of the day as labor relations, money, railroads, and trusts, the businessman generally adhered closely to the laissez-faire doctrine. He naturally looked with disfavor on attempts by workers to interfere with the *status quo*. Regarding himself as the benefactor of the community in general and of the laborer in particular, the industrialist exhorted the workingman to remain quiescent and to trust to his employer and to natural law to improve his position. The entrepreneur, he informed the worker, was entitled to a large share of the total product because he was "the most important factor in the modern economy" and made the major contribution to production. It was altogether proper for him to earn more than the laborer because he possessed "superior judgment, skill, and sagacity." Moreover, since the efforts of the few had served to raise wages and increase purchasing power, the laborer had no cause for complaint. If the worker succeeded somehow in reducing the margin of profits, the capitalist would be unable to put forth his best efforts, and the total product would be diminished, to the detriment of all.[26]

Trade unions that sought to reduce the hours of labor or to improve wage rates were reminded that matters of this sort were determined by inexorable laws of supply and demand that unions, as well as employers, were powerless to set aside.[27] Some businessmen,

---

[25] See Senate Committee on Education and Labor, *Report upon the Relations between Labor and Capital*, II, 1072; *ibid.*, I, 1072; and Thomas C. Cochran, "The Executive Mind: The Role of Railroad Leaders," *Bulletin of the Business Historical Society*, XXV (December, 1951), 236–237.

[26] Richard Rogers Bowker, *Of Work and Wealth: A Summary of Economics* (New York, 1883), p. 6; Bowker, *Of Business* (Boston, 1901), pp. 20–21; A. S. Wheeler, "The Labor Question," *Andover Review*, VI (November, 1886), 471–474; Henry Holt, "The Social Discontent—III. More Remedies," *Forum*, XIX (April, 1895), 175–176; W. J. Ashley, *Surveys Historic and Economic* (New York, 1900), pp. 409–410. Railroad entrepreneurs, Thomas Cochran tells us, were more inclined to adhere to a laissez-faire position with respect to the relations of labor and capital than with respect to any other economic problem (*Railroad Leaders*, p. 173).

[27] Wheeler, "The Labor Question," *Andover Review*, VI (November, 1886), 475–476; Henry Clews, *Fifty Years in Wall Street* (New York, 1915), p. 493; Wood, *Natural Law in the Business World*, p. 217; testimony of Danford Knowlton, Senate

indeed, insisted that trade unions not only were an "intrusion" upon the domain of natural law, but that they were withal destructive of the rights of the individual laborer and, in effect, subversive of the existing order. One manufacturer referred to unions as "fierce, cruel, arbitrary, dictatorial—in a word, tyrannical!" The *Portage Lake Mining Gazette,* reflecting the views of employers in Michigan's copper country, declared that "nothing more thoroughly un-American, in practice and in principle, can well be conceived than trades unionism." The secretary of the Southern Industrial Convention contended that "labor organizations are . . . the greatest menace to this Government that exists inside or outside the pale of our national domain." Henry Clews thought the demands of the Knights of Labor "utterly revolutionary of the inalienable rights of the citizen" and "completely subversive of social order." [28] When Carnegie's lieutenant, Henry Clay Frick, broke the Amalgamated Association of Iron and Steel Workers in the famous Homestead Strike of 1892,[29] the Pittsburgh employer Thomas Mellon applauded this action as one that all employers would sooner or later have to repeat. Employee "usurpation" of the control of business "had to be checked," he wrote Carnegie, "or industry requiring the employment of labor would have to cease." [30]

Committee on Education and Labor, *Report upon the Relations between Labor and Capital,* II, 1071; Cochran, *Railroad Leaders,* pp. 178–179. For a survey of employer opinion in the East with respect to the attempt of the American Federation of Labor to win the eight-hour day by trade-union action, see *Boston Herald,* December 9, 1889. In resisting union demands for higher wages, employers, Edward C. Kirkland maintains, insisted that business conditions and the laws of trade simply did not permit the granting of wage increases ("You Can't Win," *Journal of Economic History,* XIV [1954], 322–326, 331).

[28] See Edward L. Day, "The Labor Question," *Century,* X (July, 1886), 399; William B. Gates, Jr., *Michigan Copper and Boston Dollars: An Economic History of the Michigan Copper Mining Industry* (Cambridge, Mass., 1951), p. 113; testimony of N. F. Thompson, U. S. Industrial Commission, *Report on the Relations and Conditions of Capital and Labor* (Vol. VII of the Commission's *Reports;* Washington, D.C., 1901), p. 756; and Clews, "The Labor Crisis," *North American Review,* CXLII (June, 1886), 599.

[29] Carnegie's insistence that he favored trade unions (see, for example, Carnegie, "An Employer's View of the Labor Question," *Forum,* I [April, 1886], 118–119) should be measured against the labor record of the Carnegie enterprises and the fact that Carnegie as well as Frick wished to see the Homestead plant run on a nonunion basis. See Henry David, "Upheaval at Homestead," in Daniel Aaron, ed., *America in Crisis* (New York, 1952), pp. 140–144; Carnegie to W. L. Abbott, August 7, 1889, and Carnegie to George Lauder, Jr., July 17, 1892, Carnegie Papers.

[30] Mellon to Carnegie, January 30, 1893, Carnegie Papers.

The state as well as the trade union was cautioned by employers to entrust the labor contract to the bargaining of the individual worker and his employer. "I say the legislature has no right to encroach upon me as to whether I shall employ men eight hours, or ten, or fifteen," the clothing manufacturer Henry V. Rothschild informed a committee of the House of Representatives. "It is a matter of mutual agreement, and the legislature has no right, according to the principles of our government, according to the principles of the Declaration of Independence, to impose upon me what hours of labor I shall have between myself and my employees." [31] Jane Addams has informed us that the Illinois labor legislation of the 1890's "ran counter to the instinct and tradition, almost to the very religion of the manufacturers of the state." [32]

With respect to the great currency problems that troubled the nation in the three and one-half decades after the Civil War, the business community was in essential agreement with the laissez-faire economists. Although some businessmen were sympathetic to the cause of greenbacks, [33] businessmen in general and the banking community in particular favored specie resumption. The battle of the standards found business leaders generally arrayed on the side of gold and using the conventional arguments as to the limited role government should play in this sphere. [34]

[31] House Select Committee, *Investigation Relative to the Causes of Depression,* 45th Cong., 3d sess., H. Misc. Doc. No. 29 (Washington, D.C., 1879), p. 131. See also testimony of Thomas M. Miller and Edward H. Ammidown, Senate Committee on Education and Labor, *Report upon the Relations between Labor and Capital,* II, 24, 1133; and testimony of T. W. Baxter, House Select Committee, *Investigation Relative to the Causes of Depression,* 46th Cong., 2d sess., H. Misc. Doc. No. 5, p. 187. Some New England textile employers, worried about competition from Southern mills whose workers labored for longer hours than their New England counterparts, were prepared to accept uniform federal regulation of the hours of labor. See, for example, testimony of Andrew G. Pierce, Simeon B. Chase, and Robert T. Davis, U. S. Industrial Commission, *Report on the Relations and Conditions of Capital and Labor* (Vol. XIV of the Commission's *Reports;* Washington, D.C., 1901), pp. 545, 562, 591.

[32] Addams, *Twenty Years at Hull House* (New York, 1910), p. 206.

[33] See, for example, testimony of H. H. Bryant and David J. King, House Select Committee, *Investigation Relative to the Causes of Depression,* 46th Cong., 2d sess., H. Misc. Doc. No. 5, pp. 396, 401; and John R. Commons *et al., History of Labour in the United States* (New York, 1918–1935), II, 244.

[34] Testimony of Lyman Gage, George Schneider, William Stewart, Jesse Spalding, House Select Committee, *Investigation Relative to the Causes of Depression,* 46th Cong., 2d sess., H. Misc. Doc. No. 5, pp. 12, 20, 222, 237; Arthur B. and

The advent of the railroad and the practices which railway managers found it necessary to employ raised doubts in the minds of some businessmen regarding the virtues of a completely unregulated economic order. Merchants and shippers disadvantageously affected by personal or place discrimination or by railway-rate agreements decided that the railway business was not one that could be safely entrusted to the free play of economic forces and that in this field at least the power of the state would have to be invoked. The pro-rata movement in the East during the 1850's and 1860's was led by members of the business community; merchants and shippers played the crucial role in the framing of the so-called Granger laws in Illinois, Iowa, Wisconsin, and Minnesota; [35] and commercial elements in New York City were instrumental in securing the Hepburn investigation of the New York State Assembly and the railway legislation that the state subsequently adopted and were, according to one scholar, "the single most important group" behind the passage of the Interstate Commerce Act.[36]

Railroad officials sought for a time to stave off state and federal railroad regulation and were not at all pleased with the regulatory legislation that was enacted. Charles Elliott Perkins, of the Chicago, Burlington and Quincy, expressed the wish that the "intelligent people" could "be made to see that the let alone policy as regards railroads is the safe one and that any other policy is full of danger." [37] Confronted by the Hepburn investigation, Presidents William H. Vanderbilt of the New York Central and H. J. Jewett of the New York, Lake

---

Henry Farquhar, *Economic and Industrial Delusions* (New York, 1891), pp. 357–358, 384, 399–401, 411; Carnegie, "The A B C of Money," in *Empire of Business*, pp. 21–67; Carnegie to Grover Cleveland, April 22, 1893, and Carnegie to George C. Norton, July 4, 1896, Carnegie Papers; Henry Wood, *The Political Economy of Natural Law* (Boston, 1894), pp. 211–224; Redlich, *Molding of American Banking*, *Part II*, pp. 430–431, 433, 436–437. Bankers, and particularly New York bankers, wanted the federal government to ease the controls which it exercised over the national banking system. See Redlich, *op. cit.*, p. 117.

[35] George Hall Miller, "The Granger Laws: A Study of the Origins of State Railway Control in the Upper Mississippi Valley" (Ph.D. thesis, University of Michigan, 1951), pp. 53–72 *et passim*.

[36] Lee Edward Benson, "New York Merchants and Farmers in the Communication Revolution" (Ph.D. thesis, Cornell University, 1951), pp. 469 *et passim*; John Foord, *The Life and Public Services of Simon Sterne* (London, 1903), pp. 186–219.

[37] Perkins to Atkinson, June 15, 1881, Edward Atkinson Papers, Massachusetts Historical Society. See also Stuyvesant Fish to Atkinson, January 13, 1887, *ibid.*; and Cochran, *Railroad Leaders*, pp. 440–442.

Erie and Western Railroad spoke of the attack on the railroads as evidence of the "growth of a disregard to the rights of property in this country." "This growing tendency to socialistic principles," they declared, "is one of the most dangerous signs of the times, and if not checked, will produce scenes of disaster that would now appal the country." This was not, Vanderbilt and Jewett thought, a matter with which individual states might cope, and unless Congress could somehow interpose its authority, all concerned would have to "wait for time either to furnish a remedy or permit the great laws of trade, now trammeled by destructive competition, to work out the result."[38] When Congress finally did "interpose its authority" by enacting the Interstate Commerce Act, railroad officials were not, however, altogether satisfied with the result. The great railroad entrepreneur John Murray Forbes branded the measure "a cross between socialism and paternalism," and other railroad leaders were equally critical of the statute.[39]

Persuaded, however, to recognize the folly of unlimited competition in an industry in which fixed costs are so prominent a factor, railroad presidents became eager for federal legislation that would legalize the pooling arrangements that the roads might themselves devise. Railroad officials, nevertheless, made it clear to the United States Industrial Commission at the turn of the century that although they were prepared to accept legislation of this sort, they, like the laissez-faire economists, were firmly opposed to the grant of full rate-making authority to the Interstate Commerce Commission and to the "sublime folly" of government ownership.[40] President E. B. Thomas of the Erie Railroad was doubtless giving expression to the thought of many of these officials at this time when he asked the Commission why public authorities did not permit the railways, which had

[38] New York Legislature, Assembly, Special Committee on Railroads, *Proceedings*, I, 70, 83.

[39] Cochran, *Railroad Leaders*, pp. 197–198, 342. For additional evidence of opposition by railroad leaders to state and federal regulation of the railroads, see Chester McArthur Destler, "The Opposition of American Businessmen to Social Control during the 'Gilded Age,'" *Mississippi Valley Historical Review*, XXXIX (March, 1953), 659–665.

[40] Testimony of John K. Cowen, Stuyvesant Fish, Melville E. Ingalls, Paul Morton, E. P. Ripley, Samuel Spencer, A. B. Stickney, U. S. Industrial Commission, *Report on Transportation* (Vol. IV of the Commission's *Reports;* Washington, D.C., 1900), pp. 276–277, 279, 286–287, 299–300, 313–319, 337–338, 463–464, 491–492, 595, 598.

done so much for the country, "to work out their own solution instead of hampering them so much with investigation, legislation, and all that line of procedure." [41]

Like the advent of the railroad, the trend toward business consolidation and the growth of trusts and industrial combinations in the last decades of the nineteenth century caused many persons to question the validity of the businessman's argument that competition equitably regulates the economic life of the nation and that state intervention is therefore unnecessary. Since one of the chief reasons for the formation of trusts was the desire of the interested parties to avoid the rigors of competition,[42] there was some difficulty in fitting these combinations into the businessman's picture of the self-regulating economic order. Many merchants and small businessmen, indeed, frightened by the implications of the consolidation movement, advocated antimonopoly action that would have as its objective the destruction of the trusts and the restoration of competitive conditions that would be more favorable to them and more in consonance with the American ideal of equality of opportunity.[43] Other businessmen, however, and particularly those associated with the larger concerns, insisted that the trusts were a natural and inevitable product of industrial progress and a source of benefit to the community.[44] Most of the businessmen who argued in this fashion maintained that the trusts did not interfere with competition in any essential way. Some, however, averred that com-

[41] U. S. Industrial Commission, *Report on Transportation* (Vol. IX of the Commission's *Reports;* Washington, D.C., 1901), p. 560.

[42] U. S. Industrial Commission, *Report on Trusts and Industrial Combinations* (Vol. XIII of the Commission's *Reports;* Washington, D.C., 1901), p. v.

[43] New York merchants, for example, were prominent in the formation in 1881 of the National Anti-Monopoly League. The League dissolved in 1883 and became a state branch of the western-controlled National Anti-Monopoly Organization. See Benson, "New York Farmers and Merchants," pp. 327–332, 425–426. Incidentally, Francis B. Thurber, the New York merchant whom Benson considers the key figure in the League, decided by the end of the century that the trust was the product of natural forces and that antitrust statutes were not necessary. See U. S. Industrial Commission, *Preliminary Report on Trusts and Industrial Combinations,* pp. 6, 16.

[44] See, for example, the statement by Eugene D. Mann, in Bridge, ed., *The Trust: Its Book,* p. 180; Wood, *Natural Law in the Business World,* pp. 195–196; Perkins to Atkinson, June 7, 1881, Atkinson Papers; Carnegie, "Popular Illusions about Trusts," in *Gospel of Wealth,* pp. 85–92; and testimony of F. B. Thurber, U. S. Industrial Commission, *Preliminary Report on Trusts and Industrial Combinations,* p. 6.

petition had served its purpose and that the era of competition was being replaced by a new era of coöperation.

Those who maintained that the trust in no way violated the principles of competition generally pointed to the factor of potential competition. It was alleged that if a trust should attempt to secure more than the average return from capital, new competitors would invade the field, and this would force prices down. Competition and the natural laws of supply and demand could therefore be relied on to secure to the consumer a fair price even in areas of the economy that were dominated by industrial combinations.[45] S. C. T. Dodd, of Standard Oil, and Hermon B. Butler, of Ryerson and Son, insisted that the formation of business consolidations had actually improved the quality of competition and that any antitrust action would constitute an unwarranted restraint of trade.[46] In similar fashion, Charles Elliott Perkins argued that the experience of many industries had demonstrated that combination was "a necessary part . . . of the natural law of competition" and that its results were of benefit to the public at large.[47]

A few businessmen, however, spoke of the "debauch of competition" and extolled the trust as the harbinger of a new era of coöperation and industrial peace. The virtues of competition, these businessmen contended, had been exaggerated, and all should rejoice that industry was moving on to a higher level. The vice president of the National Bank of the Republic informed the American Bankers Association in 1896 that competition was the life of trade "within well defined limits, but beyond those limits it [was] far from profitable and wise." [48] With trusts well established, the manufacturer Otis Kendall

[45] See the statement by Paul Morton, *Chicago Conference on Trusts, 1899,* p. 253; testimony of F. B. Thurber and Charles C. Clarke, U. S. Industrial Commission, *Preliminary Report on Trusts and Industrial Combinations,* pp. 14, 187; testimony of Henry Clay Fry, U. S. Industrial Commission, *Report on the Relations and Conditions of Capital and Labor,* VII, 904; testimony of James M. Waterbury, *Report on Trusts and Industrial Combinations,* p. 137; Carnegie, "The Bugaboo of Trusts," in *Empire of Business,* pp. 159–161, 168; Carnegie, "Popular Illusions about Trusts," in *Gospel of Wealth,* pp. 100–102.

[46] Dodd, "Aggregated Capital: Its History and Influence," in Bridge, ed., *The Trust: Its Book,* pp. 64–65; testimony of Hermon B. Butler, U. S. Industrial Commission, *Report on Trusts and Industrial Combinations,* pp. 489, 497–498.

[47] Perkins to Levi Z. Leiter, December 29, 1888, cited in Cochran, *Railroad Leaders,* p. 448.

[48] Cited in Redlich, *Molding of American Banking, Part II,* p. 177. Redlich adds, however, that "the majority [of bankers], or at least very strong minorities,

Stuart argued, the "geniuses of commerce and finance" would be able to direct industry so as to secure something better and more ethical than mere individual success. "The trust," Stuart contended, "is not only the next natural step in business, it is a step in social evolution; the trust is not only a conservator of energy and of wealth, it is a conservator of morals and religion." [49]

Though businessmen who defended the trusts differed in their views as to the vitality of competition, the vast majority of them were agreed that industrial combinations were not properly the concern of the state.[50] If a particular combination effectively served the needs of the people, they maintained, it would survive; if not, it would perish. Legislation, at all events, could in no way affect the survival of the fittest business concerns.[51] Henry O. Havemeyer, president of the American Sugar Refining Company, summed up the views of many businessmen in this matter when he informed the United States Industrial Commission that "the Government should have nothing to do with them [trusts] in any way, shape, or manner." The public, he argued, needs no information about monopoly. "Let the buyer beware; that covers the whole business. You cannot wet nurse people from the time they are born until the time they die. They have got to wade in and get stuck, and that is the way men are educated and cultivated." [52]

Although the businessman was prone to argue the virtues of the negative state, he was hardly consistent in his application of laissez-faire theories. To be sure, he criticized state action that might circumscribe his activities or that would aid other groups in the com-

---

still stuck to the traditional concept of price competition as healthy or even God-ordained" (*ibid.*).

[49] Stuart, "The Value of Trusts," *Independent,* XLIX (March 4, 1897), 272–273.

[50] For the views of businessmen who were willing to accept some legislation in this field, see testimony of John D. Rockefeller, U. S. Industrial Commission, *Preliminary Report on Trusts and Industrial Combinations,* p. 797; and testimony of Archibald S. White and Hugh Campbell, U. S. Industrial Commission, *Report on Trusts and Industrial Combinations,* pp. 265, 311.

[51] See, for example, testimony of F. B. Thurber, Charles C. Clarke, and John D. Archbold, U. S. Industrial Commission, *Preliminary Report on Trusts and Industrial Combinations,* pp. 6, 16, 187, 562; and testimony of James M. Waterbury and Hugh J. Chisolm, U. S. Industrial Commission, *Report on Trusts and Industrial Combinations,* pp. 137, 438.

[52] U. S. Industrial Commission, *Preliminary Report on Trusts and Industrial Combinations,* p. 123.

munity, but he did not oppose such activities of the state as served to promote business enterprise or to enhance business profits. Andrew Carnegie regularly denounced legislative tinkering but nevertheless advocated government construction of a Lake Erie and Ohio River Ship Canal that would lower ton-mile rates from the Lakes to the Carnegie works in Pittsburgh.[53] The National Association of Manufacturers, organized in 1895, criticized the manufacture and free distribution to farmers by the Department of Agriculture of vaccine designed to combat blackleg but importuned the federal government to promote foreign trade by chartering an international American bank, subsidizing the merchant marine, enacting a protective tariff, and reforming the consular service so as to make it more solicitous of the export needs of American manufacturers.[54] Railway officials who attacked rate-making as an improper exercise of legislative authority saw nothing amiss in legislation to prevent strikes from interfering with interstate commerce, to define liabilities in case of bankruptcy, and to require tests for color blindness; and many of them had perhaps forgotten that they were speaking for railroads that had benefited from federal land grants and from the largesse of state and local governments.[55]

One of the most patent violations of the laws of trade in the period after the Civil War was the protective tariff; and yet most businessmen, and particularly industrialists, approved of this form of government bounty.[56] Henry Clews, who told the workingman not to organize but to rely on the laws of trade, was not so convinced of the benign effects of natural law when it came to the tariff: he bitterly criticized Grover Cleveland's famous tariff message of 1887. Henry Wood and Charles Flint, who thought the state should do little more than protect property and provide for the enforcement of contracts, approved the enactment of tariff legislation that afforded protection to American industries. After declaring that he did not "believe in attempting to

[53] Carnegie to John E. Shaw, July 4, 1896, Carnegie Papers.

[54] Albert K. Steigerwalt, Jr., "The National Association of Manufacturers: Organization and Policies, 1895–1914" (Ph.D. thesis, University of Michigan, 1952), pp. 83–87, 101–130, 159–161.

[55] Cochran, *Railroad Leaders,* p. 192.

[56] For a list of manufacturers of the era who were opposed to protection and who were members of the Manufacturers' Free Trade League, see Horace Kenny to Atkinson, December 10, 1894, Atkinson Papers. For other exceptions, see Farquhar and Farquhar, *Economic and Industrial Delusions,* pp. 98–122; and E. McClung Fleming, *R. R. Bowker* (Norman, Okla., 1952), pp. 90–92 *et passim.*

control the business of the citizen by legislative enactment," the banker
E. R. Chapman went on to say that he was a high protectionist. Andrew Carnegie, although an acknowledged disciple of Herbert Spencer,
was not disposed to interpret natural law in the same manner as the
English philosopher when it came to the subject of the tariff. To the
American ironmaster, the protective tariff was a necessary means of
implementing the "evident law of nature" that many nations should
enjoy "the blessings of diversified industries." [57]

At the National Tariff Convention of 1881 representatives from
virtually all the major industries of the country announced their adherence to the principle of protection. Laissez-faire economists were
denounced at this convention because of their support of free trade,
but words of praise were directed at Francis Bowen, who, although
an advocate of laissez faire, was, at the same time, a friend to protection.[58] Most of the witnesses connected with manufacturing industries who testified before the United States Industrial Commission
spoke in favor of the protective tariff and yet denounced projects for
regulating the trusts as contrary to the laws of trade.[59] The businessman thus refused to carry laissez faire to its logical conclusion. He
was quite willing to sanction state interference with the laws of trade
when that interference offered hope of higher profits. But when the
state sought to embark on programs of social reform, the businessman
became an opponent of state action, an advocate of laissez faire.

The laissez-faire philosophy of the businessman culminated, in a
sense, in Andrew Carnegie's "Gospel of Wealth." The businessman

[57] Clews, *Wall Street Point of View,* pp. 94–97; Wood, *Political Economy of
Natural Law,* pp. 228, 231–232; Flint, "Combinations and Critics," in Bridge, ed.,
The Trust: Its Book, p. 10; testimony of E. R. Chapman, U. S. Industrial Commission,
Report on Trusts and Industrial Combinations, p. 110; Carnegie, "The Manchester
School and To-Day," in *Empire of Business,* pp. 311–323; Carnegie, "What Would
I Do with the Tariff If I Were Czar?" *ibid.,* pp. 327–345. On December 20, 1901,
after his retirement, Carnegie informed the *New York Commercial* that the tariff
had "lost much of its importance" insofar as protection was concerned and that it was
henceforth "to be considered principally in regard to Revenue" (Carnegie Papers).

[58] National Tariff Convention, *Proceedings, 1881* (Philadelphia, 1882), pp. 47–
48 *et passim.* The agreement which the Pennsylvania ironmaster Joseph Wharton
made with the trustees of the University of Pennsylvania when the Wharton School
of Finance and Commerce was established stipulated that "the right and duty of
national self-protection must be firmly asserted and demonstrated." See Arnold W.
Green, *Henry Charles Carey, Nineteenth Century Sociologist* (Philadelphia, 1951),
pp. 176–177.

[59] U. S. Industrial Commission, *Preliminary Report on Trusts and Industrial
Combinations,* pp. 23 *et passim.*

had found support for his exalted position in the doctrines of social Darwinism and laissez faire and in the actual conditions of American life. He had expounded the virtues of the system of private enterprise and had pointed out that the capitalist in his pursuit of wealth necessarily serves the common good. But he was forced to recognize that social problems still existed and that the state was being called on to solve these problems. Perhaps the public, even if it would not sanction any significant state interference with the laws of trade, would demand that the state recapture some of the gains of the wealthy by way of an income tax and use the funds so obtained to advance the general welfare. As if to meet this problem, Carnegie, who considered an income tax "perhaps the most pernicious form of taxation which has ever been conceived since human society has settled into peaceful government," [60] devised his Gospel of Wealth.

Carnegie, who had pledged himself as early as 1868 to spend "for benevolent purposes" that portion of his annual income which exceeded fifty thousand dollars,[61] first set forth his philosophy of wealth in popular form in an article that appeared in the *North American Review* in June, 1889. In this statement of his position, Carnegie accepted individualism, private property, competition, and the accumulation of wealth as the highest results of human experience. He insisted that the accumulation of wealth in the hands of the few was not only the inevitable result of the basic laws of civilization but that it was "essential for the future progress of the race." Carnegie did not, however, believe that the millionaire had discharged his responsibilities to mankind simply because he had amassed a fortune. He maintained that the man who had been wise enough to accumulate wealth was under an obligation to administer that wealth wisely. To Carnegie, this meant that the millionaire should not simply bequeath his wealth to his children or to the state,[62] for that was contrary to the best interests of all concerned, but should rather utilize his fortune during his lifetime for the benefit of the community. After having provided for the legitimate wants of his dependents, the rich man was

[60] Carnegie, "What Would I Do with the Tariff If I Were Czar?" in *Empire of Business*, p. 286.

[61] Photostated copy of memorandum dated December, 1868, Carnegie Papers.

[62] Although Carnegie deprecated the bequeathal of one's fortune to the state, he regarded an inheritance tax as the wisest form of taxation. "By taxing estates heavily at death," he declared, "the state marks its condemnation of the selfish millionaire's unworthy life" ("Wealth," *North American Review*, CXLVIII [June, 1889], 659).

to treat all "surplus revenues" as "trust funds" that he was obligated "to administer in the manner which, in his judgment, is best calculated to produce the most beneficial results for the community—the man of wealth thus becoming the mere agent and trustee for his poorer brethren, bringing to their service his superior wisdom, experience, and ability to administer, doing for them better than they would or could do for themselves." "Such, in my opinion," said Carnegie, "is the true Gospel concerning Wealth." [63]

In a second article, Carnegie detailed the types of gifts he thought most advisable. He recommended the donation of funds for the establishment of universities, the founding or extension of hospitals, medical colleges, and laboratories, the creation of public parks, and the construction of music halls, swimming pools, and churches. He considered the wisest gift to a community to be a free library, provided the community would maintain it as a public institution. [64]

Carnegie's Gospel of Wealth rested on the usual laissez-faire assumptions as to the sufficiency of an unregulated economic order. However, Carnegie's program represented, in a sense, an addition to the laissez-faire doctrine of self-interest. Whereas the advocate of laissez faire ordinarily contended that the individual in seeking and acquiring wealth thereby unconsciously serves the interests of the whole, Carnegie went one step further and maintained that the individual who accumulates wealth should consciously use this wealth during his lifetime for the general welfare.

Carnegie did not regard his Gospel of Wealth as a mere sop to the general public but rather as an actual solution for the social problems of the day. He referred to his plan as "the true antidote for the temporary unequal distribution of wealth," as a solution for the problem of rich and poor. [65] As once it had been maintained that political

[63] Carnegie, "Wealth," *North American Review*, CXLVIII (June, 1889), 655–664.

[64] Carnegie, "The Best Fields of Philanthropy," *North American Review*, CXLIX (December, 1889), 682–698.

[65] Carnegie, "Wealth," *North American Review*, CXLVIII (June, 1889), 660, 663–664. In a letter to William Gladstone of November 24, 1890, Carnegie however declared: "The ideal is one thing—the practical quite another and I limit my actions (not my thoughts) to the proper use of wealth once acquired. That an ideal Commonwealth grasping something far beyond that cure, may be able to deal with the *prevention* of immense fortunes some year in the two thousandth [*sic*] when the masses become truly educated and the few become less selfish is not to be unhoped for" (Carnegie Papers).

rule should be vested in the well-to-do, so now Carnegie was saying that the promotion of the general welfare of the community should be entrusted to those who had managed to make the most money rather than to the representatives of the people. Identifying wealth with intelligence, he insisted that the millionaires would know better than the people's government how to expend funds for the common good and that resort to the paternalism of the state was therefore unnecessary. Carnegie's Gospel of Wealth was thus a challenge to the democratic service state and represented a recrudescence of the principles of aristocracy and stewardship.

Carnegie's views with respect to the uses of wealth found favor with many of the leading industrialists of the day. "I am pleased with the sentiments you give expression to," Rockefeller wrote to Carnegie. Godkin noted that a man was criticized if he did not give freely. "His stewardship is insisted on." [66] Businessmen did not seem to take seriously Francis Amasa Walker's warning that Carnegie's views with respect to the "trusteeship of capital" were really "communistic." If the owner of wealth is a trustee for the state or the people, Walker asserted, they, as beneficiary, can, if dissatisfied with the management of the property, step in and manage it themselves. [67]

Of a piece with the Gospel of Wealth were the programs of "welfare capitalism" instituted by businessmen in the last two decades of the nineteenth century. This development stemmed, to a certain extent at least, from the desire of businessmen to persuade employees to identify their best interests with their employer rather than with a trade union or the general-welfare state. To that end employers established insurance funds for sick and injured employees, provided their workers with libraries and music halls, constructed model towns, and instituted schemes of profit sharing. A study of the subject of welfare capitalism by the Department of Labor in 1900 revealed fifteen different plans of industrial betterment in operation. [68] Although

[66] See Burton J. Hendrick, *The Life of Andrew Carnegie* (New York, 1932), I, 349; and Godkin, "The Expenditure of Rich Men," in *Problems of Modern Democracy*, p. 313.

[67] Walker, *Political Economy* (New York, 1883), p. 446.

[68] Victor H. Olmstead, "The Betterment of Industrial Conditions," Department of Labor, *Bulletin*, V (1900), 1117–1118; Nicholas Paine Gilman, *Socialism and the American Spirit* (Boston, 1893), pp. 275–307; Gilman, *A Dividend to Labor: A Study of Employers' Welfare Institutions* (Boston, 1899), pp. 206–295; Ida M. Tarbell, *The Nationalizing of Business, 1878–1898* (New York, 1936), pp. 170–178; Ghent, *Our Benevolent Feudalism*, pp. 59–66.

the movement of welfare capitalism in the 1880's and 1890's in no way reached the proportions of the similar movement in the 1920's, it is none the less significant as a manifestation of the businessman's philosophy.

II

Since the businessman was the dominant figure on the American scene during the years from 1865 to 1901, his views received strong support from most elements in American life.[69] Nowhere, however, did the business spirit find greater favor than in the Protestant church. In the Gilded Age, "urban Protestantism cultivated the middle and upper classes who possessed the ultimate power in American society." Never before had wealth mattered so much to the church. Wealthy business figures were appointed to church boards in increasing numbers, and men of business ability were in demand to serve as church officials. Even the Baptists, who had prided themselves on being a poor man's denomination, ceased to express contempt for wealth and decided that the man of wealth was also "a man of talent." The churches were fast becoming "social and religious clubs for the privileged classes." [70]

Ministers who resented the "aristocratic drift of Protestantism" denounced the alliance between church and market. "No Christian minister," charged the Reverend Franklin M. Sprague, "can deny that the church is crippled, yea, bound and gagged, because of her alliance with wealth." "The simple fact," said the Reverend Arthur T. Pier-

[69] One of the most ardent supporters of laissez faire and the existing order was W. T. Harris, U. S. commissioner of education from 1889 to 1906. Harris, a right-wing Hegelian, believed strongly in individualism, laissez faire, private property, and industrial capitalism. It was his opinion that the schools should instill in their pupils a faith in the existing social and economic structure. In 1894 he told the National Education Association that in the public school, the pupil learned "first of all to respect the rights of organized industry." See Merle Curti, *The Social Ideas of American Educators* (New York, 1935), pp. 310–347.

[70] See Ralph Henry Gabriel, *The Course of American Democratic Thought: An Intellectual History since 1815* (New York, 1940), p. 157; William Warren Sweet, *The Story of Religions in America* (New York, 1930), pp. 496–497; Roy Harold Johnson, "American Baptists in the Age of Big Business," *Journal of Religion,* XI (January, 1931), 71–73; C. A. Briggs, "The Alienation of Church and People," *Forum,* XVI (November, 1893), 376–377; John Bates Clark, *The Philosophy of Wealth* (Boston, 1886), pp. 232–233; Godkin, "The Church and Good Conduct," *Reflections and Comments, 1865–1895* (New York, 1895), pp. 152–154; and William Mackintire Salter, *Ethical Religion* (Boston, 1889), p. 141.

son, "is . . . that the communion of saintliness is displaced by the communion of respectability. Our churches are becoming the quarters of a monopoly." The Reverend R. Heber Newton complained that the church had "accepted the anti-Christian dogmas of the older political economists, and in so doing, really turned traitor to the ethics of Jesus Christ." The poor man, he declared, has no use for "a church that has no better gospel than *laissez faire*, no better brotherhood than the selfish strife of competition, no kingdom of God for human society here upon the earth, but only one up in the skies." [71]

The Protestant minister, like the businessman, gave his support to laissez faire and the *status quo*. He provided religious sanction for the businessman's views with respect to property, inequality, stewardship, state aid, and labor. Property was defended by churchmen as an exclusive right. The general well-being and progress of society were declared to be in proportion to the freedom of the individual to acquire property and to be secure in its possession. Love requires the acquisition of property, declared Mark Hopkins, the eminent Congregational minister and president of Williams College, "because it is a powerful means of benefiting others." Those who have done the most for our institutions have been men with "a strong desire of property." "As men now are," Hopkins concluded, "it is far better that they should be employed in accumulating property honestly . . . than that there should be encouraged any sentimentalism about the worthlessness of property." Princeton's clergyman-president James McCosh was no less certain of the virtues of property. No one, said he, is at liberty to deprive us of our property or to interfere with it. Attempts to do so are "theft." "The laws protecting it [property] have been one of the greatest boons that can be conferred on man." [72]

Like the businessman, the churchman accepted inequalities among men as inevitable and desirable and maintained that those who had risen to the top were the men of ability whereas those who had failed had only themselves to blame.[73] "God," said Henry Ward Beecher,

[71] Sprague, *Socialism from Genesis to Revelation* (Boston, 1893), p. 470; Evangelical Alliance of the United States, *National Perils and Opportunities* (New York, 1887), p. 118; testimony of Newton, Senate Committee on Education and Labor, *Report upon the Relations between Labor and Capital*, II, 595.

[72] Hopkins, *The Law of Love and Love as a Law* (New York, 1881), pp. 169–172; Hopkins, *Lectures on Moral Science* (Boston, 1863), p. 104; McCosh, *Our Moral Nature* (New York, 1892), p. 40.

[73] "The Christian concept of the individual as a free moral agent and the not altogether consistent doctrine that God has determined the success or failure of His

"has intended the great to be great, and the little to be little." [74]   But, in Beecher's view, it was not only predestination that served to make a man poor. He thought it a "general truth" that "no man in this land suffers from poverty unless it be more than his fault—unless it be his *sin*." [75]   In the long run, said the Bishop of Massachusetts, wealth comes to the man of morality. To desire wealth is a sign of strong character and is both "natural and necessary." Religious sanction should not be given to any attempt to suppress this desire. In his celebrated lecture, *Acres of Diamonds*, the Baptist clergyman Russell Conwell preached the "gospel of success." "I say that you ought to get rich, and it is your duty to get rich." The richest people are generally those of the best character. It is wrong to be poor. [76]

The Reverend A. J. F. Behrends, who looked upon inequality as "an original, ultimate, and unalterable fact," deprecated talk of limiting individual wealth because it involved "the right of the state to regulate personal ability, to prescribe to the Almighty how much brains a man shall be permitted to have." [77]   Roswell D. Hitchcock, of Union Theological Seminary, agreed with Behrends. Capital, he stated, represents intelligence, self-denial, and control and is "finer than labor, just

---

children were again and again cited to justify the inequality of riches which prevailed under the competitive order of private and corporate enterprise" (Curti, *Growth of American Thought,* p. 636). For the religious defense of the cult of success and self-help, see Wyllie, *Self-Made Man in America,* pp. 55–74.

[74] *New York Times,* July 30, 1877. This statement was made in a sermon in which Beecher, according to Paxton Hibben, went on to say: "I do not say that a dollar a day is enough to support a working man. But it is enough to support a man! . . . Not enough to support a man and five children if a man would insist on smoking and drinking beer. . . . But the man who cannot live on bread and water is not fit to live." Hibben notes that at the time Beecher made this statement his salary was twenty thousand dollars a year. See Hibben, *Henry Ward Beecher* (New York, 1927), pp. 326–327.

[75] Cited in Henry F. May, *Protestant Churches and Industrial America* (New York, 1949), p. 69.

[76] See William Lawrence, "The Relation of Wealth to Morals," *World's Work,* I (January, 1901), 287–289; and Conwell, *Acres of Diamonds. His Life and Achievements by Robert Shackleton.* With an Autobiographical Note (New York, 1915), pp. 18–19.

[77] Behrends, *Socialism and Christianity* (New York, 1886), pp. 103–105, 148. Although Behrends had an interest in social Christianity and was aware of existing social evils, he was a conservative, who, if willing to sanction reform on an individual, voluntary basis, looked askance at the legislative remedy. The same applies to Hitchcock and Joseph Cook. See May, *Protestant Churches and Industrial America,* pp. 163–169.

as brain is finer than muscle." "At bottom, it is an immorality to fight against the inequality of condition, which simply corresponds with inequality of endowment." [78]

Carnegie's Gospel of Wealth accorded perfectly with Protestant ideas of stewardship and hence was warmly endorsed by Protestant clergymen. "If ever Christ's words have been obeyed to the letter," stated Bishop Lawrence, "they are obeyed to-day by those who are living out His precepts of the stewardship of wealth." Speaking to the American Association for the Advancement of Science, President Joseph Cummings of Wesleyan University declared that "the great remedy for social wrongs" was to "be found in the Christian use of money." The Baptist organ, the *Standard,* hailed the benefactions of the rich "as indicative of the degree in which the great idea has taken hold of wealthy men that the very highest office and privilege of wealth is service," and spoke of "a day to come when the 'faithful and wise steward' can meet the master of all, as one at whose feet it will be an infinite joy to lay down the fruits of all his giving and all his doing." [79]

The majority of Protestant churchmen, like the businessmen, took a completely negative view of social reform and state action. They considered reform a matter of individual regeneration rather than of improved social conditions. Character, they said, determines conditions more than conditions determine character.[80] Like their business friends, they were opposed to any significant legislative interference with the laws of trade. They advised the state to protect property and enforce contracts and, in effect, to ignore the general welfare.

The idea that "government should be paternal and take care of the welfare of its subjects and provide them with labor" was denounced by the eminent divine Henry Ward Beecher as "un-American." "The American doctrine," Beecher declared, "is that it is the duty of the

[78] Hitchcock, *Socialism* (New York, 1879), pp. 85–86, 92–93. Hitchcock considered intemperance to be the chief cause of inequality of condition (*ibid.,* pp. 104–106).

[79] See Lawrence, "The Relation of Wealth to Morals," *World's Work,* I (January, 1901), 289; Charles Howard Hopkins, *The Rise of the Social Gospel in American Protestantism, 1865–1915* (New Haven, 1940), p. 90; and Johnson, "American Baptists in the Age of Big Business," *Journal of Religion,* XI (January, 1931), 75.

[80] See, for example, Hitchcock, *Socialism,* pp. 107–108; Joseph Cook, *Socialism* (Boston, 1880), p. 79; Behrends, *Socialism and Christianity,* p. 143; and Fairbairn, "The Law of Labor and Capital," *Christian Thought,* 4th Ser. (1886), p. 208.

Government merely to protect the people while they are taking care of themselves—nothing more than that. 'Hands off,' we say to the Government." [81] Roswell D. Hitchcock looked on most types of state action as communistic in character. Although recognizing that social evils existed, Hitchcock thought that the remedies for these evils were not to be prescribed by the state. Government, he asserted, may not meddle with wages, limit the number of working hours (except for minors), set up labor exchanges, or run any industry. "The questions to be settled are questions of political economy, which ought, on every account, to be settled dispassionately. Men may vote as they please, but the laws of production and of trade are as inexorable as the laws of nature." [82]

The Reverend A. J. F. Behrends differed but little in his social philosophy from that great opponent of social reform, William Graham Sumner.[83] A policy that relieves individuals of "worry" or the "fear of want," he argued, "only degrades, pauperizes and brutalizes them." All that justice requires is that each individual be left free to work at his chosen task and to reap the fruits of his labor. If responsibility is "individualized" and competition unchecked, the nation will enjoy the benefits of a cheap and abundant production. Like Sumner, Behrends feared the rule of the majority and contended that what characterizes the free state is the existence of restraints imposed on the majority by the minority.[84]

Even giving aid to the poor was criticized by some clergymen as an unwarranted exercise of state authority and as a task that was more properly entrusted to private charity. Bishop Harris of Michigan attacked state poor relief as injurious to both the poor and the rich. Relief of this sort, he held, encourages improvidence in the needy and paralyzes the bounty of the wealthy, thus depriving the poor of the personal sympathy of the rich and the rich of the gratitude of the poor. The poor and the rich, he concluded, are indispensable to one another and should be brought together "by flinging all classes . . . back on the old law of mutual helpfulness and sym-

[81] *New York Times,* July 30, 1877.

[82] Hitchcock, *Socialism,* pp. 47–51, 79–85.

[83] Of Sumner's *What Social Classes Owe to Each Other,* Behrends declared: "There is here a simple faith in reason and manhood, which needs only the affirmation of faith in God, to make it Christian; and even that is present by implication" (*Socialism and Christianity,* p. 142).

[84] Behrends, *Socialism and Christianity,* pp. 81, 90–96, 141–143, 187, 236.

pathy; by discontinuing charity by law, and relying on the charity of love." [85]

The workingman received no more sympathy from most Protestant clergymen than he did from the businessman. Labor, in the view of conservative church leaders, was but a commodity and like all other commodities was to be "governed by the imperishable laws of demand and supply." "It is all right to talk and declaim about the dignity of labor," declared the *Watchman and Reflector*. "But when all has been said of it, what is labor but a matter of barter and sale." [86]

The advice offered to the laborer by clergymen was to remain passive. The Reverend W. D. Wilson told the workingman that Jesus' advice was that he be content with his wages. If he were entitled to higher wages, in the Lord's good time he would receive them. What injustice he suffered in this world would be turned to his account in the hereafter. "Be quiet," declared Wilson. "Whatsoever your hands find to do, do it, and be content with your wages. God will take care of the rest." [87]

Other clergymen also found laissez faire to be the proper nostrum for the ills of labor, and they therefore condemned all of labor's weapons: trade unions, strikes, and labor legislation. Trade unions, they alleged, served but to drag down the superior workman to the level of the inferior and to introduce class lines into American society. "The Trades' Unions," charged the *Christian Advocate*, "are despotic and revolutionary in tendency. . . . The worst doctrines of Communism are involved in these unions. . . . Legislate Trades' Unions out of existence . . . ." [88]

The Reverend Joseph Cook, who won for himself a reputation as a reformer but who was denounced by the labor editor John Swinton as a "noisy and empty-headed preacher," [89] recognized that female and child laborers required the protection of government but insisted that adult male laborers should seek to improve their competitive position

[85] Samuel Smith Harris, *The Relation of Christianity to Civil Society* (New York, 1883), pp. 159–196. See also Behrends, *Socialism and Christianity*, pp. 187, 239–240; and Hitchcock, *Socialism*, pp. 50–51.

[86] Cited in May, *Protestant Churches and Industrial America*, p. 55.

[87] Wilson, "The Relations of Labor and Capital from a Christian Point of View," in *First Principles of Political Economy* (Philadelphia, 1882), pp. 346–350. This was the same Reverend Mr. Wilson who taught political economy at Cornell.

[88] Cited in May, *Protestant Churches and Industrial America*, p. 96. See also *ibid.*, pp. 56–57.

[89] *John Swinton's Paper*, April 4, 1886.

through self-help rather than by invoking the aid of the state. Politicians who advised workers to enlist the support of the state were attacked by Cook as "enemies of social progress." [90]

An especially bitter foe of labor was the influential Princeton clergyman-economist Lyman Atwater, a frequent contributor to Presbyterian journals and "a force in public opinion only slightly below Sumner." [91] Atwater looked upon most trade unions as "conspiracies against the laws of God, the rights of man, and the welfare of society," and believed, consequently, that they must be repressed. He was similarly opposed to strikes and was virtually thrown into a panic by the great railroad strikes of 1877. "And is a free people," he asked, "about to sit tamely under such a despotism, and allow their persons, property, liberty, government to be dependent on the beck, the caprice of a junto of men, who stand ready to strike in the dark, from their secret conclave, at everything we hold dear, our very altars and our firesides, no one knows when? . . . should we rest until this monstrous usurpation, and fomenting cause of social disorganization, of mobs and riots, of evils, . . . be abated and abolished?" A foe of trade unionism and strikes, Atwater was equally opposed to labor legislation (other than that for children or for sanitary purposes) as a means of improving the position of the workingman. "Legislation," he declared, "cannot alter the laws of nature, of man, of political economics." [92]

Bishop Harris was as critical of labor's methods as was Atwater and viewed them as being essentially socialistic.[93] Labor legislation, the

[90] Cook, Socialism, pp. 85–89. Hopkins refers to Cook as a "born reformer" (Rise of the Social Gospel, pp. 39–42). Like Behrends, however, Cook tended to stress voluntary methods for improving existing conditions. Initially, Cook advocated factory acts for female and child laborers but little else in the way of legislation. In the late 1880's, however, he did move somewhat to the left. See May, Protestant Churches and Industrial America, pp. 164–166, 168; and Arthur Mann, Yankee Reformers in the Urban Age (Cambridge, Mass., 1954), pp. 80–81.

[91] Joseph Dorfman, The Economic Mind in American Civilization (New York, 1946–1949), III, 69.

[92] Atwater, "The Labor Question in Its Christian and Economic Aspects," Presbyterian Quarterly and Princeton Review, N.S., I (July, 1872), 480–482, 484–486; Atwater, "The Great Railroad Strike," ibid., VI (October, 1877), 729–730; and Atwater, "Our Industrial and Financial Situation," ibid., IV (July, 1875), 523. For Atwater's views on the currency question and the regulation of railroads, see Atwater, "The Currency Question," ibid., IV (October, 1875), 721–742; and Atwater, "The Regulation of Railroads," Princeton Review, N.S., VII (May, 1881), 406–428.

[93] Harris considered "socialistic" "all methods which call for special or class legislation, or state interference with the fixed and persistent laws of the industrial

Bishop declared, is useless because the industrial world is governed by natural laws that man cannot annul. "The best legislation in the industrial and commercial sphere of human activity has long since been enacted by the Supreme Lawgiver; and every interposition by human government is both impertinent and harmful." [94]

From the point of view of economics, the clergymen thus advocated laissez faire as the solution for existing labor difficulties. As Bishop Harris put it: "So far as economical agencies are concerned, there is no doubt that the great principle of *laissez faire*, advanced by Adam Smith, is the correct one." [95] From the religious point of view, however, the ministers proposed Christianity as a supplement to laissez faire. The capitalist was exhorted to apply Protestant ideas with respect to the stewardship of wealth, to treat his employees properly, and to adopt such "Christian" devices as profit sharing. "The power of Christian love," said one clergyman, "should smooth and sweeten all the relations of capitalists and labor." [96]

The close alliance between the Protestant church and wealth and the attitude of Protestant clergymen toward the labor struggle were among the factors that contributed to the decline in the church attendance of Protestant workingmen in the decades after the Civil War.[97] The workers, Samuel Gompers declared in response to a query as to why laborers had become alienated from the church, "have come to look upon the church and ministry as the apologists and defenders of the wrongs committed against the interests of the people, simply because the perpetrators are the possessors of wealth." Clergy-

---

and commercial world" ("Capital and Labor," *Christian Thought,* 3d Ser. [1885], p. 28).

[94] Harris, "Capital and Labor," *Christian Thought,* 3d Ser. (1885), pp. 27–30.

[95] Harris, "Capital and Labor," *Christian Thought,* 3d Ser. (1885), p. 32.

[96] See Hitchcock, *Socialism,* pp. 99–100; Harris, "Capital and Labor," *Christian Thought,* 3d Ser. (1885), pp. 35–36; and Atwater, "The Labor Question in Its Christian and Economic Aspects," *Presbyterian Quarterly and Princeton Review,* N.S., I (July, 1872), 487–495.

[97] For polls which support this view, see Washington Gladden, *Applied Christianity* (Boston, 1887), pp. 151–152; and Alexander Jackson, "The Relation of the Classes to the Church," *Independent,* XL (March 1, 1888), 258–259. For other evidences of the divorce between the Protestant church and the laboring man in the years from 1865 to 1901, see H. Francis Perry, "The Workingman's Alienation from the Church," *American Journal of Sociology,* IV (March, 1899), 621–629; Samuel Lane Loomis, *Modern Cities and Their Religious Problems* (New York, 1887), 82–83, 88, 99; and Richard T. Ely, *Social Aspects of Christianity, and Other Essays* (New York, 1889), pp. 39–49.

men, he charged, were using "their exalted positions to discountenance all practical efforts of the toilers to lift themselves out of the slough of despondency and despair." [98]   "We believe much in Jesus and in his teachings, but not much in the teachings of his pretended followers," one workingman declared. "A civilization that permits man to be the greatest enemy of man . . . is a cheat and a sham; the political economy that permits it is a falsehood and a fraud; and a religion that allows it without constant, earnest, and persistent protest is a humbug." [99]   It was from conditions such as these that the social-gospel movement sought to rescue the Protestant church.[100]

[98] Gompers, "The Church and Labor," *American Federationist*, III (August, 1896), 119–120.

[99] "Letter from a Workingman," *Christian Union*, XXXII (October 29, 1885), 8. The "workingman" was J. Willett, of Glenn, Michigan.

[100] See Chapter VI.

V

LAISSEZ FAIRE BECOMES THE LAW
OF THE LAND

IT WAS in the courts that the idea of laissez faire won its greatest victory in the three and one-half decades after the Civil War. Here, the laissez-faire views of academic and popular theorists and of practical businessmen were translated from theory into practice. Bar and bench joined forces in making laissez faire an important element of constitutional doctrine and in establishing the courts as the ultimate censors of virtually all forms of social and economic legislation.

It is, of course, resorting to an obvious fiction to maintain that judges merely apply the appropriate words of the fundamental law in settling the constitutional questions that come before them and that their social and economic philosophy and prejudices play no part in the actual shaping of the law. Most of the great issues that judges must decide are not matters of well-established law for which the Constitution provides ready answers. To resolve these questions, judges must adapt the Constitution to existing needs as they understand them. In so doing they have found it necessary to interpret such vague words and phrases as "due process of law," "liberty," "property," "equal protection," and "interstate commerce"—all of which are undefined in the Constitution. These terms, as Felix Frankfurter has pointed out, "are the foundations for judgment upon the whole appalling domain of social and economic facts." Through their interpretation judges have been able, to a considerable extent, to read into the Constitution their own notions as to the proper limits of governmental authority.[1]

[1] Frankfurter, *Mr. Justice Holmes and the Constitution: A Review of His Twenty-five Years on the Supreme Court* (Cambridge, Mass., 1927), pp. 4–5. In

Since the subjective element has played such an important part in the shaping of constitutional law, it is necessary, before considering how laissez faire was woven into the fabric of the law during the years from 1865 to 1901, to examine the views of the legal fraternity on the subject of the functions of government and thus to understand the subjective framework within which the law was fashioned. Inasmuch as there has been a constant interaction between book, bar, and bench, it is essential to take into consideration in this connection not only the views of judges but also those of lawyers and of the writers of legal textbooks. Legal textbooks provide convenient ideas and groupings of precedents for lawyers and judges to sample, and judges often find in lawyers' briefs arguments on which to base their own opinions.[2]

On the whole, the views of the legal fraternity during the decades after the Civil War were pronouncedly conservative. Training and social position combined to make lawyers and judges supporters of the *status quo* and enemies of experimentation in the realm of government.[3] In the ideological conflict between laissez faire and the general-welfare state, bench and bar were almost invariably to be found among the champions of laissez faire.

As in the era before the Civil War, higher-law beliefs in one form

---

the words of Morris Raphael Cohen, "no historian can deny the fact that in the making of our constitutional law there generally enters the personal opinion of the judge as to what is desirable or undesirable legislation" ("Constitutional and Natural Rights in 1789 and Since," in *The Faith of a Liberal* [New York, 1946], pp. 176–177). What has been said of constitutional law might just as well be said of the law in general. "The life of the law," said Oliver Wendell Holmes, "has not been logic: it has been experience. The felt necessities of the time, the prevalent moral and political theories, intuitions of public policy, avowed or unconscious, even the prejudices which judges share with their fellow-men [a belief in laissez faire, for example], have had a good deal more to do than the syllogism in determining the rules by which men should be governed" (*The Common Law* [Boston, 1881], p. 1).

[2] In *Lawyers and the Constitution: How Laissez Faire Came to the Supreme Court* (Princeton, N.J., 1942), Benjamin R. Twiss shows how laissez-faire views were transmitted from bar to bench chiefly through the medium of legal briefs. Lawyers, he declares, are closer to everyday life than judges and thus are more imbued with the *zeitgeist*. "Judges in large part depend upon lawyers for ideas" (*ibid.*, p. 16).

[3] In this connection, see John F. Dillon, *The Laws and Jurisprudence of England and America* (Boston, 1895), pp. 293–295; Twiss, *Lawyers and the Constitution*, pp.12–13; Walton H. Hamilton, "Freedom of Contract," in Edwin R. A. Seligman, ed., *Encyclopaedia of the Social Sciences* (New York, 1930–1935), VI, 451; and Oliver Wendell Holmes, "The Path of the Law," *Harvard Law Review,* X (April, 1897), 468.

or another played an important part in the antistatist outlook of lawyers and judges. The assumption that there are implied limitations on legislative power arising from the very nature of free institutions and that it is the duty of the courts to interpose their authority whenever a legislature oversteps these limitations tended in the years after the Civil War to be absorbed in the judicial translation of such constitutional words and phrases as "liberty," "property," and "due process of law,"[4] but many jurists continued to speak in terms of a law above constitutions and designed to protect property and personal rights— particularly the former—from government encroachment. As Judge Beck of the Iowa Supreme Court declared: "There is, as it were, back of the written Constitution, an *unwritten Constitution* . . . which guarantees and well protects all the absolute rights of the people. The government can exercise no power to impair or deny them."[5]

Thomas McIntyre Cooley, professor of law at the University of Michigan, justice of the Michigan Supreme Court, first chairman of the Interstate Commerce Commission, and author of the most influential legal textbook of the period,[6] was a conspicuous advocate of the concept of implied limitations. In Cooley's opinion, the courts did not have to find an express violation of the fundamental law to declare a statute invalid: he looked upon Magna Charta and the common law as implicitly limiting the exercise of powers granted by the people to their governments and insisted that acts thereby forbidden to the departments of government "cannot be considered within any grant or apportionment of power which the people in general terms have made to those departments."[7]

Justices Stephen J. Field and David Josiah Brewer and the prominent railroad attorney John Cary looked upon the Declaration of Independence as an essential part of the constitutional system and as an expression of inherent rights which were "beyond the touch of any statute or organic instrument." As they construed it, the phrase "pursuit of happiness" included among the inalienable rights guaranteed by the Declaration the right to acquire, possess, and enjoy property.[8]

[4] Charles Grove Haines, *The Revival of Natural Law Concepts* (Cambridge, Mass., 1930), pp. 121–122, 211–212; Benjamin Fletcher Wright, Jr., *American Interpretations of Natural Law* (Cambridge, Mass., 1931), pp. 298–299, 330.

[5] Hanson *v.* Vernon, 27 Ia. 28 (1869), 73.

[6] *A Treatise on the Constitutional Limitations Which Rest upon the Legislative Power of the States of the American Union* (Boston, 1868).

[7] Cooley, *Treatise on Constitutional Limitations*, pp. 174–175.

[8] Brewer, *Protection to Private Property from Public Attack* (New Haven, 1891),

An interpretation of this sort was to have been expected, since the idea of implied limitations was ordinarily invoked to shelter vested rights from legislative attack. No matter how vested rights arise, Justice Swayne declared, "they are all equally sacred, equally beyond the reach of legislative interference." [9]

The strength of the idea of implied limitations on legislative powers is attested to by the fact that the principle that taxation is valid only when it is designed for a public purpose was evolved during this period strictly on the basis of the doctrine of implied limitations and not as the result of any provision in the federal or state constitutions. The work most frequently cited by the courts to support the theory that taxes can only be levied for a public purpose was Cooley's celebrated *Treatise on Constitutional Limitations.*[10] Despite the fact that his view was "clearly against the weight of existing authority," [11] Cooley asserted that since the "only legitimate object" of taxation is "the raising of money for public purposes and the proper needs of government, the exaction of moneys from the citizens for other purposes is not a proper exercise of this power, and must therefore be unauthorized." Although he recognized that the legislature is to be given the benefit of the doubt in matters of taxation, Cooley argued that the courts must intervene whenever the legislature exceeds its authority and judicial process can afford relief. "An unlimited power to make any and everything lawful which the legislature might see fit to call taxation," he declared, "would be, when plainly stated, an unlimited power to plunder the citizen." [12]

---

pp. 4–5; Butchers' Union Co. *v.* Crescent City Co., 111 U.S. 746 (1884), 756–757; Budd *v.* New York, 143 U.S. 517 (1892), 550; Cary, "Limitations of the Legislative Power in Respect to Personal Rights and Private Property," *Report of the Fifteenth Annual Meeting of the American Bar Association, 1892,* pp. 249–251, 255.

[9] Sinking Fund Cases, 99 U.S. 700 (1879), 733. See also William F. Dana, "Federal Restraints upon State Regulation of Railway Rates of Fare and Freight," *Harvard Law Review,* IX (January, 1896), 345; and J. V. Campbell, *Taking of Private Property for Purposes of Utility* (Chicago, 1871), p. 99.

[10] Clyde E. Jacobs, *Law Writers and the Courts: The Influence of Thomas M. Cooley, Christopher G. Tiedeman, and John F. Dillon upon American Constitutional Law* (Berkeley, Calif., 1954), p. 109. Jacobs' book contains an admirable survey (pp. 98–159) of the evolution during this period of the concept of taxation for a public purpose only.

[11] Twiss, *Lawyers and the Constitution,* p. 33. See also Howard Lee McBain, "Taxation for a Private Purpose," *Political Science Quarterly,* XXIX (June, 1914), 185–213; and Haines, *Revival of Natural Law Concepts,* pp. 123–135.

[12] Cooley, *Treatise on Constitutional Limitations,* pp. 487–488. Cooley's views

Despite an attempt by Chief Justice John Forrest Dillon of the Iowa Supreme Court to associate the idea of public purpose with the due-process clause,[13] the courts that accepted the doctrine during this period did so not on the basis of any constitutional authority but on extraconstitutional grounds.[14]   The Supreme Court of Wisconsin declared that the power to tax for a private purpose "would be obviously incompatible with the genius and institutions of a free people."   The highest court of West Virginia thought that such a tax "would be clearly a subversion of the implied reservations of individual rights; it would be the exercise of an arbitrary power contrary to the theory of our government . . . and the spirit of the Constitution of the State . . . ."   The New York Court of Appeals upheld the idea of taxation for a public purpose simply "on general principles."   The Michigan Supreme Court, in the person of Judge Cooley, asserted in People *v.* Salem that the limits upon the power of taxation which are "inherent in the subject itself . . . are as inflexible and absolute in their restraints as if directly imposed in the most positive form of words."   In this same case the court, expressing a view that was to prevail, established "settled usage" as the criterion for determining whether a tax had been levied for a public purpose.   "The urgency of the public need" or even "the extent of the public benefit which is to follow" were not, in the court's opinion, valid determinants of public purpose.[15]

The United States Supreme Court also accepted the doctrine that taxation can only be for a public purpose, and, as with the state courts, its decision rested squarely on the concept of implied limitations.   In Loan Association *v.* Topeka, Justice Miller, speaking for himself and seven other justices, denounced a tax for a private purpose as an in-

---

on this subject were expanded in his *A Treatise on the Law of Taxation, Including the Law of Local Assessments* (Chicago, 1876).   John Forrest Dillon's *Treatise on the Law of Municipal Corporations* (Chicago, 1872) was another work frequently cited by the courts to uphold the public-purpose idea with respect to taxation.   See Jacobs, *Law Writers and the Courts,* p. 121.

[13] Hanson *v.* Vernon, 27 Ia. 28 (1869).   Dillon declared that a tax for private purposes would deprive the persons taxed of property without due process of law (*ibid.,* pp. 45, 50–51).

[14] By 1900, however, five state constitutions contained public-purpose provisions. See Jacobs, *Law Writers and the Courts,* 195n.

[15] Curtis's Adm'r *v.* Whipple and Others, 24 Wisc. 350 (1869), 354; Ohio Valley Iron Works *v.* Town of Moundsville, 11 W. Va. 1 (1887), 12–13; Bush *v.* Board of Supervisors, 159 N.Y. 212 (1899), 216–217; People *v.* Salem, 20 Mich. 452 (1870), 473, 485; Jacobs, *Law Writers and the Courts,* pp. 116–120.

vasion of private rights. "It must be conceded," he declared, "that there are such rights in every free government beyond the control of the State." A government that does not recognize such rights is a despotism, "a despotism of the many, of the majority . . . but . . . none the less a despotism." "The theory of our governments," Miller continued, "is opposed to the deposit of unlimited power anywhere. . . . There are limitations on such power which grow out of the essential nature of all free governments. Implied reservations of individual rights, without which the social compact could not exist, and which are respected by all governments entitled to the name." [16]

The concept of taxation solely for a public purpose constituted an important restraint on the authority of state and local governments inasmuch as it involved not only the power to tax but also, because of their obvious relationship to this power, the powers to appropriate and to borrow money. Availing themselves of this doctrine, the courts ruled against the extension by state and local governments of aid to private businesses other than railroads, against measures designed to help individuals (as, for example, those suffering from the effects of fire or drought or in need of scholarships to attend a state university), and against the establishment of municipal or state-owned enterprises.[17]

Judges who did not specifically invoke the higher law to protect private rights from legislative interference were able to attain the same objective through a liberal interpretation of existing constitutional provisions. Judge Andrews of the New York Court of Appeals pointed out that it was unnecessary to look for "principles outside of the Constitution" in order to strike down legislation that violated "fun-

---

[16] Loan Association v. Topeka, 20 Wall. 655 (1875), 662–664. Justice Clifford alone dissented and attacked the view that courts could nullify legislation because "they think it opposed to a general latent spirit supposed to pervade or underlie the constitution. . . . Such a power," he said, "is denied to the courts, because to concede it would be to make the courts sovereign over both the constitution and the people, and convert the government into a judicial despotism" (ibid., p. 669). Even William Graham Sumner objected to Miller's "extra-legal way of looking at things." "The Court has no right to bring in great a priori principles which underlie all free govts.," Sumner wrote to Wells on June 6, 1881. "This time it makes for us. Next time it will make for theirs" (David A. Wells Papers, Library of Congress). Miller's biographer, Charles Fairman, argues that Miller actually believed that the concept of taxation for a public purpose could be derived from general constitutional principles even though he made no such assertion in his opinion (Mr. Justice Miller and the Supreme Court, 1862–1890 [Cambridge, Mass., 1939], pp. 210–211).

[17] Jacobs, Law Writers and the Courts, pp. 128–153, 157–159.

damental rights." The New York judge was confident that under "the broad and liberal interpretation" then being given to the constitutional guarantees such legislation must inevitably run counter to "the express or implied prohibitions and restraints of the Constitution." [18]

The main guarantee of private rights was to Andrews, as to the bulk of his colleagues, the due-process clause of the Fourteenth Amendment and similar clauses in the constitutions of the states. Due process of law, said Justice Brown speaking for the United States Supreme Court, implies "a conformity with natural and inherent principles of justice." [19] Well might such a believer in natural rights and implied limitations as Christopher G. Tiedeman, professor of law at the University of Missouri, applaud the disposition of the courts to avail themselves of general phrases like "due process of law" to serve "as an authority for them to lay their interdict upon all legislative acts which interfere with the individual's natural rights, even though these acts do not violate any specific or special provision of the Constitution." [20]

Quite apart from any concept of the higher law and of implied limitations, bar and bench took a rather narrow view of the necessary functions of government and of the need for positive legislation on behalf of the general welfare. Taken as a whole, the legal fraternity declared its adherence to a policy of laissez faire.[21]

Lawyers were particularly vociferous in their denunciation of legislative departures from the sacred precepts of laissez faire. "The great curse of the world," declared Henry Jackson, "is too much government!" The less the state interferes with man in his business relations, the better. The state should restrict itself to protecting the life, liberty, and property of the individual, to educating him, and to guarding his right to participate in government and to worship as he pleases, and

[18] Bertholf v. O'Reilly, 74 N.Y. 509 (1878), 514–515.

[19] Holden v. Hardy, 169 U.S. 366 (1898), 390.

[20] Tiedeman, *The Unwritten Constitution of the United States* (New York, 1890), p. 81.

[21] There were of course many exceptions, one of the most conspicuous being North Carolina's Judge Walter Clark. See Aubrey Lee Brooks and Hugh Talmage Lefler, eds., *The Papers of Walter Clark* (Chapel Hill, N. C., 1948), I, 301–357, 432–441, 451–462, 467–492; and Aubrey Lee Brooks, *Walter Clark, Fighting Judge* (Chapel Hill, N. C., 1944), pp. 75–84 *et passim.* See also Eugene Wambaugh, "The Present Scope of Government," *Report of the Twentieth Annual Meeting of the American Bar Association, 1897,* pp. 307–324; and testimony of C. C. Allen, U. S. Industrial Commission, *Preliminary Report on Trusts and Industrial Combinations* (Vol. I of the Commission's *Reports;* Washington, D.C., 1900), pp. 1177–1211.

should then "launch him for weal or for woe!" Legislation which restricts the "free action" of individuals is "contrary to public policy." Speaking before the American Bar Association in 1892, the lawyer J. R. Tucker, of Lexington, Virginia, denounced virtually all forms of government action as "paternalism." "The evils which infest and menace our country," said Tucker, "will be crushed by the free and unbound and independent manhood of the American people, unhelped and unhindered by the paternal care of their governments. This must be done or liberty will perish." [22]

The New York attorney William Cook believed government to be "the most dangerous force that enters into civilization." He regarded it as utterly unfit to solve the problems of the times and, as Spencer (whom Cook considered "one of the greatest thinkers of the age") had demonstrated, unable to do more than protect life, liberty, and property. Government interference with business, Cook contended, is "disastrous, unwise, and demoralizing both to the government and to the governed." John R. Dos Passos was of a similar opinion. "Every law that you make," Dos Passos warned, "is, as it were, a nail in the coffin of natural liberty. The object of government is not to make laws; the object of government is to avoid making laws." [23]

The prominent New York attorney William Guthrie warned that if state intervention in the social and economic life of the nation were not checked, "the worst forms of socialism will breed under the superstition, so rampant, that legislation is a sovereign cure-all for social ills." John Norton Pomeroy was convinced that the state governments were surrendering to the dread spirit of communism and socialism, a spirit which was "at war with the principles of political economy upon which society rests." Joseph Choate, perhaps the outstanding lawyer of the period, saw this same "communist spirit" present in the income-tax provision of the Wilson-Gorman Tariff of 1894. Arguing before the United States Supreme Court, he referred to the measure as "communistic in its purposes and tendencies" and declared that it was "defended here upon principles as communistic, socialistic—what shall I call them—populistic as ever have been addressed to any politi-

[22] Jackson, "Indemnity the Essence of Insurance; Causes and Consequences of Legislation Qualifying This Principle," *Report of the Tenth Annual Meeting of the American Bar Association, 1887,* pp. 280–281; Tucker, "British Institutions and American Constitutions," *ibid.,* p. 243.

[23] Cook, *The Corporation Problem* (New York, 1891), pp. 131–132, 139–140; Dos Passos, *Growth and Rights of Aggregated Capital* (Washington, D.C., 1899), p. 5.

cal assembly in the world." The legal scholar John Forrest Dillon was also alarmed at the tendency of the majority to use the political state as a means of promoting the general welfare. "The era of the despotism of the monarch, or of an oligarchy, has passed away," Dillon remarked. "If we are not struck with judicial blindness, we cannot fail to see that what is now to be feared and guarded against is the despotism of the many—of the majority." [24]

Much was made even in court decisions of the principles of Spencer and the classical economists and of the laissez-faire conclusions derived therefrom. The idea of laissez faire was exalted at the expense of the rival concept of the positive state. Laissez faire might be overthrown in the state legislature, but it was still to have its day in court.

The Michigan Supreme Court, in rejecting a state law that authorized townships to pledge their credit in aid of railroads, accepted the view of the conservative economists that "a large portion of the most urgent needs of society" should be "relegated exclusively to the law of demand and supply." It is this law, said the court, "in its natural operation and without the interference of government" that determines the number of persons who shall engage in particular pursuits. "However great the need in the direction of any particular calling," the court concluded, "the interference of the government is not tolerated, because, though it might be supplying a public want, it is considered as invading the domain that belongs exclusively to private inclination and enterprise." [25]

Similar views were expressed by the justices of Maine's highest court when they informed the state legislature that it could not pass laws enabling towns to loan or grant money to aid individuals in the manufacture of various products. "The less the State interferes with industry, the less it directs and selects the channels of enterprise, the better," three of the judges declared. "There is no safer rule than to leave to individuals the management of their own affairs. Every individual knows best where to direct his labor, every capitalist where to invest his capital." Two of the other judges of the court also spoke of the "inexorable" law of demand and supply as the "safest regulator

[24] Guthrie, "Constitutionality of the Sherman Anti-Trust Act of 1890, as Interpreted by the United States Supreme Court in the Case of the Trans-Missouri Traffic Association," *Harvard Law Review*, XI (June, 1897), 94; Pomeroy, "The Supreme Court and State Repudiation: The Virginia and Louisiana Cases," *American Law Review*, XVII (September–October, 1883), 718; Pollock *v.* Farmers' Loan and Trust Co., 157 U.S. 429 (1895), 532; Dillon, "Address," *Report of the Fifteenth Annual Meeting of the American Bar Association, 1892*, p. 206.

[25] People *v.* Salem, 20 Mich. 452 (1870), 484–485.

of business." The very next year the same court expressed an opinion that was squarely in line with the views of Andrew Carnegie. "The sagacity shown in the acquisition of capital," the court asserted, "is best fitted to control its use and disposition." [26]

The judges of New York's highest court revealed on several occasions their predilection for the doctrine of laissez faire. Judge O'Brien in 1901 expressed the opinion that courts should always remember when they expounded the Constitution that the founding fathers had acted on the assumption that "the government governs best which governs the least," [27] and apparently the judges of the New York Court of Appeals were not unmindful of this consideration. In People v. Budd, for example, three of the New York judges made abundantly clear the influence of laissez-faire doctrines on their own thinking. Judge Gray argued that the government should exercise only such functions as are necessary to protect and develop private rights and to secure to all individuals "the uniform operation of the constitutional guarantees." Judge Andrews was quite certain that the legislature was without power "to regulate private business, prescribe the conditions under which it shall be conducted, fix the price of commodities or services, or interfere with freedom of contract." Under the American system of government, he thought, individuals were "to pursue and provide for their own interests in their own way, untrammeled by burdensome and restrictive regulations which, however common in rude and irregular times, are inconsistent with constitutional liberty."

Judge Peckham, later to become a member of the United States Supreme Court, compared the idea of paternal government with "the more correct ideas which an increase of civilization and a fuller knowledge of the fundamental laws of political economy, and a truer conception of the proper functions of government have given to us at the present day." He spoke of the futility of legislative interference with private concerns and with the general laws of trade and declared that legislation of this type would array "class against class" and would bring a "recurrence of legislation which, it has been supposed, had been outgrown not only as illegal, but as wholly useless for any good effect, and only powerful for evil." [28]

In the opinion he delivered for the New York Court of Appeals in

[26] Opinion of the Justices, 58 Me. 590 (1871), 598, 603, 609; Allen v. Inhabitants of Jay, 60 Me. 124 (1872), 129.

[27] People ex rel. Rodgers v. Coler, 166 N.Y. 1 (1901), 14.

[28] People v. Budd, 117 N.Y. 1 (1889), 15, 33, 47, 68–69.

the celebrated case *In re* Jacobs, Judge Earl demonstrated that he was well aware of the teachings of Spencer and the classical economists. He spoke of "the fierce competition of trade and the inexorable laws of supply and demand" and of "the unceasing struggle for success and existence which pervades all societies of men." Referring to a minor police regulation, he declared that legislation of this sort, if sanctioned, would herald the return to mercantilist days when government regulated the entire sphere of human activities. "Such governmental interferences," Earl thought, "disturb the normal adjustments of the social fabric, and usually derange the delicate and complicated machinery of industry and cause a score of ills while attempting the removal of one." The Colorado Supreme Court also was under the impression that the increasing amount of social legislation of the period marked "a distinct and emphatic return, a retrogression" to the mercantilist era "against which our ancestors rebelled, and which was one, among other causes, that prompted them to found here a government under which it would be impossible thus to interfere with the purely private affairs of the citizen." [29]

Justice David Josiah Brewer of the United States Supreme Court was another firm believer in laissez faire.[30] While a member of the highest court of Kansas, he spoke out against a Kansas statute of 1875 that authorized townships to issue bonds so as to provide relief for citizens who were in distress as a result of the drought of the previous year. Although recognizing that the state must assist those who were "entirely destitute and helpless," Brewer felt compelled to argue that it was not within its province to aid those who were "temporarily embarrassed" so that they might more profitably pursue their regular occupations. He rejected the contention that such legislation was necessary lest those "temporarily embarrassed" might otherwise become actual paupers. "Let the doorways of taxation be opened," he declared, "not merely to the relief of present and actual distress, but in anticipation of and to guard against future want, and who can declare the result." On the bench of the United States Supreme Court Brewer reaffirmed his hostility to the extension of government activities. "The paternal theory of government," he declared, "is to me

<hr/>

[29] *In re* Jacobs, 98 N.Y. 98 (1885), 104–105, 114–115; *In re* Morgan, 26 Col. 415 (1899), 431.

[30] Cf. Brewer's remarks to the students of Washburn College as reported in the *Topeka Daily Capital,* June 17, 1883, David Josiah Brewer Collection, Yale University Library.

odious. The utmost possible liberty to the individual, and the fullest possible protection to him and his property, is both the limitation and duty of government." [31]

Chief Justice John B. Gantt of the Missouri Supreme Court was no less opposed to "paternalism" than Brewer. He denounced the paternalism of the state as proceeding upon the theory that the people were unable to manage their own affairs and as "pernicious" in its tendencies. Our governments, he thought, were founded upon the contrary principle that the people should look after their own affairs, rather than seek the aid of the state. Echoing Grover Cleveland in his famous veto of the Texas seed bill in 1887, Gantt maintained that it was the duty of the citizen "to support the government, and not the government's to support him." "Paternalism," he concluded, "is a plant that should receive no nourishment upon the soil of Missouri." [32]

The laissez-faire views of influential leaders of bar and bench were further evidenced in the shocked reaction of the conservative members of the legal fraternity to Chief Justice Waite's decision in Munn v. Illinois [33] that businesses affected with a public interest (grain elevators, for example) are subject to state regulation and that the rates fixed by a state for such businesses are not subject to judicial review. John Cary, who, as general counsel for the Chicago, Milwaukee and St. Paul Railway Company, sought to have the United States Supreme Court invalidate the legislation at issue in this case, informed the American Bar Association that the fact that the public had an interest in the use being made of property in no way deprived the owner of control of that property nor did it justify state intervention. Such interference, he declared, marked a return to the paternalism of the Middle Ages. William Guthrie regarded the dicta of Waite in Munn v. Illinois as too sweeping and was of the opinion that the Court's decision had "created as much alarm as any decision ever delivered by any court." Pomeroy similarly believed that "no other decision . . . in the course of our judicial history" threatened "such disastrous consequences to the future welfare and prosperity of the country." He regarded the decision as a menace to all business and as a direct assault on the rights of private

---

[31] State ex rel. James Griffith and Others v. Osakee Township and Others, 14 Kan. 322 (1875), 324–328; Budd v. New York, 143 U.S. 517 (1892), 551.

[32] State ex rel. Garth et al. v. Switzler, 143 Mo. 287 (1898), 322–323.

[33] 94 U.S. 113 (1877). "The American Bar in general was undoubtedly startled at the sweeping character of the doctrines asserted in the decision" (Charles Warren, The Supreme Court in United States History [rev. ed.; Boston, 1937], II, 583).

property. The prominent New York lawyer Charles Marshall thought Munn *v.* Illinois rendered property insecure against the designs of the majority and that this made necessary a new constitutional amendment specifically designed to protect private property.[34]

The judges who opposed Waite's decision were no less alarmed than conservative lawyers at the implications of the decision for private property. "I think," Justice Field wrote to David Wells, "that the doctrine announced by the majority of the court practically destroys the guarantees of the Constitution intended for the protection of the rights of private property." [35] "If there be no protection . . . against such invasion of private rights," Field declared in his dissenting opinion in the case, "all property and all business in the State are held at the mercy of a majority of its legislature." [36] Justice Brewer was similarly opposed to state regulation of elevator rates and to Waite's doctrine of public interest. If a man through his own ability has made his property of considerable value to the public, declared Brewer, that fact does not deprive him of the "full dominion" over the property. Judge Peckham denounced legislation regulating elevator rates as "vicious in its nature, communistic in its tendency." Judge Gray looked on legislation of this sort as interference with the "conduct of legitimate private business enterprise." He regarded the theory of such legislation as "a startling departure from the true conception of governmental functions." [37] This criticism of the decision of the Court in Munn *v.* Illinois was not without effect: the United States Supreme Court eventually receded from the advanced position assumed by Waite.

Leading jurists were also staunchly opposed to any governmental interference with the trend toward industrial consolidation. The

[34] Cary, "Limitations of the Legislative Power in Respect to Personal Rights and Private Property," *Report of the Fifteenth Annual Meeting of the American Bar Association, 1892,* pp. 273–283; Guthrie, *Lectures on the Fourteenth Article of Amendment to the Constitution of the United States* (Boston, 1898), p. 81; Pomeroy, "The Supreme Court and State Repudiation," *American Law Review,* XVII (September–October, 1883), 712; Marshall, "A New Constitutional Amendment," *ibid.,* XXIV (November–December, 1890), 908–931.

[35] Field to Wells, June 29, 1877, David A. Wells Papers, New York Public Library. "Since the decision in the Chicago Elevator case," Field wrote to Wells on January 30, 1878, "I do not feel very confident on any question" (Wells Papers, Library of Congress).

[36] Munn *v.* Illinois, 94 U.S. 113 (1877), 140.

[37] See Budd *v.* New York, 143 U.S. 517 (1892), 548–550; and People *v.* Budd, 117 N.Y. 1 (1889), 30–34, 71.

arguments employed by the lawyers in support of the trusts were of the usual laissez-faire, social-Darwinist type. Consolidations were pictured as the natural product of industrial evolution and as controlled by the laws of trade. There was no need to fear them, since self-interest compelled their owners to serve the best interests of the community. The Sherman Anti-Trust Act and state antitrust statutes were denounced as in conflict with the natural laws of trade and the teachings of political economy and as violations of constitutional guarantees with respect to liberty and property and the equal protection of the laws. The United States Supreme Court was advised, and not without effect, either to declare the Sherman Anti-Trust Act unconstitutional or to interpret it in the narrowest possible manner.[38]

Alarmed at the increasing amount of social legislation and the disposition of government to invade the rights of private property, the lawyers considered it to be the special mission of bench and bar to defend the Constitution and the American way of life from "radical" attack and to maintain untarnished the sacred system of laissez faire.[39] William Guthrie regarded it as the task of the bar to overcome "the despotism of the majority wielding and abusing the power of legislation, and ignorantly or intentionally undermining the foundations of the Constitution itself." "We lawyers," he solemnly announced, "are delegated not merely to defend constitutional guaranties before the courts for individual clients, but to teach the people in season and out of season to value and respect individual liberty and the rights of property. . . . To-day, more than ever," he concluded, "the bar is the great conservative force in American politics. We are the guardians of the Federal Constitution." [40]

Dillon trusted to the bar and the judiciary to protect the Constitution from popular demands for laws in conflict with it. The Consti-

---

[38] Guthrie, "Constitutionality of the Sherman Anti-Trust Act of 1890," *Harvard Law Review*, XI (June, 1897), 80–94; David Willcox, "Unconstitutionality of Recent Anti-Trust Legislation," *Forum*, XXIV (September, 1897), 107–118; Albert Stickney, *State Control of Trade and Commerce by National or State Authority* (New York, 1897), pp. 5, 134, 157–158, 179–193; Charles F. Beach, Jr., "Facts about Trusts," *Forum*, VIII (September, 1889), 61–72; Dos Passos, *Growth and Rights of Aggregated Capital*, pp. 17–18, 31–35, 54–70.

[39] Tucker referred to the American Bar as "that priestly tribe to whose hands are confided the support and defence of this Ark of the Covenant of our fathers" ("British Institutions and American Constitutions," *Report of the Fifteenth Annual Meeting of the American Bar Association, 1892,* p. 213).

[40] Guthrie, *Lectures on the Fourteenth Amendment,* pp. 31–32.

tution, he averred, "is the final breakwater against the haste and passions of the people,—against the tumultuous ocean of democracy." Andrew Allison looked to the "inner Republic, formed of the Bench and Bar," to protect corporations from legislative attack. He asserted it to be the duty of the bar "to lift above the passions of the hour enterprises which are so closely and prominently connected with . . . [the legal] profession, and also with the wealth, prosperity, and glory of our common country." In his presidential address before the American Bar Association, William Allen Butler summed up the views of his colleagues in this matter when he declared: "We may be sure that any real improvement and advance towards the perfection of the best government, which in governing least legislates least, must come from our own profession." [41]

II

With large sections of bench and bar thus committed in principle to a policy of laissez faire, it is not surprising that during the period 1865–1901 laissez faire was read into state and federal constitutions and that judicial formulas were devised to limit the scope of state social and economic legislation. In effect, the courts set themselves up as the special guardians of the negative state. Through a rather free interpretation of certain terms in the Fourteenth Amendment, they considerably extended the area of private rights that the states could not "arbitrarily" invade; and, at the same time, by construing due process of law in a broad substantive sense, they placed the narrowest possible interpretation on the admitted right of the states to promote the general welfare through the exercise of the police power. Since in most cases coming before the courts during this period, judges were compelled to strike a balance between the claims of individual rights as embodied in the Fourteenth Amendment and the claims of the state governments as subsumed under the police power, the general effect of the broadening of the former concept and of the narrowing of the latter was to play havoc with the ability of the states to act on behalf of the general welfare. Although these interrelated developments applied only to the exercise of power by the state governments, it was

[41] Dillon, *Laws and Jurisprudence of England and America*, pp. 214–215; Allison, "The Rise and Probable Decline of Private Corporations in America," *Report of the Seventh Annual Meeting of the American Bar Association, 1884*, p. 256; Butler, "Address," *Report of the Ninth Annual Meeting of the American Bar Association, 1886*, p. 188.

the state governments that were the chief source of social legislation during this period.

Writing in 1898, William Guthrie correctly observed that American constitutional history during the previous thirty years had been "little more than a commentary on the Fourteenth Amendment." [42] Guthrie might well have added that the net result of this "commentary" had been to establish that amendment as the bulwark of property rights and of the doctrine of laissez faire.

As matters turned out, the most important part of the amendment was the clause declaring that no state shall "deprive any person of life, liberty, or property, without due process of law." It was this due-process clause that afforded judges an opportunity to read their own views into the amendment. When the Fourteenth Amendment was adopted in 1868, the key terms of the clause had reasonably definite and restricted meanings. Due process of law, or, its older form, the "law of the land," was generally understood to constitute only a procedural guarantee. Although there were some important precedents for a broader interpretation, the guarantee of due process was not ordinarily construed as constituting a restraint on the substance of legislation. "Liberty" in the phrase "life, liberty, and property" signified personal liberty, freedom from restraint. "Property" referred to a static right of possession and use. It suggested something material and tangible.[43] Judical interpretation, however, was to magnify considerably the meaning of these terms. Due process was converted into a substantive guarantee against "arbitrary" legislation; liberty (or property) was interpreted so as to include the right to follow any lawful calling; and the right of property was made to embrace such intangibles as exchange value and expected earning power. From these broad interpretations of liberty and property emerged the derivative right of liberty of contract.

[42] Guthrie, *Lectures on the Fourteenth Amendment,* pp. 1–2.

[43] Lewis, *A History of American Political Thought from the Civil War to the World War* (New York, 1937), pp. 63–68; Haines, *Revival of Natural Law Concepts,* pp. 104–116, 122; Louis B. Boudin, *Government by Judiciary* (New York, 1932), II, 374–396; Edward S. Corwin, "The Doctrine of Due Process of Law before the Civil War," *Harvard Law Review,* XXIV (March, April, 1911), 366–385, 460–479; Charles E. Shattuck, "The True Meaning of the Term 'Liberty' in Those Clauses in the Federal and State Constitutions Which Protect 'Life, Liberty, and Property,'" *ibid.,* IV (March, 1891), 365–392; Twiss, *Lawyers and the Constitution,* p. 257; Robert Eugene Cushman, "Due Process of Law," in Edwin R. A. Seligman, ed., *Encyclopaedia of the Social Sciences* (New York, 1930–1935), V, 265.

The work most responsible for the transformation of due process of law from a procedural into a substantive guarantee was Thomas M. Cooley's *Treatise on Constitutional Limitations.* This book was probably "more often cited in every American court during the last half of the nineteenth century than any other work on constitutional law." [44]   Cooley, who wrote in "full sympathy with all those restraints which the caution of the fathers has imposed upon the exercise of the powers of government," sought to "point out that there are on all sides definite limitations which circumscribe the legislative authority, aside from the specific restrictions which the people impose by their constitutions." [45]   Of chief significance to constitutional development was Cooley's chapter "Of the Protection to Property by 'the Law of the Land,'" for in this chapter he established due process of law as a limitation on all branches of the government and as a protector of property rights. "Cooley, almost single handed, caused a shift of emphasis from personal to property rights." [46]

In view of Cooley's rather free translation of the due-process clause as a limiting factor on governmental action, it is interesting to note that he favored no such liberal interpretation of the Constitution as a basis for positive action on the part of the state. "I cannot recognize," Cooley wrote to Christopher Tiedeman, "any 'necessity of twisting and turning Constitutional clauses away from their plain meaning in order to bring doubtful power within the grant of powers' to the federal government, and should not be inclined to take any part in endeavoring to provide for it by a short cut. I prefer the Constitution in its 'plain meaning' as Washington and his associates made it and as Jay and Marshall gave it effect in construction." [47]   Cooley was apparently willing to stretch the meaning of the Constitution if it meant a restriction on the powers of government but not if its result would be an extension of governmental authority.

Identifying due process of law with the law of the land, Cooley accepted Daniel Webster's definition of the law of the land as "general

[44] Rodney L. Mott, *Due Process of Law* (Indianapolis, Ind., 1926), p. 186.

[45] Cooley, *Treatise on Constitutional Limitations,* p. iv.

[46] Mott, *Due Process of Law,* p. 185.

[47] Cooley to Tiedeman, February 15, 1886, Thomas McIntyre Cooley Papers, Michigan Historical Collections. Cooley did not believe that under its power to provide for the general welfare Congress has unlimited authority to legislate for what it considers the general good. He held that such a grant of power would be despotic, contrary to the principles of the Constitution, and "inconsistent with regulated liberty" (*The Influence of Habits of Thought upon Our Institutions* [n. p., 1886], p. 11).

law" and, like Webster, stated that a "legislative enactment is not necessarily the law of the land." The necessity of general rules, Cooley argued, does not prevent the legislature from setting up special rules for particular cases, provided the particular cases are based on "some general rule of legislative power." Moreover, general rules may be as obnoxious as special rules when they deprive persons of vested rights. The entire community is entitled to the protection of private rights against "arbitrary interference" by the government, even though that interference be based on a general rule. "It is not the partial character of the rule, so much as its arbitrary and unusual nature, which condemns it as unknown to the law of the land." Cooley thus regarded the law of the land or due process of law not as a mere procedural guarantee but as designed " 'to exclude arbitrary power from every branch of the government.' " "The principles . . . upon which the process is based," he declared, "are to determine whether it is 'due process' or not, and not any considerations of mere form." "Due process of law in each particular case means, such an exertion of the powers of government as the settled maxims of law sanction, and under such safeguards for the protection of individual rights as those maxims prescribe for the class of cases to which the one in question belongs." [48]

In his views with respect to classification, Cooley foreshadowed later judicial interpretations of liberty and liberty of contract. He doubted the constitutionality of a regulation made for one class of citizens that, "notwithstanding its generality," was "entirely arbitrary in its character" and restricted the rights of that class of citizens in a manner previously unknown to the law. Restrictions of this type, he said, "should be based on some reason which renders them important—like the want of capacity in infants and insane persons." If the legislature, however, should forbid persons following a lawful trade or occupation from making contracts or otherwise enjoying their property in a manner permissible to others, "it can scarcely be doubted that the act would transcend the due bounds of legislative power, even if it did not come in conflict with express constitutional provisions." Those thus deprived of acquiring or enjoying property "would be deprived of *liberty* in particulars of primary importance to . . . their 'pursuit of happiness.' " [49]

The United States Supreme Court was, for a time, reluctant to

[48] Cooley, *Treatise on Constitutional Limitations,* 353–356; *ibid.* (6th ed.; Boston, 1890), p. 432.

[49] Cooley, *Treatise on Constitutional Limitations* (1868 ed.), p. 393.

accept the broad interpretation of the due-process clause of the Fourteenth Amendment suggested by Cooley. The Slaughterhouse Cases, which arose as the result of a monopolistic grant by the state legislature of Louisiana to the Crescent City Live Stock Landing and Slaughterhouse Company, presented the Court in 1873 with its first opportunity to interpret the Fourteenth Amendment. Speaking for the majority, Justice Miller upheld the state action in question as a legitimate exercise of the police power and rejected the argument of the plaintiff that the Fourteenth Amendment was not intended to apply to the Negro alone and that the monopoly abridged the privileges and immunities of citizens of the United States, deprived them of their liberty and property without due process of law, and denied them the equal protection of the laws. Miller insisted that the amendment was designed primarily for the Negro and, furthermore, that the privileges and immunities clause, which was the chief basis of the plaintiff's case, referred only to the privileges and immunities of citizens of the United States, not of citizens of the states, and that it therefore did not limit the power of a state over its own citizens. He noted that the term "due process of law" appeared in the Fifth Amendment and in most state constitutions and asserted that "under no construction of that provision" that the Court had ever seen or any that it deemed admissible could the action of the state of Louisiana be interpreted as constituting a deprivation of property without due process of law. The Court thus refused to narrow the police power through the application of the due-process clause.[50]

Four years later, in the celebrated case of Munn v. Illinois, the Supreme Court upheld the right of a state to fix charges for the storage of grain in warehouses. Chief Justice Waite, although recognizing that "under some circumstances" regulations as to the use or the price of use of private property might constitute a deprivation of property without due process of law, announced in his majority opinion that "when [as in the warehouse business] . . . one devotes his property to a use in which the public has an interest, he, in effect, grants to the public an interest in that use, and must submit to be controlled by the public for the common good, to the extent of the interest he has thus created." Waite furthermore rejected the contention that the owner of property is entitled to a reasonable compensation for its use even though his property is clothed with a public

[50] Slaughterhouse Cases, 16 Wall. 36 (1873), 69–83; Twiss, *Lawyers and the Constitution*, pp. 42–55.

interest and that "what is reasonable is a judicial and not a legislative question." That was true enough, he said, in the case of private contracts in which the public had no interest and, in the absence of state regulation, even in the case of businesses affected with a public interest. "The controlling fact," however, said Waite, "is the power to regulate at all. If that exists, the right to establish the maximum of charge, as one of the means of regulation, is implied." The legislature might, indeed, abuse its power but "for protection against abuses by legislatures the people must resort to the polls, not to the courts."[51] The Supreme Court in this case thus refused to consider the regulation of warehouse rates a deprivation of property without due process of law and declined to establish due process as a "rule of reason" requiring judicial interpretation.

In Davidson v. New Orleans (1878) the question of due process of law was once again before the Court. Plaintiff charged that an assessment of real estate in New Orleans for draining swamps constituted a deprivation of property without due process of law. Speaking for the majority, Miller recognized that the term "due process of law" remained without satisfactory definition. He noted that whereas a due-process clause had been in the Constitution for almost a hundred years as a check on federal powers, it had rarely been invoked; but that since the provision had been imposed as a restraint on the states, court dockets were jammed with cases calling for the courts to hold that state legislatures had deprived their citizens of life, liberty, or property without due process of law. Miller thought that there was "some strange misconception of the scope of this provision as found in the fourteenth amendment." He declared, however, that no definition of due process could be given that would cover all cases and that, therefore, the intent of the clause should be decided "by the gradual process of judicial inclusion and exclusion" as cases arose. He conceded that a state could not make whatever it chose due process, but in the case in question he refused to identify just compensation with due process and to bring eminent domain under the aegis of due process.[52]

The narrow interpretation given to the due-process clause by the majority of the United States Supreme Court between 1873 and 1878 was strongly challenged in the minority opinions of two of the Court's more prominent members, Stephen J. Field and Joseph P. Bradley.

[51] Munn v. Illinois, 94 U.S. 113 (1877), 125–126, 132–134.
[52] Davidson v. New Orleans, 96 U.S. 97 (1878), 100–106.

Reading their own belief in laissez faire into the Fourteenth Amendment, Field and Bradley argued for a broad interpretation of the due-process clause, and in the end it was their view that prevailed.

In the Slaughterhouse Cases, Field protested that the Fourteenth Amendment was designed not only to protect Negroes but "to protect the citizens of the United States against the deprivation of their common rights by State legislation." It sought "to give practical effect to the declaration of 1776 of inalienable rights." He conceded the broad nature of the police power but asserted that a state could not use this power as a pretext "to encroach upon any of the just rights of the citizen, which the Constitution intended to secure against abridgment." Among the privileges and immunities that belong to the citizen, he contended, is the "right to pursue a lawful employment in a lawful manner, without other restraint than such as equally affects all persons." This right Field found to be violated by the creation of the monopoly.

Unlike Field, Bradley addressed himself to the meaning of the due-process clause. Departing from standard definitions, he maintained that the "right to choose one's calling is an essential part of . . . liberty" and that "a calling, when chosen, is a man's property and right. Liberty and property are not protected where these rights are arbitrarily assailed." Bradley therefore concluded that any law depriving a "large class of citizens from adopting a lawful employment, or from following a lawful employment previously adopted, does deprive them of liberty as well as property, without due process of law." [53]

In a notable dissent in Munn *v.* Illinois, Field made a frontal assault on the Court's narrow interpretation of the due-process clause. Reading his own belief in inalienable rights into the Fourteenth Amendment, Field insisted that the due-process clause was designed to secure to the individual the essential conditions of the pursuit of happiness and that it should therefore not be construed narrowly. Liberty, he declared, means more than "mere freedom from physical restraint." It means freedom to the individual "to pursue such callings and avocations as may be most suitable to develop his capacities, and give to them their highest enjoyment." As for property, Field asserted that "all that is beneficial in property arises from its use, and the fruits of that use; and whatever deprives a person of them deprives him of all that is valu-

[53] Slaughterhouse Cases, 16 Wall. 36 (1873), 87, 89, 97, 105, 110–111, 116, 122–123.

THE LAW OF THE LAND

able in the title and possession." It is as much a deprivation of property as understood by the Fourteenth Amendment for the legislature to interfere with the use and income of property and to determine the compensation to be derived therefrom as it is actually to seize the property. Field denied that the business in question was of a public character and insisted that that designation was limited to property upon whose owner some right had been conferred by government. The Court, he complained, seemed to think that property lost its private character when it was employed so as to make it generally useful and that the price of its use was therefore a proper subject for regulation. The principle upon which the majority based its opinion was, Field thought, nothing short of "subversive of the rights of private property." [54]

Bradley resumed the attack on the Court's view of due process in his dissent in Davidson *v*. New Orleans. Private property, he asserted, can be taken without due process of law in other ways than "by mere direct enactment" or through lack of provision for judicial proceedings. If private property is taken for public use without just compensation, it is a denial of due process. Whether the taking of property be under the taxing power, eminent domain, or the power of assessment for local purposes, the nature and cause of the taking must be considered. "If found to be suitable or admissible in the special case, it will be adjudged to be 'due process of law'; but if found to be arbitrary, oppressive, and unjust, it may be declared to be not 'due process of law.'" Bradley thus insisted that any legislative act that constituted an "arbitrary" deprivation of property should be invalidated by the courts as a violation of the due-process clause.[55]

In Butchers' Union Company *v*. Crescent City Company (1884) Field and Bradley, although in agreement with the decision of the Court, embodied their arguments in separate concurring opinions that proved to be of crucial significance to the development of substantive due process and the concept of liberty of contract. Contending that the police power of a state cannot be granted away, the Supreme Court, in this case, rejected the claim of the Crescent City Company

[54] Munn *v*. Illinois, 94 U.S. 113 (1877), 136–143.

[55] Davidson *v*. New Orleans, 96 U.S. 97 (1898), 107. In the Sinking Fund Cases, Bradley, in another dissent, established due process as a general limitation on the legislative power. Both he and Field claimed that a contract is property and to destroy it in whole or in part is to take it, and to do so by arbitrary legislation is to take it without due process of law (99 U.S. 700 [1879], 746–747, 766).

that the city of New Orleans in granting the Butchers' Union Company the privilege of maintaining slaughterhouses and stock landings in New Orleans had violated the exclusive franchise previously bestowed upon the Crescent City Company. Field and Bradley maintained that the grant of the monopoly had been invalid in the first place, as they had argued in the Slaughterhouse Cases.

Field declared that the inalienable rights expressed in the Declaration of Independence are the cornerstone of free institutions and that, among these rights, the pursuit of happiness embodies the "right to pursue any lawful business or vocation, in any manner not inconsistent with the equal rights of others." The right of individuals to pursue common callings on terms of equality is, he contended, "a distinguishing privilege of citizens of the United States, and an essential element of that freedom which they claim as their birthright." He quoted Adam Smith to sustain the view that the right to pursue a calling is also a property right and that to interfere with this right is to deprive the laborer of his property.[56] "I cannot believe," Field stated, "that what is termed in the Declaration of Independence a God-given and an inalienable right can be thus ruthlessly taken from the citizen, or that there can be any abridgment of that right except by regulations alike affecting all persons of the same age, sex, and condition."

Although conceding that the Fourteenth Amendment does not limit the subjects upon which the states may legislate, Field insisted that it does inhibit "discriminating and partial enactments, favoring some to the impairment of the rights of others." The chief purpose of the first section of the Amendment, he declared, "is to prevent any arbitrary invasion by State authority of the rights of person and property, and to secure to every one the right to pursue his happiness unrestrained, except by just, equal, and impartial laws." Bradley, in his important concurring opinion, denied that the act creating the monopoly was a police regulation and contended that the monopoly deprived the citizens of Louisiana of a portion of their liberty and

[56] "The property which every man has in his own labor, as it is the original foundation of all other property, so it is the most sacred and inviolable. The patrimony of the poor man lies in the strength and dexterity of his own hands, and to hinder his employing this strength and dexterity in what manner he thinks proper without injury to his neighbor, is a plain violation of this most sacred property. It is a manifest encroachment upon the just liberty both of the workman, and of those who might be disposed to employ him. As it hinders the one from working at what he thinks proper, so it hinders the others from employing whom they think proper" (Butchers' Union Co. v. Crescent City Co., 111 U.S. 746 [1884], 757).

property without due process of law. To support this view, he repeated the argument he had advanced in the Slaughterhouse Cases to the effect that freedom of pursuit is a part of liberty and that "man's right to his calling is property." [57]

The views as to liberty, property, and due process of law that Field and Bradley had been championing in minority and concurring opinions ever since the Slaughterhouse Cases were eventually accepted by a majority of the United States Supreme Court. In Powell v. Pennsylvania (1888) Justice Harlan, speaking for the Court, declared that the Court recognized as "embodying a sound principle of constitutional law" the proposition advanced by the defendant "that his enjoyment upon terms of equality with all others in similar circumstances of the privilege of pursuing an ordinary calling or trade, and of acquiring, holding, and selling property, is an essential part of his rights of liberty and property, as guaranteed by the Fourteenth Amendment." [58] In Allgeyer v. Louisiana (1897) the Court accepted that bulwark of laissez faire, liberty of contract, as a right protected by the Fourteenth Amendment. In the person of Justice Peckham, ever an advocate of laissez faire, the Court asserted:

The liberty mentioned in that amendment means not only the right of the citizen to be free from the mere physical restraint of his person, as by incarceration, but the term is deemed to embrace the right of the citizen to be free in the enjoyment of all his faculties; to be free to use them in all lawful ways; to live and work where he will; to earn his livelihood by any lawful calling; to pursue any livelihood or avocation, and for that purpose to enter into all contracts which may be proper, necessary and essential to his carrying out to a successful conclusion the purposes above mentioned. [59]

The Court also acceded to the view that due process of law constituted something more than a procedural guarantee. In Barbier v. Connolly (1885) a unanimous Court upheld Field's view that the due-process clause intended that "there should be no arbitrary deprivation

[57] Butchers' Union Co. v. Crescent City Co., 111 U.S. 746 (1884), 746–754, 756–759, 760–765.

[58] Powell v. Pennsylvania, 127 U.S. 678 (1888), 684.

[59] Allgeyer v. Louisiana, 165 U.S. 578 (1897), 589. In Frisbie v. U.S., Justice Brewer, speaking for the Court, had included liberty of contract among the "inalienable rights of the citizen" (157 U.S. 160 [1895], 165). It is to be noted that with the death of Justice Miller in 1890, only Field and Bradley among the justices who had decided the Slaughterhouse Cases and Munn v. Illinois still remained on the Court. See Alfred H. Kelly and Winfred A. Harbison, *The American Constitution, Its Origins and Development* (New York, 1948), p. 513.

of life or liberty, or arbitrary spoliation of property," and in Mugler *v.* Kansas (1887), as will be noted later, the Court definitely accepted due process as a restriction of a substantive character on the police power of the states.[60] What was more, the Court, holding that the term "person" as stated in the due-process clause included artificial persons, extended the protection of the clause to corporations as well as to individuals.[61] Thus by judicial interpretation the area of private rights embraced within the due-process clause was widened, and the power of the states to interfere with these rights was curtailed.

The definitions of liberty, property, and due process eventually accepted by the Supreme Court were also adopted by the state courts. With Field as their chief authority, the state courts in decision after decision made it clear that liberty, property, and due process of law were not to be narrowly construed. It was asserted again and again that one could be deprived of his liberty without actually being imprisoned or physically restrained. Liberty, it was declared, implies the right to use one's faculties in all lawful ways, to pursue any lawful calling, and to live and work where one desires. It was similarly maintained that one could be deprived of his property without the physical taking of that property. Property, said the state courts, has no value unless it can be used and enjoyed, and any law which "destroys it or its value or takes away any of its essential attributes deprives the owner of property." Liberty of contract was considered an incident either to the right of liberty or of property or as a part of both. Due process of law was declared to be the same as the law of the land and, as such, opposed to all unequal and arbitrary legislation.[62] Well might the Supreme Court of Missouri declare in 1895 that "these terms, 'life,' 'liberty,' and 'property,' are representative terms and cover every right to which a member of the body politic is en-

[60] Barbier *v.* Connolly, 113 U.S. 27 (1885), 31–32; Mugler *v.* Kansas, 123 U.S. 623 (1887), 661, 669.

[61] Santa Clara County *v.* Southern Pacific Railroad Co., 118 U.S. 394 (1886), 396.

[62] Bertholf *v.* O'Reilly, 74 N.Y. 509 (1878), 515; People *v.* Marx, 99 N.Y. 377 (1885), 386–387; *In re* Jacobs, 98 N.Y. 98 (1885), 105–107; People *v.* Gillson, 109 N.Y. 389 (1888), 398–399; Kuhn *v.* Common Council, 70 Mich. 534 (1888), 536–537; State *v.* Goodwill, 33 W. Va. 179 (1889), 183–184; Commonwealth *v.* Perry, 155 Mass. 117 (1891), 121; Frorer *et al. v.* People, 141 Ill. 171 (1892), 181; Braceville Coal Co. *v.* People, 147 Ill. 66 (1893), 70–72; Ritchie *v.* People, 155 Ill. 98 (1895), 103–106; Leep *v.* Railway Co., 58 Ark. 407 (1894), 415; Gillespie *v.* People, 188 Ill. 176 (1900), 182–186; State *v.* Loomis, 115 Mo. 307 (1893), 313–316.

titled under the law," and none of these rights can be taken away without due process of law.[63]

III

The ability of state governments to interfere in the general interest with the broad area of private rights that the courts identified with liberty and property was seriously circumscribed, as has been suggested, by the judicial construction of due process of law as a restraint of a substantive character on the police power of the states. It remains to note in greater detail how judicial formulas were devised that limited the authority of state governments to fix the rates of public utilities and the exercise of the state police power in general.

The idea of the police power as a distinct group of state powers probably originated in the seventeenth century along with the concept of sovereignty. It had a firm basis in English common law and was associated with such maxims as *Sic utere tuo ut alienum non laedas* ("So use your property as not to injure the property of others") and *Salus populi suprema lex* ("Public welfare is the highest law"). The term "police power" was first used in the United States by Chief Justice Marshall in Brown *v.* Maryland (1827), but it was not in general legal use for another twenty-five years. It received its classic definition from Chief Justice Shaw of the Massachusetts Supreme Court in Commonwealth *v.* Alger (1851). Shaw referred to the police power as the power of the legislature to enact "all manner of wholesome and reasonable laws . . . not repugnant to the constitution, as they shall judge to be for the good and welfare of the commonwealth, and of the subjects of the same." [64]

A generous interpretation by the courts of the police power of the state governments might have paved the way for judicial sanction of the concept of the general-welfare state. However, in an age when the idea of laissez faire dominated both bench and bar, it was but natural that the police power should be construed in a narrow rather than in a broad sense and that private rights should be placed before the claims of society.

As with due process of law, legal textbooks played an important part in shaping the views of judges and lawyers with respect to the police power. On the basis of the number of times they were cited,

[63] State *v.* Julow, 129 Mo. 163 (1895), 172–173.

[64] See Mott, *Due Process of Law,* pp. 300–302; and Commonwealth *v.* Alger, 61 Mass. 53 (1851), 85.

it appears that the two works of greatest importance in this connection were Cooley's *Treatise on Constitutional Limitations* and Christopher G. Tiedeman's *A Treatise on the Limitations of Police Power in the United States Considered from Both a Civil and Criminal Standpoint*. Both works took an essentially negative view of the police power.

In his brief treatment, Cooley expressed the opinion that the police power of the states is designed to "insure to each the uninterrupted enjoyment of his own, so far as is reasonably consistent with a like enjoyment of rights by others." In the exercise of this power, he asserted, the state may make "extensive and varied regulations" with respect to the rights of individuals, but its actions must not conflict with constitutional provisions designed to protect private rights and private property. Also, Cooley maintained, the police power cannot be used "under the pretence of regulation" to take away any of the essential privileges conferred upon a corporation by a charter. Police regulations "must be police regulations in fact, and not amendments in curtailment of the corporate franchise." If a regulation cannot be explained on the basis of the maxim *Sic utere tuo ut alienum non laedas,* the police power cannot be invoked.[65]

Whereas the police power was but one of the themes developed by Cooley in his great work, Tiedeman's entire treatise, as its title indicates, concerns itself with that power. In the preface to his book Tiedeman expressed concern over the fact that the masses seemed intent on abandoning laissez faire in favor of a program of social reform. "The conservative classes," he declared, "stand in constant fear of the advent of an absolutism more tyrannical and more unreasoning than any before experienced by man, the absolutism of a democratic ma-

[65] Cooley, *Treatise on Constitutional Limitations*, pp. 572, 577, 597. In dealing with specific cases, Cooley was not unwilling to permit a fairly wide exercise of the police power. He would, among other things, allow the states to forbid employments deemed contrary to the public good, regulate markets, prohibit payment of wages in truck, and regulate the employment of women and children. In general, however, Cooley wished to limit state interference in this area to the "mere preservation of public order." See *ibid.* (6th ed.; Boston, 1890), pp. 707–746; and "Labor and Capital before the Law," *North American Review*, CXXXIX (December, 1884), 508–516. Although he at first opposed state regulation of the price of service of monopolies, Cooley later conceded that when competition did not enforce reasonable charges on corporations, state regulation of profits might be necessary. See Cooley, "Limits to State Control of Private Business," *Princeton Review*, N.S., I (March, 1878), 267–268; and Cooley, "State Regulation of Corporate Profits," *North American Review*, CXXXVII (September, 1883), 205–217.

jority." The principal object of his work, he stated, was to show that "democratic absolutism is impossible . . . as long as the popular reverence for the constitutions, in their restrictions upon governmental activity, is nourished and sustained by a prompt avoidance by the courts of any violations of their provisions, in word or in spirit." He expressed a desire "to awaken the public mind to a full appreciation of the power of constitutional limitations to protect private rights against the radical experimentations of social reformers."

Looking upon private rights as belonging to man in a state of nature rather than as resting upon municipal law, Tiedeman considered it the function of government to protect these rights by restraining human actions that might interfere with their preservation and enjoyment. The power of government to impose such restraints, he explained, is the police power. The police power is thus confined to the enforcement of the legal maxim *Sic utere tuo ut alienum non laedas.* Any law that transcends this principle is a "governmental usurpation, and violates the principles of abstract justice, as they have been developed under our republican institutions." Tiedeman's view of the police power was thus completely negative: he sanctioned its use only to enforce a common-law equivalent of Spencer's law of equal freedom and not to serve the general welfare in any positive manner.

Addressing himself to the subject of constitutional limitations on the police power, Tiedeman urged a broad interpretation of federal and state constitutions as a check to the "unrighteous exercise of police power." He advised judges and lawyers that they need not adhere to the strict letter of the fundamental law in seeking prohibitions on state action. In searching for limitations on the police power, they should avail themselves of "those general clauses, which have acquired the name of 'glittering generalities,'" and which may "be appealed to as containing the germ of constitutional limitation." "The unwritten law of this country," said Tiedeman, "is in the main against the exercise of police power." Naturally enough, he found the chief guarantee of private rights in the due-process clauses in federal and state constitutions, and he did not wish to see these clauses construed in any narrow sense.

In dealing with specific phases of state action, Tiedeman demonstrated how his narrow version of the police power was to be applied and, in so doing, revealed his own unmistakable laissez-faire bias. He conceded the right of the legislature to regulate trades and occupations deemed injurious to the public but maintained that it is strictly a judicial matter to decide if a trade or calling requires regulation. Moreover, he thought it the responsibility of the judiciary to determine whether a particular police regulation exceeded the necessities of the situation. He felt that these matters were better decided by the conservative courts than by legislatures that might be more amenable to the "tyranny" of democratic majorities.

Tiedeman maintained that the right to form business relations and to draw up contracts free from dictation by the state is "a part of natural and civic liberty." Except in businesses of a quasi-public nature, he argued, a man may ask for his product whatever price others are willing to pay, even if the price is exorbitant. As for quasi-public enterprises, Tiedeman considered Waite's views as expressed in Munn v. Illinois too radical, and he therefore sided with the opinions put forth in Field's dissent. Like Field, he also protested abridgments of corporate rights disguised as police regulations.

As for employer-employee relations, Tiedeman contended that since all adults are free and equal and are entitled to the equal protection of the laws, the state cannot stipulate the terms of private employment. If the employer is in a superior bargaining position, it is only because his natural powers, intellectual or moral, are greater than those of his employees, and he is therefore entitled to the profits deriving from his superiority. The most the state can do for men on a "legal plane of equality" is to prevent trespass upon their rights. For the state to do more than this for the working classes would be "to change the government from a government of freemen to a paternal government, or a despotism, which is the same thing." [66]

Tiedeman's work, which revealed a much more extreme laissez-faire bias than Cooley's treatise, supplied the courts with convenient arguments and precedents to restrict the exercise of the police power. By the time the second edition of the book appeared in 1900, Tiedeman was able to state that the first edition had been cited with approval by the courts in literally hundreds of cases.[67]

The application of substantive due process to the police power resulted in the abandonment by the Supreme Court of the position

[66] Tiedeman, *A Treatise on the Limitations of Police Power in the United States Considered from Both a Civil and Criminal Standpoint* (St. Louis, Mo., 1886), pp. vi–viii, 1–11, 194–198, 233–238, 568–602.

[67] Tiedeman, *A Treatise on State and Federal Control of Persons and Property in the United States Considered from Both a Civil and Criminal Standpoint* (St. Louis, Mo., 1900), I, ix.

assumed by Waite in Munn v. Illinois. In Stone and Others v. Farmers' Loan and Trust Company (1886), Waite himself made it clear that there are limits to the power of regulation. "The power to regulate," he declared, "is not a power to destroy," and under the pretense of regulation, the state cannot "do that which in law amounts to a taking of private property without just compensation, or without due process of law." [68]

Four years later, in Chicago, Milwaukee and St. Paul Railway Company v. Minnesota, the Court definitely reversed the portion of Waite's opinion in Munn v. Illinois that dealt with the reasonableness of rates fixed by public authorities and announced that reasonableness is "eminently a question for judicial investigation, requiring due process of law for its determination." If a company were deprived of the right to fix reasonable rates for the use of its property and if there were no provision for an investigation by the courts of this "deprivation," then the company would be deprived of the use of its property and thus, in effect, of the property itself without due process of law. [69] The Supreme Court in this way accepted the view that use, the expected earning power of property, is in itself property (as Field had asserted in Munn v. Illinois), that state regulation of the rates charged for the use of property may constitute a "taking" of the property, and that, therefore, due process requires that recourse be had to the courts to determine the reasonableness of the rates so established. Thus, although the Court did not completely take away the power of the states to regulate public utilities, by applying the due-process clause it limited the scope of that power and made the courts the final judge of its exercise.

Not only did the courts interpret due process of law so as to require that the reasonableness of rates fixed by a state be made a subject for judicial investigation, but, beginning about 1885, they sought to circumscribe the exercise of the police power in general by establishing certain criteria to which police regulations had to conform if they were to be regarded as in accordance with due process of law. In this

[68] Stone and Others v. Farmers' Loan and Trust Co., 116 U.S. 307 (1886), 331. Due process of law and just compensation were thus, in effect, made synonymous, and the view of the Court in Davidson v. New Orleans was reversed.

[69] Chicago, Milwaukee and St. Paul Railway Co. v. Minnesota, 134 U.S. 418 (1890), 458. This case dealt with rates fixed by a state commission. In the case of Smyth v. Ames, 169 U.S. 466 (1898), the Court ruled similarly with respect to railroad rates fixed by a state legislature and established a fair return upon a fair valuation of the railroad's property as the criterion for reasonableness.

way the courts set themselves up as the censors of the social and economic legislation enacted by the states and reduced considerably the discretionary power of state legislatures. The outstanding case in effecting the new court attitude toward the police power was *In re* Jacobs, decided by the New York Court of Appeals in 1885 and cited after that time "probably more than any other single state decision in practically every case where state power over individual liberty and property rights was challenged." [70] The case arose as the result of a New York act of 1884 that prohibited the manufacture of cigars in tenement houses on any floor used as living quarters. The act applied only to cities with populations of over five hundred thousand persons. [71]

A unanimous court accepted much of the argument against the act presented by William Evarts, [72] former United States attorney general and secretary of state and later to be United States senator from New York, and in an opinion loaded with laissez-faire shibboleths pronounced the measure unconstitutional. Judge Earl, arguing along lines made familiar by Field and Bradley, asserted that the act constituted a deprivation of property (since it prohibited the prosecution of a lawful trade in a tenement house) and liberty (since it limited a cigar maker in the choice of a trade and in the places where he might work and live). Earl then took up the question as to whether such an act could be passed by the legislature in the exercise of the police power. He conceded that the police power is of a broad and extensive character but declared that "in its exercise the legislature must respect the great fundamental rights guaranteed by the Constitution. If this were otherwise, the power of the legislature would be practically without limitation." Generally, the judge asserted, the legislature is to decide what regulations are necessary to protect the health and safety of the citizen, but these regulations must have some relation to the ends they are alleged to serve. "Under the mere guise of police regulations, personal rights and private property cannot be arbitrarily invaded." [73] Nor is the decision of the legislature in this

[70] Twiss, *Lawyers and the Constitution*, pp. 99–100.

[71] Young Theodore Roosevelt, then a member of the New York legislature, considered this act a dangerous departure from laissez faire and, in a sense, socialistic, but he nevertheless thought it necessary for health reasons. See Howard Lawrence Hurwitz, *Theodore Roosevelt and Labor in New York State, 1880–1900* (New York, 1943), pp. 81–82.

[72] Evarts' argument is analyzed in Twiss, *Lawyers and the Constitution*, pp. 99–106.

[73] State courts had previously declared that the police power was not without

matter "final or conclusive." If the legislature passes an act ostensibly for the public health and in so doing deprives a citizen of his property or interferes with his liberty, the courts must examine the act and "see whether it really relates to and is convenient and appropriate to promote the public health." "A law enacted in the exercise of the police power must in fact be a police law." And looking at the act in question, the court decided that it was not intended to protect the health of cigar makers. "It cannot be perceived," Earl declared, "how the cigarmaker is to be improved in his health or his morals by forcing him from his home and its hallowed associations and beneficent influences, to ply his trade elsewhere." [74]

Thus, in the Jacobs case, the New York Court of Appeals set up the following criteria by which to determine the validity of a police regulation: (1) A police regulation may not arbitrarily invade fundamental rights. (2) A police regulation must actually be such in fact, that is, the means must be substantially related and appropriate to the ends. (3) The court and not the legislature is to be the final judge as to whether a police law does in fact promote the intended object. In this way the court arrogated to itself the right to pass on the facts as well as the law insofar as the exercise of the police power was concerned.

As has already been noted, the United States Supreme Court, despite its willingness to expand the meaning of the due-process clause, was loath to interfere with the police power of the states. In a striking opinion in Barbier v. Connolly (1885), that apostle of private rights Justice Field, speaking for the Court, upheld a San Francisco ordinance prohibiting night work in laundries and asserted categorically that the Fourteenth Amendment was not designed to interfere with the police power of the states.[75] However, in Mugler v. Kansas (1887), although sanctioning a state prohibition law, the Supreme Court, speaking through Harlan, accepted the view of the New York Court of Appeals in the Jacobs case. Harlan, after asserting the extensive character of the police power, declared that the

---

limits and that state governments could not arbitrarily invade the rights of private property under the guise of enacting police regulations. See, for example, Watertown v. Mayo, 109 Mass. 315 (1872), 319; and Lake View v. Rose Hill Cemetery Co., 70 Ill. 191 (1873), 195, 197–199.

[74] *In re* Jacobs, 98 N.Y. 98 (1885), 105–115.

[75] Barbier v. Connolly, 113 U.S. 27 (1885), 31. As early as the Slaughterhouse Cases, however, Field had declared that the police power could not be used as a pretext for invading fundamental rights.

Court was not under obligation to accept as a legitimate exercise of the police power every statute ostensibly enacted to promote public morals, public health, or public safety. Although "every possible presumption" was "to be indulged in favor of the validity of a statute," the Court was bound by the Constitution to determine whether the "limits beyond which legislation cannot rightfully go" had been exceeded. "The courts are not bound by mere forms, nor are they to be misled by mere pretences," Harlan asserted. "They are at liberty —indeed, are under a solemn duty—to look at the substance of things, whenever they enter upon the inquiry whether the legislature has transcended the limits of its authority." If a statute purportedly enacted to promote one of the objects the police power is designed to serve "has no real or substantial relation to those objects, or is a palpable invasion of the rights secured by the fundamental law, it is the duty of the courts to so adjudge, and thereby give effect to the Constitution." [76]

In Powell v. Pennsylvania (1888) the Supreme Court, in upholding a Pennsylvania statute making it a misdemeanor to sell butterine as food, backtracked from Mugler v. Kansas and declared that questions of fact as regards the exercise of the police power are for the legislature to decide. If the only argument against a statute is that it is unwise or oppressive, the Court asserted, the appeal must be to the legislature or to the ballot box, not to the judiciary. The Court, however, hastened to add that it would have interfered had the fundamental rights of life, liberty, or property been invaded under the pretense of the exercise of the police power.[77]

In Holden v. Hardy (1898) the Court once again, in effect, reasserted its right to pass on the substance of police regulations. It upheld a Utah law for miners that limited their workday to eight hours as a legitimate exercise of the police power on the grounds that the facts supported the contention that the limitation of hours was essential to promote the health of the miners.[78] Thus, although throughout this period the United States Supreme Court was reluctant

[76] Mugler v. Kansas, 123 U.S. 623 (1887), 661. See also Lawton v. Steele, 152 U.S. 133 (1894).

[77] Powell v. Pennsylvania, 127 U.S. 678 (1888), 684–687. Field dissented, citing the Jacobs case and Mugler v. Kansas. He declared, in characteristic fashion, that the right to manufacture healthy food is "an inalienable right which no State can give and no State can take away except in punishment for crime. It is involved in the right to pursue one's happiness" (ibid., pp. 692–695).

[78] Holden v. Hardy, 169 U.S. 366 (1898), 395–398.

to interfere with the police power of the states, it nevertheless forged the necessary weapons with which to strike down police legislation when it so desired. The doctrines proclaimed in Mugler v. Kansas were to have their effect in Lochner v. New York.[79]

The combined effect of the courts' broad interpretation of the rights guaranteed to individuals and corporations by the Fourteenth Amendment and of their narrow interpretation of the police power was evidenced in a series of cases appearing before the state courts after 1885. These cases, arising as the result of labor legislation enacted by the state governments, involved, in essence, a contest between the doctrine of liberty of contract and the police power. In the main, the state labor acts were declared unconstitutional, since, in the view of the judges, they deprived employers and employees of liberty and property without due process of law. State acts were invalidated that required that contracts between the owners of coal mines and their employees provide for the weighing of all coal mined,[80] that required the payment of wages at some stipulated interval [81] and in cash,[82] that forbade the fining of employees for imperfect work,[83] that required the payment of overtime to laborers for every hour of work above eight hours a day,[84] that outlawed city ordinances preventing private contractors who were working on municipal projects from contracting with employees to work more than eight hours a day or from employing Chinese labor,[85] that prohibited the employment of females for more than eight hours a day in factories or workshops,[86] that prohibited employers from requiring workers not to join

[79] 198 U.S. 45 (1905). In this case the Court rejected as contrary to the due-process clause a New York law limiting the hours of labor in bakeries to sixty a week. The decision occasioned one of Justice Holmes's most memorable dissents, in which the jurist reminded the Court that the Constitution was not intended to embody the theory of laissez faire and that "the Fourteenth Amendment does not enact Mr. Herbert Spencer's Social Statics" (ibid., pp. 75–76).

[80] Millett v. People, 117 Ill. 294 (1886).

[81] Braceville Coal Co., v. People, 147 Ill. 66 (1893); Johnson v. Goodyear Mining Co., 127 Cal. 4 (1889).

[82] Godcharles and Co. v. Wigeman, 113 Pa. St. 431 (1886); Frorer et al. v. People, 141 Ill. 171 (1892); State v. Goodwill, 33 W. Va. 179 (1889); State v. Loomis, 115 Mo. 307 (1893); State v. Haun, 61 Kan. 146 (1889).

[83] Commonwealth v. Perry, 155 Mass. 117 (1891).

[84] Low v. Rees Printing Co., 41 Neb. 127 (1894).

[85] Ex Parte Kuback, 85 Cal. 274 (1890). The California court in this case cited Cooley's Constitutional Limitations as the only authority for its decision.

[86] Ritchie v. People, 155 Ill. 98 (1895).

unions [87] or from discharging workers because of union membership,[88] and that established an eight-hour day for employees in underground mines and in smelting and ore-reduction works.[89] Armed with the opinions of Field, Bradley, Earl, and Harlan, state courts were ready to strike down legislative enactments that, in their view, did not comport with the theory of laissez faire.

These cases followed a more or less similar pattern.[90] Generally, citing Field and Bradley, the judges defined liberty and property so as to include liberty of contract. Labor was declared to be property, and the worker was therefore assumed to have the same right to sell his labor and to make contracts with reference thereto as any other property owner. Attempts to interfere with the absolute freedom of employer and employee to contract were declared to constitute a deprivation of the liberty and property of both.

The judges then proceeded to show how this deprivation of liberty and property violated the requirements of due process of law. Due process of law, they explained, was synonymous with the law of the land and therefore meant general law. It was opposed to arbitrary, unequal, or partial legislation. The various acts in question, since they usually applied to one class of laborers or to laborers in a particular industry and to a corresponding class of employers, were characterized as class legislation and therefore as not in accord with due process. The courts were willing to admit that due process did not rule out all classification, but only such classification as was arbitrary and unreasonable. However, the sole classification that the courts deemed reasonable was that which distinguished between persons who were *sui juris* and those who were not, that is, between those who had a "natural capacity" to contract and those who did not. Adult male laborers were considered to be on a plane of equality with their employers, and, therefore, legislation seeking to give them special privileges was looked upon as arbitrary class legislation and hence not in conformity with due process of law. Moreover, the courts held that such legislation degraded the adult male laborer and, in effect, put him on a par with the minor, the lunatic, and the felon, who were properly under the guardianship of the state. When the matter lay

---

[87] State *v.* Julow, 129 Mo. 163 (1895).

[88] Gillespie *v.* People, 188 Ill. 176 (1900).

[89] *In re* Morgan, 26 Col. 415 (1899).

[90] For an analysis of these cases, see Roscoe Pound, "Liberty of Contract," *Yale Law Journal,* XVIII (May, 1909), 454–487.

between persons *sui juris,* it was assumed that the legislature had no right to protect one against the other.

As for the claim of a state government that the particular act at issue was passed in pursuance of the police power, the courts, citing the Jacobs case and Mugler *v.* Kansas, insisted that a police regulation must be such in fact and not a mere pretext for interfering with fundamental rights. It was for the courts to decide whether a police regulation really did promote the health, safety, or welfare of the populace as the state asserted. For the most part, the state courts did not see how the labor legislation in question furthered any of these objectives and so ruled the acts unconstitutional.

In the language used by the judges in many of these cases involving liberty of contract, one can see to what extent the legal profession was in the grip of laissez faire. The Pennsylvania Supreme Court referred to an act prohibiting the payment of wages in truck (commodities) as "an insulting attempt to put the laborer under a legislative tutelage, which is not only degrading to his manhood, but subversive of his rights as a citizen of the United States." [91] A similar enactment in West Virginia drew the following blast from the state's highest court: "It is a species of sumptuary legislation which has been universally condemned, as an attempt to degrade the intelligence, virtue, and manhood of the American laborer, and foist upon the people a paternal government of the most objectionable character, because it assumes that the employer is a knave, and the laborer an imbecile." [92]

An innocuous truck act aroused the Missouri Supreme Court to declare that such measures "introduce a system of state paternalism which is at war with the fundamental principles of government." [93] The Kansas Supreme Court rejected the argument advanced "by writers defending the doctrine of paternalism, and by some judges" that labor was engaged in an unequal struggle with capital and therefore required state aid to improve its competitive position. In words that would have done credit to J. Laurence Laughlin, the court asserted that "those who seek to put a protector over labor reflect upon the dignity and independence of the wage-earner, and deceive him by the promise that legislation can cure all the ills of which he may

[91] Godcharles and Co. *v.* Wigeman, 113 Pa. St. 431 (1886), 437.

[92] State *v.* Goodwill, 33 W. Va. 179 (1889), 186. See also State *v.* F. C. Coal and Coke Co., 33 W. Va. 188 (1889), 190–191.

[93] State *v.* Loomis, 115 Mo. 307 (1893), 320.

complain. Such legislation," the court noted ominously, "suggests the handiwork of the politician, rather than of the political economist." [94]

IV

The judicial limitations on the exercise of governmental power thus far considered have pertained only to the functions of the state governments. In the closing years of the nineteenth century, however, legal doctrines were propounded that served ultimately to keep the functions of the federal government within relatively restricted bounds. As Benjamin R. Twiss has pointed out, the judicial construction of laissez faire as applied to the exercise of power by the federal government has revolved about the concept of limited purpose. Congress, according to this doctrine, should exercise its granted powers for limited purposes only, lest in exceeding these limits it encroach upon the powers of the states as reserved to them by the Tenth Amendment.[95]

James Coolidge Carter was one of the first to argue the doctrine of limited purpose before the United States Supreme Court. On the grounds that Congress cannot use one of its granted powers to accomplish an end that exceeds its legislative authority, he urged the Court in the Postal Lottery case (1892) [96] to pronounce invalid an act of Congress of 1890 that forbade the use of the United States mails for the passage of lottery tickets. Carter protested that Congress was in reality using its power over mail facilities to encroach upon the power of the states to suppress lotteries. It was attempting to accomplish indirectly what it could not do directly. The United States Supreme Court did not, in the case in question, heed Carter's plea, but his argument, with refinements by such attorneys as William Guthrie, was to become court doctrine in the twentieth century and was to serve as an effective brake on federal social legislation.[97]

The idea of laissez faire as applied to the exercise of Congressional power did win a signal victory in 1895 in the case of United States v.

[94] State v. Haun, 61 Kan. 146 (1899), 159, 163.

[95] Twiss, *Lawyers and the Constitution*, p. 174.

[96] *In re* Rapier, *In re* Dupré, 143 U.S. 110 (1892).

[97] The concept of limited purpose was applied by the Supreme Court in the Child Labor cases to prevent Congress from regulating child labor by means of its recognized powers to regulate interstate commerce and to tax. See Hammer v. Dagenhart, 247 U.S. 251 (1918); and Bailey v. Drexel Furniture Co., 259 U.S. 20 (1922).

E. C. Knight Company.   The case originated in a suit brought by the United States government against the sugar trust for violation of the Sherman Anti-Trust Act.   Although the sugar trust enjoyed a virtual monopoly of the sugar-refining business, the Supreme Court ruled against the government and expounded the view that Congress, in the exercise of its power to regulate interstate commerce, cannot reach behind commerce to regulate manufacturing, even though the products manufactured eventually enter into the channels of interstate trade.   "Commerce," Justice Fuller declared, "succeeds to manufacture, and is not a part of it."   Thus it does not follow that an attempt to monopolize, or the actual monopoly of, the manufacture of a given commodity necessarily involves a monopoly of commerce.   Only that which belongs to commerce is within the jurisdiction of the United States government; that which is not a part of commerce falls under the police power of the states.[98]   The distinction between commerce and manufacturing that the Court drew in this case was to serve as a formidable barrier to the regulation of business by the federal government in the twentieth century and especially during the early years of the New Deal.[99]

In United States v. Trans-Missouri Freight Association (1897)[100] another attempt was made to limit the application of the Sherman Anti-Trust Act: John Forrest Dillon sought to persuade the Supreme Court that the Sherman Act does not apply to "reasonable" restraints of trade.[101]   The Court refused to accept this contention in the case in question, but in Standard Oil Company of New Jersey et al. v. United States (1911) it reversed its position and decided that the Sherman Act applies only to "unreasonable" restraints of trade.[102]

When the doctrines propounded by Carter in the Postal Lottery

[98] United States v. E. C. Knight Co., 156 U.S. 1 (1895), 12, 16–17.

[99] "In a later generation a conservative-minded Court was to invoke Fuller's distinction [between direct and indirect effects upon commerce] repeatedly in order to strike down congressional statutes attempting to assert control over some phase of the national economy" (Kelly and Harbison, The American Constitution, p. 558). See, for example, Justice Sutherland's majority opinion in Carter v. Carter Coal Co. et al., 298 U.S. 238 (1936).   The elaboration of the decision of the Court in the Knight case went a long way toward establishing a "twilight zone" where both the federal government and the state governments were debarred from action.   See Twiss, Lawyers and the Constitution, pp. 214–238.

[100] 166 U.S. 290 (1897).

[101] Twiss, Lawyers and the Constitution, p. 191.

[102] 221 U.S. 1 (1911).

case and by Dillon in the Freight Association case were adopted by the United States Supreme Court, these, together with the dictum announced in the Knight case, supplied the Court with the necessary legal impediments with which to block the federal government when it sought to travel the road of social reform. Insofar as the Court had anything to do with the matter, Congress, no more than a state legislature, was to be permitted to forget that laissez faire was the law of the land.

In the courtroom, laissez faire thus emerged from the realm of theory to become a definite stumbling block in the path of social legislation. Judges and lawyers imbued with the philosophy of the negative state and oversolicitous for the rights of property and property owners read into the federal Constitution and into the state constitutions their own version of laissez faire. As once judges had sought to protect the individual from an overbearing executive authority, so now they sought to protect him from the legislature he himself had helped to elect. In so doing, as Roscoe Pound has said, the judiciary placed itself between the public and what the public needed and helped to protect individuals who did not need protection against society, which did need it.[103]

[103] Pound, "Common Law and Legislation," *Harvard Law Review*, XXI (April, 1908), 403.

LAISSEZ FAIRE UNDER ATTACK:

*Emergence of the Concept of the
General-Welfare State*

PREFATORY NOTE

THOUGH laissez faire was strongly supported during the years from 1865 to 1901, it was at the same time vigorously opposed. Protestant clergymen imbued with the philosophy of the social gospel found fault with the ethical implications of laissez faire. New-school economists challenged the premises of classical economics that were so closely associated with the negative state. Lester Ward and his colleagues in sociology rejected the social-Darwinist version of laissez faire and were joined in their assault on Spencerian determinism by William James and John Dewey. In their analysis of the role of the state, the political scientists Woodrow Wilson and Westel Woodbury Willoughby took issue with John Burgess and revealed the inadequacies of the let-alone policy.

The opponents of the philosophy of laissez faire proposed in its stead the rival philosophy of the general-welfare state. Whereas the advocates of laissez faire contended that the government could best advance the common weal by rendering itself as inconspicuous as possible and by permitting individuals "to work out their own salvation . . . amid the free and unrestricted play of natural forces," [1] the proponents of the general-welfare state argued—and this was the essence of the concept of the general-welfare state—that the state could best promote the general welfare by a positive exertion of its powers. They regarded the democratic state not as an evil force but as an instrument that the people could and should use to further their common interests, to ameliorate the conditions under which they lived and worked, and to provide for their health and safety and, to some extent,

---

[1] B. E. Fernow, "The Providential Functions of Government with Special Reference to Natural Resources," *Proceedings of the American Association for the Advancement of Science*, XLIV (August–September, 1895), 334.

for their social and economic security.[2] They wished to see the powers of government used both in the negative sense of restraining wrongdoing and in the positive sense of securing good, and they were inclined to believe that the repressive functions of government would tend to diminish as time went on and that its positive, ameliorative functions would increase. Although they were advocates of specific reforms for their own era, they did not, as a rule, conceive of the general-welfare state in terms of this or that function but, rather, took the position that the state must act whenever its action seemed likely to further the general well-being.

Unlike the adherents of laissez faire, the proponents of the general-welfare state believed that in the industrial age in which they lived state action was necessary to make liberty effective. Whereas American liberals of the era before the Civil War had been chiefly concerned with the negative aspects of liberty, the advocates of the general-welfare state stressed the positive side of the liberal faith.

Clergymen and academicians were not alone in criticizing laissez faire and in urging the use of the state as an agency for social reform. The drift of events in the United States in the three and one-half decades after the Civil War was hardly such as to inspire the mass of the people with any particular faith in a "natural order of things" in which the state is conspicuous chiefly because of its absence. Farmers, laborers, single taxers, Nationalists, socialists, Coxeyites, anti-monopolists, and social workers were all ready to use the state to bring about the reforms they thought necessary for their own best interests or for furthering what they believed to be the general welfare. Although it would be difficult to determine the extent to which the protest against laissez faire in the period after the Civil War directly influenced the nation's lawmakers, it is nevertheless true that in the last two decades of the nineteenth century there was considerable divergence between the practice of American legislatures and the theory of laissez faire.

[2] R. M. MacIver so defines "general-welfare functions" in his *The Web of Government* (New York, 1947), p. 331. The use of the term "general-welfare state" was suggested to me by Ralph Henry Gabriel, *The Course of American Democratic Thought: An Intellectual History since 1815* (New York, 1940), Chapter 17, and by Westel Woodbury Willoughby, *An Examination of the Nature of the State* (New York, 1896), pp. 337–339.

VI

THE SOCIAL GOSPEL

TRADITIONAL Protestantism was but little concerned with the new social problems occasioned by the industrialization and urbanization of the United States in the years after the Civil War. It continued to emphasize individual regeneration and paid scant attention to social reform. Furthermore, as already noted, the Protestant church allied itself with the well-to-do and, partly for that reason, lost the support of the working class. However, a minority of influential Protestant clergymen and laymen refused to go along with these dominant trends within the church and sought to adapt Protestantism to the needs of the new age. "Their attempts to reorient the historic faith of America to an industrial society comprised the social gospel." [1]

---

[1] Charles Howard Hopkins, *The Rise of the Social Gospel in American Protestantism, 1865–1915* (New Haven, 1940), p. 12. There was no movement at this time in the Catholic church or in Judaism that was really comparable to the social-gospel movement. Catholic leaders tended to ignore the social problems resulting from industrialization until the trial of the Molly Maguires in 1876–1877 and the great railway strikes of 1877 caused them to direct their attention more closely to the "social question." Until the late 1880's, however, Catholics, although much less complacent than they previously had been and although often critical of business ethics, tended to be conservative in their outlook and in their attitude toward organized labor and state action. Even in the last ten or fifteen years of the century Catholic social thought was on the conservative side, but Catholic clergymen and laymen were beginning to evidence a greater sympathy for organized labor and a greater willingness to invoke the aid of the state as a means of avoiding the extremes of laissez faire and socialism. James Edmund Roohan tends to emphasize the positive aspects of Catholic social thought during this era, whereas Aaron I. Abell contends that Catholic social reform was "largely negative and superficial to a degree" and that church interest in the reform movement "stemmed more from a desire to Americanize the attitudes of the Church and her children than from a genuine interest in social justice." See Roohan, "American Catholics and the Social

The social-gospel movement was initiated in the 1870's; it gained strength in the eighties; and it came of age in the last ten years of the century. Throughout these three decades the movement was much occupied with the ethics of laissez-faire capitalism.[2]

The chief feature of the social gospel was "its emphasis upon the saving of society rather than upon the salvation of individuals."[3] Reacting against the excessive individualism of traditional Protestantism and the belief that individual regeneration was in itself a sufficient goal of church endeavor, social gospelers concerned themselves with the family, the nation, and social and commercial life "as fields of the manifestation of God and of the operation of the Spirit."[4] Theologians like Washington Gladden, Theodore Munger, and Josiah Strong and such Protestant laymen as the economists Richard T. Ely and John R. Commons stressed the importance of environment as a factor in sin and consequently directed their attention to the correction of social maladjustments. Social Christianity, as one of its practitioners pointed out, "refused to obey the mandate of the old political economy, and leave the individual to the fortune of the market-place. It assumed

Question, 1865–1900" (Ph.D. thesis, Yale University, 1952), *passim;* Abell, "Origins of Catholic Social Reform in the United States: Ideological Aspects," *Review of Politics,* XI (July, 1949), 294–309; Abell, "The Reception of Leo XIII's Labor Encyclical in America, 1891–1919," *ibid.,* VII (October, 1945), 464–479; Abell, "The Catholic Factor in Urban Welfare: The Early Period, 1850–1880," *ibid.,* XIV (July, 1952), 301–324; and Theodore Maynard, *The Story of American Catholicism* (New York, 1941), pp. 526–528.

In the declaration of principles of Reform Judaism, which stemmed from their Pittsburgh conference of 1885, the Reform rabbis of America announced that they considered it their "duty to participate in the great task of modern times, to solve, on the basis of justice and righteousness, the problems presented by the contrasts and evils of the present organization of society." This aspect of Reform Judaism was, however, largely deemphasized until the twentieth century, although certain highly assimilated Reform Jews, like Felix Adler, played prominent roles in the ethical-culture movement of the period, which was, in a sense, related to the social-gospel movement. See David Philipson, *The Reform Movement in Judaism* (new and rev. ed.; New York, 1931), pp. 355–357; and Eric F. Goldman, *Rendezvous with Destiny* (New York, 1952), pp. 108–110.

[2] Hopkins, *Rise of the Social Gospel, passim.*

[3] James Dombrowski, *The Early Days of Christian Socialism in America* (New York, 1936), p. 17.

[4] See Theodore T. Munger, *The Freedom of Faith* (9th ed.; Boston, 1884), pp. 22–25; J. H. W. Stuckenberg, *Christian Sociology* (London, 1881), pp. 9–14; Shailer Mathews, *The Social Teaching of Jesus* (New York, 1897), pp. 4–6; and C. F. Morse, "Regeneration as a Force in Reform Movements," *Methodist Review,* LXXIII (November, 1891), 923–931.

the right . . . to take part in the whole economic conflict according to its social significance." [5] Rejecting any distinction between sacred and secular, social gospelers sought to apply the ethical and social principles of Christianity to all the problems of the age to the end that a more just social order might be realized here on earth. Society itself was to be redeemed and Christianized, and although individuals were still to be converted, they were to be provided with a Christian society in which to live. Only if a regenerated individual were able to live in a regenerated society could he be expected to lead a Christian life.[6]

The growing concern of the church with social questions was evidenced in the formation of a number of important church and lay organizations that interested themselves in the social aspects of Christianity. The Evangelical Alliance, inspired by Josiah Strong, Congregational minister from the Midwest and author of the influential *Our Country*, took up the cause of social Christianity in a series of annual conferences, beginning in 1885. In addition, local alliances were formed in forty cities to study sociological and industrial problems and to apply Christian solutions to them. The Convention of Christian Workers, formed in 1886, numbered twenty-five hundred followers of the social gospel by the end of the century. The Ethical Culture societies, a product of the ethical-culture movement of the period, paid considerable attention to the labor question, settlement work, and social education and eventually established schools that provided instruction in religion, ethics, and economics. The Church Association for the Advancement of the Interests of Labor was formed in 1887 by communicants of the Protestant Episcopal Church to show the sympa-

[5] William Jewett Tucker, *My Generation: An Autobiographical Interpretation* (Boston, 1919), pp. 96–97.

[6] Ely, *Social Aspects of Christianity, and Other Essays* (New York, 1889), pp. 16, 30–31, 53–57, 136–161; Gladden, *Tools and the Man: Property and Industry under the Christian Law* (Boston, 1893), pp. 1–24; Newman Smyth, *Christian Ethics* (2d ed.; Edinburgh, 1893), pp. 464–467; C. H. Zimmerman, "The Church and Economic Reforms," *Arena*, X (October, 1894), 694–700; Commons, *Social Reform and the Church* (New York, 1894), pp. 33–41, 71–73; Wilbur F. Crafts, *Practical Christian Sociology* (New York, 1896), pp. 16, 26, 44–46; Evangelical Alliance of the United States, *Christianity Practically Applied* (New York, 1894), I, 254–257; Lyman Abbott, *Christianity and Social Problems* (Boston, 1896), pp. iii, 361; Francis G. Peabody, *Jesus Christ and the Social Question* (New York, 1900), pp. 20–21; Walter Lorenzo Sheldon, *An Ethical Movement* (New York, 1896), p. 15; Stuckenberg, *Christian Sociology*, pp. 16–17; and Graham Taylor, *Pioneering on Social Frontiers* (Chicago, 1930), pp. 109–110, 387–388.

thy of that denomination for labor and to apply the principles of the gospel to the labor struggle. The Episcopalians in 1891 also established the Christian Social Union (it was reorganized as the Church Social Union in 1894) to propagate the doctrines of social Christianity. Branches of the Union, set up in connection with parishes and colleges, studied various phases of the social question, and the Union itself prepared reading outlines on social problems and distributed appropriate literature.

The American Institute of Christian Sociology was founded in 1893 to consider how the principles of Christianity might be applied to the problems of the day. Seeking to achieve its objective mainly through the establishment of local institutes, the Institute sponsored conferences in various parts of the country that dealt with the social aspects of Christianity. In 1892, under the influence of Walter Rauschenbusch, a group of Baptists organized the Brotherhood of the Kingdom to propagandize the idea of the kingdom of God on earth. Christian sociology also won its way into the seminaries of the land, and by the end of the century more than thirty leading divinity schools were offering courses in sociology.[7]

II

The application of the ethics of Christianity to the social and economic problems of the era after the Civil War brought the advocates of social Christianity face to face with the principles of laissez-faire economics then prevalent. Their general attitude toward these principles was one of severe condemnation. "Christianity," declared one of the most conservative of the advocates of social Christianity, "cannot grant the adequacy of the 'laissez-faire' philosophy, cannot admit that the perfect and permanent social state is the product of natural law and of unrestricted competition." [8]

The leaders of social Christianity variously denounced the philosophy of laissez faire as "selfish," "inhumane," "unchristian," "unethical,"

---

[7] Aaron I. Abell, *The Urban Impact on American Protestantism, 1865–1900* (Cambridge, Mass., 1943), pp. 88–117, 232–245; Hopkins, *Rise of the Social Gospel*, pp. 149–170; William D. P. Bliss, ed., *Encyclopedia of Social Reform* (New York, 1897), pp. 45–46, 275–276; Rauschenbusch, "Ideals of Social Reformers," *American Journal of Sociology*, II (September, 1896), 202–203. The extent to which the social gospel influenced the various Protestant denominations is discussed in Henry F. May, *Protestant Churches and Industrial America* (New York, 1949), pp. 182–203.

[8] A. J. F. Behrends, *Socialism and Christianity* (New York, 1886), p. 6.

"immoral," and "barbaric." "The 'let alone theory of society,'" Graham Taylor, founder of the Chicago Commons, proclaimed, "bears the mark of Cain. Its theological definition is hell." To the dean of the Cambridge Episcopal Theological School, the Reverend George Hodges, Manchesterism was "the science of extortion, the gentle art of grinding the faces of the poor." He who battles for the Christianization of society, declared the prominent Congregational minister Washington Gladden, will find his strongest foe in the field of economics. Economics is, indeed, a dismal science "because of the selfishness of its maxims and the inhumanity of its conclusions," and much of the trouble of the times is the result of the attempt to adopt its laws as "maxims of conduct." "Is it not evident," asked Charles Worcester Clark, son of the Reverend N. G. Clark, "that our economic system is diametrically opposed to Christian teaching? Christianity is the religion of peace, but industrial classes are avowedly in a state of warfare. . . . Christianity means co-operation and the uplifting of the lowliest; business means competition and the survival of the strongest." [9]

The "existing competitive system," Josiah Strong wrote Richard T. Ely, "is thoroughly selfish, and therefore thoroughly unchristian." [10] Strong's views were shared by middle-of-the-road social gospelers, who tended to look upon competition as antisocial and unchristian, as a species of warfare in which the strongest win and the weakest are crushed, in which the few are enriched and the many pauperized. A Christian society, they believed, must be organized on the basis of

[9] See Charles Loring Brace, *Gesta Christi, or a History of Humane Progress under Christianity* (2d ed.; New York, 1883), p. 414; Evangelical Alliance of the United States, *National Perils and Opportunities* (New York, 1887), p. 252; Abbott, "The New Political Economy," *Christian Union*, XXXII (July 23, 1885), 3; R. Heber Newton, *The Morals of Trade* (New York, 1876), pp. 22–34, 79–82; J. H. Hyslop, "Ethics and Economics," *Andover Review*, XV (January, 1891), 66–72; Josiah Strong, *Our Country* (rev. ed.; New York, 1891), p. 259; Taylor, "The Social Function of the Church," *American Journal of Sociology*, V (November, 1899), 313; Arthur Mann, *Yankee Reformers in the Urban Age* (Cambridge, Mass., 1954), p. 110; Gladden, *Tools and the Man*, pp. 25–54; Gladden, *Applied Christianity* (Boston, 1887), pp. 243–244; Gladden, "Good Stewardship," Sermon, November 29, 1885, Washington Gladden Papers, Ohio State Archaeological and Historical Society (November 29, 1885, is the date when this sermon was first delivered in Columbus; the dates hereafter given for Gladden sermons are the dates on which the sermons were first delivered, insofar as that can be determined from the notations on the cover page of the sermons); and Charles Worcester Clark, "Applied Christianity: Who Shall Apply It First?" *Andover Review*, XIX (January, 1893), 23–24.

[10] Strong to Ely, August 8, 1889, Richard T. Ely Papers, State Historical Society of Wisconsin.

coöperation rather than competition.[11] Left-wing social gospelers, addicted to socialism, were even more extreme in their denunciation of the competitive order. "In competition," said the Reverend Franklin M. Sprague, "every man's sword is against his brother. It is a fight: get *all you can* and give the *least you can.*" George D. Herron referred to the idea that competition is the life of trade as "the most profane and foolish of social falsehoods." Competition, he declared, "is social imbecility. It is economic waste. It is the destruction of life. It is the deformity, brutality, and atheism of civilization."[12]

The doctrine of self-interest was similarly castigated by adherents of social Christianity as "anti-Christian and barbarous." Human activity, the proponents of the social gospel argued, cannot be based on pure egoism, on lack of regard for the welfare of others. When a society relies chiefly on the selfish impulses, material and intellectual growth are arrested, for it requires higher motives than self-interest to sustain progress. Society must be based on the moral integrity of men, not on their selfishness. The Bible, after all, teaches not self-interest but self-sacrifice, and how is one to reconcile the doctrine of self-interest with the Golden Rule?[13]

Unbridled individualism was also censured by the social gospelers. Lyman Abbott, who succeeded to Henry Ward Beecher's pulpit and who was editor of the influential *Christian Union,* the first religious periodical to concern itself with the industrial problem, stated that in public debates on industrial matters he was guided by the conviction that "individualism is the characteristic of simple barbarism, not of republican civilization." The Reverend George N. Boardman of Binghamton, New York, referred to individualism as a "segregating,

[11] Gladden, *Applied Christianity,* pp. 30–33, 103–105; Gladden, *Tools and the Man,* pp. 146–203; Abbott, "The Natural Law of Competition," *Christian Union,* XXXII (July 16, 1885), 3–4; Abbott, *Christianity and Social Problems,* pp. 111–113; Rauschenbusch, "Ideals of Social Reformers," *American Journal of Sociology,* II (September, 1896), 210.

[12] Sprague, *Socialism from Genesis to Revelation* (Boston, 1893), p. 130; Herron, *The New Redemption* (New York, 1893), pp. 16–17.

[13] Sprague, *Socialism from Genesis to Revelation,* pp. 5, 130; John Bascom, "Labor and Capital," *Bibliotheca Sacra,* XXV (October, 1868), 662–665; Philo W. Sprague, *Christian Socialism. What and Why* (New York, 1891), pp. 28–50; Evangelical Alliance of the United States, *National Perils and Opportunities,* pp. 239, 252–253; J. E. Scott, *Socialism. What Is It?* (San Francisco, 1895), pp. 17–20; E. A. Washburn, *The Social Law of God* (3d ed.; New York, 1875), pp. 154–156, 201; Charles H. Zimmerman, "Wanted, An Ethical Political Economy," *Methodist Review,* LXXIV (September, 1892), 739–741.

selfish, centrifugal force that dissipates society." Morality, he declared, is social, not individual. Josiah Strong looked on excessive individualism as one of the factors explaining the rise of socialism, and he deplored the individualist's disregard of the principle that duties are coextensive with rights. To the learned Lutheran minister J. H. W. Stuckenberg, individualism unduly exalted the individual at the expense of society and made the members of society "leeches which fatten on one another." [14]

Since the main problem treated by the exponents of the social gospel was the relations between capital and labor,[15] it was but natural that the dicta of classical political economy with respect to this question should be subjected to searching criticism. Indeed, it was this aspect of the preachments of laissez faire that was most severely condemned. An obvious target for social-gospel criticism was the assumption of the classical economists that labor is but a commodity to be bought in the cheapest market and sold in the dearest. The laboring man is a human being, said the social gospelers, and he is not to be measured in terms of dollars and cents. What recognition of man's immortal soul, they asked, is contained in the commodity theory of labor? The employer must remember in dealing with his employees that he is dealing not with merchandise from which he is to make a profit but with children of God, whose welfare must be his constant concern.[16]

The contention of the economists that wages are adjusted entirely as the result of competition between employer and employee also drew the fire of the adherents of social Christianity. Many of them agreed with Gladden that "the wage-system, so long as it rests wholly on competition, is fundamentally wrong." Competition, Gladden as-

[14] Abbott, *Reminiscences* (Boston, 1915), p. 440; Ira V. Brown, *Lyman Abbott, Christian Evolutionist* (Cambridge, Mass., 1953), p. 100; Boardman, "Political Economy and the Christian Ministry," *Bibliotheca Sacra*, XXIII (January, 1866), 97–98; Strong, *Our Country*, pp. 144–145; Stuckenberg, *Christian Sociology*, pp. 18–19. See also Scott, *Socialism*, p. 20; Gladden, "Socialism and Unsocialism," *Forum*, III (April, 1887), 124–125; Rauschenbusch, "Ideals of Social Reformers," *American Journal of Sociology*, II (September, 1896), 211; and George C. Lorimer, *Studies in Social Life* (London, [1886]), pp. 19, 21.

[15] Hopkins, *Rise of the Social Gospel*, p. 80.

[16] Henry C. Potter, "The Laborer Not a Commodity," *Christian Thought,* 4th Ser. (1886), pp. 289–291; Gladden, *Applied Christianity*, pp. 51–52; Sprague, *Socialism from Genesis to Revelation*, pp. 134–137; Abbott, *Christianity and Social Problems*, pp. 200–205; William Mackintire Salter, *Ethical Religion* (Boston, 1889), pp. 147–151.

serted, introduces hostility where there should be coöperation, discord where there should be harmony. To establish competition as the regulator of the affairs of capital and labor is, in effect, to declare war between employer and employee, and in this war, labor, which is weaker than capital, will always go down to defeat.[17]

In place of a wage determined by competition, the social gospelers called on employers to pay a just wage, one that would enable the laborer to maintain a decent standard of living. They advised management to forget about Ricardo when it came to paying wages and to heed the Golden Rule. Also, although they generally did not go so far as to propose the complete abolition of the wage system, social gospelers urged its modification through the introduction of schemes of industrial partnership, profit sharing, or coöperation. Plans of this sort, they thought, accorded with Christian ethics.[18]

Critical of the principles of classical political economy as unethical, the social gospelers called for the formulation of a new ethical political economy. They advocated an economics that would make Christianity the guiding force in the conduct of man in the pursuit of wealth, that would substitute the Golden Rule for economic man, that would concern itself more with "welfare" and less with wealth, and that would endorse what ought to be as well as what is. They denied that ethics and economics can be separated in practice, that data of a moral character can be excluded in the formulation of economic law. As Gladden put it: "Economics without ethics is a mutilated science,—the play of Hamlet without Hamlet." [19] Social gospelers also contended that experience had indicated that what is ethically unjust is not economically wise, whereas a policy which pro-

[17] Gladden, *Applied Christianity*, pp. 31–33, 102–145; Gladden, *Tools and the Man*, pp. 176–184. See also Salter, *Ethical Religion*, pp. 149–151; and Clark, "Applied Christianity: Who Shall Apply It First?" *Andover Review*, XIX (January, 1893), 30–31.

[18] Salter, *Ethical Religion*, pp. 137–138, 155–158; Abbott, *Christianity and Social Problems*, pp. 194–196, 203–205; Gladden, *Applied Christianity*, pp. 33, 136–139; Gladden, *Tools and the Man*, pp. 183–241; Tucker, "Social Problems in the Pulpit," *Andover Review*, III (April, 1885), 299; Potter, "The Laborer Not a Commodity," *Christian Thought*, 4th Ser. (1886), pp. 289–291; Robert R. Roberts, "Economic and Political Ideas Expressed in the Early Social Gospel Movement, 1875–1900" (Ph.D. thesis, University of Chicago, 1952), pp. 62, 91, *et passim*. Herron believed economic justice unattainable under the wage system and therefore urged its overthrow. "The wages system," he declared, "is economic slavery; it is a profane traffic in human flesh and blood" (*New Redemption*, p. 64).

[19] Gladden, *Tools and the Man*, p. 53.

motes the welfare of the community is well-advised from the standpoint of both ethics and economics. "The precepts of Jesus Christ," the social gospelers asserted, "and the principles of sound political economy coincide." [20]

The argument for laissez faire from the social-Darwinist standpoint also came under the attack of the social gospel. The survival of the fittest as expounded by Spencer and the ethics of Christianity were, after all, quite incompatible. Social gospelers were willing to admit that the doctrine of struggle for existence, natural selection, and the survival of the fittest might apply to the animal world, but they repudiated as unchristian the unqualified application of this hypothesis to man. Extermination of the weak, they asserted, would perhaps result in material progress, but it would give us a cruel society in which the elements of kindness and compassion would be absent. Through the application of higher spiritual laws, Christianity, they believed, counteracts and restrains the operation of natural selection.[21]

The proponents of social Christianity also rejected Spencer's social determinism, his contention that social evolution is the product of natural forces alone. The main elements in progress, the Reverend Franklin M. Sprague argued, are not blind evolution, competition, and survival of the fittest but "Christian churches, Christian schools, Christian governments, Christian ethics and economics." "The social organism," he asserted, "is the creation of man. Its evolution is the product of human intelligence and volition." [22]

Since Carnegie's addition to the ideological structure of laissez-faire capitalism, the Gospel of Wealth, was but a reaffirmation of

[20] See Zimmerman, "Wanted, An Ethical Political Economy," *Methodist Review*, LXXVIII (September, 1892), 737–744; Hyslop, "Ethics and Economics," *Andover Review*, XV (January, 1891), 66–83; Washburn, *Social Law of God*, pp. 207–208; Taylor, "The Social Function of the Church," *American Journal of Sociology*, V (November, 1899), 314–316; Edward H. Rogers, *The Relations of Christianity to Capital and Labor* (Boston, 1870), p. 14; and Abbott, *Christianity and Social Problems*, pp. 223–224.

[21] Rogers, *Relations of Christianity to Capital and Labor*, p. 13; Nicholas Paine Gilman, *Socialism and the American Spirit* (Boston, 1893), pp. 21–22; Gladden, *Tools and the Man*, pp. 275–278; Franklin M. Sprague, *The Laws of Social Evolution* (Boston, 1895), pp. 24–25, 33; Zimmerman, "The Church and Economic Reforms," *Arena*, X (October, 1894), 700.

[22] Sprague, *Laws of Social Evolution*, pp. 40–41, 165–166. Sprague referred to Spencer's law of equal freedom as the "gospel of muscle" (*Socialism from Genesis to Revelation*, p. 173). The social gospel's criticism of social Darwinism is discussed in May, *Protestant Churches and Industrial America*, pp. 145–147.

Protestant ideas of stewardship, it was not subjected to the same degree of criticism by the social gospelers as were the teachings of the
classical economists and the social Darwinists. There were, however, a few dissenting voices. The Christian Socialist William Dwight
Porter Bliss referred to Carnegie's gospel as a "blasphemous libel on
Christ's Gospel of Brotherhood." [23]   The practical-minded Richard T.
Ely, one of the most important lay advocates of the social gospel,
pointed out that private philanthropy can, at best, be only an auxiliary
to "established, regularly working institutions" in serving the cause of
social reform. Philanthropic effort, he argued, is in itself unable to
deal adequately with such problems as poverty, education, sanitation,
and housing. A single sanitary law, for example, can accomplish
more for tenement-house dwellers than "all the achievements of private
philanthropy in a generation." Whereas private philanthropy, moreover, concerns itself with results, the "coercive philanthropy" of the
state deals with causes and anticipates harm. Thus, said Ely, philan-
thropists render a public service when they support hospitals and reformatories, but more important ends are served when, by child-labor
laws and safety and sanitary legislation, the power of the state is invoked to diminish the need for such institutions. [24]

The most searching analysis of Carnegie's Gospel of Wealth came
from Professor William Jewett Tucker of Andover Theological Seminary. Tucker complained that discussion of Carnegie's proposal had
centered about the question of the disposition of the rich man's wealth
and that Carnegie's argument justifying the existence of so much
wealth in a few hands, which Tucker believed to be the real point
at issue, had been overlooked. Should the people, he warned, accept Carnegie's proposal and entrust the improvement of society to
the charity of the few under the assumption that the rich can do more
for the community than the community can do for itself, public spirit
and self-respect would deteriorate. Society, Tucker maintained, cannot afford thus to be patronized and to permit charity to do the work
of justice. It must itself accept the responsibility for the public uses
of wealth and must advance through its own efforts rather than through
any "gospel of patronage." [25]

[23] Bliss, "What to Do Now," *Dawn*, II (July–August, 1890), 114.
[24] Ely, *The Social Law of Service* (Cincinnati, 1896), pp. 193–205; Ely, *Social
Aspects of Christianity*, pp. 85–112; Ely, "Philanthropy," *Chautauquan*, IX (October,
1888), 16–18.
[25] Tucker, " 'The Gospel of Wealth,' " *Andover Review*, XV (June, 1891), 631–
645; Tucker, *My Generation*, p. 180.

III

Although most of the important figures in the social-gospel movement challenged the premises upon which laissez faire was based and recognized the need for greater church concern with the social problems of the day, they did not, generally speaking, envision the solution of these problems by the action of the state. They dismissed laissez faire as unethical, but in its stead they offered not the general-welfare state but Christianity. As the Reverend Nicholas Paine Gilman put it: "Only a small portion of the Kingdom of Heaven cometh through legislation." [26] The Kingdom of God was rather to be attained by Christian individuals following in the steps of Jesus, by Christian individuals applying the Golden Rule in their everyday life. "It is the personal element that Christian discipleship needs to emphasize," declared the most famous of social-gospel novelists.[27]

The social gospelers, it is true, stressed the need for social regeneration, but, paradoxically, many of them thought that this objective could best be achieved through the individual. Rather than seek state aid to attack directly the social and economic wrongs that they so clearly recognized, they called for personal self-sacrifice, for a broader application of the principle of stewardship, for the voluntary adoption of such "Christian" devices as profit sharing and coöperation.[28] For the special problems of the city, their major solutions were the institutional church and the religious social settlement, rather than remedial social legislation.[29]

[26] Gilman, *Socialism and the American Spirit*, p. 364. Gilman himself, however, favored a modest extension of the functions of the state. See *ibid.*, pp. 252–268, 312–318; and Mann, *Yankee Reformers*, pp. 83–84, 98–99.

[27] Charles M. Sheldon, *In His Steps: What Would Jesus Do?* (Chicago, 1898), p. 275. This book was written in 1896, and by June, 1897, one hundred thousand copies had been sold. Sheldon estimated in 1933 that total sales had reached the twenty-three-million mark. See Hopkins, *Rise of the Social Gospel*, pp. 142–143. Sheldon's central idea was that individuals in their everyday life should act as they believe Jesus would have acted in similar circumstances.

[28] See, for example, Mathews, *Social Teaching of Jesus*, pp. 210–217; Mathews, "The Significance of the Church to the Social Movement," *American Journal of Sociology*, IV (March, 1899), 615–620; Gilman, *Socialism and the American Spirit*, pp. 275–307, 335, 346–347; F. D. Huntington, "Social Problems and the Church," *Forum*, X (October, 1890), 141; Peabody, *Jesus Christ and the Social Question*, pp. 115–119; Strong, *Our Country*, pp. 230–232, 259–261; Washburn, *Social Law of God*, pp. 169, 198. The church, Abell correctly points out, hoped to solve the social problems of the day "by insisting that all classes acknowledge spiritual allegiance to Jesus Christ" (*Urban Impact on American Protestantism*, p. 86).

[29] Hopkins, *Rise of the Social Gospel*, p. 319. Social gospelers did advocate

Despite the general lack of enthusiasm for the state as an agency of reform, an increasing number of social gospelers came to realize that exhortation to follow the Golden Rule was in itself an insufficient means of bringing about needed changes and that state action might serve as an important ancillary to Christian ethics in effecting the regeneration of society. For the most part, the leaders of the social gospel who advocated state action were middle-of-the-roaders who wished to secure the adoption of certain reforms within the framework of the existing order. There was, however, a radical wing of the movement that believed that the existing order was in itself opposed to Christian principles and that it should therefore be replaced by a socialist state in which Christian ideas of brotherhood could more readily be applied.

In calling upon the state to buttress the cause of social Christianity, the middle-of-the-roaders were seeking a golden mean between laissez faire on the one hand and socialism on the other. "Between the extreme view of those who would have the state let industry alone," declared the founder of the American Sabbath Union, the Reverend Wilbur F. Crafts, "and those who would have the state monopolize it, the Christian sociologist should impartially seek the golden mean."[30] In similar fashion, the Reverend J. H. W. Stuckenberg argued that since individualism sought to elevate the individual without consideration of, or even at the expense of, society and since socialism, per contra, was insufficiently concerned with the rights of the individual, Christian social science should seek a middle ground between these extremes by reconciling the interests of the individual and the interests of society and showing the proper relationship between them.[31]

Lay adherents of the social gospel were instrumental in urging upon the church a more realistic view of the potentialities of state action. The economists Richard T. Ely and John R. Commons were of special significance in this respect. Ely, who believed that "Christianity which is not practical is not Christianity at all," advised the church to utilize the state as a means of securing necessary reforms. "God," he declared, "works through the State in carrying out His purposes more universally than through any other institution." It is, indeed, just as much religious work to pass good laws as to preach ser-

municipal ownership of public utilities as one means of dealing with the problem of the city. See Roberts, "Economic and Political Ideas Expressed in the Early Social Gospel Movement," p. 151.

[30] Crafts, *Practical Christian Sociology*, p. 183.

[31] Stuckenberg, *Christian Sociology*, pp. 18–21.

mons, just as holy to combat filth and disease as to send out missionaries to convert the heathen. The state, Ely argued, is "religious in its essence," and only religious measures such as factory acts, educational laws, and laws providing for the honest administration of justice should be enacted. He suggested that the church interest itself in such pressing problems of the day as child, female, and Sunday labor, housing, provision of urban recreational facilities, corruption in government, the distribution of wealth, charities and corrections, and social settlements. He believed that the church should establish goals for the state to attain, and he urged it to combat the optimistic philosophy of the age, which constituted an intellectual barrier to needed improvements.[32]

Commons wished both clergy and laity to study the facts of sociology so that they might become more familiar with the nature of society, but he thought that the Christian love of humanity would have to be applied to these facts to ensure their proper utilization. Science and Christianity, he asserted, must be united "to save the world." Once they had gathered the necessary facts and infused them with Christian ethics, Christians, Commons believed, would have to address themselves to the essentially religious task of bettering social conditions. They would soon discover that voluntary effort in the form of charity and philanthropy was by itself an insufficient means of dealing with the problem and that to effect essential reforms, it would be necessary to resort to the coercive power of the state. Few Christians, Commons held, comprehended "the strategic position held by government as the key to all social reforms and the Christianization of society." "Government," he declared, "is the only supreme authority among men . . . the only means whereby refractory, obstructive, and selfishly interested elements of society may be brought into line with social progress." He therefore urged Christians to take an active part in politics and to fight for the reforms necessary to improve social conditions. Among such reforms he included the regulation of corporations, municipal ownership of public utilities, factory legislation, sanitary regulations, and the improvement of tenement-house conditions.[33]

Among the ranks of the clergymen, a number of social-gospel lead-

[32] Ely, "The Next Things in Social Reform," *Christian Union*, XLIII (April 23, 1891), 531; Ely, "Person and Property," *Christian Advocate*, LXVI (March 19, 1891), 186; Ely, "The State," *ibid.*, LXVI (June 11, 1891), 386; Ely, *Social Aspects of Christianity*, pp. 73–77; Ely, *Social Law of Service*, pp. 173–174.

[33] Commons, *Social Reform and the Church*, pp. 3–63, 72–114, 123–151.

ers also subscribed to the view that a certain amount of state action would be necessary to establish the Kingdom of God. The Reverend George N. Boardman was of the opinion that there was "something repulsive in the thought that it [government] should disregard the social relations which God has established, and should consider itself as simply the minister of cold justice." Government, he declared, must have the necessary power to protect the weak and to safeguard interests without which society cannot exist. The Reverend Newman Smyth of New Haven, who thought that socialism was impractical and that it assigned too many functions to the state, nevertheless believed that some change in the existing order was necessary. "There is scientific social work to be done," he declared, "both in keeping the avenues of preferment wide open to individual talent and enterprise, and also in restricting the accumulation and use of wealth to an extent which threatens the public welfare." Smyth's criterion for all legislation was its social utility: he did not believe that any a priori theories should be permitted to stand in the way of needed reforms.[34]

The Reverend Wilbur F. Crafts referred to the let-alone theory of government as "discredited and discarded" and contended that the industrialization and urbanization of society made necessary an extension of the functions of the state. Specifically, he recommended that Christians support municipal ownership of public utilities, national ownership of railways, mines, and the telegraph, and legislation to remove the evils of child labor and sweatshops. The Reverend G. H. Dryer of Rochester, New York, advocated a similar program of state action and declared that the police state would have to give way to the general-welfare state. It is the weak state rather than the strong state that we have to fear, Dryer asserted.[35]

Lyman Abbott, who considered the primary function of the church to be the rebuilding of men rather than the reform of the social organization, was nevertheless an advocate of a great number of social reforms. Laissez faire, he thought, was inadequate to the needs of the time and would have to be replaced by "a new conception of the functions of government and consequent enlargement of its powers, and the sphere of its operations." Government was, indeed, on the

[34] Boardman, "Political Economy and the Christian Ministry," *Bibliotheca Sacra,* XXIII (January, 1866), 100–104; Smyth, *Christian Ethics,* pp. 448–462.

[35] Crafts, *Practical Christian Sociology,* pp. 168–173, 177–183; Dryer, "Tendencies in American Economics," *Methodist Review,* LXXIII (March, 1891), 247–252.

way to becoming "a league of men combined . . . for the better development of its wealth, the better reward of its industry, the better promotion of its welfare." Looking to coöperative action rather than to natural laws for the correction of the inequities of the existing system, Abbott urged the regulation of tenement houses by law, municipal ownership of street-light facilities and street-car lines, state regulation of mines and oil wells, federal ownership of the telegraph and the telephone, federal regulation of interstate railroads, prohibition of child labor, regulation of the working conditions of women, legal recognition of trade unions, the enactment of a national forest-conservation law, and federal appropriations for public education. The ultimate reform for which he campaigned was the establishment of industrial coöperatives that would be managed by the workers themselves.[36]

Another prominent clergyman who looked to the state to take positive action on behalf of the common weal was the liberal Episcopalian minister R. Heber Newton. Striking out at those who "make a fetish of natural law," Newton argued that man "can largely command the natural law of society just as he so largely commands the natural law of the physical world." He also rejected that companion "fetish" of natural law, laissez faire, and asserted that "the state's first concern is to see her citizens healthful, vigorous, wealth-producing factors." His program of reform embraced postal-savings banks, factory laws, a national bureau of labor to serve the workingman, government aid to cope with unemployment, possible government aid to producers' coöperatives, tenement legislation, regulation of the railroads, public ownership of all newly discovered mineral resources, and use of the taxing power to limit private fortunes. Newton thought that ultimately competition would give way to association, individualism to coöperation, planless production to "systematic and intelligent production and distribution, according to the capacities of the market," but he advocated a gradualist approach to these goals "without now writing the final edition of the astronomy of the new heavens." He recognized the danger inherent in the increase of state functions that the reforms he advocated involved, but he was even more concerned about what

[36] Abbott, "Christianity versus Socialism," North American Review, CXLVIII (April, 1889), 447–453; Abbott, "Danger Ahead," Century, N.S., IX (November, 1885), 57–58; Abbott, Christianity and Social Problems, pp. 112–113, 119–121, 124–133; Abbott, Reminiscences, pp. 395–412, 422–423, 441–442; Abbott, "Industrial Democracy," Forum, IX (August, 1890), 668; Brown, Abbott, pp. 104–108.

might occur should the state avoid its responsibilities in these matters.[37]

The ethical religionists were also willing to use the state to further the general interest.[38] Government, they argued, is not a necessary evil, but a potential force for good. It exists not only to protect life but also to make it tolerable. Indeed, it should aim at making life something more than tolerable. It should stand for justice and seek actively to promote the general welfare. When government partakes of this nature, its goal and that of religion are one and the same.[39]

The most influential and the most famous of the clergymen who during this period were seeking some middle ground between laissez faire and socialism was Washington Gladden. A graduate of Williams College, Gladden from 1871 to 1875 served on the editorial board of the influential religious weekly, the *Independent*. In 1875 he became pastor of the North Congregational Church of Springfield, Massachusetts, and remained there until 1882. In that year he was called to the First Congregational Church of Columbus, Ohio, where he served as pastor and pastor emeritus until his death in 1918. Throughout his long and honorable career he was one of the leading exponents of social Christianity.

In his first work in the field of social Christianity, *Working People and Their Employers*, published in 1876, Gladden rejected trade unionism, government interference, and the teachings of political economy as solutions for the industrial problem. Given the wage system, he declared, only the application of the Golden Rule could bring industrial peace. As the means of coping with the existing depression, he proposed the cultivation of simpler tastes and of the virtues of industry and frugality, a greater sense of contentment, and

[37] U. S. Congress, Senate, Committee on Education and Labor, *Report upon the Relations between Labor and Capital* (Washington, D.C., 1885), II, 535–596; Newton, "Nationalism," *Dawn*, I (July 15, 1889), 2–3. Newton eventually became president of the New York chapter of the Society of Christian Socialists and associate editor of the *Dawn*, a journal of Christian Socialism.

[38] "If all men were brothers (i.e. thought themselves so)," the ethical religionist William Salter wrote, "the solution would not be so difficult. But to many, most perhaps,—that is idealism, moonshine. The question is, then, how far by law we can make them *act* so, even if they don't feel so?" (Salter to Lloyd, February 6, 1888, Henry Demarest Lloyd Papers, State Historical Society of Wisconsin).

[39] Salter, *Ethical Religion*, pp. 131–133, 211–214; Sheldon, *An Ethical Movement*, pp. 268–269, 280–283; John Lovejoy Elliott, "The Relation of the Ethical Ideal to Social Reform," in Horace J. Bridges, ed., *Aspects of Ethical Religion: Essays in Honor of Felix Adler* (New York, 1926), pp. 332–333.

faith in God. He did not even consider the responsibility of government in this matter. Indeed, Gladden showed himself to be no friend of state action. He spoke of the "vice of depending on the nation, instead of depending on themselves," as "one to which far too many of our citizens have been addicted" and declared that, "as a general rule," this had not "proved a very efficient method of developing high character." He quoted Herbert Spencer's "Over-Legislation" to refute the arguments of the socialists.[40]

Gladden, however, did not remain an opponent of the state. In his subsequent writings in the 1880's and 1890's he rejected the argument for laissez faire and pointed to the state as an important aid to Christian ethics in effecting the Christianization of society. Desirous of striking a balance between socialism and laissez faire, he became an earnest advocate of the general-welfare state.

In proclaiming his divergence from the let-alone policy, Gladden repudiated the arguments upon which the doctrine of laissez faire was based. He conceded that individualism had been a necessary weapon in the fight against feudalism, but he did not think it a sound basis on which to establish a healthy society. He agreed with the socialists that starvation wages, depression, and the growth of plutocracy were "the natural issues of an industrial system whose sole motive power is self-interest, and whose sole regulative principle is competition." He regarded the overthrow of classical political economy as "the first business of the Christian church," for "no other dragon is devouring so many precious lives." [41] Gladden also refused to accept the materialistic conception of the laissez-faire economists and the social Darwinists that man is powerless to direct social forces to beneficent ends. "The environment," he asserted, "is not our master . . . it is our medium." "Christian morality assumes that the wills of men are free." "We are not hopelessly drifting in the current of social progress; we may shape our own course and choose our own port." [42]

But though Gladden repudiated laissez faire and individualism, he

[40] Gladden, *Working People and Their Employers* (Boston, 1876), pp. 37–73, 166–210, 213–214, 218. In his *Recollections* (Boston, 1909), pp. 255–257, Gladden declared that this was "not an important book" and that he was "not proud of the achievement."

[41] Gladden, "Socialism and Unsocialism," *Forum*, III (April, 1887), 124–125; Gladden, *Applied Christianity*, pp. 58–70, 175–176.

[42] Gladden, *Social Facts and Forces* (New York, 1897), p. 2; Gladden, Sermon, May 29, 1892, Gladden Papers; Gladden, "Can Our Social Ills Be Remedied?" *Forum*, VIII (September, 1889), 18–27; Gladden, *Tools and the Man*, pp. 35–37.

refused to embrace what he considered the opposite extreme: socialism. Although he accepted the socialist indictment of the existing order, he criticized the socialist solution. He considered the socialists' theory of labor value a false doctrine. He thought that socialism undervalued self-help and self-interest just as laissez faire overvalued them, that it would severely limit the freedom and independence of the individual, and that it would eventually lead to dictatorship. He was certain that the socialist attempt to regulate the social and industrial life of the nation through a centralized bureaucracy would collapse under its own weight. Furthermore, he believed that socialism would paralyze private enterprise; and it was his view that, in the last analysis, private enterprise had reared America's great civilization and was essential, albeit in modified form, to its future progress.[43]

Gladden, therefore, sought some halfway house between socialism and laissez faire. Midway between these "two opposing errors" he saw "the safe path of social progress," a path that would unite and coördinate individualism and socialism, liberty and love, and "the perfection of each with the welfare of all."[44] To attain this middle ground, to bring about the Christianization of society, Gladden thought it necessary that Christian principles and methods be applied by individuals to the problems of the day, but he was also ready to enlist the aid of the state. He did not believe that the state could cure all mischief, yet he thought that there was much that it could do. "New occasions," he declared, "bring new duties; the functions of the state must be broadened to meet the exigencies of our expanding civilization. We may go far beyond Mr. Spencer's limits and yet stop a great way this side of socialism."[45]

Gladden thought that Christians should invoke the power of the state not only to protect life and property but also to promote "to some extent, the general welfare." Government, he advised, should exercise both the negative police function of safeguarding individual rights and punishing wrongdoing and the positive function of promoting the general welfare through the economic and social coöperation of all the people; and, as Gladden saw it, with the advance of civiliza-

[43] Gladden, *Applied Christianity*, pp. 71–72, 87–98, 129–130; Gladden, *Tools and the Man*, pp. 256–274.

[44] Gladden, *Tools and the Man*, pp. 273–274; Gladden, *Applied Christianity*, p. 98; Gladden, Sermon, May, 1891, Gladden Papers.

[45] Gladden, *Applied Christianity*, pp. 100–101.

tion the activities of government would be increasingly of the latter type.

To Gladden, the promotion of the general welfare meant that government should aid "the humblest and poorest and weakest" and that the weak and downtrodden should be given a "fair start in the race of life." It meant also "the co-operation of all of us, through the State, in improving the conditions of life for all men . . . ." He did not wish the state "to be turned into a good fairy" who would "empty the horn of plenty at every man's door," nor did he believe that it should seek to relieve individuals of the responsibility of caring for themselves, but he did think of government as "a great co-operative agency" through which the people could "supply many of their wants and provide for many of their necessities" and which could promote the "health, the comfort, the innocent enjoyment, and the prosperity of its citizens." [46]

Gladden rejected the contention of the proponents of laissez faire that whatever the state does beyond mere protection it does poorly. He recognized this as an argument he himself had used on occasion but as one whose validity he had come to question. He thought it possible that the federal and the state governments might actually be improved if heavier tasks were assigned them. Extension of the functions of government would lead the people to pay greater attention to their political duties and to exercise greater care in the selection of public officials. At any rate, Gladden was willing to test this theory. "If we have not yet attained to that lofty morality by which we should be fitted for the tremendous tasks imposed upon us by Socialism, we are ready," he thought, "to assume larger responsibilities, and to undertake greater services." [47]

To implement his views regarding the proper role of the state, Gladden proposed an extensive program of social reform. His recommendations comprised the establishment of compulsory public education, suppression of speculation, abolition of the saloon, government regulation of property in land to ensure the use of the land in the general interest, prohibition of Sunday labor, passage of child-labor

[46] Gladden, *Tools and the Man*, pp. 281–282; Gladden, "The Philosophy of Anarchism," *Outlook*, LXIX (October, 19, 1901), 453–454; Gladden, "The Gospel of the Kingdom," Sermon, January 27, 1889, Gladden Papers; Gladden, Sermons, April 12, 1891, May 27, 1894, 1896 (no month or day given), *ibid.*; Gladden, "The City That Ought to Be," Sermon, April 4, 1897, *ibid.*

[47] Gladden, *Tools and the Man*, pp. 284–286.

laws, limitation of hours in certain occupations—if not in all of them —inspection for sanitary purposes of factories, workshops, and mines, provision of work by public authorities for those unemployed through no fault of their own, arbitration between labor and management (compulsory arbitration in the case of quasi-public corporations), government regulation of the corporate form of organization, rigid supervision and control of trusts, strict state control and ultimate state ownership of natural monopolies, a heavy inheritance tax, and a progressive income tax.[48] Gladden, however, thought that this program would be of little value unless the individual were regenerated and persuaded to live on a higher moral plane. In Gladden's view, what was needed was not only a better world, but also better men to live in it.[49]

IV

Whereas Gladden and some of his colleagues hoped to effect the reform and Christianization of society within the framework of the existing capitalist order, a small band of left-wing social gospelers who believed that the teachings of Christ could not be applied within the capitalist scheme of things proposed the establishment of a socialist state. Only in such a state, they thought, could the Christian ideal of brotherhood be realized. The socialism of the left-wing social gospelers was, on the whole, of a very vague sort, and only slightly resembled the Marxian version. Christian Socialists derived their main inspiration from Jesus Christ and borrowed from socialist philosophy only what comported with their ideals of brotherhood and social justice. They were socialists, in short, not because they believed in socialism but because they believed in Christianity.[50]

The first of the Christian organizations that supported the cause of socialism in this period was the Christian Labor Union, established in 1872. The leaders of this tiny group were the Reverend Jesse H. Jones, a Congregational minister, Edward H. Rogers, a Methodist lay preacher, and T. Wharton Collens, a Catholic judge.

[48] Gladden, *Tools and the Man*, pp. 71–81, 287–302; Gladden, *Applied Christianity*, p. 101; Gladden, *Social Facts and Forces*, pp. 39–43, 82–154; Gladden, Sermons, September 1, 1889, May 20, 1890, January 23, 1898, February 27, 1898, Gladden Papers.

[49] Gladden, *Tools and the Man*, pp. 304–306.

[50] For an interesting analysis of Christian Socialism, see Paul Monroe, "English and American Christian Socialism: An Estimate," *American Journal of Sociology*, I (July, 1895), 50–68. See also Hopkins, *Rise of the Social Gospel*, pp. 171–183; and Dombrowski, *Christian Socialism in America*, pp. 99–106.

The Christian Labor Union was at the outset but little concerned with the relation of the state to industrial society and with the political aspects of socialism, and its members devoted their principal attention to educational work. They sought to persuade the churches to set up mutual-benefit societies to aid the poor, to encourage all forms of industrial coöperation, to withdraw support from the "maxims of trade," and to accept the socialist theory of labor value. They condemned the existing order as "one of embodied falsities" and urged the abolition of interest, profit, and the wage system as unchristian.

During its early years the Union endorsed only such specific reforms as shorter hours, coöperative banks, workshops, and stores, and provision of a home for every worker, but it eventually endorsed the complete program of socialism, proposing public ownership of machinery, the means of transportation, the media of exchange, and the products of industry before their final distribution. Only with this type of industrial democracy in force, thought the leaders of the Union, could the Kingdom of God be realized on earth. The ideals of the Christian Labor Union, however, found but little support either inside or outside the church (". . . nobody will look at us i.e. nobody of the 'comfortable classes,'" Jones complained to David Wells), and the organization passed out of existence in 1878.[51]

After the demise of the Christian Labor Union the cause of Christian Socialism was moribund in the United States until 1889, when, chiefly as the result of the efforts of William Dwight Porter Bliss— Episcopalian clergyman, member of the Knights of Labor, enthusiastic follower, for a time, of Henry George and Edward Bellamy, and indefatigable social reformer—the Society of Christian Socialists was formed in Boston. A chapter of the Society was soon thereafter created in New York City, and state organizations were formed in Ohio, Kansas, and Illinois.[52]

The ideals of the founders of the Society of Christian Socialists were set forth in the Declaration of Principles adopted by the Boston group. "All social, political, and industrial relations," the declaration proclaimed, "should be based ón the fatherhood of God and the brother-

[51] Dombrowski, *Christian Socialism in America*, pp. 77–83; Hopkins, *Rise of the Social Gospel*, pp. 42–49; Evangelical Alliance of the United States, *National Perils and Opportunities*, pp. 235–236; Jones to Wells, July 27, 1874, David A. Wells Papers, Library of Congress. May considers Jesse Jones a Christian Communist rather than a socialist (*Protestant Churches and Industrial America*, pp. 75–79).

[52] Hopkins, *Rise of the Social Gospel*, pp. 171–175; Dombrowski, *Christian Socialism in America*, pp. 100–101.

hood of man, in the spirit and according to the teachings of Jesus Christ." The existing capitalist order, however, was, in the view of the declaration, based on economic individualism rather than on the teachings of Christ, and this had resulted in the proliferation of such moral evils as mammonism, overcrowding, intemperance, prostitution, and crime. It was therefore the obligation of Christianity to protest against the capitalist system and to demand a reconstructed social order that would be beneficial to society and that would be based on the Christian principle " 'We are members one of another.' " The belief was expressed that the economic circumstances then giving rise to trusts and business consolidations, combined with the development of individual character, would necessarily bring about a social order that would be both Christian and socialist. The Declaration of Principles concluded with a statement of the Society's objectives, which were: (1) "To show that the aim of socialism is embraced in the aim of Christianity"; and (2) to awaken the church to the fact that Christ's teachings lead directly to socialism and that therefore the church must "apply itself to the realization of the social principles of Christianity." [53]

The views of the Society of Christian Socialists and particularly of Bliss were amplified principally in the pages of the *Dawn*, edited by Bliss and the chief organ of Christian Socialism. Christian Socialism was proposed as the embodiment of the social law of God and as the cure for the social ills of the day. It was represented as a middle way between extreme individualism and narrow socialism, a form of social organization based on the sacrifice of the individual but one whose outcome would be "the highest individuality." Yet it was not really, said the Christian Socialists, a particular scheme of social organization but rather "a principle of social action" that involved the gradual transfer of more and more capital from private into public hands and the replacement of competition by "fraternal combination." The economic objectives of Christian Socialism were thus declared to be akin to those of political socialism, but these objectives were to be fulfilled *"by starting from Christ"* and by instituting the Kingdom of God here on earth.[54]

[53] "Christian Socialism," Bliss, ed., *Encyclopedia of Social Reform*, p. 258; *Dawn*, I (May 15, 1889), 3.

[54] Bliss, "What to Do Now," *Dawn*, II (July–August, 1890), 110–111; Bliss, "What Is Christian Socialism?" *ibid.*, IV (June, 1892), 12; "What Socialism Is," *ibid.*, VII (February, 1896), 9; Bliss, "Why Am I a Christian Socialist?" *Twentieth Century*, V (October 2, 1890), 4–6; Bliss, *What Christian Socialism Is* (reprinted from the *Dawn*; Boston, 1894), pp. 9–11, 18; "Christian Socialism," Bliss, ed., *Encyclopedia of Social Reform*, pp. 259–260. See also Sprague, *Christian Socialism*,

Vague as to the nature of the socialism they favored, Christian Socialists were equally vague as to how the reconstructed social order that they advocated could be established. The Society regarded its main task as educational, and Bliss was wont to proclaim that the most practical thing that Christian Socialists could do was to inform the public of the truths of Christian Socialism; [55] yet Bliss agreed with Edward Bellamy that what was needed was "not goody, goody church-talk but plain advocacy of what to do." [56] "What to do" almost inevitably involved state action, and Christian Socialists seemed agreed that "a deeper, wider, diviner conception of the State" was required to counteract the previous overemphasis of the church on the individual. "In the caucus, we may find our cross," Bliss declared, "in the State we may find our Calvary. There to-day is the battle for human right; there must we give ourselves for the brethren."

Although proclaiming themselves state socialists, insisting that the state has "a Divine function to fulfill in the social life," and contending that the danger in a democracy is that the state will do too little rather than too much, Christian Socialists nevertheless maintained that they were not doctrinaire on the question of state functions but regarded the problem as one to be decided by circumstances and experience. "We are not in haste to turn property over to Uncle Sam, trusting to Uncle Sam to realize God's kingdom in the United States. With every respect for Uncle Sam we still believe in the necessity of the development of the individual." "I am very little of a paternalist," Bliss informed Richard T. Ely, "and believe that we must begin with the people, at the very foundations, ethically and democratically, and that although this may be slower, it is the only lasting way." [57]

Though not altogether lucid in their discussion of the role of the

pp. 51–142, 159–166, 183–184; Vida Dutton Scudder, "Socialism and Spiritual Progress,—A Speculation," *Andover Review*, XVI (July, 1891), 49–67; and Scudder, *On Journey* (New York, 1937), p. 163.

[55] Bliss, "Be Practical," *Dawn*, I (August 15, 1889), 1–2; Bliss, "What to Do Now," *ibid.*, II (July–August, 1890), 111, 114; "What to Do Now. A Socialistic Programme," *ibid.*, VII (October, 1895), 5–6; Hopkins, *Rise of the Social Gospel*, p. 176.

[56] Bliss to Bellamy, April 23, 1897, Edward Bellamy Papers, Houghton Library, Harvard University.

[57] Bliss, "A Symposium upon the Relation of the State to the Individual," *Dawn*, II (November, 1890), 281–283, 284, 289–290; Bliss, "What Is Christian Socialism?" *ibid.*, IV (June, 1892), 12; Bliss, "What to Do Now," *ibid.*, II (July–August, 1890), 110–111; Bliss, *What Christian Socialism Is*, p. 18; Bliss to Ely, March 30, 1891, Ely Papers.

state,[58] Christian Socialists did announce their support of a great many reforms (Christian Socialism "is not one reform. It is many reforms on *one principle*") that involved an extension of state activities for what was presumed to be the general welfare. Indeed, judging from the broad character of their demands and the vagueness of their general social and religious philosophy, one does not find it too difficult to understand the comment of a critical contemporary that the Society of Christian Socialists was "something like a society for the propagation of virtue in general." [59] Specifically, the Christian Socialists endorsed the eight-hour day, provision of free technical education and a midday meal for every student, direct legislation, emancipation of women, public employment of the unemployed, municipal public-housing and slum-clearance projects, municipal ownership of public utilities, national ownership of railroads, the telegraph, the telephone, and newly discovered mines, postal-savings banks, the issuance of money by the government directly to the people, and a graduated tax on land values that would ultimately result in the appropriation for the people of the entire value of the nation's natural resources. Christian Socialists, of course, hastened to point out that they placed their main reliance not on legislation but on the divine spirit and that their appeal was principally to the church rather than to the state.[60]

In accordance with his view that the principles of Christian Social-

[58] More explicit is his appraisal of the role of the state in the Christian Socialist scheme of things was the Reverend Franklin M. Sprague of Springfield, Massachusetts, who was apparently unconnected with the Boston group of Christian Socialists. Sprague pointed to the state as the only power capable of introducing and sustaining Christian Socialism. He contended that there were two opposing theories with respect to the functions of the state, one emphasizing individual liberty, the other social justice. Individual liberty, he argued, had been a necessary slogan with which to combat political despotism, but it was being used to justify the rapacity of the few. The state that stands for social justice, Sprague contended, serves the general welfare, and its functions must be sufficient unto this end. The only question to be raised with respect to the action of the state in any instance is, "will it conserve the public welfare?" See Sprague, *Socialism from Genesis to Revelation*, pp. 138–181.

[59] Nicholas Paine Gilman, "Christian Socialism in America," *Unitarian Review*, XXXII (October, 1889), 351.

[60] *Dawn*, I (May 15, 1889), 2; *ibid.*, I (July 15, 1889), 2; *ibid.*, III (June, 1891), 2; "What Christian Socialists Believe Should Be Done Now," *ibid.*, IV (October, 1892), 7–8; "What to Do Now. A Socialistic Programme," *ibid.*, VII (October, 1895), 5–6; Bliss, *What Christian Socialism Is*, pp. 19–20; "Christian Socialism," Bliss, ed., *Encyclopedia of Social Reform*, pp. 259–260.

ism must be implemented within the church, Bliss in 1890 founded the Mission of the Carpenter. The first meeting of the Mission led to the establishment of the Brotherhood of the Carpenter to consider the social applications of Christianity, and, as Charles H. Hopkins has pointed out, "the Society of Christian Socialists gradually became the Church of the Carpenter."

The Mission closed its doors in 1896, but Bliss's activities on behalf of socialism and reform continued undiminished. In order to propagate his beliefs with respect to Fabian Socialism, he projected an American Fabian League in 1895 and was, until its demise in 1900, the editor of the *American Fabian*. In 1897 he brought out his *Encyclopedia of Social Reform*, and followed up this significant effort to describe the diverse strands of the reform movement with fruitless attempts to provide organizational unity for that movement. He served as organizing secretary and later as traveling secretary of the Christian Social Union and was able in that capacity to expound the social teachings of Christ across the land. Until his death in 1926 Bliss continued to serve the cause of Christian Socialism.[61]

To the left of Bliss and the Society of Christian Socialists was the Congregational minister George D. Herron, without a doubt the most dramatic figure of the social-gospel movement in the 1890's. Herron first gained prominence in 1890, as the result of an address entitled "The Message of Jesus to Men of Wealth" that he delivered before the Minnesota Congregational Club. The next year he accepted a position at the First Congregational Church of Burlington, Iowa, and here his sermons attracted national attention. In 1893 he was called to Iowa College (now Grinnell College) to fill the chair of Applied Christianity endowed for him by Mrs. E. D. Rand, one of his wealthy Burlington parishioners. In addition to meeting his classes and writing for the religious weekly the *Kingdom*, Herron, who felt himself "overwhelmingly pursued by the conviction" that he "must . . . show what Christianity really is" and "must extricate the social ideals of Jesus from the mazes and tangles of traditional religion, and raise the ideal before the people," [62] lectured throughout the land on his version of the social gospel and called upon the church

---

[61] Hopkins, *Rise of the Social Gospel*, pp. 177–180; Howard H. Quint, *The Forging of American Socialism* (Columbia, S. C., 1953), pp. 117–118, 122–126; Thomas P. Jenkin, "The American Fabian Movement," *Western Political Quarterly*, I (June, 1948), 113–123.

[62] Herron to Lloyd, September 20, 1895, Lloyd Papers.

to reconstruct society in accord with the ideals of Christ. His increasingly radical pronouncements made him the subject of controversy wherever he went, and his attack on marriage as a "coercive institution" only added to his reputation as a social rebel. To save Iowa College authorities embarrassment, Herron resigned his position late in 1899.[63]

Without equivocation, Herron condemned existing conditions in market, state, and church. *"The worst charge that can be made against a Christian,"* he asserted, *"is that he attempts to justify the existing order."* It is an order based on the anarchic and atheistic principles of self-interest and competition and one in which it is impossible to attain social justice. It concentrates wealth in the hands of the few and impoverishes the many. It makes appeal to the lowest qualities of man and results in the survival of the unfit.[64] Herron denounced the church for its "manifest subservience to wealth" and repudiated church efforts to reconcile laissez-faire capitalism with Christianity as "treason to the kingdom of God." He referred to Protestantism as "practically a caste religion" that would rather keep the social movement within the bounds of Mammon than seek to implement the social ideals of Jesus.[65]

Herron's solution for the problems of the day was the cross, self-sacrifice. Moral progress, he declared, can come only through sacrifice. "Sacrifice, not self-interest, is the life of the individual, of society, of the nation." Only through suffering will society learn obedience to the ideals of Jesus and hence be regenerated. Everything must therefore be devoted to the service of man; fellowship must replace competition; service must replace greed; the cross must be made the standard of all values.[66]

Although "he was mainly an interpreter of Jesus—a religious

[63] Herron's career and views are discussed in Hopkins, *Rise of the Social Gospel,* pp. 184–200; Dombrowski, *Christian Socialism in America,* pp. 171–193; Quint, *Forging of American Socialism,* pp. 126–141; and Robert T. Handy, "George D. Herron and the Kingdom Movement," *Church History,* XIX (June, 1950), 97–115.

[64] Herron, *New Redemption,* p. 143; Herron, "The Message of Jesus to Men of Wealth," *Christian Union,* XLII (December 11, 1890), 804–805; Herron, *The Christian Society* (Chicago, 1894), p. 125; Herron, *The Christian State* (New York, 1895), pp. 87–102. An especially scathing indictment of the existing order can be found in Herron, *Between Caesar and Jesus* (New York, 1899), pp. 13–40 *et passim.*

[65] Herron, "The Opportunity of. the Church," *Arena,* XV (December, 1895), 42–48.

[66] Herron, "The Message of Jesus to Men of Wealth," *Christian Union,* XLII (December 11, 1890), 805; Herron, *New Redemption,* pp. 20–21, 39–43.

crusader rather than a political or social reformer," [67] Herron was fully conscious of the role the state might play in bringing into being the new social order that, in his view, obedience to Christ required. The state, he said, must be "the medium through which the law and order of God are received and wrought out in progress." It must become Christian and must translate the sacrifice of Christ into its laws. Indeed, the state can save itself only by following Christ. Its sociology and political economy should be that of the Sermon on the Mount. It must give up the worship of property and must abandon laissez faire, individualistic theories of freedom, and commercial theories of government. It can prove its right to exist only if it secures a greater measure of social justice. "It is the duty of the state to so reconstruct itself as to procure for every man full opportunity to develop all his powers, and to see that no member of society suffers for the want of work and bread."

Not only must the state become Christian, but Christianity must become political. Christianity needs the state for its realization as much as the state needs Christianity for its redemption and perfection. If Christianity supplies the only force that can procure social justice, the state is the only means whereby this force can reach all the people. "The state is the only organ through which the people can act collectively in the search for justice." [68]

The attainment of political democracy, Herron contended, is only the first step in the struggle for democracy. Democracy, if it is to survive, must become social and must take possession of the industrial world. The industrial well-being of the people must not depend on the will of a few men as it does now. Absolutism in industry must give way to industrial democracy, just as political absolutism has given way to political democracy. The individualistic theory of private property, in effect, makes private ownership impossible for the great majority of the people and results in the definition of human worth in terms of property rather than in terms of social righteousness. Society, however, does not exist to protect property, but, rather, property exists to support society. The rule of the people by property must therefore be replaced by the rule of property by the people. The people must take over the great industrial monopolies and must own and distribute the products of their labor. Through the agency of the state they can create an economy grounded in justice that will

[67] Abell, *Urban Impact on American Protestantism*, p. 80.

[68] Herron, *Christian State*, pp. 31, 53–65, 107–109; Herron, *New Redemption*, pp. 29–31, 34–35.

provide sustenance to all who work. Industrial democracy, "the social actualization of Christianity," can be achieved if the people will coöperate to secure a few basic reforms: proportional representation, civil-service reform, government ownership of the railways, and government control of certain sources of production.[69]

Only the selfish and the ignorant, Herron thought, would stand in the way of the extension of the industrial and economic functions of the state. Those who challenged state control on the grounds of economic liberty were, in his view, blind to the fact that the competitive system had already destroyed economic liberty. He was certain that association and collectivism would provide a hundred times more liberty than was provided by the existing order.[70]

Privately an adherent of the Socialist Labor party throughout the period, Herron in 1900 openly gave his support to Debs and the Social Democratic party. Whatever influence in religious circles he still enjoyed was, however, dissipated the next year, when, after being divorced by his wife for "cruelty, culminating in desertion," he married Mrs. Rand's daughter Carrie in a highly unconventional ceremony and was promptly expelled from the ministry of the Congregational Church for "immoral and unchristian conduct." Shortly thereafter Herron quit the United States for Italy. "Such," says Hopkins, "was the tragic end of the most brilliant episode in social-gospel history."[71]

V

The social-gospel movement was related to the subject of laissez faire and the general-welfare state in several important respects. Its most significant contribution to that subject was its attack on the philosophy of laissez faire. Striking at one of the most vulnerable points of this philosophy, social-gospel leaders stressed the fact that the argument for laissez faire was based on unethical and unchristian premises, that classical political economy and social Darwinism were morally incompatible with Christianity. In so contending, the proponents of social Christianity helped to discredit the let-alone policy and to clear away a formidable obstacle in the path of the general-welfare state.[72]

[69] Herron, *Christian State*, pp. 55–56, 86–105; Herron, *New Redemption*, pp. 31–35.

[70] Herron, *Christian State*, pp. 105–107.

[71] Hopkins, *Rise of the Social Gospel*, p. 200.

[72] Merle Curti contends that "no arguments against *laissez faire*, private enter-

The social-gospel movement also served as an important educational force. The educational work carried on by the various social-gospel organizations stimulated public interest in a number of problems of the day and helped to build up the necessary public support for a program of social and economic reform. Although the social gospel failed to win the unqualified adherence of labor or to convert any considerable number of conservatives,[73] it did exert a significant influence on the thought of the Progressive era. As Ralph H. Gabriel has noted, the social gospel constituted "the religious phase of the progressive movement." [74] Not only was its influence apparent in the thought of such Progressive leaders as Theodore Roosevelt, Robert La Follette, Tom Johnson, and "Golden Rule" Jones, but the philosophy of social Christianity also made a profound impression on those middle-class citizens who supported and sustained Progressivism. The social gospel made it possible for Progressives to "justify social change in terms of Christian doctrine" and thus gave to their cause "authority, power and a link with tradition." [75]

As for the concept of the general-welfare state, social gospelers, on the whole, were not overconcerned with that matter. Although they were effective critics of the existing order, their criticism was in the main destructive rather than constructive. They pointed to various maladjustments in the social and economic order, but other than a plea that individuals be better Christians, they generally had little that was positive to offer in the way of a solution. However, a few practical-minded leaders of the social-gospel movement, such as Richard T. Ely and Washington Gladden, saw that the state could be an effective ally of Christianity in attaining social justice and in promoting the general welfare. It was the influential lay advocate of the social gospel Richard T. Ely who took the lead in the formulation of a new ethical political economy that consigned laissez faire to the junk pile, that stressed welfare rather than wealth, and that proclaimed the virtues of the positive rather than the negative state. It is to this new political economy that we now turn our attention.

---

prise, and corporate wealth caused more concern to the champions of the existing order than those advanced in the name of Christ" (*The Growth of American Thought* [New York, 1943], p. 632). See also Godkin, "The Economic Man," in *Problems of Modern Democracy* (New York, 1897), pp. 174–178.

[73] May, *Protestant Churches and Industrial America*, pp. 213–224.

[74] Gabriel, *Course of American Democratic Thought*, p. 332.

[75] May, *Protestant Churches and Industrial America*, pp. 224–231. See also Roberts, "Economic and Political Ideas Expressed in the Early Social Gospel Movement," pp. 203–204, 207–208, 210–211.

VII

THE NEW POLITICAL ECONOMY

THE tenets of classical political economy so strongly held in the nineteenth century by professional and popular economists both in Europe and America were subjected to vigorous attack in the middle years of the century by the historical school of political economy. The most prominent members of the historical school were the German economists Wilhelm Roscher, Bruno Hildebrand, and Karl Knies. These men did not believe that there was anything immutable about the economic laws elucidated by the classical economists: economic truth, they maintained, is relative rather than absolute. Since the progress of history gives rise to new facts and new conditions that completely alter the economic environment, economic theory and economic laws must be adjusted to the conditions of a particular age and a particular locale.

The historical school also found the psychology of the classical economists to be inadequate. Man, they asserted, cannot be regarded as a creature who is completely absorbed in the pursuit of gain and who is constantly motivated by self-interest. Other motives than self-interest are present in the economic world, and these cannot be ignored in the formulation of economic theory. The historical-minded economists were likewise critical of the methodology of the classicists and insisted that economic principles must be based primarily on inductive rather than deductive reasoning. In place of the deductive logic employed by Malthus and Ricardo, they proposed the study of economic history and the use of statistics as the means of arriving at a proper understanding of the existing economic order.

The principles of Roscher, Knies, and Hildebrand were further developed by a second generation of German historical economists, the so-called younger historical school. Like their predecessors, these economists stressed the relativity of economic truth, the need for historical study and statistics, and the use of the inductive method. However, such leaders of the younger group as Gustav von Schmoller and Adolf Wagner were more concerned than the earlier historical economists with ethical and humanitarian ideals and with the necessity for emphasis on the moral element in economic study. They also evidenced a greater interest than the first generation of historical economists in the potentialities of state action and tended to regard the state as a means of solidifying national feeling and of promoting social justice. Through the use of state power they hoped to bring about a more equitable distribution of wealth and a greater degree of well-being for the working classes. Their activity led to the calling of a congress in 1872 at Eisenach at which leading figures in academic and public life proclaimed their opposition to the Manchester School and laissez faire. From the deliberations of this congress emerged the *Verein für Sozialpolitik*, an organization designed to gather the scientific material necessary to further the cause of social reform in Germany.[1]

The views of the German leaders of the historical school of political economy reached the United States through the medium of a group of young American economists who, in the 1870's and 1880's, went to Germany to further their academic education. Most prominent among these economists were Richard T. Ely, Henry Carter Adams, Edmund J. James, Simon Nelson Patten, John Bates Clark, Edwin R. A. Seligman, and Richmond Mayo-Smith. In Germany these men were taught a new scientific approach to the study of economics. They were impressed by the ethical view of economics and the humanitarianism of such economists as Karl Knies, Johannes Conrad, and Adolf Wagner, and they observed in Germany that an efficient state could do much for the general welfare. As a group they became dissatisfied with the doctrines of classical economics and laissez faire. They were determined to "break the 'crust'" that had formed over the study of political economy in the United States and to formulate a

---

[1] Charles Gide and Charles Rist, *A History of Economic Doctrines from the Time of the Physiocrats to the Present Day* (Boston, n. d.), pp. 379–407, 436–448; Harry Elmer Barnes, ed., *The History and Prospects of the Social Sciences* (New York, 1925), pp. 378–381; John Kells Ingram, *A History of Political Economy* (New York, 1897), pp. 200–215; Philip Charles Newman, *The Development of Economic Thought* (New York, 1952), pp. 183–192, 207–208.

new political economy that would be more compatible with the realities of the age in which they lived.[2]   In accord with this desire, they attempted to divorce political economy from laissez faire and to associate it more closely with the general-welfare state.

In common with the historical school of political economy in Europe, the new school of political economy in the United States, which was the American equivalent of the historical school, repudiated the basic tenets of classical political economy that lay at the core of the doctrine of laissez faire.   The leaders of the new school maintained that there is a close relationship between ethics and economics, considered economic truth relative rather than absolute, championed the inductive method, and criticized the assumptions of the laissez-faire credo with respect to self-interest and competition.

New-school economists were critical of the attempt of the classical economists to divorce economics from ethics and of their contention that the economist should not permit his analysis of the laws governing the production, exchange, and distribution of wealth to be influenced by any consideration of what ought to be.   To economists of the new school, it appeared that ethics was very much a part of economics.[3]   Their concern with the ethical implications of economic phenomena stemmed, primarily, from two sources.   As already noted, the relationship between ethics and economics had been impressed upon them by their German teachers, but more important than the German influence was the impulse of social Christianity.   Leading members of the new school, such as Richard T. Ely, John R. Commons, Edward W. Bemis, Henry Carter Adams, and John Bates Clark, were also important figures in the social-gospel movement, or were at least influenced by its point of view.[4]   They carried over to economics the

[2] J. F. Normano, *The Spirit of American Economics* (New York, 1943), pp. 134–135; Richard T. Ely, *Ground under Our Feet: An Autobiography* (New York, 1938), pp. 44, 58, 121, 132, 145–146; Joseph Dorfman, "The Role of the German Historical School in American Economic Thought," *American Economic Review*, XLV (May, 1955), 17–28.

[3] Ely considered the emphasis on ethics the most marked characteristic of the new school of political economy (*An Introduction to Political Economy* [New York, 1889], p. 119).   Speaking of the members of the new school, Godkin declared: "Their clothes are economical, but their talk is ethical" ("The Economic Man," in *Problems of Modern Democracy* [New York, 1897], p. 166).

[4] The role of Ely and Commons in the social-gospel movement was discussed in Chapter VI.   For Bemis' views on the subject, see Bemis, "The Relation of the Church to the Social Question," *Dawn*, II (July–August, 1890), 148–158.   Adams originally intended to enter the ministry and actually did enroll in Andover Theological Seminary in 1875, but he abandoned the ministry for economics "not so much

message of the social gospel that Christian ethics must be applied to all branches of human endeavor. The economics they propounded was scientific, but it was also ethical. It is thus easy to understand why a proponent of social Christianity such as the Reverend Josiah Strong should have hailed the new school as "a Christian school of political economy" and why twenty-three clergymen, including Washington Gladden, Lyman Abbott, R. Heber Newton, and Newman Smyth, were charter members of the American Economic Association, which was founded by new-school economists in 1885.[5]

In line with its ethical predilections, the new school of political economy placed man rather than wealth in the center of the economic stage and subordinated everything to his welfare. Pointing to the human factor as the leading element in production, new-school economists condemned the principle of self-interest as unchristian and advocated brotherhood and a regard for one's fellows in its stead. They called on such ethical agencies as the church, the school, and the state to help guide economic development.[6]

Although a regard for ethics was characteristic of the new school as a whole, it was most apparent in the thought of Richard T. Ely, the founder and the most influential figure of the new school. To Ely, the establishment of the new school of political economy denoted "a return to the grand principles of common sense and Christian precept." He believed that "love, generosity, nobility of character, self-sacrifice, and all that is best and truest in our nature have their place in economic life." Since he was convinced that man, to a certain extent,

---

for itself as constituting an avenue through which to reach his goal of ethical reform." Adams lectured for several summers at the Plymouth School of Applied Ethics. See "Memorial to Former President Henry C. Adams," *American Economic Review*, XII (September, 1922), 403–406. See also the references in n. 6.

[5] Strong to Ely, November 17, 1888, Ely Papers, State Historical Society of Wisconsin; Ely, "Report of the Organization of the American Economic Association," *Publications of the American Economic Association*, I (1886), 8, 43–46. (Henceforth, *Publications of the American Economic Association* will be referred to as *A. E. A. Publications*.)

[6] "It is now on all hands silently taken for granted," E. Benjamin Andrews declared, "that the actual subject-matter of our science is *weal*, whereas in its classical days *wealth*, a very different notion, held that post of honor" ("Political Economy, Old and New," *Andover Review*, VI [August, 1886], 139). See also Adams, *Christianity as a Social Force* (Ann Arbor, Mich., 1892); Clark, "Christianity and Modern Economics," *New Englander and Yale Review*, XLVII (July, 1887), 50–51; Andrews, "Individualism as a Sociological Principle," *Yale Review*, II (May, 1893), 16–18; and Mayo-Smith, " 'The Dismal Science,' " *Craftsman*, VII (November 9, 1889), 1.

is capable of directing economic development, he thought that the economist must have an ethical ideal in mind as the goal of economic effort and must show how this goal can be attained. As Ely saw it, the ethical ideal consisted in "the most perfect development of all human faculties in each individual." To promote this ideal, he favored such a production and distribution of economic goods as would subserve the purpose of existence of all members of society, and he believed that all economic facts should be measured by this ethical standard. Thus, to Ely, low wages and long working hours, which served to diminish the ability of the worker to participate in the benefits of civilization, stood condemned as ethically unjust. He did not expect industrial society to achieve the ethical ideal immediately, but he did think that it should point its efforts in that direction.[7]

Ely's ethical views led him away from an economic philosophy interested primarily in the individual to a concern for society and the general well-being. He rejected the view that each man must look out for himself and that social classes owe nothing to one another. Regarding the interests of men to be "inextricably intertwined" and believing the law of brotherhood applicable to the economic field, he espoused the idea of social solidarity. Our welfare, he asserted, is a social matter; "our weal is a common weal."[8]

Impressed with the Darwinian hypothesis, the new school of political economy refused to grant to the doctrines of classical economics the immutability that was sometimes claimed for them. They insisted on the relativity of economic truth and the necessity of adjusting economic thought to the conditions of a particular time and a particular society. "The modern school," Columbia's Edwin Seligman declared, ". . . holds that the economic theories of any generation must be regarded primarily as the outgrowth of the peculiar conditions of time, place, and nationality, under which the doctrines were evolved, and that no particular set of tenets can arrogate to itself the claim of immutable truth, or the assumption of universal applicability to all countries or epochs."[9]

[7] Ely, "The Past and the Present of Political Economy," *Johns Hopkins University Studies in Historical and Political Science*, II (1884), 186, 202; Ely, *Social Aspects of Christianity, and Other Essays* (New York, 1889), pp. 115–132; Ely, "Ethics and Economics," in Ely *et al.*, *Science Economic Discussion* (New York, 1886), pp. 44–56; Ely, *The Labor Movement in America* (New York, 1886), pp. 311–313, 320–322; Ely, *Introduction to Political Economy*, pp. 84–86.

[8] Ely, *The Social Law of Service* (Cincinnati, 1896), p. 127.

[9] Seligman, "Continuity of Economic Thought," in Ely *et al.*, *Science Economic*

Applying this view to the doctrine of laissez faire, Seligman pointed out that the plea of laissez faire had originated essentially as a protest against the excessive restrictions of the mercantilist era. The physiocrats and Adam Smith had rightly objected to the regulations that in their day obstructed the artisan, the farmer, and the merchant. They had been correct in calling for an end to paternal government and for the adoption of a policy of laissez faire. Seligman, however, argued that the industrial revolution, which was in its infancy when Smith wrote his great work, had ushered in a host of new problems that did not exist in 1776 and had made society so complex that laissez faire was no longer a tenable policy. Edmund James, who was professor of public finance and administration at the Wharton School of Finance and Economy between 1883 and 1896 and was the founder of the American Academy of Political and Social Science, similarly contended that in Smith's day the best interest of the public required that government activity be curtailed and that private enterprise be set free but that in his own day the same public interest made it imperative that the government be called on to regulate private enterprise. "It is an historical rule of wide application," declared Henry Carter Adams, in words to which none of the new-school economists would have taken exception, "that as countries become more populous, and the social and industrial relations more complex, the functions of government must necessarily extend to continuously new objects." A laissez-faire economist such as David A. Wells, who refused to recognize this "historical rule," was dismissed by Simon Patten as "an eighteenth century man commenting on nineteenth century facts." [10]

Since the new school emphasized the evolution of economic truth rather than the fixed character of economic laws,[11] it is quite obvious

Discussion, pp. 1–2, 21–22. See also Adams, *Outline of Lectures upon Political Economy* (2d ed.; Ann Arbor, Mich., 1886), p. 4; Patten, *The Economic Basis of Protection* (2d ed.; Philadelphia, 1895), p. 10; James, Preface, in Ingram, *History of Political Economy*, pp. vii–xiii.

[10] Seligman, "Continuity of Economic Thought," in Ely *et al., Science Economic Discussion*, pp. 9–13; James, "The Relation of the Modern Municipality to the Gas Supply," *A. E. A. Publications*, I (1886), 53–54; Adams, *Public Debts* (New York, 1887), p. 394; Patten, "Wells' Recent Economic Changes," *Political Science Quarterly*, V (March, 1890), 102.

[11] The brilliant Thorstein Veblen complained that the economics of the historical school fell far short of being an evolutionary science. The historical school, he maintained, had provided "a narrative survey of phenomena, not a genetic account of an unfolding process." "An evolutionary economics," he contended, "must be the theory of a process of cultural growth as determined by the economic interest, a theory of a cumulative sequence of economic institutions stated in terms of the

that it found the deductive method of reasoning inadequate for its purposes. It championed the inductive method, which proceeds from the observation of facts to general rules and principles. It rejected all a priori principles and looked to history and statistics to provide the facts of economic life. With the information thus obtained, the young economists approached economic problems in a pragmatic spirit, judging each case on its individual merits. In this way they sought to prevent economic science from degenerating into a few abstract formulas divorced from the realities of the age.[12]

The basic assumptions of the laissez-faire faith with respect to competition and self-interest were also discarded by the new school of political economy. New-school economists, as will be noted in greater detail later, did not believe that competition exists in all spheres of the economy, nor did they regard unrestricted competition as necessarily a beneficent force even within the area of the economy that is subject to its sway. Competition, Seligman declared, "does not exist universally," and it "does not always work evenly; it often secures undue advantages to the unscrupulous; it has given birth to great abuses in the factory system and the fraudulent speculation of modern society." [13]

The psychology of the classical economists also came in for severe criticism. New-school economists insisted that self-interest is not necessarily the chief motive in economic life. They maintained that

process itself" ("Why Is Economics Not an Evolutionary Science?" *Quarterly Journal of Economics*, XII [July, 1898], 375, 386–388, 393).

Although Veblen was critical of the various schools of economists (and particularly of the preconceptions of the classical economists), he did not interest himself directly in the question of the role of the state in promoting the general welfare. His only "canon of welfare," as Paul T. Homan has indicated, was the "maximum output of goods." See Veblen, "The Preconceptions of Economic Science," *Quarterly Journal of Economics*, XIII (January, July, 1899), 121–150, 396–426; XIV (February, 1900), 240–269; and Homan, *Contemporary Economic Thought* (New York, 1928), pp. 108, 176–177.

[12] Mayo-Smith, "Methods of Investigation in Political Economy," in Ely *et al.*, *Science Economic Discussion*, pp. 104–122; Ely, "The Past and the Present of Political Economy," *Johns Hopkins University Studies*, II (1884), 183–185, 202. Ely referred to this method as the "look and see" method (*Ground under Our Feet*, p. 186). Henry Carter Adams praised the "method of study and skill of systemization" of the German historical school but rejected the "centralizing tendency" of German economics ("The Position of Socialism in the Historical Development of Political Economy," *Penn Monthly*, X [April, 1879], 293–294).

[13] Seligman, "Railway Tariffs and the Interstate Commerce Law. II," *Political Science Quarterly*, II (September, 1887), 370.

considerations of national honor, devotion to principle, and altruistic regard for one's fellow men figure prominently in the action of individuals in pursuit of a livelihood, and they did not regard as adequate any psychology of economic activity that did not take account of these social considerations. Furthermore, the new-school economists were unwilling to assume that the individual knows his own best interests and that, if left free, will act accordingly. It is an obvious fact, they asserted, that the individual will sacrifice what is ultimately to his own advantage for the sake of some immediate pleasure.[14]

The new-school economists were particularly critical of the assumption of Adam Smith that the individual in following his own self-interest unconsciously serves the best interests of society and that, therefore, state intervention is both unwise and unnecessary. They categorically denied that the interests of the individual and the interests of society are necessarily identical and repudiated the notion that when any particular individual advances his own interests, he automatically furthers the permanent interests of society. As evidences of their contention, new-school economists pointed to the improvident exploitation of the natural resources of the country and to the construction of railroads beyond the existing needs of the nation. "Private self-interest," they therefore concluded, "is too powerful, or too ignorant, or too immoral to promote the common good without compulsion." [15]

New-school economists also rejected the standard argument of some of the exponents of laissez faire that although theoretically there were some things the state might do for the general welfare, existing governments were too inefficient and corrupt to assume the added burden of new duties. Adams, Ely, James, and others asserted that if existing governments left so much to be desired, it was precisely because their duties had been restricted within the narrowest possible

[14] Ely, "The Past and the Present of Political Economy," *Johns Hopkins University Studies,* II (1884), 173–176; Ely, *Introduction to Political Economy,* pp. 151–153; Adams, "Relation of the State to Industrial Action," *A. E. A. Publications,* I (1887), 484–486; George B. Newcomb, "Political Economy in Its Relations to Ethics," *Christian Thought,* 3d Ser. (1885), p. 279; Andrews, "Individualism as a Sociological Principle," *Yale Review,* II (May, 1893), 19–21.

[15] See Adams, "Relation of the State to Industrial Action," *A. E. A. Publications,* I (1887), 481–484; Newcomb, "Political Economy in Its Relations to Ethics," *Christian Thought,* 3d Ser. (1885), pp. 274–275; Ely, *Introduction to Political Economy,* pp. 98–99; and John R. Commons, *The Distribution of Wealth* (New York, 1893), p. 61.

limits. This had persuaded men of talent to offer their services to private corporations rather than to the state [16] and had caused the citizenry to pay but scant attention to the functioning of government. Weakened, the state had become a prey to the assaults of private interests and powerful corporations. If the state were given more important duties, however, better men would be attracted to the public service, and the voters would evidence a greater interest in government and would exercise greater care in the selection of public officials. A strong state would also be able to resist the corrupting influence of special interests. Thus, whereas laissez faire had resulted in the degradation of the public service, enlargement of government functions would result in its improvement.[17]

Having rejected the basic postulates of classical economics upon which the philosophy of laissez faire was founded, the new-school economists saw no logical necessity for adhering to laissez faire either as a principle of universal application or as a maxim with a presumption in its favor.[18] Furthermore, their study of the practice of states, past and present, convinced them that not only was laissez faire false as a theory but that, in fact, no government had ever been able to conform to its requirements.[19] Thus impressed with the inadequacies of laissez faire both as a scientific theory and as a practice and impelled by their appreciation of the complexities of the industrial age in which they lived and by their desire to fulfill the requirements of

[16] Adams insisted that it was the failure of society properly to "correlate public and private activity" that had produced public corruption. Social harmony could prevail, he believed, only if equal inducements were offered in both the private and public spheres of activity. See Adams, *Public Debts,* pp. 367–375; and Adams, "Relation of the State to Industrial Action," *A. E. A. Publications,* I (1887), 528–540.

[17] Ely, *Socialism: An Examination of Its Nature . . . with Suggestions for Social Reform* (New York, 1894), p. 284; Ely, *Problems of To-day: A Discussion of Protective Tariffs, Taxation, and Monopolies* (New York, 1890), p. 237; Ely, Introduction, in William E. Barns, ed., *The Labor Problem* (New York, 1886), p. 16; James, "The State as an Economic Factor," in Ely *et al., Science Economic Discussion,* pp. 32–33; Adams, "Relation of the State to Industrial Action," *A. E. A. Publications,* I (1887), 528–540.

[18] Adams criticized as unscientific the point of view of such economists as Francis Amasa Walker who denied the validity of the premises of laissez faire and yet claimed that there was a presumption in its favor ("Relation of the State to Industrial Action," *A. E. A. Publications,* I [1887], 487–490).

[19] See, for example, Ely, "The Past and the Present of Political Economy," *Johns Hopkins University Studies,* II (1884), 161–162.

the ethical ideal, the economists of the new school worked out a new philosophy of the general welfare that, for the greater part, required the action of the state for its realization.

As Ely has said, those who thought that the new school was interested only in methodology or the gathering of facts did not see beyond the surface. The young economists wanted to promote the welfare of the mass of the people and thus to bring about a better world. By a study of "life itself," they hoped to gather the necessary information with which to mold the forces at work in society and to improve existing conditions. They were quite certain that the individual is not a mere pawn of the environment, that progress consists not in man's subjection to natural laws but rather in his subjugation of nature. They believed that "within certain limits we can have just such a kind of economic life as we wish." As economists, they therefore felt that they had a responsibility for shaping "the character of the national economy" and for promoting the general welfare. "In a certain sense," declared Richard T. Ely, "the political economist is to the general public what the attorney is to the private individual." [20]

As "attorneys" for the general public, the new-school economists called on the state to take positive action in behalf of the general well-being. They rejected unequivocally the laissez-faire theory of the state. "We do not regard it [the state] as a merely negative factor, the influence of which is most happy when it is smallest," declared Edmund James, "but we recognize that some of the most necessary functions of a civilized society can be performed only by the state, and some others most efficiently by the state; that the state, in a word, is a permanent category of economic life, and not merely a temporary crutch which may be cast away when society becomes more perfect." "We do not need a new world nor a new man," Simon Patten declared, "but we do need a new society and a state whose power will be superior to that of any combination of selfish individuals, and whose duties will be commensurate with human wants." "That is not the

[20] Ely, *Ground under Our Feet*, pp. 153–155; Ely, *Introduction to Political Economy*, pp. 37–38, 96, 99–100, 109; Ely, "Political Economy in America," *North American Review*, CXLIV (February, 1887), 119; Ely, "Socialism," *Andover Review*, V (February, 1886), 161. "I do not believe that this is the best of all possible worlds," Mayo-Smith wrote to Atkinson on June 20, 1890. "I do believe that it can be made a good deal better than it is and what we are trying to discover is how to adjust institutions more perfectly to human needs" (Edward Atkinson Papers, Massachusetts Historical Society).

best government which governs least, but which governs the most wisely," asserted Henry Carter Adams.[21]

And from the new-school point of view, the government "which governs the most wisely" is the one that addresses itself to the amelioration of the conditions under which its citizens live and work, that performs general-welfare functions. "The State," Henry Carter Adams contended, "exists for its citizens, and its chief service is to provide conditions under which the activities of citizens may prosper." [22] "Government," asserted James, "should interfere in all instances where its interference will tell for better health, better education, better morals, greater comfort of the community." It should coöperate with private enterprise in seeking to extend to as many people as possible "the benefits of . . . modern civilization," and it should "assist to the extent of its power in bettering the conditions under which the great mass of the people have to earn their living." [23] The state, new-school economists thought, should minister to the social and economic needs of the people not only by restraining antisocial activities but also by assuming functions of a positive, fostering type. It should be an agency both for regulation and for service.[24] They would, indeed, permit no arbitrary limit to be imposed on the right of the state to act "save its ability to do good." The government, said the president

[21] Statement by James, in Ely, "Report of the Organization of the American Economic Association," *A. E. A. Publications,* I (1886), 26; Patten, "The Consumption of Wealth," in Ely *et al., Science Economic Discussion,* p. 135; Adams, "An Interpretation of the Social Movements of Our Time," *International Journal of Ethics,* II (October, 1891), 43.

[22] Adams, *The Science of Finance: An Analysis of Public Expenditures and Public Revenues* (New York, 1899), pp. 31–32.

[23] James, "State Interference," *Chautauquan,* VIII (June, 1888), 535–536. See also James, "Factory Laws," in John J. Lalor, ed., *Cyclopaedia of Political Science, Political Economy, and of the Political History of the United States* (Chicago, 1883–1884), II, 154–155.

[24] Analyzing the role of the state as an economic factor, James concluded that state action of a fostering type as well as of a restraining type had ever been a condition of economic development. He believed that "compulsory associative action" by the state was necessary to build highways and to undertake drainage projects, to care for the forests, to encourage the building of railroads, and, in general, to undertake tasks that did not appear profitable to the individual ("The State as an Economic Factor," in Ely *et al., Science Economic Discussion,* pp. 26–31, 33–34). See also James, "The Government in Its Relation to the Forests," Department of Agriculture, Forestry Division, *Bulletin No. 2* (1888), pp. 23–31; Ely, *Introduction to Political Economy,* p. 262; and Mayo-Smith, "Social Problems: How They Arise . . . ," *Christian Thought,* 5th Ser. (1888), pp. 427–428.

of Brown University, E. Benjamin Andrews, "should do at any time and place all that it is then and there for the true and permanent weal of society at large that it should do." [25]

Ely made it clear that the state action on behalf of the general welfare that new-school economists advocated was not to be construed as paternalism. In a democratic state, he explained, the government is not something apart from the people. It *is* the people. In fact, it is the only institution that stands for all of the people, not just some of the people. When the people, therefore, use the democratic state to promote their own interests, they are not subjecting themselves to paternalism but are merely helping themselves. The proper term to apply to such governmental action is fraternalism, not paternalism. [26]

Although the tendency of nineteenth-century liberalism had been to associate liberalism with laissez faire, new-school economists did not regard their plea for increased state action as antithetical in any way to the liberty of the individual or to the tenets of liberalism. Their aim, like that of earlier liberals, was to secure individual freedom and equality of opportunity for individual development. Liberty, however, they argued, has its positive as well as its negative aspects. It means not only absence of restraint but the "presence of conditions which make possible the unfolding of our faculties." As a matter of fact, in the prevailing industrial society, the emphasis on the negative aspects of liberty, on the policy of laissez faire, resulted, they believed, not in liberty and the realization of liberal ideals but rather in the abuse of liberty, in "a degrading dependence of some men upon others and consequently social degradation." It meant a narrowing of opportunity, excessive inequalities in the distribution of wealth, and the abuse of the weak by the strong. [27]

[25] See Ely, *Introduction to Political Economy*, p. 92; and Andrews, "Individualism as a Sociological Principle," *Yale Review*, II (May, 1893), 27. Although Andrews believed that there was a presumption in favor of laissez faire, he was closer in his thought to Ely than to Francis Walker. He recognized that "automatism" was insufficient in the economic sphere and that "wits and planning" were essential (*ibid.*, pp. 25–27).

[26] Ely, "Fraternalism *vs.* Paternalism in Government," *Century*, N.S., XXXIII (March, 1898), 781–784; Ely, *Introduction to Political Economy*, p. 89; Ely, Introduction, in Barns, ed., *Labor Problem*, p. 12.

[27] Sherwood, "Tendencies in American Economic Thought," *Johns Hopkins University Studies in Historical and Political Science*, XV (December, 1897), 597–598; Ely, "A Programme for Labor Reform," *Century*, N.S., XVII (April, 1890), 951; Ely, "The Next Things in Social Reform," *Christian Union*, XLIII (April 23,

If freedom were actually to be preserved in an industrial society, new-school economists contended, some degree of regulation by the state was necessary. "The multiplying relations of men with one another" that characterize an industrial society, Richard T. Ely told the Madison Literary Society in an address in 1897, make "regulation by the power of the state . . . a condition of freedom." The state action that he advocated might perhaps "lessen the amount of theoretical liberty," but he was confident that it would "increase control over nature in the individual, and promote the growth of practical liberty."

Like Ely, E. Benjamin Andrews was also of the opinion that the individual does not automatically become less free simply because the government increases its functions. State action might actually "increase the average net freedom of all men who come within the scope of its power." John R. Commons, in similar fashion, argued that state action of the proper sort constituted the means of implementing a higher individualism. "If governmental control serves to stimulate the self-reliant energies of the people, if it opens up new avenues for private enterprise, if it equalizes and widens the opportunity for employment, if it prevents injustice, oppression, and monopoly, if it stimulates a noble ambition, inspires hopefulness, and vouchsafes rewards where they are earned, then," Commons declared, "government is not socialistic but rather is supplementing the highest individualism." [28] Thus did new-school economists advocate a positive brand of liberalism to replace the negative liberalism of the Manchester School and of Jefferson.

Although new-school economists did not fear state action and al-

---

1891), 532; Ely, "The Nature and Significance of Corporations," *Harper's Monthly Magazine,* LXXIV (May, 1887), 970; Ely, Introduction, in Barns, ed., *Labor Problem,* pp. 13–14; Ely, "The Evolution of Industrial Society" (an address to the Madison Literary Society, 1897), Ely Papers; Ely, "Liberty a Social Product," *Our Day,* XVI (December, 1896), 671–672; Mayo-Smith, "Social Problems," *Christian Thought,* 5th Ser. (1886), pp. 428–429.

[28] See Ely, "The Evolution of Industrial Society," Ely Papers; Ely, "Liberty a Social Product," *Our Day,* XVI (December, 1896), 672; Ely, "The Growth of Corporations," *Harper's Monthly Magazine,* LXXV (June, 1887), 78–79; Andrews, "A Symposium upon the Relation of the State to the Individual," *Dawn,* II (November, 1890), 299; and Commons, "Progressive Individualism," *American Magazine of Civics,* VI (June, 1895), 565. See also Seligman, "The Living Wage," *Gunton's Institute Bulletin,* I (March 26, 1898), 264; Sherwood, "Tendencies in American Economic Thought," *Johns Hopkins University Studies,* XV (December, 1897), 597–598; and Mayo-Smith, "Social Problems," *Christian Thought,* 5th Ser. (1888), pp. 428–429.

though they placed the welfare of society above that of any individual, they did not indulge in any Hegelian worship of the state. They did not wish to see the state encroach upon the legitimate sphere of the individual or to dull "the spur of individual initiative." They wanted rather to harmonize public and private activity, to determine by scientific investigation the proper bounds of each.[29] Through state action and social reform, they hoped to find some middle ground between a rigid conservatism and an uncompromising radicalism, between laissez faire and socialism. Thus Ely, who, as we shall see, wished to steer a middle course between a conservatism that resisted social reform and a radicalism that would destroy all that had already been achieved, declared: "I condemn alike that individualism which would allow the state no room for industrial activity, and that socialism which would absorb in the state the functions of the individual."

Like Ely, Edward W. Bemis, who taught economics at various institutions in the 1880's and 1890's and then became Cleveland's superintendent of water works in the first decade of the twentieth century, sought a "golden mean" between laissez faire and socialism and found it in "moderate State action, less, indeed, than demanded by the socialist, but greater than at present." Henry Carter Adams, who was also looking for a middle course between unrestrained individualism and complete government control, spoke of "the tyranny of German socialism and . . . the yet greater tyranny of anarchy." "It is my wish," Adams asserted in a letter to President James B. Angell of the University of Michigan in which he set forth his basic social philosophy, "that our civilization may be saved from the sterility of what is commonly called socialism, and to that end I advocate a further development of proprietary rights and a further development of the science of government." [30]

[29] Seligman, "Continuity of Economic Thought," in Ely *et al., Science Economic Discussion,* p. 23; Andrews, "A Symposium upon the Relation of the State to the Individual," *Dawn,* II (November, 1890), 300; Andrews, *Wealth and Moral Law* (Hartford, Conn., 1894), pp. 111–112; Smith, "Social Problems," *Christian Thought,* 5th Ser. (1888), pp. 428–429; statements by Ely, Adams, and James, in Ely, "Report of the Organization of the American Economic Association," *A. E. A. Publications,* I (1886), 17, 21–22, 26–27; William W. Folwell, "Protective Tariffs as a Question of National Economy," in Albert Shaw, ed., *The National Revenues: A Collection of Papers by American Economists* (Chicago, 1888), pp. 37–38.

[30] Ely, "The Economic Discussion in Science," in Ely *et al., Science Economic Discussion,* p. 69; Bemis, "Socialism and State Action," *Journal of Social Science,* XXI (September, 1886), 56; Adams *et al.,* "The 'Labor Problem,'" *Scientific American Supplement,* XXII (August 21, 1886), 8863; Adams to Angell, March 25, 1886,

Although new-school economists believed that there is much the state can and should do, their view of state action was essentially a pragmatic one. They did not regard the state as necessarily evil or as necessarily "a worker of righteousness"; nor did they think that there was any necessary presumption in favor of state action or in favor of individual action. They believed that each proposition to expand the functions of government should be examined on its own merits "in the light of history and experience" and of the demonstrated needs of the time "rather than in the light of doubtful deductions from imperfect premises." State aid, they thought, should be invoked "wherever it promises to produce more good than harm for the society concerned."[31] They recognized that there were many ways in which the state could serve the general welfare, and so they did not hesitate to enlist its aid. They supported increased action, however, not out of any desire to glorify the state but rather because they thought that such action would improve and enrich the life of the individual and of the society in which he lived.

II

As a means of implementing their ideas with respect to the necessity for objective research and for a new view of the responsibilities of the state in relation to the general welfare, the economists of the new school turned to organization. Interest in this direction culminated in 1885 with the formation of the American Economic Association. The protest against laissez faire, at least insofar as the founders of the organization were concerned, was an important aspect of the early history of the American Economic Association.[32] However, this feature of the Association became progressively less important, and

---

Angell Papers, Michigan Historical Collections. For similar statements, see Seligman, "Continuity of Economic Thought," in Ely *et al.*, *Science Economic Discussion*, p. 23; and James, "State Interference," *Chautauquan*, VIII (June, 1888), 534.

[31] See Andrews, *Wealth and Moral Law*, p. 112; Andrews, "A Symposium upon the Relation of the State to the Individual," *Dawn*, II (November, 1890), 300; statement by Adams, in Ely, "Report of the Organization of the American Economic Association," *A. E. A. Publications*, I (1886), 21; Adams, "Relation of the State to Industrial Action," *ibid.*, I (1887), 494–495; Henry S. Green, "Mr. Godkin and the New Political Economy," *Arena*, XX (July, 1898), 37; James, "Relation of the Modern Municipality to the Gas Supply," *A. E. A. Publications*, I (1886), 81–83; and James, "State Interference," *Chautauquan*, VIII (June, 1888), 536.

[32] Ely, "The American Economic Association 1885–1909 . . . ," *A. E. A. Publications*, 3d Ser., XI (1910), 71–72; Ely, *Ground under Our Feet*, pp. 132–133.

by 1892 the American Economic Association had become simply a scholarly organization, without any direct interest in state policy and social reform.

First of the new-school economists to attempt to form an organization of economists to promote the causes of economic research and social reform were Simon Nelson Patten and Edmund J. James. Both men had studied under Johannes Conrad at the University of Halle, and he had convinced them that if American students of political economy were to have any influence on practical politics, it would be necessary for them to form in the United States an organization similar to the German *Verein für Sozialpolitik*.[33] In the winter of 1884–1885 Patten and James drew up a constitution for a Society for the Study of National Economy, an organization designed to resemble the *Verein für Sozialpolitik*. As the constitution indicated, the two economists thought that the proposed organization should not only "encourage the careful investigation and free discussion of the special problems of our national economy," but that it should also "combat the widespread view that our economic problems will solve themselves, and that our laws and institutions which at present favor individual instead of collective action can promote the best utilization of our material resources and secure to each individual the highest development of all his faculties."

The platform that Patten and James included in the constitution so as to indicate the attitude of the proposed organization toward existing social and economic problems boldly asserted that the state "is a positive factor in material production," that it therefore "has legitimate claims to a share of the product," and that the best interests of the public require that the state should appropriate this share and apply it to the promotion of the general welfare.

The platform repudiated the notion that true economy in government consists in the reduction of public revenues rather than in an efficient use of public funds to "promote public ends." It declared that it was idle to expect good administration "in a society where the people view the state as a merely negative factor in national life, and . . . therefore . . . attempt to remedy administrative evils by limiting government action instead of purifying and rendering efficient government service." The best way to attain "purity and economy in our administration," the platform asserted, was to have the state assume its proper functions. The consequent importance of govern-

[33] Statement by James, *A. E. A. Publications*, 3d Ser., XI (1910), 108.

ment service would focus public attention on public affairs and would result in an economical administration.

The existing educational system was pronounced a failure because it had not succeeded in maintaining the proper standards of "intelligence and industrial efficiency." The blame for this was placed on local authorities, and it was therefore proposed that the national government "protect the rights and interests of the whole against the short-sightedness and selfishness of the parts" by supplementing local revenue for education with national grants in aid.[34]

The platform asserted that the problems that had arisen as a result of the struggle between labor and capital would have to be studied and solved with reference to the best interests of the community. The public interest required that the sanitary and industrial conditions of the laborer be such as to enable him and his family to become useful citizens. Such conditions could be realized only if the workingman received adequate compensation and if he had sufficient leisure time for mental and moral growth. Also, if the nation's material resources were to be utilized effectively, "the qualities upon which the accumulation of capital depend" would have to be developed in all classes of society. Existing laws, however, hindered the growth of these qualities because they encouraged the consolidation of capital and industry in a few hands "instead of that system which would naturally grow up in our national economy of smaller industries so distributed as best to utilize our material resources." The state was therefore advised to "enforce those measures which will assist in realizing all the conditions of a sound industrial system against both the greed of capitalists and the shortsightedness of the laborer." The government was also urged to put an end to the discriminatory practices of the railroads, which, it was charged, violated the rights of individuals and communities and tended to distribute labor and capital in an unnatural manner.

The final two planks of the platform dealt with the subject in which Patten and James were most interested: national planning to attain the most effective utilization of the nation's resources. The platform announced that it was the duty of the state to reserve sufficient forest lands in each locality to subserve public needs. A change in existing land laws was called for so as to encourage the acquisition of land by a class of farmers whose "interests in management" would

[34] James's ideas in this regard are developed in greater detail in his article "National Aid to Popular Education," *Andover Review*, V (March, 1886), 250–262.

coincide with the public interest, that is, farmers who would use the best machinery, rotate their crops so as to get the most out of the soil, and utilize the best breeds of livestock. The interests of the nation as a whole, the platform declared, could best be promoted if each section concentrated on developing the resources for which it was most suited and relied on other sections for the commodities that it could not advantageously produce.

As means for furthering the common interests of the various sections, the platform suggested the collection and dissemination of information with respect to national industries and the most effective ways of developing them, a survey of the mineral and agricultural resources of the nation, the establishment of experimental stations, and the sponsorship of fairs and expositions and the employment of bounties and exemptions to encourage the use of approved practices and the most suitable crops and livestock. To achieve this program of balanced regional development, Patten and James looked to the state. "While individuals and societies," they explained, "may contribute something toward these results, yet, owing to the haphazard character of their effort, no adequate assistance can be expected from them. It is, therefore, not only beneath the dignity of a great nation, but also contrary to its interests, to rely upon the charity of its individual members for the promotion of so necessary an end as the symmetrical development of its material resources." [35]

The constitution of the Society for the Study of National Economy drawn up by Patten and James clearly indicates the views of some of the "bolder" new-school economists with respect to the use of the state as an instrument to promote the general welfare. In proposing the outlines of a program of national planning, Patten and James were anticipating, to a certain extent, the ideas of latter-day advocates of a planned economy; and in considering the responsibility of the federal government for the nation's system of public education, they were coping with a problem that remains without adequate solution to the present day. They also took issue with the economy advocates, and their analysis of economy and efficiency in government and the relationship of these problems to the functions of government represents an early defense of government spending for social reform. The attempt to form an organization of economists committed to these propositions, however, came to naught. The program Patten and James

[35] The Constitution of the Society for the Study of National Economy is given in its entirety in Ely, *Ground under Our Feet*, pp. 296–299.

proposed was far too advanced to attract the support of any great number of economists in the United States of the 1880's.[36]

When it became evident that the project for a Society for the Study of National Economy would fall through, young Richard T. Ely, who was then teaching at Johns Hopkins and who had been thinking of forming an association of American economists even before the idea of Patten and James took shape,[37] drew up a prospectus for an organization to be called the American Economic Association.[38] Ely, favoring an organization that would be broad enough to enlist the support of all the "younger progressive" economists who were interested in objective research, and yet wishing to exclude "men of the Sumner type,"[39] emphasized the need for the inductive approach and, although rejecting laissez faire, placed less stress than Patten and James on government intervention.

The Ely prospectus set forth as the basic objectives of the proposed association the encouragement of objective research and freedom of discussion in the sphere of political economy and the dissemination of economic knowledge. The platform for the organization embodied some of the basic views of the new school, as Ely understood them.

First of all, Ely proposed an unequivocal repudiation of laissez faire. "We regard the state as an educational and ethical agency whose positive aid is an indispensable condition of human progress. While we recognize the necessity of individual initiative in industrial life, we hold that the doctrine of *laissez-faire* is unsafe in politics and unsound in morals; and that it suggests an inadequate explanation of the relations between the state and the citizens." The second point of the platform stressed the need for inductive study of the conditions

[36] Statement by James, *A. E. A. Publications*, 3d Ser., XI (1910), 109–110; Ely, *Ground under Our Feet*, pp. 134–135.

[37] A letter from Francis Amasa Walker to Richard T. Ely, dated April 30, 1884, clearly indicates that Ely had already by that time suggested the possibility of forming a "society composed of economists who repudiate laissez faire as a scientific doctrine" (Ely Papers).

[38] The account of the organization of the American Economic Association is based on Ely, "Report of the Organization of the American Economic Association," *A. E. A. Publications*, I (1886), 5–46; and Ely, "The American Economic Association 1885–1909," *ibid.*, 3d Ser., XI (1910), 47–92. In drawing up the prospectus Ely received the aid of James, Seligman, and the historian Herbert Baxter Adams.

[39] Ely to Seligman, June 23, 1885, in Dorfman, "The Seligman Correspondence II," *Political Science Quarterly*, LVI (June, 1941), 281. In the same letter Ely assured Seligman that he believed in "individual initiative and effort" and did not wish that "the State should everywhere interfere."

of economic life, past and present, so as to further the scientific development of political economy. The third point gave expression to Ely's belief that the cure for social problems necessitated a blending of ethics, science, and state action. "We hold," it declared, "that the conflict of labor and capital has brought to the front a vast number of social problems whose solution is impossible without the united efforts of Church, state and science." In the final point of the platform Ely, unlike Patten and James, did not attempt to commit the proposed organization to a specific program of state action but, rather, asserted that the American Economic Association would not assume any "partisan attitude" on questions of government policy, particularly with regard to the protective tariff and "restrictions on trade." The belief was expressed that the readiness of economists "to assert themselves as advocates" had been a major reason for the lack of harmony among them. The platform, therefore, merely recommended changes in policy to correspond with the "progressive development of economic conditions."

A mimeographed circular of the prospectus was distributed among economists believed to be in sympathy with the ideas expressed, and it was proposed that those who were interested should meet at Saratoga, New York, in September, 1885, in conjunction with the American Historical Association (to which most of the economists belonged). On September 8, 1885, a call signed by Ely, Henry Carter Adams, and John Bates Clark was read at a meeting of the Historical Association, and interested persons were invited to meet that day to formulate plans for the establishment of an American Economic Association. Those present at the first meeting included Richard T. Ely, Henry Carter Adams, John Bates Clark, Edmund J. James, Andrew D. White, E. Benjamin Andrews, Washington Gladden, Edward Bemis, Edwin Seligman, Herbert Baxter Adams, and Alexander Johnston.

Ely was elected temporary secretary and was assigned the task of explaining the aims of the organization. He contended that a platform was necessary because the organization was designed to influence public opinion as well as to investigate and study.[40] He wanted to

[40] In letters to Seligman of June 9 and June 23, 1885, Ely expressed the hope that the A. E. A. would "exercise influence on public opinion" and declared that its purpose was "to accomplish in America what the Verein für Sozialpolitik has done in Germany—not necessarily accepting all the doctrines of the Germans" (Dorfman, "The Seligman Correspondence II," *Political Science Quarterly*, LVI [June, 1941], 280–281). Twenty-five years later, in reviewing the founding of the Association, Ely stated that the aim of the founders was "two-fold,—scientific and practical"

bring the views of the Association before the public so as to distinguish the new school from the old school. It was necessary, he said, to indicate the proper province of the state because there were certain functions that government would have to perform in order to maintain equality of opportunity. The platform, he asserted, emphasized the mission of both the state and the individual, and it was one of the purposes of the organization to determine the proper functions of each.[41] Ely explained the interest of the new school in social ethics and declared that the aid of the church was sought because the work of the Association lay in the field of practical Christianity.

Discussion of the platform centered about its formal denial of laissez faire. Seligman, E. Benjamin Andrews, and Alexander Johnston did not think that the organization should take sides on this matter, and even Henry Carter Adams feared that Ely's repudiation of laissez faire might be construed as an acceptance of the German view of social relations and its glorification of the state. There was also some discussion concerning Ely's appeal for the intervention of moral forces in the solution of social problems. The platform was then referred to a committee consisting of H. C. Adams, Ely, Gladden, Johnston, and Clark. In deference to the objections already noted, the wording of the statement with respect to state action and laissez faire was weakened by the committee to read: "We regard the state as an agency whose positive assistance is one of the indispensable conditions of human progress." The other points in Ely's original proposal were not altered. However, in order that the views ex-

---

("The American Economic Association 1885–1909," *A. E. A. Publications,* 3d Ser., XI [1910], 71). On the other hand, in seeking to persuade the conservative Edward Atkinson to join the Association, Ely declared, "We are not *advocates*—but students —men of science who are searching for truth. We do not think we know it all and we welcome all who desire to aid in research" (Ely to Atkinson, April 28, 1887, Atkinson Papers). It was vainly expected by the founders of the organization that the reports and recommendations of the standing committees of the Association and the debates on them would influence both public opinion and legislation. See Ely, "The American Economic Association 1885–1909," *A. E. A. Publications,* 3d Ser., XI (1910), 71–72; and Ely, *Ground under Our Feet,* pp. 132–133, 142–145, 148.

[41] Speaking of laissez faire, Ely declared: "It is difficult to define *laissez-faire* categorically, because it is so absurd that its defenders can never be induced to say precisely what they mean. Yet it stands for a well-known, though rather vague set of ideas, to which appeal is made every day in the year by the bench, the bar, the newspapers and our legislative bodies" ("Report of the Organization of the American Economic Association," *A. E. A. Publications,* I [1886], 17).

pressed should not deter any interested economist from joining the organization, the committee accepted a suggestion by H. B. Adams and affixed a note to the document declaring that the platform represented the views of the founders of the organization and was "not to be regarded as binding upon individual members." In this form the "statement of principles" was accepted by the organization and incorporated into its constitution.

As Ely has said, the statement of principles that was finally adopted represented "a compromise on behalf of catholicity." However, it was still too strong for some of the more conservative economists: J. Laurence Laughlin, William Graham Sumner, and Arthur Twining Hadley refused to join the new organization. Laughlin, for one, was displeased because the Association "seemed desirous of excluding Prof. Sumner," and he declared that he would not join any organization of economists unless it were committed to naught save "love of truth." He had no desire, he informed Seligman, "to be another rag tied on to Ely's kite to steady his erratic movements." [42]

Francis Amasa Walker was elected president of the Association, and Ely was chosen secretary. Ely served in this capacity for seven years, and during that time his office at Johns Hopkins was truly a bureau of information for the Association's members. To what extent the organization influenced the development of social control in the United States during the early years of its history, as Ely hoped it would, it is difficult to say. One contemporary writer looked on the Association as "the investigator, advocate, idealist, educator, of American life" and believed that it had not only stimulated research but had also influenced legislation.[43] Certain it is that the many monographs

[42] See Bemis to Ely, September 29, 1886, Ely Papers; and Laughlin to Seligman, July 11, 1890, Edwin R. A. Seligman Papers, Columbia University Library. Hadley and Laughlin both refused to accept positions on the council of the A. E. A. to which they had been elected. See James to Ely, April 27, 1887, copy in Seligman Papers. Sumner spoke of the arguments of the German historical school as "Dutch drivel" (Sumner to Newcomb, January 19, 1886, Simon Newcomb Papers, Library of Congress). Frank Taussig did not join the organization until 1886, but this delay was occasioned by "personal reasons." In 1885 Taussig had not yet decided whether he wished to devote his life to the teaching of political economy. When he finally made up his mind, he joined the Association (Taussig to Ely, October 10, 1886, Ely Papers). Taussig thought that there was "much truth in the qualifications which they [the historical school] suggest to accepted economic principles" (Taussig to Wells, May 23, 1884, David A. Wells Papers, Library of Congress).

[43] Lyman P. Powell, "The American Economic Association," *Chautauquan*, XV (August, 1892), 602.

published under the auspices of the Association, such as Henry Carter Adams' "Relation of the State to Industrial Action," Edmund James's "Relation of the Modern Municipality to the Gas Supply," and B. E. Fernow's "Practicability of American Forest Administration," stimulated discussion of a host of problems concerning the relation of the state to economic life. These publications, according to Ely, "went to . . . persons in a position to exercise influence, and they went at the right juncture and produced an impression that was out of all proportion to the number of our [American Economic Association] members." Branches of the Association were formed in Springfield, Massachusetts, Washington, D.C., Buffalo, Kansas City, and elsewhere, and these too served as centers of discussion of important economic problems.[44]

The members of the new school of political economy were, however, to realize only in part their hopes as regards the role to be played by an association of American economists. Their desire for an organization that would facilitate freedom of discussion among economists and would stimulate the objective study of economic problems was indeed satisfied; but their efforts to have this organization repudiate laissez faire and support a program of state action were destined ultimately to fail. As noted, the initial attempt in this direction by Patten and James elicited almost no favorable response. Ely's platform for the American Economic Association, which, although it supported state action in a general way, did not spell out any specific program of social reform, also did not find favor with very many economists and, as a result, had to be modified in the manner already indicated. A strong movement developed within the Association soon after its founding to drop the statement of principles altogether and thereby to remove a deterrent to the entry of more "conservative" elements into the organization.[45] At the 1888 convention of the Association, the statement of principles was abandoned, and it was announced that the Association would "take no partisan attitude" nor would it

[44] Ely, *Ground under Our Feet,* pp. 161–162. The most important of the subsidiary organizations was the Connecticut Valley Economic Association, formed at Springfield, Massachusetts, in 1886. John Bates Clark, Franklin Giddings, and Edward Bemis were its most prominent members. Its constitution is reprinted in Ely, "Proceedings of the Second Annual Meeting of the American Economic Association," *A. E. A. Publications,* III (1888), 217–218.

[45] See letters of Clark to Seligman, April 25, 1887, and Walker to Seligman, September 24, [1887?], in Dorfman, "The Seligman Correspondence I," *Political Science Quarterly,* LVI (March, 1941), 108–111.

"commit its members to any position on practical economic questions." [46]

As the years went by, the old-school economists were welcomed into the organization, and, for all practical purposes, they were in command by 1892. [47]   In that year Charles F. Dunbar of the old school replaced the slightly less conservative Francis Walker as president, and Edward A. Ross replaced Ely as secretary.   Although Ross, who had been a student of Ely's, was in sympathy with his teacher's views, the end of Ely's secretaryship more or less symbolized the declining influence of the new-school point of view in the American Economic Association and marked the end of new-school hopes that the Association would in some way help to promote the cause of social reform. [48]

III

Although the leaders of the new school of political economy failed to build an association of economists committed to the support of the positive state, they continued as individuals to advocate state action on behalf of the general welfare.   Most notable in this respect were Henry Carter Adams, Richard T. Ely, and Simon Nelson Patten. Adams set forth certain general principles to guide the state in its relation to industrial action; Ely spelled out in detail a concrete program of social reform; and Patten, less interested than Ely and Adams in ameliorative measures, advocated conscious state planning.

In 1878 Henry Carter Adams received the first degree of doctor of philosophy in political economy conferred by Johns Hopkins University.   After continuing his studies for a little more than a year in Europe, he taught briefly at Cornell University and at Johns Hopkins. Between 1881 and 1886 he divided his time between the University of

[46] Ely, "Report of the Proceedings at the Third Annual Meeting," *A. E. A. Publications*, IV (1889), 314.

[47] "I have a feeling," Ely's student David Kinley complained to Henry Demarest Lloyd in a letter of December 5, 1899, "that, for the past few years, the reactionary tendency in the association has been predominent" (Lloyd Papers, State Historical Society of Wisconsin).   Note the membership list published in the *Handbook of the American Economic Association* (Baltimore, 1890), pp. 27–64; and see also Laughlin, "The Study of Political Economy in the United States," *Journal of Political Economy*, I (December, 1892), 11.

[48] Ely, *Ground under Our Feet*, pp. 163–164.   Ely served as president of the organization during the year 1899–1900.   For evidence that even Ely had become reconciled to the changing character of the Association, see his letter to Seligman of October 22, 1890, in Dorfman, "Seligman Correspondence II," *Political Science Quarterly*, LVI (June, 1941), 282.

Michigan (where he had first lectured in the fall of 1880) and Cornell, teaching for part of the academic year at each institution. A speech on the relations of capital and labor delivered by Adams in March, 1886, in which the young economist proposed that laborers be afforded a proprietary right in industry,[49] antagonized the chairman of the board of trustees of Cornell and apparently influenced that university to dispense with Adams' services. In 1887 he accepted a professorship at Michigan, where he remained until his death in 1921. From 1888 to 1911, in addition to his work at Michigan, Adams served as statistician for the Interstate Commerce Commission.

In 1887 the American Economic Association published one of Adams' most significant contributions to American economic thought, "Relation of the State to Industrial Action." In this work Adams criticized the theory of laissez faire and set forth certain general principles to guide the state in its actions with respect to private enterprise. His analysis of the fallacies inherent in the theory of laissez faire was in consonance with the general new-school point of view in this matter, as has been indicated earlier. Adams, however, did not remain satisfied with destructive criticism of the let-alone policy: he thought it necessary "to search for those principles to which industrial legislation should conform."

Adams believed that the confusion in his day concerning the proper sphere of government resulted from a failure to distinguish between "*laissez-faire* as a dogma and free competition as a principle." He took issue with the assumption that competition is always a force for good and that it operates effectively only when the state adheres to a policy of laissez faire. "Competition," he asserted, "is neither malevolent nor beneficent, but will work malevolence or beneficence according to the conditions under which it is permitted to act." If the benefits deriving from competition are to be attained and the disadvantages resulting therefrom to be avoided, competition, Adams thought, must be regulated by the state.[50]

Three basic evils result, Adams pointed out, when competition operates under a regime of laissez faire. In the first place, unrestricted competition tends to force the moral sentiments and business practices in any particular trade down to the level of the worst man who can

[49] The speech is reprinted in *Scientific American Supplement*, XXII (August 21, 1886), 8861–8863.

[50] Adams, "Relation of the State to Industrial Action," *A. E. A. Publications*, I (1887), 495–499.

maintain himself in that trade. In order to meet competition, the "good men" in the trade must follow in the path of the worst man. Secondly, unregulated competition makes it impossible for society to realize the benefits to be derived from monopoly. Thirdly, too great a dependence on competition on the one hand and a policy of restricting public powers on the other result in a weak and corrupt government and upset the harmony that should properly prevail in society.

To remedy these defects, Adams set forth three basic guiding principles. As already noted, he proposed to combat the evils of weak and corrupt government by an extension of the functions of the state. To prevent competitive conditions in any trade from degenerating to the level of practice of the least ethical person in that trade, he advised that the state determine the plane upon which competition may operate. When the majority of competitors are agreed as to a given procedure but cannot enforce their desires because a few men in the same business refuse to abide by the proposed regulation, the state, Adams contended, must intervene and embody the sentiments of the majority in law. By so doing, the state establishes "a legal plane of competition" that is higher than the one that prevailed before the enactment of the statute. Adams asserted that government in thus raising the level of competition in no sense restricts competitive action but merely determines the manner in which it shall take place. Thus if the state prohibits child labor, competition is simply raised to the level of adult labor. In this way the benefits of private initiative are preserved, and its evils eradicated.[51]

Turning his attention to the question of monopoly, Adams expressed the belief that it was not so much monopoly that the public feared as that the power of monopoly would be used to serve purely private ends. Monopoly, he argued, presents the possibility of cheap and efficient operation, but some means must be devised to ensure that the potential advantages of monopoly will actually be realized by society. Since a monopoly represents "a business superior to the regulating control of competition," it cannot be assumed that the forces of competition will compel it to set a fair price for its products. On the contrary, if left to its own devices, a monopoly will charge the highest price possible, and the public will derive no benefit from its efficient operation. The state must therefore intervene to ensure

[51] Adams, "Relation of the State to Industrial Action," *A. E. A. Publications*, I (1887), 502–511.

that society is not oppressed by monopolies but is, rather, benefited by them.

Having decided that the state must somehow enable the people to realize the benefits of monopoly, Adams proceeded to classify the different types of industries so that statesmen would be able to determine readily which industries should be subjected to public control. Basing his classification on the increment of the product resulting from a given increment of capital and labor, Adams divided industries into three categories: industries of constant returns, industries of diminishing returns, and industries of increasing returns.

When industries are characterized by constant returns, Adams explained, a proportional increase in capital and labor is required to obtain a given increment in the amount of the product. In businesses of this type—a retail grocery, for example—success depends to a great extent on the personal ability of the businessman and his attention to detail, and price is determined by the average cost of production. No regulation by law is required for businesses of this category other than that necessary to determine the plane of competition. In industries of the second class—farming, for example—an increment of the product calls for a proportionally greater increment of capital and labor. Since the struggle for success in industries of this type, as with the first type, is mainly a struggle to depress the cost of rendering services, no state intervention is necessary.

Unlike the situation that prevails when industries are characterized by constant or diminishing returns, in the case of industries of increasing returns (natural monopolies), a given increment of capital and labor produces a proportionally greater increment of the product. In businesses of this type—railroads and public utilities, for example —success depends on the amount of business done rather than on individual management. Competition cannot exercise a healthy regulative influence because it is easier for an established business to expand its facilities than for a new concern to offer competition. In industries of this type, therefore, monopoly is inevitable, and "the only question at issue is, whether society shall support an irresponsible, extra-legal monopoly, or a monopoly established by law and managed in the interests of the public." Only if the second method is adopted, Adams concluded, will the benefits of monopoly be realized by the people.[52]

[52] Adams, "Relation of the State to Industrial Action," *A. E. A. Publications,* I (1887), 511–528.

Adams thus recognized two spheres of economic activity, a competitive sphere and a noncompetitive sphere. As he saw it, all that is required of the state in the noncompetitive sphere is that it determine the plane upon which competition may operate. Once this has been done, competition can be relied on to secure to the public the greatest possible benefits. When competition gives way to monopoly, however, state intervention is necessary, Adams thought, to ensure that the public will be served.[53]

In establishing his general rule with respect to noncompetitive industries, Adams did not specify whether state intervention was to take the form of carefully guarded franchises, regulatory commissions, public competition with private industry, or public ownership. However, although he did not commit himself in his "Relation of the State to Industrial Action," there is reason to believe that, for a time at least, Adams, like most members of the new school of political economy, regarded public ownership as the best method of dealing with the natural monopolies.[54]

The most comprehensive analysis by a new-school economist of the supposed advantages of public ownership of natural monopolies over private ownership (subject to public control) was made by Edmund James in his important study of the relationship of the municipality to the gas supply. James rejected the argument that the state has no right to engage in industrial enterprise as a proposition advanced by those who stood to benefit from the *status quo* or who had inadequate knowledge of government action. He also found himself

[53] For the similar views of Ely on the subject of competition, see Ely, *Introduction to Political Economy*, pp. 84–85; Ely, "Competition: Its Nature, Its Permanency, and Its Beneficence," *A. E. A. Publications*, 3d Ser., II (1901), 55–70; and Ely, *Natural Monopolies and Local Taxation* (Boston, 1889), p. 2.

[54] In his letter to President Angell of March 25, 1886, Adams declared that he favored federal ownership of the telegraph and parcel post, state ownership of mines, and municipal "control" of gas and water works and street railways (Angell Papers). Where municipal monopolies were not publicly owned, Adams proposed that the portion of their profit which was represented by unearned increment be appropriated by the people in the form of taxation ("Suggestions for a System of Taxation," *Publications of the Michigan Political Science Association*, I [May, 1894], 59–60). With respect to railroads, Adams wrote in 1898 that the experience of the Interstate Commerce Commission during the first ten years of its history did not constitute a valid test of the adequacy of the commission type of control and that it was still not clear to him whether the railroads should be regulated by the government or publicly owned ("A Decade of Federal Railway Regulation," *Atlantic Monthly*, LXXXI [April, 1898], 443).

unable to agree with the assertion that private management could manufacture such an item as gas more cheaply than the government could. This claim, he contended, was based on the assumptions that employees of a privately owned enterprise were more honest than employees of the public and that a private owner had a greater immediate interest in his business than a public officer had and would therefore attend more closely to the details of the business. In James's view, however, the first assumption did not hold true where there was a proper civil-service system in effect, and, however valid the second assumption might be in the case of a small business of which the owner himself was the manager, it was not applicable to businesses that were operated for their owners by paid managers.

The advantages in terms of economical operation of natural monopolies, James argued, were actually on the side of public rather than private enterprise. There was less danger of overcapitalization in the case of public ownership. The state could obtain money at a lower rate of interest than private enterprise could, and so its fixed charges would be less than those of a private concern. Also, since privately owned monopolies were always under public attack, they found it necessary to compensate for the risks involved by charging high rates for their services. To support his views as to the superiority of public ownership, James pointed out that a study of gas works in private and public hands in Europe and America revealed that public ownership had provided better service at lower prices to the consumer than had private ownership under public control.[55]

James also rejected the argument that a public utility should be left in private hands because this kept a potential source of public corruption out of politics. He maintained that private ownership in no way altered the fact of public corruption; it merely altered the form. Did not franchise holders attempt to buy votes and legislators, to influence regulatory commissions, and to use pressure to prevent necessary investigations? James thought that the real problem was to improve the character of the nation's administrative system, and he believed that this could be achieved only if the government assumed important functions. If this were done, the people would insist on honest administration. Quite apart from all the reasons already

[55] Commons reached the same conclusion with respect to municipal electric-light plants. See Commons, "Municipal Electric Lighting," in Edward W. Bemis, ed., *Municipal Monopolies: A Collection of Papers by American Economists and Specialists* (New York, 1899), pp. 173–174.

noted, James favored public ownership because he believed that no prime necessity of life such as gas, water, or electricity should be entrusted to a private concern, regardless of how carefully the conduct of that concern might be watched.[56]

Bemis and Ely advanced other reasons why natural monopolies should be in public hands. They looked to public ownership to increase civic consciousness and to help attract better men into government service. Publicly owned monopolies, they believed, would treat their employees better than privately owned businesses, would pay them higher wages, and have them work fewer hours, and, as a result, there would be fewer strikes. Farmers would also benefit in that they would be charged lower rates for moving their crops. Ely thought that in the event of government ownership of natural monopolies there would be less fluctuation in industrial life, crises would be mitigated, technological improvements would be more readily utilized, unearned income would be reduced to the lowest possible point, and, as a consequence, there would be a better distribution of wealth.[57]

Seligman believed that government ownership should be confined to those natural monopolies in whose operation there was widespread social interest, which required a relatively small capital investment, and in which the tasks of management were relatively simple. These circumstances applied, he thought, to the parcel post, the telephone, and municipal electric-light and water industries, but he was undecided as to whether municipal gas works belonged in the same category. Because of the great amount of capital invested and the complexity of the management, Seligman believed that the railroad industry should remain in private hands. Government control of this industry, he thought, should seek "to preserve the advantages of com-

[56] James, "Relation of the Modern Municipality to the Gas Supply," *A. E. A. Publications*, I (1886), 80–122.

[57] Bemis, "Regulation or Ownership?" in Bemis, ed., *Municipal Monopolies*, pp. 660–667; Ely, *Socialism and Social Reform*, pp. 266–291; Ely, *Monopolies and Trusts* (New York, 1900), pp. 258–264; Ely, "Public Control of Private Corporations," *Cosmopolitan*, XXX (February, 1901), 430–433; Ely, "The Advantages of Public Ownership and Management of Natural Monopolies," *ibid.*, XXX (March, 1901), 557–560. Even John Bates Clark favored the public ownership of gas, water, and electric-light plants. See Clark to Ely, February 1, 1888, Ely Papers. Bemis, although endorsing public ownership, informed the United States Industrial Commission that he was not at all certain that the public was as yet prepared for the task. See U. S. Industrial Commission, *Report on Transportation* (Vol. IX of the Commission's *Reports;* Washington, D.C., 1901), p. 99.

petition in facilities while doing away with that of competition in rates." [58]

In addition to proposing new principles to guide state action, Adams argued for the revision of the code of social ethics underlying the existing system of jurisprudence. The code of ethics conceived for a simple, nonindustrial society Adams found utterly inapplicable to an industrial society where localism in industry had disappeared and simplicity in organization was disappearing. In an industrial system dominated by corporations, Adams contended, old rules of business conduct that identified personal interest with social morality were inappropriate.[59] The system of jurisprudence, he thought, would therefore have to be modified so that "the social interest and the rights of individuals in associated industry" might find their proper expression. Believing that the fundamental principle of Anglo-Saxon liberty is that property is essential to liberty, Adams maintained that we would have to devise a new theory of property that gave to the workingman some proprietary right in industry. He thought that this right would be clarified as a result of the evolution of collective bargaining and the labor contract.[60]

In suggesting that the state attempt by appropriate legislation to establish a more ethical plane of competition and to capture for society the benefits of monopoly and that laborers be afforded proprietary rights in industry, Adams was plotting a course for the future. As Joseph Dorfman has so aptly remarked, "Adams was in a very real sense the philosophical parent of much of the political-economic legislation of the next fifty years. His influence was certainly both powerful and pervasive." [61]

[58] Seligman, "Government Ownership of Quasi-Public Corporations," *Gunton's Magazine,* XX (April, 1901), 305–322; Seligman to Thomas McIntyre Cooley, November 16, 1886, Cooley Papers, Michigan Historical Collections.

[59] Adams came to contend that corporations, unlike individuals, are "superior to the satisfactory control of competition." He therefore believed that provision must be made for "complete and perfect publicity in corporate affairs." He also thought that the privilege of incorporation should be limited to businesses "in which the interests of the public are relatively greater than the interests of the individual incorporators" ("Publicity and Corporate Abuses," *Publications of the Michigan Political Science Association,* I [May, 1894], 109–120).

[60] Adams, "Economics and Jurisprudence," *A. E. A. Economic Studies,* II (1897), 7–35; Adams et al., "The 'Labor Problem,'" *Scientific American Supplement,* XXII (August 21, 1886), 8861–8863.

[61] Dorfman, *The Economic Mind in American Civilization, 1606–1918* (New York, 1946–1949), III, p. 174. For an understanding evaluation of Adams'

IV

Whereas Adams formulated a set of principles to guide state action, Richard T. Ely concentrated his attention on the blocking out of a fairly complete program of social reform.[62] Believing that the mission of government is to secure "the good life," [63] Ely called on the state to enact a series of ameliorative measures designed to promote the livelihood and welfare of its citizens.

Ely was graduated from Columbia College in 1876. He received his Ph.D. at Heidelberg in 1879, and in 1881, after a discouraging period of unemployment, was appointed to a teaching position at Johns Hopkins. The eleven years he spent at Johns Hopkins were among the most fruitful of his long life. In addition to his regular teaching, he found time to write numerous books and articles, to participate actively in the Chautauqua program, to serve on the Baltimore Tax Commission and on the Maryland Tax Commission, and to organize and serve as secretary of the American Economic Association. Disappointed over a failure to secure a promotion, however, Ely left Johns Hopkins in 1892 to become director of the school of economics, political science, and history at the University of Wisconsin, where he was to remain for over thirty years. He died on October 4, 1943, at the age of eighty-nine.

As already noted, Ely hoped to steer a middle course between a rigid conservatism and socialism. No socialist himself,[64] he found

thought and his influence, see Dorfman, ed., *Relation of the State to Industrial Action and Economics and Jurisprudence: Two Essays by Henry Carter Adams* (New York, 1954), pp. 3–55.

[62] The ideas expressed in this section are developed in much the same way in Sidney Fine, "Richard T. Ely, Forerunner of Progressivism, 1880–1901," *Mississippi Valley Historical Review,* XXXVII (March, 1951), 599–624.

[63] Ely, "Person and Property," *Christian Advocate,* LXVI (March 19, 1891), 186.

[64] On July 12, 1894, the *Nation,* under the heading "The College Anarchist," carried a letter from Oliver E. Wells, Wisconsin's superintendent of public instruction, which charged that Ely believed "in strikes and boycotts, justifying and encouraging the one while practising the other." "Prof. Ely, director of the School of Economics," Wells stated, "differs from Ely, the socialist, only in the adroit and covert method of the advocacy." The general acceptance of his teachings would "furnish a seeming moral justification of attacks upon life and property." The regents of the University of Wisconsin appointed a three-man investigating committee to examine Wells's charges. In a communication to the committee, Wells complained that Ely's work would not only fail to teach the young proper "reverence for law" but would also fail "to leave an impression of the immutability and dominance of

that socialist agitation had, to a certain extent, been a force for good. Socialism, he believed, had helped arouse the social conscience and had made men sensitive to the plight of the unfortunate. It had familiarized people with the idea of social change and progress and had placed a needed emphasis on the social rather than the individual side of economic life. Furthermore, it had given rise to a critical examination of institutions once taken for granted. Ely, however, was unwilling to accept the socialist solution. Socialism, he thought, was both too pessimistic with respect to the present and too optimistic with respect to the future. The concentration of power in the hands of government that it required posed a threat to individual liberty. Ely regarded vast areas of production, such as agriculture, commerce, and most lines of manufacturing, as unsuited to socialism, and also felt that the socialist state would be unable to establish a standard of distributive justice that would be generally acceptable and that would at the same time enlist the services of the talented members of society. Socialist theories of value would also, he believed, make it difficult for a socialist state to maintain an equilibrium between demand and supply.[65]

Opposed both to unrestricted individualism and to socialism, Ely sought some middle position that would avoid the danger of these extremes. "Is there not," he asked, "a golden mean between the too little; namely, rigid, obstructive, and revolutionary conservatism, . . . and the too much; namely, reckless radicalism, which in reaching out for improvement, risks the treasures accumulated during so many ages, treasures so painfully gathered together?" Is it not possible to add the good of socialism to the existing order and yet to keep that order intact? Ely thought that it was possible, that there was some golden mean. The solution, he felt confident, lay in a program of government-sponsored social reform, in the implementation of the philosophy of

---

natural and economic laws." Ely's books not only abounded in "quotations favorable to lawlessness and disorder," but they also contained a "comprehensive bibliography of such writings." Ely was, furthermore, a representative of the new school of political economy, the essence of whose system was to teach "reliance upon state-help rather than self-help." There was no substance to Wells's ridiculous charges, and the investigation resulted in a complete exoneration for Ely. See *Nation,* LIX (July 12, 1894), 27; *The Ely Investigation. Communications of Superintendent Wells to the Investigating Committee* (n. p., 1894); Ely, *Ground under Our Feet,* pp. 218–233; and Merle Curti and Vernon Carstensen, *The University of Wisconsin, 1848–1925* (Madison, Wisc., 1949), I, 508–527.

[65] Ely, *Socialism and Social Reform,* pp. 113–249.

the general-welfare state. Through a multiplicity of ameliorative measures effecting changes "within the framework of existing society," the state, he believed, could both stave off the threat of socialism and yet serve the common weal.[66]

Ely's program of reform was particularly concerned with the problem of monopoly. He defined monopoly as "that substantial unity of action on the part of one or more persons engaged in some kind of business which gives exclusive control, more particularly, although not solely, with respect to price."[67] Avoiding the hysterical lack of discrimination usually associated with the subject, he was careful to point out that not every business operating on a large scale and not every combination was a monopoly. He recognized two broad categories of monopoly: social and natural. The first comprised in the main monopolies established by the government in the general interest, as, for example, patents, copyrights, trade-marks, and public-consumption monopolies, and Ely saw little necessity for altering existing arrangements as they applied to this category of monopoly.[68]

Vastly different, however, was the problem of the natural monopolies, defined by Ely as monopolies arising from properties inherent in a particular business, from a limited supply of a raw material, or as the result of secrecy.[69] Most important among these, in Ely's view, were the monopolies arising from properties inherent in the business—railroads, the telegraph and telephone, local rapid-transit agencies, municipal water works, gas works, electric-light plants, and the like. Whereas in the 1880's Ely, following Adams, had maintained that such monopolies were the consequence of the operation of the law of increasing returns, by the turn of the century he was arguing, in more general terms, that it was chiefly the "increment in gain" resulting from combinations of this sort that produced the monopoly. This situation, he pointed out, obtained where businesses occupied peculiarly favored locations or furnished services or commodities that had to be used in

[66] *Ibid.*, pp. 255–257, 350–351; Ely, "Recent American Socialism," *Johns Hopkins University Studies in Historical and Political Science,* III (1885), 295; Ely, *Ground under Our Feet,* pp. 152–153.

[67] Ely, *Monopolies and Trusts,* p. 14.

[68] Ely, *Monopolies and Trusts,* pp. 42–55. Ely at one time referred to these monopolies as "artificial monopolies" (*Socialism and Social Reform,* pp. 293–294).

[69] Ely regarded anthracite coal as an example of a monopoly arising from a limited supply of a raw material and the manufacture of certain chemicals or gunpowder as examples of monopolies arising from secrecy (*Monopolies and Trusts,* pp. 56–58, 74–75).

connection with the plant itself. In any event, it was Ely's contention that businesses of this sort were not subject to competition and
inevitably became monopolies.[70]

Ely consistently refused to recognize the existence of true monopolies outside the categories of natural and social monopolies that he
had established. Where monopolistic tendencies apparently existed
in industries not included in these categories, he maintained that it
was not the result of properties inherent in the business, as was the
case with the natural monopolies, but was, rather, occasioned by
some special factor, such as aid afforded to favored concerns by the
natural monopolies (especially the railroads). Mere mass of capital
or mere combination without external aid could not in themselves, in
Ely's view, produce monopoly. Apart from the field of natural monopoly and the problem of concentration of wealth, it was therefore
his contention that the so-called trust problem merely referred to the
"tendency to do business on a large scale," and in this he saw no harm.
Size in itself did not frighten him. On the contrary, he believed that
where concentration of production was the result of the free play of
economic forces, it was a good thing, and although it was necessary to
remove any attendant abuses, it was foolish to attempt to proceed
against the combination itself. Ely was thus an opponent of the
Sherman Anti-Trust Act and thought that it could "produce nothing
but harm." [71]

Natural monopolies, however, were another matter, and, as previously indicated, Ely's solution for this problem was government
ownership.[72] He regarded such a policy as eminently superior to
regulation by commission, which, in his view, represented a vain
attempt to harmonize two essentially antagonistic elements: private
property and government regulation.[73] In addition to public owner-

[70] Ely, *Monopolies and Trusts,* pp. 55–75.

[71] Ely, *Monopolies and Trusts,* pp. 141–144, 168–174, 212–213; Ely, "The Nature
and Significance of Monopolies and Trusts," *International Journal of Ethics,* X
(April, 1900), 282–283.

[72] In the case of natural monopolies resulting from a limited supply of a raw
material, Ely favored government ownership but private operation (*Socialism and
Social Reform,* pp. 292–293).

[73] Ely was ultimately to change his views with respect to public ownership,
mainly because it did not appear to him that public ownership had increased popular
interest or pride in government, nor had it attracted men of talent to government
service. He therefore came to believe that regulation by commission was preferable.
See Ely, "Government in Business and the General-Welfare," *Review of Reviews,*
LXXXIV (October, 1931), 46; and Ely, *Ground under Our Feet,* pp. 251–265.

ship of natural monopolies, Ely suggested various other reforms to limit factors promotive of monopoly and to curb such evils as were incidental to large-scale production. He advocated reform of the tariff where it aids monopoly and reform of the patent law where patents constitute the basis of objectionable monopolies. Taxation of bequests and inheritances so as to break up large fortunes would, he believed, result in a more equitable distribution of wealth and the partial absorption by society of the surplus value already accumulated by monopoly.

Much could also be accomplished, Ely anticipated, through reform of the law of private corporations. The purpose of such reform, he thought, should be to protect the public against fraudulent practices. He proposed that persons wishing to form corporations be required to issue a prospectus containing full information about the business to be pursued. According to Ely's plan, those signing the prospectus would be held responsible to the investors and to the general public for the accuracy of their statements. Persons connected with the promotion of the corporation would be subject to unlimited liability for "a term of years" and the directors of the corporation, to double liability. Full and complete publicity would be the rule with respect to the operation of corporations. To enforce these provisions, Ely favored the establishment of bureaus of corporations in the various states and a federal bureau of corporations. But this was as far as he thought it necessary to go. He opposed the establishment of a commission to regulate the "trusts" and plans for the "detailed public control of private business in general." [74]

Whereas Ely believed that public activity must be the dominant force in the field of monopoly, he thought that the area of the economy where competition obtains should be left to private enterprise. However, although he regarded competition as a beneficent force within its sphere, he was not satisfied that it should remain completely without regulation. Like Henry Carter Adams, he advocated state action to establish a more ethical plane of competition. Most of the reforms Ely believed necessary to attain this end were in the category of labor legislation: establishment of boards of arbitration and conciliation, enactment of safety and sanitary legislation, abolition of sweatshops, the passage of employers' liability acts and of acts providing for the eight-hour day and one day of rest in seven, restrictions on

[74] Ely, *Monopolies and Trusts*, pp. 264–271; Ely, "The Future of Corporations," *Harper's Monthly Magazine*, LXXV (July, 1887), 265–266.

child and female labor, and the payment of wages in lawful money. In addition, Ely suggested the inspection of markets and the enactment of pure-food legislation.[75]

With regard to the nation's money supply, Ely, like most of the new-school economists, was opposed on economic grounds to the free coinage of silver at 16 to 1 and to the unrestricted issue of fiat money.[76] He suggested that the pressing need for a more elastic currency be met by permitting a central bank to issue currency beyond the amount regularly authorized, the extra currency being subject to tax. Other monetary reforms suggested by Ely were a government guarantee of bank issues and the establishment of postal-savings banks. He also thought the government should find means to extend credit to individuals, particularly to farmers.[77]

Ely was one of the pioneers of the conservation movement.[78] He was especially interested in the problem of forestry and in the necessity of government action to conserve the nation's forest resources. He envisioned the creation of an extensive system of forest reserves, the planting of trees on suitable land, and the training and organizing by the state of a large body of foresters.[79] By the end of the century

[75] Ely, *Natural Monopolies and Local Taxation*, p. 2; Ely, "Fundamental Beliefs in My Social Philosophy," *Forum*, XVIII (October, 1894), 180; Ely, *Socialism and Social Reform*, pp. 317–322.

[76] Ely to Henry Demarest Lloyd, June 2, 1896, Lloyd Papers; Ely to H. B. Fay, December 24, 1897, Ely Papers; Patten, "Wells' Recent Economic Changes," *Political Science Quarterly*, V (March, 1890), 86; Mayo-Smith, "Money and Prices," *ibid.*, XV (June, 1900), 211; Mayo-Smith, "Free Silver and Wages," *ibid.*, XI (September, 1896), 464–477; Clark, "The After Effects of Free Coinage of Silver," *ibid.*, XI (September, 1896), 493–501. Ely also regarded the Populists' subtreasury scheme as "visionary and unworthy of attention" (Ely to Lloyd, June 2, 1896, Lloyd Papers).

[77] Ely, *Socialism and Social Reform*, pp. 329, 335; Ely to Lyman J. Gage, May 24, 1897, Ely Papers; Ely, "The Next Things in Social Reform," *Christian Union*, XLIII (April 23, 1891), 532.

[78] Patten, James, and Adams were also conspicuous advocates of conservation measures. The views of Patten and James in this regard have already been discussed. For Adams, see *Science of Finance*, pp. 242–247. Ely believed that "it was the work of economists in preparing the public mind throughout the length and breadth of the land that helped to make possible the later work of the conservationists" (Ely *et al.*, *The Foundations of National Prosperity: Studies in the Conservation of Permanent Natural Resources* [New York, 1917], p. 16).

[79] Ely, *Introduction to Political Economy*, pp. 90–92; Ely *et al.*, *Foundations of National Prosperity*, pp. 15–16.

he was also suggesting measures necessary to conserve the nation's mineral resources.[80]

Ely was, for a time, an advocate, although not a particularly zealous one, of those innovations in the political machinery that the Progressives fondly hoped would place the reins of government more securely in the hands of the people. He favored the initiative and referendum, the Australian ballot, proportional representation, and a corrupt-practices act that would impose limits on the expenses candidates might incur in their quest for office and that would require complete publicity with respect to party accounts. So that the various units of government could be staffed with efficient personnel, Ely recommended the establishment of a federal civil academy and the provision by the state universities of suitable training for government positions.[81]

Ely was also much concerned with the problem of the city, that "one conspicuous failure" of American democracy that the Progressive movement sought to convert into a success. He was confident that the evils connected with city government could be dispelled by a combination of those elements to which he attached such great importance: religion and increased government action. What was required, he thought, was a religious revival strong enough to modify man's character and to pervade every aspect of political life, and an expansion of the functions of city government that would not only serve to meet social and economic needs but that would also help to attract better men into public life and to increase civic consciousness. Specifically, Ely urged that city governments extend their public-education system, improve their sanitary legislation and sanitary administration, provide free public baths, gardens, parks, and playgrounds and other recreational facilities, improve the housing conditions of the poor and make medical facilities available to them, organize poor relief more effectively, provide stricter regulation of the liquor traffic, establish municipal savings banks, municipalize markets and slaughterhouses, and, of course, take over all public utilities.

---

[80] Ely, *Foundations of National Prosperity*, p. 16.

[81] Ely, *Socialism and Social Reform*, pp. 344–349. Ely later opposed initiative, referendum, and recall and referred to the first two as "suitable only to a primitive rural democracy" ("Progressivism, True and False—An Outline," *Review of Reviews*, LI [February, 1915], 210). For Ely's recommendations for the extension of the public-education system, see *Socialism and Social Reform*, pp. 324–326.

Reforms of this sort, he thought, were more likely to provide a solution for the social and economic problems of the city than any "trifling readjustment of political machinery." [82]

In addition to the general categories of reform already noted,[83] Ely advocated a host of other social-reform measures, many of them to be realized in the next century, many of them closely associated with the general-welfare state. To meet the problem of improved housing for the poor, he recommended not only sanitary laws but also public housing. He urged that municipalities be given the authority to tear down unfit tenements and to construct improved dwellings. He also declared himself in favor of a program of social insurance and suggested that the government supplement private and voluntary insurance so that economic protection against death, old age, sickness, and accidents might be extended to all.[84] Ely also wished the state to assume a greater responsibility with respect to the problem of unemployment by establishing public employment offices, providing public work for the unemployed, leasing public lands to farmers, and perhaps even guaranteeing the right to a job.[85]

With Ely we also note a new friendliness of the economist for organized labor. "I have wandered about the streets of New York

[82] Ely, *Problems of To-Day*, pp. 231–245; Ely, "The Improvement of Municipal Government," *Christian Union*, XLII (October 9, 1890), 460–461.

[83] Ely was an important advocate of reform of the tax structure. He made many interesting suggestions as to methods by which units of local government might capture the unearned increment from real estate. He was also an early supporter of state income taxes. Ely wished to see the tariff simplified and tariff rates reduced, but he thought that the importance of the tariff had been exaggerated and that this had served to divert attention from necessary reforms. In 1888 he suggested that a portion of the Treasury surplus, accumulating partly as the result of tariff revenues, be expended for public improvements. For Ely's views on taxation and the tariff, see Ely, *Taxation in American States and Cities* (New York, 1888); Ely, "Reforms in Taxation," *Cosmopolitan*, XXX (January, 1901), 307–309; Ely, "The Next Things in Social Reform," *Christian Union*, XLIII (April 23, 1891), 532; Ely, *Socialism and Social Reform*, pp. 300–305, 334; Ely, *Problems of To-Day*, pp. 214–222; Ely, *Introduction to Political Economy*, pp. 208–210; and Ely, "The Tariff and Trusts—Expenditures for Internal Improvements," in Shaw, ed., *National Revenues*, pp. 56–67.

[84] Ely, *Socialism and Social Reform*, pp. 328, 330–331. Ely complained that the American people did not realize the importance of social insurance. "It is bound," he said prophetically, "to receive a great extension and to become one of the problems of the future" (*Monopolies and Trusts*, pp. 272–273).

[85] Ely, *Socialism and Social Reform*, pp. 331–333; Ely, "The Next Things in Social Reform," *Christian Union*, XLIII (April 23, 1891), 532.

without money for board bills and in a most wretched desperate state," Ely wrote to the Detroit anarchist and labor leader Joseph A. Labadie on August 14, 1885. "It was once when in such a condition that I took upon myself a vow to write in behalf of the laboring classes."[86] Ely made good his vow when in 1886 he brought out *The Labor Movement in America,* a work that initiated the scientific study of labor in the United States. Ely looked on the labor movement as the realization of the Golden Rule and contended that it represented mankind better than any other movement. "The labor movement, . . . in its broadest terms," he wrote, "is the effort of men to live the life of men. . . . Half conscious though it may be, the labor movement is a force pushing on towards the attainment of the purpose of humanity; . . . namely, the full and harmonious development in each individual of all human faculties. . . . And this development of human powers in the individual is not to be entirely for self, but it is to be for the sake of their beneficent use in the service of one's fellows in a Christian civilization."

Labor organizations, Ely asserted, are not an artificial product but "the natural and inevitable outcome of existing industrial conditions." He argued that when there is no labor union present to insist on collective bargaining, the terms of the labor contract are, in effect, determined by the employer alone. He upheld labor's right to strike and repudiated the notion that strikes are always foolish.[87]

In addition to the labor union, Ely looked to the church, the school, and especially the state to ameliorate the position of the workingman. He rejected the contention of the classical economists that the state discharges its responsibility to the laborer when it removes restraints on his activity and eschews all interference with his freedom to contract. He asserted that this view was based on the false assumption of the natural equality of men and the equally false assumption that labor, like any other commodity, always moves to the best market for its services. As essential "conditions of industrial peace," Ely stressed the enactment of appropriate labor legislation, a wide diffusion of knowledge about social, political, and economic problems, and the application of the principles of Christianity. He upheld legislation on behalf of the laborer as important to society as a whole

[86] Sidney Fine, ed., "The Ely-Labadie Letters," *Michigan History,* XXXVI (March, 1952), 17.

[87] Ely, *Labor Movement in America,* pp. 3–4, 92–119, 149; Ely, "Labor Organizations," *Christian Advocate,* LXVI (September 10, 1891), 602.

inasmuch as he believed the welfare of society to be dependent on the existence of a strong wage-earning class.[88]

The numerous reforms advocated by Ely in his attempt to develop a positive brand of liberalism and to steer a middle course between laissez faire and socialism read like a catalogue of measures sponsored by the twentieth-century liberal.[89] The implementation of this program, the implementation, in effect, of the concept of the general-welfare state, would, Ely anticipated, usher in "a society with real, not merely nominal, freedom, to pursue the best; a society in which men shall work together for common purposes, and in which this wholesome co-operation shall take place largely through government, but through a government which has become less repressive and has developed its positive side." [90] He had no fear that he was attempting to make progress too rapidly. It is impossible, he said, "to go too fast in the attainment of right social relations." The danger in the United States, as he saw it, was "not that we shall go too rapidly, but that we shall not go at all." [91]

No ivory-tower scholar, Ely exercised a pervasive influence on social thought and the course of social reform both during the eighties and the nineties and during subsequent periods of reform. His numerous publications attracted a considerable amount of attention, and, as one writer declared in 1892, they "exercised a wider and more positive influence on American legislation than the works of any other economist of the . . . generation." [92] Of special importance among Ely's books was the *Introduction to Political Economy* (later editions were titled *Outlines of Political Economy*). Originally distributed through the Chautauqua Literary and Scientific Circle, this work sold thirty

[88] Ely, *Labor Movement in America*, pp. 96–100, 295–332; Ely, "Conditions of Industrial Peace," *Forum*, III (August, 1887), 638–644.

[89] Ely, of course, was not alone among new-school economists in advocating social-reform measures. For the reform proposals of other new-school economists, see Adams to Angell, March 25, 1886, Angell Papers; Commons, *Distribution of Wealth, passim;* Commons, "Progressive Individualism," *American Magazine of Civics,* VI (June, 1895), 561–574; James, "State Interference," *Chautauquan,* VIII (June, 1888), 534–536; and Bemis, "The Complaint of the Poor," *Independent,* XL (May 24, 1888), 645.

[90] Ely, *Socialism and Social Reform*, p. 352.

[91] Ely, "Are We Going Too Fast?" *Christian Advocate*, LXVII (March 31, 1892), 206; Ely, "Report of the Proceedings of the American Economic Association at the Fifth Annual Meeting," *A. E. A. Publications*, VIII (1893), 55.

[92] Powell, "The American Economic Association," *Chautauquan,* XV (August, 1892), 604.

thousand copies in a decade and an estimated five hundred thousand copies in all. Significant for its attention to the cause of social reform, Ely's text, as Joseph Dorfman has said, exerted "a considerable influence on the thought of Americans." [93]

Although a layman, Ely was one of the most influential figures in the social-gospel movement of the 1880's and 1890's. His books enjoyed such wide circulation that they "tended to become the norm for all endeavor in the field of social Christianity. Wherever religion was concerned with social problems his work usually was used as a text." He was a frequent speaker to church groups and religious gatherings, and his Chautauqua lectures were often concerned with social-gospel themes. He was also prominently connected with some of the important social-gospel agencies, serving for a time as secretary of the Christian Social Union and being founder and first president of the American Institute of Christian Sociology. [94]

As a teacher at Johns Hopkins and at the University of Wisconsin, Ely trained and influenced an enormous number of persons who were later to occupy important positions in American life. As G. C. Sellery wrote in 1939, "it is common knowledge, among those who know the field, that Dr. Ely has a greater 'gallery' than any other economics professor in the country." The most famous of Ely's pupils was Woodrow Wilson, though Ely always felt that Wilson was little influenced, at least immediately, by the instruction he received from him at Johns Hopkins. The same, however, can hardly be said for others among the distinguished group of Ely's students. It was Ely who converted John R. Commons to the new economics and who was to influence the thinking of the prominent sociologist Edward A. Ross and the important reformers of the Progressive period, Frederic C. Howe and Albert Shaw. The historian Frederick Jackson Turner, John Finley, who became editor of the *New York Times*, David Kinley, who became president of the University of Illinois, and Dr. Henry Taylor, who

[93] See Ely, *Ground under Our Feet*, pp. 81–82; *Publishers' Weekly*, CXLIV (October 16, 1943), 1530; and Dorfman, *Economic Mind in American Civilization*, III, 164. The correspondence in the Ely Papers attests to the influence of other works by Ely, particularly *The Labor Movement in America* and *Social Aspects of Christianity*.

[94] James Dombrowski, *The Early Days of Christian Socialism in America* (New York, 1936), p. 53; Charles Howard Hopkins, *The Rise of the Social Gospel in American Protestantism, 1865–1915* (New Haven, 1940), pp. 113, 116, 163–164; Aaron I. Abell, *The Urban Impact on American Protestantism, 1865–1900* (Cambridge, Mass., 1943), pp. 106–111; Ely, *Ground under Our Feet*, p. 78.

became chief of the Bureau of Agricultural Economics, were also among the Ely "gallery." Howe has testified that those "who came under his [Ely's] influence learned to look at the world with inquiring minds and to challenge the finality of established things." The "entire tendency and work of my life," Howe wrote to Ely, "was altered by the new chemical combination which your influence and teaching suggested, and I fancy, in fact I know, that this must be true of a large number of men the country over." [95]

Both the Progressive movement and the New Deal were to attest to Ely's significance as a precursor of twentieth-century reform. Not only did he exert an influence on Albert Shaw and Frederic Howe, who were to play subsidiary, albeit important, roles during the Progressive era, but his ideas were also to have their effect upon two of the giant figures of Progressivism: Robert La Follette and Theodore Roosevelt. La Follette, although never one of Ely's students, always referred to Ely as his teacher, and both La Follette and Charles McCarthy have attested to the influence of Ely and Ely's thought on the "Wisconsin Idea." [96] Ely believed that he influenced Theodore Roosevelt both through his writings and through Albert Shaw, who was one of Roosevelt's advisors. Ely reports an occasion when Roosevelt declared: "I know Dr. Ely. He first introduced me to radicalism in economics and then he made me sane in my radicalism." [97] As for the New Deal, Monsignor John A. Ryan, whose plan of industrial democracy had a "tremendous influence" on New Deal thought,[98] has testified that Ely's contribution to his social education was "very large indeed." Ryan was particularly impressed by Ely's *Social Aspects of Christianity* and his *Socialism . . . with Suggestions for Social Reform.* The program of social reform that Ely set forth in the latter volume was the "first systematic program" of its sort that

[95] See Sellery, Review of Ely's *Ground under Our Feet*, in *Wisconsin Magazine of History*, XXII (June, 1939), 463–464; Ely, *Ground under Our Feet*, pp. 104–119 *et passim;* Commons, *Myself* (New York, 1934), pp. 40, 42–44; "Communication from Frederick Jackson Turner to Constance Lindsay Skinner," *Wisconsin Magazine of History*, XIX (September, 1935), 100; Howe, *The Confessions of a Reformer* (New York, 1925), p. 28; and Howe to Ely, December 31, 1900, Ely Papers.

[96] See La Follette, *La Follette's Autobiography* (6th ed.; Madison, Wisc., 1913), pp. 30–32; McCarthy, *The Wisconsin Idea* (New York, 1912), pp. 27–31; and Ely, *Ground under Our Feet*, p. 216.

[97] Ely, *Ground under Our Feet*, pp. 277–279.

[98] Dwight Lowell Dumond, *America in Our Time, 1896–1946* (New York, 1947), p. 461.

had come to Ryan's attention, and Ryan informs us that he never ceased to believe in it.[99]

V

In common with other new-school economists, Simon Nelson Patten rejected laissez faire and affirmed the need for state action on behalf of the general welfare. But, unlike most of his colleagues, Patten believed that the state could best promote the commonweal by a program of conscious planning designed to secure a better adjustment of the American people to their environment. Patten, it is true, did not present a detailed blueprint of the planned society, but he did provide the theoretical foundation upon which such a society could be established.

Patten's views were conditioned to a great extent by the environment in which he spent the formative years of his life. He grew up amid the lush prairie lands of Illinois and so became aware at an early age of the possibility of an economy of abundance. After a few months' study at Northwestern University in 1875, he went to Germany to continue his education under Johannes Conrad at the University of Halle, and he was greatly impressed by the character of the German economy and the intelligent use the Germans made of their resources. Some years after his return from Germany, Patten, as has been noted, collaborated with Edmund James in a vain effort to establish an organization of economists committed to the support of a definite program of state planning for the general welfare. In 1888 Patten became professor of political economy at the University of Pennsylvania, and he continued his association with that institution until his retirement in 1917.[100]

Patten's rather abstruse economic thought differed markedly in its essentials from the thought of the classical economists.[101] Where they concentrated on the objective environment, he concentrated on the subjective environment. Where they emphasized production, he emphasized consumption. Where they talked of a static economy, he talked of a dynamic one.

[99] Ryan, *Social Doctrine in Action* (New York, 1941), pp. 52–54.

[100] Henry Rogers Seager, Introduction, in Patten, *Essays in Economic Theory*, ed. Rexford Guy Tugwell (New York, 1924), p. xiii; Broadus Mitchell, "Simon Nelson Patten," in Allen Johnson and Dumas Malone, eds., *Dictionary of American Biography* (Authors ed.; New York, 1937), XIV, 298–299.

[101] See, especially, Patten, *The Premises of Political Economy* (Philadelphia, 1885).

Patten thought it possible to start economic investigations from the point of view either of nature or of man. Whereas the classical economists, as he saw it, had generally taken the former position and had made objective differences in nature their first premises, Patten preferred that economic investigations begin with man. The progress of civilization, he maintained, had led to the supremacy of man over nature, and, as a result, differences in men had become more important in explaining economic phenomena than had differences in nature.[102]

Patten contended that the classical economists thought in terms of a static economy precisely because they focused their attention on the objective environment. This, he argued, led them to believe that nature is so niggardly and the surplus it yields so small that no radical change in social relations is possible. If they had made man rather than nature the object of their concern, Patten asserted, they would have come to an altogether different conclusion. When man is made the center of attention, one sees that industrial activities and consumption are directed by the wants of men rather than by obstacles imposed by nature. The economic environment, indeed, changes with changes in men. Different classes of men view the world in different ways, and the environment they find depends on their mental characteristics. "The objective laws of a given society," therefore, "are not simply the laws of nature; they are laws derived from the particular combination of natural forces of which the society makes use." Changes in race psychology thus rather obviously give rise to a new economic environment. This new economic environment, through changes in consumption, modifies the standard of life. The standard of life, in turn, acts on the race psychology and in so doing creates new motives in production. This interaction between the subjective and objective environments makes for a dynamic, progressive economy.

A theory of production, Patten thought, must take cognizance both of the mental qualities of producers and of the conditions of nature that tend to develop higher intelligence in men. Improvements in production indicate a change in race psychology and give evidence that a higher type of man has been utilizing some force of nature beyond the reach of lower types of men. The progress in race psychology is most apparent in the ideal it creates of state activity. As race psychology develops, the welfare of society, rather than the welfare of

---

[102] Patten, *The Theory of Dynamic Economics* (Philadelphia, 1892), pp. v–vi.

the individual, becomes the ideal. New wants are created that can be satisfied only by the concerted action of society. When these wants become stronger than the wants of a selfish nature, production is modified, and natural forces can be used to greater advantage.

The causes for the high price of food, low wages, and reduction in the rate of interest do not lie in the objective environment, in the niggardliness of nature, but rather in the subjective condition of producers, in race psychology. Every advance in race psychology serves to open up new fields of employment, to modify wants so as to lower the cost of production, and to change poor land into good land by increasing the demand for a variety of crops. The law of diminishing returns need not, therefore, apply "so long as new avenues are open for the psychical development of the race and the growth of social ideas and feelings." [103]

That strong social feelings are not as yet sufficiently active in guiding production is indicated by the failure of the nation to use the surplus income of society collectively. The rapid increase in the nation's productive power has driven down costs of production and created a surplus revenue over and above the minimum sums that must go to rent, wages, and interest; but this surplus tends to be absorbed by the static classes among the producers, the classes, apparently, that enjoy monopoly power. These static classes not only give back to society less in prosperity than they take from it in surplus, but they also impose their own view of things upon society as a whole. The result is that only certain mental qualities of the individual are encouraged, and a class psychology is formed that is antagonistic to the general welfare. Thus it is that strong social feelings and an active interest in the future welfare of the race, motives that contribute as much to production as natural advantages or the efforts of individuals, are neglected.

Public ends would be better served and a higher standard of living assured, Patten believed, if the state were permitted to capture the surplus revenue by means of taxation and to utilize the funds so obtained to provide such public conveniences as parks, places of amusement, good roads, and efficient systems of drainage and sanitation in the cities and, above all, to establish a system of education that would seek to develop all the productive qualities in man and that

[103] Patten, *Theory of Dynamic Economics,* pp. 36–38, 138–141, 146–147; Patten to Franklin H. Giddings, August 27, 1897, Giddings Papers, Columbia University Library.

would eventually cause every individual to be prompted by the same social feelings and to look upon production from the standpoint of the general welfare.[104]

Subjective factors are perhaps of even greater importance in the field of consumption than in the field of production. Most men refuse to modify habits of consumption formed in the past so as to bring these habits into harmony with a changed environment. Because of the strength of their appetites, they are willing to work hard for a little food, and they avoid forms of production where long series of efforts are required. Although "cheap" men of this sort are in demand for work in factories where skill is no longer necessary, their habits of consumption lead to their destruction. They sacrifice their permanent interests to gratify present feelings. They are intemperate in their use of strong drink and tobacco and are indifferent to the wholesomeness of their food. They crowd together in tenements and disregard the necessity for cleanliness. Some laborers will modify their habits of consumption and will survive, but those who refuse to make the essential adjustments will be exterminated. Natural forces will in this way eventually produce a higher class of laborer; and, although the employer will continue to seek the cheapest man, the cheapest man of one age will be a better man than the cheapest man of an earlier age. Society, however, cannot stand by and permit the lowest classes to be destroyed. It must educate these classes to the necessity of adjusting their habits of consumption to the environment. Society must act to bring as large a part of the population as possible into harmony with the environment.[105]

Convinced that the American people had not adjusted their habits of consumption to American conditions and that they were not employing the nation's land and resources to the best advantage,[106] Pat-

[104] Patten, "The Stability of Prices," *A. E. A. Publications,* III (1889), 408–428; Patten, *Theory of Dynamic Economics,* pp. 148–153; Patten, "The Scope of Political Economy," *Yale Review,* II (November, 1893), 271–272; James Lane Boswell, *The Economics of Simon Nelson Patten* (Philadelphia, 1933), pp. 70–71.

[105] Patten, "The Consumption of Wealth," *Publications of the University of Pennsylvania Political Economy and Public Law Series,* No. 4 (1889), pp. 62–70. Patten believed that society was under a special obligation to the laborer inasmuch as large-scale production and the high price of land had diminished whatever opportunity he had to advance into the ranks of the self-employed (*ibid.,* pp. 68–69).

[106] "If the people here would stop howling about silver and develop their many real resources," Patten wrote to Franklin H. Giddings from Colorado on August 19, 1895, "they could make it a grand country and we would all want to summer here" (Giddings Papers). See also Patten, "The Consumption of Wealth," *Pub-*

ten called on government to institute an "active policy" to bring the people into closer harmony with their environment. The main element in his proposed active policy was the protective tariff. He regarded protection not as a temporary expedient but as part of a "consistent endeavor to keep society dynamic and progressive," as an element in a fixed national policy designed to increase the productive power and value of labor and to bring people into adjustment with their environment. When a nation follows a passive policy, Patten argued, it does not create new opportunities for labor as rapidly as the population increases but, rather, allows the increase of population to find employment on poorer land. This crowding of individuals onto poorer land and into the existing fields of labor serves to increase rents and depress wages and results in a great waste of capital and of productive power. A nation that pursues an active policy can anticipate and obviate this increase in rent and hence in the price of products by bringing new lands into cultivation at public expense and by overcoming the obstacles to the extension of the field of employment. It must, at the same time, adopt a policy of protection, since, otherwise, its rate of wages will be determined by the least progressive nation with which it trades.[107]

In a dynamic society, moreover, individuals are constantly changing with their environment. The new conditions they confront give rise to new wants, and, therefore, new opportunities for labor and industry are continually being created which are superior to those originally put to use. A nation in a dynamic condition will consequently always have infant industries brought into being to supply the demand of the people for new articles. These new industries must

---

lications of the University of Pennsylvania Political Economy and Public Law Series, No. 4 (1889), p. 62; and Patten, *Economic Basis of Protection*, pp. 12, 96–97.

[107] Patten, *Economic Basis of Protection*, pp. 7–8, 54–80, 103–105; Patten, *Premises of Political Economy*, pp. 237–241. Patten also looked to government to maintain high wages and a high rate of interest so as to prevent a few men with skill and surplus capital from combining with those having only their labor to offer and hence being able to undersell competitors who had to combine their own skill and capital with their own labor. The combination of low interest rates and low wages, Patten argued, tended to concentrate capital in the hands of the few, was favorable neither to the increase of capital funds nor to the maintenance of a high standard of living, and discouraged the progress of individuals who otherwise would have saved for themselves and would have utilized opportunities not yet developed by large-scale production. See Patten, *Premises of Political Economy*, pp. 217–237.

be encouraged in every way, and all obstacles in the path of their development must be removed. If we are to have "an orderly, consistent development of our country and its resources," the state must "encourage the introduction of new industries with every change in the tastes, habits, or environment of the people." [108]

An active policy can also be employed to bring the habits of consumption of the people into harmony with the environment. To ensure that those crops will be grown for which the soil is best fitted, the government should create in the vicinity of each class of lands a demand for all that range of products necessary for the best use of the land. Also, through a policy of temporary high prices, the government can encourage the scientific production of desirable articles now crudely produced. Ultimately, scientific production and changed consumption habits will lead to cheaper production costs and lower prices.[109]

In addition to the protective tariff and government intervention to modify consumption habits, Patten regarded internal improvements as a vitally important part of an active policy. He also believed that the industrial development of the South should receive special encouragement. "The key to national prosperity," he declared, "lies in Southern prosperity." The South is the natural market of the West, and until the South itself is developed, the West cannot attain to that prosperity which its natural conditions permit. Patten also placed special stress on education as a means of helping Americans adjust to their surroundings. He thought that there was a great need for manual-training courses to increase the efficiency of the individual laborer, and he considered instruction of this sort "the most efficient means of leading to an adjustment to the new conditions of the country." [110]

The structure of Patten's thought as evidenced in the books and articles he wrote during the 1880's and 1890's was much too complicated and theoretical to win him any great following. What influence he had derived from his ability as a teacher. It was in the classroom that he drove home his ideas about the general welfare and the need for an active policy of government.[111] One can perhaps best

[108] Patten, *Economic Basis of Protection,* pp. 94–98.

[109] Patten, *Economic Basis of Protection,* pp. 31, 112–113, 121–125.

[110] Patten, *Economic Basis of Protection,* pp. 143–144; Patten, *Premises of Political Economy,* pp. 241–244.

[111] Mitchell, "Simon Nelson Patten," in *Dictionary of American Biography,* XIV,

see the influence of Simon Nelson Patten in the work of two of his most famous pupils: Walter Weyl, author of *The New Democracy* and one of the theorists of Progressivism, and Rexford G. Tugwell, a member of Franklin D. Roosevelt's "brain trust" and the director of the New Deal's Resettlement Administration.

VI

It was for only a relatively brief period that the new-school point of view, with its emphasis on the inductive method and the positive state, governed the thought of American economists. In the last decade of the nineteenth century, partly as the result of the influence of English and Austrian economists, there was a trend back to classical economic theory and the deductive method and to a modified form of laissez faire. In America this partial return to classicism was most clearly evidenced in the work of John Bates Clark, greatest of the country's neoclassicists.[112]

Clark was the first of the young American economists who traveled to Germany in the 1870's and 1880's to sit at the feet of the German economists. It was from Karl Knies that Clark, like Ely, learned the approach of the historical school to economic inquiry. In the 1880's Clark was one of the most prominent figures in the new school, and he was active in the establishment of the American Economic Association. But Clark was not to remain in the ranks of the new-school economists.

Clark's economic thought went through a rather curious evolution. In his first important work, *The Philosophy of Wealth*, which appeared in 1886,[113] Clark was extremely critical of classical theory. He insisted that the objective of political economy is not only a quantitative increase of wealth but also a more just distribution. He stressed the necessity for uniting ethics and economics and asserted that "economic man" is more selfish and mechanical than the reality, that "in the last analysis the sense of right in men is a supreme motive, in the market as elsewhere." [114]

299; Dorfman, *Economic Mind in American Civilization*, III, 187–188. Scott Nearing states that Patten always set up one standard in the classroom: the public welfare (*Educational Frontiers: A Book about Simon Nelson Patten and Other Teachers* [New York, 1925], p. 17).

[112] Normano, *Spirit of American Economics*, pp. 139–145.

[113] Most of the essays in this work had been published previously.

[114] Clark, *The Philosophy of Wealth* (Boston, 1885), pp. 48–49, 56, 157–158, 205. See also Clark, "Christianity and Modern Economics," *New Englander and*

In view of his later work, Clark's attitude during this early period as regards competition is of particular interest. He spoke of "competition of the individualistic type" as "rapidly passing out of existence," as giving way to consolidation and monopoly. "The principle which is at the basis of Ricardian economics," he declared, "is ceasing to have any general application to the system under which we live." Clark held that this was as it should be, since competition had become "incapable of working justice." He spoke of moral force as an "alternative regulator." "Competition without moral restraints," he insisted, "is a monster." "Nothing could be wilder or fiercer than an unrestricted struggle of millions of men for gain, and nothing more irrational than to present such a struggle as a scientific ideal." Clark also recognized the necessity for a province of noncompetitive economics: he did not believe that competition worked well in the case of railroads and regarded it as perhaps an ineffective means of adjusting the differences between capital and labor. However, he thought that the competitive system, despite its faults, was superior to other economic systems and that competition was still needed as a guiding principle for distribution. Competition, he declared, should be tolerated insofar as it prevents still greater injustice; but whenever it fails to do this, a superior power should stand ready to abolish it. Where competition survives, it should be recognized as "the imperfect agent of moral law." [115]

Clark, however, although continuing to express sympathy for the cause of social reform,[116] was eventually to abandon his criticism of the competitive system. The year after the publication of *The Philosophy of Wealth* he was already arguing that "pure profit" is annihilated by competition and that the rewards of business life are connected

---

Yale Review, XLVII (July, 1887), 50–51. The religious aspects of Clark's economic thought (and that of Ely and Patten) are discussed in John Rutherford Everett, *Religion in Economics* (New York, 1946).

[115] Clark, *Philosophy of Wealth*, pp. 147–151, 203–208, 219–220.

[116] Clark informed Ely that the latter had "some very excellent reforms in hand. I sympathize with them," he declared, "and wish them all success." He advised Ely, however, not to give the appearance of seeking to merge "the practical augmentation of state functions with doctrinaire socialism, and endorsing the latter." He feared that Ely failed to distinguish between "the natural enlargement of state functions, and the doctrinarian [*sic*] policy of pushing such enlargement toward a goal" (Clark to Ely, November 3, 1890, and March 17, 1891, Ely Papers). Clark informed Lester Ward that his (Clark's) views were closer to those of Ward than to the "antique orthodoxy" (Clark to Ward, February 22, 1893, Lester F. Ward Papers, John Hay Library of Brown University).

with service. In 1893 he asserted that "true competition" can never be suppressed, and the next year we find him declaring that laws that reveal any distrust of the competitive method of adjusting shares of distribution are socialistic. Competition, Clark proclaimed in 1896, is the "social guarantor of progress." [117]

Clark's dissent from the views expressed in *The Philosophy of Wealth* and his complete acceptance of the existing "natural" order are best evidenced in his magnum opus, *The Distribution of Wealth,* published in 1899. In the preface to this work Clark declared that it was his purpose "to show that the distribution of the income of society is controlled by a natural law, and that this law, if it worked without friction, would give to every agent of production the amount of wealth which that agent creates." In a rather remarkable display of deductive reasoning, he attempted to prove that "free competition tends to give to labor what labor creates, to capitalists what capital creates, and to *entrepreneurs* what the co-ordinating function creates." [118] Since the existing scheme of things thus appeared to him to be inherently just, Clark rejected the argument that labor was being exploited and insisted that there was no necessity for government interference with the essentials of the competitive system.

Although his theory of distribution led him directly to laissez faire, Clark, in fact, believed that the government should do a bit more than preserve order and enforce contracts. He was convinced, it is true, that the existing system was fundamentally sound and that the competitive process tended to provide for each individual his "natural share" of the product, but he recognized that there were obstructions in the path of competition that resulted in inequities, and he believed that these obstructions must be removed by government so that "natural economic law" might "have its way." Competition, he de-

---

[117] Clark, "Profits under Modern Conditions," *Political Science Quarterly,* II (December, 1887), 603–619; Clark to Ward, February 22, 1893, Ward Papers; Clark, "The Modern Appeal to Legal Forces in Economic Life," *A. E. A. Publications,* IX (1894), 483–484, 501–502; Clark, "The Theory of Economic Progress," *A. E. A. Economic Studies,* I (1896), 8.

[118] Clark, *The Distribution of Wealth* (New York, 1899), pp. v, 3. Clark dealt only with the static forces in distribution. He recognized that society is always dynamic, but he believed that despite this, the forces at work at any particular moment fix the rates to which prices, wages, and interest tend to conform (*ibid.,* pp. vi, 61). For Veblen's criticism of Clark's thesis that each individual receives in remuneration what he contributes in productivity, see "Industrial and Pecuniary Employments," *A. E. A. Publications,* 3d Ser., II (1901), 190–235.

clared, "is now interfered with. The task of the state is to stop these interferences." State action with this objective in view would constitute "a new and higher type of *laissez-faire,* for it is compelling powers of evil to let beneficent nature alone. . . . Hinder not the grand dynamics of nature," Clark concluded, "but lay hands on whatever perverse agent may now presume to offer hindrances." [119]

Clark's view that the government must enforce competition was reflected particularly in his approach to the trust problem, which for him became the key economic problem of the age. Clark, who looked favorably on the centralization of business but was opposed to monopoly, was convinced that consolidation would not lead to monopoly if competition were kept free, if big business were forbidden to employ unfair methods of competition. In dealing with the trust problem, the state, he advised, must not attempt to limit the size of corporations or to break up large corporations, abolish the tariff suddenly, fix prices, tax profits out of existence, or experiment with schemes of state socialism. The central task of government with respect to this problem, as Clark saw it, was to protect the independent producer. If the trusts were unable to eliminate him, they could not mulct the consumer, pay farmers low prices for raw materials, or depress wages. The efficient little fellow, Clark thought, could take care of himself in a fair struggle, but he was being crushed by unfair methods of competition, by "refined forms of robbery," and these, Clark advised, the state must suppress. It must proscribe factors' agreements, local price cutting, and the "breaking of a general scale of prices" for predatory purposes. Protected against unfair methods of competition, the small businessman, Clark believed, would be able to hold his own. As for the trusts, if they were forbidden to employ unfair methods of competition, potential competition could be relied upon to keep them in line and to prevent them from exercising monopoly power.[120]

As another example of what he intended by the concept of regulated competition, Clark proposed that the railroads be forbidden to

[119] Clark, "The Scholar's Political Opportunity," *Political Science Quarterly,* XII (December, 1897), 590–591, 593–600; Clark, "The Modern Appeal to Legal Forces in Economic Life," *A. E. A. Publications,* IX (1894), 481–501; Clark, "Theory Lecture," January 29, 1896, manuscript in Clark Papers, in possession of John Maurice Clark.

[120] Dorfman, *Economic Mind in American Civilization,* III, 204; Clark, *The Control of Trusts* (New York, 1901), pp. 6–16, 21–88; Clark, "How to Deal with Trusts," *Independent,* LIII (May 2, 1901), 1001–1004; Clark, "Theory Lecture," January 29, 1896, Clark Papers.

discriminate in favor of particular industries but that they be allowed to combine to provide lower rates and better service. He believed that factory legislation for women and children was essential and that workers should be permitted to combine to determine their wages, but he thought that a line must be drawn beyond which trade unions should not be authorized to go. And recognizing the nature of the "corporation problem," Clark pointed out that not only must the public be protected against the corporations but that the owners of corporations must be protected against management.[121]

Clark's intellectual ideal was essentially the competitive society of the classical economists: in the competitive system of private enterprise he saw the best guarantee of the general welfare. But Clark interpreted the policeman role of the state somewhat more broadly than his orthodox predecessors had. Although he did not believe that the state should do anything creative, that it should seek to modify the existing social and economic order in any essential way, he did think that it should clear away whatever obstructs the perfect operation of that order. Let the state act in this way, Clark asserted, and competition will secure justice for all.[122]

The new-school economists and their neoclassical successors thus proposed three basic methods of employing the state as an agency to combat the problems of an industrial age and to promote the general welfare. Ely and Adams advocated a program of social reform consisting of ameliorative measures designed to raise the level of competition to a higher moral plane, to vest in the state the ownership of natural monopolies, and, in general, to minister to the education, health, and general well-being of the citizenry. Simon Nelson Patten urged the necessity of national planning to bring the people into proper adjustment to their environment. John Bates Clark proposed that the state enforce competition and then trust to competition to ensure social progress. The reform movements of the twentieth century were to witness the implementation in varying degrees of each of these approaches to the age-old problem of the relationship of the state to the individual and to the economy.

[121] Clark, "The Scholar's Political Opportunity," *Political Science Quarterly,* XII (December, 1897), 600–601.

[122] "It is interesting," Paul T. Homan remarks, "that a system reminiscent of the earlier advocates of *laissez-faire* should end upon a note of government regulation" (*Contemporary Economic Thought,* p. 92). See also Ely, "A Decade of Economic Theory," *Annals of the American Academy of Political and Social Science,* XV (March, 1900), 249–250.

VIII

SOCIOLOGY, POLITICAL SCIENCE, AND PRAGMATISM

INSOFAR as sociology existed as a recognized body of knowledge in the United States after the Civil War and before 1883, it was dominated by the thought of Herbert Spencer.[1] In 1883, however, Lester Frank Ward completed his monumental *Dynamic Sociology* and gave to sociology a new orientation. Ward's work exerted an important influence on Albion W. Small and Edward A. Ross and a lesser influence on Franklin H. Giddings, and these three men, like Ward, played important roles in the fashioning of American sociological thought. Ward, Ross, and Small parted from laissez faire and sought to ally sociology with the general-welfare state. Giddings was unwilling to follow this course, but though his sympathies were with laissez faire, he was considerably less an opponent of state action than were Spencer and Sumner.

The sociology that emerged in America in the 1880's and 1890's had important ties with the developments in political economy and religion already noted. Ward, Ross, Small, and Giddings were all members at one time or another of the American Economic Association, and Ross in 1892 became the secretary of that organization. Ross and Small learned their economics from Richard T. Ely, and both, for a

[1] In 1883 the only college course that went by the name of sociology was that offered by Yale's William Graham Sumner. The field of the social sciences was completely undefined. Sociological subjects were dealt with in courses in philanthropy, the history of civilization, the philosophy of history, and social science. See Jesse Bernard, "The History and Prospects of Sociology in the United States," in George A. Lundberg *et al.*, eds., *Trends in American Sociology* (New York, 1929), pp. 5–12.

time, taught economics in the Ely manner.[2]   Giddings was an associate
of John Bates Clark and was co-author with him of a work on economic
theory.[3]   Significantly, with respect to the functions of the state, the
sociology of Ross and Small bears a strong resemblance to the economics of Ely, whereas there is a similar correspondence between the
sociology of Giddings and the economics of Clark.

The social-gospel movement also left its impress on sociological
thought during this period.   Although Ward evidenced no interest
in the subject of social Christianity, Small, Ross, and Giddings were
much concerned with the relationship of ethics and social progress.
Small, who had been trained in theology, was particularly sympathetic
to the ideals of the social gospel and hoped to see the church become a
more effective social factor.[4]

II

Greatest of the American sociologists in the last two decades of
the nineteenth century and the true founder of American sociology
was Lester Frank Ward.   In Ward, Herbert Spencer found one of his
most formidable critics.   It was Ward, as much as any individual,
who undermined the Spencerian do-nothing social philosophy and
laid the scientific basis for the positive state.[5]

Born in 1841 in Joliet, Illinois, and brought up under frontier conditions, Ward was impressed at an early age with the ability of man
to cope with the forces of nature.   After having served for twenty-
seven months with the Union forces and having been wounded at
Chancellorsville, Ward in 1865 obtained a position in the United States
Treasury Department.   Eventually becoming chief paleontologist, he

[2] Ross, *Seventy Years of It: An Autobiography* (New York, 1936), pp. 40, 56;
Small to Ely, November 3, 1889, Richard T. Ely Papers, State Historical Society of
Wisconsin; James Dombrowski, *The Early Days of Christian Socialism in America*
(New York, 1936), p. 9.

[3] *The Modern Distributive Process* (Boston, 1888).

[4] Small to Ward, April 10, 1895, in Bernhard J. Stern, ed., "The Letters of
Albion W. Small to Lester F. Ward," *Social Forces*, XII (December, 1933), 171.

[5] James P. Lichtenberger refers to Ward as "the spokesman for his generation in
the overthrow of the *laissez faire* theory, and in the emphasis upon the possibility of
the conscious control and direction of social forces in the interest of human welfare
through the dissemination of scientific knowledge" (*Development of Social Theory*
[New York, 1923]), p. 357.   An understanding account of Ward's social thought
and influence is contained in Henry Steele Commager, *The American Mind: An
Interpretation of American Thought and Character since the 1880's* (New Haven,
1950), pp. 203–216.

remained in government employ in one capacity or another for forty-one years and observed that there were many positive ways in which the state could serve the individual and society. Ward began work on his *Dynamic Sociology* in 1869 and completed the task in 1883. In numerous books and articles published during the remaining years of the century, he clarified and amplified his sociological views and reiterated his plea for an extension of social controls.[6]

It was Ward's belief that sociology must serve a utilitarian purpose: he disagreed with those who contended that sociology was a pure science and that its laws and principles did not have to be applied to contemporaneous social movements. Ward felt that the widespread discontent of the age in which he lived should be diverted into proper channels by those who understood the laws that had generated it, and he thought that catastrophe would result were not science and reform united. "The problem of to-day," he remarked, "is how to help on a certain evolution by averting an otherwise equally certain revolution."[7] The supreme purpose of sociology in Ward's view was thus "the betterment of society." "Dynamic Sociology," he declared, "aims at the organization of happiness."[8]

Ward recognized two types of social progress: genetic (passive dynamic) and telic (active dynamic). Genetic progress, he explained, refers to the unconscious working of the social forces. Society is considered completely passive and is acted upon by the forces of nature. This is the type of progress that has taken place in the animal and vegetable worlds and in the inorganic kingdoms of nature, and it cannot be denied that this process has also resulted in some sort of social development. As a matter of fact, genetic progress is the only type of social progress that most social scientists recognize. What they understand by social evolution is the "blind, unconscious working

[6] Ward did not enter academic ranks until 1906, when he became professor of sociology at Brown University.

[7] Ward, "The Utilitarian Character of Dynamic Sociology," in *Glimpses of the Cosmos* (New York, 1913–1918), IV, 312–315. (*Glimpses of the Cosmos* contains all of Ward's "minor papers and addresses" and some autobiographical notes.) See also Ward, *Outlines of Sociology* (New York, 1898), pp. 193–194; and Ward, *Dynamic Sociology* (New York, 1883), I, 54–56.

[8] Ward, *Outlines of Sociology*, pp. 203–207; Ward, *Dynamic Sociology*, II, 159; Ward, "Sociology and Economics," *Annals of the American Academy of Political and Social Science*, XIII (March, 1899), 233. (Henceforth, the *Annals* will be referred to simply by that term.)

of the social forces making for human perfectionment in the collective state." [9]

Human evolution, however, involves something more than the blind working of the social forces. The development of the intellectual faculty results in an entirely new type of social progress, which may be called "telic," and the greater part of human evolution is of this sort.[10] Telic progress results from the application of the intellect to nature. Man uses his mind power in conjunction with his will power to guide the forces of nature to his advantage. Progress of this sort is absolutely necessary inasmuch as genetic progress, although it has resulted in considerable material advance, works too slowly to keep pace with the wants of an increasing population.[11]

Refuting the central tenet of the Spencer-Sumner school of sociologists that nature's way is superior to man's way and that human interference with nature invariably results in evil, Ward demonstrated the effectiveness of man's method, the telic, as compared to nature's, the genetic. There is enormous waste in nature, he contended. Nature utterly disregards the amount of energy required to produce a given result and often pays an extravagant price for a small return. Consider, for example, nature's prodigality with respect to reproduction. The octopus must lay fifty thousand eggs to maintain itself. A codfish must hatch one million young fish a year so that two will survive. In the vegetable kingdom, a single plant has been found to contain more than three million spores. The very terms "natural selection" and "survival of the fittest" imply that the bulk of things are not selected and that only the few survive.

The apparent peace in nature is, moreover, illusory. There is constant strife going on in the natural world, and this strife, far from resulting in the survival of the fittest possible, causes a comparatively low level of development for all forms that do survive. As a result, only the actually fittest, not the fittest possible, survive.[12]

[9] Ward, *Dynamic Sociology*, I, 56–57; Ward, *Outlines of Sociology*, pp. 179, 220–223.

[10] Ward criticized Spencer for resting his sociology on biology rather than on psychology ("The Political Ethics of Herbert Spencer," *Annals*, IV [January, 1894], 595–604).

[11] Ward, *Dynamic Sociology*, I, 28–30; Ward, *Outlines of Sociology*, pp. 179–182, 235; Ward, *The Psychic Factors of Civilization* (Boston, 1893), pp. 242–244; Ward, "Mind as a Social Factor," in *Glimpses of the Cosmos*, III, 367–369.

[12] Ward, "Scientific Basis of Positive Political Economy," in *Glimpses of the*

Contrast with the wasteful genetic method the method of man, the telic method. Telic phenomena, which are produced when mind interferes with nature, are characterized by will and purpose, are psychical rather than physical, and produce effects at a distance from, and of a greater value than, the causes themselves. Only with man is there true economy, for to do things economically requires foresight and design. Whereas the environment transforms the animal, man transforms the environment. Whereas nature gives us only the actually fittest species, man works toward the fittest possible. He removes competition in favor of one species, and that species then outstrips all others. It is man's interference with the competition in nature that has produced horticulture and breeding and has given us cereals and fruit trees and domesticated animals. Through the process of invention man has controlled the natural forces and made them serve his needs. It is man's intellect that has guided the natural forces and given us our civilization. It is the mind factor that has devised institutions to mitigate the harshness of the struggle for existence and to protect the weak. Whenever man places his artificial stamp upon things, he improves them. Thus it is that human progress has been the result chiefly of artificial selection rather than of natural selection.[13]

In the main, however, the telic method has thus far been employed only by the individual (individual telesis) rather than by society as a whole (collective telesis) and has been applied chiefly to physical and mechanical phenomena rather than to social phenomena. "The functions of society are performed in a sort of random chance manner," with the result that the same waste is evident in the social and economic world as occurs when nature is uncontrolled. Natural resources are squandered without any regard for the future; the soil is exhausted; forests are plundered; the population distributes itself poorly; cities grow up unplanned; transportation facilities are duplicated; there is strife between labor and capital and an inequitable distribution of wealth; millions are overworked and other millions are unemployed in the "soulless struggle for existence and scramble for

Cosmos, III, 33–34; Ward, Dynamic Sociology, I, 72–73, and II, 86–88; Ward, Psychic Factors of Civilization, pp. 251–252, 260–261.

[13] Ward, "Scientific Basis of Positive Political Economy," in Glimpses of the Cosmos, III, 36–37, 47–48; Ward, "Mind as a Social Factor," ibid., pp. 369–374, 376–377; Ward, Dynamic Sociology, I, 33–35; II, 205–206; Ward, Psychic Factors of Civilization, pp. 256–257, 260–262. Spencer, of course, found fault with this view. "I regard social progress [he wrote to Ward] as mainly a question of character, and not of knowledge or enlightenment" (Glimpses of the Cosmos, III, 213).

gain." Moreover, the unrestrained competition postulated by the natural laws of trade, far from distributing the favors of the world according to merit, as Sumner contends it does,[14] brings only waste and disorder and consequently invites unrestrained combination. Combination in turn leads to monopoly and higher prices and the stifling of free individual activity.[15]

Rather than entrust social and economic development to the wasteful operation of "unregulated natural forces," Ward called on society as a whole to apply the active-dynamic—the telic—method and to subject social phenomena to intelligent social control in the public interest. He regarded such action as eminently practicable because he believed that the movement of society is controlled by a particular set of natural forces, the social forces, which are as capable of direction as any of the natural forces. "Society itself," he asserted, "is the domain of law and . . . its movements, so far from being sporadic, irregular, and incapable of classification or prediction, are the strict determinable products of antecedent causes, which can be studied and known by man in the same way that the causes of physical phenomena have been studied and learned by him—by the scientific method." If man can subjugate and control all other natural forces, he is perfectly capable of controlling the social forces. Why should these forces alone be left to chance? There is no more reason to presume that the social forces, of themselves, will produce grand results than to believe that unguided physical forces would have produced the printing press and the cotton gin.[16]

But the defenders of laissez faire maintain that society always does better when left alone, that social legislation not only fails to improve matters but has in most cases resulted in positive harm. The social engineer need not, however, be deterred by this argument. If social legislation had been completely inoperative, that, truly, would be a

[14] Ward referred to Sumner's *What Social Classes Owe to Each Other* as "a sort of final wail against the modern practices of states and peoples which run counter to . . . current theories" ("Professor Sumner's Social Classes," in *Glimpses of the Cosmos,* III, 301).

[15] Ward, "Scientific Basis of Positive Political Economy," in *Glimpses of the Cosmos,* III, 34–36; Ward, "The Sociological Basis of Protection and Free Trade," *ibid.,* IV, 186–189; Ward, *Dynamic Sociology,* I, 29–30; Ward, *Psychic Factors of Civilization,* pp. 263–276.

[16] Ward, *Dynamic Sociology,* I, vi, 35–36, 50–51, 54, 57–59; Ward, *Outlines of Sociology,* pp. 186–187; Ward, "Scientific Basis of Positive Political Economy," in *Glimpses of the Cosmos,* III, 48.

cause for discouragement; but if legislative measures have produced harmful consequences, this at least proves that law can accomplish something, and the problem, therefore, is simply to ensure that it accomplishes what is desired.[17]

True legislation is, after all, but a form of invention by which the legislator seeks to control the social forces in the interests of society in the same manner as the inventor attempts to control certain natural forces. If government has thus far failed in its efforts to promote the general welfare, it is merely because it has been ill-adapted to the ends that it should serve and because legislators, ignorant of the forces they have been trying to control, have bungled the job. If government is to control the social forces successfully, legislators must become sociologists, and the art of government must be treated as an applied social science. "Before progressive legislation can become a success, every legislature must become, as it were, a polytechnic school, a laboratory of philosophical research into the laws of society and of human nature." "No legislator," Ward asserted, "is qualified to propose or vote on measures designed to affect the destinies of millions of social units until he masters all that is known of the science of society." [18]

Ward suggested various means that might be employed to make government more scientific in character. He favored the establishment of a national university that would provide instruction in the science and art of government and whose graduates would staff the administrative offices of the federal government.[19] Scientific legislation, he thought, could be promoted through a more extensive use of the committee system, through enlargement of the administrative jurisdiction of government, and especially through a wise use of statistics. He suggested that "every movement of whatever nature going on in the country" be reported regularly to a central bureau of statistics, which would systematize the facts and then submit them to Congress. Armed with this information, Congress would be able to plan for the sound operation of the national economy.[20]

[17] Ward, *Dynamic Sociology*, I, 36–37; Ward, "The Political Ethics of Herbert Spencer," *Annals*, IV (January, 1894), 601–605.

[18] Ward, *Dynamic Sociology*, I, 37, and II, 249–252.

[19] The Ward Papers afford abundant evidence of Ward's interest in the establishment of a university of this type. See also "A National University, Its Character and Purpose," in *Glimpses of the Cosmos*, IV, 324–325.

[20] Ward, *Psychic Factors of Civilization*, pp. 310–312; Ward, "The Way to Scientific Lawmaking," in *Glimpses of the Cosmos*, II, 168–171.

Government would take on a more scientific character, Ward thought, if it made greater use of "attractive" rather than "compulsory" legislation. Existing laws, he contended, were mainly of the coercive type ("We are living in the 'stone age' of the art of government") in that they appealed to the fear of punishment rather than holding out inducements for beneficent action. Attractive legislation, Ward believed, would make it possible to divert human desires into socially useful channels. Such legislation, employing the indirect, intellectual method, would make it advantageous to the individual to do what is for the good of society. As examples of attractive legislation, Ward pointed to the protective tariff, subsidies to railroads, and bounties to steamship lines. He regarded such legislative schemes as appropriate means of inducing individuals to exert themselves in a manner that benefits society; and he thought that sociologist and statesman should coöperate to devise additional legislation of this sort.[21]

To Ward, however, popular scientific education was the real key to collective telesis, to social planning. If sociological knowledge were confined to the select few, they might use this information for purposes of self-aggrandizement, but if the knowledge of the principles of sociology were diffused throughout society, it would then be possible for society to make intelligent use of the forces and materials existing in nature and to achieve greater progress than could be wrought by natural selection alone. Popular scientific education, Ward therefore concluded, is the great panacea, "the one clear, overshadowing and immediate social duty to which all others are subordinate." [22]

Ward was not unmindful of the criticism of government and government practice by the advocates of laissez faire, and, indeed, he conceded that this criticism was, on the whole, justified. It was his contention, however, that the shortcomings of government were basi-

---

[21] Ward, *Dynamic Sociology*, I, 39–45, and II, 249–250; Ward, *Outlines of Sociology*, pp. 187–189, 272–277; Ward, "The Sociological Position of Protection and Free Trade," in *Glimpses of the Cosmos*, IV, 182–184.

[22] Ward, *Dynamic Sociology*, I, 12–27, and II, 593–607, 625–633; Ward, Preface to the Second Edition, in *Dynamic Sociology* (2d ed.; New York, 1897), I, xvii. See also Ward, "Broadening the Way to Success," *Forum*, II (December, 1886), 340–350. Early in his career Ward planned a book to be entitled *The Great Panacea* which was to demonstrate the importance of education to social progress. This projected work eventually developed into the *Dynamic Sociology*. See Elsa Peverly Kimball, *Sociology and Education: An Analysis of the Theories of Spencer and Ward* (New York, 1932), pp. 253–254.

cally the result of the unscientific character of existing governments and that with the general increase of sociological knowledge and the application of the telic method, the evils of government would fall by the way, and government would, as a result, become a great force for good.[23]

As Ward saw it, government has four main functions: restraint, protection, accommodation, and the improvement or amelioration of society. Ward looked upon protection and restraint as complementary functions. When the government protects some individuals in their rights, he explained, it restrains others, at the same time, from interfering with these rights. The protection offered by government is based on the idea that men living without government will injure one another far more than government injures them. Governments have always appealed for support on the basis of the protective function, and it must be admitted that protection is still a necessary function of government even in the most enlightened countries. The function of accommodation is based on the relationship of principal to agent. Society, the principal, employs government, the agent, to perform certain tasks of common interest to the members of society. Ward thought this "the most simple and legitimate sphere of government," but felt that it was one to which scant attention had been paid by political theorists in their discussion of the functions of government. He regarded the accommodative function as a step in the direction of the ameliorative function, but he did not think that government was yet aware of its responsibilities as regards the latter. Nor did he believe that government would be able to perform the all-important ameliorative function adequately until it became more scientific in character.[24]

Ward saw that in his own day there was a marked discrepancy between theory and practice with respect to the functions of the state. Whereas all civilized nations were increasing the scope of their activities, the dominant social philosophy, laissez faire, condemned the bulk of the action taken. Ward, who believed that government should be limited in its functions only by its ability to serve the general welfare, was unwilling to accept the argument of some of the advocates of laissez faire that the disposition of the people to use the state as an instrument of reform was but a temporary madness that would soon

[23] Ward, *Dynamic Sociology*, I, 53–55, and II, 224–227; Ward, *Psychic Factors of Civilization*, pp. 301–302.

[24] Ward, *Dynamic Sociology*, II, 214–217, 231–250.

subside. He saw no reason to anticipate that there would be a return to laissez faire.[25]

Ward regarded the arguments against state action that were being employed in his day as utterly anachronistic. He thought that there was good reason to have advanced these arguments when it was necessary for society to rid itself of an onerous oligarchical control, but the use of the same arguments to combat the activities of a representative government seemed to him to be rather wide of the mark. In a representative government, he declared, the state is not something apart from the people but is simply the agency through which society "expresses and enforces its collective will." So-called state interference is but a case of society managing its own affairs. It is, indeed, this very conception that somehow society must manage its own affairs that underlies the trend toward increased government action.[26]

Ward repudiated the contention of the theorists of laissez faire that the state is incapable of managing great enterprises. He pointed to the government-owned Post Office, the nation's public-education system, the local fire department, the Naval Observatory, the United States Geological Survey, and the success of state ownership schemes in Europe as evidence of the ability of the state to perform important tasks. Such acknowledged functions of government as control of finances, criminal jurisprudence, customs regulation, postal affairs, and education, he pointed out, had at one time been in the domain of private enterprise, but society had determined that these important activities must be assumed by the state. The state, Ward believed, had demonstrated its superiority to private enterprise in the management of large projects of a public character.[27]

Despite the increasing amount of state regulation, big business, Ward argued, had succeeded in creating a public sentiment that was opposed to state interference. Those who profited by the *status quo* had capitalized on the popular faith in individual liberty and the widespread distrust of government stemming from governmental abuses of

[25] Ward, "Politico-Social Functions," in *Glimpses of the Cosmos*, II, 335–338; Ward, *Psychic Factors of Civilization*, pp. 302–303.

[26] Ward, "Politico-Social Functions," in *Glimpses of the Cosmos*, II, 339–341; Ward, "The Political Ethics of Herbert Spencer," *Annals*, IV (January, 1894), 606–607; Ward, *Psychic Factors of Civilization*, pp. 317–318; Ward, "False Notions of Government," *Forum*, III (June, 1887), 364–367; Ward, *Outlines of Sociology*, p. 264.

[27] Ward, *Dynamic Sociology*, II, 578–593; Ward, "Politico-Social Functions," in *Glimpses of the Cosmos*, II, 346–350.

bygone days and had nursed along the negative view of the state. Yet the businessmen who upheld laissez faire and denounced paternalism were the same businessmen who invoked the aid of the state to further their own interests. Indeed, if there was any paternalism about which to complain, it was the protection and aid which the state afforded to wealth. The government, which failed signally to defend the weak, seemed to devote its principal energies to protecting the strong. It legalized trusts, subsidized corporations, sustained speculations, granted valuable franchises, and "creates, defends, and protects a vast array of purely parasitic enterprises." It was government that made the possession of wealth possible, government that afforded business activities the protection of the law. "Those who denounce state interference," Ward asserted, "are the ones who most frequently and successfully invoke it. The cry of *laissez faire* mainly goes up from the ones who, if really 'let alone,' would instantly lose their wealth-absorbing power."

Business elements kept alive the antigovernment sentiment, Ward contended, not because they believed in laissez faire but because they feared that if the laissez-faire philosophy were abandoned, government would consider the unequal distribution of wealth, which was the greatest evil of society, as within its purview and, in coping with this problem, would trench on the domain of those who benefited most from the *status quo*. When big business cried paternalism, it was therefore merely referring to government action that would recognize the claim of "the defenceless laborer and artisan" to a share of the state protection afforded business.[28]

Ward was convinced that the America of his day was ruled by a plutocracy and that government, in neglecting to protect the people against the abuses of wealth, was failing in its most important duty. Not wishing to see society submit to the power of wealth, he advocated the establishment of a "genuine people's government, with ample power to protect society against all forms of injustice, . . . coupled with a warm and dutiful regard for the true interests of each and all, the poor as well as the rich." [29]

[28] Ward, "Plutocracy and Paternalism," *Forum*, XX (November, 1895), 304–309; Ward, *Psychic Factors of Civilization*, pp. 319–321.

[29] Ward, *Psychic Factors of Civilization*, p. 322; Ward, "Plutocracy and Paternalism," *Forum*, XX (November, 1895), 309–310; Ward, "False Notions of Government," *ibid.*, III (June, 1887), 369–372.

Society, Ward believed, should take over from the individual and should consciously direct the social forces so as to shape its own destiny. To this "scientific control of the social forces by the collective mind of society," he gave the name "sociocracy." Sociocracy, he explained, "is the symbol of positive social action as against the negativism of the dominant *laissez faire* school of politico-economic *doctrinaires.*" Once sociocracy was established, Ward felt certain that all irrelevant issues would be set aside and that society, through government, would concentrate on advancing its own interests. Sociocracy would be free from the errors of both individualism and socialism. Whereas individualism had created artificial inequalities and socialism sought to create artificial equalities, sociocracy would recognize natural inequalities but would abolish artificial inequalities. Whereas the system of individualism conferred benefits only on the intelligent, the cunning, or the fortunate, and socialism sought to bestow equal benefits on all, sociocracy would confer benefits according to merit and would insist on equality of opportunity as the means of determining the degree of merit.[30]

Unlike Richard T. Ely, Lester Ward had no concrete program of social reform to submit to the public: he was, to be sure, less interested in individual measures of reform than in providing the scientific basis for the planned society, for sociocracy. However, Ward, as noted, believed that sociocracy could not be instituted unless knowledge of the social forces were diffused throughout society, and until this scientific stage was attained he looked to social reform to keep society and the state from lagging behind the march of events.[31]

Although Ward was not really well-known as a sociologist until near the close of the nineteenth century,[32] he was by no means an insignificant figure during the eighties and nineties. Not only did he exert a tremendous influence on his fellow sociologists, Ross and Small, but his views on laissez faire and the state found great favor with such prominent individuals as Andrew D. White, Richard T. Ely,

[30] Ward, *Psychic Factors of Civilization*, pp. 323–327; Ward, *Dynamic Sociology*, I, 60; Ward, "Politico-Social Functions," in *Glimpses of the Cosmos*, II, 353; Ward, *Outlines of Sociology*, pp. 292–293.

[31] Ward, *Psychic Factors of Civilization*, pp. 99–101.

[32] Samuel Chugerman blames the neglect of Ward on the general neglect of sociology in his age, Ward's refusal to meddle in practical politics, his agnosticism, and his "radicalism" (*Lester F. Ward, the American Aristotle* [Durham, N. C., 1939], pp. 68–76).

Washington Gladden, and Westel Woodbury Willoughby.[33]   A series of semipopular articles that he wrote for the *Forum* elicited a wide and mostly favorable response.[34]   Although he was doubtless considerably oversanguine as to the potentialities of popular education and the ability and willingness of society to control the social forces and although his hopes with respect to sociocracy have not been altogether realized, Ward, as one contemporary historian has remarked, "was the prophet of . . . all those movements looking to that reconstruction of society and economy through government intervention which is the most striking development in the political history of the last half-century in America." [35]

III

Ward's *Dynamic Sociology* was virtually an unknown work until its merit was recognized in 1890 by Albion Woodbury Small, then president of Colby University (now Colby College).   Son of a Baptist minister and a graduate of Newton Theological Seminary, Small in 1879 made the scholar's pilgrimage to Germany to continue his studies.   He taught history and political economy at Colby from 1881 to 1888 and the next year took his Ph.D. at Johns Hopkins University. Soon afterward he became president of Colby.   Small also taught part time at that institution, and in 1890 introduced a course in sociology. In 1892 he was called to the University of Chicago to head the department of sociology, the first of its kind anywhere in the world.

Small regarded the sociology of Ward as marking "an immeasurable advance upon that of Spencer."   Spencer's sociology, he maintained, ended where sociology should begin.   It reduced sociology to mere description and ignored the whole field of active social dynamics.   "Such sociology," Small declared, "can have no more direct

[33] White thought that Ward's "Psychological Basis of Social Economics" showed "the weak basis of the whole *laissez-faire* system."   Ely drew on Ward's *Dynamic Sociology* to buttress his views on labor organizations and coöperatives.   Gladden accepted Ward's arguments with respect to social determinism.   See White to Ward, March 31, 1893, Ward Papers, John Hay Library of Brown University; Ely to Ward, November 10, 1887, July 30, 1890, *ibid.*; Gladden, "Can Our Social Ills Be Remedied?" *Forum*, VIII (September, 1889), 18–19; and Willoughby, *An Examination of the Nature of the State* (New York, 1896), pp. 329–333.

[34] See letters to Ward, 1886–1887, 1895, in Ward Papers.

[35] Commager, *American Mind*, pp. 215–216.   See also James Q. Dealey *et al.*, "Lester Frank Ward," *American Journal of Sociology*, XIX (July, 1913), 65; and Harry Elmer Barnes, Foreword, in Chugerman, *Ward*, p. 11.

influence upon human progress than a census of the waves of the ocean could have upon the speed of ships." On the other hand, Ward, in Small's view, made sociology teleological rather than descriptive and demonstrated that social evolution was a distinctly psychical product.[36]

Small's sociological viewpoint was primarily ethical. He looked on Christian ideals and precise social science as complementary and sought to combine knowledge with love, a thorough analysis of the complexities of existing social conditions with a study of the ethics of the New Testament. He was not interested in the mere gathering of facts apart from their use for social improvement. There is something better than science, he declared, and that is "prevision by means of science, and . . . intelligent direction of endeavor to realize the vision." Although descriptive sociology, Small maintained, must be a synthesis of the facts concerning the society of the past and the present, social statics is "the science of social ideals . . . a qualitative and approximate account of the society which ought to be. . . . Social Statics is, in brief, Social Ethics." [37] To Small, it was the ultimate purpose of sociology "to discover the principles of coöperation by application of which human society may adopt the most effective means of securing happiness." He dedicated the *American Journal of Sociology*, which he edited, to the support of "every wise endeavor to insure the good of men." [38]

In his consideration of questions involving state action and individual rights, Small, like Ward, rejected laissez faire and looked upon the proper expansion of state functions as conducive to the general welfare. His views in this regard are clearly illustrated in his analysis of the relation of the state to property in general and to the corporation in particular.

[36] Small and George E. Vincent, *An Introduction to the Study of Society* (New York, 1894), pp. 46, 50–51. This volume was "perhaps the first elementary textbook in sociology prepared for popular use as a college text" (Howard W. Odum, *American Sociology* [New York, 1951], p. 104).

[37] Small, "Sanity in Social Agitation," *American Journal of Sociology*, IV (November, 1898), 348–349; Small, "Scholarship and Social Agitation," *ibid.*, I (March, 1896), 564; Small, "Static and Dynamic Sociology," *ibid.*, I (September, 1895), 207–209; Small and Vincent, *Introduction to the Study of Society*, pp. 19–20, 66–67.

[38] Small, "The Relation of Sociology to Economics," *Journal of Political Economy*, III (March, 1895), 183; Small, "The Era of Sociology," *American Journal of Sociology*, I (July, 1895), 15.

With respect to claims upon property, Small distinguished between "ownership" and "proprietorship." He applied the term "ownership" to "claims that are practically absolute" and the term "proprietorship" to claims with "institutionalized limits," and he thought it necessary to distinguish sharply between these two types of claims. He believed that the right of exclusive ownership should be limited to "one's just portion of the fruits of one's labor" and contended that as soon as partnership is involved in production or consumption, absolute ownership ends, and proprietorship begins. Thus he insisted that natural resources, accumulated capital, perfected methods and processes, and chemical and medical discoveries are not properly the object of individual ownership: they "belong to man, not to men." When they are permitted to become the absolute possession of individuals, other members of the community are deprived of their ethical claim to a share of the social heritage. Small had no desire to see private property abolished, but he did look forward to the socialization of both property and the individual, and it was to this end that he advocated a careful distinction between different types of property rights.[39]

In similar fashion, Small thought that the rights of corporations must be subordinated to the general welfare. Corporations, he contended, should be regarded as servants of the public and should be taken to task whenever they fail to serve public ends. Not only should legislation be passed that defines the manner in which corporate action must recognize the public interest, but the public should be permitted to alter corporate charters whenever it thinks that it is in the general interest to do so. Small anticipated the "progressive public absorption of corporate and monopolistic advantages" and believed that the town that did not own its gas and electric works, its water supply, and its street railway was "presumably a town of low grade both in economic intelligence and in civic virtue."[40]

IV

When young Edward A. Ross transferred his major interest from economics to sociology, he, like Small, enlisted under the banner of Lester Ward. Finding the sociology of Spencer completely unsatis-

[39] Small, "Scholarship and Social Agitation," *American Journal of Sociology,* I (March, 1896), 571–578. See also Small, "Private Business Is a Public Trust," *ibid.,* I (November, 1895), 282.

[40] Small, "The State and Semi-Public Corporations," *American Journal of Sociology,* I (January, 1896), 398–410.

factory, Ross introduced his sociology class at Stanford to Ward's *Dynamic Sociology*. The students, he wrote to Ward, were "wildly enthusiastic over it." [41]

Ross, like Ward, found it impossible to accept the basic assumptions of the social Darwinists. He refused to identify competition with natural selection. He did not think that the struggle for existence was helping the abler members of society to multiply more rapidly than the less able, and he therefore saw no reason for giving the "fittest" free rein.[42] He also found fault with Spencer's distinction between the voluntary coöperation that obtains in industrial life and the compulsory coöperation of government. He argued that whereas government had formerly implied the rule of one, or of the few, it had come to mean the rule of the majority. On the other hand, the rule of the individual that prevailed at one time in industry had been replaced by the rule of the majority or of the few responsible to the majority (as in the corporation and the labor union). In this way, government had become liberalized and industry centralized so that they met at a common point: majority rule. There was therefore no sociological difference between private activity and state activity, and in any particular case the only valid question to be asked was whether the state or the individual could perform the task more cheaply and more efficiently.[43]

In the conflict between laissez faire and sociocracy, Ross aligned himself with Ward.[44] "In order to protect ourselves against the lawlessness, the insolence, and the rapacity of over-grown private interests," he declared, "we shall have to develop the state, especially on its administrative side." He referred to "social welfare" as "merely a synonym for the gain that comes through joint action," and he looked to social control as one means of securing this objective.[45]

[41] Ross to Ward, January 28, 1892, Ward Papers.

[42] Ross to Ward, November 25, 1894, Ward Papers; Ross, *Seventy Years of It*, pp. 55–56.

[43] Ross to Ward, December 13, 1891, in Stern, ed., "The Ward-Ross Correspondence, 1891–1896," *American Sociological Review*, III (June, 1938), 364.

[44] The ethical-minded Ross did not, however, believe that education alone was sufficient to attain the progress that Ward envisioned. "Should there not," he asked Ward, "along with developing intelligence to give us command over natural and social forces, go increasingly a developing sympathy to prevent the (socially) costly pursuit of individual gain?" (Ross to Ward, February 22, 1892, in Stern, ed., "The Ward-Ross Correspondence, 1891–1896," *American Sociological Review*, III [June, 1938], 368).

[45] Ross, *Social Control* (New York, 1901), pp. 88, 418–419. Among the

V

The revolt against the Spencer-Sumner brand of laissez faire and social determinism that was inspired by Lester Ward and that received the strong and able support of Albion Small and Edward Ross did not gain the adherence of Franklin Henry Giddings. However, although Giddings' sociological writings bear the heavy impress of the thought of Herbert Spencer, he was considerably less an opponent of state action than was Spencer. He did not subscribe to Ward's sociocracy, but neither did he endorse a policy of complete laissez faire.

Like Small and Ross, Giddings came to sociology by way of economics. Giddings' economics, however, was not of the new-school variety. Long an intimate friend and associate of John Bates Clark, Giddings adhered rather strictly to the classical tradition. The faith in the natural order of things, so evident in Giddings' sociology, was also a hallmark of his economic thought.

Unimpressed by the attack of the new-school economists on classical theory, Giddings continued to believe that the "essential Ricardian principles" were as true in his day as they had ever been. He spoke of a "natural rate of wages" which is fixed by competition and is at the same time the ethical and the economic rate and contended that legislation and trade-union activity can modify the rate of wages only where competition is imperfect.[46] He believed that even the trusts were ruled by economic law and that potential competition would prevent them from gouging the public. "Economic law," said Giddings, "is as inexorable as the law of gravitation, and business will never cease to be controlled by it." [47]

---

specific reforms which Ross advocated were "radical limitation" of the work of children and married women, the establishment of legal standards of safety, health, and decency for factories and workshops, reservation by state governments in the charters of industrial corporations of the right to compel arbitration in labor disputes, the supplying of cheap municipal water, light, and transportation or else the taxing of monopoly profits to provide public improvements, and the implementation of a policy designed to secure " 'reasonable' prices" for everyday items manufactured by trusts. See Kansas Bureau of Labor and Industry, *Eleventh Annual Report, 1895* (Topeka, Kan., 1896), p. 198.

[46] Giddings, "The Persistence of Competition," in Giddings and Clark, *Modern Distributive Process*, p. 34; Giddings, "The Natural Rate of Wages," *ibid.*, pp. 52–69; Giddings, "Industrial Democracy," in *Democracy and Empire* (New York, 1900), pp. 122–125.

[47] Giddings, "The Trusts and the Public," in *Democracy and Empire*, pp. 137–143.

Although Giddings' theory of social evolution ostensibly represented an attempt to harmonize the determinism of Spencer with the telesis of Ward, the emphasis was primarily on the former. "I think I can show," Giddings wrote to Seligman, "that his [Spencer's] interpretation of the physical aspect of social development is essentially true, but it must be restated in new terms, and reillustrated and enforced by material drawn from the fresher researches in economics, politics, and so on." [48]

Social aggregations, Giddings maintained, are formed at the outset as the result of such external conditions as food supply, temperature, and the like. This process is entirely physical. Eventually, however, a consciousness of kind appears in like individuals within the aggregation and develops into association. Association presently reacts favorably on the pleasures and "life chances" of individuals, and as they become aware of this, the volitional process is initiated. Thenceforth, the associated individuals consciously attempt "to extend and to perfect their social relations." In this way, the choices of individuals and societies become important elements in social causation. But now the physical process sets in again. Choices have various consequences, some harmful, some beneficial. Natural selection operates upon the choices, and those choices and their resulting activities that are harmful are eliminated, "perhaps through the subordination or the extinction of individuals, perhaps through the disappearance of whole societies. . . . Thus the cycle of social causation begins and ends in the physical process. Between beginning and completion is the volitional process of artificial selection or of conscious choosing as determined by the consciousness of kind. But this is by no means a substitution of an artificial for a natural process, as Mr. Ward contends. It is merely an enormous multiplication of the variations on which natural selection finally acts." [49]

Giddings thus placed much less stress than Ward on the psychical process, on the ability of man individually and of society collectively to direct and shape the social forces to the greatest human advantage. Satisfied that the volitional process is primarily conditioned by physical facts, Giddings looked on social action as a "reaction, and, as such, definitely limited and conditioned." "The group, like the individual," he declared, "can will what it wills; but what it does will is deter-

[48] Giddings to Seligman, March 21, 1890, Edwin R. A. Seligman Papers, Columbia University Library.

[49] Giddings, *The Principles of Sociology* (New York, 1896), pp. 19–20.

mined by conditions that man did not create, and whether the group will keep on willing this thing or that thing, will depend on whether the thing willed conduces to social survival. If it does not, there is presently an end of social willing along those lines." [50] Lester Ward would have none of this determinism. Giddings, he declared, regarded society as "something absolutely passive to be analyzed and dissected like the carcass of a dead animal." [51] The young sociologist Charles H. Cooley was also unimpressed with Giddings' sociology and linked Giddings and Spencer in his journal as "dogmatic system-makers." [52]

Regarding the choices of men and of society as definitely limited, Giddings saw no such extensive field for state action as was envisioned

[50] Giddings, *The Theory of Sociology* (Philadelphia, 1894), pp. 71–72.

[51] Ward, "Principles of Sociology," *Annals,* VIII (July, 1896), 5. Curiously enough, on November 12, 1896, Giddings wrote to Ward: "I am convinced that you are right in the one supreme contention that you have most at heart,—namely, that in the civilization of today 'collective telesis' is the supremely important social process, and that education is the supremely important method" (Ward Papers).

[52] Journal of Charles H. Cooley, January 14, 1897, Charles H. Cooley Papers, Michigan Historical Collections. Charles H. Cooley, the son of Thomas M. Cooley, received a Ph.D. in economics from the University of Michigan in 1894. He taught his first course in sociology during the academic year 1894–1895 at the University of Michigan, where since 1892 he had held a half-time instructorship in the department of political economy. Although impressed with Spencer's "general conception of the progressive organization of life," Cooley was not in sympathy with Spencer's "more specific views on society." He thought that Spencer tended to confuse success with survival and that his "multitude of facts" were really "only illustrations of *a priori* conclusions." Cooley's own sociological work in the 1890's was concerned with competition as the "mechanism of social selection." He argued that the only alternative to competition in determining a person's place in the social system is status, "some fixed, mechanical rule." Competition, he thought, must continue as long as society moves and lives, but its quality can be improved by legislation which seeks to equalize and better competitive conditions (as, for example, appropriate factory and railroad legislation) and its efficiency increased by the "development of rational organization," in the form of such selective agencies as education, "to supplement and in part to replace the somewhat blind and irrational competition that accompanies rapid change." See Edward C. Jandy, *Charles Horton Cooley* (New York, 1942), pp. 9–58; Cooley Journal, July 21, 1895, January 14, 1897, Cooley Papers; Cooley, "The Development of Sociology at Michigan," in *Sociological Theory and Social Research* (New York, 1930), pp. 4–5; Cooley, "Competition and Organization," *Publications of the Michigan Political Science Association,* I (December, 1894), 33–45; and Cooley, "Personal Competition . . . ," *A. E. A. Economic Studies,* IV (April, 1899), 80, 93–99, 106–107, 162–166.

by Ward and his disciples.   In a letter to David A. Wells in 1877, while his interest was still economics rather than sociology, he announced himself "a firm believer in Herbert Spencer's doctrine which limits state functions to the enforcement of contracts and preservation of the peace," but he was ultimately to abandon this extreme position and by the end of the century was criticizing political philosophers who unqualifiedly approved laissez faire as well as those who unqualifiedly condemned it.[53]   He regarded laissez faire as the proper procedure to follow when "contemplating the possibility of restraining the spontaneous activity of mature and normal men," but he thought it a very bad policy for society to employ in its conduct toward the "immature and degenerate."   Defective and untrained human beings, who are poorly equipped to cope with the vicissitudes of life, Giddings maintained, must be aided when they suffer and restrained and disciplined when they do wrong.[54]

Giddings saw that social advance was always attended by human suffering as the unprogressive elements of society were pushed to the wall.   Whenever the constructive reorganization of society fails to keep pace with the rate of social activity, he declared, there is an increase of suffering.   However, the ethical consciousness of society is aroused by this unfortunate concomitant of social progress, and there is a demand for public and private philanthropy.   The advocates of laissez faire must learn that this is a perfectly sound development and that in order to preserve social cohesion, society must assume the costs of its progress and, insofar as possible, provide for the displaced. The socialists, on the other hand, must learn that industrial derangements cannot be prevented in a progressive world.   There will always be a part of the community which is relatively useless as far as society is concerned, and the fullest benefit can be derived from this group only when its members are kept in practical subjection to other individuals or to the state.[55]

Giddings suggested that a distinction be drawn between the activities of the state that increase social burdens and decrease the power of the people to bear them and state action that lessens social burdens

[53] Giddings to Wells, December 4, 1877, David A. Wells Papers, Library of Congress; Giddings, *Principles of Sociology*, p. 353.

[54] Giddings, *Principles of Sociology*, pp. 353–354.

[55] Giddings, "The Ethics of Social Progress," in Jane Addams *et al.*, *Philanthropy and Social Progress* (New York, 1893), pp. 219, 233–234, 242–248; Giddings, *Principles of Sociology*, pp. 351–353.

and develops individual enterprise. He classified government functions of the latter type as "societarian," including in this category such activities as public ownership of the post office and taxation for schools and sanitary improvements. Government action of this sort, he argued, "recognizes the state and the individual as coordinate powers" and aims "to make society serve its individual members, and to make individuals better members of society." [56]

Although Giddings accorded his approval to the principle of societarian action, he favored its application only in the most restricted manner and was greatly disturbed by the measures of social reform enacted in his own day. He feared that social democracy, or socialism, was already at hand and that its method, which was to compel everyone "to meddle with everything that is none of his business" and to forbid him, "under any circumstances, to mind his own business," had already gained acceptance.[57]

Giddings, like Spencer, thought that in the struggle for existence natural selection results in the survival of the fittest. But whereas Spencer was content to see the unfit perish, Giddings, arguing from the ethical standpoint, believed that society must shelter those who have fallen behind. This, however, was the extent to which he would invoke the power of the state. He did not wish the state to interfere in any essential way with the basic conditions of the struggle for existence and attempt to modify these conditions in the interests of the general welfare. Placing his major emphasis on the physical rather than on the psychic factors of civilization, Giddings held that, in the main, the state must follow, not direct, the course of social evolution.[58]

VI

As compared to Ward, Small, Ross, and Giddings, John Bascom was of but little significance to the development of sociological thought in the United States in the 1880's and 1890's. Sociology, as a matter of fact, was only one of Bascom's many interests. At various times a

[56] Giddings, "Industrial Democracy," in *Democracy and Empire*, pp. 112–114.

[57] Giddings, "The Relation of Social Democracy to the Higher Education," *ibid.*, pp. 220–221.

[58] Joseph J. Spengler is nevertheless correct in his estimate that a "comparison of the social theory of Giddings with that of Spencer furnishes a conservative measure of the decline of Social Darwinism" ("Evolutionism in American Economics, 1800–1946," in Stow Persons, ed., *Evolutionary Thought in America* [New Haven, 1950], p. 231).

student of theology, a writer on political economy, a teacher of rhetoric and oratory, esthetics, and English literature, and a college president, Bascom did not contribute a work on sociology, or, more properly, social ethics, until 1887.[59] Today, his sociological writings are little remembered, and, judged solely from the viewpoint of sociology, they are, indeed, of minor importance. However, they do serve as significant examples of the manner in which the new currents of thought in religion, economics, and sociology were contributing in the last decades of the nineteenth century to the formulation of the concept of the general-welfare state.

In his initial writings on political economy in the 1850's and 1860's, Bascom adhered rather closely to the basic principles of the English classical economists. He described what he then regarded as the inexorable laws of trade, deprecated any legislative interference with liberty of contract, and condemned strikes as economically unsound.[60]

Bascom, however, was ultimately to deviate considerably from the economics of laissez faire. A study of sociology and a concern for ethics and social Christianity [61] served to convince him that economic principles are modified at every turn by the circumstances under which they operate and that, in any event, they must be subordinated to higher ethical considerations. Bascom saw that habit, custom, local attachments, fear of change, lack of intelligence, and lack of mobility prevented the worker from moving promptly to the best market for his services. He noted that competition usually did not work as indicated, that it did not prevent the growth of monopoly and the concentration of wealth, and that, because of the superior bargaining power of the employer, it generally brought hardship to the laborer.

[59] Bascom was a student at both Auburn Theological Seminary and Andover Theological Seminary. From 1852 to 1874, except for the year 1855, he taught at Williams College. His *Political Economy* was published in 1859. He was president of the University of Wisconsin from 1874 to 1887. After resigning his Wisconsin post, he lectured on sociology at Williams, and in 1891 became professor of political science at the same institution. See Ernest Sutherland Bates, "John Bascom," in Allen Johnson and Dumas Malone, eds., *Dictionary of American Biography* (Authors ed.; New York, 1937), II, 32–33.

[60] Bascom, "Labor and Capital," *Bibliotheca Sacra*, XXV (October, 1868), 678–683; Dorfman, *The Economic Mind in American Civilization, 1606–1918* (New York, 1946–1949), II, 752–755.

[61] For Bascom's views on the social gospel, see Bascom, *Sociology* (New York, 1887), pp. 239–243.

From a study of sociology he concluded that individuals are not always aware of their best interests, that they are guided by motives other than self-interest, and that individual well-being is often in conflict with the general welfare. Since it appeared to him that the laws of economics failed to operate perfectly and to ensure justice under all circumstances, Bascom decided that the economist must invoke the moral law ("the most pervasive and potent law in society") to correct the inequities of the existing order and to enable society to pass from the industrial stage to a higher moral stage.[62]

The state, Bascom advised, must not stand idly by and permit natural developments to run their course, for when social movements are left exclusively to natural tendencies, they inevitably gravitate toward tyranny. The state is not a mere spectator whose aid is to be invoked only to repress crime but is rather a constructive and humane force. We must reject the argument from the past that the state is "a blind, hopeless bungler, to be crowded as much as possible into the background." When this argument prevails and the state does not interfere with the social forces, the poor and the weak are crushed and the strong are enthroned. Just as the strong once used the state to perpetuate their rule, so now they attack the state for the same purpose. The state must therefore reassert itself. In the interests of the general welfare, it must regain the powers that it has permitted individuals to exercise and that they have employed for purposes of self-aggrandizement.[63]

When it comes to positive questions of law, the chief consideration must not be what is best for the individual but what is most conducive to the general welfare. The state has a moral responsibility to do whatever it actually can do for the general welfare. This means that the state should give aid as well as protection and should assume such functions as are necessary to express the collective power. The advocates of laissez faire deny that the state can further the general welfare by positive action and claim that such action will derange the operation of natural law. However, if the state can do evil, it can also do good. "If it is potent enough to embarrass the laws of nature,

[62] Bascom, *Things Learned by Living* (New York, 1913), pp. 155–158; Bascom, *Sociology,* pp. 57, 58–79, 147–148; Bascom, *Social Theory* (New York, 1895), pp. 122, 134–165. Cf. Bascom, "Competition, Actual and Theoretical," *Quarterly Journal of Economics,* XIV (August, 1900), 537–542.

[63] Bascom, *Sociology,* pp. 210–211, 225–227.

it should be potent enough to aid them." The lesson of experience is "not one of non-interference but of wise guidance, a careful study of all the forces with which we have to do, and a handling of them according to their nature." [64]

In the interests of the whole, the state must constantly address itself to the task of equalizing competitive conditions. Although men have equal rights, they are unequal in ability, and, as a result, some men are always falling behind in the struggle for survival. If the state, therefore, limits itself to the mere protection of equal rights, as Spencer advises, extreme inequalities in society will be the inevitable result. The best interests of the community demand "a constant transfer of advantages from competitor to competitor." When an individual has lost out in the struggle for existence, he must be put back on his feet. "The state must aim at a perpetual renewal of the opportunities of life in every man and class of men. No misfortune must be complete, no disposition final." "The race is to be renewed, noon and night, on equal terms." [65]

Neither the extreme individualism of Spencer nor the socialism of Marx, Bascom thought, is a safe guide to state action. The state should not shackle individual enterprise, but neither must individual enterprise be permitted to encroach upon the general welfare. If society is to move forward, individual rights and collective rights must be harmonized, and this can best be achieved by "restraints assigned and powers conferred by the general welfare." [66]

VII

In the field of political science, as in economics and sociology, the trend of thought in the 1880's and 1890's was away from laissez faire. Although such writers on the science of government as John Burgess disapproved of state intervention in the social and economic life of the nation, Woodrow Wilson and Westel Woodbury Willoughby,

[64] See Bascom, *Ethics* (New York, 1879), pp. 257–259, 274–277; Bascom, *Sociology,* pp. 54–57; and Bascom, *Social Theory,* pp. 298–301.

[65] Bascom, *Sociology,* pp. 37–40, 43–47.

[66] Bascom, *Social Theory,* pp. 304–305; Bascom, *Sociology,* pp. 216–217. Among the specific measures of state action advocated by Bascom were a graduated income tax, regulation of the labor contract, strict control over franchises, outlawry of speculative sales, control of trusts, and government assumption of responsibility for the problem of pauperism. See Bascom, *Sociology,* pp. 213–217, 223–229; and Bascom, *Social Theory,* pp. 342–345, 412–417.

building on the arguments of sociologists and economists critical of laissez faire and on their own investigations of state practice, concluded that in the interests of the general welfare, the state must perform certain functions beyond those that the advocates of laissez faire believed necessary.[67]

During his student and professorial years Woodrow Wilson looked with some favor on the essential elements of the laissez-faire creed. From his Princeton teacher Lyman Atwater and his favorite magazine editor, Edwin Lawrence Godkin, he learned about the efficacy of the natural laws of trade and the unwisdom of government intervention in social and economic affairs. In keeping with his inclinations, young Wilson greatly admired the British statesmen Cobden, Bright, and Gladstone for their devotion to, and practical application of, the ideals of nineteenth-century liberalism. But Wilson was also exposed to the new developments in the economic thought of the era after the Civil War. He was cheered by the "moderation" and "Christianity" of John Bates Clark's *Philosophy of Wealth,* and Francis Walker's economic writings made a profound impression upon him. At Johns Hopkins, although Wilson did not subscribe to Richard T. Ely's comparatively advanced views on social reform and labor, he was nevertheless won over to the historical, inductive approach, and it is thus not altogether surprising that the list of members of the first

[67] Although the political thought of Theodore Dwight Woolsey was also at variance with the doctrine of laissez faire, Woolsey's analysis of the state was primarily a product of scholarship before the Civil War and, except in date, hardly belongs to the intellectual history of the postwar era. In addition to its absolutely essential duties of providing redress for wrongs and preventing any trespass on individual rights, the state, Woolsey contended, may also include within its sphere of action "a certain degree and kind of care of the *outward welfare of the community*" and the "cultivation of the spiritual nature by educating the religious nature, the moral sense, the taste, the intellect." As society advances, it becomes evident that the state cannot limit itself to its jural duties but must undertake certain tasks of essential interest to the general welfare that it alone can effectively accomplish, such as the protection of labor against capital and the enactment of sanitary legislation. Latter-day Federalist that he was, Woolsey would entrust the state with ample power to prevent and punish immorality and went so far as to sanction the establishment of a state church. He wished to see the poor kept down as much as possible and insisted that justice did not require the state to do anything on their behalf. He feared popular rule and was much more concerned that there be no interference by the state with the activities of the individual than that the state be obstructed in its actions on behalf of the general welfare. See Woolsey, *Political Science or the State* (New York, 1878), I, 208–242, and II, 392–438.

council of the American Economic Association includes the name of Woodrow Wilson.[68]

The clearest expression of Wilson's thought during the closing years of the nineteenth century with respect to the functions of government is to be found in his treatise *The State*, which was published in 1889. Wilson divided state functions into "constituent" and "ministrant." He defined the former category as comprising those functions that every government must perform, even according to uncompromising advocates of laissez faire. Among these indispensable functions he included the protection of persons and property from violence and robbery, the determination of contractual rights between individuals, the definition and punishment of crime, the administration of justice, and the conduct of foreign relations. Wilson explained that the ministrant functions, unlike the constituent functions, are not indispensable to the very existence of government or social organization but are, rather, optional functions that convenience or expediency determine shall be carried on by government so as to enhance the general welfare. As examples of ministrant functions he cited the regulation of commerce, industry, and labor, the maintenance of means of transportation and communication, the ownership of public utilities, the care of the poor, and the establishment of a system of public education.

Although history, Wilson declared, is full of warnings not to give the state too much power to interfere with the lives of its citizens, government, far from being an evil, is actually "the indispensable organ of society." "Every means . . . by which society may be perfected through the instrumentality of government, every means by which individual rights can be fitly adjusted and harmonized with public duties . . . ought certainly to be diligently sought, and, when found, sedulously fostered by every friend of society."

The schemes of the socialists, Wilson asserted, are fanciful, but the socialists are on firm ground in their desire to harmonize individual and social interests. The socialist protest against individualism is also

---

[68] William Diamond, *The Economic Thought of Woodrow Wilson* (Baltimore, 1943), pp. 20–37; *John Bates Clark: A Memorial* (New York, 1938), p. 20; Ely, *Ground under Our Feet: An Autobiography* (New York, 1938), pp. 108–115; Ely, "Report of the Organization of the American Economic Association," *A. E. A. Publications,* I (1886), 40. For Wilson's reaction to the events of the 1890's and for an analysis of his political thought during his academic period, see Arthur S. Link, *Wilson: The Road to the White House* (Princeton, N.J., 1947), pp. 23–28, 31–35. Link stresses the essential conservatism of Wilson's thought.

not without some basis, for there is much about modern individualism "that is hateful, too hateful to last." Competition has become so distorted under the existing economic order as sometimes to concentrate power and wealth in the hands of the few to the disadvantage of the poor and the weak. Self-interest has become synonymous with "grasping selfishness," and not only love and compassion, but free competition in part, also, have been set aside.

Between individualism and socialism a middle ground must be found that provides ample freedom for individual self-development but protects this freedom against unfair competition and reduces to a minimum the conflict between the individual and society. In order to attain this desired result, the aid of government is necessary. Through the equalization of competitive conditions, government can ensure that the necessary opportunity will be present for the self-development of the individual. To this end, to equalize competitive conditions, government must regulate natural monopolies,[69] forbid child labor, limit the hours of female labor and of all laborers in certain trades, supervise the conditions of sanitation in factories, and test the quality and purity of goods.

It must always be remembered, however, that society is something bigger and more important than the state, that the state is a means and not an end, and that it exists for the sake of society and not vice versa. There are "natural and imperative limits to state action." The aid of the state should be invoked only when public action is indispensable to the equalization of "conditions of endeavor" and to "the maintenance of uniform rules of individual rights and relationships." If public coöperation is not absolutely required by the general welfare and is merely a convenience, government should surrender the field to private enterprise. Although it is very difficult to draw the line between voluntary and state action, the state should definitely not engage in activities that can just as well be carried on by "optional associations." The state, at all events, "must not lead. It must create conditions, but not mould individuals." [70]

Wilson was a firm believer in the competitive system, in the system of individual enterprise. However, like John Bates Clark, he looked to government to enforce competition, to ensure that the conditions

[69] Unlike the new-school economists, Wilson preferred government regulation to outright government ownership. See Wilson, *The State* (rev. ed.; Boston, 1898), pp. 633–635.

[70] Wilson, *The State,* pp. 613–615, 629–639.

necessary to the most effective operation of the competitive order are always maintained. If the state acted in this manner, Wilson thought, there would be equality of opportunity for all. Thus in 1889 Wilson was already giving expression to ideas that were to mature in the New Freedom.

The analysis of the functions of the state by the Johns Hopkins political scientist Westel Woodbury Willoughby was similar in most respects to that of Woodrow Wilson. Willoughby's views as regards the role of government were influenced considerably by the new school's repudiation of the premises of classical political economy and by Lester Ward's criticism of the sociology and political ethics of Herbert Spencer. It was chiefly on the basis of these new currents of thought in economics and sociology that Willoughby rejected laissez faire and advocated that the state undertake certain limited functions on behalf of the general welfare.[71]

Like Wilson, Willoughby divided the functions of the state into the essential and the nonessential or common-welfare functions. By the latter designation, he meant functions other than those necessary for the mere existence of the state and for the maintenance of order. The state performs functions of this sort because they are deemed to be advantageous to the people. The determination of just what these functions shall be is a matter of expediency. In each case it must be decided whether the proposed activity promotes the general welfare, whether the benefits to be derived from public control outweigh the possible disadvantages. At all events, Willoughby maintained, "there is no valid objection to the use of the political power for the performance of any function that will beneficially affect the social welfare." [72]

State common-welfare activities, Willoughby thought, should be designed to provide freedom of opportunity for each individual to develop his capacities to the utmost and to reap the full rewards of his efforts. This suggests the abandonment by the state of the cruder forms of interference but the extension of its educational and regulatory functions. The state should provide free education in all branches of knowledge and should disseminate whatever information can be of value and aid to the people. The state is justified in seeking to raise the ethical plane of competition, in taking over industries in which competition cannot be maintained, in acting to prevent individuals

[71] Willoughby, *Examination of the Nature of the State*, pp. 323–337; Willoughby, *Social Justice* (New York, 1900), pp. 269–293.

[72] Willoughby, *Examination of the Nature of the State*, pp. 310–350.

from oppressing one another, and in assuming essential duties that would otherwise not be performed.[73]

VIII

The psychology and philosophy of William James and John Dewey, which culminated in the formulation of the philosophy of pragmatism, did not in the period preceding the twentieth century issue in any concrete plans for state action, but they served nevertheless, like the sociology of Lester Ward, to challenge a social Darwinism that reduced man to a mere automaton in a world where the laws of nature ruled supreme and to encourage a belief in the efficacy of ideas as instruments for manipulating the environment. As Richard Hofstadter has pointed out, this was "a position necessary to any philosophically consistent theory of social reform."[74] To James, to be sure, pragmatism was a philosophy of individualism, but John Dewey's instrumentalism, first explicitly proclaimed in 1903, supplied pragmatism with a social conscience and made it the philosophy of Progressivism.

Born to wealth and an individualist to the core, William James was an admirer of Herbert Spencer during the 1860's and actually felt "spiritually wounded, as by the defacement of a sacred image or picture," when he heard the philosopher Charles S. Peirce attack Spencer's *First Principles*. By the time he began teaching classes at Harvard in 1872, however, James had already rejected Spencer, and he was ultimately to conclude that the English philosopher was "absolutely worthless in all *fundamental* matters of thought." He came to regard Spencer's *First Principles* as "almost a museum of blundering reason" and his philosophy of social and intellectual progress as an "obsolete anachronism, reverting to a pre-Darwinian type of thought." To be sure, he assigned Spencer's works to his Harvard classes as textbooks, but he used them principally as "source books for the illustration of philosophical error."[75] Although sympathetic to Spencer's

[73] Willoughby, *Social Justice*, pp. 304–311.

[74] Hofstadter, *Social Darwinism in American Thought, 1860–1915* (Philadelphia, 1944), p. 105.

[75] See Ralph Barton Perry, *The Thought and Character of William James* (Boston, 1935), I, 474–477; and James, "Great Men and Their Environment," in *The Will to Believe and Other Essays in Popular Philosophy* (New York, 1897), p. 254. James wrote in 1892: " 'He left a Spencer's name to other times, linked with one virtue and a thousand crimes.' The one virtue is his belief in the universality of evolution—the 1000 crimes are his 5000 pages of absolute incompetence to work it out in detail." See Perry, *James*, I, 475.

brand of individualism, William James had no desire to share in Spencer's "vast dream of universal fatalism." [76]

Fundamental to all of James's thought was "the idea of the essentially active and interested character of the human mind." [77] In an article written in 1878 he took issue with Spencer's definition of mind as "correspondence," of mental evolution as the "adjustment of inner to outer relations." In limiting mind to the perception of fact, Spencer's definition, James contended, omits the vast range of mental activity that in no sense corresponds with what is but is, rather, dictated by "subjective interests," the concern of the mind with the ideal, with beauty, wit, morals, and logic. Survival, which Spencer seems to regard as the dominating interest of mind as correspondence, is but one of many interests of man, and individuals who possess talents that society regards as desirable, as for example, artists, philosophers, and religious leaders, will be permitted to survive even if they are poorly adapted to the natural environment.

Spencer's description of right thinking as that which conforms to outward relations is, James asserted, simply another "teleological affirmation," like that of other men. The truth of the matter is that every individual can frame his own "private categorical imperative" of what constitutes correctness in thought, "and these different ideals, instead of entering upon the scene armed with a warrant . . . appear only as so many brute affirmations left to fight it out upon the chessboard among themselves. They are, at best, postulates, each of which must depend on the general concensus of experience as a whole to bear out its validity. The formula which proves to have the most massive destiny will be the true one." "Thought will be coerced away" from the erroneous postulates, and those that survive will constitute "the right way of thinking." [78]

As he had rejected Spencer's definition of mind as correspondence, so James, in his *Principles of Psychology*, repudiated as antipsychological the "conscious automaton-theory," which attributed human behavior to purely physical events over which consciousness, although present, had no control. James insisted that consciousness is efficacious, that it is "a selecting agency" that chooses and emphasizes one of the several materials presented to it. The mere body that houses

---

[76] James, "Spencer's 'Data of Ethics,'" in *Collected Essays and Reviews* (London, 1920), p. 150.

[77] Perry, Preface, in *Collected Essays and Reviews*, p. ix.

[78] James, "Remarks on Spencer's Definition of Mind as Correspondence," in *Collected Essays and Reviews*, pp. 44–46, 52–54, 58–61, 65.

the brain cannot be said to have any interests in the absence of a "superadded commenting intelligence." With respect to survival, one can say that, physically speaking, if certain actions occur survival will result, but the bodily organs and the rest of the physical world for that matter are indifferent to all this. Survival enters the discussion "only as an *hypothesis made by an onlooker* about the future." It is consciousness that transforms survival from a hypothesis into an "imperative decree." Only with the introduction of consciousness do real ends appear. "Every actually existing consciousness seems to itself at any rate to be a *fighter for ends,* of which many, but for its presence, would not be ends at all." [79]

Far then from accepting the role of passive adjustment that Spencer assigned to mind, James viewed mind as fundamentally active and creative.

> I, for my part, [he declared] cannot escape the consideration, . . . that the knower is not simply a mirror floating with no foot-hold anywhere, and passively reflecting an order that he comes upon and finds simply existing. The knower is an actor, and co-efficient of truth on one side, whilst on the other he registers the truth which he helps to create. Mental interests, hypotheses, postulates, so far as they are bases for human action—action which to a great extent transforms the world—help to *make* the truth which they declare. In other words, there belongs to mind, from its birth upward, a spontaneity, a vote. It is in the game, and not a mere looker-on . . . .[80]

James rebelled not only against Spencer's view of mind but also against his monistic, determinist conception of the world as "one unbending unit of fact." The arch-individualist James could not abide a "block-universe" philosophy whose categories were necessity and impossibility and in which chance and novelties were ruled out *ab initio.* The world he saw was "a pluralistic, restless universe, in which no single point of view can ever take in the whole scene." It was a world in which alternative possibilities were present and where the issue was to be decided *"here and now."* [81] He envisioned "a zone of insecurity in human affairs," and it was in this zone, so far as he was concerned, that the whole dramatic interest of life lay. However

[79] James, *The Principles of Psychology* (New York, 1890), I, 138–141.

[80] James, "Remarks on Spencer's Definition of Mind as Correspondence," in *Collected Essays and Reviews,* p. 67.

[81] James, "The Dilemma of Determinism," in *Will to Believe,* pp. 151–153, 176–179, 183.

confined the area of this "dynamic belt of quivering uncertainty," it was "roomy enough to lodge the whole range of human passions." And, on the contrary, however wide "the sphere of the race's average," it was "a dead and stagnant thing, an achieved possession, from which all insecurity had vanished." The social-Darwinist concern for "averages and general laws and predetermined tendencies" and their "undervaluing of the importance of individual differences" were to James "the most pernicious and immoral of fatalisms. Suppose," he said, "there is a social equilibrium fated to be, whose is it to be,—that of your preference, or mine? There lies the question of questions, and it is one which no study of averages can decide." [82]

That James should have become the philosopher of pragmatism is not at all surprising when one considers his views with respect to the active role of mind in an unfinished universe and his frequent assertions that if the "drift of thinking" confirmed a hypothesis, that hypothesis was true.[83] Although pragmatism was long implicit in James's thought,[84] the pragmatist movement was not officially launched until August 26, 1898, when James addressed the Philosophical Union of the University of California on "Philosophical Conceptions and Practical Results." Acknowledging his indebtedness to Charles Peirce, James announced as "the principle of pragmatism" the thesis that "the ultimate test for us of what a truth means is . . . the conduct it dictates or inspires. But it inspires that conduct because it first foretells some particular turn to our experience which shall call for just that conduct from us." [85] As it turned out, James's lecture attracted but little attention until reprinted in 1904 as "The Pragmatic Method," and pragmatism itself did not occupy "the centre of the philosophical stage" until after the appearance in 1907 of James's *Pragmatism.*[86]

Although James repudiated the fundamental assumptions of the social Darwinists, he continued to admire the "antique spirit of English individualism" to which Spencer gave expression. A devotee of Ed-

[82] James, "The Importance of Individuals," in *Will to Believe,* pp. 257–262.

[83] See, for example, James, "The Will to Believe," in *Will to Believe,* p. 17; James, "Spencer's 'Data of Ethics,'" in *Collected Essays and Reviews,* pp. 148–149; and James, "Remarks on Spencer's Definition of Mind as Correspondence," *ibid.,* pp. 60–61, 65.

[84] Perry, *James,* II, 448–451.

[85] James, "Philosophical Conceptions and Practical Results," in *Collected Essays and Reviews,* pp. 410, 412.

[86] Perry, *James,* II, 371.

win Godkin and a Mugwump in politics,[87] James was not interested in the problem of social reform, and his thought, despite its possible implications for social invention and control, was devoid of real social content. His attacks on closed systems of thought and determinist philosophies were presented in terms of what they signified for the individual and his role in the universe and not in terms of their possible meaning for the general-welfare state. "The solid meaning of life," James announced, "is always the same eternal thing,—the marriage, namely, of some unhabitual ideal, however special, with some fidelity, courage, and endurance; with some man's or woman's pains." [88]

The Jamesian emphasis on the individual as innovator was nowhere more graphically demonstrated than in James's theory with respect to the role of great men in social evolution. Whereas Spencer and his cohorts insisted that the changes which take place in communities from generation to generation are the inevitable product of environment and circumstance, James contended that "the difference is due to the accumulated influences of individuals, of their examples, their initiatives, and their decisions." The great man, he insisted, must be accepted as a datum in the same way as Darwin recognizes spontaneous variations. The environment may adopt or reject the great man, but if it does adopt him, it becomes modified by his influence in some original and special way.[89]

The social content that was missing from James's pragmatism was supplied by John Dewey, who, in his formulation of instrumentalism, advised the application to social problems of the scientist's technique of hypothesis verified by experiment and experience.[90] Although the philosophy of instrumentalism was first explicitly set forth by Dewey in 1903 in *Studies in Logical Theory*, the various ingredients of the theory were more or less evident in Dewey's thought before the turn of the century.[91]

[87] Perry, *James*, I, 487; II, 290–299.

[88] James, *Talks to Teachers on Psychology: and to Students on Some of Life's Ideals* (New York, 1899), pp. 298–299.

[89] James, "Great Men and Their Environment," in *Will to Believe*, pp. 216–254.

[90] Merle Curti, *The Social Ideas of American Educators* (New York, 1935), pp. 507–508.

[91] See, for example, Dewey, *The Study of Ethics* (Ann Arbor, Mich., 1897), p. 11; Dewey, *My Pedagogic Creed* (New York, 1897), p. 14; and Dewey, "The Significance of the Problem of Knowledge," in *The Influence of Darwin on Philosophy and Other Essays in Contemporary Thought* (New York, 1910), pp. 271–304.

Unlike William James, John Dewey "from an early period" had an interest in social problems. "Social interests and social problems," he later wrote, "had to me the intellectual appeal and provided the intellectual sustenance that many seem to have found primarily in religious questions." The social emphasis in Dewey's thought was as apparent in the 1880's when, as a graduate student at Johns Hopkins and as an instructor at the University of Michigan, he was under the influence of the conservative-minded Hegel, as it was in the 1890's, after James's *Psychology,* with its biological approach to psychology, "acted as a ferment to transform old beliefs." [92]

Dewey's writings in the field of ethics in the 1880's and 1890's revealed rather clearly their author's marked interest in social affairs and social change. In describing the ethics of democracy, Dewey argued that democracy must be the controlling factor in the market place, as it is in civil and political affairs. "A democracy of wealth," he said, "is a necessity"; industrial organization must become "a *social* function." [93] He deplored the fact that the emphasis on altruism was tending to enthrone charity as a moral principle, "in a sense which implies continued social inequality, and social slavery, or undue dependence of one upon another." Better than to give charity was to secure for one's fellow men the conditions of freedom that would make it unnecessary for them to depend on the altruism of others. "The moral end," as Dewey saw it, was "wholly social," and he regarded the paramount duty of the age to be "the socializing of intelligence—the realizing of its bearing on social practice." [94]

Like William James, Dewey stressed the active role of mind in relationship to a changing environment. When he declared in 1902 that "the biological point of view commits us to the conviction that mind, whatever else it may be, is at least an organ of service for the control of environment in relation to the ends of the life process," [95] he was neatly summing up views to which he had been giving expression for some time. In his *Psychology,* published in 1887, while he was still under the influence of Hegel, Dewey asserted that habit

[92] See Dewey, "From Absolutism to Experimentalism," in George P. Adams and Wm. P. Montague, eds., *Contemporary American Philosophy* (New York, 1930), II, 20, 23–24; and Curti, *Social Ideas of American Educators,* pp. 502–504, 508–509.

[93] Dewey, *The Ethics of Democracy* (Ann Arbor, Mich., 1888), pp. 25–28.

[94] Dewey, *Outlines of a Critical Theory of Ethics* (Ann Arbor, Mich., 1891), pp. 108, 118, 127.

[95] Dewey, "Interpretation of Savage Mind," *Psychological Review,* IX (May, 1902), 219.

creates a mechanism that attends automatically to the routine elements of experience and thus leaves mind "free to control new and
variable factors." The power to adjust to new circumstances and to
grow, he noted, "requires the conscious effort of intelligence and the
active direction of will." [96]

Unless it led to action, philosophy itself appeared to be of little
value to Dewey. "As the philosopher has received his problem from
the world of action," Dewey insisted, "so he must return his account
there for auditing and liquidation." Knowledge must become a tool,
and the dominating interest of philosophy must be the use of knowledge to direct conduct. Believing that philosophy should become a
method, Dewey applauded what he thought was the transfer of interest from metaphysics to social ethics and psychology. The concern
of social ethics, he pointed out, was not the nature of value in general
but "the *particular* values that ought to be realized in the life of every
one" and the conditions that made that realization possible. Psychology was an attempt to describe "the machinery of the individual
considered as the instrument and organ through which social action
operates." The development of psychology betokened an awareness
that the existing world was the product neither of fate nor of chance
but was, rather, "based on law and order, on a system of existing
stimuli and modes of reaction, through knowledge of which we can
modify the practical outcome." [97] Although Dewey found the psychology of Lester Ward's *Psychic Factors of Civilization* outmoded, he
could agree with Ward on the necessity for employing mind power to
control the environment in man's interest. [98]

Disagreeing with the social Darwinists, Dewey did not believe that
man played a completely passive role in the evolutionary process of
struggle for existence, natural selection, and survival of the fittest.
In an article published in 1898, Dewey, whose desire to reconcile
science and morality was an influential factor in the formulation of
instrumentalism, took issue with Huxley's contention that there is an
inevitable conflict between the cosmic process and the ethical process.
The ethical process, Dewey argued, is itself a part of the cosmic
process. To maintain the ethical order, man must interfere with

[96] Dewey, *Psychology* (New York, 1887), pp. 113–115.

[97] Dewey, "Significance of the Problem of Knowledge," in *Influence of Darwin,*
pp. 274, 299–303; Dewey, *Psychology and Social Practice* (Chicago, 1901), pp.
38–39, 41–42.

[98] Dewey, "Social Psychology," *Psychological Review,* I (July, 1894), 400–408.

conditions as they are. In so doing, he does not attempt to oppose the entire natural environment but rather makes over one part of it by relating that part to the environment as a whole.

There was no conflict, in Dewey's view, between the ethical process and the natural process with respect to the survival of the fittest. Fitness, he asserted, must be defined in terms of all the conditions that obtain, which includes the social structure, and since the environment is now social and is constantly undergoing change, fitness must be judged with reference to social adaptation and the flexibility necessary to adjust to sudden changes in the environment.

The struggle for existence is just as much a part of the ethical process as of the cosmic process. It consists essentially in the adaptation of impulses and promptings to changing conditions. The tension is between an organ adjusted to past conditions and the functions required by present conditions, and the solution lies in reconstruction and readaptation to conditions. The animal does this by chance, but man can anticipate the problem by intelligence and foresight. He is able to maintain the institutions that have come down to him but can make them over to suit existing conditions. "The problem," said Dewey, in words reminiscent of Richard T. Ely, "is the reconciliation of unbridled radicalism and inert conservatism, in a movement of reasonable reform."

Dewey also argued that natural selection is a part of the ethical process as well as of the cosmic process. The view that natural selection does not operate in the ethical order, he declared, derives from the mistaken assumption that there is only one type of selection, "ordeal by death." In the world of man, however, selection may take place as the result of education or of public opinion, both of which encourage certain types of action and discourage others. Actually, there is no essential difference between the type of adjustment that takes place in the cosmic process and in the ethical process. Every living being adjusts dynamically, not statically, to its environment, and subjects existing conditions to its needs, thus creating what is for it a more favorable environment. "The unwritten chapter in natural selection is that of the evolution of environments."

In man, the power to discover new environments reaches its climax. Because of scientific progress, the application of invention to industry, and improved transportation and communication, the environment has become variable and unstable. The "supreme condition of success" therefore lies in "flexibility of function, the enlargement of the

range of uses to which one and the same organ . . . may be put,"
and "any change in that direction is a favorable variation which must
be selected." The difference between the ethical and the cosmic
process is thus not that selection no longer operates but rather that
with man selection "along the lines of variations which enlarge and
intensify the environment" is "active as never before." Thus having
rejected Huxley's thesis of the conflict between the ethical process and
the cosmic process in all its essential respects, Dewey concluded that
the real distinction between the two was simply that "the processes
and forces bound up with the cosmic have come to consciousness in
man." [99]

Although Dewey did not hesitate to lend his support to social
reforms effected by legislation, it was to education that he looked as
"the fundamental method of social progress and reform." "I believe,"
he stated in 1897, "that education is a regulation of the process of
coming to share in the social consciousness; and that the adjustment
of individual activity on the basis of this social consciousness is the
only sure method of social reconstruction." Through education,
Dewey believed, society could orient itself in the direction in which
it desired to move.[100]

In assigning to intelligence a creative role in the universe, Dewey
and James, though their emphasis was quite different, contributed importantly to the mounting intellectual assault on the fortress of social
Darwinism and, in effect, helped to ally philosophy and psychology
with the emerging social sciences—economics, sociology, and political
science—in providing scientific sanction for the demands of the advocates of social reform. To the ideology of conservatism, there was
now opposed an ideology of reform.

[99] Dewey, "Evolution and Ethics," *Monist*, VIII (April, 1898), 321–341.
[100] Dewey, *My Pedagogic Creed*, p. 16.

IX

IN QUEST OF REFORM

DISSATISFACTION with laissez faire and the *status quo* and a willingness to use the state as an instrument for social reform and the general welfare were not confined to academic circles in the decades after the Civil War. Disturbed because the remarkable expansion of the American economy in this period was attended by increasing inequalities in the distribution of wealth, a drift toward monopoly, railway abuses of various sorts, unemployment on an unprecedented scale, and health and housing problems in the rapidly growing cities, reformers and humanitarians rejected the "gospel of inaction" and turned to the state to rectify existing abuses and to help usher in a more just social order. Farmers and laborers, dissatisfied with their economic plight, also did not hesitate to enlist the aid of the state in their efforts to improve their position. Whether impelled by theoretical considerations or hard economic facts, the elements that clamored for reform agreed, in effect, with the veteran reformer George W. Julian that the solution of the problems of the age could not be entrusted to the operation of natural law but must come about largely as "the result of efforts consciously put forth for the purpose." [1]

II

"The true patriot, the true philanthropist, the true social reformer," Henry George wrote to David A. Wells in 1871, "is the man who strives . . . to replace bad economic laws with good ones." [2] Actually, the task of the "true patriot" and the "true reformer," as George came to

[1] Julian, "Is the Reformer Any Longer Needed?" *North American Review,* CXXVII (September–October, 1878), 237–260.

[2] George to Wells, September 19, 1871, David A. Wells Papers, Library of Congress.

see it, was to explain the "increase of want" that unfortunately seemed to be associated with the "increase of wealth." A visit to New York in the winter of 1868–1869 had impressed George with "the shocking contrast between monstrous wealth and debasing want," and he pledged himself to find the explanation for this unhappy phenomenon. Two years later, in California, where since 1857 the Philadelphia-born George had been eking out a living as a printer and newspaperman, he saw in the land speculation of the day the answer to his question. His analysis of the problem was first presented to the public, in brief, in *Our Land and Land Policy*, published in 1871, and then, definitively, in 1879 in *Progress and Poverty*.[3]

"If I live," George had written his mother late in 1876, "I will make myself known, even in Philadelphia."[4] When he had completed *Progress and Poverty*, he was convinced that he had authored a work which would indeed make him known "even in Philadelphia." To his father, he wrote, ". . . it will ultimately be considered a great book, —will be published in both hemispheres, and be translated into different languages."[5] George's expectations were fulfilled to the letter, for the publication of *Progress and Poverty* made its author a figure of world-wide renown. George's hopes that his book "would be intelligible to those who never read and thought on such subjects before" were also to be realized. As Richard T. Ely declared, tens of thousands of persons who had never before read a book on economics read *Progress and Poverty*. By 1905, according to the estimate of George's son, more than two million copies had been printed.[6]

In many respects the economic thought of Henry George resembled that of the classical economists. George regarded political economy as based on the "truth" that "men seek to gratify their desires with the

[3] Henry George, Jr., *The Life of Henry George* (25th anniv. ed.; New York, 1905), pp. 191–193, 219–235. It should be noted that George did not attack the private ownership of land in *Our Land and Land Policy*. On this point, see Charles Albro Barker's definitive biography of George, *Henry George* (New York, 1955), pp. 151–152.

[4] Henry George to his mother, November 13, 1876, Henry George Collection, New York Public Library.

[5] Henry George to his father, September 15, 1879, George Collection.

[6] Henry George to Charles Nordhoff, December 21, 1879, George Collection; Ely, "Recent American Socialism," *Johns Hopkins University Studies in Historical and Political Science*, III (1885), 249; Laughlin, "The Study of Political Economy in the United States," *Journal of Political Economy*, I (December, 1892), 13; George, Jr., "How the Book Came to Be Written," in George, *Progress and Poverty* (Modern Library ed.; New York, n. d.), p. xii.

least exertion" and believed that a true science of political economy must be deductive. He looked upon production and distribution as being governed by natural laws as constant as those that operate in the physical world and accepted the adage that "competition is the life of trade." Like the classical economists, he was also "a free trader pure and absolute." [7] However, George's predilection for the economics of laissez faire was tempered by a concern for the ethical implications of economic phenomena and by a warm humanitarianism. There was no place in his thought for an economics that did not explain the poverty that existed alongside unparalleled progress and that inveighed against the efforts of the workingman to better his lot. [8] Nor would George tolerate any divorce between ethics and economics. Politico-economic theory, he thought, must fall within the scope of a higher moral law and must embody the teachings of Christ. The "golden rule of morals" and "the golden rule of the science of wealth" must be one and the same. [9] Like the social gospelers, he believed that the intelligence to solve social problems and to right social wrongs must be animated by religious sentiments. He was highly critical of a church that "in all its branches" was "offering men stones instead of bread, and thistles instead of figs," and was "ignoring the simple remedy of justice." Only a Christianity that attacks vested wrongs, George declared, has the power to regenerate the world. [10]

Henry George, like the *philosophes* of the eighteenth century and like Thomas Jefferson, was a firm believer in the doctrine of natural

[7] George, *Progress and Poverty* (4th ed.; New York, 1883), pp. 10–11; George, *The Science of Political Economy* (New York, *c.* 1898), pp. 87–88, 92–104, 207–208, 402–403, 444, 450–453; George to Wells, October 12, 1886, Wells Papers, Library of Congress; George, *Protection or Free Trade* (Garden City, N. Y., [1911?]), *passim.*

[8] George, *Progress and Poverty*, pp. 11–12; George, Jr., *Life of Henry George*, pp. 277–278. George did not agree with Atkinson that the movement for the eight-hour day represented an attempt to substitute a statute for a steam engine. It was rather "an attempt to utilize for the masses some portion of the benefits of the steam engine" (George to Wells, September 19, 1871, Wells Papers, Library of Congress). George similarly rejected Spencer's social determinism. See George, *A Perplexed Philosopher* (Garden City, N. Y., [1911?]), pp. 132–135.

[9] George, *Progress and Poverty*, pp. 473–474; George, *Protection or Free Trade*, p. 8; George, Jr., *Life of Henry George*, pp. 278–279.

[10] George, *Social Problems* (Chicago, 1884), pp. 20–21; George, "Thou Shalt Not Steal," *The Land and Labor Library*, I (June 18, 1887), 3; George to Mills, May 18, 1891, George Collection; George, *The Land Question* (Garden City, N. Y., [1911?]), p. 96. See also George Raymond Geiger, *The Philosophy of Henry George* (Grand Forks, N. D., 1931), pp. 13, 281–286.

rights. Legitimate government, he thought, must be based on a conception of natural rights such as is embodied in the Declaration of Independence. George, however, widened the concept of natural rights as expressed in the Declaration of Independence to include economic rights as well as political and social rights. The rights of life, liberty, and the pursuit of happiness, he insisted, cannot be realized when the inalienable equal right of each individual to the bounty of nature is denied.[11] It was in the denial of this right, in the existence of private ownership of land, that George saw the explanation of that "great enigma," the association of poverty with progress.

Rephrasing Ricardo's famous law of rent, George declared that "the ownership of a natural agent of production will give the power of appropriating so much of the wealth produced by the exertion of labor and capital upon it as exceeds the return which the same application of labor and capital could secure in the least productive occupation in which they freely engage." The law of rent, George argued, is also the law of wages and interest, since all that labor can secure as wages and capital as interest is what they could have obtained from land that yields no rent. Their share is determined by what remains after rent, "that part of the produce which accrues to the owners of land or other natural capabilities by virtue of their ownership," receives its share of the product. Consequently, even though the productive power of society should increase, if the increase of rent keeps pace with the gain in productivity, the share going to wages and interest cannot be augmented. Actually, as a result of the increase in population, improvement in the arts of production, and land speculation, every gain in productive power results in a more than proportionate increase in the share taken by rent and a consequent decrease in the share of wages and interest. Rent, which is essentially "a value, or return, collectively created," "swallows up the whole gain and pauperism accompanies progress."

To abolish the poverty that was associated with progress, what was required, George therefore concluded, was to substitute a common ownership of land for individual ownership. Although he recognized the right of the government to abolish private property in land, he proposed as "a simpler, easier, and quieter way" of attaining the same objective that the state appropriate economic rent by taxation, that it confiscate the entire return derived from the ownership of bare land

[11] George, *Social Problems*, pp. 130–146, 234; George, *Progress and Poverty*, pp. 303–306, 489–490.

IN QUEST OF REFORM

as distinguished from improvements. The imposition of the tax on economic rent would not only yield the state sufficient revenue to permit it to abolish all other forms of taxation, but it would also "raise wages, increase the earnings of capital, extirpate pauperism, abolish poverty, give remunerative employment to whoever wishes it, afford free scope to human powers, lessen crime, elevate morals, and taste, and intelligence, purify government and carry civilization to yet nobler heights." Through this one important action, this "single tax" as it came to be known,[12] the state could extirpate poverty once and for all.[13]

Although George looked to the confiscation of economic rent as the solution for the problem of poverty, it does not follow, as has sometimes been suggested, that save for this one great reform he supported a policy of laissez faire. George, to be sure, spoke harshly of government restrictions and regulations that interfered with the free play of individual action. He believed that activities of a repressive sort that went beyond the mere protection of individual rights generally defeated the ends that they were intended to serve, and he wished to see government functions of this type curtailed. At the same time, however, George thought that it was necessary to extend the coöperative functions of government, the social side of government. He was aware that government must increasingly assume positive functions in order to keep pace with social progress. Only in the early stages of social development, he pointed out, is it possible to limit government to such functions as are necessary to provide for the common defense and to protect the weak against the strong. As society progresses, the state, in order to preserve equal individual rights, must add coöperative functions to its basic restrictive duties.[14]

The single tax fitted neatly into Henry George's conception of the true role of government. The adoption of this tax, George thought, would considerably reduce the operations of government on the repressive side. There would be no other taxes for the state to collect and no need for police agencies to check tax evasions; and litigation concerning the ownership of land would cease. With wealth more equi-

[12] The term "the single tax" was first used as a slogan for George's panacea in 1887, by George's disciple, Thomas G. Shearman. See Arthur Nichols Young, *The Single Tax Movement in the United States* (Princeton, N. J., 1916), pp. 109–111; and Barker, *Henry George*, p. 518.

[13] George, *Progress and Poverty*, pp. 148–154, 198–201, 205–266, 295–296, 362–366; George to Josephine Shaw Lowell, October 5, 1883, George Collection.

[14] George, *Social Problems*, pp. 234–240, 251, 260–261; George, *Progress and Poverty*, pp. 287–289.

tably distributed, there would be fewer criminals and a decreasing need for the coercive organs of government. "Society would thus approach the ideal of Jeffersonian democracy, the promised land of Herbert Spencer, the abolition of government." The abolition of government of which George spoke, however, was of government "only as a directing and repressive power." As the state, owing to the adoption of the single tax, curtailed its restrictive activities, it would be enabled to assume "certain other functions" that were "pressing for recognition."

By "certain other functions" George had reference to general-welfare functions. He proposed that the revenues to be derived from the single tax be distributed to the community in the form of public benefits. He would have government provide free medical facilities for the public, establish museums, libraries, lecture rooms, music and dance halls, technical schools, theaters, public baths, playgrounds, and gymnasiums, and support all forms of intellectual and scientific endeavor. In addition, George thought that the state, so as to protect the natural rights and equal liberties of each individual, should extend its jurisdiction over all businesses of a monopolistic character and should actually take over those that are complete monopolies. In the interests of the general welfare, the government, he believed, must assume ownership of the railroads, the telegraph and telephone, and municipal public utilities. A government that acted in this way could "realize the dreams of socialism." It would become "the administration of a great co-operative society . . . the agency by which the common property was administered for the common benefit." [15]

Although a foe of socialism and suspicious even of social reformers like Richard T. Ely who did not endorse the single tax,[16] George was not an advocate of laissez faire. Where the proponents of laissez faire, such as Spencer, would extend the functions of government, on the "negatively regulative" side, George would curtail them; and where they would curtail the functions of government, on the positive, coöperative side, he would extend them.

After the publication of *Progress and Poverty*, George devoted the remaining years of his life to propagating the gospel of the single tax.

[15] See George, *Progress and Poverty*, pp. 395–396, 408–410; George, *Social Problems*, pp. 241–242, 252–260; and George to Lowell, October 5, 1883, George Collection.

[16] George, *Protection or Free Trade*, pp. 304–308; George to Thomas F. Walker, September 9, 1884, September 25, 1890, George Collection; George to Edmund Yardley, February 26, 1895, *ibid.*

He was not only active as a lecturer and writer in the United States, but his trips abroad did much to stimulate the land-reform movements in England, Ireland, and Australia. In 1886 he became labor's candidate for mayor of New York, primarily because he thought that his entry into the campaign would, as he wrote to his friend Dr. Edward Taylor, "bring the land question into practical politics and do more to popularize its discussion than years of writing could do." In a bitterly fought campaign, George ran second to the Democrats' Abram S. Hewitt but ahead of the Republican candidate, Theodore Roosevelt. The next year George ran for secretary of state of New York on the United Labor party ticket but was decisively defeated. In 1897, despite the advice of his physician, he made a second attempt to win the New York mayoralty, this time as an independent Democrat. Five days before the election, however, he succumbed to an apoplectic stroke.[17]

Although the legislative accomplishments of the single-tax movement have been meager indeed, Henry George had not fought his battle in vain. Not only did he establish himself as an important figure in the realm of American economic thought and as an influence on the movement for tax reform, but, as the era of Progressivism was to demonstrate, his ideas served as a stimulant to the reform movement as a whole. Progressives such as Tom Johnson, Peter Witt, Newton D. Baker, and Frederic C. Howe in Cleveland, Golden Rule Jones and Brand Whitlock in Toledo, W. S. U'Ren in Oregon, L. F. C. Garvin in Rhode Island, George Record and Mark Fagan in New Jersey, Congressman William Kent of California, Congressman Warren Worth Bailey of Pennsylvania, Woodrow Wilson's assistant secretary of labor, Louis F. Post, Wilson's secretary of the interior, Franklin K. Lane, Wilson's secretary, Joseph Tumulty, and even Lincoln Steffens and Clarence Darrow were all influenced to a greater or lesser extent, by the ideas of Henry George.[18]

III

Whereas Henry George affirmed the inalienable equal right of each individual to the bounty of nature, Edward Bellamy emphasized

[17] George, Jr., *Life of Henry George,* pp. 335–438, 459–503, 513–541, 593–611; George to Taylor, September 10, 1886, George Collection.

[18] Young, *Single Tax Movement,* pp. 285–286, 312–319; Ransom E. Noble, Jr., "Henry George and the Progressive Movement," *American Journal of Economics and Sociology,* VIII (April, 1949), 259–263, 269; Barker, *Henry George,* pp. 621–635.

the equal right of all persons to the entire human inheritance. Believing that the social machinery gives an unearned increment not only to the value of land but to the value of all forms of labor, Bellamy concluded that the social organism is the inheritance of all and must belong to society generally. Unlike most critics of laissez faire during this period, Bellamy saw no middle ground between a laissez-faire economy and the complete nationalization of the means of production and distribution.

A newspaperman and novelist whose work had previously attracted but little attention, Bellamy vaulted into public prominence in 1888 with the publication of the utopian novel *Looking Backward, 2000–1887,* a book that achieved a sale in every way comparable with *Progress and Poverty.* Two hundred and ten thousand copies of *Looking Backward* had been sold by the end of December, 1889; in the early 1890's one million copies were in "active circulation." [19] The views that he had expounded in *Looking Backward* were amplified by Bellamy in a second novel, *Equality,* published in 1897, and in the pages of the *Nationalist* and the *New Nation,* journals founded largely to propagate Bellamy's doctrine of Nationalism.[20]

Whereas Henry George found much to praise in the system of private enterprise, Bellamy denounced the existing economic order as "radically wrong in morals and preposterous economically." He spoke of its "excessive individualism" as "inconsistent with much public spirit." Self-interest he considered synonymous with selfishness and as making an appeal "solely to the anti-social and brutal side of human nature." He regarded competition as an "immoral, wasteful, brutal scramble for existence" that permits each individual to work for his own maintenance at the expense of the community. There can be real competition, Bellamy contended, only between parties of equal strength. What passes for competition in the capitalist system is simply a "brutal and cowardly slaughter of the unarmed and overmatched by bullies in armor." [21]

[19] See John Hope Franklin, "Edward Bellamy and Nationalism," *New England Quarterly,* XI (December, 1938), 754; and Charles A. Madison, "Edward Bellamy, Social Dreamer," *ibid.,* XV (September, 1942), 457.

[20] The *Nationalist* appeared from May, 1889, to April, 1891; the *New Nation* from January 31, 1891, to February 3, 1894.

[21] *New Nation,* I (January 31, 1891), 13; Bellamy, *Looking Backward, 2000–1887* (Tower Books ed.; Cleveland, 1945), pp. 48, 222–225, 265–271; Bellamy, *Equality* (New York, 1897), pp. 333, 394–395.

Bellamy also struck hard at the lack of planning that, he believed, characterized the system of private enterprise of his day. He referred to the existing system of production as, in effect, a system for preventing production. He pointed to industrial warfare, idle men and machines, and economic depressions as the necessary concomitants of the capitalist order and ridiculed the contention that these phenomena are to be endured as inevitable.[22]

The laissez-faire view of the state was also subjected to Bellamy's trenchant criticism. He saw little logic in a political philosophy that sanctioned the use of force to combat the foreign foe and the domestic brigand but that did not approve state action to cope with the real enemies of the people: cold, hunger, and nakedness. Because the system of laissez faire places the production and distribution of wealth, upon which the well-being of society depends, outside the sphere of government control, the possessors of great wealth, Bellamy contended, are able to dictate to the government, the laborer, the farmer, and the small businessman; and government by the people and for the people gives way to government by the capitalists and for the capitalists.[23]

To remedy the defects that he believed inherent in the capitalist system, Bellamy proposed the establishment of a new economic order based on nationalized industries and economic equality. He was confident that the people would realize the danger of permitting the industry and commerce of the nation to be run by capitalists who were not responsible to the general public for their actions and, in the interests of self-government, would take over the economic plant of the nation as once they had assumed control of the political machinery.[24] He envisioned a utopia where the state would be the sole monopoly and the employer of all labor. In the new economic order, all citizens who were physically able would be responsible to the state for industrial or intellectual service from the ages of twenty-one to forty-five. Through a system of national planning, labor would be utilized to its best advantage.[25]

The profits to be derived from the national industries would, in

[22] Bellamy, *Looking Backward*, pp. 217–235.

[23] *Ibid.*, pp. 64–65; Bellamy, *Equality*, pp. 7–13; Bellamy, "Nationalism—Principles, Purposes," *Nationalist*, II (April, 1890), 174–176.

[24] For a time the motto of the *New Nation* was, "The industrial system of a nation, as well as its political system, ought to be a government of the people, by the people, for the people."

[25] Bellamy, *Looking Backward*, pp. 61–62, 66–68, 314–315.

Bellamy's scheme, be shared equally by all the people. To Bellamy, the only adequate guarantee of life, liberty, and the pursuit of happiness was economic equality. He repudiated the suggestion that the state discharges its responsibility to its citizens when it provides them with equality of opportunity and then simply umpires the ensuing struggle among them. To accept such a position, he wrote in one of his notebooks, would make it appear as though "we objected to men eating those they conquered in battle, not because we objected to men eating men on principle, but merely because the individuals on the scrimmage line did not start fair. Give them each a club and match them according to weight, so that all will be fair play, and then let the eating go on. Thus," said Bellamy, "we will not have nor tolerate any talk of a reform that stops here." [26]   In the Nationalist state, the government would provide the means of labor and life on equal terms to all. Solicitous for the social and economic security of its inhabitants, it would also guarantee "the nurture, education, and comfortable maintenance of every citizen, from the cradle to the grave." [27]

Bellamy brushed aside arguments that his proposals involved an undue extension of the powers of government. He insisted that in the Nationalist scheme of things there would actually be less interference with personal liberty than there was in the existing order. Once economic equality was established, the elaborate restrictive machinery of government designed to protect persons and property and to wage war would be rendered superfluous, and there would be no further need for punitive and coercive regulations. The government would merely serve as the "co-ordinating directory" of the associated industries, and the positive rather than the negative aspects of its work would be developed. It was not sufficiently realized by the people, Bellamy thought, that the transfer of government from monarchic or aristocratic control to popular control made possible a new positive view of the state as an agency for the general welfare. Nationalism, he declared, "aims to put an end to the present irresponsible control of the economic interests of the country by capitalists pursuing their private ends, and to replace it by responsible public agencies acting

[26] Notebook No. 7, pp. 12–14, Bellamy Papers, Houghton Library, Harvard University. "We object to a state of society," Bellamy wrote, "which makes it possible for any man to use his superior strength to stand on his fellow's shoulders, or which causes him to suffer indignity and cruelty because he is weak" (*ibid.*).

[27] Bellamy, *Equality,* pp. 17–18, 76–87; Bellamy, *Looking Backward,* pp. 91–92.

for the general welfare." "Government by a few for a few" was to be replaced by "Government by all for all." [28]

To Bellamy, Nationalism was but the realization of the social teachings of the Gospel. He referred to his utopia as the "Republic of the Golden Rule," and he looked to a "great revival" that would emphasize the social aspects of Christianity to provide the necessary impulse for the adoption of his plan. This religious movement, he thought, would engender "a tide of enthusiasm for the social, not the personal, salvation, and for the establishment in brotherly love of the kingdom of God on earth which Christ bade men hope and work for." He believed the nation would awaken "to the profoundly ethical and truly religious character and claims of the movement for an industrial system which should guarantee the economic equality of all the people." [29]

The ethical character of Nationalism appealed to many clergymen: twenty-one ministers were affiliated with the various Nationalist clubs. The Society of Christian Socialists developed in 1889 out of a meeting of Boston clergymen who were members of a Nationalist club, and Bellamy referred to its journal, the *Dawn*, as "devoted to the Christian Socialistic side of Nationalism." [30] Clergymen who followed in the path of Bellamy no doubt concurred in the opinion of the Reverend W. D. P. Bliss that "Nationalism means essentially the application of ethics and equity through government to business. Its development means the development of righteousness in social order. And righteousness *is* Christianity." [31]

Convinced of the justice of his cause and the inevitability of its success, Bellamy came to believe that his entire program could be realized within fifty years by a gradual and orderly application of the principle of public ownership.[32] As a first step, he proposed the acquisition by the federal government of the railroads, the telegraph

[28] Bellamy, *Looking Backward*, pp. 64–65, 117, 201–203; Bellamy, *Equality*, pp. 406–409; Bellamy, "The Programme of the Nationalists," *Forum*, XVII (March, 1894), 81, 91.

[29] Bellamy, *Equality*, pp. 1, 340–345.

[30] See James Dombrowski, *The Early Days of Christian Socialism in America* (New York, 1936), pp. 93–95; Charles Howard Hopkins, *The Rise of the Social Gospel in American Protestantism, 1865–1915* (New Haven, 1940), pp. 173–174; Bellamy to Ely, November 13, 1889, Richard T. Ely Papers, State Historical Society of Wisconsin.

[31] Bliss, "Christianity and Nationalism," *Nationalist*, I (August, 1889), 99.

[32] "Editorial Notes," *Nationalist*, I (May, 1889), 21.

and telephone, the express business, and the coal mines, assumption by the state governments of the liquor business and the fire- and life-insurance business, and the municipalization of local public utilities. The advantages of public ownership would then be demonstrated for all to observe. Laborers in the state-owned industries would work short hours for good wages and would be provided with working conditions superior to those prevailing in the private sectors of the economy. They would receive support in sickness and pensions in the event of disabling accidents and when they became too old to work. Public stores would furnish them with their necessities at cost, and government cotton farms and food farms would be established to provide the supplies for these stores. Bellamy believed that the nationalization of these few basic industries would bring approximately one and one-half million to two million workers within the orbit of Nationalism and would provide a "bulwark" against the capitalist order and a nucleus for further nationalization. He was certain that the superiority of the nationalized section of the economy to the non-nationalized part would become so apparent that the people would call for the general adoption of Nationalism.[33]

The popularity of Bellamy's scheme was attested to not only by the wide circulation of *Looking Backward* but also by the formation of Nationalist clubs throughout the land. The first of these clubs was established in Boston in December, 1888. It included in its membership such prominent figures as Edward Everett Hale, W. D. P. Bliss, Rabbi Solomon Schindler, William Dean Howells, Hamlin Garland, Julia Ward Howe, and Frances Willard. From Boston the movement spread to other parts of the country, and by October, 1890, one hundred and fifty Nationalist clubs had come into being in twenty-seven states.[34] Bellamy's Nationalist followers endorsed his gradualist approach to the

---

[33] Bellamy, *Equality*, pp. 353–362; Bellamy, "Nationalism—Principles, Purposes," *Nationalist*, II (April, 1890), 177–178; Bellamy, "First Steps toward Nationalism," *Forum*, X (October, 1890), 174–184; Bellamy, "The Programme of the Nationalists," *ibid.*, XVII (March, 1894), 81–91. The plans for gradual nationalization presented by Bellamy in the sources noted differ in detail but not in their essence. In the *Forum* article of 1894 Bellamy contended that it was necessary for the states to enter the forestry business and for the federal government to operate the fisheries. If the public also assumed the ownership of all monopolies, a giant stride would be taken in the direction of Nationalism. Bellamy proposed that public authorities pay present costs of reproduction to the owners of businesses that were made public property.

[34] Arthur E. Morgan, *Edward Bellamy* (New York, 1944), pp. 249–253; Fred E. Haynes, *Social Politics in the United States* (Boston, 1924), p. 146.

problem of nationalization of the economy and subscribed to his view that the state, in the general interest, must enlarge the sphere of its activities and must guarantee the social and economic security of its citizens.[35]

In terms of practical accomplishments, the success of the Nationalists was small indeed. In 1891 they induced the Massachusetts legislature to pass a law that gave cities and villages of the state the authority to own and operate electric and gas works. A similar law applying to coal yards, which was passed the next year, ran afoul of the state courts. Nationalists were also instrumental in getting the Populist party to espouse public ownership of the railroads, telegraph, and telephone. By 1895, however, Nationalism as an independent movement was dead. Its proposals involved far too radical a change in existing institutions to appeal to any great number of Americans. But, as Bellamy's biographer maintains, the great achievement of Bellamy and his Nationalist followers was not so much in the direction of bringing about specific social reforms as in helping to create a public attitude that was favorable to social change in general.[36]

IV

The years from 1865 to 1896 were largely years of agrarian discontent in the United States. Farm prices, which had risen sharply during the Civil War, went the way of all prices when the inflationary spiral came to an end, and despite occasional spurts upward, the secu-

[35] Sylvester Baxter, "What Is Nationalism?" *Nationalist,* I (June, 1889), 8–12; Edward Everett Hale, "The Best Government," *ibid.,* p. 37; Hale, "New England Nationalism," in *Addresses and Essays in Subjects of History, Education, and Government* (Boston, 1900), pp. 391–392; Frederick M. Willis, "The Sphere of the State," *Nationalist,* II (April, 1890), 155–162; "What the Government Can Do," *Craftsman,* VI (September 28, 1889), 2; Solomon Schindler, "Insurance and the Nation," *Arena,* X (August, 1894), 383–385; Arthur Mann, "Solomon Schindler: Boston Radical," *New England Quarterly,* XXIII (December, 1950), 467–469, 474–475.

[36] Morgan, *Edward Bellamy,* pp. 275–298. See also Howard Quint, *The Forging of American Socialism* (Columbia, S. C., 1953), pp. 89–102; "How Cleveland's Victory Prepares the Way for Nationalism," *New Nation,* II (November 19, 1892), 686; Franklin, "Edward Bellamy and Nationalism," *New England Quarterly,* XI (December, 1938), 764–772; Katherine Pearson Woods, "Edward Bellamy: Author and Economist," *Bookman,* VII (July, 1898), 398–401; and Haynes, *Social Politics in the United States,* pp. 146–151. Interest in Bellamy and Nationalism was revived during the depression years after 1929 and during the era of the New Deal. On this development, see Elizabeth Sadler, "One Book's Influence," *New England Quarterly,* XVII (December, 1944), 544–549.

lar trend of farm prices from the late 1860's to the Bryan-McKinley campaign of 1896 was decidedly downward. The farmer complained not only that farm prices were too low but that middleman costs and railroad charges were too high, that he was compelled to purchase manufactured goods at monopolistic prices, and that farm credit, whether long term or short term, was difficult to obtain and altogether too expensive. At the same time as farm prices were declining, the rising price of farm land and the increased investment of farmers in agricultural machinery tended to drive the fixed costs of the farmer upward. The large fixed investment of the farmer per dollar output was responsible for an alarming increase in the farm-mortgage debt and in the percentage of farms operated by tenants.[37]

Beset by economic difficulties and troubled over both the decline in their political power and the relatively greater social and educational advantages available to the city dweller, the farmers attempted to promote their common interests by organizing. The Grange and its political offshoots in the late 1860's and early and middle 1870's, the Greenback party, which was active from 1876 to 1884, and the Alliances and the People's party of the late eighties and the nineties became the media through which the farmers registered their protest and sought to effect the social, economic, and political changes they deemed necessary.

As indicated by the efforts of the Grange and the Alliances to establish farm coöperatives of various sorts, the organized farmers attempted, to a certain extent at least, to improve their lot by their own endeavors. Increasingly, however, they looked to the state as the only agency capable of introducing the reforms that they believed were needed to restore farm prosperity. Driven to invoke the aid of the state by agricultural depression rather than by political theory, the farmers nevertheless blended their voices with those of the theorists of reform in asserting that government, in the interests of the general welfare, must assume a greater responsibility for the successful functioning of the economy and must aid in the establishment of a more just social order. "It is the paramount duty of the government, in all its legislation," declared the Independent party (Greenback) platform of 1876, "to keep in view the full development of all legitimate

[37] Solon Justus Buck, *The Granger Movement* (Cambridge, Mass., 1913), pp. 3–39; John D. Hicks, *The Populist Revolt* (Minneapolis, 1931), pp. 54–95; E. A. J. Johnson and Herman E. Krooss, *The Origins and Development of the American Economy* (New York, 1953), pp. 270–273.

business, agricultural, mining, manufacturing, and commercial." [38] "We believe," the Populists asserted in their platform of 1892, "that the powers of government—in other words, of the people—should be expanded (as in the case of the postal service) as rapidly and as far as the good sense of an intelligent people and the teachings of experience shall justify, to the end that oppression, injustice, and poverty shall eventually cease in the land." [39]

In his utopian novel *Caesar's Column,* the colorful and influential Granger, Greenbacker, and Populist, Ignatius Donnelly, proclaimed that "government is intended to be merely a plain and simple instrument, to insure to every industrious citizen not only liberty, but an educated mind, a comfortable home, an abundant supply of food and clothing, and a pleasant, happy life." "We have but to expand the powers of government," he declared, "to solve the enigma of the world." In his utopia, the government would employ the surplus income of society to construct great public works to benefit the laborer and would fix the rate of compensation so as to afford all workers not only "a comfortable living" but also a surplus to set aside for their old age. It would provide farmers with non-interest-bearing loans so that they might establish themselves, would supply doctors and lawyers for all, and would see that "no man is plundered, and no man starved, who is willing to work." [40]

Although the difficulties of the farmer in the decades after the Civil War were largely the result of the increase of farm production at a more rapid rate than the increase of the nation's population, the farmer tended to see in the practices of the railroads and, increasingly, in the nation's monetary and banking system the source of his troubles, and it was primarily in these areas that he sought the assistance of the government. The Grange and the state Anti-Monopoly or Reform parties of the 1870's, to whose formation the members of the avowedly nonpartisan Grange often contributed, addressed themselves principally to the solution of the railroad problem; and if it is now evident that the so-called Granger laws enacted in the states of the upper Mississippi Valley at this time to provide for the regulation of railroad rates and practices were less the result of Granger activity than was

[38] Edward Stanwood, *A History of the Presidency from 1788 to 1897* (Boston, 1898), p. 367.

[39] Hicks, *Populist Revolt,* p. 441.

[40] Donnelly, *Caesar's Column* (Chicago, 1891), pp. 120–122, 129–130, 358–359.

once believed, it is nonetheless true that the organized farmers contributed to the general movement for railroad regulation in the 1870's.[41]
Although state legislation providing for the regulation of railroads was
enacted during the period when the Grange was active, that organization failed to persuade the federal government that it could aid the
farmers in obtaining lower rates to the seaboard and the Gulf by con-
structing a double-track freight railroad from some point in the Mississippi Valley to the Atlantic coast and by establishing a workable
water route from the Great Lakes to the Gulf of Mexico.[42]

The modification or outright repeal of the Granger laws soon after
their enactment and the general failure of railroad regulation to
achieve the results anticipated by the farmers eventually induced the
agrarian forces to press for a more radical solution of the railroad problem.   The Greenback party in 1880 and 1884, it is true, called only for
Congressional regulation of interstate commerce, but the Populists
Omaha platform of 1892 demanded that the federal government assume the ownership of the nation's railroads, and of the telegraph and
telephone as well.[43]   Only in this fashion, thought the Populists, could
the railroads be made to serve the public interest.

The Greenback and Populist forces were, all in all, less interested
than the Grangers in the railroad problem.   Their concern was primarily the money problem, and they saw in the inflation of the currency either by means of greenbacks or free silver, or both, the obvious
method of driving up the price of farm commodities and thus easing
the crushing burden of farm debt.   The steady appreciation in the
value of the dollar after the Civil War was explained by the farmer
largely in terms of the inadequacy of the money supply, and he pointed
to the decrease in the per capita amount of paper money and coin in
circulation ($30.35 in 1865; $21.10 in 1896 [44]) as evidence for his contention.   Taking a position diametrically opposed to that of the advocate of thoroughgoing laissez faire, the farmer insisted that the federal government assume exclusive control over the coinage and currency

[41] Buck, *Granger Movement*, pp. 80–101, 123–205; George Hall Miller, "The
Granger Laws: A Study of the Origins of State Railway Control in the Upper
Mississippi Valley" (Ph.D. thesis, University of Michigan, 1951), *passim*.

[42] Buck, *Granger Movement*, pp. 111–114.

[43] Stanwood, *History of the Presidency from 1788 to 1897*, pp. 410, 425; Hicks
Populist Revolt, p. 443.   The Greenback party platform of 1884 did approve federal
construction of national railroads if that proved necessary to correct abuses.

[44] Paul Studenski and Herman E. Krooss, *Financial History of the United States*
(New York, 1952), pp. 160, 239.

and that it issue money in sufficient quantity to meet the needs of the economy in general and of agriculture in particular.

The greenback movement of the era after the Civil War was influenced to a considerable extent by the monetary theories of Edward Kellogg and was, down to the early 1870's at least, less the result of agrarian concern than of labor interest. The monetary ideas advanced in the 1840's by Edward Kellogg, a New York dry-goods merchant who had suffered financial embarrassment as a result of the panic of 1837, attributed poor labor conditions and monetary fluctuations to excessive interest rates. The value of money as a medium of exchange, Kellogg argued, is determined by the interest rate, and as this rate increases, the price of property, which is represented by money, falls, and capital tends to accumulate in the hands of the few. The remedy for this situation proposed by Kellogg was the establishment of a national bank that would issue legal-tender currency to persons borrowing on real-estate security. The interest charged was not to exceed 1.1 per cent, which, according to Kellogg, was the labor cost of manufacturing and loaning money; and since money in his view served a public use but was not a productive agent, he believed that its cost should be no greater than the labor-cost of supplying it. Kellogg further proposed that the legal-tender currency issued be made interconvertible with government bonds bearing 1 per cent interest: if the market rate of money fell below 1 per cent, the mortgagor could convert his currency into bonds; if the market rate exceeded 1 per cent, the bondholder could exchange his bonds for currency. In this way the interest rate could be kept at approximately 1 per cent, and the currency would have uniform value throughout the United States, would not be subject to overissue, and would be adjusted to business requirements.[45]

Kellogg's scheme was adapted to the monetary conditions resulting from the Civil War by the businessman, politician, and labor reformer Alexander Campbell, who proposed in 1864 that the federal government convert its war debt into bonds bearing 3 per cent interest, estimated by Campbell as the rate of national savings, and intercon-

[45] Joseph Dorfman, *The Economic Mind in American Civilization, 1606–1918* (New York, 1934), II, 678–681; Chester McArthur Destler, "The Influence of Edward Kellogg upon American Radicalism, 1865–1896," in *American Radicalism, 1865–1901: Essays and Documents* (New London, Conn., 1946), pp. 51–55; John R. Commons *et al.*, *History of Labour in the United States* (New York, 1918–1935), II, 119–120.

vertible with greenbacks, the irredeemable legal-tender currency issued by the Union government during the war. Campbell dropped Kellogg's land-loan idea and suggested merely that the government issue currency to meet its obligations.[46]

It was in the form proposed by Campbell that Kellogg's ideas were accepted by the National Labor Union, an amorphous federation of labor and reform organizations founded in 1866. Interested in the establishment of producers' coöperatives, the National Labor Union saw in the Kellogg-Campbell scheme the means of obtaining credit at low rates of interest for coöperative ventures. At its 1867 convention the organization accepted the view that the rate of interest determines the shares of the product that go to labor and capital and proposed therefore that the federal government abolish the national banking system and pay its debts with legal-tender treasury notes convertible at the option of the holder into government bonds bearing 3 per cent interest. The result, it was proclaimed, would be the equitable distribution of the products of labor between labor and "non-producing" capital. This idea, modified only in that the proposed rate of interest on the bonds was increased to 3.65 per cent, was carried into politics by the National Labor Reform party, which was organized in 1871 by the National Labor Union and was overwhelmingly defeated in the presidential election of 1872.[47]

Although the Industrial Congresses of 1873 and 1874 accepted a version of the National Labor Union's monetary plan and although the Knights of Labor favored the abolition of the national banking system and government issue of greenbacks and even flirted briefly with Kelloggism in 1885, the defeat of the National Labor Reform party in 1872 more or less marked the end of the wage-earner period of greenbackism. Western sentiment for greenback inflation had been gathering force ever since 1867, and although former members of the National Labor Union were instrumental, along with the agrarian Independent party of Indiana, in the establishment in 1876 of the Independent (Greenback) party and in the drawing up of its platform, such voting strength as the greenback forces were able to muster in 1876

[46] Dorfman, *Economic Mind in American Civilization,* II, 978–980; Destler, "Influence of Edward Kellogg," in *American Radicalism,* p. 56.

[47] Commons *et al., Documentary History of American Industrial Society* (Cleveland, 1910–1911), IX, 179–181; Commons *et al., History of Labour,* II, 120–121; Destler, "Influence of Edward Kellogg," in *American Radicalism,* 56–59; Stanwood, *History of the Presidency from 1788 to 1897,* p. 336.

and afterward was largely drawn from agricultural areas; and the interest of the farmer was not so much the rate of interest as it was inflation. "Inflate the currency," declared Solon Chase, chairman of the Maine Greenback-Labor convention of 1878, "and you raise the price of my steers and at the same time pay the public debt." [48]

The platform of the Independent party in 1876 still retained ties with Kelloggism: it called not only for the repeal of the recently passed Specie Resumption Act, which pledged the federal government to redeem greenbacks dollar for dollar and to limit their amount, but also demanded the issuance of United States notes to the people by the government, such notes to be full legal tender and to be interconvertible with United States bonds bearing 3.65 per cent interest.[49] The party's candidate, the eighty-five-year-old ironmaster and reformer, Peter Cooper, believed, like all the greenbackers, that the government must exercise exclusive control over the money supply. By the time of his nomination, he had come to accept the idea of the interconvertible bond and was proposing that the federal government restore the full amount of money that had been in circulation at the end of the Civil War and that it then increase this amount to match increases in the population and the volume of exchanges, the currency as a whole to be interconvertible with government bonds bearing a rate of interest slightly above the average annual increase in the value of the property of the nation. Ultimately, Cooper was to suggest that the federal government put additional currency into circulation in the form of payments for the construction of fifty ocean steamers and two double-track railroads from the Atlantic to the Pacific and also that it loan money at 1 per cent interest to each state according to its population, the states to loan the money to counties at 2 per cent, and the counties to individuals at 3 per cent on real-estate security. To suggestions that his proposals involved too great an extension of the functions of government, Cooper responded that the government would have to become more paternal if it were to serve its true object, the "promotion of human welfare." [50]

[48] See Destler, "Influence of Edward Kellogg," in *American Radicalism*, pp. 60–67; Destler, "Western Radicalism, 1865–1901: Concepts and Origins," *ibid.*, p. 7; Commons *et al.*, *History of Labour*, II, 121; and Buck, *The Agrarian Crusade* (New Haven, 1921), pp. 87, 90–91.

[49] Stanwood, *History of the Presidency from 1788 to 1897*, pp. 367–368.

[50] See Cooper, *Ideas for a Science of Good Government in Addresses, Letters and Articles on a Strictly National Currency, Tariff and Civil Service* (2d ed.; New York, 1883), pp. 37–40, 103–104, 107–108, 121–122, 143–145, 173, 178, 229;

The interconvertible bond proposal, which appeared in the platform of the Independent party in 1876, disappeared from the greenback program once the inflationary forces, wedded to the quantity theory of money, gained firm control of the movement. They desired the federal government to abolish the national banking system, to assume exclusive control of the coinage and of the currency, and to issue legal-tender currency in amounts sufficient to maintain a fully functioning economy. The Independent party changed its name in 1878 to the National (Greenback-Labor) party, but despite the inclusion of some labor planks in its platform and the presence of labor elements in the party, control of the organization was in the hands of farmers, lawyers, and radical businessmen. The platform adopted in 1878 omitted all mention of the interconvertible bond and asserted merely that Congress should provide currency "adequate to the full employment of labor, the equitable distribution of its products, and the requirements of business, fixing a minimum amount *per capita* of the population as near as may be, and otherwise regulating its value by wise and equitable provisions of law, so that the rate of interest will secure to labor its just reward." [51]   In its platforms of 1880 and 1884 the Greenback party dropped the reference to the rate of interest and called for the substitution of greenbacks for national bank notes, the free coinage of silver, and, in the words of the 1884 platform, government issuance of currency "in sufficient quantities to supply the actual demand of trade and commerce, in accordance with the increase of population and the development of our industries." [52]

---

testimony of Cooper, U. S. Congress, House, Select Committee, *Investigation Relative to the Causes of the General Depression in Labor and Business, etc.*, 46th Cong., 2d sess., H. Misc. Doc. No. 5 (Washington, D.C., 1879), pp. 383–384; Edward C. Mack, *Peter Cooper, Citizen of New York* (New York, 1949), pp. 358–359, 366, 370–372, 379–380; and Allan Nevins, *Abram S. Hewitt; with Some Account of Peter Cooper* (New York, 1935), pp. 284–286. Although Cooper had at one time been an opponent of government paternalism, his espousal of greenbackism led him to an acceptance of a broader view of state functions, and he became, in Mack's words, "very nearly an advocate of the social service state." His recommendations for government action included the provision of public work for the unemployed, the establishment of publicly supported industrial schools, government construction of Western railroads, and the organization of postal-savings banks. See Mack, *Cooper*, pp. 374–380; Cooper, *Ideas for a Science of Good Government*, pp. 121–122, 178; and Nevins, *Hewitt*, pp. 287–288.

[51] See Commons *et al.*, *History of Labour*, II, 244; and *Appletons' Annual Cyclopaedia and Register of Important Events of the Year 1878* (New York, 1879), p. 807.

[52] Stanwood, *History of the Presidency from 1788 to 1897*, pp. 409, 425.

As a political movement, greenbackism never mustered sufficient strength to secure the adoption of its program. The party's best showing was in the off-year elections of 1878, when it garnered approximately one million votes. In the 1876 election, it polled but 81,737 votes; in 1880 but 308,578 votes; and in 1884, in conjunction with the Anti-Monopoly party, 175,370 votes.[53] Defeat in 1884 signaled the end of the Greenback party, but greenbackism itself lived on, in one form or another, in the programs of the Alliances, North and South, and of the People's party.

Alliance men and Populists were, for the most part, advocates of the quantity theory of money and tended to see in the increase of the circulating medium to fifty dollars per capita, at a time when per capita circulation was approximately half that amount, the answer to low farm prices and the burden of farm debt. As the key means of putting the added money into circulation, the Southern Alliance proposed the subtreasury plan, which involved loans by the federal government of legal-tender currency, at 1 or 2 per cent interest, on nonperishable farm crops deposited in government warehouses. Since the subtreasury scheme, suggestive in some respects of present-day crop-loan programs of the federal government, appeared to work best with cotton, the Northern Alliance did not find it as enticing a proposal as the Southern Alliance did, and recommended, for its part, that the government put legal-tender currency into circulation by extending long-term loans at low rates of interest to farmers offering real estate as security.[54]

The land-loan idea of the Northern Alliance was popularized in S. F. Norton's *Ten Men of Money Island*, which had appeared much earlier in serial form in the Chicago *Sentinel* and which was "the one greenback treatise that appears to have enjoyed a tremendous audience,"[55] and also in the writings of the Populist senator from Kansas, W. A. Peffer. Contending that the chief problem that confronted the nation was the "money power," Peffer insisted that the government must supply money to the people on reasonable terms. He endorsed the subtreasury plan and federal land loans at 1 per cent interest and

[53] Stanwood, *History of the Presidency from 1788 to 1897*, pp. 383, 417, 448; Buck, *Agrarian Crusade*, p. 90.

[54] See N. A. Dunning, *The Philosophy of Price, and Its Relation to Domestic Commerce* (Chicago, 1887), pp. 30–105, 219–220, 233–236; Hicks, *Populist Revolt*, pp. 186–200; S. M. Scott, *The Sub-Treasury Plan and the Land and Loan System* (Topeka, Kan., 1891); and Destler, "Influence of Edward Kellogg," in *American Radicalism*, pp. 69–73.

[55] Dorfman, *Economic Mind in American Civilization*, III, 115.

proposed also that the national banks, as agents of the federal government, should provide short-term loans at 2 per cent interest.[56]

In its "Ocala Demands" of December, 1890, the Southern Alliance combined the plans of North and South by calling for the adoption of both the subtreasury and the land-loan schemes. The same proposal was incorporated in the Cincinnati platform of the People's party, the political organization of the Populists. The Omaha platform of 1892, upon which the Populists campaigned for the presidency, called, however, merely for the issuance by the federal government of a flexible legal-tender currency to be distributed directly to the people at a tax not to exceed 2 per cent as provided either in the subtreasury plan or in "a better system" and also in the form of payments for "public improvements." The Omaha platform also contained the usual demand that the amount of money in circulation be increased to fifty dollars per capita, and, as had most of the earlier Alliance and Populist pronouncements, it called for the free and unlimited coinage of silver at 16 to 1.[57]

The free-silver movement had been gaining in strength ever since the middle seventies, at which time the market price of silver, demonetized to all intents and purposes by the Coinage Act of 1873, fell below the legal ratio of 16 to 1. Free silver enjoyed more formidable political support than had the greenback movement, but orthodox Populists tended to regard unlimited silver coinage at 16 to 1 as insufficient in itself to produce the desired level of circulation of fifty dollars per capita. However, as silverites joined their ranks in increasing numbers, the Populists placed greater and greater emphasis on free silver as a solution for the money question, and finally in 1896 they accepted as their own presidential candidate the Democratic candidate, William Jennings Bryan, who was running on a platform that espoused free silver but that ignored the other monetary demands of the Populists.[58] Bryan's defeat ensured the triumph of the gold standard, and the farmers themselves lost interest in the money question as farm prices began a steady upward climb after 1896.

Although the farmers emphasized the railroad and the money questions, they did not confine their legislative demands to these two prob-

[56] Peffer, The Farmer's Side (New York, 1891), pp. 148–149, 185–210, 218–219, 227–228, 242–256. Cf. Peffer, "The Cure for a Vicious Monetary System," Forum, XXII (February, 1897), 728–730.

[57] Hicks, Populist Revolt, pp. 200–204, 430, 433, 442–443.

[58] Hicks, Populist Revolt, pp. 316–320, 340–379.

lems. Grangers urged their state legislatures to establish state boards of agriculture, to provide for the collection of agricultural statistics, to appropriate money for agricultural colleges and to introduce agricultural subjects in the public schools, to supply textbooks to school children free of charge or at cost, to tax mortgages and at the same time reduce proportionately the tax on mortgaged property, to reduce the legal rate of interest, and, in the case of California, to establish a system of irrigation under the control of the state. They importuned the federal government to reform the patent laws, to advance the Department of Agriculture to cabinet rank, to stamp out pleuropneumonia among cattle, to regulate weights and measures, and to provide greater security for bank deposits.

In its various platforms, the Greenback party called for the reservation of public lands for actual settlers, a graduated income tax, a government postal-telegraph system, and appropriate legislation to ameliorate labor conditions. The Populists, in addition to their railroad and monetary demands, recommended a graduated income tax, postal-savings banks, use of the public lands for actual settlers, rigid enforcement of the federal eight-hour-day law, and abolition of the Pinkerton system.[59] As Solon Buck has observed, "in general it may be said that the farmers' organizations and parties stood for increased governmental activity; they scorned the economic and political doctrine of *laissez faire;* they believed that the people's governments could and should be used in many ways for promoting the welfare of the people, for assuring social justice, and for restoring and preserving economic as well as political equality." [60]

The attention that historians have focused on the greenback problem and the battle of the standards, on the efforts of farmers to inflate the currency and the resistance that these efforts encountered, has tended to obscure the proposals of economists and reformers of the late nineteenth century that pointed neither to inflation nor deflation but rather to the maintenance by government action of a dollar of constant purchasing power. Believing that fluctuations in the price level contributed importantly to industrial and financial disturbances,

[59] Buck, *Granger Movement,* pp. 102–122; Stanwood, *History of the Presidency from 1788 to 1897,* pp. 409–410, 425–426; *Appletons' Annual Cyclopaedia and Register of Important Events of the Year 1878,* p. 807; Hicks, *Populist Revolt,* pp. 443–444.

[60] Buck, *Agrarian Crusade,* pp. 199–200. See also Frederick Jackson Turner, *The Frontier in American History* (New York, 1920), pp. 276–277, 305–306; and Destler, "Western Radicalism, 1865–1901," in *American Radicalism,* pp. 17–20.

advocates of a dollar of uniform value spoke of the "ideal dollar" as one that would always buy the same average amount of commodities.[61]

Proponents of the "commodity dollar" assumed the validity of the quantity theory of money and saw a direct relationship between the amount of money in circulation and the price level. By increasing or decreasing the amount of money in circulation, the government, they believed, could raise or lower prices as it saw fit. Some of them were aware of the criticism that the quantity theory as usually expressed limited itself to money in circulation and conveniently ignored the fact that 90 per cent of the business of the nation was conducted on credit; but they either assumed that manipulation of the amount of money in circulation was in itself sufficient to control the movement of prices, or they suggested that the government, if such action proved necessary to stabilize the dollar, could supplement its management of money in circulation by extending its control over bank credit as well, and thus over the money supply as a whole.[62]

The essential contention of the advocates of a dollar of constant purchasing power was that the most stable standard of value was neither a monometallic gold or silver standard nor even a bimetallic standard but rather a "composite commodity standard," a multiple standard. They proposed in general that the federal government create an expert nonpartisan commission whose task it would be to collect price statistics for a large list of standard commodities,[63] to construct a properly weighted price index or simply to decide the total sum required to purchase these commodities, and to report the

[61] E. Benjamin Andrews, "An Honest Dollar," *A. E. A. Publications,* IV (November, 1889), 404; Commons, "Economic Reform," *Voice,* September 14, 1893; J. Allen Smith, "The Multiple Money Standard," *Annals,* VII (March, 1896), 176–181; Frank Parsons, *Rational Money* (Philadelphia, 1898), pp. iii–v; Henry Winn, "Multiple-Standard Money," *Arena,* XIX (May, 1898), 639.

[62] Commons, "Economic Reform," *Voice,* September 14, 1893; Thomas Elmer Will, "Stable Money," *Journal of Political Economy,* VII (December, 1898), 87–89; Parsons, *Rational Money,* pp. iii, ix–xi, 100–102; Winn, "Multiple-Standard Money," *Arena,* XIX (May, 1898), 650; Eltweed Pomeroy, "The Multiple Standard for Money," *ibid.,* XVIII (September, 1897), 323–324.

[63] Will argued that there was a double movement of prices, an oscillatory short-term movement and a secular downward trend, and he proposed that a government commission present an accurate statistical description of both of these movements ("Stable Money," *Journal of Political Economy,* VII [December, 1898], 86–87). Parsons wanted the standard eventually to include not only commodities but also "goods, services, privileges and all manner of purchaseable things" (*Rational Money,* pp. 124, 128–129).

results periodically. On the basis of this information, the proper authorities of the federal government could then take the necessary action to maintain price stability.[64]

Those who proposed the adoption of the multiple standard of value suggested various means by which an authorized agency of the federal government could increase or decrease the amount of money in circulation or make other necessary adjustments to maintain the uniform value of the dollar. Some of the advocates of the multiple standard, such as the economists Simon Newcomb, J. Allen Smith (eventually to become famous as a political scientist), E. Benjamin Andrews, and John R. Commons, believed that the government could attain the desired results without abandoning specie backing for its currency. Newcomb, who was one of the first American economists to concern himself with this subject, proposed that paper money be issued that would be redeemable not in gold dollars of a fixed weight but rather in gold and silver bullion of sufficient amount to purchase at average wholesale prices a definite number of commodities.[65]

J. Allen Smith, who discussed the multiple standard in a doctoral thesis that he wrote under the direction of Henry Carter Adams, agreed with Newcomb that the government should issue legal-tender currency that would be convertible into specie whose price would vary inversely

[64] Newcomb, "The Standard of Value," *North American Review*, CXXIX (September, 1879), 226–228; Newcomb to A. J. Warner, June 26, 1885, Newcomb Letterbooks, Simon Newcomb Papers, Library of Congress; Andrews, "An Honest Dollar," *A. E. A. Publications*, IV (November, 1889), 430–433, 439–440; Commons, "Economic Reform," *Voice*, September 14, 1893; Smith, "The Multiple Money Standard," *Annals*, VII (March, 1896), 196–207; Parsons, *Rational Money*, pp. 124–126, 128–137; Winn, "Multiple-Standard Money," *Arena*, XIX (May, 1898), 647–648; Pomeroy, "The Multiple Standard for Money," *ibid.*, XVIII (September, 1897), 331–333; George H. Shibley, "Who Shall Control the Price Level?" *ibid.*, XXIII (January, 1900), 85. Andrews proposed a seven-man commission consisting of the secretary of the treasury, the director of the mint, the comptroller of the currency, the nation's ablest statistician, the ablest banker, and the two ablest specialists in monetary science, the first three to serve ex officio and the other four to be appointed by the president.

[65] Newcomb, "The Standard of Value," *North American Review*, CXXIX (September, 1879), 234–235. Cf. Newcomb, "Has the Standard Gold Dollar Appreciated?" *Journal of Political Economy*, I (September, 1893), 503–512. Francis Amasa Walker thought that the use of the multiple standard could be justified only insofar as it was necessary to safeguard the property of charitable institutions, retired persons, trust funds, and widows' estates and that it might also be made applicable to loans to governments and corporations (*Money* [New York, 1878], pp. 161–163).

with general prices: if general prices rose, the government would lower the price of gold and silver and thus contract the currency, and if prices fell it would increase the price of the two metals and thus expand the currency.   Anticipating the open-market operations of the Federal Reserve System, Smith also suggested that the government could increase the amount of currency in circulation and thus raise prices by purchasing on the open market certain approved securities, such as government or industrial bonds, and could then sell these securities when it wished to contract the currency.   Ultimately, Smith pointed out, the expansion and contraction of the currency is effected by the relationship between taxation and expenditures.   When income from taxation exceeds disbursements, the money supply is contracted, whereas deficit financing has a reverse effect.[66]

E. Benjamin Andrews thought that the federal government could inflate the currency and raise prices by purchasing silver that could be coined into tokens taking the form of certificates.   To reduce the currency supply and prices, the government could sell call bonds that would be redeemable in silver certificates.   These bonds could be called in when it was necessary to replenish the supply of money.[67] John R. Commons, who supported gold as the international standard of value and was an opponent of free silver, proposed a scheme to provide an elastic currency that involved the use of silver as a money of redemption at its market value.   He recommended the establishment of a national monetary commission that would purchase silver bullion with legal-tended bullion notes when it was necessary to expand the currency and then would sell the silver bullion for the bullion notes outstanding when it desired to contract the currency. To prevent corners and speculation, the commission might also issue a restricted number of bullion notes without a corresponding purchase of silver and place them on deposit, subject to call, in approved banks, where they would form the basis for credit expansion.   If these banks overextended themselves creditwise, the commission could withdraw its deposit and thus force a contraction of credit.   Commons also suggested that the government might expand the currency by extending loans to farmers on the security of their crops, the money being redeemable in silver at its market value.[68]

[66] Smith, "The Multiple Money Standard," *Annals,* VII (March, 1896), 205–213.

[67] Andrews, "An Honest Dollar," *A. E. A. Publications,* IV (November, 1889), 433–434.

[68] Commons, "Economic Reform," *Voice,* September 14, 1893.

Proponents of a multiple standard of value and a managed currency such as Frank Parsons, professor of law at Boston University and a notable advocate of public ownership of natural monopolies, Thomas Elmer Will, president of Kansas State Agricultural College (now Kansas State College of Agriculture and Applied Sciences) during the brief period when the Board of Regents was Populist controlled, Henry Winn, Populist candidate for governor of Massachusetts in 1891 and 1892, and Eltweed Pomeroy, champion of direct legislation, argued that the stability of prices could best be achieved by money magic if the currency were completely divorced from specie. Whereas a specie-backed currency was affected by unpredictable changes in mining conditions and by the actions of foreign governments, a government-issued legal-tender currency that had no relationship to specie was fully subject to public regulation and was thus a suitable instrument for the control of prices. Such a currency could be expanded so as to raise prices by the government purchase of call bonds or securities, by loans extended at low rates of interest on good security at federal postal banks, and by new issues of currency to pay for federal public improvements or to be loaned to states and municipalities for similar purposes. The money supply could be contracted by the sale of call bonds and securities and by raising the interest rate at the postal banks so as to encourage saving and discourage borrowing. Proponents of a multiple standard and an irredeemable currency also recognized the role that surplus and deficit financing could play in changing the money supply.[69]

In effect, the advocates of the multiple standard of value proposed to substitute the action of government for the play of the market place in the regulation of the money supply and hence, in their view, of the price level. " 'Nature,' unassisted by reason," declared E. Benjamin Andrews, "is elsewhere proving a tricky guide: why follow her so blindly in the dark forest of monetary science?" "A truly elastic currency," John R. Commons declared in similar vein, "can be obtained only by substituting scientific human design for nature's unconscious lottery." [70] The advice of the advocates of the multiple standard fell on deaf ears in the late nineteenth century, but their

[69] Parsons, *Rational Money*, pp. vii–viii, 102–104, 119, 126–128; Will, "Stable Money," *Journal of Political Economy*, VII (December, 1898), 89–92; Winn, "Multiple-Standard Money," *Arena*, XIX (May, 1898), 639–641, 647, 649–650; Pomeroy, "The Multiple Standard of Money," *ibid.*, XVIII (September, 1897), 318–331, 333–336.

[70] Andrews, "An Honest Dollar," *A. E. A. Publications*, IV (November, 1889), 439; Commons, "Economic Reform," *Voice*, September 14, 1893.

ideas were to take on some significance in the early days of the New Deal, when Franklin D. Roosevelt seemed for a time to be moving in the direction of a commodity dollar.

V

Although his real wages increased materially between 1865 and 1900, the workingman was not altogether content with his lot. Made to feel insecure by increasing mechanization, the nationalization of the labor market, the consolidation of industry, the pressure of the immigrant, and the specter of unemployment, industrial laborers turned to organization to strengthen their bargaining power and to promote their common interests. Numerous national trade unions were organized by the various crafts, and ambitious attempts were made to establish national labor federations to represent the labor movement as a whole. The chief products of the latter sort of efforts were the National Labor Union, the Knights of Labor, and the American Federation of Labor. Although these organizations differed in their approach to the labor problem, their formation testified to the fact that laborers were no more willing than farmers to permit the laws of trade to be the arbiters of their fate and that they looked to positive action to give substance to their hopes.

The entry of workingmen into labor unions indicated a desire on their part to help themselves, but the workers did not rely on unionization alone to reach their goals. Like the organized farmers, the organized laborers did not hesitate to invoke the power of the state when it suited their interests to do so. The National Labor Union and the Knights of Labor placed far greater emphasis on winning legislative victories than did the job-conscious American Federation of Labor, but even the A.F.L. was not averse to supplementing its own efforts with state action.

In itself the outgrowth of labor's political campaign to secure the eight-hour day,[71] the National Labor Union, founded in 1866, was from the beginning of its history deeply involved in political action of one sort or another. Such leaders of the organization as William Sylvis, president of the Iron Molders' International Union, and Andrew Cameron, editor of the Chicago *Workingman's Advocate*, had become skeptical of the benefits to be derived from trade unionism and looked to political action as the proper method for promoting labor's cause. "I

[71] Commons *et al., History of Labour*, II, 91–96; Commons *et al., Documentary History*, IX, 126–127.

have long since come to the conclusion that no permanent reform can ever be established through the agency of trades unions as they are now and have been conducted," Sylvis declared. "All the evils under which we groan are legislative; that is, they are the result of bad laws, and there is no way to reach the matter and effect a cure but by repeal of those laws, and this can only be done through political action." [72] The evils of society, Cameron said in a similar vein, "are legislative in character," and "the remedy must therefore be legislative." [73] It is thus not altogether surprising that the National Labor Union should have established a five-man labor lobby in Washington in 1868, the first permanent national lobby of an American labor organization, that it should have decided at its 1867 convention that its "very existence" depended "upon the immediate organization of an independent labor party," and that when the National Labor Reform party was finally organized in 1871, the National Labor Union virtually ceased to function.[74]

During the first year of its existence, the National Labor Union was primarily interested in securing legislation to achieve the eight-hour day. The philosopher of the eight-hour movement of the 1860's was the Boston machinist Ira Steward, sometimes referred to as the "eight-hour monomaniac." Steward argued that the rate of wages is not determined by the amount of capital or the number of workers but rather by the standard of living of the workingman. The leisure time that would result from a reduction of the hours of labor would serve to increase the wants and appetites of laborers and would impel them to demand higher wages. Because of the ever-increasing productivity of capital stemming from the wider use of machinery, employers would find no difficulty in acceding to the workers' demands. The result of the universal adoption of the shorter workday would thus be an increase in the wages of labor. Eventually, a further reduction in the hours of labor would persuade the worker to demand still higher pay, a process that would continue until the existing order gave way to the coöperative commonwealth.[75]

[72] See Jonathan Grossman, *William Sylvis, Pioneer of American Labor: A Study of the Labor Movement during the Era of the Civil War* (New York, 1945), pp. 189, 232; and Terence V. Powderly, *Thirty Years of Labor, 1859 to 1889* (Columbus, Ohio, 1889), pp. 78–79.

[73] Commons *et al.*, *Documentary History*, IX, 165–166.

[74] Commons *et al.*, *Documentary History*, IX, 204, 232, 263–265, 270–273; Commons *et al.*, *History of Labour*, II, 130, 145–146, 153–155.

[75] Commons *et al.*, *History of Labour*, II, 89–90; Commons *et al.*, *Documentary*

Proclaiming the eight-hour day "the first and grand desideratum of the hour," the National Labor Union sought to persuade Congress and the state legislatures to enact the necessary legislation. The chief product of the movement was an eight-hour law passed by Congress in 1868, but, like the legislation of the states on the subject, the United States statute was largely ineffective.[76] By the time the federal eight-hour law was enacted, however, the National Labor Union had already relegated the shorter workday to a secondary position among its demands and had espoused greenbackism as the true nostrum for the ailments of labor. As previously noted, the National Labor Union saw in the schemes of Edward Kellogg and Alexander Campbell a practicable means of financing the producers' coöperatives that leaders of the organization like William Sylvis hoped would eventually supplant the wage system.[77]

Although greenbackism dominated the thinking of the National Labor Union after 1867 and constituted the chief interest of the short-lived National Labor Reform party, it did not represent the sum of the National Labor Union's demands. In an effort to mitigate the competition of cheap labor, the National Labor Union called for the exclusion of Chinese labor, the repeal of the contract labor law of 1864, and restrictions on the use of convict labor. In addition, the organization demanded the reservation of public lands for actual settlers and the provision of free transportation to these lands for persons wishing to settle there, government regulation of the railroad and the telegraph, establishment of a federal department of labor, a census of manufactures, occupations, and incomes, enactment of mechanics'

History, IX, 279–305. Steward's ideas were later taken up by George Gunton, editor for a time of the Christian Labor Union's *Labor Standard,* founder of the Institute of Social Economics, and charged ultimately with having been in the "pay of a great corporation." Gunton argued that the increase of wages resulting from the eight-hour day would extend the market for the products of industry and would bring lower prices and higher profits. See Dorfman, *Economic Mind in American Civilization,* III, xxx; Gunton, *Wealth and Progress: A Critical Examination of the Wages Question* (7th ed.; New York, 1897), pp. 228–273 *et passim;* Gunton, *Principles of Social Economics* (New York, 1891), pp. 203–217, 236, 436–437; and Gunton, *The Economic and Social Importance of the Eight-Hour Movement* (Washington, D.C., 1889).

[76] Commons *et al., History of Labour,* II, 102–110, 124–125; Commons *et al., Documentary History,* IX, 136, 184; Marion C. Cahill, *Shorter Hours: A History of the Movement since the Civil War* (New York, 1932), pp. 69–72.

[77] Grossman, *Sylvis,* pp. 191–194.

lien laws, and provision of better housing for workingmen.[78]   When the National Labor Union and the National Labor Reform party collapsed after the election of 1872, these demands were still largely unfulfilled.

Although the Noble Order of the Knights of Labor, like the National Labor Union, espoused coöperation as a means by which laborers could help themselves to escape the wage system and although the leaders of the organization pinned their hopes for success on work of an educational character rather than on political action or, for that matter, on the methods of trade unionism, the demands of the organization as embodied in the preamble of 1878 and subsequent amendments to it were largely of a sort that required the action of the state for their implementation.   In addition to its endorsement of coöperative institutions and the substitution of arbitration for strikes, the preamble called for the establishment of bureaus of labor statistics in the various states, the adoption of measures providing for the health and safety of laborers and for the indemnification of those injured because of lack of necessary safeguards, abrogation of all laws not bearing equally upon capital and labor, payment of wages weekly and in cash, equal pay to both sexes for equal work, mechanics' lien laws, abolition of the contract system on public works, abolition of the system of contract convict labor, prohibition of the import of contract labor, prohibition of child labor under fourteen, reservation of public lands for actual settlers and the taxation at their full value of lands held for speculative purposes, issuance by the national government of legal-tender currency directly to the people without the intervention of the banks, government purchase of the railroads, telegraph, and telephone, denial to corporations of licenses and contracts that would authorize the "construction or operation of any means of transporting intelligence, passengers or freight," and a graduated income tax.[79]

[78] Commons *et al.*, *Documentary History*, IX, 138–140, 188, 204–206, 221–226, 233–239.

[79] Powderly, *Thirty Years of Labor*, pp. 243–245, 285–286, 306, 337–343, 362–370, 387, 396–410, 452–460; Norman J. Ware, *The Labor Movement in the United States, 1860–1895* (New York, 1929), p. xiii; *Constitution of the General Assembly, District Assemblies, and Local Assemblies of the Order of the Knights of Labor of America*—adopted at Reading, Pa. Jan. 1–4, 1878, . . . revised at Hamilton, Ont., October 5–12, 1885 (n. p., n. d.), pp. 2–4.   See also H. W. K. Eastman, *The Science of Government* (Lawrence, Mass., 1888), pp. 29–66, 80–81, 87–90.

In an effort to attain their objectives, the Knights lobbied for the legislation they favored, and local and district assemblies and individual leaders of the organization engaged in extensive independent political activity. The national organization successfully avoided involvement in partisan politics until 1889, after which Western agrarians and New York socialists infiltrated the Knights of Labor, then very much on the decline, and associated it with the Alliance movement and the People's party.[80]

Whereas the National Labor Union and the Knights of Labor, in theory at least, placed relatively little emphasis on the use of the economic weapons of trade unionism, the most successful of the national labor federations formed during this period, the A.F.L.,[81] accepted the view that organized labor must rely principally on its economic power to realize its goals. Rejecting such nostrums as coöperation and greenbackism, which had been popular with earlier labor organizations and which were designed to elevate the laborer into the middle class, the leaders of the job-conscious A.F.L. sought to build up their organization on the basis of the methods of trade-unionism. They were less interested in winning victories for labor at the polls or in the halls of Congress and of the state legislatures than in securing trade agreements that would improve the position of the worker on the job.[82] Thus, significantly, when the A.F.L. between 1888 and 1891 staged its great campaign to attain the eight-hour day, it demanded eight-hour legislation only for government employees and sought to secure the eight-hour rule for private employees by agreements between management and organized labor.[83]

Although the leaders of the A.F.L. tended to place less emphasis than their predecessors in the labor movement on political action as a weapon of labor, this did not mean an acceptance on their part of the philosophy of laissez faire. They rejected the natural laws of the classical economists and particularly the iron law of wages and were

[80] Ware, *Labor Movement in the United States,* pp. 354–370.

[81] The A.F.L., although formed in 1886, traces its origin to the Federation of Organized Trades and Labor Unions of the United States and Canada, formed in 1881. The latter supported the standard legislative demands of labor during this period and, in 1886, strongly endorsed independent political action. See Commons et al., *History of Labour,* II, 319–320, 324, 331, 463–465.

[82] The philosophy of job-conscious unionism is brilliantly analyzed in Selig Perlman, *A Theory of the Labor Movement* (New York, 1928).

[83] Sidney Fine, "The Eight-Hour Day Movement in the United States, 1888–1891," *Mississippi Valley Historical Review,* XL (December, 1953), 443–444.

convinced that the welfare of the workingman could be enhanced by positive action.[84] Where they differed from more politically minded labor leaders was in their belief that the positive action required should largely take the form of trade-union activity rather than the legislative measures of the general-welfare state.

As a matter of fact, although it emphasized the economic approach to labor problems, the A.F.L., at least during the years from 1886 to 1901, was not so much opposed to labor legislation and to political activity by laborers as it was opposed to "party political action" and to the establishment of an independent labor party like the National Labor Reform party. At different times after 1886 Samuel Gompers, the president of the A.F.L., advised laborers that they "should more largely encompass their thoughts and actions in entering into the sphere and affairs of government," insisted that workingmen had a right to demand legislation in their interest, and claimed that by "an intelligent use of the ballot" the workers could very well "lighten the burdens of our economic struggles." [85]

Prodded by the socialist element in its midst, the A.F.L. voted at its 1893 convention to submit a rather advanced eleven-point political program to the consideration of the affiliated unions. The measures proposed comprised compulsory education, the initiative, the referendum, the eight-hour day, government inspection of mines and workshops, abolition of the sweating system, employers' liability laws, abolition of the contract system on public works, municipal ownership of public utilities, nationalization of the telegraph, telephone, railroads, and mines, and "collective ownership by the people of all means of production and distribution."

At the 1894 convention the various proposals were voted on one by one, and all but the collective-ownership plank were accepted. However, the motion to adopt the amended platform as a whole was

[84] See, for example, Samuel Gompers, *Seventy Years of Life and Labor: An Autobiography* (New York, 1925), II, 1–3.

[85] See A.F.L., *Report of Proceedings of the Second Annual Convention, 1887* (Bloomington, Ill., 1906), p. 10; A.F.L., *Report of Proceedings of the Twelfth Annual Convention, 1892* (Bloomington, Ill., 1906), p. 13; A.F.L., *Report of Proceedings of the Thirteenth Annual Convention, 1893* (Bloomington, Ill., 1906), p. 12; A.F.L., *Report of Proceedings of the Fourteenth Annual Convention, 1894* (Bloomington, Ill., 1906), p. 14; A.F.L., *Report of Proceedings of the Sixteenth Annual Convention, 1896* (Bloomington, Ill., 1906), pp. 21–22; and A.F.L., *Report of Proceedings of the Eighteenth Annual Convention, 1898* (Bloomington, Ill., 1905), p. 15.

defeated. At the next annual convention the delegates decided that the platform had not been officially adopted but did agree nevertheless that, as amended, it embodied the legislative demands of the Federation. For several years thereafter the platform (minus the collective-ownership plank) was regularly published in the *American Federationist* as the "Legislative Platform" of the A.F.L.[86] Even the job-conscious and conservative A.F.L. was not unwilling in the 1890's to enlist the aid of the state to further the cause of the workingman.

As the depression years following the panics of 1873 and 1893 were to demonstrate, one of the most serious problems confronting laborers in the industrial society emerging in the United States after the Civil War was unemployment. Advocates of laissez faire and social Darwinism contended, of course, that those who were out of work had only themselves to blame and that society was under no obligation to provide them with jobs, but it was obvious to many persons that the ranks of the unemployed were filled to a considerable extent by persons who were willing but unable to find work. Although the A.F.L. thought that the problem of unemployment would largely be solved if only the trade unions were successful in their attempt to persuade employers to grant the shorter workday,[87] an increasing number of reformers came to contend that if the state were adequately to serve the general interest, it must assume the burden of unemployment and provide work for the jobless.

During the depression after the panic of 1873, a few of the leaders of the greenback movement sought to convince the federal government that it should take action to cope with the problem of unemployment. Peter Cooper, the Independent party presidential candidate in 1876, advised President Hayes that the federal government could aid unemployed laborers by providing them with unoccupied lands in the West or by putting them to work in the construction of such "great and obvious public improvements" as a northwestern or southwestern railroad. The federal government, he suggested, could enlist the aid of state and municipal governments in dealing with unemployment by issuing them legal-tender currency in exchange for their bonds

---

[86] Quint, *Forging of American Socialism,* pp. 65–71; Commons *et al., History of Labour,* II, 509–513; Haynes, *Social Politics in the United States,* pp. 104–107.

[87] The principal argument employed by the A.F.L. in the 1880's and 1890's in its efforts to attain the eight-hour day was that the shorter workday was a necessary means of dealing with the problem of unemployment.

so that they might employ labor profitably on public improvements.[88]

In similar fashion, William A. Carsey, secretary of the general committee of the Greenback-Labor party, in 1878 informed a committee of the House of Representatives that was investigating the causes of the depression that the government could solve the problem of unemployment by transporting the jobless to the public lands of the West and loaning them money at low rates of interest and by initiating a large-scale program of public works to be paid for by the issuance of greenbacks. The government, he declared, must ensure that every man who is willing to work is provided with employment. "It is the best government," Carsey maintained, "that takes the best care of its people." [89] Proposals akin to those of Cooper and Carsey were embodied in three separate bills introduced during the sessions of the forty-fifth Congress (1877–1878) that called upon the federal government to aid the settlement of the jobless in the West by extending them loans in the form of greenbacks and, in the case of two of the bills, by also providing them with free transportation.[90]

One of the more conspicuous advocates during the 1870's and 1880's of the view that government must provide jobs for the unemployed and must seek to maintain full employment was William Godwin Moody. Since idleness in Moody's view was "the sum of all social evils," he believed that government should take such measures as were necessary to ensure that unemployment did not occur. Every man, he insisted, should have both the right and the opportunity to work at good wages. As Moody saw it, unemployment existed because production had outstripped consumption. Full employment could be attained, he thought, if the hours of labor were substantially reduced by law (in 1883 he proposed a six-hour day) and if sufficient additional machinery were employed to provide for the increased number of workers and to meet the consequent increase in consumption needs. In addition, Moody proposed the establishment of a national bureau of labor to gather statistics relative to the state of the economy that would serve as a guide to the federal government in its actions to maintain full em-

[88] Cooper, *Ideas for a Science of Good Government*, p. 121.

[89] U. S. Congress, House, Select Committee, *Investigation Relative to the Causes of Depression*, 45th Cong., 3d sess., H. Misc. Doc. No. 29 (Washington, D.C., 1879), pp. 51–52, 55, 57.

[90] Albert V. House, Jr., "Proposals of Government Aid to Agricultural Settlement during the Depression of 1873–1879," *Agricultural History*, XII (January, 1938), 46–66.

ployment. If the reports of the bureau revealed that there was unemployment in the nation even though consumption demands were being met, the hours of labor could be shortened so as to provide employment for all. However, if in the event of full employment, there was still insufficient production of the necessities and conveniences of life, the hours of labor could be lengthened so as to provide the necessary production.[91] Although Moody's conception of the legislation necessary to provide full employment was limited to the area of the hours of labor, he was, in a sense, an early advocate of the policy that culminated in the enactment of the Employment Act of 1946 and the establishment of the Council of Economic Advisers.

A few years after Moody proposed the six-hour day as the means of guaranteeing full employment, a somewhat different approach to the problem of unemployment was set forth by the Reverend John M. Gregory of Illinois Industrial University (now the University of Illinois). Gregory viewed unemployment as an inevitable concomitant of industrialism. Rejecting the policy of laissez faire as "dangerous . . . weak and cruel," he argued that it was the task of government to care for the involuntarily idle by providing them with work or by advancing them wages or loaning them money without interest. So as to anticipate and make provision for the inevitable periods of unemployment, Gregory suggested that workers be encouraged to save money during periods of employment and that society or government should establish postal-savings banks in which deposits would be protected against loss, should institute a program of social insurance to insure the worker against unemployment, accidents, illness, and old age, and should provide him with free dispensaries, hospitals, and asylums, which would be financed by employer and employee contributions.[92]

The heavy industrial unemployment that followed in the wake of the panic of 1893 brought to the fore once again the question of the responsibility of public authorities in the matter of aid for the jobless.

[91] Moody, *Land and Labor in the United States* (New York, 1883), pp. 215–258; Moody, *Our Labor Difficulties* (Boston, 1878), pp. 9–11, 31–34, 38–42, 65–66, 70–72; House Select Committee, *Investigation Relative to the Causes of Depression,* 45th Cong., 3d sess., H. Misc. Doc. No. 29, pp. 160–161; U. S. Congress, Senate, Committee on Education and Labor, *Report upon the Relations between Labor and Capital* (Washington, D.C., 1885), I, 983–987; Dorfman, *Economic Mind in American Civilization,* III, 28.

[92] Gregory, "The Problem of the Unemployed," *Independent,* XXXIX (November 10, 1887), 1443; Dorfman, *Economic Mind in American Civilization,* III, 76–77.

However, although municipal governments expanded their public works and local agencies, private and public, made extensive use of the principle of work relief for the first time in American history, state governments and the federal government refused to make any direct assault on the problem of unemployment.[93]

The belief of some Americans that it was the responsibility of the federal government as well as of local government to provide work for the unemployed was demonstrated in a graphic way during the depression year of 1894, when "armies" of the unemployed descended upon Washington and demanded that the government supply them with jobs. The most famous of the industrial armies was that led by Jacob S. Coxey, a wealthy businessman from Massillon, Ohio. In his scheme for aiding the unemployed, Coxey combined an interest in greenbacks (he went so far as to name one of his children "Legal Tender") and in good roads with a humanitarian desire to provide work for the involuntarily unemployed. Coxey's views were expressed in their most elaborate form in the Non-Interest-Bearing Bond Bill, which Coxey devised early in 1894. The measure stipulated that whenever any unit of local government desired to make improvements, it should deposit with the secretary of the treasury of the United States a twenty-five year non-interest-bearing bond in an amount not to exceed one half of the assessed valuation of its property. The Treasury was then to supply the local-government unit with legal-tender currency equal to the value of the bond, which was to be retired at the rate of 4 per cent per annum. When the bill became law, all units of local government were to be required to give employment at the rate of $1.50 per day for eight hours of work to all men applying for work.[94]

To impress his ideas on Congress, Coxey led a band of the unemployed to Washington, arriving there April 30, 1894. The "petition in boots" failed, however, to win the sympathy of either the nation's lawmakers or the Washington police. Coxey was unceremoniously jailed for twenty days for illegally carrying banners and fined five dollars for walking on the grass.[95]

[93] Leah Hannah Feder, *Unemployment Relief in Periods of Depression: A Study of Measures Adopted in Certain American Cities, 1857 through 1922* (New York, 1936), pp. 71–188.

[94] Donald L. McMurry, *Coxey's Army* (Boston, 1929), pp. 302–303. The Non-Interest-Bearing Bond Bill was designed to replace the Good Roads Bill that Coxey had devised in 1892. See *ibid.*, pp. 26–27, 301–302.

[95] McMurry, *Coxey's Army*, pp. 49–123. Coxey's Army was known as "The Commonweal of Christ." It was given a semireligious character by Coxey's

"Coxey's Army" was but one of the armies of the unemployed that descended upon Washington in the spring and early summer of 1894. From California and the Pacific Northwest, from the Rocky Mountain states and the Middle West, and from New England, small bands of the unemployed marched to the nation's capital and called upon the federal government to supply them with work. For the most part, the industrial armies were intent upon but one thing: some action by the federal government to provide the unemployed with jobs. Only the small army from New England, which was led by the socialist-minded Massachusetts journalist Morrison I. Swift, proposed that Congress initiate wide-sweeping reforms. The New Englanders demanded that the federal government furnish the unemployed with work on the highways and that it provide them with farms and factories, that the Constitution be amended so as to affirm the right of every man to a job, that interest-bearing bonds be withdrawn, that land not actually in use be opened to cultivation, that the railroads, the telegraph, and the mines be nationalized, and that a commission be established to investigate the desirability of nationalizing the trusts.[96]

The number of those who actually attempted to march upon Washington was small indeed. It is estimated that not more than ten thousand persons were engaged in the various industrial armies at any one time and that there were never more than one thousand of the unemployed in Washington.[97] The movement, however, attracted considerable interest and focused attention on the question of the responsibility of government for the victims of economic crises. Labor and farm journals applauded the Coxeyites, but the conservative press, for the most part, denounced them as "dangerous characters" and insisted that it was not the business of government to provide jobs for the unemployed.[98]

The march to Washington of the industrial armies was but a spectacular manifestation of the view to which many reformers were sub-

---

associate, Carl Browne. The Commonweal's banner contained the following incongruous declaration: "Peace on Earth Good Will to Men. He Hath Risen, but Death to Interest on Bonds." See *ibid.*, pp. 38–39.

[96] McMurry, *Coxey's Army,* pp. 127–241.

[97] McMurry, *Coxey's Army,* pp. 242, 262.

[98] For digests of newspaper opinion on the Coxeyites, see *Public Opinion,* XVII (April 5, 12, 19, 26; May 3, 10, 1894), 24, 43–44, 69–70, 95, 115–116, 137–138. See also [Edwin L. Godkin], "Who Is Responsible for Coxey?" *Nation,* LVIII (May 3, 1894), 322–323; and [Godkin], "The Coxey 'Problem,'" *ibid.,* LVIII (May 17, 1894), 358.

scribing in more quiet fashion during the hard times after 1893, namely, that the state had an obligation to its unemployed citizens. At its annual convention in 1893 the A.F.L., although commending the efforts of private individuals to aid "the terrible distress of the unemployed," insisted that "it is the province, duty and in the power of our city, state and national governments to give immediate and adequate relief," and it endorsed Coxey's Good Roads Bill, which called for the issuance by the federal government of five hundred million dollars in legal-tender currency for the construction of good roads.[99]   Samuel M. Jones, Toledo's famous reform mayor of the late 1890's and the early years of the twentieth century, maintained that society must recognize the right of every individual to a job and must provide work for the unemployed,[100] and this view was endorsed by such reformers as Frank Parsons, Thomas Elmer Will, and B. O. Flower, editor of the *Arena*.   "The first duty of the government," Will declared, "is to care for the people—to see that each is provided with the opportunity for useful labor, rational development, and the living of a complete life."   Flower argued that the general-welfare clause of the Constitution was sanction enough for the federal government to put the unemployed to work on such tasks as reclaiming the arid lands of the West or building levees on the banks of the Mississippi.[101]

The economist John R. Commons, who considered unemployment "the most serious of all our industrial problems," affirmed that in an age when monopoly circumscribed the right to "freedom of industry" (defined as "the right to free access to nature for the production and acquisition of wealth"), the right to life and liberty was of little importance unless recognition were similarly afforded to the right to work.   "There is . . . pressing upon us," he asserted, "the claim for recognition of this new and higher right, belonging to man as a man, by virtue of the very dignity of the manhood that is in him. . . .

[99] A.F.L., *Proceedings, 1893,* pp. 37, 47–48.   The A.F.L. reaffirmed this endorsement, in substance, in 1894.   See A.F.L., *Proceedings, 1894,* p. 31.

[100] Harvey S. Ford, "The Life and Times of Golden Rule Jones," (Ph.D. thesis, University of Michigan, 1953), pp. 290, 422.   Jones's book on this subject was entitled *The New Right* (New York, 1899).

[101] Parsons, "The Philosophy of Mutualism," *Arena,* IX (May, 1894), 808; Will, Parsons, and James M. Brown, "The Unemployed: A Symposium," *ibid.,* X (October, 1894), 714–715; Flower, "How to Increase National Wealth by the Employment of Paralyzed Industry," *ibid.,* XVIII (August, 1897), 200–210; Flower *et al.,* "An Army of Wealth Creators vs. an Army of Destruction," *ibid.,* XXV (May, 1901), 538.

The right to work, for every man that is willing, is the next great human right to be defined and enforced by law." This right could be implemented, Commons thought, if security of tenure against arbitrary discharge were afforded all workers who were honest and efficient, and if government provided work for the unemployed and aided them in other ways. Through appropriate civil-service regulations government could provide secure tenure for its own employees; and it could protect employees in private industry by setting up courts of arbitration that would take action against employers who discharged workers for any cause other than inefficiency or dishonesty and that would adjudicate problems involving hours, wages, and working conditions. It could aid the unemployed by establishing employment bureaus, by devising a system of taxation that would compel the owners of unimproved lands and natural resources who were holding them off the market for speculative purposes to make them available to laborers, by providing public works, and, perhaps, by instituting a system of unemployment insurance.[102]

Like Commons, Charles A. Tuttle, a professor of history and political economy at Wabash College, insisted at the 1901 meeting of the American Economic Association that it was one of the "'fundamental industrial rights'" of the worker to be indemnified for the loss of his job resulting from technological progress. This indemnification, Tuttle suggested, might take the form of free public employment bureaus or, perhaps, free railroad transportation (presumably to a new job); and the cost could be met from the general tax revenues and by a special tax on employers. Of the economists who joined in the discussion following the reading of Tuttle's paper, only John R. Commons saw real merit in this proposal.[103]

The prominent social gospeler Washington Gladden was another of the advocates of social reform who in the final years of the nineteenth century championed the idea of state aid for the unemployed.

---

[102] U. S. Industrial Commission, *Report on the Relations and Conditions of Capital and Labor* (Vol. XIV of the Commission's *Reports;* Washington, D.C., 1901), pp. 34, 41–42; Commons, *The Distribution of Wealth* (New York, 1893), pp. 79–85; Commons, "The Right to Work," *Arena,* XXI (February, 1899), 131–142.

[103] Tuttle, "The Workman's Position in the Light of Economic Progress," *A. E. A. Publications,* 3d Ser., III (February, 1902), 206–211. The discussion of the paper is on pages 213–234 of the same volume. For the views of economists and others as to how best to cope with the problem of unemployment and the problem of improving the conditions of laborers in general, see Kansas Bureau of Labor and Industry, *Eleventh Annual Report, 1895* (Topeka, Kan., 1896), pp. 185–211.

The unemployables, Gladden pointed out, are properly the concern of either private or public charity. As for the able-bodied unemployed, those who are unwilling to work should be disciplined in workhouses and farm colonies; those who are incompetent should be placed in trade schools; and those who are well and able to work but unable to find jobs in private industry should be provided work by public authorities. Such action by the state, Gladden said, might constitute socialism, but in his view it was infinitely preferable to pauperism. Like so many of the reformers of his own day, and like the New Dealers and Fair Dealers of a later era, Gladden believed that the state that is actively concerned with the welfare of its citizens must protect the workingman against the menace of unemployment.[104]

VI

During the three and one-half decades after the Civil War, socialism in the United States was more important as a negative than as a positive force. Although but few Americans subscribed to its tenets, many of them were impelled by the socialist argument to reëxamine the basic principles of the capitalist-democratic faith and to ponder the necessity for some degree of social change. Social gospelers and advocates of social reform in general, notwithstanding their rejection of the socialist solution, believed that there was a good deal of truth in the socialist critique of the existing order, and many of them sought to meet this criticism and to stave off the threat of socialism itself by sponsoring reforms that, they believed, would correct the inequities of the capitalist regime without destroying its essentials.

Modern socialism of the Marxian variety did not really develop in America until after the Civil War: it was not until after Appomattox that the utopian socialism of an earlier, predominantly agrarian order gave way to the Marxian socialism of an industrial age. Whereas the utopian variety depended chiefly on voluntary coöperation for its actualization, Marxian socialism tended to look to the state to introduce the socialist order.

Of the socialist parties formed in the United States after the Civil War, the two most important and the two that were destined to sur-

[104] Gladden, "What Can the State Do for the Man Who Works," Sermon, February 6, 1898, Washington Gladden Papers, Ohio State Archaeological and Historical Society; Gladden, "What to Do with the Workless Man," Sermon, 1898, *ibid.*; Gladden, "What to Do with the Workless Man," *Proceedings of the National Conference of Charities and Correction, 1899*, pp. 141–152.

vive were the Socialist Labor party and the Socialist party. The Socialist Labor party traces its history back to 1876, when three small socialist organizations merged to form the Workingmen's Party of the United States.[105] The party was weak in numbers, and its leadership and membership were recruited largely from among the foreign-born. The peak electoral strength of the organization was registered in the off-year elections of 1898, when 82,204 votes were cast for its candidates, but the enrolled membership of the party was far below that figure.[106] Although the ultimate goal of the Socialist Labor party was the collective ownership of "all the means of production, transportation, and distribution . . . and the substitution of the co-operative commonwealth for the present state of planless production, industrial war, and social disorder," the party until 1900 included in its platform a set of immediate demands designed to ameliorate the conditions of the workingman and to win the organization the support of laborers and reformers. These demands were similar to the standard legislative proposals of organized labor during this era, but, in addition, the party called for free justice in the law courts, government organization of the banking and insurance business, and compulsory education to the age of fourteen, with all materials and books to be furnished free of charge.[107]

In seeking to win a wider audience for their doctrines among the American people, Socialist Laborites affirmed that the extension of the scope of government that their program involved was both necessary and proper. Government, one of the pamphlets of the Socialistic Tract Association of Detroit announced, is "an institution devoted to the exclusive purpose of furthering the well-being and happiness of the people individually and collectively." Since man's happiness consists in enjoying the products of science, art, and industry, the chief duty of government, the pamphlet stated, is to provide the citizen with

---

[105] The Workingmen's Party changed its name to "Socialistic Labor Party" at its convention of December, 1877. "Socialistic" was subsequently changed to "Socialist." See Quint, *Forging of American Socialism*, pp. 13–15.

[106] Morris Hillquit, *History of Socialism in the United States* (4th ed.; New York, 1906), pp. 213–214, 226–228, 238, 283–284; Ira Kipnis, *The American Socialist Movement, 1897–1912* (New York, 1952), pp. 22, 36n.

[107] Hillquit, *History of Socialism*, pp. 352–353; House Select Committee, *Investigation Relative to the Causes of Depression*, 46th Cong., 2d sess., H. Misc. Doc. No. 5, pp. 153–154. The immediate demands included such items as the eight-hour day, establishment of bureaus of labor statistics, restrictions on child, female, and convict labor, and employer liability for industrial accidents.

the opportunity to procure these objects by giving his labor in exchange.[108] The Brooklyn socialist C. Osborne Ward, brother of Lester Ward, commented that socialism simply involved the application to industry of the same principle of democracy that had already been applied to the political machinery. In similar vein, the Socialistic Tract Association maintained that just as the post office and the fire department had been deemed too vital to the public interest to be entrusted to private hands, so the means of production, upon which the very existence of the worker depended, must be collectively controlled.[109]

The socialists were intent on pointing out that the object of government was to provide the citizen not only with protection, but with security as well. The socialist state, it was said, would replace "the present employing class," would provide jobs for all, and would ensure that each worker received the full proceeds of his labor either in personal remuneration or in public benefits. It would plan production carefully so as to bring it into balance with consumption and would thus avoid the imbalance that produced depressions.[110]

The most comprehensive analysis of Marxian socialism for an American audience during the 1880's was that presented by the Danish immigrant Laurence Gronlund in his book *The Cooperative Commonwealth.* Attempting to adjust socialism to American conditions, Gronlund specifically rejected the class-conflict thesis of the Marxists and represented socialism as achieving its ends by peaceful, evolutionary means.

[108] Socialistic Tract Association, "Government," *Tracts on Socialism, No. 2* (Detroit, [1879]), pp. 1–2.

[109] Ward, *A Labor Catechism of Political Economy* (New York, 1878), pp. 5–7; Socialistic Tract Association, "Who Should Be Socialists?" *Tracts on Socialism, No. 4* (Detroit, [1879]), p. 4. See also testimony of T. J. Morgan, House Select Committee, *Investigation Relative to the Causes of Depression,* 46th Cong., 2d sess., H. Misc. Doc. No. 5, pp. 144–145, 149–150.

[110] Socialistic Tract Association, "What Is Socialism?" *Tracts on Socialism, No. 1* (Detroit, [1879]), p. 2; Socialistic Tract Association, "What Socialism Means," *ibid., No. 3* (Detroit, [1879]), p. 2; Socialistic Tract Association, "Governmental Control," *ibid., No. 7* (Detroit, [1879]), p. 1; Ward, *Labor Catechism,* pp. 65, 164–165; testimony of Robert H. Bartholomee and Adolph Douai, House Select Committee, *Investigation Relative to the Causes of Depression,* 45th Cong., 3d sess., H. Misc. Doc. No. 29, pp. 19–20, 30–41; testimony of Benjamin Sibley, *ibid.,* 46th Cong., 2d sess., H. Misc. Doc. No. 5, 157–158; testimony of Douai, Senate Committee on Education and Labor, *Report upon the Relations between Labor and Capital,* II, 718.

Gronlund charged that the let-alone system had permitted the few to monopolize the means of production and to appropriate for themselves the share of the product attributable to the increasing productivity of labor. Private enterprise had, however, run its course and was destined to be replaced by social coöperation: the state was to become the steward of the nation's wealth.

Government, Gronlund argued, is not a necessary evil but "man's greatest good." Its objective is not merely the greatest good of the greatest number but the greatest good of every citizen, and in its pursuit of this end it can take whatever steps are expedient, including the appropriation of the instruments of production. The coöperative commonwealth of the future will not, however, mean the end of self-help but rather will provide the conditions that make self-help possible. "The future Commonwealth," Gronlund declared, "will *help* every individual to attain the highest development he or she has capacity for. It will lay a cover for every one at Nature's table." [111]

In the early 1890's Gronlund suggested the formation of an American Socialist Fraternity, to consist of a small number of educated young men who could be persuaded to believe that socialism was "*providentially destined* to be our future social system" and who would then convert the nation to this view. The only qualification for membership, Gronlund wrote to Richard T. Ely, is "*a disposition to welcome the extension of the functions of government.*" [112]

At the same time as Gronlund was preparing to receive into the American Socialist Fraternity those who had "a disposition to welcome the extension of the functions of government," the Socialist Labor party was falling under the control of a new leader, who was bent upon expelling from the party's ranks all those whose understanding of socialism differed from his own interpretation of Marxism. Daniel De Leon, born in Curaçao in 1852, graduate of the University of Leyden and of Columbia Law School, and lecturer in Latin-Ameri-

[111] See Gronlund, *The Cooperative Commonwealth in Its Outlines: An Exposition of Modern Socialism* (Boston, 1884), pp. 7–11, 34–52, 74–88, 95–97, 104–105; and Quint, *Forging of American Socialism,* pp. 28–30. Gronlund became a member of the executive committee of the Socialist Labor party in 1888. See W. Ellison Chalmers, "Laurence Gronlund," in Allen Johnson and Dumas Malone, eds., *Dictionary of American Biography* (Authors ed.; New York, 1937), VII, 14–15.

[112] Gronlund to Ely, April 16, 1891, enclosing printed circular dated February 22, 1891, Ely Papers. Gronlund advised Ely that the qualification for membership would exclude followers of Henry George and Herbert Spencer. He hoped that his organization would be an effective force by the year 1900.

can diplomacy at Columbia University from 1883 to 1889, entered the Socialist Labor party in 1890 and soon became the dominant power in the organization. Intransigent to a degree, he not only drove from the Socialist Labor party all save simon-pure De Leonists but sought to mold the organization into a class-conscious, revolutionary party that would make no compromise with capitalism and would not associate itself with middle-class reform groups in seeking the adoption of ameliorative measures that fell short of outright socialism. At its national convention in 1900, the Socialist Labor party dropped the immediate demands from its platform and thus, in effect, proclaimed the incompatibility of social reform and socialism.[113]

While De Leon was trying in the 1890's to fashion the Socialist Labor party in his own image, other activities were taking place in the area of American socialism that were to culminate in 1901 in the formation of the Socialist Party of America. In 1897 Eugene V. Debs transformed the then decadent American Railway Union into the Social Democracy of America. Joining the ranks of the new organization were many members of the Brotherhood of the Co-operative Commonwealth, a utopian-minded socialist group for which Debs had at one time served as national organizer and whose immediate objective was to colonize a Western state, to capture control of its government, and to convert it to socialism. In addition to urging the collective ownership of land and the means of production, distribution, and transportation, the Declaration of Principles of the Social Democracy of America, bespeaking the colonization interest of some of the organization's members, called for the colonization of a Western state, the introduction therein of coöperative industry, and then the gradual extension of operations "until the National Co-operative Commonwealth shall be established." The immediate demands set forth in the declaration included the public ownership of all industries controlled by monopolies, government ownership of the means of transportation and communication and of mines and mineral and oil deposits, construction of public works to ease unemployment, postal-savings banks, and the initiative, referendum, recall, and proportional representation. The immediate demands of the Social Democracy reflected the middle-class American background of many

[113] Quint, *Forging of American Socialism*, pp. 142–168, 371; Daniel Bell, "The Background and the Development of Marxian Socialism in the United States," in Donald Drew Egbert and Stow Persons, eds., *Socialism and American Life* (Princeton, N. J., 1952), I, 244–248; Kipnis, *American Socialist Movement*, p. 42.

of the organization's members and their interest in reformism as well as in socialism.[114]

There was division within the ranks of the Social Democracy between the advocates of colonization and the advocates of political action, and when the former gained control of the organization in 1898, the latter, led by Victor Berger and Eugene Debs, seceded and formed the Social Democratic party. The immediate demands of the Social Democratic party were substantially those stated in the Declaration of Principles of the Social Democracy of America. Unlike the Socialist Labor party, the Social Democrats, many of whom had previously allied themselves with Populism or Nationalism, were prepared to support piecemeal reform and piecemeal nationalization as a prelude to the establishment of socialism. Thus the party's platform of 1898 even contained demands designed to win support for the Social Democrats among the farmers. The "farmers' demands" called for the lease of public lands to farmers in portions not to exceed 640 acres, state control of forests and waterways, public construction of grain elevators, magazines, and cold-storage buildings and their use by farmers at cost, extension of telephone service to farmers at cost, uniform railroad rates for the transportation of agricultural products, and extension of public credit to towns and counties for the purpose of soil improvement and the construction of roads and irrigation and drainage systems. These demands were, however, eliminated from the party platform as the result of a referendum taken in 1899.[115]

For purposes of the presidential campaign of 1900 the Social Democrats and a dissident faction of the Socialist Labor party, headed by Morris Hillquit, Job Harriman, and others, agreed on a coalition ticket of Debs for president and Harriman for vice president. In July, 1901, several months after the election, the two groups finally merged to form the Socialist Party of America. Unlike the Socialist Labor party, which had but recently dropped the immediate legislative proposals from its platform, the Socialist party refused to separate itself completely from the main stream of American reform and in-

[114] Quint, *Forging of American Socialism*, pp. 282–307; Bell, "Development of Marxian Socialism," in Egbert and Persons, eds., *Socialism and American Life*, I, 259–264; Kipnis, *American Socialist Movement*, pp. 51–60.

[115] Quint, *Forging of American Socialism*, pp. 307–323; Bell, "Development of Marxian Socialism," in Egbert and Persons, eds., *Socialism and American Life*, I, 264–266; Kipnis, *American Socialist Movement*, pp. 60–73; Ray Ginger, *The Bending Cross: A Biography of Eugene Victor Debs* (New Brunswick, N. J., 1949), pp. 197–199.

cluded a list of immediate demands in its platform. These comprised public ownership of the means of transportation and communication and other public utilities and of industries controlled by trusts, reduction of the hours of labor and an increase in the wages of all laborers, state or national insurance of workers to cover accidents, illness, unemployment, and old age, inauguration of a system of public industries, public education of children to the age of eighteen (state and municipal aid to be provided for books, clothing, and food), equal civil and political rights for men and women, and the initiative, referendum, recall, and proportional representation. Unlike such advocates of the general-welfare state as Richard T. Ely, who proposed social reform as an antidote to both laissez faire and socialism, the socialists were willing to support reforms to be effected within the framework of the existing order because action of this sort, they believed, might be conducive to the eventual introduction of socialism and because they wished to gain adherents in the capitalist world of today while working for what they hoped would be the socialist world of tomorrow.[116]

VII

The consolidation of business in the decades after the Civil War probably more than any other single factor caused Americans to concern themselves with the problem of the relationship of the state to the economic order. Traditionally hostile to monopoly, the bulk of the American people viewed with alarm the formation of gigantic business concerns in the *post-bellum* era.[117] They tended to refer to these concerns as "trusts" or "monopolies" and made little attempt to distinguish between the trust, properly speaking, and other forms of consolidation, or between the centralization of business and actual monopoly. As John Bates Clark pointed out, the term "trust" was

[116] Quint, *Forging of American Socialism*, pp. 332–388; Bell, "Development of Marxian Socialism," in Egbert and Persons, eds., *Socialism and American Life*, I, 273–275; Kipnis, *American Socialist Movement*, pp. 81–106; Ginger, *Bending Cross*, pp. 208–213; Hillquit, *History of American Socialism*, pp. 349–351.

[117] William Cook declared that "the great majority of the American people look upon corporations and their colossal aggregations of capital as dangerous to the republic. A vague and indescribable dread and suspicion of them pervade the minds of men" (*The Corporation Problem* [New York, 1891], p. 253). John Bates Clark thought that the antitrust movement in the South and the West bore a "remote resemblance" to the antislavery movement (*The Control of Trusts* [New York, 1901], p. 3).

popularly defined as "any corporation that is big enough to be menacing."[118] Although influential persons in the world of business (and their attorneys) and intransigent social Darwinists saw no cause for concern, the prevailing view was that something must be done about the trusts. The remedies proposed were numerous indeed, but, in the main, they involved the use of state power in one form or another.[119] Only the state, it appeared, could cope effectively with the problem of business consolidation.

Although the great majority of the people appeared to believe that natural law and potential competition would not in themselves protect the public from the dangers of monopoly, Americans were divided in their opinion as to the proper course for public authorities to pursue in dealing with the trust problem. A strongly held view, particularly among farmers and small businessmen, was that the trusts were incompatible with free competition and that they should therefore be smashed. Those who espoused this view insisted that free competition was essential to the public welfare and that it was being throttled by the trusts. They denied that the trust was "an orderly development from preceding conditions" and insisted rather that the combination movement was "an artificially stimulated movement, solely prompted by ordinary, vulgar human motives." If the process of "trustification" were not checked, there would be an end to the equality of economic opportunity that was the boast of America, and control of the government would pass from the people to the monopolies. Proponents of this view therefore regarded it as the duty of the state to interpose its authority and to protect the people against the menace of the trusts by providing for their "complete and prompt annihilation." The "trust-busters" wished, in the main, to restore the competitive conditions that had prevailed in the United States before the rise of large-scale aggregations of capital, and it was to this end that they invoked the power of the state.[120] Legislative policy during this period tended

[118] *Chicago Conference on Trusts* . . . , *1899* (Chicago, 1900), p. 404.

[119] This whole subject is discussed in Arthur P. Dudden, "Antimonopolism, 1865–1890: The Historical Background and Intellectual Origins of the Antitrust Movement in the United States" (Ph.D. thesis, University of Michigan, 1950).

[120] W. Scott Morgan, *History of the Wheel and Alliance, and the Impending Revolution* (St. Louis, Mo., 1891), pp. 16–17; D. C. Cloud, *Monopolies and the People* (Davenport, Iowa, 1873), pp. 335, 343–345; A. B. Nettleton, ed., *Trusts or Competition?* (Chicago, 1900), pp. 13, 59, 75–78, 170–174; speeches of Dudley Wooten, G. W. Atkinson, E. C. Crow, P. E. Dowe, Hazen Pingree, Jefferson Davis, John W. Hayes, and John I. Yellott, *Chicago Conference on Trusts, 1899,* pp. 42–53

to accord with their view: the antitrust statutes of the state governments and the federal government's Sherman Anti-Trust Act did not aim at the regulation of the trusts but rather at their destruction.

Some of the opponents of the trusts believed that they were the product of such artificial stimulants as the protective tariff, patents, and discriminatory railroad rates and that they would disappear once these favors were denied them. It was therefore unnecessary for public authorities to make a frontal assault on the trusts themselves: what was required was tariff reform, changes in the patent law, and the outlawing of discriminatory railroad rates.[121]

In contrast to those who viewed the trusts as unnatural and dangerous, an increasing number of persons tended to argue that the consolidation of business was a natural and inevitable development and that it could not be reversed. Potentially, moreover, the trusts, these persons held, were a force for good in that their relatively lower costs of production as compared to smaller business units enabled them to offer their products to the public at lower prices. Since the trusts, however, were not compelled by competition to share with the public the economies of large-scale production and were, indeed, relatively free to employ such extortionate practices as they pleased, it was necessary for the state to take the place of competition and to regulate the trusts in the public interest.[122] "While monopolies are inevitable," said the associate editor of the *Engineering News,* Charles Whiting Baker, "our *subjection* to them is not inevitable." Monopolies cannot be abolished, but they can be regulated by the state so that any benefits deriving from their operation will redound to the public. "The only remedy for monopoly is control; the only power that can control is government." [123]

---

et passim. Wooten and Crow went so far as to recommend that the right of incorporation be limited to concerns established for a quasi-public purpose.

[121] See, for example, speeches of Lawson Purdy, Byron W. Holt, Horatio W. Seymour, S. H. Greeley, and J. Sterling Morton, *Chicago Conference on Trusts, 1899,* pp. 166–171 *et passim.*

[122] At the Chicago Conference on Trusts, held in 1899, the opinion most frequently expressed by the delegates, who included in their number representatives from many segments of American life, was that trusts were inevitable, that they had certain economic advantages, and that they must be regulated by the state to ensure that these advantages were realized by the public. See note 126 and Henry Rand Hatfield, "The Chicago Conference on Trusts," *Journal of Political Economy,* VIII (December, 1899), 5–6.

[123] Baker, *Monopolies and the People* (New York, 1889), pp. 159–161, 181, 238, 263.

Members of the new school of political economy identified themselves for the most part with the view that trusts should be regulated rather than destroyed. Defining a monopoly as any business large enough to control the price of its product with little reference to the law of supply and demand, such economists as E. Benjamin Andrews, Jeremiah W. Jenks, John R. Commons, and Edward W. Bemis rejected the view of Henry Carter Adams and Richard T. Ely that monopoly could exist only in the case of businesses characterized by decreasing costs and insisted that massed capital alone could produce a monopoly. They were inclined to argue that competition "in its ancient and familiar form" was "passing away never to reappear" and that this was not to be regretted, because monopoly had in it "the power to be immeasurably superior to that which it supplants." To realize the potential advantages of monopoly, however, society would have to "substitute its own conscious control over the work of production for the spontaneous action of economic forces." [124] "We must recognize the monopolies as existing facts," Seligman noted, "but hold them under control. . . . To legislate against them and fall back on the specific of free competition would be absolutely futile. Competition has had its day and has proved ineffective. Let us be bold enough to look the facts straight in the face and not shrink from the logical conclusions of our premises. Recognize the combinations but regulate them." [125]

There was relatively little agreement among those who believed that trusts should be controlled rather than destroyed as to the proper method of implementing this idea. The various solutions proposed included public ownership of all monopolies or, at least, of natural monopolies, a tax on the surplus profits of trusts, publicity for corporate practices, government supervision of the security issues of trusts,

[124] See Andrews, "The Economic Law of Monopoly," *Journal of Social Science,* XXVI (February, 1890), 1–12; Andrews, "Trusts According to Official Investigations," *Quarterly Journal of Economics,* III (January, 1889), 136–137; Andrews, *Wealth and Moral Law* (Hartford, Conn., 1894), pp. 32–38, 46–49; Jenks, "Capitalistic Monopolies and Their Relation to the State," *Political Science Quarterly,* IX (September, 1894), 486–505; Commons, *Distribution of Wealth,* pp. 103–107; Seligman, "Railway Tariffs and the Interstate Commerce Law. II," *ibid.,* II (September, 1887), 370–373; speech of Bemis, *Chicago Conference on Trusts, 1899,* pp. 394–404; and Bemis, "The Trust Problem—Its Real Nature," *Forum,* XXVIII (December, 1899), 412–420.

[125] Seligman, "Railway Tariffs and the Interstate Commerce Law. II," *Political Science Quarterly,* II (September, 1887), 374.

government control of the prices of products manufactured by the trusts, federal incorporation, and a government audit of the accounts of corporations.[126]

The belief that natural monopolies should be publicly owned was particularly attractive to reformers in the last decade of the nineteenth century.[127] This was the view of the leading members of the new school of political economy, and it enjoyed widespread support among reformers outside their ranks. Frank Parsons, who became an expert on the subject, was a particularly zealous advocate of public ownership and was appropriately enough president of the National League for Promoting the Public Ownership of Monopolies. The roster of officers of this organization reads like a "Who's Who" of reformers of the late nineteenth century. Among the vice presidents were Hazen Pingree, William Dean Howells, John R. Commons, J. Allen Smith, E. Benjamin Andrews, Senator Marion Butler, and the religious leaders Washington Gladden, George D. Herron, Edward Everett Hale, and B. Fay Mills. The membership of the executive council included Thomas E. Will, Henry D. Lloyd, B. O. Flower, and George Gates, and among the "distributing secretaries" were Graham Taylor, W. D. P. Bliss, and "Golden Rule" Jones.[128]

Public ownership of all monopolies (not just natural monopolies)

[126] Speeches of William Fortune, Azel F. Hatch, Robert S. Taylor, Stephen P. Corliss, Joseph Nimmo, Jr., John M. Stahl, Charles Foster, George Gunton, George R. Gaither, Jr., Francis G. Newlands, Thomas J. Morgan, Henry White, Edward Bemis, A. E. Rogers, C. D. Willard, Laurence Gronlund, S. A. Martin, Samuel M. Jones, F. E. Haley, Emerson McMillin, in *Chicago Conference on Trusts, 1899*, pp. 53–57 *et passim;* Jenks, "Capitalistic Monopolies and Their Relation to the State," *Political Science Quarterly*, IX (September, 1894), 506–509; Andrews, "A Symposium upon the Relation of the State to the Individual," *Dawn*, II (November, 1890), 300–301; Commons, *Distribution of Wealth*, p. 258; Bemis, "The Trust Problem—Its Real Nature," *Forum*, XXVIII (December, 1899), 420–426.

[127] Many persons, of course, believed that natural monopolies should be publicly owned but that all other trusts or monopolies should be destroyed.

[128] Parsons, *The Public Ownership of Monopolies* (Boston, 1894); Parsons, *Our Country's Need* (Boston, 1894), pp. 74–84; Parsons, "The People's Highways," *Arena*, XII (April, 1895), 218; Parsons, *The City for the People* (Philadelphia, [1900]), pp. 17–254; Parsons to [Marietta] Holley, [November 24, 1890], Frank Parsons Collection, Yale University Library; U. S. Industrial Commission, *Report on Transportation* (Vol. IX of the Commission's *Reports;* Washington, D.C., 1901), pp. 123–193, 883–890. For Parsons' advanced social and economic views, see Arthur Mann, "Frank Parsons: The Professor as Crusader," *Mississippi Valley Historical Review*, XXXVII (December, 1950), 471–490; Parsons, "The Philosophy of Mutualism," *Arena*, IX (May, 1894), 783–815; and Parsons, *Our Country's Need*.

was the solution for the trust problem proposed by the man whose name is perhaps most closely associated with the antitrust movement of the late nineteenth century, Henry Demarest Lloyd. After having been admitted to the New York bar in 1869, Lloyd was active for a time in the American Free Trade League and in the Liberal Republican movement of 1872. Following the collapse of the latter movement, he turned his attention to journalism and, settling in the Chicago area, served from 1874 to 1885 as financial editor and editorial writer for the *Chicago Tribune*. Lloyd became particularly concerned with the problem of monopoly, and his writings on the subject in the *Tribune* and the journals of the day attracted widespread attention. In 1894 he published his now-classic exposition of the evils of monopoly in general and the Standard Oil Company in particular, *Wealth against Commonwealth*. It is principally on this work, hailed by B. Fay Mills as "the Uncle Tom's cabin of the social movement," that Lloyd's fame as an antimonopolist rests.[129]

Lloyd was bitterly critical of the premises of the social Darwinists and the classical economists and of the theory of laissez faire. He could not agree with Spencer that in the existing order the struggle for existence resulted in the survival of the fittest "in any sense moral or profitable to the community." "It is a race to the bad," he declared, "and the winners are the worst. A system in which the prizes go to meanness invariably marches with the meanest men at the head." That such men as Rockefeller and Vanderbilt "survived" was but an indication of "the character of the current civilisation." Like Lester Ward, Lloyd believed that the natural and social environment could be molded so that "a better kind of fittest" rather than the most selfish would survive. "There is no surer test of the title of scholars to be called cultivated," he declared, "than whether they have mastered the fact that in social science the 'laws' that rule men are the laws that men make." [130]

Lloyd also objected to the central principles of classical economics. "These doctrines of the desire of wealth, of exclusive regulation by

[129] Caro Lloyd, *Henry Demarest Lloyd, 1847–1903* (New York, 1912), I, 18–166; Destler, "Wealth against Commonwealth, 1894 and 1944," in *American Radicalism*, pp. 136–138; Mills to Lloyd, November 12, 1895, Henry Demarest Lloyd Papers, State Historical Society of Wisconsin.

[130] Notebook 19, 1890, p. 502, Lloyd Papers; Card Notes, p. 143, *ibid.;* Lloyd, *Wealth against Commonwealth* (New York, 1894), p. 513; Lloyd, "A New Political Economy Predicting a New Wealth," in *Man, the Social Creator* (New York, 1906), pp. 218–220.

competition, and of the irresistible laws of trade," he declared, "have been a royal road for shifting responsibility for injustice and legal selfishness from human shoulders upon the back of Nature." The theories of the classical economists, he wrote in one of his notebooks, were "utterly, eternally, helplessly wrong—mere covers for fraud and robbery." On the other hand, Lloyd liked the ideas of the new school of political economy "very much" and thought that he might someday join the American Economic Association, although he confessed the very word "'Economic' gives me a shudder—I have come to detest so deeply the irreligious, and I think unscientific, doctrines which the Economists have put forward, with such Calvinistic logic and cruelty." [131]

The laissez-faire economists, Lloyd contended, ignored the fundamental facts of economic life. Their conclusions were invalid because they were based on the assumption of the existence of free competition, whereas the great reality of the age was not competition but combination. "When combination comes in at the door, this political economy of competition flies out of the window." [132] The principle of self-interest, with its assumption that the social interest can be made secondary to the individual interest, Lloyd branded as "one of the historic mistakes of humanity," as the theory of political anarchy operating in the field of industry. It had resulted in the exploitation of the nation's resources, the monopolization of industry, and the conversion of the free farmer into a tenant and of the workingman into "the fixture of the locomotive or the factory." [133]

Defining laissez faire as the argument of businessmen that they are to be free from interference "on the ground that they have superior rights as a reward and superior abilities as a cause," Lloyd insisted that such a contention "won't bear examination." "A study of the facts would easily show," he declared, "that business success is won by a sort of predatory over-reaching, down-treading quality." The businessman simply tries to "'hog down'" what others have accomplished.

[131] Lloyd, "The Political Economy of Seventy-three Million Dollars," in *Lords of Industry* (New York, 1910), p. 61; Notebook 12, November, 1888, p. 310, Lloyd Papers; Lloyd to William M. Salter, October 30, 1885, *ibid.*

[132] Lloyd, "The Political Economy of Seventy-three Million Dollars," in *Lords of Industry*, pp. 61–65.

[133] Lloyd, *Wealth against Commonwealth*, pp. 494–499. Lloyd charged that the economists who taught that there was a dichotomy between "market freedom" and "moral freedom" were "the most mischievous and most truly anarchistic teachers of our age" (Notebook 16, 1889, pp. 437–438, Lloyd Papers).

He does not seek to develop the great potential of the earth and to put men to work. He is "ignorant, narrow, selfish." [134]

Critical of social Darwinism, classical economics, and laissez faire, Lloyd attacked the church as still another bulwark of the existing order. Explaining to the Reverend Quincy Dowd the reason why he did not join a church, he declared:

The Church has so far adopted the economic ideas of the age of trade —in competitive pew rents, paid preachers, etc.,—that it is dependent for its support on those men who are making the money, and (therefore?) does not attack their sins, although these go to the very root of the social and individual disorders of our times. Trade, or business, has now become a system by which the powerful are those who best organize wholesale lying, theft, killing, Sabbath breaking, idolatry, covetousness, but against these Cyclopean transgressors of the Ten Commandments the Church is silent.[135]

Like the advocates of the social gospel, Lloyd pleaded for "a church of the deed as well of the creed . . . a church which will make every social wrong a moral wrong, and every moral wrong a legal wrong . . . a church in which no man will have a right to do with his own what he will, but only a right to do what is right." "Every question between men," he insisted, "is a religious question, a question of moral economy before it becomes one of political economy." Industrial problems must therefore be discussed from the ethical point of view, and the Golden Rule must prevail in the market place as elsewhere.[136]

As Lloyd saw it, the alternative before the American people was "Reform or Revolution." Redress for existing wrongs would have to be brought about through the action of the state or by anarchy. If

[134] Notebook 10, 1888, p. 253, and Notebook 14, 1889, pp. 394–395, Lloyd Papers.

[135] Lloyd to Dowd, April 6, 1890, Lloyd Papers.

[136] Lloyd, "The New Conscience," *North American Review*, CXLVII (September, 1888), 337–339; Lloyd to Gladden, April 14, 1896, Gladden Papers; Lloyd, *Wealth against Commonwealth*, pp. 503–505. Lloyd said that he wrote *Wealth against Commonwealth* "with the most constructive hope of helping in the application of ethical and religious principles to the business administration of the industrial resources of our common humanity" (cited in C. Lloyd, *Lloyd*, I, 183). Lloyd considered the labor movement the most religious movement of the age because it was based on the Golden Rule. He looked to the labor movement to overthrow the teachings of the classical economists and to free mankind from the "superstitions and sins of the market" ("The Labour Movement," in *Men, the Workers* [New York, 1909], pp. 14–16, 18–20).

reform were to be successfully accomplished, the people would have "to take upon themselves through the State, for the common good, the powers now misused by the few." The "noblest, strongest, best passion and force" in the development of society, he contended, "is that which acts through the State, through government, to cure the too strong and to protect the weak [and] to preserve the common weal." [137]

"The true *laissez-faire*," Lloyd asserted, "is let the individual do what the individual can do best, and let the community do what the community can do best." Wherever the common interest is concerned, the state must act. It must act, however, for the interests of all and must consult "*all* welfares" in what it does.[138]

Like the new-school economists, Lloyd interpreted liberalism in a positive rather than in a negative sense. "Liberty," he declared, "is not escape from law, but the use of law, for one's protection and advantage." The true path to individual freedom as he saw it was through collective action, and he believed that the "higher faculties" of the individual would be "set free for higher activity, growth and enjoyment" as the state relieved its citizens of "common wants and perils." [139]

Lloyd contended that the existing system of laissez faire had culminated in monopoly. "The race to overrun," he declared, "is being succeeded by the struggle to divide, and combinations are reappearing on all sides." To Lloyd, monopoly was "the greatest social, political, and moral fact of the age." He looked upon the tendency to combination as "one of those revolutions which march through history with giant strides." It had vested control over the necessaries of life in the hands of the few, who regulated the production and consumption of wealth not in the interests of the general welfare but solely to obtain maximum profits. Lloyd was not so much alarmed at the forms monopoly assumed as at the fact that it signified arbitrary control, "control without consent," "rule without representation." All business, he insisted, was tending in this direction. "Our rising issue is with business. Monopoly is business at the end of its journey. It has

[137] Lloyd to Henry Carter Adams, December 6, 1886, Lloyd Papers; Lloyd to Ely, April 2, 1896, *ibid.*; Notebook G, p. 84, *ibid.*
[138] Lloyd, *Wealth against Commonwealth*, p. 497; Notebook 16, 1889, p. 436, Lloyd Papers; Card Notes, 1896, p. 8, and Card Notes after 1897, p. 126, *ibid.*
[139] Notebook 13, November, 1888, pp. 341, 350, and Notebook 14, 1889, p. 383, Lloyd Papers.

got there.   The irrepressible conflict is now as distinctly with business as the issue so lately met was with slavery." [140]

Although Lloyd was convinced that the existing trusts had attained their power by illegal means and that "every important man in the Oil, coal and many other trusts ought to-day to be in some one of our penitentiaries," he nevertheless thought that it would be futile to attempt to break up the trusts and restore the regime of competition. "Let me say," he wrote to a friend, ". . . that I wrote my book [*Wealth against Commonwealth*] not with any desire to create such a feeling against the combinations as to lead the public back upon their path to re-establish competition, but only to draw such a realistic picture of the ruin and wickedness which attended our present commercial methods as to revolt the people into passing on to a better system." [141]

The "better system" of which Lloyd wrote was not government regulation, which he regarded as a compromise with the very evil of which the people complained, but rather public ownership.   In his view, public ownership simply involved the extension of the principle of democracy to the market place.   Industry, like government, he maintained, exists through the coöperation of all the people and must therefore, like government, be directed by the people for the general welfare.   The coöperative methods of the public school and the post office must be applied "to all toils in which private sovereignty has become through monopoly a despotism over the public."   "Liberty," Lloyd concluded, "recast the old forms of government into the Republic, and it must remould our institutions of wealth into the Commonwealth." [142]

Although the public ownership of monopolies was the essential reform for which he campaigned, Lloyd, as his notebooks suggest, wished to see the movement of reform pushed along many fronts. In one of his blueprints for reform, he advocated, among other things, that all workers be enrolled and licensed in their particular trade, that industries be classified into guilds, and that all contracts for employment be made with the various guilds.   He suggested that every citizen be guaranteed against exposure and starvation and that no un-

[140] Lloyd, "Lords of Industry," in *Lords of Industry*, pp. 117, 143; Lloyd, *Wealth against Commonwealth*, pp. 6, 511–512.

[141] Lloyd to Frederick H. Gillett, November 30, 1896, Lloyd Papers.

[142] Lloyd, *Wealth against Commonwealth*, pp. 516–523, 532–535; Lloyd to H. R. Meyer, January 5, 1899, Lloyd Papers.

skilled laborer be dismissed from a job or suffer a reduction in pay "except under cognizance of some representative of state." He favored a system of pensions for disabled and aged workers, the eight-hour day, abolition of child labor and "wife" labor, strict regulation of safety and sanitary conditions in tenements, employer responsibility for industrial accidents resulting from defective or poorly guarded machinery, national technical and art schools, legislation proscribing all forms of fraud and adulteration, a proportional or a progressive income tax, repeal of all laws granting special privileges to banks and railroads, recapture of all forfeitable government land grants, imposition of high taxes on idle lands, "confiscatory, and inquisatorial [sic] taxation of all lines of luxury," and "complete reconstruction of our great cities." [143]

Lloyd was always concerned with striking a proper balance between the claims of the individual and the claims of society,[144] but unlike such men as Washington Gladden, Lester Ward, and Richard T. Ely, he espoused the philosophy of Fabian socialism as the proper method of attaining this goal. He was not, however, a "sectarian socialist," and he refused to join the Socialist Labor party. The ultimate aim of socialism, he insisted, was not the "communization of all production and distribution and the distinct prohibition of all individual competitive effort." Believing that a dualism prevailed in the economic sphere as elsewhere, he argued that "private ownership for private gain and competitive and individual initiative" were "entirely consistent with public and private morality and welfare under certain circumstances." "To me," Lloyd wrote to E. B. Gaston, "socialism presents itself not so much as a new doctrine as the entrance of the doctrine of mercy, justice and the common good into the new fields of modern wealth." He interpreted social evolution as a "continual struggle for equilibrium between the individual and society, between power and the people," and since he believed that the "power of money" had come to overshadow the power of the community, he saw it as the task of his age "to apply to this economic tyrant and this money power the same social restraints that in previous ages we have

[143] Notebook G, pp. 69–73, Lloyd Papers; C. Lloyd, *Lloyd*, I, 110–112.

[144] See, for example, the following in Lloyd's notebooks: Notebook 2, [1887], p. 4; Notebook 4, [1887 or 1888], p. 58; Notebook 10, October, 1888, pp. 241, 261; Notebook 13, November, 1888, pp. 350–351; Notebook 16, May, 1889, pp. 428–429; Lloyd to W. T. Harris, December 17, 1897, Lloyd Papers; and C. Lloyd, *Lloyd*, I, 292–295.

applied to the power of the church and the power of the kings. But let us beware," he cautioned, "lest we create a new power to oppress." [145]

Although he was no friend to free silver,[146] Lloyd for a time saw in the People's party a possible vehicle for the implementation of his social and political views. In July, 1894, he played a part in bringing about a coalition of Populist and labor and reform forces in Illinois on a platform that called for "the collective ownership by the people of all such means of production and distribution as the people elect to operate for the commonwealth." However, not only did this alliance fail to produce any significant electoral results in Illinois, but Lloyd was completely unsuccessful in seeking to make of the national People's party the radical reform organization he believed the times required.[147] Lloyd's ideas were, indeed, to the left of the road the American movement of reform was destined to follow; but, like George and Bellamy, he nevertheless helped to arouse the urban middle class, which was to play so large a part in the Progressive movement, to the need for social and economic reform. As one student of Lloyd has indicated, such writings of Lloyd's as *Wealth against Commonwealth* were "of prime importance in shocking professional men, intellectuals, liberal clergy, and intelligent readers into a realistic attitude toward contemporary social and economic problems, and in opening minds to reform proposals that involved an enlargement of governmental powers." [148]

[145] Lloyd to E. B. Gaston, August 7, 1899, Lloyd Papers; C. Lloyd, *Lloyd*, I, 301–304.

[146] "Although I am not at all, as you know," Lloyd wrote to Atkinson, "a gold man, I am perfectly willing to hold your knives while you stab the silver folly" (Lloyd to Atkinson, December 3, 1897, Edward Atkinson Papers, Massachusetts Historical Society).

[147] Destler, "Consummation of a Labor-Populist Alliance in Illinois, 1894," in *American Radicalism*, pp. 162–174; Destler, "The Labor-Populist Alliance of Illinois in the Election of 1894," *ibid.*, pp. 175–211; "The People's Party Convention at Springfield, Illinois, July 4, 1894," draft of proposed platform in Lloyd Papers; Lloyd to Clarence Darrow, November 23, 1894, *ibid.*; Quint, *Forging of American Socialism*, pp. 227–237.

[148] Destler, "Wealth against Commonwealth, 1894 and 1944," in *American Radicalism*, p. 161. For the appeal of George and Bellamy to middle-class persons, see Daniel Aaron, *Men of Good Hope: A Story of American Progressives* (New York, 1951), pp. 79–80, 113–114; Quint, *Forging of American Socialism*, pp. 84–86, 95; and Barker, *Henry George*, pp. 511 ff.

VIII

The doctrine of laissez faire, and particularly the Spencer-Sumner variety of individualism, was attacked on still another front during the last two decades of the nineteenth century by the men and women who participated in the work of the social settlements. The first of the social settlements in the United States was the Neighborhood Guild, which was founded in New York in 1886 by Dr. Stanton Coit. Fourteen years later there were approximately one hundred social settlements in existence, and they were engaged in a variety of activities designed to meet the problems of urban life.[149]

The most famous of the social settlements was Hull House, founded in Chicago in 1889 by Jane Addams and Ellen Starr. Whereas Sumner declared that social classes owe nothing to one another, Hull House emphasized the reciprocal dependence of social classes and sought to add the "social function" to democracy. It proclaimed the "solidarity of the human race" and tried to "express in social service and in terms of action the spirit of Christ." [150]

Settlement workers were quick to see that the problems with which they dealt were in themselves the product of antecedent social and economic causes, a fact that induced them to campaign for such measures of social and economic betterment as factory legislation, public-health reform, and improved housing. As Jane Addams expressed it, the social workers were "bound to see the needs of their neighborhood as a whole, to furnish data for legislation, and to use their influence to secure it." [151]

The concern for problems of social welfare evidenced in the es-

[149] Arthur Meier Schlesinger, *The Rise of the City, 1878–1898* (New York, 1933), pp. 351–352.

[150] See Addams, *Twenty Years at Hull House* (New York, 1910), pp. 91, 124, 126; and Addams, "Hull House, Chicago: An Effort toward Social Democracy," *Forum*, XIV (October, 1892), 226. "Although its influence cannot be measured," the Beards declared of Hull House, "the guess may be hazarded that no other single institution of the period did as much to counteract the dogma of individualism and restore the social principle to thought about civilization" (*The American Spirit* [New York, 1942], p. 475).

[151] See Addams, *Twenty Years at Hull House,* pp. 126, 198–230; Julia C. Lathrop, "What the Settlement Work Stands For," *Proceedings of the National Conference of Charities and Correction, 1896,* pp. 108–109; testimony of Robert A. Woods, U. S. Industrial Commission, *Report on the Relations and Conditions of Capital and Labor,* XIV, 198–203; Josephine Goldmark, *Impatient Crusader* (Urbana, Ill., 1953), pp. 34–36; and Schlesinger, *Rise of the City,* p. 353.

tablishment of settlement houses was also manifest in the work of the American Social Science Association and the National Conference of Charities and Correction. The American Social Science Association was formed in 1865 as the result of a conference called by the Massachusetts Board of State Charities at the behest of the Boston Social Science Association. Its work was allocated to four departments, of which the Department of Social Economy was concerned, among other things, with such matters as pauperism, workhouses, intemperance, the relation of idleness to female crime, intemperance, and prostitution, and the relation of the "gifted and educated classes toward the weak, the witless and the ignorant." Interested in "fostering . . . the spirit of science in relation to social problems," the organization hoped to furnish legislators with "data basic to social reform." [152]

As Franklin B. Sanborn, general secretary of the American Social Science Association, indicated, the Association sought "to learn patiently what *is*—to promote diligently what *should* be." "Our friends of the pessimistic school," he asserted, "dwell with grim satisfaction on their doctrine that teaches the 'survival of the fittest;' but, if the fittest do survive, they must make the world a better place to live in. It is the survival and not the extirpation upon which the student of social science fastens his attention." Sanborn spoke caustically of "the chimera of non-interference by government . . . which has been conjured up so many times to thwart wise statesmanship and a decent public policy, in the ethical relations of government." The same restraints and assistance that parents exercise toward their children must, he insisted, be extended by the "virtuous community toward its weak, vicious and rebellious members." The American Social Science Association from the first, he said, had sought to correct the evils of the existing order so as to promote the best interests of society as a whole. It had done so in the "settled conviction that human society is, in fact, a whole; . . . a composite unity, so contrived by its Creator that nothing can long be hurtful to a part which is profitable to the aggregate." [153]

The National Conference of Charities and Correction, one of

---

[152] Luther Lee Bernard and Jessie Bernard, *Origins of American Sociology* (New York, 1943), pp. 540–544, 559–570. The Department of Social Economy originally concerned itself with economic as well as social problems, but in 1874 the economic subjects were assigned to a new Department of Trade and Finance.

[153] Sanborn, "The Social Sciences. Their Growth and Future," *Journal of Social Science*, XXI (September, 1886), 5–6, 10; Sanborn, "Society and Socialism," *ibid.*, XXXIII (November, 1895), 24.

many organizations fathered by the American Social Science Association, was established in 1874 under the auspices of the Association and remained within its fold until 1879, when it became an independent agency. An outgrowth of the Department of Social Economy, the new organization was concerned with such problems as treatment of the insane and the feeble-minded, protection of children, poor relief, penal reform, charity organizations, and social settlements.[154] It worked closely with the state boards of charities, and its committee on legislation recommended in 1901 the establishment of a federal Bureau of Charities and Corrections whose principal task would be to collect and diffuse information pertaining to social welfare. This, the committee thought, represented "a limited and modest extension of the general welfare policy of the federal government." [155]

IX

Ever the organizer, the indefatigable William Dwight Porter Bliss decided in 1897 that the time had come to unite the reform forces of the country into a national organization whose purpose would be to educate the public with respect to those measures upon which the advocates of reform were agreed. On September 3, 1897, in San Francisco, Bliss met with a small group of persons, mostly Christian Socialists, and founded the Union Reform League. The League's platform called for direct legislation, the direct primary, civil-service reform, public works for the jobless, public ownership and operation of natural monopolies, postal-savings banks, express, and telegraph, reduction of the hours of labor, limitations on child and female labor, income and inheritance taxes, issuance of money by the government rather than the banks, and a program of social insurance. Although Bliss hoped to make the organization national in character, it proved to be of importance only in California and Ohio.[156]

Anxious to make the influence of the reformers felt in the election of 1900, Bliss proposed that the spokesmen for reform meet to draft

[154] Frank J. Bruno, *Trends in Social Work as Reflected in the Proceedings of the National Conference of Social Work, 1874–1946* (New York, 1948), pp. 3–7, 26–27, 55–119. Until 1879 the organization was known as the Conference of Boards of Public Charities. It became the National Conference of Social Work in 1917.

[155] Committee on Legislation, "Special Field of National Legislation," *Proceedings of the National Conference of Charities and Correction, 1901*, pp. 115–116.

[156] Quint, *Forging of American Socialism*, pp. 256–261; Bliss, "Union Reform League Activities," *Arena*, XXII (July, 1899), 111–114.

a program that would then be submitted to the Democratic party for incorporation in its platform. If the Democrats accepted the program, the reformers would rally to the party's support, but if the Democrats refused to coöperate, the Union Reform League would itself form a new political party.[157] With this in mind, Bliss joined several other reformers in issuing a call for a National Social and Political Conference to meet in Buffalo late in July, 1899.

The Buffalo conference, in Bliss's view "the best and most representative conference of reformers ever held in this country," resulted in the transformation of the Union Reform League into the Social Reform Union and the adoption of a five-point program calling for direct legislation and proportional representation, the public ownership of public utilities or monopolies deriving from natural resources or the existence of society, direct taxation so that the values society creates may benefit all equally, complete control by the government of the medium of exchange, and anti-imperialism. The convention voted to support any political party that would adopt these principles, but it was recognized that the chief purpose of the organization was educational and that it would seek to affect politics without actually entering the political arena. Bliss was appointed president of the organization, and Eltweed Pomeroy, Frank Parsons, and Edward Bemis were made secretaries. The vice presidents included Henry Demarest Lloyd, Eugene Debs, Laurence Gronlund, Samuel Gompers, William Dean Howells, Golden Rule Jones, Hazen Pingree, Edwin Markham, George D. Herron, George E. McNeill, Judge Walter Clark, John Peter Altgeld, and Florence Kelley.[158]

To promote its educational objectives, the Social Reform Union set up a College of Social Science to conduct correspondence courses dealing with social, economic, and political subjects. Thomas E. Will was president of the College, and its staff included Edward Bemis, John R. Commons, and Frank Parsons. In addition, the Social Reform Union established a library department, whose task it was to place

---

[157] Bliss, "Unite or Perish," *Arena*, XXII (July, 1899), 78–89. Bliss believed the Democratic party to be more inclined to reform than the Republican party.

[158] Bliss, "A Plea for Union or What Is the Social Reform Union?" *Social Forum*, I (September 1, 1899), 128–130; Bliss, "The Social Reform Union," *Arena*, XXII (August, 1899), 272–275; "Statement of Objects, Results and Action of the National Social and Political Conference Held at Buffalo, N. Y., June 28th to July 4th, 1899," copy in Ely Papers; Eltweed Pomeroy, "The National Social and Political Conference," *Social Forum*, I (August, 1899), 272–275; Quint, *Forging of American Socialism*, pp. 261–264.

works on economics in the libraries of small towns and villages, and issued publications, prepared by the staff of the College, that explained the chief reforms that the Union espoused.[159]

Although the Social Reform Union's membership of approximately five hundred exceeded that of the Union Reform League, the organization was represented in only eight states, and it was neither a cohesive nor a particularly influential force. The members of the Union did not present a common front during the election of 1900, and after a second National Social and Political Conference, held in Detroit in June, 1901, the Social Reform Union passed from the scene.[160]

The failure of Bliss to establish an effective national organization of reformers in the last years of the nineteenth century was less an indication of the relative strength of reform sentiment in the United States at that time than it was of the diverse character of the reformers and of their inability to agree on, or to support, a common program of reform. As subsequent events were to demonstrate, the reformers had not been crying in the wilderness: many of their proposals were to be taken up by the major parties and, eventually, to be incorporated into law.

Although the reformers and reform groups of the 1880's and 1890's differed in their estimate of the reforms that the existing situation required, they tended to agree that the functions of the state should be expanded and that a more positive use of the powers of government was essential to promote what in their view was the common interest. Thus did the quest for reform lead away from laissez faire and toward the general-welfare state.

[159] Quint, *Forging of American Socialism*, pp. 264–266; Bliss, "A Plea for Union or What Is the Social Reform Union?" *Social Forum*, I (September 1, 1899), 130–131.

[160] Quint, *Forging of American Socialism*, pp. 266–270.

X

THE LEGISLATIVE RECORD

AS AN eminent sociologist has pointed out, whenever the structure of society becomes more complex and private business extends the range of its activities, new tasks are likely to be imposed on government regardless of "the particular philosophies that governments cherish." [1] Thus it was that despite the vigorous assertion of the theory of laissez faire in the era between Appomattox and the accession of Theodore Roosevelt to the presidency, the changing character of the American economy and of American society compelled the state governments and the federal government to assume a variety of new duties not sanctioned by the advocates of the negative state.

The general lack of correspondence between the theory of laissez faire and the practice of governments, state and national, did not escape the attention of discerning observers of the American scene. James Bryce, for example, noted that although Americans imagined themselves wedded to the theory of laissez faire, they were, in practice, no more reluctant than the English to extend the functions of government "into ever-widening fields." In similar vein, Albert Shaw remarked to Edwin Seligman in a letter of 1887 that "the tendency to appeal to legislation in our western farming states is remarkably strong, and, strangely enough, our politicians all regard themselves as orthodox economists, opposed to the increase of state functions." [2]

Although disciples of Herbert Spencer were already complaining

[1] R. M. MacIver, *The Web of Government* (New York, 1947), p. 314.

[2] Bryce, *The American Commonwealth* (London, 1888), III, 273; Shaw to Seligman, September 15, 1887, Edwin R. A. Seligman Papers, Columbia University Library. See also Shaw, "The American State and the American Man," *Contemporary Review*, LI (May, 1887), 695–711; and Allen Johnston Going, *Bourbon Democracy in Alabama, 1874–1890* (University, Ala., 1951), pp. 109–110.

in the 1860's of what they considered evidences of "over-legislation," [3] it was chiefly in the 1880's and 1890's that the wide gulf between theory and practice with respect to laissez faire became evident. The comptroller of the state of New York lamented in 1897 that state expenditures in New York between 1881 and 1896 had increased four times as much as the increase in the state's population.[4] According to Albert Shaw, the "one striking and common characteristic" of the five thousand general laws or amendments to general laws enacted by state legislatures in 1885 was their "utter disregard of the *laissez-faire* principle."[5] After examining 1,191 of the thirteen thousand laws of all types enacted by the states and territories in 1889 and 1890, the attorney F. J. Stimson concluded that only seventeen of the statutes embodied notions of individualism. Twenty-nine per cent of the laws were, in Stimson's view, "socialistic" in that they limited personal and civic freedom in some essential, and he placed the remainder in the category of "allowable socialism" because they recognized the right of private property although they regulated its use.[6]

Reflecting the apprehension in conservative business circles at the drift away from laissez faire, Comptroller of the United States James Eckels cried out in 1897 against "the menace of legislation." "The most insignificant subjects," he declared, "have not been too trivial to be legislated upon, while the most important have received constant attention." Congress and the state legislatures, he complained, "proceed upon the theory that every business principle and business enterprise must be regulated by legislative act."[7]

II

State and local governments were, on the whole, less reluctant than the federal government to extend the scope of their activities in the last three and one-half decades of the nineteenth century. Not only did they seek to promote economic development by favorable

---

[3] See, for example, "Sociological Record," *New York Social Science Review,* II (August, 1866), 97–104.

[4] Comptroller of the State of New York, *Annual Report, 1897* (Albany, N. Y., 1897), pp. x–xi.

[5] Shaw, "The American State and the American Man," *Contemporary Review,* LI (May, 1887), 698.

[6] Stimson, "The Ethics of Democracy: Liberty," *Scribner's Magazine,* XV (May, 1894), 648–656; Stimson, *Popular Law-Making* (New York, 1910), p. 127.

[7] Eckels, "The Menace of Legislation," *North American Review,* CLXV (August, 1897), 241–244.

legislation, as they had done before the Civil War, but they also assumed new or added responsibilities with respect to the regulation of business and labor conditions, the ownership of public utilities, the conservation of natural resources, and the problems of education, health, and social welfare.

Although the decade of the 1840's had witnessed a partial reaction against the policy of state aid for internal improvements, state and local governments continued to assist in the construction of railroads during the period after the Civil War. Massachusetts provided loans to spur the construction of the Boston, Hartford and Erie Railroad and, after first supporting private enterprise in the task, undertook itself the completion of the Hoosac Tunnel, which was opened to traffic in 1875. The state of Maine and the city of Bangor provided land and money to facilitate the construction of a railroad between Bangor and St. John, and local aid for railroad construction continued in Maine as late as the 1890's. Indianapolis in 1876 made its credit available for the construction of a Belt Railroad around the city, and between 1874 and 1884 Cincinnati built the Cincinnati Southern Railway. The panic of 1873 led in many states to the enactment of statutes and the approval of constitutional provisions that severely restricted the right of state and local governments to help private corporations such as railroads, but this did not bring a halt to state interest in the construction of internal improvements. In the 1890's, as a result of the prodding of the League of American Wheelmen, state governments turned their attention to a long-neglected problem and began to provide aid for the improvement of existing roads and the construction and maintenance of new roads.[8]

In addition to their attempts to promote the construction of internal improvements, state and local governments sought to assist and encourage the economic pursuits of their citizens, particularly those who were engaged in agriculture. Most states subsidized agricul-

[8] Carter Goodrich, "The Revulsion against Internal Improvements," *Journal of Economic History*, X (November, 1950), 149–152, 158–159; Edward Chase Kirkland, *Men, Cities and Transportation: A Study in New England History, 1820–1900* (Cambridge, Mass., 1948), I, 387–432, 466–493; II, 36–64; Charles J. Bullock, "Historical Sketch of the Finances and Financial Policies of Massachusetts from 1780 to 1905," *A. E. A. Publications*, 3d Ser., VIII (1907), 339–344; Fred Eugene Jewett, *A Financial History of Maine* (New York, 1937), p. 45; Otto Dorner, "Good Roads and State Aid," *Forum*, XXVI (February, 1899), 668–672; Don C. Sowers, "The Financial History of New York State from 1789 to 1912," *Columbia University Studies in History, Economics and Public Law*, LVII (1914), 543–544.

tural fairs, and many contributed to the support of agricultural societies and farmers' institutes. By 1901 eleven states had established departments of agriculture, which provided a variety of services to farmers, and every state had its agricultural experiment station. By means of bounties and tax exemptions, state governments sought to encourage the production of beet sugar, jute, flax, hemp, silk, potato starch, salt, and such nonagricultural products as canaigre leather, Portland cement, and iron and iron pipe.[9]

The states did not confine their interest in the economy to promotional activities, and, as industry grew in power, state governments found it necessary to regulate business and labor conditions in order to protect the weaker members of society. Thus when the railroads failed to usher in an economic utopia and railway abuses became prevalent, state governments turned from the promotion of railroad construction to the regulation of railroad rates and practices. By the end of the century virtually every state had provided for the regulation of its railroads, with regulatory powers generally vested in a state railroad commission.[10] The states also extended their supervisory control over banks and insurance companies. The banks of twenty-six states were subject to supervision by 1900, and by the same date twenty-one states had independent departments of insurance.[11] Massachusetts in 1885 established a Gas and Electric Light Commission,

[9] Shaw, "The American State and the American Man," *Contemporary Review*, LI (May, 1887), 700–702; Bryce, *American Commonwealth*, II, 276–277; William F. Willoughby, "State Activities and Politics," *Papers of the American Historical Association*, V (January, April, 1891), 121; Fred A. Shannon, *The Farmer's Last Frontier: Agriculture, 1860–1897* (New York, 1945), pp. 269, 280–282; Edward Wiest, *Agricultural Organization in the United States* (*University of Kentucky Studies in Economics and Sociology*, Vol. II) (Lexington, Ky., 1923), pp. 295–296; Stimson, *Popular Law-Making*, p. 135; Ivan L. Pollock, *History of Economic Legislation in Iowa* (Iowa City, Iowa, 1918), pp. 69–70; Sowers, "Financial History of New York State," *Columbia University Studies in History, Economics and Public Law*, LVII (1914), 522–523.

[10] Balthasar Henry Meyer, *Railway Legislation in the United States* (New York, 1903), pp. 108–186; Solon Justus Buck, *The Granger Movement* (Cambridge, 1913), pp. 123–205; Merle Fainsod and Lincoln Gordon, *Government and the American Economy* (New York, 1941), pp. 227–229.

[11] U. S. National Monetary Commission, "State Banks and Trust Companies since the Passage of the National-Bank Act," by George E. Barnett (Vol. VII of the Commission's *Publications*), 61st Cong., 3d sess., S. Doc. No. 659 (Washington, D.C., 1911), pp. 178–179; Edwin Wilhite Patterson, *The Insurance Commissioner in the United States* (Cambridge, Mass., 1927), pp. 525–537; Pollock, *Economic Legislation in Iowa*, pp. 139–167, 187–206.

and North Carolina in 1899 created the nation's first state corporation commission and assigned it jurisdiction over railroads, banks, loan and trust companies, and public utilities.[12]

Despite the actions of Massachusetts and North Carolina, state governments, ordinarily, did not themselves assume the burden of regulating public utilities in the period before 1900 but, rather, assigned that task to municipal authorities.[13] Although the latter generally ignored the pleas of such persons as Frank Parsons for public ownership, the public-ownership movement did make a little headway during this era. Whereas in 1865 but 42 per cent of the city waterworks were publicly owned, in 1896 the figure had risen to 53.2 per cent; and this total included forty-one of the fifty largest cities of the nation. The municipalization of electric lighting was, for the most part, confined to the smaller cities: in 1898 there were 353 public electric-light plants, as compared with two hundred such plants in 1892; but the 1898 figure represented only 13.5 per cent of the total number of plants and only 4.8 per cent of the total population. Thirteen cities (including Wheeling, Toledo, and Duluth) were operating their own gas works in 1899, as compared with three such cities in 1865. Municipal authorities were particularly reluctant to extend their sway over street railways, with the result that in 1899 the only street railway owned and operated by public authorities consisted of the two miles of single track across the Brooklyn Bridge.[14]

Quite apart from the problem of railroads and of public utilities in general, the consolidation of business in the decades after the Civil War was productive of state legislation on the subject of trusts and monopolies. Twenty-one states and territories had enacted antitrust measures (in constitutional or legislative form) by July 2, 1890, the date of the passage of the federal Sherman Anti-Trust Act, and by the end of the century nine additional states and territories had fallen into

[12] Clyde Lyndon King, *The Regulation of Municipal Utilities* (New York, 1912), p. 253; C. Vann Woodward, *Origins of the New South, 1877–1913* (Baton Rouge, La., 1951), p. 380.

[13] Parsons, "The Legal Aspects of Monopoly," in Edward W. Bemis, ed., *Municipal Monopolies: A Collection of Papers by American Economists and Specialists* (New York, 1899), pp. 478–479.

[14] Bemis, ed., *Municipal Monopolies*, pp. 16, 20–21, 27, 59, 187–188, 565, 607–621, 673. For the capitalization of publicly owned and privately owned public utilities at the turn of the century, see testimony of Bemis, U. S. Industrial Commission, *Report on Transportation* (Vol. IX of the Commission's *Reports;* Washington, D.C., 1901), p. 88.

line. Reflecting the wishes of the trust busters, the state antitrust statutes generally outlawed combinations in restraint of trade and proscribed practices that were deemed promotive of monopoly. Taken as a whole, these measures implied a "general recognition of the right of the state to proscribe that which is opposed to public policy." [15]

The growing power of industry as compared to labor and the demands of laborers for legislative assistance persuaded state governments after 1885 to pay increasing attention to the labor problem. Between 1887 and 1897, the various states and territories enacted 1,639 laws pertaining to labor,[16] and by the end of the century labor had received legislative recognition of many of its demands.[17]

Regulations pertaining to hours and wages were abundant by the end of the century. The right to rest one day in seven was guaranteed to practically all employees. Thirteen states stipulated the length of the workday in the absence of contracts to the contrary. Twelve states and the District of Columbia fixed the hours of labor, generally eight a day, on public-works projects. Utah and Wyoming limited the hours of miners to eight a day. Four states fixed the hours of bakery workers, and twelve states, the hours of railroad workers. Fifteen states limited the hours of women in factories and in special occupations. Five states forbade the employment of females in all mines, and an additional four forbade the employment of women in coal mines. Twenty-four states prohibited the employment in factories of children under a certain age (usually fourteen), and twenty-two states regulated the hours of employment of such children as could be employed. In addition, most states limited child labor by various educational requirements.

With respect to wages, three states forbade the imposition of fines on factory employees for imperfect work. Laws stipulating the time of payment were enacted by twenty-three states. Payment in lawful money was required by most states. Company stores were outlawed in three states, and eleven states decreed that business concerns were

[15] See Henry R. Seager and Charles A. Gulick, *Trust and Corporation Problems* (New York, 1929), pp. 341–348; and J. D. Forrest, "Anti-Monopoly Legislation in the United States," *American Journal of Sociology*, I (January, 1896), 419–424.

[16] F. J. Stimson, "Democracy and the Laboring Man," *Atlantic Monthly*, LXXX (November, 1897), 606.

[17] The following summary of labor legislation is based on U. S. Industrial Commission, *Report on Labor Legislation* (Vol. V of the Commission's *Reports;* Washington, D.C., 1900).

not to compel their employees to deal with company stores. Seventeen states provided for the fair weighing of coal at the mines or required that coal be weighed before screening and credited to the miners in determining their wages. In addition, various state laws prohibited the attachment of wages, protected the assignment of wages, gave preference or priority to wage debts, or made corporation stockholders individually liable for corporation debts to laborers.

Eight states did away with the common law of conspiracy insofar as it was applicable to combinations of workingmen. The common law as applied to industrial accidents was modified by other state enactments. The fellow-servant doctrine, which relieved the employer of liability for injuries sustained as the result of negligence by a fellow employee, was dispensed with in eleven states (in eight of these states this applied only to railroad employees), and ten states made employers liable for injuries to employees resulting from defective machinery.

Twenty-one states provided for the inspection of factories and workshops for safety and sanitation.[18] Antisweatshop laws were enacted in nine states. Sixteen states outlawed the "yellow-dog" contract and prohibited discrimination against employees because of union membership. Most states proscribed blacklisting. Six forbade the importation of "Pinkerton men," and eight stipulated that sheriffs were not to employ deputy sheriffs (for strike-breaking) from outside the state. Nearly all the states had labor bureaus or commissioners, and about half made provision for boards of conciliation and arbitration. Public employment offices were provided by five states. In addition to all these regulations, there were elaborate regulations dealing with convict labor and with mine safety.

Taken as a whole, the labor laws enacted by the various state governments in the last fifteen years of the century marked a departure from laissez-faire views with respect to freedom of contract. Although many of the laws were declared unconstitutional and although they were generally poorly enforced,[19] they nevertheless constituted the

[18] Only thirteen of these states made it obligatory upon factory owners to take certain precautions against accidents. See W. F. Willoughby, "Accidents to Labor as Regulated by Law in the United States," Department of Labor, *Bulletin*, VI (1901), 20–21.

[19] The ineffectiveness of much of this legislation is discussed in W. J. Ghent, *Our Benevolent Feudalism* (New York, 1902), pp. 83–101.

real beginning of attempts by the states to improve the competitive position of the workingman. As one observer noted, the labor laws of the era asserted the right of government "to interfere with the natural laws of the business world" and were designed "to secure the liberty of one class by curbing the license of another." [20]

The state governments also assumed new responsibilities in the years after the Civil War for education, health, and social welfare. One of the most striking developments in the field of public education was the growth of the public high school. In 1878 there were less than eight hundred public high schools in the country, and the total enrollment in these schools was about one hundred thousand. By 1900 there were over six thousand such schools, serving a total of approximately 520,000 pupils. The growth of the public high school was accompanied by the enactment of compulsory attendance laws, especially in the North and the West: by 1898 thirty-one states had accepted the principle of compulsory attendance.[21] The state governments during this period assumed obligations with respect to the supplying of textbooks. By 1891 eight states had adopted a free textbook system in whole or in part. California in 1884 decided to set up its own publishing plant to provide for the textbook needs of the state's public-education system. Other states arranged for the adoption of uniform textbooks throughout the common schools and for the mass purchase of textbooks at fixed prices.[22] The era after the Civil War also witnessed the extension of the system of public libraries: between 1878 and 1898 eighteen states authorized the use of taxation for the establishment of such libraries.[23]

The first state board of health was established by Louisiana in 1867, and by the end of the century such boards were in existence in forty-two states. Four states passed pure-food laws in 1881, and by 1895 twenty-three others had acted in similar fashion. By 1900 the principal cities of the nation and twenty-nine of the states had enacted pure-milk laws, and various states had taken action, ostensibly

[20] George W. Alger, "The Courts and Factory Legislation," *American Journal of Sociology*, VI (November, 1900), 397.

[21] Arthur Meier Schlesinger, *The Rise of the City, 1878–1898* (New York, 1933), pp. 161–162; U. S. Commissioner of Education, *Report for the Year 1899–1900* (Washington, D.C., 1900), I, liv.

[22] Jeremiah W. Jenks, "School-Book Legislation," *Political Science Quarterly*, VI (March, 1891), 90–125.

[23] Schlesinger, *Rise of the City*, p. 175.

for reasons connected with health, to discourage the production of butter substitutes.[24]

Although the first state board for the supervision of charities was set up in Massachusetts in 1863, the movement to establish public supervisory agencies over state charitable institutions did not develop until after the Civil War. By 1900 boards or commissions of charities were operating in twenty-five states. Some of these agencies had powers of supervision and report only, but in such states as Rhode Island, Kansas, and Wisconsin, the board exercised actual control over state charitable institutions.[25]

Apparently not impressed by Spencer's dire warnings, the states considerably increased the number of public institutions designed to care for the "unfit." Reports by forty-three states and territories to the National Conference of Charities and Correction in 1894 revealed the existence of 363 state benevolent, penal, and reformatory institutions.[26] Taxpayers of the state of New York in the late 1890's, to cite one instance, supported an institution for blind children, an institution for deaf mutes, an institution for orphans and for destitute Indian children, two reform schools for juvenile delinquents and two reformatories for older youths, an institution for feeble-minded children, an institution for feeble-minded women, an institution for idiots, three houses of refuge for criminal women, a colony of epileptics, a home for old soldiers and sailors, and another home for old soldiers and their wives, mothers, and widows and for destitute army nurses, eleven hospitals for the pauper insane and two hospitals for the criminal insane, and three state prisons. The state comptroller complained that the state provided for "sufferers from nearly every ailment . . . that flesh is heir to" and that it dispensed charity "with an almost lavish hand." [27] An important precedent in the welfare area was set by the Ohio legis-

---

[24] Allan Nevins, *The Emergence of Modern America, 1865–1878* (New York, 1927), pp. 322–323; Schlesinger, *Rise of the City*, pp. 133–134, 244–245; Willoughby, "State Activities and Politics," *Papers of the American Historical Association*, V (January, April, 1891), 118–119; Mazÿck P. Ravenel, ed., *A Half Century of Public Health* (New York, 1921), pp. 138–155, 214–215, 285–286; Bryce, *American Commonwealth*, III, 413–414.

[25] Leontine Lincoln, "State Boards and Commissions," *Proceedings of the National Conference of Charities and Correction, 1900*, p. 169; Amos G. Warner, *American Charities* (New York, 1894), pp. 359–360.

[26] *Proceedings of the National Conference of Charities and Correction, 1894,* pp. 259–269.

[27] See Comptroller of the State of New York, *Annual Report, 1897*, pp. vii–viii; and *ibid., 1898* (Albany, N. Y., 1898), p. vii.

lature in 1898, when it enacted the first state law providing pensions for the blind.[28]

The "restrictive" regulation of housing in the United States began in 1867, with the enactment of a New York tenement-house law. This was but the first of a series of tenement laws in New York that culminated in 1901 in the passage of a model statute that established "fairly high" minimum standards of structure and sanitation for new buildings and newly altered buildings, somewhat lower standards for existing dwellings, and uniform standards of maintenance for all dwellings. Massachusetts passed a tenement-house law for Boston in 1871, and Pennsylvania did so for Philadelphia in 1895. These laws, like the New York legislation, were of the restrictive variety. Constructive housing legislation, providing for the public erection of low-cost dwellings, had to await a later era.[29]

In an effort to give effect to the view that it is a proper function of government to provide not only for the immediate welfare of its citizens but also for their future welfare and the welfare of their descendants,[30] the state governments in the period after the Civil War demonstrated an increasing interest in the conservation of natural resources. A multitude of state laws were enacted for the purpose of conserving fish and game. To administer these laws, fish commissions were set up in the 1860's and 1870's in virtually all of the states, and by the end of the century game agencies had been established in thirty states and territories, usually in conjunction with the state fish commission. Between 1885 and 1900 forestry agencies were created in thirteen states and territories in order to care for state forests and to encourage the cultivation of trees. These same years witnessed the establishment of five state park systems; but only New York and Massachusetts had central administrative agencies to manage

[28] U. S. Federal Security Agency, Social Security Administration, *Social Security in the United States* (new ed.; Washington, D.C., 1952), p. 45.

[29] Edith Elmer Wood, *The Housing of the Unskilled Wage Earner* (New York, 1919), pp. 29–45, 60, 75–78, 82; Mary Stevenson Callcott and Willoughby C. Waterman, *Principles of Social Legislation* (New York, 1932), pp. 109–111; Nevins, *Emergence of Modern America*, pp. 322–323; Schlesinger, *Rise of the City*, pp. 110–111.

[30] B. E. Fernow, the great forestry expert, referred to government functions such as conservation as the "providential functions" ("The Providential Functions of Government with Special Reference to Natural Resources," *Proceedings of the American Association for the Advancement of Science*, XLIV [August–September, 1895], 335–336).

their parks. Minor gains were also registered in the conservation of mineral products. By 1900 ten states had provided for geological surveys on a permanent basis. Between 1879 and 1900 eight states passed laws designed to prevent waste in oil products, and two extended their regulations to include gas as well.[31]

In addition to their other activities, state governments did not hesitate to invade the field of private morality. This tendency was most apparent with respect to the liquor traffic. State-wide prohibition, already in existence in 1875 in Vermont, New Hampshire, Maine, and Kansas, was adopted by Iowa in 1882, Rhode Island in 1886, and North Dakota and South Dakota in 1889. Iowa, Rhode Island, and South Dakota, however, abandoned prohibition before the end of the century. Fourteen states had made provision for local option by 1896, and licensing laws were generally in effect in other states. South Carolina in 1893 set up exclusive state liquor dispensaries.[32] The state governments also sought to protect their inhabitants from "evils" other than drink. State laws proscribed the publication and sale of obscene literature, gambling, lotteries, and even prize fighting. Kentucky prohibited the sale and publication of books and periodicals whose chief purpose was to record the commission of crime. Iowa subjected to fine and imprisonment persons who manufactured, sold, or gave away cigarettes or cigarette papers.[33]

III

Although the disparity between theory and practice with respect to laissez faire in the three and one-half decades after the Civil War was most apparent on the level of state and local government, the

[31] Clifford J. Hynning, *State Conservation of Resources* (Washington, D.C., 1939), pp. 23–26, 29, 32, 41–43, 52–56, 105; Ralph M. Van Brocklin, "The Movement for the Conservation of Natural Resources in the United States before 1901" (Ph.D. thesis, University of Michigan, 1952), pp. 22–25, 27, 35–36, 47–48, 50–65, 86–108, 182–183; Eugene T. Petersen, "The History of Wild Life Conservation in Michigan, 1859–1921" (Ph.D. thesis, University of Michigan, 1952), pp. 11–133, 166–172; Pollock, *Economic Legislation in Iowa*, pp. 102–104; Sowers, "Financial History of New York State," *Columbia University Studies in History, Economics and Public Law*, LVII (1914), 366–367.

[32] Ernest H. Cherrington, *The Evolution of Prohibition in the United States of America* (Westerville, Ohio, 1920), pp. 158–269; Schlesinger, *Rise of the City*, pp. 357–358.

[33] Shaw, "The American State and the American Man," *Contemporary Review*, LI (May, 1887), 707–709; Bryce, *American Commonwealth*, III, 423; John E. Briggs, *History of Social Legislation in Iowa* (Iowa City, Iowa, 1915), pp. 134, 136–137, 141–142.

federal government was no slave to the doctrine of the negative state. The exigencies of the time and the pressure of politics compelled it to do considerably more than most proponents of laissez faire thought necessary. It promoted the interests of businessmen and farmers and also undertook the regulation of certain business activities. It initiated a national conservation policy and sought to promote the education, health, and morality of its citizens.

The federal government was most solicitous for the welfare of the businessman. Between 1866 and 1871 it granted over fifty million acres of public lands directly to railroad companies.[34] To the delight of manufacturers, it maintained a high tariff policy throughout the period. From 1865 to 1874 it granted subsidies to steamship companies carrying mail to Brazil, Hawaii, and the Far East. Contracts were terminated in 1874, but in 1891 the Ocean Mail Act revived merchant-marine mail subsidies on a somewhat reduced scale.[35]

The farmer, also, was not neglected by the federal government. The Department of Agriculture, created in 1862, functioned as a service agency for the farmer. The Homestead Act of 1862, although its effects on the settlement of the West have been grossly exaggerated, provided the agriculturist with an opportunity to acquire 160 acres of land in the public domain practically free of charge. The Morrill Act of the same year granted public lands to the states to maintain colleges which, among other things, would provide instruction in agricultural subjects. In 1890 Congress voted additional aid for agricultural education in the form of direct annual grants to the states. The Hatch Act of 1887 provided funds for state agricultural experiment stations. In 1886, in the interests of the dairy farmer, the federal government placed a heavy tax on the manufacture, sale, and importation of oleomargarine, and in 1899 a similar tax was placed on filled cheese. Having provided for the elimination of the import duty on raw sugar, the McKinley Tariff of 1890 extended a subsidy of two cents a pound to the growers of domestic sugar.[36]

[34] Lewis H. Haney, *A Congressional History of Railways in the United States* (Madison, Wisc., 1908–1910), II, 19–20.

[35] Fainsod and Gordon, *Government and the American Economy*, pp. 87–88, 94–95.

[36] Shannon, *Farmer's Last Frontier*, pp. 53–58, 270–277, 281–290; A. W. Harris, "What the Government Is Doing for the Farmer," *Century*, N.S., XXII (July, 1892), 465–472; Fainsod and Gordon, *Government and the American Economy*, pp. 110–111. For evidence of the varied activities of the Department of Agriculture on behalf of the farmer, see U. S. Department of Agriculture, *Yearbook, 1899* (Washington, D.C., 1900).

With respect to the regulation of business, the most important step taken by the federal government during this period was the enactment in 1887, after nineteen years of discussion, of the Interstate Commerce Act.[37] This measure not only provided for the regulation of certain practices of the nation's railroads but also established the first of the important regulatory commissions of the federal government. Like the railroads, the nation's merchant marine was also subjected to government regulation. Between 1874 and 1899 eighty-five statutes pertaining to navigation and the merchant marine were enacted, and in 1899 the statutes in force dealing with this subject filled 423 pages of closely printed type. Among other things, these measures provided for the registration and inspection of vessels, the regulation of passenger and freight traffic, the wages of merchant seamen, the liability of owners, masters, and shippers, and the licensing of officers, engineers, and pilots.[38] In an attempt to cope with the trust problem, Congress in 1890 enacted the Sherman Anti-Trust Act, a measure that outlawed combinations in restraint of trade between the states or with foreign nations.

Federal legislation dealing with the conditions of labor was hardly as extensive as the labor legislation of the states. An act of 1868 established eight hours as the legal day's work for persons employed by or on behalf of the federal government, but the measure was loosely drawn and poorly enforced, and it was not until 1892 that an effective federal eight-hour law was passed. In 1885 an anti-contract-labor law was adopted that proscribed the importation of immigrants under contract to work. In addition to providing for the voluntary mediation and arbitration of labor disputes involving interstate carriers, the Erdman Act of 1898 stipulated that employees of railroads operating in interstate commerce were not to be discriminated against because of union membership.[39]

[37] For the legislative history of the Interstate Commerce Act, see Haney, *Congressional History of Railways*, II, 240–312. In presenting the bill to the Senate, Senator Shelby M. Cullom declared: "I believe I am justified in saying that there is no subject of a public nature that is before the country about which there is so great unanimity of opinion as there is upon the proposition that the National Government ought in some way to regulate interstate commerce" (*Fifty Years of Public Service* [Chicago, 1911], pp. 319–320).

[38] U. S. Bureau of Navigation, *Laws of the United States Relating to Navigation and the Merchant Marine* (Washington, D.C., 1899), *passim;* Bryce, *American Commonwealth*, III, 419.

[39] John R. Commons and John B. Andrews, *Principles of Labor Legislation* (4th rev. ed., New York, 1936), pp. 117–118, 348, 433.

Although the federal government during this period placed few obstacles in the path of those engaged in exploiting the rich natural resources of the nation, it did nevertheless initiate measures designed to promote conservation. In 1872 Yellowstone became the first national park, and by the end of the century five additional national parks had been created. The United States Fish Commission was created in 1871 and was given the authority the next year to propagate food fish artificially and to distribute them. A fish-culture station was established at Woods Hole, Massachusetts, in 1883, and fish hatcheries were set up during the period in various parts of the country. Congress also provided in the 1880's for the construction of three railroad cars to transport fish to the various sections of the country for distribution. Federal legislation was devised to protect the Alaskan salmon fisheries and the shad and the herring in that part of the Potomac River within the District of Columbia; and game birds and animals within the District were also made the subject of protective federal legislation. By the Lacey Act of 1900, the federal government prohibited the interstate transmission of wild game killed in violation of state laws and regulated the import of wild animals and birds from foreign lands.[40]

Action was also initiated during this period to preserve the nation's forest resources. A forestry agency was established in the Department of Agriculture after Congress in 1876 authorized the commissioner of agriculture to arrange for a study of the nation's forest resources. This agency was reorganized in 1881 as the Division of Forestry. In 1891, in an action hailed by the great conservationist Gifford Pinchot as "the most important legislation in the history of Forestry in America" and as "the beginning and basis of our whole National Forest System," Congress empowered the president to withdraw forest lands from public entry. Under the authority of this measure, Harrison, Cleveland, and McKinley created forty-five million acres of forest reserves.[41]

Although the federal government evidenced some interest in the irrigation of the arid lands of the West, little of importance was accomplished before the turn of the century. An Irrigation Division

[40] Van Brocklin, "Conservation of Natural Resources in the United States before 1901," pp. 109–118, 222–233.

[41] Jenks Cameron, *The Development of Governmental Forest Control in the United States* (Baltimore, 1928), pp. 187–191; Van Brocklin, "Conservation of Natural Resources in the United States before 1901," pp. 34–35, 71–81; Pinchot, *Breaking New Ground* (New York, 1947), p. 85; Fainsod and Gordon, *Government and the American Economy*, pp. 737–738.

was established in the Geological Survey in 1888, and Congress appropriated funds in the 1880's for the drilling of artesian wells on the plains to determine whether these lands could be irrigated.[42]   Congress sought by the Desert Land Act of 1877 to encourage individuals to irrigate their own land and by the Carey Act of 1894 to enlist the aid of the states in this work,[43] but it was clear by the end of the century that the task of irrigation and reclamation would have to be undertaken directly by the federal government. The Republican platform of 1900 recommended the adoption of "adequate National legislation to reclaim the arid lands of the United States," [44] a proposal that was implemented by the Reclamation Act of 1902.

To promote the cause of public education, the federal government in 1867 created a Department of Education (it became the Office of Education in 1868) to serve as a national clearing house for matters pertaining to education. A forward-looking measure sponsored by Senator Blair of New Hampshire that called for the distribution of federal funds to the states in proportion to the illiteracy of their population passed the Senate three times during the 1880's only to meet defeat in the House of Representatives.[45]

In 1892 Congress evidenced its first real interest in the housing question by appropriating twenty thousand dollars for an investigation of slum conditions in cities of over two hundred thousand population.[46]   Prodded by Anthony Comstock, Congress sought to protect the morals of the people by means of a federal law of 1873 that provided penalties for the sending of obscene pictures or printed matter through the mails.[47]

The federal government in the decades after the Civil War also expanded the scope of its activities relating to the health of the nation. The surgeon general of the United States was required by a law of

[42] Van Brocklin, "Conservation of Natural Resources in the United States before 1901," pp. 198–199, 202–203.

[43] The Desert Land Act permitted land entries in the arid states of 640 acres at $1.25 an acre by persons who would irrigate their land.   The Carey Act permitted the arid states to obtain one million acres of desert land from the federal government provided that the land was irrigated and occupied within ten years.

[44] Edward Stanwood, *A History of the Presidency from 1897 to 1916* (Boston, 1916), p. 49.

[45] Schlesinger, *Rise of the City,* pp. 161, 164–165.

[46] U. S. Congress, House, *Your Congress and American Housing: The Actions of Congress on Housing from 1892 to 1951,* by Jack Levin, 82d Cong., 2d sess., H. Doc. No. 532 (Washington, D.C., 1952), p. 1.

[47] Schlesinger, *Rise of the City,* pp. 270–271.

1878 to draft appropriate rules and regulations for the quarantine treatment of vessels arriving from foreign ports. In 1882 Congress appropriated money for the establishment of a fund to aid local authorities in dealing with epidemics. In 1890 it passed a quarantine law designed to prevent the interstate transmission of certain infectious diseases, and in 1900 it authorized the Bureau of Chemistry in the Department of Agriculture to examine imported shipments of food and to exclude adulterated and misbranded products.[48] Action was also taken by the federal government to cope with the problem of diseased cattle: the Bureau of Animal Industry, established in the Department of Agriculture in 1884, was assigned the task of eradicating contagious diseases among domestic animals, and acts of 1890 and 1891 empowered the secretary of agriculture to inspect animals and meats intended for export or for interstate commerce.[49] It was but a step from the measures of the 1880's and 1890's to the enactment of the Pure Food and Drug Act of 1906 and the Meat Inspection Act of the same year.

At the turn of the century it was becoming apparent to many congressmen that the times called for the federal government to embark on an extensive program of social and economic reform. This view was evidenced in the final recommendations of the United States Industrial Commission, created by Congress in 1898 to survey the economic life of the nation.[50] After listening to testimony for four years, the commission advised the Congress to enact a comprehensive set of measures designed to promote the social and economic well-being of the nation. Although Congress did not comply with the wishes of the commission in every respect, it is nevertheless true that the commission's legislative recommendations anticipated in large measure the principal reforms of the Progressive era.

The Industrial Commission urged that agriculture "should receive as much direct benefit from legislation as any other industry." It sug-

[48] Ravenel, ed., *Half Century of Public Health,* pp. 121–123, 215–216.

[49] Shannon, *Farmer's Last Frontier,* p. 271; George F. Thompson, "Administrative Work of the Federal Government in Relation to the Animal Industry," U. S. Department of Agriculture, *Yearbook, 1899,* pp. 441–464; Harris, "What the Government Is Doing for the Farmer," *Century,* N.S., XXII (July, 1892), 469.

[50] The Commission consisted of five senators, five representatives, and nine other men appointed by the president with the consent of the Senate. It was instructed to investigate matters pertaining to immigration, labor, agriculture, manufacturing, and business and then to report to Congress and to suggest necessary legislation.

gested that the secretary of agriculture be given authority to inspect agricultural products intended for export, to halt the interstate shipment of diseased meat, and to fix standard grades for cereals. It recommended the establishment in the Department of Agriculture of a pure food and drug section with the necessary authority to prevent the interstate shipment of impure food and drugs. Congress was advised to extend the system of rural free delivery and to encourage state and local highway construction by appropriating money for the building of sample stretches of improved roads. The commission suggested that the federal government reclaim arid public lands and that the policy of setting aside forest reserves be continued.

The Industrial Commission called for the strengthening of the Interstate Commerce Commission and recommended that it be given the power, on complaint, to pass on the reasonableness of freight and passenger rates. It also urged that steps be taken to prevent the watering of railroad stock.

With respect to industrial combinations, the Industrial Commission advised the strict enforcement of the antitrust statutes, the legislative proscription of such discriminatory practices as local price-cutting, and the enactment of legislation to give publicity to the issue of securities. It called on the states to exercise strict control over public-service corporations and to assume the power either to recommend or to regulate their rates. It urged Congress to regulate and tax all corporations engaged in interstate commerce and to establish a special bureau of corporations in the Treasury Department and assign it the power to register corporations engaged in interstate or foreign commerce, to gather reports from these corporations and to examine their accounts, and to collect information regarding registered corporations and the general industrial condition of the country as a basis for future Congressional legislation.

The commission deemed both state and federal action necessary to promote the interests of labor. It recommended to the states that they enact uniform child-labor laws, make eight hours the legal working day on public works, follow the example of the Utah eight-hour law for miners, enact antisweatshop laws and antitruck laws, and establish state bureaus of labor. It was further recommended that commissioners from the various state bureaus of labor meet in annual conferences to exchange information and to recommend necessary labor legislation to Congress and the states. Congress was advised to regulate the interstate movement of private detectives for strike-breaking purposes, to check the importation of convict-made goods into any state without its consent, to draft a code of laws for railway labor, and to enact legislation to protect the union label.[51]

IV

To the person living in the present era of "big" government, the legislative accomplishments of state and nation in the years between 1865 and 1901 appear to be meager indeed. It must be remembered, however, that this was a period of transition during which government officials were confronted with a multitude of new problems occasioned by the rapid industrialization and urbanization of the country. Although public authorities had hardly played a passive role with respect to the economy in the era before the Civil War, governmental responsibility in the postwar years had to be recognized in areas where there had been little or no awareness of such responsibility previously, and new techniques of regulation and control had to be devised. In their efforts to deal with conservation, public health, the relations of capital and labor, the practices of corporations, and the special problems presented by the public-service corporation, public authorities were, therefore, more or less breaking new ground. However, their practice lagged far behind the legislative recommendations of such advocates of the general-welfare state as Richard T. Ely and Washington Gladden. The result was that when the nineteenth century drew to a close, the philosophy of the general-welfare state had still to be applied. That task, as it turned out, fell to the movements of reform of the twentieth century.

[51] U. S. Industrial Commission, *Final Report* (Vol. XIX of the Commission's *Reports;* Washington, D.C., 1902), pp. 197–200, 481–484, 649–652, 947–953, 1083–1084.

CONCLUSION: THE YEARS
SINCE 1901

XI

THE GENERAL–WELFARE STATE IN THE
TWENTIETH CENTURY

THE years between the end of the Civil War and the accession
of Theodore Roosevelt to the presidency were years of transition
and change in the United States. During this period a nation of farms
was in the process of becoming a nation of cities and factories. The
changes in social, economic, and political institutions wrought by this
development produced controversy in the world of thought as new
ideas rose to challenge established faiths. With respect to the functions of the state, the conflict of ideas took the form of a struggle between the doctrine of laissez faire and the concept of the general-welfare state. "This battle between State-interference and *laissez-faire*,"
one writer noted in 1884, "is now upon us; it will be waged through
all the near future." [1]

Though the doctrine of laissez faire was strongly held during the
years from 1865 to 1901, it was at the same time subjected to a determined attack. A variety of individuals and organizations joined
in the assault upon the negative state, but their criticism of laissez
faire stemmed from certain common considerations. To an important
extent, the opponents of laissez faire were motivated by a concern for
the ethical implications of the arguments commonly advanced in support of the doctrine of noninterference. [2] They tended to stress what

[1] John Stahl Patterson, *Reforms: Their Difficulties and Possibilities* (New York,
1884), p. 213.

[2] In Great Britain also, according to Viscount Goschen, laissez faire lost favor
"chiefly owing to moral considerations." "It has become . . . a matter of conscience with the public," declared Goschen, "that it cannot stand aside when
calamities occur; that the indirect action of other influences is too slow, or too un-
certain; that in its own action alone it can find the satisfaction of its conscientious

to them appeared to be the unethical nature of natural selection, unbridled competition, and the doctrine of self-interest and were disinclined to remain passive in the face of suffering and to trust to natural law to cure the diseases that afflicted society. As Christian individuals, they considered it their moral responsibility to attempt to reform social abuses and to improve social conditions. The ethical element in the protest against laissez faire was most conspicuous in the thought of the social gospelers, but it was also a very prominent feature of the economics of the new school of political economy, the sociology of Albion Small, Edward Ross, and John Bascom, and the reformism of Henry George, Edward Bellamy, Henry Demarest Lloyd, and Jane Addams.

The protest against laissez faire was not only ethical in character, it was also scientific: the critics of laissez faire, as Richard T. Ely declared, brought "science to the aid of Christianity." [3]   The emerging social sciences—economics, sociology, and political science—and the philosophy and psychology of William James and John Dewey all contributed to this development. The protagonists of these bodies of thought disputed the validity of the tenets of classical economics and social Darwinism and helped to undermine the theoretical foundations upon which the structure of laissez faire had been reared.

A third major causative factor in the repudiation of laissez faire by social gospelers, social scientists, and social reformers was their growing realization that the criticisms the advocates of laissez faire directed at the state were indeed applicable to a state ruled by an absolute monarch or by an oligarchy but did not obtain in a democracy. In a democratic state, the critics of laissez faire asserted, government is not something apart from the people but is merely their agent and is employed by them to accomplish such purposes as they have in view. Popular resort to state action, therefore, partakes of the nature of self-help and is not to be construed as paternalism.

Lastly, those who disapproved of laissez faire believed that although laissez faire was sufficient unto the needs of an earlier agricultural age, it was a dangerous policy to pursue in a complex industrial society. "I have long been convinced," Andrew White, for example, declared in 1893, "that, while the laissez-faire theory rendered good service by clearing the modern world of the worst in the cum-

---

scruples" ("Laissez Faire and Government Interference," in *Essays and Addresses on Economic Questions* [*1865–1893*] [London, 1905], pp. 297–298, 300).

[3] Ely declared this to be the purpose of the American Economic Association (*Social Aspects of Christianity, and Other Essays* [New York, 1889], p. 25).

brous system of the last century, it is utterly inadequate as regards the great problems now pressing upon the world." [4] Only the state, the critics of laissez faire contended, was capable of dealing with such typical problems of an industrialized, urbanized society as railroads, monopoly, substandard labor conditions, slums and tenements, and the public health.

The opponents of the negative state did not, for the most part, confine themselves to mere criticism of the premises of laissez faire. From the social philosophy of such foes of the let-alone policy as Washington Gladden, Richard T. Ely, Lester F. Ward, and Henry Demarest Lloyd, there emerged, on the constructive side, the concept of the general-welfare state, of the state that seeks to promote the general welfare not by rendering itself inconspicuous but by taking such positive action as is deemed necessary to improve the conditions under which its citizens live and work. Its proponents did not conceive of the general-welfare state in terms of certain specific functions of government, such as social security or the maintenance of full employment,[5] nor were they, generally, very much concerned whether a particular task of government was performed by the states or by the federal government. They simply assumed that government could promote the public interest by appropriate positive action and that its authority should therefore be invoked whenever the circumstances indicated that such action would further the common weal. They did not fear the state, nor did they look upon it as "a power omniscent, omnipotent and morally perfect, the intervention of which needs only to be secured to remedy every social evil." [6] Essentially, they viewed the state as servant rather than as master and were prepared, as Frank Parsons suggested, to utilize its authority not only to "restrain evil" but also to "secure good." [7]

For the most part, the advocates of the general-welfare state hoped

[4] White to Ward, March 31, 1893, Lester F. Ward Papers, John Hay Library of Brown University.

[5] Contemporary critics and analysts of the "welfare state" tend to equate that concept with social security, or a government commitment to maintain full employment, or both.   See Jules Abels, *The Welfare State* (New York, 1951), p. 20; Harry K. Girvetz, *From Wealth to Welfare: The Evolution of Liberalism* (Stanford, Calif., 1950), pp. 230–258; and Donald R. Richberg, "Liberalism, Paternalism, Security, and the Welfare State," in Sheldon Glueck, ed., *The Welfare State and the National Welfare* (Cambridge, Mass., 1952), p. 252.

[6] Gilman, *Socialism and the American Spirit* (Boston, 1893), p. 309.

[7] Parsons, "The Purposes of Government," *Industrialist,* XXIV (May, 1898), 296.

to steer a middle course between the known evils of laissez faire and the anticipated evils of socialism. They thought the philosophy of laissez faire incompatible with the needs of the age, but they were equally opposed to any solution for existing problems that would do away altogether with private property, competition, and free enterprise and that might lead to the establishment of a totalitarian state. They sought a moderate, democratic solution that would somehow reconcile the interests of the individual and the interests of society, that would preserve the essentials of the capitalist system while removing the attendant abuses. Fearful of the extremes of laissez faire and of socialism, the theorists of the general-welfare state proposed the golden mean of social reform.

Those who advocated the general-welfare state were in no way abandoning the cause of liberalism. They sought rather to convert liberalism from a negative faith into a positive one. They wholeheartedly accepted the liberal ideals of individual freedom, fair play, and equality of opportunity; but whereas liberals of an earlier age looked to the absence of state restraint as the best means of reaching these goals, the proponents of the general-welfare state believed that the industrial revolution had so altered the economic environment that liberal aims could be attained only if the aid of the state was invoked.

Although some historians have looked upon the period from the end of the Civil War to the turn of the century as a time when laissez faire ruled supreme and have attributed the decline of that doctrine to a later era,[8] there seems to be little doubt that both as a practice and as a theory laissez faire was losing ground during the last two decades of the nineteenth century. The practice of state legislatures during these years certainly did not conform to the principles of abstract individualism; and though the national government was less inclined than the state governments to deviate from the policy of laissez faire, the nation's lawmakers did extend the functions of the federal govern-

[8] Harold Underwood Faulkner, for example, maintains that it was not until the early years of the twentieth century that the people realized that laissez faire was a failure. He insists that the discontent of the eighties and nineties was "chiefly a restlessness of the city proletariat over low wages and of the farmers over declining prices" and that it involved no general protest against laissez faire and the *status quo* (*The Quest for Social Justice, 1898–1914* [New York, 1931], p. 111). Louis M. Hacker and Benjamin B. Kendrick, although recognizing the existence of earlier complaints against laissez faire, refer to the protest against laissez faire during the first fifteen years of the twentieth century as "new" (*The United States since 1865* [New York, 1939], p. 413).

ment in several important ways and, at the end of the century, appeared ready to increase further the scope of federal activity.

It was chiefly as a theory, however, that laissez faire was losing ground during the closing decades of the nineteenth century. Religious leaders in increasing numbers were abandoning the traditional individualism of Protestant theology and enlisting under the banners of the social gospel. Classical economics was discredited to a degree by the new school of political economy; and even the neoclassicists modified somewhat the laissez-faire views of their orthodox predecessors. The social Darwinism of Spencer and Sumner was strongly challenged by the arguments of William James and John Dewey and the sociology of Ward, Small, and Ross; and although the sociology of Giddings was greatly influenced by the views of Spencer, Giddings did not subscribe to Spencer's ideas with respect to laissez faire. Woodrow Wilson and W. W. Willoughby were by no means advocates of extensive state activity, but they nevertheless took issue with John Burgess and led political science away from laissez faire.

Laissez faire was also losing favor with the public at large. Farmers and organized laborers and the numerous followers of Henry George, Edward Bellamy, Henry Demarest Lloyd, and other reformers appeared unimpressed by the philosophy of the negative state and showed little inclination to entrust their fate to the laws of nature.

Informed observers in the last decade of the nineteenth century were convinced that the doctrine of laissez faire had ceased to enjoy public support and that the people were not at all reluctant to use the state to further the general interest. "It is required of the government to-day," said W. F. Willoughby in 1891, "that it shall not be content with the mere exercise of its essential functions, but that it shall take advantage of its optional powers to better the material conditions of its citizens." Nicholas Paine Gilman noted that "the doctrine that the welfare of all deserves first consideration" (which he equated with socialism) was "commending itself more and more strongly to thoughtful minds." "The laissez-faire doctrine," asserted Albion Small in 1896, "is today as fast in the limbo of political impotence as is the Queen of the Sandwich Islands." "Popular judgment," he felt, was "intoxicated with the splendid half truth that society is what men choose to make it." "The State is viewed in an entirely different light from that of a century ago," Francis Thorpe declared in the same year. "The individualism of 1776 complained of too much government; to-day it complains of too little." As he looked upon the

American scene in the final year of the century, Francis G. Peabody thought that never before had so many people been moved by the "recognition of inequality in social opportunity, by the call to social service, by dreams of a better social world." [9]

As Henry Steele Commager has pointed out, Lester Ward in the early 1880's had spoken of the drift toward increased government regulation as "an impulse without a philosophy, an instinct rather than a conviction." "By the turn of the century," Commager accurately notes, "the philosophy had been formulated, the instinct had crystallized into popular conviction, and statesmen were preparing to translate that conviction into legislation." [10]

II

Although many of the measures proposed by the forces of reform in the 1880's and 1890's were enacted into law before the close of the nineteenth century, the concept of the general-welfare state was primarily in the discussion stage in the years preceding 1901. [11] It was largely owing to the Progressive movement, the New Deal, and the Fair Deal of the twentieth century that theory was translated into practice and that the concept of the general-welfare state was embodied in legislation. As the result of these reform movements and of the impact on the American economy of two world wars, the scope of government activity in twentieth-century America has been enlarged tremendously. Whereas government held 7 per cent of the nation's capital assets in 1900, it held 20 per cent of such assets in 1950. Twelve per cent of the nation's labor force was employed by government in 1950 as compared to 4 per cent in 1900. Government in 1950 added

[9] Willoughby, "State Activities and Politics," *Papers of the American Historical Association,* V (January, April, 1891), 118; Gilman, *Socialism and the American Spirit,* pp. 16–18, 99; Small, "The State and Semi-Public Corporations," *American Journal of Sociology,* I (January, 1896), 407; Small, "The Era of Sociology," *ibid.,* I (July, 1895), 3; Thorpe, "The Dominant Idea of American Democracy," *Harper's Monthly Magazine,* XCIII (November, 1896), 841; Peabody, *Jesus Christ and the Social Question* (New York, 1900), p. 3.

[10] Commager, *The American Mind: An Interpretation of American Thought and Character since the 1880's* (New Haven, 1950), p. 217.

[11] "Every idea I hear mooted now," Vida Scudder declared in 1936, "all revulsions from Civilization As Is, and pretty much all schemes of social betterment . . . were discussed—I had almost said *ad nauseam*—fifty years ago." But, noted Miss Scudder, "schemes have crept nearer; they have changed from dreams to programs. . . . Proposed reforms have entered practical politics to a degree unimagined in the last century" (*On Journey* [New York, 1937], pp. 169–170).

twelve billion dollars, or 6 per cent, to the income of individuals through transfer payments and subtracted eighteen billion dollars, or 9 per cent, from such income in the form of the income tax; in 1900, transfer payments amounted to less than 1 per cent of the total income, and there was no income tax. The federal government spent five million dollars for social welfare, health, and security in 1900 and almost two billion dollars for the same purposes in 1949. Expenditures for labor during the same period increased from two hundred thousand dollars to $193,000,000; expenditures for agriculture, from three million dollars to $2,512,000,000; and expenditures for natural resources, from nine million dollars to $1,512,000,000.[12]

The reform movements of the twentieth century were in many ways related to and affected by the men and ideas associated with the development of the concept of the general-welfare state in the late nineteenth century. Richard T. Ely, John R. Commons, and Edward A. Ross aided Robert La Follette in introducing Progressivism in Wisconsin,[13] and Ely, as has already been noted, exerted an important influence on the Progressive movement and a lesser influence on the New Deal. The concepts of Henry Carter Adams are evident in much of the factory legislation of the twentieth century and in the attempts of the Federal Trade Commission to raise the ethical level of competition; and the New Freedom of Woodrow Wilson afforded legislative recognition to John Bates Clark's concept of regulated competition. The ideas of Simon Nelson Patten, as previously indicated, found expression in the writings of Walter Weyl, a student of Patten's and an important theorist of Progressivism, and in the writings and activities of Rexford Guy Tugwell, another Patten student and one of the members of Franklin D. Roosevelt's original "brain trust." Patten, moreover, would doubtless have acclaimed the actions of the New Deal that aimed at the planned use of the land.

Lester Ward and W. Godwin Moody would surely have applauded the Employment Act of 1946 and the role that it assigned to the Council of Economic Advisers, and Jacob S. Coxey and many other reformers of the late nineteenth century would have regarded the work-relief and public-works programs of the New Deal as in accord with policies they had recommended at a much earlier date. The

[12] Solomon Fabricant, *The Trend of Government Activity since 1900* (New York, 1953), pp. 9, 242–243.

[13] Charles McCarthy, *The Wisconsin Idea* (New York, 1912), pp. 27–29, 316–317.

social-security program of the New Deal and the Fair Deal represented a partial fulfillment of the proposals of Bellamy and the Nationalists, and certainly J. Allen Smith, E. Benjamin Andrews, Frank Parsons, Thomas E. Will, and John R. Commons may be regarded as early advocates of the idea of the commodity dollar that was briefly espoused by Franklin D. Roosevelt and the New Deal.

Those who in the last decades of the nineteenth century proposed that the trusts be smashed and those who proposed that the trusts be regulated would have found exponents of their points of view among the reformers of the twentieth century, and members of the new school of political economy would have been gratified to learn that it was generally recognized in the twentieth century that natural monopolies must be either publicly owned or strictly regulated. Many of the proposals of the Populists and of the various Socialist parties of the 1890's have been enacted into law, and Populists would have recognized in the crop loans of the Commodity Credit Corporation something very akin to their much-maligned subtreasury scheme.

Although the Progressive movement, the New Deal, and the Fair Deal differed in several essential respects, as reform movements they had many characteristics in common. Progressives, New Dealers, and Fair Dealers, like most reformers of the late nineteenth century, were essentially pragmatic in their approach to the use of state power and were inclined to decide whether or not to invoke the aid of the state in coping with any particular problem on the merits of the case rather than in accordance with some preconceived plan or idea. John Dewey's view that ideas would enable men to reach their goals when these ideas led to the creation of an environment that would be favorable to the attainment of the goals epitomized the liberal philosophy of the Progressive era,[14] and Dewey's pragmatism, however crudely it was expressed, was only slightly less influential during the period of the New Deal and the Fair Deal. Franklin D. Roosevelt nicely summarized the approach of the reformers of the 1930's, in particular, when he declared in a speech at Oglethorpe University on May 22, 1932: "The country needs and, unless I mistake its temper, the country demands bold, persistent experimentation. It is common sense to take

[14] Eric F. Goldman, *Rendezvous with Destiny* (New York, 1952), pp. 158–159. "A re-reading of the books and speeches of the Progressive Era makes clear the influence of pragmatism upon the thinking of those who proudly attached to themselves the designation, liberal" (Ralph Henry Gabriel, *The Course of American Democratic Thought: An Intellectual History since 1815* [New York, 1940], p. 336).

a method and try it. If it fails, admit it frankly and try another. But above all, try something."[15]

A concern for ethics and for the social implications of Christianity, which constituted so important a part of the protest against laissez faire and of the reform movements of the late nineteenth century, was also a vital ingredient of twentieth-century reform. As has already been noted, the social gospel exerted a significant influence on the leaders and the rank and file of Progressivism and was, in a sense, the religion of the Progressive movement. The social gospel attained maturity during the Progressive era with the establishment of social-service commissions and agencies by the large Protestant denominations and with the formation in 1908 of the Federal Council of the Churches of Christ. The latter organization, representing thirty Protestant denominations, was not only a product of the social-gospel movement but became, in effect, the institutional embodiment of the social-gospel point of view in American Protestantism. Significantly, the social creed that it adopted in 1908 and amended in 1912 was in perfect accord with the legislative objectives of Progressivism.[16]

Individual New Dealers of importance were also influenced by the teachings of social Christianity. As a student at Grinnell College, Harry Hopkins had been particularly impressed by Edward A. Steiner's course in Applied Christianity.[17] When asked by a reporter to state his philosophy, Franklin D. Roosevelt responded, "I am a Christian and a Democrat—that's all."[18] As Ralph H. Gabriel has noted, Henry Wallace, like Richard T. Ely, was "a lay prophet of the social gospel." Wallace, during the New Deal era, spoke of religion as "the most practical thing in the world" and doubted that the reforms of the New Deal would prove successful unless they were "inspired by men who in their hearts catch a larger vision than the hard driving profit-motives of the past." "The time is ripe right here in the United States today," Wallace declared in 1938, "for a practical yet religious acceptance of the doctrine of the general welfare."[19]

[15] Samuel I. Rosenman, comp., *The Public Papers and Addresses of Franklin D. Roosevelt* (New York, 1938–1950), I, 646.

[16] Charles Howard Hopkins, *The Rise of the Social Gospel in American Protestantism, 1865–1915* (New Haven, 1940), pp. 280–317.

[17] Robert E. Sherwood, *Roosevelt and Hopkins* (Bantam Books; rev. and enlarged ed.; New York, 1950), I, 22.

[18] Cited in Frances Perkins, *The Roosevelt I Knew* (New York, 1946), p. 330.

[19] See Gabriel, *Course of American Democratic Thought,* p. 306; and Wallace, *Democracy Reborn,* ed. Russell Lord (New York, 1944), pp. 72–74, 144.

Like most of the advocates of the general-welfare state of the late nineteenth century, Progressives, New Dealers, and Fair Dealers rejected both laissez faire and socialism and sought to strengthen the free-enterprise system by introducing essential reforms and by equalizing opportunity. "It is difficult to say more," Edward R. Lewis has noted, "than that the progressive movement was a program for a newer individualism, a mean between socialism and laissez faire, an attempt to make an adjustment of the forces then impinging on our national life." [20]   Theodore Roosevelt, as he so often said, believed neither in unrestricted individualism nor in socialism, and he espoused social reform as "a corrective to Socialism and an antidote to anarchy." "A blind and ignorant resistance to every effort for the reform of abuses and for a readjustment of society to modern industrial conditions," he informed Congress, "represents not true conservatism, but an incitement to the wildest radicalism; for wise radicalism and wise conservatism go hand in hand, one bent on progress, the other bent on seeing that no change is made unless in the right direction." [21] Wilson, like Roosevelt, insisted that he was a progressive because "to be progressive was to preserve the essentials of our institutions." "If you want to oust socialism," Wilson wrote in 1912, "you have got to propose something better. . . . You cannot oppose hopeful programs by negations." [22]

The New Deal and the Fair Deal resulted in much more extensive government intervention in the economic sphere than had occurred during the Progressive era, but New Dealers and Fair Dealers regarded their reforms as designed to strengthen rather than to destroy capitalism. The New Deal, Robert Sherwood has declared, "was, in fact, as Roosevelt conceived it and conducted it, a revolution of the Right, rising up to fight its own defense." Referring to the many reforms of the New Deal, President Roosevelt declared in 1937: "Action

[20] Lewis, *History of American Political Thought from the Civil War to the World War* (New York, 1937), p. 364.

[21] Hermann Hagedorn, ed., *The Works of Theodore Roosevelt* (Memorial ed.; New York, 1923–1926), XVII, 428–429, 586–587; XIX, 371. See also Henry F. Pringle, *Theodore Roosevelt* (New York, 1931), pp. 413, 427, *et passim;* and Richard Hofstadter, *The American Political Tradition and the Men Who Made It* (New York, 1948), pp. 203–233.

[22] See Wilson, *The New Freedom* (New York, 1913), p. 44; Joseph Dorfman, *The Economic Mind in American Civilization, 1606–1918* (New York, 1946–1949), III, 338; Ray Stannard Baker, *Woodrow Wilson, Life and Letters* (Garden City, N. Y., 1927–1939), IV, 376.

was necessary to remove the sore spots which had crept into our economic system, if we were to keep the system of private property for the future. To preserve we had to reform." [23] Although the Fair Deal was criticized by its opponents as "creeping socialism," Harry Truman argued that one of the principal purposes of the Fair Deal was to "improve the environment in which private enterprise works." [24]

The reformers of the twentieth century believed as did the theorists of the general-welfare state of the late nineteenth century that the ends of liberalism could be attained in a complex industrial society only by positive state action. In one of his 1912 campaign speeches, Woodrow Wilson, for example, declared: "I feel confident that if Jefferson were living in our day he would see what we see: that the individual is caught in a great confused nexus of all sorts of complicated circumstances, and that to let him alone is to leave him helpless as against the obstacles with which he has to contend; and that, therefore, law in our day must come to the assistance of the individual. . . . Freedom to-day is something more than being let alone. The program of a government of freedom must in these days be positive, not negative merely." [25] In similar vein, Franklin D. Roosevelt proclaimed at a later time that "the liberal party insists that Government has the definite duty to use all its powers and resources to meet new social problems with new social controls—to insure to the average person the right to his own economic and political life, liberty, and the pursuit of happiness." [26]

III

Although as it manifested itself in the states of the Midwest, Progressivism was largely in the tradition of the Grange and the Populists and owed much of its strength to agrarian elements, the national Progressive movement in its leadership and in its most characteristic support was an urban, middle-class phenomenon. Middle-class citizens were alarmed at the concentration of wealth at the top of the economic pyramid and tended to believe that the giant corpora-

[23] See Sherwood, *Roosevelt and Hopkins,* I, 90; and *Public Papers and Addresses of Franklin D. Roosevelt,* II, 3.

[24] *New York Times,* January 15, 1953 (text of Truman's Seventh Annual Economic Report to Congress).

[25] Wilson, *New Freedom,* p. 284.

[26] *Public Papers and Addresses of Franklin D. Roosevelt,* VII, xxix. See also Roosevelt's redefinition of the rights of man as expressed in the Declaration of Independence, *ibid.,* I, 753–755.

tions were not only limiting the opportunity of the small businessman to get ahead but that they were creatures of special privilege that corrupted public officials and had altogether too much political influence. Just as it feared the power of the trusts at the top, so the middle class was also alarmed at the threat to its position from below posed by the increasing influence of socialism and, to some extent, by the growing strength of organized labor. In order to curb the power of big business and to equalize opportunity and, at the same time, to stave off the threat of socialism and to drain discontent into more moderate channels, the middle class was prepared to enlist the aid of the state and to embark upon a program of social and economic reform.[27]

The legislation resulting from the impulse of Progressivism was more than anything else regulatory in its character and was designed, as Charles McCarthy said of the legislation that implemented the Wisconsin Idea, to equalize the position of the strong and the weak by "a powerful state intervention." [28] Thus city governments during the Progressive era assumed the ownership of municipal public utilities or subjected them to strict regulation; state governments strengthened their control over railroads and brought public utilities under state supervision; and the federal government increased the power of the Interstate Commerce Commission over railroads, strengthened federal control over the banking system, and sought by means of new legislation to arrest the development of trusts. The state governments, in particular, added extensively to the existing body of labor laws by enacting measures that placed additional restrictions on the use of child labor, limited the hours of female labor and of adult male labor in certain occupations, and, beginning with Massachusetts in 1912, established minimum wages for female labor. The federal government limited somewhat the use of injunctions in labor disputes by the Clayton Act, improved the working conditions of merchant seamen by the La Follette Seamen's Act, and established a basic eight-hour day for the employees of interstate railroads by the Adamson Act. It provided for the inspection of meat destined for interstate commerce and sought to protect consumers against impure food and

[27] Russel B. Nye, *Midwestern Progressive Politics* (East Lansing, Mich., 1951), pp. 237–239, 276–277; Goldman, *Rendezvous with Destiny*, pp. 74–77; George E. Mowry, *The California Progressives* (Berkeley, Calif., 1951), pp. 86–104; William Diamond, *The Economic Thought of Woodrow Wilson* (Baltimore, 1943), pp. 63–64.

[28] McCarthy, *Wisconsin Idea*, p. 46.

drugs and, in the interests of the farmer, regulated the sale of cotton for future delivery and established grades and standards in the marketing of grains. Important progress was also made by state and city governments during the Progressive era with respect to the problem of slum housing.

In addition to providing legislation of an essentially regulatory nature, the Progressives increased the services that government rendered to the people. Most cities not only drew up milk codes but also established milk depots that sold milk at cost or provided it free of charge to needy persons. City governments established public playgrounds, baby clinics, and day nurseries and provided free medical and dental examinations for school children and free meals for impecunious school children. Legislation of the federal government and the state governments evidenced an increasing interest on the part of public authorities in the conservation and wise use of natural resources, and by the Reclamation Act of 1902 the federal government initiated a vast program designed to irrigate and reclaim the arid lands of the West. The federal government enlarged the services of the post office to include postal savings and parcel post, extended aid to the states for the construction of highways, subsidized agricultural extension work and the teaching of agricultural and vocational subjects in the high schools, and provided for the extension to farmers of short-term and long-term credit and for the issuance to farmers of warehouse receipts that could be used as collateral for loans.

Important beginnings were made during the Progressive era in the field of social security. By 1917 forty states and territories had enacted workmen's compensation laws, thus, in effect, shifting the burden of industrial accidents from the injured employee to society. Arizona in 1914 enacted the first state old-age pension law, but the measure was declared unconstitutional by the state supreme court two years later. Illinois and Missouri in 1911 instituted the program of "mothers' aid" by providing pensions for mothers with dependent children.[29]

To a certain extent at least, Progressive reform had as its objective the restoration of conditions that had existed before the development

[29] The reform legislation of the Progressive era can be traced in Harold Underwood Faulkner, *The Decline of Laissez Faire, 1897–1917* (New York, 1951), *passim;* Faulkner, *Quest for Social Justice, passim;* and U. S. Federal Security Agency, Social Security Administration, *Social Security in the United States* (new ed.; Washington, D.C., 1952), pp. 45–46.

of large-scale industry and the combination movement. Many Progressives, as John Chamberlain has indicated, thought of reform in terms of "return" and looked to government intervention to revive the economic individualism and free competition that, they believed, had prevailed in the simpler economy of bygone days.[30] Having restored competition and provided equality of opportunity for all, the government, Progressives of this view believed, should serve as an umpire to ensure that the competitive game was cleanly played and that those who violated the rules of fair play were punished.

Something of this nostalgic quality was present in Woodrow Wilson's New Freedom, which, as William Diamond has written, was designed "to restore the American economy to a Golden Age of competitive capitalism: an age in which every man had been his own employer or could hope to become one, an age in which the small business class had been free from the pressure of monopoly."[31] Wilson believed that the success of the American scheme depended on the opportunity of the little fellow to rise in the economic scale and upon the ability of the small businessman to hold his own against large aggregations of wealth. He was confident that as long as competition remained free and unfettered, the chance to get ahead would be present to all men, and each would prosper according to his abilities.

As Wilson saw it, however, the fact of the matter was that free competition did not prevail in the economy. The tariff afforded special privileges to the protected industries and was a boon to monopoly; the concentration of the sources of credit in the hands of the few, revealed in the report of the Pujo committee, made it difficult for the small businessman to obtain the capital funds that he needed; and, above all, the trusts limited the opportunity of the little fellow to get ahead.[32] In these circumstances, Wilson argued, it was necessary for government to step in and to make sure that competition remained free and fair and that "all forms of unjust handicaps against the little man" were eliminated. Like John Bates Clark, Wilson proposed regulated competition as the proper solution for the nation's economic

[30] Chamberlain, *Farewell to Reform. The Rise, Life and Decay of the Progressive Mind in America* (2d ed.; New York, 1933), pp. 310–311; Nelson Manfred Blake, *A Short History of American Life* (New York, 1952), pp. 556–557.

[31] Diamond, *Economic Thought of Woodrow Wilson*, p. 125.

[32] Wilson insisted that he was not opposed to big business, which had forged ahead as a result of its superior efficiency, but that he was opposed to the trusts, which in his view had attained their power only because they had employed unfair methods of competition (*New Freedom*, p. 180).

problems. The life of the nation, he declared, must "be sustained, or at least supplemented" by government action. The government must "set the stage . . . for the doing of justice to men in every relationship of life." It was its task "to equalize conditions, to make the path of right the path of safety and advantage, to see that every man has a fair chance to live and to serve himself, to see that injustice and wrong are not wrought upon any." "All the fair competition you choose," Wilson declared, "but no unfair competition of any kind." [33]

Wilson was unusually successful in securing the legislation he thought necessary to implement the philosophy of the New Freedom. The Underwood Tariff struck at the special advantages that high tariff rates afforded to the protected industries. The Federal Reserve Act sought to break up the "money trust" and to provide the nation with a more elastic currency. The Clayton Act proscribed certain unfair methods of competition that were deemed promotive of monopoly, and the Federal Trade Commission Act gave to the Federal Trade Commission the power to issue cease-and-desist orders against unfair methods of competition in interstate commerce, with the expectation that the Commission would not only be able to maintain a more competitive economic structure but that it would also be able to raise the ethical level of competition. In addition to these measures, which constituted the heart of the New Freedom, the Wilson administrations secured the legislation for the laborer and the farmer already noted.

Not all Progressivism, however, had the "return" quality that characterized the New Freedom of Woodrow Wilson. Many of the Progressives who stood with Theodore Roosevelt at Armageddon in 1912 and battled for the Lord subscribed to Roosevelt's view that the concentration of wealth was natural and inevitable and that it was the task of government, not to seek by its intervention to recapture an earlier age of small business units and untrammeled competition, but rather to accept "bigness" and to attempt to control it in the national interest. This was a view that Roosevelt proclaimed in his first annual message to Congress in December, 1901, and one that he was to reiterate with varying degrees of consistency throughout the remainder of his career.

As president, Roosevelt, despite his reputation as a "trust-buster" and his seeming willingness to use the Sherman Anti-Trust Act against

[33] See Wilson, *New Freedom*, pp. 14–17, 19–20, 163–191, 217–219, 222, 262, 284, 292, 294; and Diamond, *Economic Thought of Woodrow Wilson*, pp. 87–130.

certain "bad" trusts, made it abundantly clear that he regarded combination and concentration as both natural and inevitable and as potentially of benefit to society, but that he felt it was necessary to subject all corporations operating in interstate commerce to national regulation to ensure that they actually served the common weal. He insisted again and again that he was against misconduct but not against wealth and that legislation should seek to combat only the former. Roosevelt was never altogether clear as to the methods that might be employed by the federal government to guarantee that the large corporations served the public interest, but at various times during his presidential years he suggested, as means to this end, federal control over the capitalization of interstate corporations, full publicity for corporate practices, a national license law, federal incorporation, and prohibition of methods leading to improper combination. "We hold," said Roosevelt, "that the government should not conduct the business of the nation, but that it should exercise such supervision as will insure its being conducted in the interest of the nation." [34]

Roosevelt's views on reform and the role of government in relationship to the general welfare broadened and deepened after he left the presidency, partly as the result of the influence on his thinking of Herbert Croly's *Promise of American Life*.[35] The former president proclaimed his acceptance of Croly's doctrine of the New Nationalism in his famous speech at Osawatomie on August 31, 1910, and it was on a platform that embodied his version of the New Nationalism and, to be sure, of the general-welfare state that Roosevelt ran for the presidency in 1912 as the candidate of the Progressive party.

Progressives, Roosevelt the New Nationalist announced, sought "to use the government as an efficient agency for the practical betterment of social and economic conditions throughout this land": they advocated an extension rather than a limitation of governmental power. At one time, he asserted, the limitation of the authority of government had meant "increasing liberty for the people." It had now come to mean "enslavement of the people by the great corporations who can only be held in check through the extension of governmental power." "We propose," Roosevelt proclaimed, "to use the

[34] *Works of Theodore Roosevelt*, XVII, 100–107, 164–166, 199–200, 315–320, 427–430, 493–495, 577–586; XVIII, 78–79, 95–96.

[35] Pringle, *Roosevelt*, pp. 540–541; Goldman, *Rendezvous with Destiny*, pp. 204–205, 207.

government as the most efficient instrument for the uplift of our people as a whole. We propose to give a fair chance to the workers and to strengthen their rights. We propose to use the whole power of the government to protect all those who, under Mr. Wilson's *laissez-faire* system [a reference to a statement by Wilson that the history of liberty was a history of the limitation rather than of the increase of governmental power] are trodden down in the ferocious scrambling of an unregulated and purely individualistic industrialism."

The square deal to which he was committed did not, Roosevelt declared, mean simply fair play under the existing rules of the game but such changes in the rules as were essential to produce greater equality of opportunity. He insisted that the conditions must be altered that enabled individuals to hold and to exercise power in a manner that injured the general welfare. The powers of production bequeathed by the nineteenth century to the twentieth should, he declared, "be made to administer to the needs of the many rather than be exploited for the profits of the few." "The man who wrongly holds that every human right is secondary to his profit," Roosevelt boldly proclaimed, "must now give way to the advocate of human welfare, who rightly maintains that every man holds his property subject to the general right of the community to regulate its use to whatever degree the public welfare may require it." He advised the delegates to the Ohio Constitutional Convention of 1912 to see to it in their work that no restriction was placed on the power of the legislature to enact laws "under which your people can promote the general welfare, the common good." [36]

Roosevelt the New Nationalist continued to argue as had Roosevelt the president that it was impossible to restore the competitive conditions of the nineteenth century, that the nation must accept the fact that the great combinations were here to stay, and that it was the task of the federal government to control them in the public interest. "The way out," he said in his Osawatomie speech, "lies, not in attempting to prevent such combinations, but in completely controlling them in the interest of the public welfare." Although the Sherman Act, Roosevelt argued, could be employed against monopolies or against businesses guilty of antisocial practices, to rely on it alone to deal

[36] See *Works of Theodore Roosevelt*, XIX, 169, 176–177, 361, 409, 420–429; and Roosevelt, *The New Nationalism* (New York, 1910), pp. 11–13, 17–18, 23–24, 27–28, 54, 126.

with the problem of bigness constituted "Toryism and reaction." He recommended the establishment of a "national industrial commission" to control the great corporations in approximately the same manner as the Interstate Commerce Commission controlled the railroads. Such a commission could compel publicity for the acts of corporations that it supervised, ensure honest capitalization, and check unwarranted price boosts, restrictions on production, and any other unfair practices. The federal government, Roosevelt asserted, should seek to preserve competition wherever it is practicable to do so, but where competition has been eliminated and cannot be restored, "the government must step in and itself supply the needed control on behalf of the people as a whole." [37]

The public interest, Roosevelt insisted, required not only the regulation of the uses of wealth but also of the terms and conditions of labor. He suggested the establishment of "minimum occupational standards" below which work should not be performed. To this end, he advised that employers be required to file with public authorities such data with respect to working conditions as the public interest decreed. He recommended the establishment of minimum-wage commissions by the state governments and the federal government to determine the wage standards that the public should sanction as the minimum, and he urged that minimum-wage laws for female workers should immediately be enacted by the states and the federal government. The federal government, he thought, should investigate industries with a view to establishing standards of safety and sanitation, and he advised that mine and factory inspection be standardized by an interstate agreement or by the enactment of a federal statute.

Roosevelt favored the prohibition of manufacturing in tenements and the regulation of sanitation in temporary construction camps. He thought that standards of compensation for industrial accidents, disease, and death should be established by federal and state legislation, and he wished to see further restrictions placed on the employment of women and children. Anticipating the New Deal, he recommended that the hazards of sickness, accidents, invalidism, unemployment, and old age should be met by insurance, the costs to be borne by employer and employee and, perhaps, also by the public. The Progressives, Roosevelt said, supported the idea of the "living wage," which meant a wage sufficient to promote morality and to enable the worker to

[37] See Roosevelt, *New Nationalism*, pp. 14–16; and *Works of Theodore Roosevelt,* XIX, 170–176, 379–392.

provide for education and recreation, to care for his children, and to save against sickness and old age.[38]

The Progressive platform of 1912 accepted the Roosevelt program of reform *in toto* and announced the new party's approval of the doctrine of the general-welfare state. The platform proclaimed that the resources, business, institutions, and laws of the country should be "utilized, maintained, or altered in whatever manner will best promote the general interest. It is time to set the public welfare in the first place." The Progressive party offered itself "as the instrument of the people to sweep away old abuses, to build a new and nobler commonwealth." It promised to bring under "effective national jurisdiction" the problems that had "expanded beyond the reach of the individual states." It endorsed Roosevelt's view of the need to devise "minimum safety and health standards for the various occupations," prohibit child labor, establish minimum-wage standards for female laborers, provide for a living wage, prohibit night work for women, institute an eight-hour day for female and juvenile workers, provide for one day of rest in seven for all wage workers, establish the eight-hour day in industries in continuous twenty-four-hour operation, abolish the convict contract-labor system, secure publicity in regard to wages, hours, and conditions of labor, and establish a Department of Labor of cabinet rank.

The party promised to spur the development of agricultural credit and coöperation, to promote agricultural education, and to unite in a single department the various agencies of the federal government dealing with public health. It pledged itself to secure for the Interstate Commerce Commission the power "to value the physical property of railroads." The platform insisted that the control of the currency should be in the hands of the federal government rather than of private banking agencies. It expressed the view that the federal government should coöperate with private business to expand the nation's foreign trade.

The principle of the conservation of natural resources was strongly endorsed, and the party promised to protect the national forests, to retain for the federal government the withdrawn mineral lands and waterpower sites and to open them for use under laws that would encourage their development and yield the people some return, and to enact legislation providing for the lease of the public grazing lands.

[38] Roosevelt, *New Nationalism*, pp. 24–25, 128–129; *Works of Theodore Roosevelt*, XIX, 177, 371–376.

The Progressives announced their intention to aid in the extension of good roads and to support the construction of national highways. Anticipating the Tennessee Valley Authority and similar projects, the platform declared it to be "a national obligation to develop our rivers, and especially the Mississippi and its tributaries, without delay, under a comprehensive general plan covering each river system from its source to its mouth, designed to secure its highest usefulness for navigation, irrigation, domestic supply, water-power, and the prevention of floods." The Progressives also promised appropriate legislation to provide government supervision over security issues, with a view to protecting the public against false information disseminated by issuing concerns.

With regard to the vital trust question, the Progressive platform endorsed the Roosevelt position and demanded "strong national regulation of interstate corporations." It urged the establishment of a "strong, federal administrative commission" with the power to secure publicity for corporate transactions that were of public interest, to attack unfair competition, false capitalization, and special privilege, and "to keep open, equally to all, the highways of American commerce." [39]

Although Roosevelt in the election of 1912 made a remarkable showing for a third-party candidate, the New Freedom rather than the New Nationalism emerged the victor. The Bull Moose party was scuttled in 1916, and Roosevelt returned to the Republican fold; but the death of the party did not mean the demise of the policies for which it had fought. Some of the party's proposals were enacted into law by the Wilson administration, and many more were later put into effect by the New Deal. It is not at all surprising that Bull Moosers such as Harold Ickes, Edward P. Costigan, and Bronson Cutting should also be found among the supporters of the New Deal. [40]

Legislative endorsement of Woodrow Wilson's program of reform marked the end of the Progressive movement in the sphere of national politics. The cause of social reform was pushed into the background after 1917 as the nation devoted its energies first to the prosecution of war and then to the enjoyment of "normalcy." When normalcy gave way to depression, however, a new administration was summoned to

[39] Edward Stanwood, A History of the Presidency from 1897 to 1916 (Boston, 1916), pp. 288–295.

[40] George E. Mowry, Theodore Roosevelt and the Progressive Movement (Madison, Wisc., 1946), pp. 145–146, 381.

Washington that promised to give the people a "new deal" and to use all the resources of the government to revive the faltering economy.

In some aspects of its thought and in many of its objectives the New Deal was related to earlier movements of reform in the United States, and particularly to the Progressive movement. "The word 'Deal,' " Roosevelt commented in 1937, "implied that the Government itself was going to use affirmative action to bring about its avowed objectives rather than stand by and hope that general economic laws alone would attain them. The word 'New,' " as Roosevelt defined it, "implied that a new order of things designed to benefit the great mass of our farmers, workers and business men would replace the old order of privilege in a Nation which was completely and thoroughly disgusted with the existing dispensation." [41] Inconsistent in many respects, the New Deal was consistent in its view that government should help the people "to gain a larger social justice." It believed, as Frances Perkins has said, that "all the political and practical forces of the community should and could be directed to making life better for ordinary people." [42]

The New Deal resulted in a considerable extension of the regulatory functions of the federal government.[43] The federal government not only strengthened its controls over banks and railroads, but it enlarged the scope of its regulatory authority to include securities issues and the securities exchanges, public-utility holding companies, motor carriers, and agricultural and industrial production. It forbade employers to interfere with their employees' right to organize and to designate representatives for collective bargaining, and it established standards with respect to minimum wages, maximum hours, and child labor that had to be observed by most concerns engaged in interstate commerce and by concerns working on government contracts.

More than the Progressives, the New Dealers emphasized the services that a benevolent government could render to its citizens. The result was that the federal government during the New Deal period provided relief and jobs for the needy and the unemployed, constructed

[41] *Public Papers and Addresses of Franklin D. Roosevelt*, II, 5.

[42] See *Public Papers and Addresses of Franklin D. Roosevelt*, I, xiii; and Perkins, *The Roosevelt I Knew*, p. 167. For an analysis of the New Deal's views as regards the role of government, see Thomas Paul Jenkin, "Reactions of Major Groups to Positive Government in the United States, 1930–1940," *University of California Publications in Political Science*, I (1945), 251–297.

[43] For the legislation of the New Deal, see Broadus Mitchell, *Depression Decade: From New Era through New Deal, 1929–1941* (New York, 1947), *passim*.

dwellings for low-income families, supplied certain areas with cheap electric power, brought electricity to the farm through the Rural Electrification Administration, furnished a variety of services to marginal and tenant farmers through the Resettlement Administration and the Farm Security Administration, extended loans to banks, railroads, insurance companies, mortgage companies, industrial concerns, farmers, homeowners, and states and municipalities, and greatly expanded the whole program of conservation of natural resources.

Building to a certain extent on the experience of the Hoover administration, the New Deal assigned to the federal government the full responsibility for coping with the problems of the depression and for spurring the forces of recovery. The federal government provided direct and work relief for the unemployed and instituted a large-scale program of public works. It tinkered with the nation's currency in an effort to raise prices and came to the aid of various types of debtors. It initiated programs with respect to industry, agriculture, and transportation that were designed to restore prosperity to those sectors of the economy and sought by its various reform measures to remedy the conditions that had led the nation to economic disaster.

Prodded by such persons as Marriner S. Eccles, special assistant for a time to Secretary of the Treasury Morgenthau and eventually chairman of the Board of Governors of the Federal Reserve System, the New Deal in its battle with the depression moved toward an acceptance of the idea that the government should pursue a compensatory fiscal policy to ensure the successful functioning of the economy. In time of depression and depressed national income, unemployment, and insufficient production, deficit financing by the government, according to Eccles, was necessary to put idle men, money, and machines to work. Money had to be placed in the hands of persons who would spend it and thus stimulate production and employment. Relief payments and social-security payments were justified since, in addition to other reasons that made them necessary, they increased mass purchasing power and hence served to spur the economy. Similarly, government expenditures for public works and public housing were warranted in that not only did such expenditures provide employment directly but they also served to encourage the entire construction industry.

Tax policy was also related to this general program insofar as taxation served to compel those with idle funds to put their money to work or brought such funds into the federal treasury to be redistributed by means of government expenditures to persons who would spend. New Dealers also believed that the government could stimulate private sectors of the economy to borrow, produce, and employ by maintaining low interest rates and by the activities of such organizations as the Federal Housing Administration, which extended government guarantees to banks so as to induce them to loan money for the construction and repair of homes.

Eccles regarded deficit spending as a temporary policy designed in periods of deflation and depression to compensate for the relative inactivity of private sectors of the economy. For boom times, he favored a government compensatory fiscal policy that involved a balanced budget or surplus financing and the use of fiscal powers to restrain spending by private sectors of the economy. He did not subscribe to the thesis of the mature economy and to the view that private enterprise would never again be able to generate sufficient investment to maintain full employment and that therefore a permanent policy of large-scale government spending and deficits was necessary. He simply wanted the government to serve as a balance wheel, compensating for the lack of private economic activity in time of depression and curbing inflation in boom times.[44]

Roosevelt was reluctant to accept Eccles' views with respect to deficit financing and did not endorse the thesis until after the recession of 1937–1938. In his message to Congress of April 14, 1938, the president justified deficit spending as a temporary policy "to supplement the normal processes" and "to drive the economic system at higher speed." [45]

Whereas the nation in the era before 1933 had looked to competition to maintain balance in the economy, the Roosevelt administration, particularly during the period of the first New Deal (1933–1935), accepted the view that it was the task of government to coöperate with private sectors of the economy in maintaining a balanced economy. "Our task now," Roosevelt declared in his famous Commonwealth

[44] Eccles, *Beckoning Frontiers: Public and Personal Recollections* (New York, 1951), pp. 37–38, 71–87, 104–113, 130–132, 148–152, 183–187, 254–265, 294–323, 393–397. Eccles states that the ideas which he expressed, frequently attributed to Lord Keynes, "were not abstracted from his [Keynes's] books, which I have never read. My conceptions were based on naked-eye observation and experience . . . ." (*ibid.*, pp. 131–132).

[45] See Eccles, *Beckoning Frontiers*, pp. 96–99, 117–118, 311; and *Public Papers and Addresses of Franklin D. Roosevelt*, VII, 221–233.

Club address during the 1932 campaign, "is not discovery or exploitation of natural resources, or necessarily producing more goods. It is the soberer, less dramatic business of administering resources and plants already in hand, of seeking to reestablish foreign markets for our surplus production, of meeting the problem of underconsumption, of adjusting production to consumption, of distributing wealth and products more equitably, of adapting existing economic organizations to the service of the people. The day of enlightened administration has come." Two years later Roosevelt announced that what the New Deal sought was "balance in our economic system—balance between agriculture and industry, and balance between the wage earner, the employer and the consumer." [46]

To this end, the New Deal pushed through the National Industrial Recovery Act (N.I.R.A.) and established the first Agricultural Adjustment Administration (A.A.A.). The N.I.R.A. program, some of whose aspects would no doubt have delighted Theodore Roosevelt and the New Nationalists, had the long-range objective of stabilizing private enterprise through the coöperation of government, business, and labor.[47] It afforded the status of law to the codes of fair competition drawn up by trade or industrial associations and approved by the president, suspended the antitrust laws with respect to actions taken in conformity with the codes, and, as implemented, provided for the administration of the codes by code authorities primarily representative of the firms in the particular coded industry or trade. In return for these concessions to industry, labor was guaranteed the right of collective bargaining, and employers were required to observe certain minimum labor standards in regard to hours, wages, and child labor. The principal objective of the A.A.A. program was to reëstablish farm prices at a level that would give farm commodities a purchasing power with respect to nonfarm articles equal to the purchasing power of farm commodities in the period 1909–1914. For this purpose, the farmer was offered a subsidy to reduce the acreage that he devoted to

[46] See *Public Papers and Addresses of Franklin D. Roosevelt*, I, 751–752; III, 125; Raymond Moley, *After Seven Years* (New York, 1939), pp. 23–24, 48, 184, 194; and Rexford Guy Tugwell, "The Preparation of a President," *Western Political Quarterly*, I (June, 1948), 144–145.

[47] Roosevelt declared that the N.I.R.A. represented "a supreme effort to stabilize for all time the many factors which make for the prosperity of the Nation, and the preservation of American standards" (*Public Papers and Addresses of Franklin D. Roosevelt*, II, 246).

the growing of the basic agricultural commodities. The money for the payments to the farmer was raised by a tax on processors.

When the N.I.R.A. was declared unconstitutional in 1935, the New Deal abandoned the alliance with business that was implicit in that program, departed from the camp of Theodore Roosevelt and the New Nationalists, and began to move in the direction of Wilson and Brandeis and the antimonopolists.[48] Laborers and farmers, however, continued to be the beneficiaries of New Deal legislation. The federal government, after the N.I.R.A. was invalidated by the Supreme Court, reaffirmed in the Wagner Act the right of laborers to organize and bargain collectively through representatives of their own choosing, and by the Fair Labor Standards Act of 1938 it established standards with respect to hours, wages, and child labor that were designed to protect the unorganized laborer in particular. Although the first A.A.A. was declared unconstitutional in 1936, New Deal farm legislation after that date continued to have as its objective the attainment of parity prices for the basic farm commodities.

Coming into office in the midst of a great depression and at a time when the appalling results of the lack of a program of social security were apparent for all to see, New Dealers, more than the reformers of any previous period, came to believe that government must not only provide opportunity for its citizens but also a measure of economic and social security. The Social Security Act of 1935 constituted the most obvious and important legislative recognition of this view, but one may also note in the same connection the adoption of a plan for deposit insurance, the Railroad Retirement Acts of 1934 and 1935, the activities of the Farm Security Administration, the attempt to provide the farmers with parity prices, the program of wheat insurance initiated by the Agricultural Adjustment Act of 1938, and similar measures. "Security," Clinton L. Rossiter has noted, "was the bright word in Franklin Roosevelt's lexicon." [49]

In his State of the Union message of 1944, many years after the last of the important New Deal reforms had been adopted, Roosevelt, in seeking to chart a domestic program for postwar America, emphasized the fact that true freedom could not exist in the absence of eco-

---

[48] Goldman, *Rendezvous with Destiny*, pp. 333–337, 340–342, 361–367.

[49] See Goldman, *Rendezvous with Destiny*, pp. 370–371; and Clinton Rossiter, "The Political Philosophy of F. D. Roosevelt: A Challenge to Scholarship," *Review of Politics*, XI (January, 1949), 90.

nomic security. He thought that the nation had come to accept a "second Bill of Rights," which established "a new basis of security and prosperity." Among these rights, Roosevelt included the right to a useful and remunerative job, the right of the individual to earn enough to provide adequate food, clothing, and recreation, the right of the farmer to sell his products at prices that would give him and his family a decent living, the right of the businessman to trade without the hindrance of unfair competition or monopoly, the right of every family to a decent home, the right to adequate medical care and the opportunity to achieve and enjoy good health, the right to adequate protection against the fear of old age, sickness, accidents, and unemployment, and the right to a good education. All these rights, the president concluded, spelled security, and he looked forward to their further legislative realization after the war.[50]

In the event, the task of securing legislative recognition for Roosevelt's second bill of rights fell to his successor in office, Harry S. Truman. Roosevelt would no doubt have subscribed to the objectives of Truman's Fair Deal, for the Fair Deal was largely a continuation of the policies of the New Deal, and, like the second bill of rights, its emphasis was on economic security. Asserting that "we have pledged our common resources to help one another in the hazards and struggles of individual life," Truman, in his State of the Union message of 1949, set forth as the principal elements of the Fair Deal the protection of the economy against the cycle of "boom and bust," the repeal of the Taft-Hartley Act and the reënactment of the Wagner Act but with jurisdictional strikes and "unjustifiable" secondary boycotts prohibited and provision made for preventing strikes in industries vital to the public interest, the strengthening of the antitrust laws, the improvement of the nation's farm program so as to achieve abundant production and parity of income for agriculture, application of the lessons of the T.V.A. to other river valleys, approval of the St. Lawrence seaway and power project, expansion of the social-security program both as to size of benefits and extent of coverage, a system of prepaid medical insurance, a program of low-rent public housing, slum clearance, farm housing, and housing research, and the enactment of appropriate civil-rights legislation.[51] Some of the president's recommendations were enacted into law by Congress, but when Truman

---

[50] *Public Papers and Addresses of Franklin D. Roosevelt*, XIII, 41.

[51] *Congressional Record*, 81st Cong., 1st sess., pp. 74–76.

left office in January, 1953, the principal proposals of the Fair Deal were still to be realized.

Of the legislative accomplishments of the Truman era, the most significant by far was the Employment Act of 1946. The New Deal, to be sure, had affirmed that the government must protect the people against the consequences of depression; and, as Walter Lippman had pointed out in 1935, if it was the responsibility of the government "to protect the people against the consequences of depression, then inevitably the government must regulate the prosperity which precedes depression and produces it. If government is responsible for the downward phase of the business cycle, it has a responsibility in the whole business cycle." [52] This responsibility was recognized by the Employment Act, which established a three-man Council of Economic Advisers that was to make continuous studies of the economy and was to report to the president and through him to Congress on the policies required to avoid economic fluctuations and to maintain maximum production, employment, and purchasing power.

The Employment Act, as Truman pointed out in his final annual economic report, rejected the view of the laissez-faire economists that "we are the victims of unchangeable economic laws, that we are powerless to do more than forecast what will happen to us under the operations of such laws" and asserted rather that "our economy within reasonable limits will be what we make it, and that intelligent human action will shape our future." It committed the federal government to supplement the activities of private enterprise not only to prevent depressions but "to maintain as a matter of continuing policy a full, bountiful and growing economy." [53] Certainly, the Employment Act of 1946 is as striking a legislative victory for the philosophy of the general-welfare state as is to be found in American history.

As the mid-point of the twentieth century was reached, Americans would appear to have rejected the admonition that that government is

[52] Walter Lippman, "The Permanent New Deal," *Yale Review*, XXIV (June, 1935), 665.

[53] *New York Times*, January 15, 1953. In an address of October 18, 1954, Arthur F. Burns, the Eisenhower administration's chairman of the Council of Economic Advisers, declared that "it is no longer a matter of serious controversy whether the Government should play a positive role in helping to maintain a high level of economic activity. What we debate nowadays is not the need for controlling business cycles, but rather the nature of governmental action, its timing and its extent" (*ibid.*, October 19, 1954).

best which governs least and to have endorsed the view that in the interests of the general welfare the state should restrain the strong and protect the weak, should provide such services to the people as private enterprise is unable or unwilling to supply, should seek to stabilize the economy and to counteract the cycle of boom and bust, and should provide the citizen with some degree of economic security. It had come to be recognized that the state had a responsibility with respect to the welfare of each of its citizens and each group of citizens and that this responsibility was to be discharged by such positive action as was warranted in any particular case rather than by the invocation of the doctrines of laissez faire and natural law.[54]   Thus had the ideological conflict of the late nineteenth century between the advocates of laissez faire and the advocates of the general-welfare state been resolved in theory, in practice, and in public esteem in favor of the general-welfare state.

[54] In this connection, see Merle Curti *et al.*, *An American History* (New York, 1950), II, 430–431.   For a description of the anti-statism of conservatives at mid-century, see Clinton Rossiter, *Conservatism in America* (New York, 1955), pp. 187, 193–198.

BIBLIOGRAPHY · INDEX

BIBLIOGRAPHY

Primary Sources

MANUSCRIPT MATERIALS

James B. Angell Papers. Michigan Historical Collections, University of Michigan.

Edward Atkinson Papers. Massachusetts Historical Society.

Edward Bellamy Papers. Houghton Library, Harvard University.

David Josiah Brewer Collection. Yale University Library.

John W. Burgess Papers. Columbia University Library.

Andrew Carnegie Papers. Library of Congress.

John Bates Clark Papers. In possession of John Maurice Clark, John Bates Clark Professor of Political Economy, Columbia University.

Grover Cleveland Papers. Library of Congress.

Charles H. Cooley Papers. Michigan Historical Collections, University of Michigan.

Thomas McIntyre Cooley Papers. Michigan Historical Collections, University of Michigan.

Richard T. Ely Papers. State Historical Society of Wisconsin.

Henry George Collection. New York Public Library.

Franklin H. Giddings Papers. Columbia University Library.

Washington Gladden Papers. Ohio State Archaeological and Historical Society.

Joseph A. Labadie Collection. University of Michigan Library.

James L. Laughlin Papers. University of Chicago Library.

Henry Demarest Lloyd Papers. State Historical Society of Wisconsin.

Hugh McCulloch Papers. Library of Congress.

Simon Newcomb Papers. Library of Congress.

Frank Parsons Collection. Yale University Library.

Edwin R. A. Seligman Papers. Columbia University Library.

Lester F. Ward Papers. John Hay Library of Brown University.

David A. Wells Papers.   Library of Congress.
David A. Wells Papers.   New York Public Library.

UNITED STATES DOCUMENTS

Congressional Record, 81st Cong., 1st sess.

JAMES, EDMUND J. "The Government in Its Relation to the Forests,"
United States Department of Agriculture, Forestry Division, *Bulletin
No. 2* (1888), pp. 23–39.

OLMSTEAD, VICTOR H.   "The Betterment of Industrial Conditions," Department of Labor, *Bulletin,* V (1900), 1117–1156.

THORPE, FRANCIS NEWTON, comp.   *The Federal and State Constitutions,
Colonial Charters, and Other Organic Laws of the States, Territories,
and Colonies Now or Heretofore Forming the United States of America.*
Washington, 1909.   7 vols.

U. S. BUREAU OF THE CENSUS.   *Abstract of the Twelfth Census of the
United States, 1900.*   Washington, 1904.

—— *Fifteenth Census of the United States,* I (*Population*).   Washington,
1931.

U. S. BUREAU OF FOREIGN AND DOMESTIC COMMERCE.   *Statistical Abstract of the United States, 1921.*   Washington, 1922.

U. S. BUREAU OF NAVIGATION.   *Laws of the United States Relating to
Navigation and the Merchant Marine.*   Washington, 1899.

U. S. CONGRESS. HOUSE. SELECT COMMITTEE.   *Investigation Relative
to the Causes of the General Depression in Labor and Business, etc.*
45th Cong., 3d sess., H. Misc. Doc. No. 29; 46th Cong., 2d sess.,
H. Misc. Doc. No. 5.   Washington, 1879.

—— —— SPECIAL COMMISSIONER OF THE REVENUE.   *Report, 1869.*   41st
Cong., 2d sess., H. Exec. Doc. No. 27.   Washington, 1870.

—— —— *Your Congress and American Housing: The Actions of Congress
on Housing from 1892 to 1951,* by Jack Levin.   82 Cong., 2d sess.,
H. Doc. No. 532.   Washington, 1952.

—— SENATE. COMMITTEE ON EDUCATION AND LABOR.   *Report upon the
Relations between Labor and Capital, and Testimony Taken by the
Committee.*   Washington, 1885.   4 vols.

—— —— MONETARY COMMISSION.   *Report and Accompanying Documents.*
44th Cong., 2d sess., S. Rept. No. 703.   Washington, 1877.

U. S. DEPARTMENT OF THE INTERIOR. UNITED STATES COMMISSIONER OF
EDUCATION.   *Report for the Year 1899–1900.*   Washington, 1900.   2
vols.

U. S. FEDERAL SECURITY AGENCY, SOCIAL SECURITY ADMINISTRATION.
Social Security in the United States.   New ed.   Washington, 1952.

U. S. INDUSTRIAL COMMISSION.   *Reports.*   Washington, 1900–1902.   19
vols.

U. S. NATIONAL MONETARY COMMISSION.   "State Banks and Trust Companies since the Passage of the National-Bank Act," by George E. Barnett (Vol. VII of the Commission's *Publications*), 61st Cong., 3d sess., S. Doc. No. 659 (Washington, D.C., 1911).

WILLOUGHBY, W. F. "Accidents to Labor as Regulated by Law in the United States," Department of Labor, *Bulletin,* VI (1901), 1–28.

STATE DOCUMENTS

CONNECTICUT. BUREAU OF LABOR STATISTICS. *First Annual Report, 1885* (Second Series); *Second Annual Report, 1886.* Hartford, 1885–1886.

KANSAS. BUREAU OF LABOR AND INDUSTRY. *Eleventh Annual Report, 1895.* Topeka, 1896.

MASSACHUSETTS. LEGISLATURE. *Documents Printed by Order of the House of Representatives of the Commonwealth of Massachusetts during the Session of the General Court, A.D. 1845.* H. Doc. No. 50. Boston, 1845.

NEW YORK. COMPTROLLER. *Annual Reports, 1897–1898.* Albany, 1897–1898.

—— LEGISLATURE. ASSEMBLY. SPECIAL COMMITTEE ON RAILROADS. *Proceedings.* Albany, 1879. 5 vols.

OTHER PRIMARY SOURCES

ABBOTT, LYMAN. *Christianity and Social Problems.* Boston, 1896.

—— "Christianity versus Socialism," *North American Review,* CXLVIII (April, 1889), 447–453.

—— "Danger Ahead," *Century,* N.S., IX (November, 1885), 51–59.

—— "Industrial Democracy," *Forum,* IX (August, 1890), 658–669.

—— "The Natural Law of Competition," *Christian Union,* XXXII (July 16, 1885), 3–4.

—— "The New Political Economy," *Christian Union,* XXXII (July 23, 1885), 3–4.

—— *Reminiscences.* Boston, 1915.

ADAMS, HENRY CARTER. *Christianity as a Social Force.* Ann Arbor, Mich., 1892.

—— "A Decade of Federal Railway Regulation," *Atlantic Monthly,* LXXXI (April, 1898), 433–443.

—— "Economics and Jurisprudence," *American Economic Association Economic Studies,* II (1897), 1–35.

—— "An Interpretation of the Social Movements of Our Time," *International Journal of Ethics,* II (October, 1891), 32–50.

—— *Outline of Lectures upon Political Economy.* Prepared for the use of students at the University of Michigan and Cornell University. 2d ed. Ann Arbor, Mich., 1886.

—— "The Position of Socialism in the Historical Development of Political Economy," *Penn Monthly,* X (April, 1879), 285–294.

ADAMS, HENRY CARTER. *Public Debts: An Essay in the Science of Finance.* New York, 1887.

—— "Publicity and Corporate Abuses," *Publications of the Michigan Political Science Association,* I (May, 1894), 109–120.

—— "Relation of the State to Industrial Action," *Publications of the American Economic Association,* I (1887), 465–549.

—— *The Science of Finance: An Analysis of Public Expenditures and Public Revenues.* New York, 1899.

—— "Suggestions for a System of Taxation," *Publications of the Michigan Political Science Association,* I (May, 1894), 49–74.

—— ET AL. "The 'Labor Problem,'" *Scientific American Supplement,* XXII (August 21, 1886), 8861–8863.

ADAMS, OSCAR FAY. "Aristocratic Drift of American Protestantism," *North American Review,* CXLII (February, 1886), 194–199.

ADDAMS, JANE. "Hull House, Chicago: An Effort toward Social Democracy," *Forum,* XIV (October, 1892), 226–241.

—— *Twenty Years at Hull House.* With autobiographical notes. New York, 1910.

—— ET AL. *Philanthropy and Social Progress.* New York, 1893.

ALGER, GEORGE W. "The Courts and Factory Legislation," *American Journal of Sociology,* VI (November, 1900), 396–406.

ALLISON, ANDREW. "The Rise and Probable Decline of Private Corporations in America," *Report of the Seventh Annual Meeting of the American Bar Association, 1884,* pp. 241–256.

AMERICAN FEDERATION OF LABOR. *Proceedings, 1881–1901.* Bloomington, Ill., 1905–1906. 5 vols.

"American Political Ideas," *North American Review,* CI (October, 1865), 550–566.

ANDREWS, E. BENJAMIN. "The Economic Law of Monopoly," *Journal of Social Science,* XXVI (February, 1890), 1–12.

—— "Economic Reform Short of Socialism," *International Journal of Ethics,* II (April, 1892), 273–288.

—— "An Honest Dollar," *Publications of the American Economic Association,* IV (November, 1889), 395–444.

—— "Individualism as a Sociological Principle," *Yale Review,* II (May, 1893), 13–27.

—— *Institutes of Economics.* Boston, 1889.

—— "Political Economy, Old and New," *Andover Review,* VI (August, 1886), 130–148.

—— "Trusts According to Official Investigations," *Quarterly Journal of Economics,* III (January, 1889), 117–152.

—— *Wealth and Moral Law.* Hartford, Conn., 1894.

Appletons' Annual Cyclopaedia and Register of Important Events of the Year 1878. New York, 1879.

ASHLEY, CHARLES S. "The Relation of Evolution to Political Economy," *Popular Science Monthly*, XLIV (February, 1894), 458–461.

ASHLEY, W. J. *Surveys Historic and Economic.* New York, 1900.

ATKINSON, EDWARD. *The Distribution of Products, or the Mechanism and Metaphysics of Exchange.* New York, 1885.

—— "The Eight-Hour Question," *Bradstreet's*, XIII (April 24, 1886), 260–262.

—— "The Hours of Labor," *North American Review*, CXLII (May, 1886), 507–515.

—— *The Industrial Progress of the Nation: Consumption Limited, Production Unlimited.* New York, 1890.

—— "Inefficiency of Economic Legislation," *Journal of Social Science*, IV (1871), 123–132.

—— *Labor and Capital Allies Not Enemies.* New York, 1879.

—— *The Margin of Profits.* New York, 1887.

—— *On the Collection of Revenue.* Rev. ed. New York, 1869.

—— "The Philosophy of Money," *Monist*, VI (April, 1896), 337–350.

—— *The Railway, the Farmer and the Public.* New York, 1885.

—— "Veto of the Inflation Bill of 1874," *Journal of Political Economy*, I (December, 1892), 117–119.

—— AND EDWARD T. CABOT. "Personal Liberty," *Popular Science Monthly*, XL (February, 1892), 433–446.

ATWATER, LYMAN H. "The Currency Question," *Presbyterian Quarterly and Princeton Review*, N.S., IV (October, 1875), 721–742.

—— "The Great Railroad Strike," *Presbyterian Quarterly and Princeton Review*, N.S., VI (October, 1877), 719–744.

—— "The Labor Question in Its Economic and Christian Aspects," *Presbyterian Quarterly and Princeton Review*, N.S., I (July, 1872), 468–495.

—— "The Regulation of Railroads," *Princeton Review*, N.S., VII (May, 1881), 406–428.

BAKER, CHARLES WHITING. *Monopolies and the People.* New York, 1889.

BARNS, WILLIAM E., ed. *The Labor Problem. Plain Questions and Practical Answers.* With an introduction by Richard T. Ely and special contributions by James A. Waterworth and Fred Woodrow. New York, 1886.

BASCOM, JOHN. "Competition, Actual and Theoretical," *Quarterly Journal of Economics*, XIV (August, 1900), 537–542.

—— *Ethics or Science of Duty.* New York, 1879.

—— "Labor and Capital" ("The Natural Theology of Social Science," No. IV), *Bibliotheca Sacra*, XXV (October, 1868), 645–686.

—— *Social Theory: A Grouping of Social Facts and Principles.* New York, 1895.

—— *Sociology.* New York, 1887.

—— *Things Learned by Living.* New York, 1913.

BASTIAT, FRÉDÉRIC. *Harmonies of Political Economy.* Tr. from the French, with a notice of the life and writings of the author, by Patrick James Stirling. London, 1860.

BAXTER, SYLVESTER. "What Is Nationalism?" *Nationalist,* I (June, 1889), 8–12.

BEACH, CHARLES F., JR. "Facts about Trusts," *Forum,* VIII (September, 1889), 61–72.

BEHRENDS, A. J. F. *Socialism and Christianity.* New York, 1886.

BELLAMY, EDWARD. *Equality.* New York, 1897.

—— "First Steps toward Nationalism," *Forum,* X (October, 1890), 174–184.

—— *Looking Backward, 2000–1887.* Tower Books ed. Cleveland, 1945.

—— "Nationalism—Principles, Purposes," *Nationalist,* II (April, 1889), 174–180.

—— "The Programme of the Nationalists," *Forum,* XVII (March, 1894), 81–91.

BEMIS, EDWARD W. "The Complaint of the Poor," *Independent,* XL (May 24, 1888), 645.

—— ed. *Municipal Monopolies: A Collection of Papers by American Economists and Specialists.* New York, 1899.

—— "The Relation of the Church to Social Questions," *Dawn,* II (July–August, 1890), 148–158.

—— "Socialism and State Action," *Journal of Social Science,* XXI (September, 1886), 33–68.

—— "The Trust Problem—Its Real Nature," *Forum,* XXVIII (December, 1899), 412–426.

BIGELOW, ERASTUS B. "The Relations of Capital and Labor," *Atlantic Monthly,* XLII (October, 1878), 475–487.

"Bimetallic Theory," *Nation,* LVII (July 13, 1893), 22–23.

BLISS, W. D. P., ed. *The Encyclopedia of Social Reform.* New York, 1897.

—— "Nationalism and Christianity," *Nationalist,* I (August, 1890), 97–99.

—— "A Plea for Union or What Is the Social Reform Union?" *Social Forum,* I (September 1, 1899), 128–132.

—— "The Social Reform Union," *Arena,* XXII (August, 1899), 272–275.

—— "Union Reform League Activities," *Arena,* XXII (July, 1899), 111–114.

—— "Unite or Perish," *Arena,* XXII (July, 1899), 78–89.

—— *What Christian Socialism Is.* Reprinted from *Dawn.* Boston, 1894.

—— "What Is Christian Socialism?" Rev. ed., *Dawn,* IV (June, 1892), 8–12.

—— "What to Do Now," *Dawn,* II (July–August, 1890), 109–114.

—— "Why Am I a Christian Socialist?" *Twentieth Century,* V (October 2, 1890), 5–6.

—— "Why We Prefer Socialism to Nationalism," *Dawn,* III (February 12, 1891), 3–5.

BOARDMAN, GEORGE N. "Political Economy and the Christian Ministry," *Bibliotheca Sacra*, XXIII (January, 1866), 73–107.

BOLLES, ALBERT S. *Chapters in Political Economy.* New York, 1874.

BONHAM, JOHN M. *Industrial Liberty.* New York, 1888.

BOWEN, FRANCIS. *American Political Economy; Including Strictures on the Management of the Currency and the Finances since 1861.* New York, 1870.

BOWKER, RICHARD ROGERS. *Economics for the People.* New York, 1886.

—— *Of Business.* Boston, 1901.

—— *Of Work and Wealth: A Summary of Economics.* New York, 1883.

BRACE, CHARLES LORING. *Gesta Christi, or a History of Humane Progress under Christianity.* 2d ed. New York, 1883.

BREWER, DAVID JOSIAH. *Protection to Private Property from Public Attack.* New Haven, 1891.

BRIDGE, JAMES H., ed. *The Trust: Its Book.* New York, 1902.

BRIGGS, C. A. "The Alienation of Church and People," *Forum*, XVI (November, 1893), 366–378.

BROOKS, AUBREY LEE, AND HUGH TALMAGE LEFLER, eds. *The Papers of Walter Clark.* Chapel Hill, N.C., 1948. 2 vols.

BRYCE, JAMES. *The American Commonwealth.* London, 1888. 3 vols.

BURGESS, JOHN W. "The Ideal of the American Commonwealth," *Political Science Quarterly*, X (September, 1895), 404–425.

—— *Political Science and Comparative Constitutional Law.* Boston, 1891. 2 vols.

—— "Private Corporations from the Point of View of Political Science," *Political Science Quarterly*, XIII (June, 1898), 201–212.

—— *Reminiscences of an American Scholar: The Beginnings of Columbia University.* New York, 1934.

CAMPBELL, J. V. *Taking of Private Property for Purposes of Utility.* Chicago, 1871.

CANFIELD, JAMES H. *Taxation: A Plain Talk for Plain People.* New York, 1883.

CAREY, HENRY C. *Principles of Social Science.* Philadelphia, 1858–1860. 3 vols.

CARNEGIE, ANDREW. *Autobiography of Andrew Carnegie.* Boston, 1920.

—— "The Best Fields for Philanthropy," *North American Review*, CXLIX (December, 1889), 682–698.

—— *The Empire of Business.* New York, 1902.

—— *The Gospel of Wealth and Other Timely Essays.* New York, 1900.

—— *Problems of To-day.* New York, 1908.

—— *Triumphant Democracy, or Fifty Years' March of the Republic.* New York, 1886.

—— "Wealth," *North American Review*, CXLVIII (June, 1889), 653–664.

CARTER, JAMES C. "The Ideal and Actual in the Law," *Report of the*

Thirteenth Annual Meeting of the American Bar Association, 1890, pp. 217–245.

CARY, JOHN W. "Limitations of the Legislative Power in Respect to Personal Rights and Private Property," *Report of the Fifteenth Annual Meeting of the American Bar Association, 1892,* pp. 245–285.

CHAPIN, AARON L. "The Relations of Labor and Capital," *Transactions of the Wisconsin Academy of Sciences, Arts, and Letters,* I (1870–1872), 45–61.

Chicago Conference on Trusts. . . , 1899. Chicago, 1900.

CLARK, CHARLES WORCESTER. "Applied Christianity: Who Shall Apply It First?" *Andover Review,* XIX (January, 1893), 18–33.

CLARK, JOHN BATES. "Christianity and Modern Economics," *New Englander and Yale Review,* XLVII (July, 1887), 50–59.

—— *The Control of Trusts.* New York, 1901.

—— *The Distribution of Wealth: A Theory of Wages, Interest and Profits.* New York, 1899.

—— "How to Deal with Trusts," *Independent,* LIII (May 2, 1901), 1001–1004.

—— "The Modern Appeal to Legal Forces in Economic Life," *Publications of the American Economic Association,* IX (1894), 479–502.

—— "Natural Law in Political Economy," *Christian Science Register,* LXX (December 3, 1891), 791–793.

—— *The Philosophy of Wealth.* Boston, 1886.

—— "Profits under Modern Conditions," *Political Science Quarterly,* II (December, 1887), 603–619.

—— "The Scholar's Political Opportunity," *Political Science Quarterly,* XII (December, 1897), 589–602.

—— "The Theory of Economic Progress," *American Economic Association Economic Studies,* I (1896), 1–22.

—— "The Trust Conference at Chicago," *Independent,* LI (September 28, 1899), 2602–2604.

—— AND FRANKLIN H. GIDDINGS. *The Modern Distributive Process: Studies of Competition and Its Limits . . . in the Industrial Society of Today.* Boston, 1888.

CLEWS, HENRY. *Fifty Years in Wall Street.* New York, 1915.

—— "The Labor Crisis," *North American Review,* CXLII (June, 1886), 598–602.

—— *The Wall Street Point of View.* New York, c. 1900.

CLOUD, D. C. *Monopolies and the People.* Davenport, Iowa, 1873.

COFFIN, CHARLES CARLETON. "Labor and the Natural Forces," *Atlantic Monthly,* XLIII (May, 1879), 553–566.

COLTON, CALVIN, ed. *The Works of Henry Clay; Comprising His Life, Correspondence and Speeches.* Federal ed. New York, 1904. 10 vols.

COMMONS, JOHN R. *The Distribution of Wealth.* New York, 1893.

—— "Economic Reform," *Voice,* September 14, 1893.

—— *Myself.* New York, 1934.

—— "Progressive Individualism," *American Magazine of Civics,* VI (June, 1895), 561–574.

—— "The Right to Work," *Arena,* XXI (February, 1899), 131–142.

—— *Social Reform and the Church.* New York, 1894.

—— ET AL. *Documentary History of American Industrial Society.* Cleveland, 1910–1911. 11 vols.

"Communication from Frederick Jackson Turner to Constance Lindsay Skinner," *Wisconsin Magazine of History,* XIX (September, 1935), 95–103.

"Competition," *Popular Science Monthly,* XXXIV (March, 1889), 699–700.

Constitution of the General Assembly, District Assemblies, and Local Assemblies of the Order of the Knights of Labor of America. Adopted at Reading, Pa., Jan. 1–4, 1878; . . . revised at Hamilton, Ont., October 5–12, 1885. n. p., n. d.

CONWELL, RUSSELL. *Acres of Diamonds. His Life and Achievements by Robert Shackleton.* With an autobiographical note. New York, 1915.

COOK, JOSEPH. *Labor; with Preludes on Current Events.* Boston, 1880.

—— *Socialism; with Preludes on Current Events.* Boston, 1880.

COOK, WILLIAM W. *The Corporation Problem: The Public Phases of Corporations . . . and Political Questions to Which They Have Given Rise.* New York, 1891.

COOLEY, CHARLES H. "Competition and Organization," *Publications of the Michigan Political Science Association,* I (December, 1894), 33–45.

—— "Personal Competition. Its Place in the Social Order and Effect upon Individuals; with Some Considerations on Success," *American Economic Association Economic Studies,* IV (April, 1899), 71–173.

—— *Sociological Theory and Social Research. Being Selected Papers of Charles Horton Cooley.* With an introduction and notes by Robert Cooley Angell. New York, 1930.

COOLEY, THOMAS MCINTYRE. "The Fundamentals of American Liberty," *Michigan Law Journal,* III (June, 1894), 149–156.

—— *The Influence of Habits of Thought upon Our Institutions.* n. p., 1886.

—— "Labor and Capital before the Law," *North American Review,* CXXXIX (December, 1884), 503–516.

—— "Limits to State Control of Private Business," *Princeton Review,* N.S., I (March, 1878), 233–271.

—— "State Regulation of Corporate Profits," *North American Review,* CXXXVII (September, 1883), 205–217.

—— *A Treatise on the Constitutional Limitations Which Rest upon the Legislative Power of the States of the American Union.* Boston, 1868. 6th ed., Boston, 1890.

COOLEY, THOMAS MCINTYRE. *A Treatise on the Law of Taxation, Including the Law of Local Assessments.* Chicago, 1876.

COOPER, PETER. *Ideas for a Science of Good Government in Addresses, Letters and Articles on a Strictly National Currency, Tariff and Civil Service.* 2d ed. New York, 1883.

CORBIN, AUSTIN. "The Tyranny of Labor Organizations," *North American Review*, CLXIX (October, 1889), 413–420.

CRAFTS, WILBUR F. *Practical Christian Sociology.* New York, 1896.

CULLOM, SHELBY M. *Fifty Years of Public Service.* Chicago, 1911.

DANA, WILLIAM F. "Federal Restraints upon State Regulation of Railroad Rates of Fare and Freight," *Harvard Law Review*, IX (January, 1896), 324–345.

DAY, EDWARD L. "The Labor Question," *Century*, N.S., X (July, 1886), 397–403.

DENSLOW, VAN BUREN. *Principles of the Economic Philosophy of Society, Government and Industry.* New York, 1885.

DEWEY, JOHN. *The Ethics of Democracy.* Ann Arbor, Mich., 1888.

—— "Evolution and Ethics," *Monist*, VIII (April, 1898), 321–341.

—— *The Influence of Darwin on Philosophy and Other Essays in Contemporary Thought.* New York, 1910.

—— "Interpretation of Savage Mind," *Psychological Review*, IX (May, 1902), 217–230.

—— *My Pedagogic Creed.* New York, 1897.

—— *Outlines of a Critical Theory of Ethics.* Ann Arbor, Mich., 1891.

—— *Psychology.* New York, 1887.

—— *Psychology and Social Practice.* Chicago, 1901.

—— "Social Psychology," *Psychological Review*, I (July, 1894), 400–411.

—— *The Study of Ethics.* Ann Arbor, Mich., 1897.

DILLON, JOHN F. *The Laws and Jurisprudence of England and America.* Boston, 1895.

—— *Treatise on the Law of Municipal Corporations.* Chicago, 1872.

DODD, S. C. T. *Combinations: Their Uses and Abuses, with a History of the Standard Oil Trust.* New York, 1888.

DONNELLY, IGNATIUS. *Caesar's Column: A Story of the Twentieth Century.* Chicago, 1891.

DORFMAN, JOSEPH, ed. *Relation of the State to Industrial Action and Economics and Jurisprudence: Two Essays by Henry Carter Adams.* New York, 1954.

—— "The Seligman Correspondence I, II, III, IV," *Political Science Quarterly*, LVI (March, June, September, December, 1941), 107–124, 270–286, 392–419, 573–599.

DORNER, OTTO. "Good Roads and State Aid," *Forum*, XXVI (February, 1899), 668–672.

DOS PASSOS, JOHN R. *Growth and Rights of Aggregated Capital.* Argument of John R. Dos Passos of New York before the U. S. Industrial Commission. Washington, D.C., 1899.

DRYER, G. H. "Tendencies in American Economics," *Methodist Review*, LXXIII (March, 1891), 244–252.

DUNNING, N. A. *The Philosophy of Price, and Its Relation to Domestic Commerce.* Chicago, 1887.

EASTMAN, H. W. K. *The Science of Government: A True Assay of the Crude Ore of Political Economy.* Lawrence, Mass., 1888.

ECCLES, MARRINER S. *Beckoning Frontiers: Public and Personal Recollections.* New York, 1951.

ECCLES, R. G. "The Labor Question," *Popular Science Monthly*, XI (September, 1877), 606–611.

ECKELS, JAMES H. "The Menace of Legislation," *North American Review*, CLXV (August, 1897), 240–246.

ELDER, WILLIAM. *Questions of the Day: Economic and Social.* Philadelphia, 1871.

ELY, RICHARD T. "The Advantages of Public Ownership and Management of Natural Monopolies," *Cosmopolitan*, XXX (March, 1901), 557–560.

—— "The American Economic Association 1885–1909. With Special Reference to Its Origins and Early Development. An Historical Sketch," *Publications of the American Economic Association*, 3d Series, XI (1910), 47–92.

—— "Competition: Its Nature, Its Permanency, and Its Beneficence," *Publications of the American Economic Association*, 3d Series, II (1901), 55–70.

—— "Conditions of Industrial Peace," *Forum*, III (August, 1887), 638–644.

—— "A Decade of Economic Theory," *Annals of the American Academy of Political and Social Science*, XV (March, 1900), 236–256.

—— "The Founding and Early History of the American Economic Association," *American Economic Review*, XXVI (Supplement) (March, 1936), 140–150.

—— "Fraternalism vs. Paternalism in Government," *Century*, N.S., XXXIII (March, 1898), 781–785.

—— "Fundamental Beliefs in My Social Philosophy," *Forum*, XVIII (October, 1894), 173–183.

—— "Government in Business and the General Welfare," *Review of Reviews*, LXXXIV (October, 1931), 44–47.

—— *Ground under Our Feet: An Autobiography.* New York, 1938.

—— "The Improvement of Municipal Government," *Christian Union*, XLII (October 9, 1890), 460–461.

—— *An Introduction to Political Economy.* New York, 1889.

—— *The Labor Movement in America.* New York, 1886.

—— "Liberty a Social Product," *Our Day*, XVI (December, 1896), 671–672.

ELY, RICHARD T. *Monopolies and Trusts.* New York, 1900.

—— *Natural Monopolies and Local Taxation.* Boston, 1889.

—— "The Nature and Significance of Monopolies and Trusts," *International Journal of Ethics,* X (April, 1900), 273–288.

—— "The Next Things in Social Reform," *Christian Union,* XLIII (April 23, 1891), 531–532.

—— "The Past and the Present of Political Economy," *Johns Hopkins University Studies in Historical and Political Science,* II (1884), 137–202.

—— "Philanthropy," *Chautauquan,* IX (October, 1888), 16–18.

—— "Political Economy in America," *North American Review,* CXLIV (February, 1887), 113–119.

—— *Problems of To-day: A Discussion of Protective Tariffs, Taxation, and Monopolies.* New York, 1890.

—— "Proceedings of the Second Annual Meeting of the American Economic Association," *Publications of the American Economic Association,* III (1888), 193–225.

—— "A Programme for Labor Reform," *Century,* N.S., XVII (April, 1890), 938–951.

—— "Progressivism True and False—An Outline," *Review of Reviews,* LI (February, 1915), 209–211.

—— "Public Control of Private Corporations," *Cosmopolitan,* XXX (February, 1901), 430–433.

—— "Recent American Socialism," *Johns Hopkins University Studies in Historical and Political Science,* III (1885), 231–304.

—— "Reforms in Taxation," *Cosmopolitan,* XXX (January, 1901), 307–309.

—— "Report of the Organization of the American Economic Association," *Publications of the American Economic Association,* I (1886), 5–46.

—— "Report of the Proceedings at the Third Annual Meeting," *Publications of the American Economic Association,* IV (1889), 269–321.

—— "The Situation and the Remedy," *Independent,* XLIX (March 4, 1897), 268–271.

—— *Social Aspects of Christianity, and Other Essays.* New York, 1889.

—— *The Social Law of Service.* Cincinnati, 1896.

—— *Socialism: An Examination of Its Nature, Its Strength, and Its Weakness, with Suggestions for Social Reform.* New York, 1894.

—— "Suggestions on Social Topics," *Christian Advocate,* LXVI (February 12—December 3, 1891); LXVII (February 16—March 31, 1892).

—— *Taxation in American States and Cities.* Assisted by John H. Finley. New York, 1888.

—— ET AL. *The Foundations of National Prosperity: Studies in the Conservation of Permanent Natural Resources.* New York, 1917.

—— —— *Science Economic Discussion.* New York, 1886.

The Ely Investigation. Communications of Superintendent Wells to the Investigating Committee. n. p., [1894].

EMERSON, RALPH WALDO. *Essays, First and Second Series.* Boston, 1883. 2 vols. in one.

"Encroachments of the State," *Popular Science Monthly,* XXXI (October, 1887), 847–848.

EVANGELICAL ALLIANCE OF THE UNITED STATES. *Christianity Practically Applied.* New York, 1894. 2 vols.

—— *National Perils and Opportunities.* New York, 1887.

FAIRBAIRN, ROBERT B. "The Law of Labor and Capital," *Christian Thought,* 4th Series (1886), 196–210.

FARQUHAR, ARTHUR B., AND HENRY FARQUHAR. *Economic and Industrial Delusions.* New York, 1891.

FERNOW, B. E. "The Providential Functions of Government with Special Reference to Natural Resources," *Proceedings of the American Association for the Advancement of Science,* XLIV (August–September, 1895), 325–344.

FINE, SIDNEY, ed. "The Ely-Labadie Letters," *Michigan History,* XXXVI (March, 1952), 1–32.

FISK, ETHEL F., ed. *The Letters of John Fiske.* New York, 1940.

FLOWER, B. O. "How to Increase National Wealth by the Employment of Paralyzed Industry," *Arena,* XVIII (August, 1897), 200–210.

—— ET AL. "An Army of Wealth Creators vs. an Army of Destruction," *Arena,* XXV (May, 1901), 521–546.

FORREST, J. D. "Anti-Monopoly Legislation in the United States," *American Journal of Sociology,* I (January, 1896), 411–425.

"Functions of the State," *Popular Science Monthly,* XXX (April, 1887), 699–702.

GEORGE, HENRY. *The Land Question; What It Involves, and How Alone It Can be Settled (The Complete Works of Henry George,* Vol. III). Garden City, N.Y., [1911?].

—— *A Perplexed Philosopher: Being an Examination of Mr. Herbert Spencer's Various Utterances on the Land Question . . . (The Complete Works of Henry George,* Vol. V). Garden City, N.Y., [1911?].

—— *Progress and Poverty: An Inquiry into the Cause of Industrial Depressions and of Increase of Want with Increase of Wealth. The Remedy.* 4th ed. New York, 1883. Modern Library ed., New York, n.d.

—— *Protection or Free Trade: An Examination of the Tariff Question, with Especial Regard to the Interests of Labor (The Complete Works of Henry George,* Vol. IV). Garden City, N.Y., [1911?].

—— *The Science of Political Economy.* New York, *c.* 1898.

—— *Social Problems.* Chicago, 1884.

—— "Thou Shalt Not Steal," *The Land and Labor Library,* I (June 18, 1887), 1–6.

GIDDINGS, FRANKLIN HENRY. *Democracy and Empire; with Studies of Their*

Psychological, Economic, and Moral Foundations. New York, 1900.

GIDDINGS, FRANKLIN HENRY. *The Principles of Sociology: An Analysis of the Phenomena of Association and of Social Organization.* New York, 1896.

—— *The Theory of Sociology.* Philadelphia, 1894.

GILMAN, NICHOLAS PAINE. "Christian Socialism in America," *Unitarian Review,* XXXII (October, 1889), 345–357.

—— *A Dividend to Labor: A Study of Employers' Welfare Institutions.* Boston, 1899.

—— *Socialism and the American Spirit.* Boston, 1893.

GLADDEN, WASHINGTON. *Applied Christianity: Moral Aspects of Social Questions.* Boston, 1887.

—— "Can Our Social Ills Be Remedied?" *Forum,* VIII (September, 1889), 18–27.

—— *Recollections.* Boston, 1909.

—— *Social Facts and Forces.* New York, 1897.

—— "Socialism and Unsocialism," *Forum,* III (April, 1887), 122–130.

—— *Tools and the Man: Property and Industry under the Christian Law.* Boston, 1893.

—— "What to Do with the Workless Man," *Proceedings of the National Conference of Charities and Correction, 1899,* pp. 141–152.

—— *Working People and Their Employers.* Boston, 1876.

[GODKIN, EDWIN L.] "The Coxey 'Problem,'" *Nation,* LVIII (May 17, 1894), 358.

[——] "The Eight-Hour Movement," *Nation,* I (November 16, 1865), 615–616.

[——] "Labor and Politics," *Nation,* XIV (June 13, 1872), 386–387.

—— *Problems of Modern Democracy.* New York, 1897.

—— *Reflections and Comments, 1865–1895.* New York, 1895.

—— *Unforeseen Tendencies of Democracy.* Boston, 1898.

[——] "Who Is Responsible for Coxey?" *Nation,* LVIII (May 3, 1894), 322–323.

GOMPERS, SAMUEL. "The Church and Labor," *American Federationist,* III (August, 1896), 119–120.

—— *Seventy Years of Life and Labor: An Autobiography.* New York, 1925. 2 vols.

GOSCHEN, GEORGE JOACHIM, VISCOUNT. *Essays and Addresses on Economic Questions (1865–1893); with Introductory Notes (1905). . . .* London, 1905.

"Government—Parts I and II," *New York Social Science Review,* I (January, July, 1865), 1–29, 288–308.

"The Granger Decisions," *Nation,* XXIV (March 8, 1877), 143–144.

GREEN, HENRY S. "Mr. Godkin and the New Political Economy," *Arena,* XX (July, 1898), 27–38.

GREGORY, JOHN M. "The Problem of the Unemployed," *Independent,* XXXIX (November 10, 1887), 1443.

GRONLUND, LAURENCE. *The Cooperative Commonwealth in Its Outlines: An Exposition of Modern Socialism.* Boston, 1884.

GROSVENOR, W. M. *Does Protection Protect? An Examination of the Effect of Different Forms of Tariff upon American Industry.* New York, 1871.

"The Growth of Corporate and Decline of Governmental Power," *Nation,* XVI (May 15, 1873), 328–329.

GUNTON, GEORGE. *The Economic and Social Importance of the Eight-Hour Movement.* Washington, D.C., 1889.

—— *Principles of Social Economics Inductively Considered and Practically Applied with Criticisms on Current Theories.* New York, 1891.

—— *Wealth and Progress: A Critical Examination of the Wages Question.* 7th ed. New York, 1897.

GUTHRIE, WILLIAM D. "Constitutionality of the Sherman Anti-Trust Act of 1890, as Interpreted by the United States Supreme Court in the Case of the Trans-Missouri Traffic Association," *Harvard Law Review,* XI (June, 1897), 80–94.

—— *Lectures on the Fourteenth Article of Amendment to the Constitution of the United States.* Boston, 1898.

HADLEY, ARTHUR TWINING. "American Railroad Legislation," *Harper's Monthly Magazine,* LXXV (June, 1887), 141–150.

—— *Economics: An Account of the Relations between Private Property and Public Welfare.* New York, 1896.

—— *The Education of the American Citizen.* New York, 1902.

—— "Ely's 'Socialism and Social Reform,'" *Forum,* XVIII (October, 1894), 184–191.

—— "The Formation and Control of Trusts," *Scribner's Magazine,* XXVI (November, 1899), 604–610.

—— "Francis A. Walker's Contributions to Economic Theory," *Political Science Quarterly,* XII (June, 1897), 295–308.

—— "The Good and Evil of Industrial Combination," *Atlantic Monthly,* LXXIX (March, 1897), 377–385.

—— "Government Administration of Industrial Enterprise," *Yale Review,* IV (February, 1896), 398–408.

—— "Private Monopolies and Public Rights," *Quarterly Journal of Economics,* I (October, 1886), 28–44.

—— *Railroad Transportation: Its History and Its Laws.* New York, 1885.

—— "Some Difficulties of Public Business Management," *Political Science Quarterly,* III (December, 1888), 572–591.

HAGEDORN, HERMANN, ed. *The Works of Theodore Roosevelt.* Memorial ed. New York, 1923–1926. 24 vols.

HALE, EDWARD EVERETT. *Addresses and Essays on Subjects of History,*

Education, and Government (*The Works of Edward Everett Hale*, Library ed., Vol. III). Boston, 1900.

HALE, EDWARD EVERETT. "The Best Government," *Nationalist*, I (June, 1889), 37–40.

HAMILTON, SAMUEL M. "The Christian Use of Wealth," *Christian Thought*, 4th Series (1886), pp. 211–214.

Handbook of the American Economic Association. Baltimore, 1890.

HARRIS, A. W. "What the Government Is Doing for the Farmer," *Century*, N.S., XXII (July, 1892), 465–472.

HARRIS, SAMUEL SMITH. "Capital and Labor," *Christian Thought*, 3d Series (1885), pp. 20–37.

—— *The Relation of Christianity to Civil Society*. New York, 1883.

HARVEY, W. H. *Coin's Financial School*. Chicago, 1894.

HATFIELD, HENRY RAND. "The Chicago Trust Conference," *Journal of Political Economy*, VIII (December, 1899), 1–18.

HAWLEY, FREDERICK B. "Edward Atkinson's Economic Theories," *Forum*, VII (May, 1889), 292–304.

HERRON, GEORGE D. *Between Caesar and Jesus*. New York, 1899.

—— *The Christian Society*. Chicago, 1894.

—— *The Christian State: A Political Vision of Christ*. New York, 1895.

—— "The Message of Jesus to Men of Wealth," *Christian Union*, XLII (December 11, 1890), 804–805.

—— *The New Redemption: A Call to the Church to Reconstruct Society According to the Gospel of Christ*. New York, 1893.

HITCHCOCK, ROSWELL D. *Socialism*. New York, 1879.

HOLMES, OLIVER WENDELL. *The Common Law*. Boston, 1881.

—— "The Path of the Law," *Harvard Law Review*, X (April, 1897), 457–478.

HOLT, HENRY. *Garrulities of an Octogenarian Editor; with Other Essays Somewhat Biographical and Autobiographical*. Boston, 1923.

—— *On the Civic Relations*. 3d ed. of *Talks on Civics*. Boston, 1907.

—— "The Social Discontent—II. Some Remedies," *Forum*, XIX (March, 1895), 68–82.

—— "The Social Discontent—III. More Remedies," *Forum*, XIX (April, 1895), 169–186.

HOPKINS, MARK. *The Law of Love and Love as a Law; or, Christian Ethics*. New York, 1881.

—— *Lectures on Moral Science*. Boston, 1863.

"How Cleveland's Victory Prepares the Way for Nationalism," *New Nation*, II (November 19, 1892), 686.

HOWE, FREDERIC C. *The Confessions of a Reformer*. New York, 1925.

HUNTINGTON, F. D. "Social Problems and the Church," *Forum*, X (October, 1890), 125–141.

HYSLOP, J. H. "Ethics and Economics," *Andover Review*, XV (January, 1891), 66–83.

JACKSON, ALEXANDER. "The Relation of the Classes to the Church," *Independent*, XL (March 1, 1888), 258–259.

JACKSON, HENRY. "Indemnity the Essence of Insurance; Causes and Consequences of Legislation Qualifying This Principle," *Report of the Tenth Annual Meeting of the American Bar Association, 1887*, pp. 261–287.

JAMES, EDMUND J. "State Interference," *Chautauquan*, VIII (June, 1888), 534–536.

—— "The Relation of the Modern Municipality to the Gas Supply," *Publications of the American Economic Association*, I (1886), 47–122.

JAMES, WILLIAM. *Collected Essays and Reviews*. London, 1920.

—— *Memories and Studies*. New York, 1917.

—— *The Principles of Psychology*. New York, 1890. 2 vols.

—— *Talks to Teachers on Psychology: And to Students on Some of Life's Problems*. New York, 1899.

—— *The Will to Believe and Other Essays in Popular Philosophy*. New York, 1897.

JENKS, JEREMIAH W. "Capitalistic Monopolies and Their Relation to the State," *Political Science Quarterly*, IX (September, 1894), 486–509.

—— "School-Book Legislation," *Political Science Quarterly*, VI (March, 1891), 90–125.

JONES, SAMUEL M. *The New Right: A Plea for Fair Play through a More Just Social Order*. New York, 1899.

JULIAN, GEORGE W. "Is the Reformer Any Longer Needed?" *North American Review*, CXXVII (September–October, 1878), 237–260.

LA FOLLETTE, ROBERT MARION. *La Follette's Autobiography*. 6th ed. Madison, Wisc., 1913.

LALOR, JOHN J., ed. *Cyclopaedia of Political Science, Political Economy, and of the Political History of the United States*. Chicago, 1883–1884. 3 vols.

LATHROP, JULIA C. "What the Settlement Work Stands For," *Proceedings of the National Conference of Charities and Correction, 1896*, pp. 106–110.

LAUGHLIN, J. LAURENCE. *The Elements of Political Economy*. New York, 1887.

—— *Facts about Money*. Chicago, 1895.

—— "Protection and Socialism," *International Review*, VII (October, 1879), 427–435.

—— "The Study of Political Economy in the United States," *Journal of Political Economy*, I (December, 1892), 1–19.

LAVELEYE, ÉMILE DE. *The Elements of Political Economy*. Tr. Alfred W. Pollard. With an introduction and supplementary chapter by F. W. Taussig. New York, 1884.

LAWRENCE, WILLIAM. "The Relation of Wealth to Morals," *World's Work*, I (January, 1901), 286–292.

LESLIE, T. E. C.   "Political Economy in the United States," *Fortnightly Review*, XXXIV (October 1, 1880), 488–509.

LIEB, HERMANN.   *The Protective Tariff.   What It Does for Us!*   4th and rev. ed.   Chicago, 1888.

LINCOLN, LEONTINE.   "State Boards and Commissions," *Proceedings of the National Conference of Charities and Correction, 1900*, pp. 167–172.

LIPSCOMB, ANDREW A., ed.   *The Writings of Thomas Jefferson.*   Library ed.   Washington, D.C., 1903–1904.   20 vols.

LLOYD, HENRY DEMAREST.   *Lords of Industry.*   New York, 1910.

—— *Man, the Social Creator.*   New York, 1906.

—— *Men, the Workers.*   New York, 1909.

—— "The New Conscience," *North American Review*, CXLVIII (September, 1888), 325–339.

—— *Wealth against Commonwealth.*   New York, 1894.

LODGE, HENRY CABOT, ed.   *The Works of Alexander Hamilton.*   New York, 1885.   9 vols.

LOOMIS, SAMUEL LANE.   *Modern Cities and Their Religious Problems.*   New York, 1887.

LORIMER, GEORGE C.   *Studies in Social Life: A Review of the Principles, Practices, and Problems of Society.*   London, [1886].

LOWELL, A. LAWRENCE.   *Essays on Government.*   Boston, 1889.

McCOSH, JAMES.   *Our Moral Nature.*   New York, 1892.

MACVANE, SILAS M.   *The Working Principles of Political Economy in a New and Practical Form.   A Book for Beginners.*   2d ed., rev.   New York, 1897.

MALONE, DUMAS, ed.   *Correspondence between Thomas Jefferson and Pierre Samuel du Pont de Nemours, 1798–1817.*   Boston, 1930.

MALTHUS, T. R.   *An Essay on the Principle of Population . . . .*   6th ed.   London, 1826.   2 vols.

—— *Principles of Political Economy Considered with a View to Their Practical Application.*   2d ed.   London, 1836.

MARSHALL, CHARLES C.   "A New Constitutional Amendment," *American Law Review*, XXIV (November–December, 1890), 908–931.

MARTINEAU, HARRIET.   *Illustrations of Political Economy.*   Nos. I–XXV.   London, 1832–1834.

MATHEWS, ROBERT.   "Ethics and Economics," *Popular Science Monthly*, XXXIII (October, 1888), 771–783.

MATHEWS, SHAILER.   "The Significance of the Church to the Social Movement," *American Journal of Sociology*, IV (March, 1899), 603–620.

—— *The Social Teaching of Jesus: An Essay in Christian Sociology.*   New York, 1897.

MAYO-SMITH, RICHMOND.   "Free Silver and Wages," *Political Science Quarterly*, XI (September, 1896), 464–477.

—— "Money and Prices," *Political Science Quarterly*, XV (June, 1900), 196–216.

—— "Social Problems: How They Arise, What They Are, and How Modern Political Economy Views Them," *Christian Thought*, 5th Series (1888), pp. 417–429.

MEANS, D. McG. "The Dangerous Absurdity of State Aid," *Forum*, XVII (May, 1894), 287–296.

MILL, JOHN STUART. *Essays on Some Unsettled Questions of Political Economy.* London, 1844.

—— *Principles of Political Economy; with Some of Their Applications to Social Philosophy.* From the 5th London ed. New York, 1881. 2 vols.

—— *Principles of Political Economy.* Abridged by J. Laurence Laughlin. New York, 1885.

MILLER, WARNER. "Business Men in Politics," *North American Review*, CLI (November, 1890), 576–581.

MOLEY, RAYMOND. *After Seven Years.* New York, 1939.

MONETARY COMMISSION OF THE INDIANAPOLIS CONVENTION OF BOARDS OF TRADE, CHAMBERS OF COMMERCE, COMMERCIAL CLUBS, AND OTHER SIMILAR BODIES OF THE UNITED STATES. *Report.* Chicago, 1898.

MOODY, WILLIAM GODWIN. *Land and Labor in the United States.* New York, 1883.

—— *Our Labor Difficulties: The Cause, and the Way Out; Being a Practical Solution of the Labor Problem.* Boston, 1878.

MORGAN, W. SCOTT. *History of the Wheel and Alliance, and the Impending Revolution.* St. Louis, Mo., 1891.

MORSE, C. M. "Regeneration as a Force in Reform Movements," *Methodist Review*, LXXIII (November, 1891), 923–931.

MUNGER, THEODORE T. *The Freedom of Faith.* 9th ed. Boston, 1884.

NATIONAL TARIFF CONVENTION. *Proceedings, 1881.* Philadelphia, 1882.

NEARING, SCOTT. *Educational Frontiers: A Book about Simon Nelson Patten and Other Teachers.* New York, 1925.

NETTLETON, A. B., ed. *Trusts or Competition? Both Sides of the Great Question in Business, Law and Politics.* Chicago, 1900.

"The New Socialism," *Nation*, XLVIII (June 13, 1889), 478–479.

NEWCOMB, GEORGE B. "Political Economy in Its Relation to Ethics," *Christian Thought*, 3d Series (1885), pp. 262–285.

NEWCOMB, SIMON. *The ABC of Finance; or, the Money and Labor Questions Familiarly Explained to Common People, in Short and Easy Lessons.* New York, 1877.

—— "Has the Standard Gold Dollar Appreciated?" *Journal of Political Economy*, I (September, 1893), 503–512.

—— "The Let-Alone Principle," *North American Review*, CX (January, 1870), 1–33.

NEWCOMB, SIMON. "The Organization of Labor. II. The Interest of the Laborer in Production," *Princeton Review*, N.S., VI (September, 1880), 231–246.

—— *A Plain Man's Talk on the Labor Question.* New York, 1886.

—— *Principles of Political Economy.* New York, 1885.

—— "The Problem of Economic Education," *Quarterly Journal of Economics*, VII (July, 1893), 375–399.

—— *The Reminiscences of an Astronomer.* Boston, 1903.

—— "The Standard of Value," *North American Review*, CXXIX (September, 1879), 223–237.

—— "The Two Schools of Political Economy," *Princeton Review*, N.S., XIV (November, 1884), 291–301.

NEWTON, R. HEBER. *The Morals of Trade.* New York, 1876.

NORTON, S. F. *Ten Men of Money Island, or the Primer of Finance.* Rev. ed. Girard, Kan., 1902.

Our Revenue System and the Civil Service. New York, c. 1872.

PARSONS, FRANK. *The City for the People, or the Municipalization of the City Government and of Local Franchises.* Philadelphia, [1900].

—— *Government and the Law of Equal Freedom: An Examination of Herbert Spencer's Theories of Government and Individual Liberty.* Boston, 1892.

—— "The New Political Economy," *Bibliotheca Sacra*, LVI (January, 1899), 120–139.

—— *Our Country's Need.* Boston, 1894.

—— "The People's Highways," *Arena*, XII (April, 1895), 218–232.

—— "The Philosophy of Mutualism," *Arena*, IX (May, 1894), 783–815.

—— *The Public Ownership of Monopolies.* Boston, 1894.

—— "The Purposes of Government," *Industrialist*, XXIV (January, February, March, May, 1898), 22–34, 100–106, 162–174, 289–298.

—— *Rational Money: A National Currency Intelligently Regulated in Reference to the Multiple Standard.* Philadelphia, 1898.

PARSONS, GEORGE FREDERIC. "The Labor Question," *Atlantic Monthly*, LVIII (July, 1886), 97–113.

PATTEN, SIMON N. "The Consumption of Wealth," *Publications of the University of Pennsylvania Political Economy and Public Law Series*, No. 4 (1889), pp. 1–70.

—— *The Economic Basis of Protection.* 2d ed. Philadelphia, 1895.

—— *Essays in Economic Theory.* Ed. Rexford Guy Tugwell. With an introduction by Henry Rogers Seager. New York, 1924.

—— *The Premises of Political Economy; Being a Re-examination of Certain Fundamental Principles of Economic Science.* Philadelphia, 1885.

—— "The Scope of Political Economy," *Yale Review*, II (November, 1893), 264–287.

—— "The Stability of Prices," *Publications of the American Economic Association,* III (1889), 365–428.

—— *The Theory of Dynamic Economics.* Philadelphia, 1892.

—— *The Theory of Social Forces.* Philadelphia, 1896.

—— "Wells' Recent Economic Changes," *Political Science Quarterly,* V (March, 1890), 84–103.

PATTERSON, JOHN STAHL. *Reforms: Their Difficulties and Possibilities.* New York, 1884.

PEABODY, FRANCIS G. *Jesus Christ and the Social Question: An Examination of the Teaching of Jesus in Its Relation to Some of the Problems of Modern Social Life.* New York, 1900.

PEFFER, W. A. "The Cure for a Vicious Monetary System," *Forum,* XXII (February, 1897), 722–730.

—— *The Farmer's Side. His Troubles and Their Remedy.* New York, 1891.

PERKINS, FRANCES. *The Roosevelt I Knew.* New York, 1946.

"A Pernicious Political Tendency," *Popular Science Monthly,* XXVII (July, 1885), 410–412.

PERRY, ARTHUR LATHAM. *Elements of Political Economy.* 7th ed. rev. and enlarged. New York, 1872.

—— *Introduction to Political Economy.* New York, 1880.

—— *Political Economy.* 18th ed. of *Elements of Political Economy.* New York, 1883.

—— "Preparation for Citizenship. IV. At Williams College," *Education,* IX (April, 1889), 513–521.

—— *Williamstown and Williams College.* New York, 1899.

PERRY, H. FRANCIS. "The Workingman's Alienation from the Church," *American Journal of Sociology,* IV (March, 1899), 621–629.

PINCHOT, GIFFORD. *Breaking New Ground.* New York, 1947.

POMEROY, ELTWEED. "The Multiple Standard for Money," *Arena,* XVIII (September, 1897), 318–338.

—— "The National and Social Political Conference," *Social Forum,* I (August 1, 1889), 81–92.

POMEROY, JOHN NORTON. "The Supreme Court and State Repudiation: The Virginia and Louisiana Cases," *American Law Review,* XVII (September–October, 1883), 684–734.

POTTER, HENRY C. "The Laborer Not a Commodity," *Christian Thought,* 4th Series (1886), pp. 289–291.

POWDERLY, TERENCE V. *Thirty Years of Labor, 1859 to 1889.* Columbus, Ohio, 1889.

POWELL, LYMAN P. "The American Economic Association," *Chautauquan,* XV (August, 1892), 601–607.

RAUSCHENBUSCH, WALTER. "The Ideals of Social Reformers," *American Journal of Sociology,* II (September, 1896), 202–219.

RAYMOND, DANIEL. *The Elements of Political Economy.* 2d ed. Baltimore, 1823. 2 vols.

"The Recent Strikes," *Popular Science Monthly,* I (September, 1872), 623–624.

REECE, BENJAMIN. "Law as a Disturber of Social Order," *Popular Science Monthly,* XXIV (March, 1889), 631–643.

"Regulation and Confiscation," *Nation,* XLVII (September 6, 1888), 185–186.

RENO, CONRAD. "The Wage-Contract and Personal Liberty," *Popular Science Monthly,* XLI (September, 1892), 644–652.

RICARDO, DAVID. *On the Principles of Political Economy and Taxation.* 3d ed. London, 1821.

RICH, GEORGE A. "Trusts Their Own Corrective," *Popular Science Monthly,* XLIV (April, 1894), 740–743.

RICHARDSON, JAMES D., comp. *A Compilation of the Messages and Papers of the Presidents, 1789–1902.* New York, 1903. 10 vols.

ROCKEFELLER, JOHN D. *Random Reminiscences of Men and Events.* London, 1909.

ROGERS, EDWARD H. *The Relations of Christianity to Labor and Capital.* Boston, 1870.

ROOSEVELT, THEODORE. *The New Nationalism.* New York, 1910.

ROSENMAN, SAMUEL I., comp. *The Public Papers and Addresses of Franklin D. Roosevelt.* New York, 1938–1950. 13 vols.

ROSS, EDWARD A. "Recollections of a Pioneer in Sociology," *Social Forces,* XX (October, 1941), 32–35.

—— *Seventy Years of It: An Autobiography.* New York, 1936.

—— *Social Control: A Survey of the Foundations of Order.* New York, 1901.

RYAN, JOHN A. *Social Doctrine in Action: A Personal History.* New York, 1941.

SALTER, WILLIAM MACKINTIRE. *Ethical Religion.* Boston, 1889.

SANBORN, FRANKLIN B. "The Social Sciences. Their Growth and Future," *Journal of Social Science,* XXI (September, 1886), 1–12.

—— "Society and Socialism," *Journal of Social Science,* XXXIII (November, 1895), 20–28.

SAY, JEAN BAPTISTE. *A Treatise on Political Economy; or the Production, Distribution, and Consumption of Wealth.* Tr. from the 4th ed. of the French by C. R. Prinsep. London, 1821. 2 vols.

SCHINDLER, SOLOMON. "Insurance and the Nation," *Arena,* X (August, 1894), 379–385.

SCOTT, J. E. *Socialism. What Is It? Is It Christian? Should the Church Take Any Interest in It?* San Francisco, 1895.

SCOTT, S. M. *The Sub-Treasury Plan and the Land and Loan System.* Topeka, Kan., 1891.

SCUDDER, VIDA DUTTON. *On Journey.* New York, 1937.

—— "Socialism and Spiritual Progress," *Andover Review,* XVI (July, 1891), 49–67.

SEARING, EDWARD W. "The Reign of the Huckster," *New Nation,* II (January 2, 1892), 5–9.

SELIGMAN, EDWIN R. A. "Government Ownership of Quasi-Public Corporations," *Gunton's Magazine,* XX (April, 1901), 305–322.

—— "The Living Wage," *Gunton Institute Bulletin,* I (March 26, 1898), 257–268.

—— "Railway Tariffs and the Interstate Commerce Law. II," *Political Science Quarterly,* II (September, 1887), 369–413.

SHAW, ALBERT. "The American State and the American Man," *Contemporary Review,* LI (May, 1887), 695–711.

—— ed. *The National Revenues: A Collection of Papers by American Economists.* Chicago, 1888.

SHELDON, CHARLES M. *In His Steps: What Would Jesus Do?* Chicago, 1898.

SHELDON, WALTER LORENZO. *An Ethical Movement: A Volume of Lectures.* New York, 1896.

SHERWOOD, SIDNEY. "Tendencies in American Economic Thought," *Johns Hopkins University Studies in Historical and Political Science,* XV (December, 1897), 567–608.

SHIBLEY, GEORGE H. "Who Shall Control the Price Level?" *Arena,* XXIII (January, 1900), 68–87.

"Sketch of William Graham Sumner," *Popular Science Monthly,* XXXV (June, 1889), 261–269.

SMALL, ALBION W. "The Era of Sociology," *American Journal of Sociology,* I (July, 1895), 1–15.

—— "The Meaning of the Social Movement," *American Journal of Sociology,* III (November, 1897), 340–354.

—— "Private Business Is a Public Trust," *American Journal of Sociology,* I (November, 1895), 276–289.

—— "The Relation of Sociology to Economics," *Journal of Political Economy,* III (March, 1895), 169–184.

—— "Sanity in Social Agitation," *American Journal of Sociology,* IV (November, 1898), 335–351.

—— "Scholarship and Social Agitation," *American Journal of Sociology,* I (March, 1896), 564–582.

—— "The State and Semi-Public Corporations," *American Journal of Sociology,* I (January, 1896), 398–410.

—— "Static and Dynamic Sociology," *American Journal of Sociology,* I (September, 1895), 195–209.

—— AND GEORGE E. VINCENT. *An Introduction to the Study of Society.* New York, 1894.

SMITH, ADAM. *An Inquiry into the Nature and Causes of the Wealth of Nations.* Ed. Edwin Cannan. With an introduction by Max Lerner. New York, 1937.

SMITH, E. PESHINE. *A Manual of Political Economy.* New York, 1868.

SMITH, FRANKLIN. "An Apostate Democracy," *Popular Science Monthly,* LII (March, 1898), 654–674.

—— "The Despotism of Democracy," *Popular Science Monthly,* LI (August, 1897), 489–507.

—— "An Object Lesson in Social Reform," *Popular Science Monthly,* L (January, 1897), 305–311.

—— "Politics as a Form of Civil War," *Popular Science Monthly,* LIV (March, 1899), 588–604.

—— "Real Problems of Democracy," *Popular Science Monthly,* LVI (November, 1899), 1–13.

—— "A State Official on Excessive Taxation," *Popular Science Monthly,* LVI (April, 1900), 645–659.

SMITH, J. ALLEN. "The Multiple Money Standard," *Annals of the American Academy of Political and Social Science,* VII (March, 1896), 173–232.

SMYTH, NEWMAN. *Christian Ethics.* 2d ed. Edinburgh, 1893.

"The Social Science Association," *Popular Science Monthly,* V (July, 1874), 367–369.

SOCIALISTIC TRACT ASSOCIATION. *Tracts on Socialism.* Detroit, [1879].

"Sociological Record," *New York Social Science Review,* II (August, 1866), 97–112.

SPENCER, HERBERT. *An Autobiography.* New York, 1904. 2 vols.

—— *The Data of Ethics.* New York, 1883.

—— *Essays: Moral, Political and Aesthetic.* New York, 1865.

—— *First Principles of a New System of Philosophy* (*A System of Synthetic Philosophy,* Vol. I). New York, 1876.

—— *The Man versus the State.* New York, 1885. Ed. Truxton Beale, New York, 1916.

—— *The Principles of Ethics* (*A System of Synthetic Philosophy,* Vols. IX–X). New York, 1897. 2 vols.

—— *The Principles of Sociology* (*A System of Synthetic Philosophy,* Vols. VI–VIII). New York, 1880–1897. 3 vols.

—— *Social Statics.* London, 1851. Abridged and rev. ed., together with *The Man versus the State,* New York, 1896.

—— *The Study of Sociology.* New York, 1896.

"Spencer's Impressions of America," *Popular Science Monthly,* XXII (December, 1882), 268–273.

SPRAGUE, FRANKLIN M. *The Laws of Social Evolution: A Critique of Benjamin Kidd's 'Social Evolution' and a Statement of the True Principles Which Govern Social Progress.* Boston, 1895.

—— *Socialism from Genesis to Revelation.* Boston, 1893.

Sprague, Philo W. *Christian Socialism. What and Why.* New York, 1891.

"The State and Social Organization," *Popular Science Monthly*, XXXIII (July, 1888), 411–412.

"State Education," *Popular Science Monthly*, XXXI (May, 1887), 124–127.

Stern, Bernhard J., ed. "Giddings, Ward, and Small: An Interchange of Letters," *Social Forces*, X (March, 1932), 305–318.

—— "The Letters of Albion W. Small to Lester F. Ward," *Social Forces*, XII (December, 1933), 163–173; XIII (March, 1935), 323–340; XV (December, 1936), 174–186.

—— "The Ward-Ross Correspondence, 1891–1896," *American Sociological Review*, III (June, 1938), 362–401.

Stickney, Albert. *State Control of Trade and Commerce by National or State Authority.* New York, 1897.

Stimson, F. J. "Democracy and the Laboring Man," *Atlantic Monthly*, LXXX (November, 1897), 605–619.

—— "The Ethics of Democracy," *Scribner's Magazine*, I (June, 1887), 661–671.

—— "The Ethics of Democracy: Liberty," *Scribner's Magazine*, XV (May, 1894), 649–656.

Strong, Josiah. *Our Country. Its Possible Future and Its Present Crisis.* Rev. ed. New York, 1891.

Stuart, Otis Kendall. "The Value of Trusts," *Independent*, XLIX (March 4, 1897), 272–273.

Stuckenberg, J. H. W. *Christian Sociology.* London, 1881.

Sturtevant, Julian M. *Economics, or the Science of Wealth.* New York, 1881.

—— Review of Prof. Perry's *Political Economy*, *New Englander*, XXXVIII (January, 1879), 19–33.

Sumner, William Graham. *The Challenge of Facts and Other Essays.* Ed. Albert Galloway Keller. New Haven, 1914.

—— *Earth Hunger and Other Essays.* Ed. Albert Galloway Keller. New Haven, 1913.

—— *Essays of William Graham Sumner.* Ed. Albert Galloway Keller and Maurice R. Davie. New Haven, 1934. 2 vols.

—— *War and Other Essays.* Ed. Albert Galloway Keller. New Haven, 1911.

—— *What Social Classes Owe to Each Other.* New York, 1883.

—— "Why I Am a Free Trader," *Twentieth Century*, IV (April 24, 1890), 8–10.

"Tariff Legislation," *Popular Science Monthly*, XXXVII (September, 1890), 696–698.

Taussig, Frank W. "The Silver Situation in the United States," *Publications of the American Economic Association*, VII (1892), 1–118.

TAUSSIG, FRANK W. *Wages and Capital: An Examination of the Wages Fund Doctrine.* New York, 1896.

—— "Workmen's Insurance in Germany," *Forum,* VIII (October, 1889), 159–169.

TAYLOR, GRAHAM. *Pioneering on Social Frontiers.* Chicago, 1930.

—— "The Social Function of the Church," *American Journal of Sociology,* V (November, 1899), 305–321.

THOMPSON, ROBERT ELLIS. *Political Economy; with Special Reference to the Industrial History of Nations.* Rev. ed. of *Social Science and National Economy.* Philadelphia, 1882.

THOREAU, HENRY DAVID. *The Writings of Henry David Thoreau.* Riverside ed. Boston, 1894. 10 vols.

THORPE, FRANCIS N. "The Dominant Idea of American Democracy," *Harper's Monthly Magazine,* XCIII (November, 1896), 838–842.

TIEDEMAN, CHRISTOPHER G. *A Treatise on the Limitations of Police Power in the United States Considered from Both a Civil and Criminal Standpoint.* St. Louis, Mo., 1886.

—— *A Treatise on State and Federal Control of Persons and Property in the United States Considered from Both a Civil and Criminal Standpoint.* 2d ed. of *A Treatise on the Limitations of Police Power.* . . . St. Louis, Mo., 1900. 2 vols.

—— *The Unwritten Constitution of the United States: A Philosophical Inquiry into the Fundamentals of American Constitutional Law.* New York, 1890.

TUCKER, BENJAMIN R., W. D. P. BLISS, AND E. B. ANDREWS. "A Symposium upon the Relation of the State to the Individual," *Dawn,* II (November, 1890), 265–301.

TUCKER, J. RANDOLPH. "British Institutions and American Constitutions," *Report of the Fifteenth Annual Meeting of the American Bar Association, 1892,* pp. 213–244.

TUCKER, WILLIAM JEWETT. "'The Gospel of Wealth,'" *Andover Review,* XV (June, 1891), 631–645.

—— *My Generation: An Autobiographical Interpretation.* Boston, 1919.

TUGWELL, REXFORD G. "The Preparation of a President," *Western Political Quarterly,* I (June, 1948), 131–153.

TUTTLE, CHARLES A. "The Workman's Position in the Light of Economic Progress," *Publications of the American Economic Association,* 3d Series, III (February, 1902), 199–212.

VEBLEN, THORSTEIN. "Industrial and Pecuniary Employments," *Publications of the American Economic Association,* 3d Series, II (1901), 190–235.

—— "The Preconceptions of Economic Science," *Quarterly Journal of Economics,* XIII (January, July, 1899), 121–150, 396–426; XIV (February, 1900), 240–269.

—— "Why Is Economics Not an Evolutionary Science?" *Quarterly Journal of Economics*, XII (July, 1898), 373–397.

"Wages, Capital and Rich Men," *Popular Science Monthly*, XXV (October, 1884), 788–795.

WALKER, AMASA. "Legal Interference with the Hours of Labor," *Lippincott's*, II (November, 1868), 527–533.

—— *The Science of Wealth: A Manual of Political Economy Embracing the Laws of Trade, Currency, and Finance.* 2d ed. Boston, 1866.

WALKER, FRANCIS AMASA. *Bimetallism: A Tract for the Times.* Boston, 1894.

—— *Discussions in Economics and Statistics.* Ed. Davis R. Dewey. New York, 1899. 2 vols.

—— *First Lessons on Political Economy.* New York, 1893.

—— *Money.* New York, 1878.

—— *Political Economy.* New York, 1883.

—— "Recent Progress of Political Economy in the United States," *Publications of the American Economic Association*, IV (1889), 243–268.

—— "The Tide of Economic Thought," *Publications of the American Economic Association*, VI (1891), 15–38.

—— *The Wages Question: A Treatise on Wages and the Wages Class.* New York, 1876.

WALLACE, GEORGE M. "Governmental Aid to Injustice," *Popular Science Monthly*, XXXVI (December, 1889), 191–193.

WALLACE, HENRY A. *Democracy Reborn.* Selected from public papers and edited with an introduction and notes by Russell Lord. New York, 1944.

WAMBAUGH, EUGENE. "The Present Scope of Government," *Atlantic Monthly*, LXXXI (January, 1898), 120–130.

WARD, [C.] OSBORNE. *A Labor Catechism of Political Economy. A Study for the People.* New York, 1878.

WARD, LESTER F. "Broadening the Way to Success," *Forum*, II (December, 1886), 340–350.

—— *Dynamic Sociology, or Applied Social Science as Based upon Statical Sociology and the Less Complex Sciences.* New York, 1883. 2 vols. 2d ed., New York, 1897.

—— "False Notions of Government," *Forum*, III (June, 1887), 364–372.

—— *Glimpses of the Cosmos.* New York, 1913–1918. 6 vols.

—— *Outlines of Sociology.* New York, 1898.

—— "Plutocracy and Paternalism," *Forum*, XX (November, 1895), 300–310.

—— "The Political Ethics of Herbert Spencer," *Annals of the American Academy of Political and Social Science*, IV (January, 1894), 582–619.

—— "Principles of Sociology," *Annals of the American Academy of Political and Social Science*, VIII (July, 1896), 1–31.

WARD, LESTER F. *The Psychic Factors of Civilization.* Boston, 1893.

—— "Sociology and Economics," *Annals of the American Academy of Political and Social Science,* XIII (March, 1899), 230–234.

WARNER, AMOS G. *American Charities: A Study in Philanthropy and Economics.* New York, 1894.

WASHBURN, E. A. *The Social Law of God: Sermons on the Ten Commandments.* 3d ed. New York, 1875.

WAYLAND, FRANCIS. *The Elements of Political Economy.* 3d ed. Boston, 1840. Recast by Aaron L. Chapin, New York, 1881.

WEBSTER, DANIEL. *The Works of Daniel Webster.* 11th ed. Boston, 1858. 6 vols.

—— *The Writings and Speeches of Daniel Webster.* National ed. Boston, 1903. 18 vols.

WELLS, DAVID AMES. "The Creed of Free Trade," *Atlantic Monthly,* XXXVI (August, 1875), 204–220.

—— *The Cremation Theory of Specie Resumption.* Reprinted from the *New York Herald,* February 13, 1875. New York, 1875.

—— *Free Trade Essential to Future National Prosperity and Development.* New York, 1882.

—— "How Will the United States Supreme Court Decide the Granger Railroad Cases?" *Nation,* XIX (October 29, 1874), 282–284.

—— *Practical Economics: A Collection of Essays Respecting Certain of the Recent Economic Experiences of the United States.* New York, 1894.

—— *A Primer of Tariff Reform.* London, 1885.

—— *Recent Economic Changes and Their Effect on the Production and Distribution of Wealth and the Well-Being of Society.* New York, 1890.

—— *Robinson Crusoe's Money.* New York, 1876.

"What Socialism Is," *Dawn,* VII (February, 1896), 8–10.

"What the Government Can Do," *Craftsman,* VI (September, 1889), 2.

"What to Do Now. A Socialistic Programme," *Dawn,* VII (October, 1895), 5–6.

WHEELER, A. S. "The Labor Question," *Andover Review,* VI (November, 1886), 467–478.

WHITE, HORACE. *Coin's Financial Fool. A Reply to Coin's Financial School.* New York, 1895.

[——] "Communistic Features of the Chicago Platform," *Nation,* XXXVIII (June 26, 1884), 540.

—— *Money and Banking Illustrated by American History.* Boston, 1895.

WHITE, WILLIAM ALLEN. *The Autobiography of William Allen White.* New York, 1946.

WILL, THOMAS ELMER. "Stable Money," *Journal of Political Economy,* VII (December, 1898), 85–92.

—— FRANK PARSONS, AND JAMES M. BROWN, "The Unemployed: A Symposium," *Arena,* X (October, 1894), 701–720.

WILLCOX, DAVID. "Unconstitutionality of Recent Anti-Trust Legislation," *Forum*, XXIV (September, 1897), 107–118.

WILLETT, J. "Letter from a Workingman," *Christian Union*, XXXII (October 29, 1885), 7–8.

WILLIS, FREDERICK M. "The Sphere of the State," *Nationalist*, II (April, 1890), 155–162.

WILLOUGHBY, WESTEL WOODBURY. *An Examination of the Nature of the State: A Study in Political Philosophy.* New York, 1896.

—— *Social Justice: A Critical Essay.* New York, 1900.

WILLOUGHBY, WILLIAM F. "State Activities and Politics," *Papers of the American Historical Association*, V (January, April, 1891), 111–127.

WILSON, W. D. *First Principles of Political Economy; with Reference to Statesmanship and the Progress of Civilization.* Philadelphia, 1882.

WILSON, WOODROW. *The New Freedom: A Call for the Emancipation of the Generous Energies of a People.* New York, 1913.

—— *The State: Elements of Historical and Practical Politics.* Rev. ed. Boston, 1898.

WINN, HENRY. "Multiple-Standard Money," *Arena*, XIX (May, 1898), 639–657.

WOOD, BENJAMIN. *The Successful Man of Business.* 2d ed. Rev. and enlarged. New York, 1899.

WOOD, HENRY. *Natural Law in the Business World.* Boston, 1887.

—— *The Political Economy of Natural Law.* Boston, 1894.

WOOLSEY, THEODORE D. *Political Science or the State, Theoretically and Practically Considered.* New York, 1878. 2 vols.

YOUMANS, EDWARD L., ed. *Herbert Spencer on the Americans and the Americans on Herbert Spencer.* New York, 1883.

ZIMMERMAN, CHARLES H. "The Church and Economic Reforms," *Arena*, X (October, 1894), 694–700.

—— "Wanted, An Ethical Political Economy," *Methodist Review*, LXXIV (September, 1892), 737–744.

Secondary Sources

AARON, DANIEL, ed. *America in Crisis.* New York, 1952.

—— *Men of Good Hope: A Story of American Progressives.* New York, 1951.

ABELL, AARON I. "The Catholic Factor in Urban Welfare: The Early Period, 1850–1880," *Review of Politics*, XIV (July, 1952), 289–324.

—— "Origins of Catholic Social Reform in the United States: Ideological Aspects," *Review of Politics*, XI (July, 1949), 294–309.

—— "The Reception of Leo XIII's Labor Encyclical in America, 1891–1919," *Review of Politics*, VII (October, 1945), 464–495.

ABELL, AARON I. *The Urban Impact on American Protestantism, 1865–1900.* Cambridge, Mass., 1943.

ABELS, JULES. *The Welfare State: A Mortgage of America's Future.* New York, 1951.

ADAMS, GEORGE P., AND WM. PEPPERELL MONTAGUE, eds. *Contemporary American Philosophy.* New York, 1930. 2 vols.

BAKER, RAY STANNARD. *Woodrow Wilson, Life and Letters.* Garden City, N.Y., 1927–1939. 8 vols.

BARKER, CHARLES ALBRO. *Henry George.* New York, 1955.

BARNES, HARRY ELMER, ed. *The History and Prospects of the Social Sciences.* New York, 1925.

—— "Two Representative Contributions of Sociology to Political Theory: The Doctrines of William Graham Sumner and Lester Frank Ward," *American Journal of Sociology,* XXV (July, September, 1919), 1–23, 273–288.

BARROWS, CHESTER L. *William M. Evarts, Lawyer, Diplomat, Statesman.* Chapel Hill, N.C., 1941.

BEARD, CHARLES A. "The Idea of Let Us Alone," *Virginia Quarterly Review,* XV (Autumn, 1939), 500–514.

—— "The Myth of Rugged American Individualism," *Harper's Magazine,* CLXIV (December, 1931), 13–22.

—— *Public Policy and the General Welfare.* New York, 1941.

—— AND MARY R. BEARD. *The American Spirit: A Study of the Idea of Civilization in the United States (The Rise of American Civilization,* Vol. IV). New York, 1942.

BECKER, CARL L. *Freedom and Responsibility in the American Way of Life.* New York, 1945.

BENSON, LEE EDWARD. "New York Merchants and Farmers in the Communication Revolution, 1873–1887." Ph.D. thesis, Cornell University, 1952.

BERNARD, LUTHER LEE, AND JESSIE BERNARD. *Origins of American Sociology: The Social Science Movement in the United States.* New York, 1943.

BIDWELL, PERCY WELLS, AND JOHN I. FALCONER. *History of Agriculture in the Northern United States, 1620–1860.* Washington, D.C., 1925.

BLAKE, NELSON MANFRED. *A Short History of American Life.* New York, 1952.

BLEASE, W. LYON. *A Short History of English Liberalism.* London, 1913.

BORNEMANN, ALFRED. *J. Laurence Laughlin: Chapters in the Career of an Economist.* Washington, D.C., 1940.

BOSWELL, JAMES LANE. *The Economics of Simon Nelson Patten.* Philadelphia, 1933.

BOUDIN, LOUIS B. *Government by Judiciary.* New York, 1932. 2 vols.

BRIDGES, HORACE J., ed. *Aspects of Ethical Religion: Essays in Honor of*

Felix Adler on the Fiftieth Anniversary of His Founding of the Ethical Movement, 1876. New York, 1926.

BRIGGS, JOHN E. *History of Social Legislation in Iowa.* Iowa City, Iowa, 1915.

BROOKS, AUBREY LEE. *Walter Clark, Fighting Judge.* Chapel Hill, N.C., 1944.

BROWN, BERNARD EDWARD. *American Conservatives: The Political Thought of Francis Lieber and John W. Burgess.* New York, 1951.

BROWN, IRA V. *Lyman Abbott, Christian Evolutionist: A Study in Religious Liberalism.* Cambridge, Mass., 1953.

BRUNO, FRANK J. *Trends in Social Work as Reflected in the Proceedings of the National Conference of Social Work, 1874–1946.* New York, 1948.

BRYSON, GLADYS. "The Emergence of the Social Sciences from Moral Philosophy," *International Journal of Ethics,* XLII (April, 1932), 304–323.

BUCK, SOLON JUSTUS. *The Agrarian Crusade: A Chronicle of the Farmer in Politics (The Chronicles of America,* Vol. XLV). New Haven, 1921.
—— *The Granger Movement: A Study of Agricultural Organization and Its Political, Economic and Social Manifestations.* Cambridge, Mass., 1913.

BULLOCK, CHARLES J. "Historical Sketch of the Finances and Financial Policies of Massachusetts from 1780 to 1905," *Publications of the American Economic Association,* 3d Series, VIII (1897), 268–412.

CAHILL, MARION C. *Shorter Hours: A History of the Movement since the Civil War.* New York, 1932.

CALLCOTT, MARY STEVENSON, AND WILLOUGHBY C. WATERMAN. *Principles of Social Legislation.* New York, 1932.

CALLENDER, GUY S. "The Early Transportation and Banking Enterprises of the States in Relation to the Growth of Corporations," *Quarterly Journal of Economics,* XVII (November, 1902), 111–162.

CAMERON, JENKS. *The Development of Governmental Forest Control in the United States.* Baltimore, 1928.

CAMPBELL, W. W. "Simon Newcomb," *Memoirs of the National Academy of Sciences,* XVII (1924), 1–18.

CAREY, ROBERT LINCOLN. *Daniel Webster as an Economist.* New York, 1929.

CHAMBERLAIN, JOHN. *Farewell to Reform. The Rise, Life and Decay of the Progressive Mind in America.* 2d ed. New York, 1933.

CHERRINGTON, ERNEST H. *The Evolution of Prohibition in the United States of America: A Chronological History of the Liquor Problem and the Temperance Reform in the United States from the Earliest Settlements to the Consummation of National Prohibition.* Westerville, Ohio, 1920.

CHUGERMAN, SAMUEL. *Lester F. Ward, the American Aristotle: A Summary and Interpretation of His Sociology.* Durham, N.C., 1939.

CLARK, JOHN MAURICE, ET AL. *Adam Smith, 1776–1926.* Chicago, 1928.

COCHRAN, THOMAS C. "The Executive Mind: The Role of Railroad Leaders, 1845–1890," *Bulletin of the Business Historical Society,* XXV (December, 1951), 230–241.

—— "The Faith of Our Fathers," *Frontiers of Democracy,* VI (1939), 17–19.

—— *Railroad Leaders, 1845–1890: The Business Mind in Action.* Cambridge, Mass., 1953.

—— AND WILLIAM MILLER. *The Age of Enterprise: A Social History of Industrial America.* New York, 1942.

COHEN, MORRIS R. *The Faith of a Liberal.* New York, 1946.

COLE, ARTHUR CHARLES. *The Irrepressible Conflict, 1850–1865 (A History of American Life,* Vol. VII), New York, 1934.

COMAN, KATHARINE. *Economic Beginnings of the Far West: How We Won the Land beyond the Mississippi.* New York, 1912. 2 vols.

COMMAGER, HENRY STEELE. *The American Mind: An Interpretation of American Thought and Character since the 1880's.* New Haven, 1950.

COMMONS, JOHN R., ET AL. *History of Labour in the United States.* New York, 1918–1935. 4 vols.

—— AND JOHN B. ANDREWS. *Principles of Labor Legislation.* 4th rev. ed. New York, 1936.

COONS, ARTHUR G., ed. *Government Expansion in the Economic Sphere (Annals of the American Academy of Political and Social Science,* Vol. CCVI). Philadelphia, 1939.

CORWIN, EDWARD S. "The Doctrine of Due Process of Law before the Civil War," *Harvard Law Review,* XXIV (March, April, 1911), 366–385, 460–479.

—— "The Supreme Court and the Fourteenth Amendment," *Michigan Law Review,* VII (June, 1909), 643–672.

CUNNINGHAM, W. *The Growth of English Industry and Commerce in Modern Times.* Cambridge, England, 1917–1919. 2 vols.

CURTI, MERLE. *The Growth of American Thought.* New York, 1943.

—— *The Social Ideas of American Educators.* New York, 1935.

—— ET AL. *An American History.* New York, 1950. 2 vols.

—— AND VERNON CARSTENSEN. *The University of Wisconsin: A History, 1848–1925.* Madison, Wisc., 1949. 2 vols.

CUSHMAN, ROBERT EUGENE. "The Social and Economic Interpretation of the Fourteenth Amendment," *Michigan Law Review,* XX (May, 1922), 737–764.

DEALEY, JAMES Q., et al. "Lester Frank Ward," *American Journal of Sociology,* XIX (July, 1913), 61–78.

DEMILLE, ANNA GEORGE. *Henry George, Citizen of the World.* Ed. Don C. Shoemaker. Chapel Hill, N.C., 1950.

DESTLER, CHESTER MCARTHUR. *American Radicalism, 1865–1901: Essays and Documents.* New London, Conn., 1946.

—— "The Opposition of American Businessmen to Social Control during the 'Gilded Age,'" *Mississippi Valley Historical Review,* XXXIX (March, 1953), 641–672.

DEYRUP, FELICIA JOHNSON. *Arms Makers of the Connecticut Valley: A Regional Study of the Economic Development of the Small Arms Industry, 1798–1870 (Smith College Studies in History,* Vol. XXXIII). Northampton, Mass., 1948.

DIAMOND, WILLIAM. *The Economic Thought of Woodrow Wilson.* Baltimore, 1943.

DOMBROWSKI, JAMES. *The Early Days of Christian Socialism in America.* New York, 1936.

DORFMAN, JOSEPH. *The Economic Mind in American Civilization, 1606–1918.* New York, 1946–1949. 3 vols.

—— "The Role of the German Historical School in American Economic Thought," *American Economic Review,* XLV (May, 1955) 17–28.

—— *Thorstein Veblen and His America.* New York, 1934.

DORSEY, EMMETT E. "The Evolution of the Concept of the Welfare State in the United States since 1890." Ph.D. thesis, American University, 1953.

DUDDEN, ARTHUR P. "Antimonopolism, 1865–1890: The Historical Background and Intellectual Origins of the Antitrust Movement in the United States." Ph.D. thesis, University of Michigan, 1950.

DUMOND, DWIGHT LOWELL. *America in Our Time, 1896–1946.* New York, 1947.

DUNBAR, CHARLES F. "Economic Science in America, 1776–1876," *North American Review,* CXXII (January, 1876), 124–154.

DUNCAN, DAVID. *Life and Letters of Herbert Spencer.* New York, 1908. 2 vols.

EGBERT, DONALD DREW, AND STOW PERSONS, eds. *Socialism and American Life.* Princeton, N.J., 1952. 2 vols.

EVERETT, JOHN RUTHERFORD. *Religion in Economics: A Study of John Bates Clark, Richard T. Ely, Simon N. Patten.* New York, 1946.

FABRICANT, SOLOMON. *The Trend of Government Activity since 1900.* New York, 1953.

FAINSOD, MERLE, AND LINCOLN GORDON. *Government and the American Economy.* New York, 1941.

FAIRMAN, CHARLES. *Mr. Justice Miller and the Supreme Court, 1862–1890.* Cambridge, Mass., 1939.

FARNAM, HENRY W. *Chapters in the History of Social Legislation in the United States to 1860.* Washington, D.C., 1938.

FAULKNER, HAROLD UNDERWOOD. *The Decline of Laissez Faire, 1897–1917 (The Economic History of the United States,* Vol. VII). New York, 1951.

FAULKNER, HAROLD UNDERWOOD. *The Quest for Social Justice (A History of American Life,* Vol. XI). New York, 1931.

FEDER, LEAH HANNAH. *Unemployment Relief in Periods of Depression: A Study of Measures Adopted in Certain American Cities, 1857 through 1922.* New York, 1936.

FERLEGER, HERBERT RONALD. *David A. Wells and the American Revenue System, 1865–1870.* New York, 1942.

FINE, SIDNEY. "The Eight-hour Day Movement in the United States, 1888–1891," *Mississippi Valley Historical Review,* XL (December, 1953), 441–462.

—— "Richard T. Ely, Forerunner of Progressivism," *Mississippi Valley Historical Review,* XXXVII (March, 1951), 599–624.

FISH, CARL RUSSELL. *The Rise of the Common Man, 1830–1850 (A History of American Life,* Vol. VI). New York, 1927.

FISHER, IRVING. "Why Has the Doctrine of Laissez Faire Been Abandoned?" *Science,* N.S., XXV (January 4, 1907), 18–27.

FISKE, JOHN. *Edward Livingston Youmans, Interpreter of Science for the People.* New York, 1894.

FLEMING, E. McCLUNG. *R. R. Bowker, Militant Liberal.* Norman, Okla., 1952.

FOORD, JOHN. *The Life and Public Services of Simon Sterne.* London, 1903.

FORD, HARVEY S. "The Life and Times of Golden Rule Jones." Ph.D. thesis, University of Michigan, 1953.

FRANKFURTER, FELIX. *Mr. Justice Holmes and the Constitution: A Review of His Twenty-five Years on the Supreme Court.* Cambridge, Mass., 1927.

FRANKLIN, JOHN HOPE. "Edward Bellamy and Nationalism," *New England Quarterly,* XI (December, 1938), 739–772.

FREUND, ERNST. *The Police Power, Public Policy and Constitutional Rights.* Chicago, 1904.

GABRIEL, RALPH HENRY. *The Course of American Democratic Thought: An Intellectual History since 1815.* New York, 1940.

GATES, WILLIAM B., JR. *Michigan Copper and Boston Dollars: An Economic History of the Michigan Copper Mining Industry.* Cambridge, Mass., 1951.

GEIGER, GEORGE RAYMOND. *The Philosophy of Henry George.* Grand Forks, N.D., 1931.

GEORGE, HENRY, JR. *The Life of Henry George.* Twenty-fifth anniv. ed. New York, 1905.

GHENT, W. J. *Our Benevolent Feudalism.* New York, 1902.

GIDE, CHARLES, AND CHARLES RIST. *A History of Economic Doctrines from the Time of the Physiocrats to the Present Day.* Authorised translation from the second revised and augmented edition of 1913 by R. Richards. Boston, n. d.

GINGER, RAY. *The Bending Cross: A Biography of Eugene Victor Debs.* New Brunswick, N.J., 1949.

GIRVETZ, HARRY K. *From Wealth to Welfare: The Evolution of Liberalism.* Stanford, Calif., 1950.

GLUECK, SHELDON, ed. *The Welfare State and the National Welfare: A Symposium on Some of the Threatening Tendencies of Our Times.* Cambridge, Mass., 1952.

GOING, ALLEN JOHNSTON. *Bourbon Democracy in Alabama, 1874–1890.* University, Ala., 1951.

GOLDMAN, ERIC F. *Rendezvous with Destiny.* New York, 1952.

GOLDMARK, JOSEPHINE. *Impatient Crusader.* Urbana, Ill., 1953.

GOODRICH, CARTER. "The Revulsion against Internal Improvements," *Journal of Economic History,* X (November, 1950), 145–169.

GREEN, ARNOLD W. *Henry Charles Carey, Nineteenth Century Sociologist.* Philadelphia, 1951.

GRIMES, ALAN PENDLETON. *The Political Liberalism of the New York Nation, 1865–1932.* Chapel Hill, N.C., 1953.

GROSSMAN, JONATHAN. *William Sylvis, Pioneer of American Labor: A Study of the Labor Movement during the Era of the Civil War.* New York, 1945.

HACKER, LOUIS M., AND BENJAMIN B. KENDRICK. *The United States since 1865.* New York, 1939.

HADDOW, ANNA. *Political Science in American Colleges and Universities, 1636–1900.* New York, 1939.

HADLEY, MORRIS. *Arthur Twining Hadley.* New Haven, 1948.

HAINES, CHARLES GROVE. *The Revival of Natural Law Concepts: A Study of the Establishment and of the Interpretation of Limits on Legislatures with Special Reference to the Development of Certain Phases of American Constitutional Law.* Cambridge, Mass., 1930.

HANDLIN, OSCAR, AND MARY FLUG HANDLIN. *Commonwealth: A Study of the Role of Government in the American Economy: Massachusetts, 1774–1861.* New York, 1947.

HANDY, ROBERT T. "George D. Herron and the Kingdom Movement," *Church History,* XIX (June, 1950), 97–115.

HANEY, LEWIS H. *A Congressional History of Railways in the United States.* Madison, Wisc., 1908–1910. 2 vols.

HARRIS, SEYMOUR, ed. *Saving American Capitalism: A Liberal Economic Program.* New York, 1948.

HARTZ, LOUIS. *Economic Policy and Democratic Thought: Pennsylvania, 1776–1860.* Cambridge, Mass., 1948.

—— *The Liberal Tradition in America: An Interpretation of American Political Thought since the Revolution.* New York, 1955.

HAVENS, R. M. "The Laissez-Faire Theory in Presidential Messages," *Tasks* of Economic History (A Supplemental Issue of Journal of Economic History), I (December, 1941), 86–95.

HAYES, CARLETON J. H. A Political and Cultural History of Modern Europe. New York, 1936. 2 vols.

HAYNES, FRED E. Social Politics in the United States. Boston, 1924.

HEARNSHAW, F. C. J., ed. The Social and Political Ideas of Some Representative Thinkers of the Victorian Age. London, 1933.

HEATH, MILTON SYDNEY. Constructive Liberalism: The Role of the State in Economic Development in Georgia to 1860. Cambridge, Mass., 1954.

HENDRICK, BURTON J. The Life of Andrew Carnegie. New York, 1932. 2 vols.

HIBBARD, BENJAMIN HORACE. A History of the Public Land Policies. New York, 1924.

HIBBEN, PAXTON. Henry Ward Beecher: An American Portrait. New York, 1927.

HICKS, JOHN D. The Populist Revolt: A History of the Farmers' Alliance and the People's Party. Minneapolis, 1931.

HILLQUIT, MORRIS. History of Socialism in the United States. 4th ed. New York, 1906.

HOBHOUSE, L. T. Liberalism. London, [1911].

HOFSTADTER, RICHARD. The American Political Tradition and the Men Who Made It. New York, 1948.

—— Social Darwinism in American Thought, 1860–1915. Philadelphia, 1944.

HOLLANDER, JACOB H. Economic Liberalism. New York, 1925.

HOLLENBACH, JOHN WILLIAM. "A Study of Economic Individualism in the American Novel from 1865 to 1888." Ph.D. thesis, University of Wisconsin, 1941.

HOMAN, PAUL T. Contemporary Economic Thought. New York, 1928.

HOPKINS, CHARLES HOWARD. The Rise of the Social Gospel in American Protestantism, 1865–1915. New Haven, 1940.

HOUSE, ALBERT V., JR. "Proposals of Government Aid to Agricultural Settlement during the Depression of 1873–1879," Agricultural History, XII (January, 1938), 46–66.

HOXIE, RALPH GORDON. "John W. Burgess, American Scholar. Book I: The Founding of the Faculty of Political Science." Ph.D. thesis, Columbia University, 1950.

HURWITZ, HOWARD LAWRENCE. Theodore Roosevelt and Labor in New York State, 1880–1900. New York, 1943.

HYNNING, CLIFFORD J. State Conservation of Resources. Washington, D.C., 1939.

INGRAM, JOHN KELLS. A History of Political Economy. Preface by Edmund J. James. New York, 1897.

JACOBS, CLYDE E. *Law Writers and the Courts: The Influence of Thomas M. Cooley, Christopher G. Tiedeman, and John F. Dillon upon American Constitutional Law.* Berkeley, Calif., 1954.

JANDY, EDWARD C. *Charles Horton Cooley. His Life and His Social Theory.* New York, 1942.

JENKIN, THOMAS P. "The American Fabian Movement," *Western Political Quarterly*, I (June, 1948), 113–123.

—— "Reactions of Major Groups to Positive Government in the United States, 1930–1940: A Study in Contemporary Political Thought," *University of California Publications in Political Science*, I (1945), 243–408.

JEWETT, FRED EUGENE. *A Financial History of Maine.* New York, 1937.

John Bates Clark: A Memorial. New York, 1938.

JOHNSON, ALLEN, AND DUMAS MALONE, eds. *Dictionary of American Biography.* Authors Edition. New York, 1937. 21 vols.

JOHNSON, E. A. J., AND HERMAN E. KROOSS. *The Origins and Development of the American Economy. An Introduction to Economics.* New York, 1953.

JOHNSON, EMORY R., ET AL. *History of the Domestic and Foreign Commerce of the United States.* Washington, D.C., 1915. 2 vols.

JOHNSON, ROY HAROLD. "American Baptists in the Age of Big Business," *Journal of Religion*, XI (January, 1931), 63–85.

JOSEPHSON, MATTHEW. *The Politicos, 1865–1896.* New York, 1938.

JOYNER, FRED B. *David Ames Wells, Champion of Free Trade.* Cedar Rapids, Iowa, 1939.

KAPLAN, A. D. H. *Henry Charles Carey: A Study in American Economic Thought.* Baltimore, 1931.

KELLER, ALBERT G. "The Discoverer of the Forgotten Man," *American Mercury*, XXVII (November, 1932), 257–270.

KELLY, ALFRED H., AND WINFRED A. HARBISON. *The American Constitution, Its Origins and Development.* New York, 1948.

KEYNES, JOHN MAYNARD. *Laissez-Faire and Communism.* New York, 1926.

KIMBALL, ELSA PEVERLY. *Sociology and Education: An Analysis of the Theories of Spencer and Ward.* New York, 1932.

KING, CLYDE LYNDON. *The Regulation of Municipal Utilities.* New York, 1912.

KIPNIS, IRA. *The American Socialist Movement, 1897–1912.* New York, 1952.

KIRKLAND, EDWARD C. *Business in the Gilded Age: The Conservative's Balance Sheet.* Madison, Wisc., 1952.

—— *A History of American Economic Life.* 3d ed. New York, 1951.

—— *Men, Cities and Transportation: A Study in New England History, 1820–1900.* Cambridge, Mass., 1948. 2 vols.

KIRKLAND, EDWARD C. "You Can't Win," *Journal of Economic History*, XIV (1954), 321–332.

LEWIS, EDWARD R. *A History of American Political Thought from the Civil War to the World War.* New York, 1937.

LICHTENBERGER, JAMES P. *Development of Social Theory.* New York, 1923.

LINK, ARTHUR S. *Wilson: The Road to the White House.* Princeton, N.J. 1947.

LIPPMAN, WALTER. "The Permanent New Deal," *Yale Review*, XXIV (June, 1935), 649–667.

LLOYD, CARO. *Henry Demarest Lloyd, 1847–1903. A Biography.* New York, 1912. 2 vols.

LOEWENBERG, BERT J. "Darwinism Comes to America, 1865–1900," *Mississippi Valley Historical Review*, XXVIII (December, 1941), 339–368.

LUNDBERG, GEORGE, ET AL., eds. *Trends in American Sociology.* New York, 1929.

LYON, LEVERETT S., ET AL. *Government and Economic Life: Development and Current Issues of American Public Policy.* Washington, D.C., 1939–1940. 2 vols.

MCBAIN, HOWARD LEE. "Taxation for a Private Purpose," *Political Science Quarterly*, XXIX (June, 1914), 185–213.

MCCARTHY, CHARLES. *The Wisconsin Idea.* New York, 1912.

MCCLOSKEY, ROBERT GREEN. *American Conservatism in the Age of Enterprise: A Study of William Graham Sumner, Stephen J. Field, and Andrew Carnegie.* Cambridge, Mass., 1951.

MACGILL, CAROLINE E., ET AL. *History of Transportation in the United States before 1860.* Washington, D.C., 1917.

MACGREGOR, D. H. *Economic Thought and Policy.* London, 1949.

MACIVER, R. M. *The Web of Government.* New York, 1947.

MACK, EDWARD C. *Peter Cooper, Citizen of New York.* New York, 1949.

MCMURRY, DONALD L. *Coxey's Army: A Study of the Industrial Army Movement of 1894.* Boston, 1929.

MADISON, CHARLES A. "Edward Bellamy, Social Dreamer," *New England Quarterly*, XV (September, 1942), 444–466.

MANN, ARTHUR. *Yankee Reformers in the Urban Age.* Cambridge, Mass., 1954.

—— "Frank Parsons: The Professor as Crusader," *Mississippi Valley Historical Review*, XXXVII (December, 1950), 471–490.

—— "Solomon Schindler: Boston Radical," *New England Quarterly*, XXIII (December, 1950), 453–476.

MARTIN, JAMES J. *Men against the State: The Expositors of Individualist Anarchism in America, 1827–1908.* DeKalb, Ill., 1953.

MAY, HENRY F. *Protestant Churches and Industrial America.* New York, 1949.

MAYNARD, THEODORE. *The Story of American Catholicism.* New York, 1941.

"Memorial to Former President Henry C. Adams," *American Economic Review,* XII (September, 1922), 401–416.

MENDELSON, WALLACE. "Mr. Justice Field and Laissez-Faire," *Virginia Law Review,* XXXVI (February, 1950), 45–58.

MERRIAM, CHARLES EDWARD. *American Political Ideas: Studies in the Development of American Political Thought, 1865–1917.* New York, 1920.

MEYER, BALTHASAR HENRY. *Railway Legislation in the United States.* New York, 1903.

MILLER, GEORGE HALL. "The Granger Laws: A Study of the Origins of State Railway Control in the Upper Mississippi Valley." Ph.D. thesis, University of Michigan, 1951.

MITCHELL, BROADUS. *Depression Decade: From New Era through New Deal, 1929–1941 (The Economic History of the United States, Vol. IX).* New York, 1947.

MONROE, PAUL. "English and American Christian Socialism: An Estimate," *American Journal of Sociology,* I (July, 1895) 50–68.

MORGAN, ARTHUR E. *Edward Bellamy.* New York, 1944.

MOTT, RODNEY L. *Due Process of Law: A Historical and Analytical Treatise of the Principles and Methods Followed by the Courts in the Application of the Concept of the Law of the Land.* Indianapolis, Ind., 1926.

MOWRY, GEORGE E. *The California Progressives.* Berkeley, Calif., 1951.

—— *Theodore Roosevelt and the Progressive Movement.* Madison, Wisc., 1946.

MUDGE, EUGENE TENBROECK. *The Social Philosophy of John Taylor of Caroline: A Study in Jeffersonian Democracy.* New York, 1939.

MUNROE, JAMES PHINNEY. *A Life of Francis Amasa Walker.* New York, 1923.

NEVINS, ALLAN. *Abram S. Hewitt; with Some Account of Peter Cooper.* New York, 1935.

—— *The Emergence of Modern America, 1865–1878 (A History of American Life, Vol. VIII).* New York, 1927.

NEWMAN, PHILIP CHARLES. *The Development of Economic Thought.* New York, 1952.

NOBLE, RANSOM E., JR. "Henry George and the Progressive Movement," *American Journal of Economics and Sociology,* VIII (April, 1949), 259–269.

NORMANO, J. F. *The Spirit of American Economics: A Study in the History of Economic Ideas in the United States prior to the Great Depression.* New York, 1943.

NYE, RUSSEL B. *Midwestern Progressive Politics: A Historical Study of Its Origins and Development, 1870–1950.* East Lansing, Mich., 1951.

O'CONNOR, MICHAEL J. L. *Origins of Academic Economics in the United States.* New York, 1944.

ODUM, HOWARD W., ed. *American Masters of Social Science: An Approach to the Study of the Social Sciences through a Neglected Field of Biography.* New York, 1927.

—— *American Sociology: The Story of Sociology in the United States through 1950.* New York, 1951.

OGDEN, ROLLO, ed. *Life and Letters of Edwin Lawrence Godkin.* New York, 1907. 2 vols.

PALGRAVE, R. H. INGLIS, ed. *Dictionary of Political Economy.* London, 1894–1901. 3 vols.

PARRINGTON, VERNON LOUIS. *The Beginnings of Critical Realism in America (Main Currents in American Thought, Vol. III).* New York, 1930.

PATTERSON, EDWIN WILHITE. *The Insurance Commissioner in the United States: A Study in Administrative Law and Practice.* Cambridge, Mass., 1927.

PERLMAN, SELIG. *A Theory of the Labor Movement.* New York, 1928.

PERRY, CARROLL. *A Professor of Life: A Sketch of Arthur Latham Perry of Williams College.* Boston, 1923.

PERRY, RALPH BARTON. *The Thought and Character of William James.* Boston, 1935. 2 vols.

PERSONS, STOW, ed. *Evolutionary Thought in America.* New Haven, 1950.

PETERSEN, EUGENE T. "The History of Wild Life Conservation in Michigan, 1859–1921." Ph.D. thesis, University of Michigan, 1952.

PHELPS, WILLIAM L. "When Yale Was Given to Sumnerology," *Literary Digest International Book Review,* III (1925), 661–663.

PHILIPSON, DAVID. *The Reform Movement in Judaism.* New and rev. ed. New York, 1931.

POLLOCK, IVAN L. *History of Economic Legislation in Iowa.* Iowa City, Iowa, 1918.

POUND, ROSCOE. "Common Law and Legislation," *Harvard Law Review,* XXI (April, 1908), 383–407.

—— "Liberty of Contract," *Yale Law Journal,* XVIII (May, 1909), 454–487.

PRIMM, JAMES NEAL. *Economic Policy in the Development of a Western State: Missouri, 1820–1860.* Cambridge, Mass., 1954.

PRINGLE, HENRY F. *Theodore Roosevelt. A Biography.* New York, 1931.

QUINT, HOWARD. *The Forging of American Socialism: Origins of the Modern Movement.* Columbia, S.C., 1953.

RAVENEL, MAZŸCK P., ed. *A Half Century of Public Health.* New York, 1921.

READ, CONYERS, ed. *The Constitution Reconsidered.* New York, 1938.

REDLICH, FRITZ. *The Molding of American Banking: Men and Ideas, Part II: 1840–1910*. New York, 1951.

ROBBINS, LIONEL. *The Theory of Economic Policy in English Classical Political Economy*. London, 1952.

ROBERTS, ROBERT R. "Economic and Political Ideas Expressed in the Early Social Gospel Movement, 1875–1900." Ph.D. thesis, University of Chicago, 1952.

ROOHAN, JAMES EDMUND. "American Catholics and the Social Question, 1865–1900." Ph.D. thesis, Yale University, 1952.

ROSSITER, CLINTON. *Conservatism in America*. New York, 1955.

—— "The Political Philosophy of F. D. Roosevelt: A Challenge to Scholarship," *Review of Politics*, XI (January, 1949), 87–95.

ROWE, KENNETH WYER. *Mathew Carey: A Study in American Economic Development*. Baltimore, 1933.

SADLER, ELIZABETH. "One Book's Influence," *New England Quarterly*, XVII (December, 1944), 530–555.

SCHAPIRO, J. SALWYN. *Liberalism and the Challenge of Fascism: Social Forces in England and France (1815–1870)*. New York, 1949.

SCHLESINGER, ARTHUR MEIER. *The Rise of the City, 1878–1898 (A History of American Life, Vol. X)*. New York, 1933.

SCHLESINGER, ARTHUR M., JR. *The Age of Jackson*. Boston, 1945.

SEAGER, HENRY R., AND CHARLES A. GULICK, JR. *Trust and Corporation Problems*. New York, 1929.

SELIGMAN, EDWIN R. A., ed. *Encyclopaedia of the Social Sciences*. New York, 1930–1935. 15 vols.

SHANNON, FRED A. *The Farmer's Last Frontier: Agriculture, 1860–1897 (The Economic History of the United States, Vol. V)*. New York, 1945.

SHATTUCK, CHARLES E. "The True Meaning of the Term 'Liberty' in Those Clauses in the Federal and State Constitutions Which Protect 'Life, Liberty, and Property,'" *Harvard Law Review*, IV (March, 1891), 365–392.

SHERWOOD, ROBERT E. *Roosevelt and Hopkins*. Rev. and enlarged ed. Bantam Books. New York, 1950. 2 vols.

SHIELDS, CURRIN V. "The American Tradition of Empirical Collectivism," *American Political Science Review*, XLVI (March, 1952), 104–120.

SHULTZ, WILLIAM J., AND M. R. CAINE. *Financial Development of the United States*. New York, 1937.

SMALL, ALBION W. "Fifty Years of Sociology in the United States (1865–1915), *American Journal of Sociology*, XXI (May, 1916), 721–864.

SMITH, MORTIMER. "W. G. Sumner: The Forgotten Man," *American Mercury*, LXXI (September, 1950), 357–366.

SORENSON, LLOYD R. "Some Classical Economists, Laissez Faire, and the

Factory Acts," *Journal of Economic History,* XII (Summer, 1952), 247–262.

SOWERS, DON C. "The Financial History of New York State from 1789 to 1912," *Columbia University Studies in History, Economics and Public Law,* LVII (1914), 325–670.

STANWOOD, EDWARD. *A History of the Presidency from 1788 to 1897.* Boston, 1898.

—— *A History of the Presidency from 1897 to 1916.* Boston, 1916.

STARR, HARRIS E. *William Graham Sumner.* New York, 1925.

STEIGERWALT, ALBERT K., JR. "The National Association of Manufacturers: Organization and Policies, 1895–1914." Ph.D. thesis, University of Michigan, 1952.

STIMSON, F. J. *Popular Law-Making: A Study of the Origin, History, and Present Tendencies of Law-Making by Statute.* New York, 1910.

STUDENSKI, PAUL, AND HERMAN E. KROOSS. *Financial History of the United States.* New York, 1952.

SWEET, WILLIAM WARREN. *The Story of Religions in America.* New York, 1930.

SWISHER, CARL BRENT. *Stephen J. Field, Craftsman of the Law.* Washington, D.C., 1930.

TARBELL, IDA M. *The Nationalizing of Business, 1878–1898 (A History of American Life,* Vol. IX). New York, 1936.

TAYLOR, GEORGE ROGERS. *The Transportation Revolution, 1815–1860 (The Economic History of the United States,* Vol. IV). New York, 1951.

TEILHAC, ERNEST. *Pioneers of American Economic Thought in the Nineteenth Century.* Tr. E. A. J. Johnson. New York, 1936.

TOYER, FRANCES AURELIA. "The Economic Thought of John Bates Clark." Ph.D. thesis, New York University, 1951.

TRIMBLE, WILLIAM. "The Social Philosophy of the Loco-Foco Democracy," *American Journal of Sociology,* XXVI (May, 1921), 705–715.

TUGWELL, REXFORD G. "Notes on the Life and Work of Simon Nelson Patten," *Journal of Political Economy,* XXXI (April, 1923), 153–208.

TURNER, FREDERICK JACKSON. *The Frontier in American History.* New York, 1920.

TWISS, BENJAMIN R. *Lawyers and the Constitution: How Laissez Faire Came to the Supreme Court.* Princeton, N.J., 1942.

VAN BROCKLIN, RALPH M. "The Movement for the Conservation of Natural Resources in the United States before 1901." Ph.D. thesis, University of Michigan, 1952.

VOLIN, LAZAR. "Henry Carter Adams: Critic of Laissez-Faire," *Journal of Social Philosophy,* III (April, 1938), 235–250.

WALKER, KENNETH O. "The Classical Economists and the Factory Acts," *Journal of Economic History,* I (November, 1941), 168–177.

WARE, NORMAN J. *The Labor Movement in the United States, 1860–1895: A Study in Democracy.* New York, 1929.

WARREN, CHARLES. *The Supreme Court in United States History.* Rev. ed. Boston, 1937. 2 vols.

WHITE, MORTON G. *Social Thought in America: The Revolt against Formalism.* New York, 1949.

WIEST, EDWARD. *Agricultural Organization in the United States (University of Kentucky Studies in Economics and Sociology,* Vol. II). Lexington, Ky., 1923.

WILLIAMSON, HAROLD F. *Edward Atkinson: The Biography of an American Liberal.* Boston, 1934.

WILTSE, CHARLES MAURICE. *The Jeffersonian Tradition in American Democracy.* Chapel Hill, N.C., 1935.

WINSTON, GEORGE TAYLOE. *A Builder of the New South: Being the Story of the Life Work of Daniel Augustus Tompkins.* Garden City, N.Y., 1920.

WOOD, EDITH ELMER. *The Housing of the Unskilled Wage Earner. America's Next Problem.* New York, 1919.

WOODS, KATHERINE PEARSON. "Edward Bellamy: Author and Economist," *Bookman,* VII (July, 1898), 398–401.

WOODWARD, C. VANN. *Origins of the New South, 1877–1913 (A History of the South,* Vol. IX). Baton Rouge, La., 1951.

WRIGHT, BENJAMIN FLETCHER, JR. *American Interpretations of Natural Law: A Study in the History of Political Thought.* Cambridge, Mass., 1931.

WYLLIE, IRVIN G. *The Self-Made Man in America: The Myth of Rags to Riches.* New Brunswick, N.J., 1954.

YOUNG, ARTHUR NICHOLS. *The Single Tax Movement in the United States.* Princeton, N.J., 1916.

INDEX

(The superior figures indicate footnotes on the pages specified.)

Selected Ann Arbor Paperbacks
Works of enduring merit

For a complete list of Ann Arbor Paperback titles write:
THE UNIVERSITY OF MICHIGAN PRESS ANN ARBOR